Metahistory

Metahistory

THE HISTORICAL IMAGINATION
IN NINETEENTH-CENTURY EUROPE

Hayden White 🕮

THE JOHNS HOPKINS UNIVERSITY PRESS
Baltimore & London

Originally published, 1973
Johns Hopkins Paperbacks edition, 1975
05 04 03 02 01 00 99 98 97   13 12 11 10 9

The Johns Hopkins University Press
2715 North Charles Street
Baltimore, Maryland 21218-4319
The Johns Hopkins Press Ltd., London

Library of Congress Cataloging-in-Publication Data

White, Hayden   1928–
   Metahistory: the historical imagination in
nineteenth-century Europe.

   Bibliography: pp. 443–48.
   1. Historiography—History. 2. History—Philosophy. I. Title.
D13.W565   907´.2   73-8110
ISBN 0-8018-1469-3

ISBN 0-8018-1761-7 (pbk.)

A catalog record for this book is available from the British Library.

One can study only what one has first dreamed about.

Bachelard

THE PSYCHOANALYSIS OF FIRE

CONTENTS

PREFACE

This analysis of the deep structure of the historical imagination is preceded by a methodological Introduction. Here I try to set forth, explicitly and in a systematic way, the interpretative principles on which the work is based. While reading the classics of nineteenth-century European historical thought, it became obvious to me that to consider them as representative forms of historical reflection required a formal theory of the historical work. I have tried to present such a theory in the Introduction.

In this theory I treat the historical work as what it most manifestly is: a verbal structure in the form of a narrative prose discourse. Histories (and philosophies of history as well) combine a certain amount of "data," theoretical concepts for "explaining" these data, and a narrative structure for their presentation as an icon of sets of events presumed to have occurred in times past. In addition, I maintain, they contain a deep structural content which is generally poetic, and specifically linguistic, in nature, and which serves as the precritically accepted paradigm of what a distinctively "historical" explanation should be. This paradigm functions as the "metahistorical" element in all historical works that are more comprehensive in scope than the monograph or archival report.

The terminology I have used to characterize the different levels on which a historical account unfolds and to construct a typology of historiographical styles may prove mystifying. But I have tried first to identify the manifest—epistemological, aesthetic, and moral—dimensions of the historical work and then to penetrate to the deeper level on which these theoretical operations found their implicit, precritical sanctions. Unlike other analysts of historical writing, I do not consider the "metahistorical" understructure of the historical work to consist of the theoretical concepts explicitly used by the historian to give to his narratives the aspect of an "explanation." I believe that such concepts comprise the manifest level of the work inasmuch as they appear on the "surface" of the text and can usually be identified with relative ease. But I distinguish among three kinds of strategy that can be used by historians to gain different kinds of "explanatory affect." I call these different strategies explanation by formal argument, explanation by emplotment, and explanation by ideological implication. *Within* each of these different strategies I identify four possible modes of articulation by which the historian can gain an explanatory affect of a specific kind. For arguments there are the modes of Formism, Organicism, Mechanism, and Contextualism; for emplotments there are the archetypes of Romance, Comedy, Tragedy, and Satire; and for ideological implication there are the tactics of Anarchism, Conservatism, Radicalism, and Liberalism. A specific combination of modes comprises what I call the historiographical "style" of a particular historian or philosopher of history. I have sought to explicate this style in my studies of Michelet, Ranke, Tocqueville, and Burckhardt among the historians, and of Hegel, Marx, Nietzsche, and Croce among the philosophers of history, of nineteenth-century Europe.

In order to relate these different styles to one another as elements of a single tradition of historical thinking, I have been forced to postulate a deep level of consciousness on which a historical thinker chooses conceptual strategies by which to explain or represent his data. On this level, I believe, the historian performs an essentially *poetic* act, in which he *pre*figures the historical field and constitutes it as a domain upon which to bring to bear the specific theories he will use to explain "what was *really* happening" in it. This act of prefiguration may, in turn, take a number of forms, the types of which are characterizable by the linguistic modes in which they are cast. Following a tradition of interpretation as old as Aristotle, but more recently developed by Vico, modern linguists, and literary theorists, I call these types of prefiguration by the names of the four tropes of poetic language: Metaphor, Metonymy, Synecdoche, and Irony. Since this terminology will in all probability be alien to many of my readers, I have explained in the Introduction why I have used it and what I mean by its categories.

One of my principal aims, over and above that of identifying and interpreting the main forms of historical consciousness in nineteenth-century Europe, has been to establish the uniquely *poetic* elements in historiography and philosophy of history in whatever age they were practiced. It is often said that history is a mixture of science and art. But, while recent analytical philosophers have succeeded in clarifying the extent to which history may be regarded as a kind of science, very little attention has been given to its artistic components. Through the disclosure of the linguistic ground on which a given idea of history was constituted, I have attempted to establish the ineluctably poetic nature of the historical work and to specify the prefigurative element in a historical account by which its theoretical concepts were tacitly sanctioned.

Thus I have postulated four principal modes of historical consciousness on the basis of the prefigurative (tropological) strategy which informs each of them: Metaphor, Synecdoche, Metonymy, and Irony. Each of these modes of consciousness provides the basis for a distinctive linguistic protocol by which to prefigure the historical field and on the basis of which specific strategies of historical interpretation can be employed for "explaining" it. I contend that the recognized masters of nineteenth-century historical thinking can be understood, and that their relations to one another as participants in a common tradition of inquiry can be established, by the explication of the different tropological modes which underlie and inform their work. In short, it is my view that the dominant tropological mode and its attendant linguistic protocol comprise the irreducibly "metahistorical" basis of every historical work. And I maintain that this metahistorical element in the works of the master historians of the nineteenth century constitutes the "philosophies of history" which implicitly sustain their works and without which they could not have produced the kinds of works they did.

Finally, I have tried to show that the works of the principal philosophers of history of the nineteenth century (Hegel, Marx, Nietzsche, and Croce) differ from those of their counterparts in what is sometimes called "proper history" (Michelet, Ranke, Tocqueville, and Burckhardt) only in emphasis, not in content. What remains implicit in the historians is simply brought to the surface and systematically defended in the works of the great philosophers of history. It is no accident that the principal philosophers of history were also (or have lately been discovered to have been) quintessentially philosophers of language. That is why they were able to grasp, more or less self-consciously, the poetic, or at least linguistic, grounds on which the putatively "scientific" theories of nineteenth-century historiography had their origins. Of course, these philosophers sought to exempt themselves from the charges of linguistic determinism with which they charged their opponents. But it is undeniable, in my view, that all of them understood the essential point I have tried to make: that, in any field of study not yet reduced (or elevated) to the status of a genuine science, thought remains the captive of the linguistic mode in which it seeks to grasp the outline of objects inhabiting its field of perception.

The general conclusions I have drawn from my study of nineteenth-century historical consciousness can be summarized as follows: (1) there can be no "proper history" which is not at the same time "philosophy of history";

(2) the possible modes of historiography are the same as the possible modes of speculative philosophy of history; (3) these modes, in turn, are in reality *formalizations* of poetic insights that analytically precede them and that sanction the particular theories used to give historical accounts the aspect of an "explanation"; (4) there are no apodictically certain theoretical grounds on which one can legitimately claim an authority for any one of the modes over the others as being more "realistic"; (5) as a consequence of this, we are indentured to a *choice* among contending interpretative strategies in any effort to reflect on history-in-general; (6) as a corollary of this, the best grounds for choosing one perspective on history rather than another are ultimately aesthetic or moral rather than epistemological; and, finally, (7) the demand for the scientization of history represents only the statement of a preference for a specific modality of historical conceptualization, the grounds of which are either moral or aesthetic, but the epistemological justification of which still remains to be established.

In presenting my analyses of the works of the master historical thinkers of the nineteenth century in the order in which they appear, I have tried to suggest that their thought represents the working out of the possibilities of tropological prefiguration of the historical field contained in poetic language in general. The actual elaboration of these possibilities is, in my view, what plunged European historical thinking into the Ironic condition of mind which seized it at the end of the nineteenth century and which is sometimes called "the crisis of historicism." The Irony of which this "crisis" was the phenomenal form has continued to flourish as the dominant mode of professional historiography, as cultivated in the academy, ever since. This, I believe, is what accounts both for the theoretical torpor of the best representatives of modern academic historiography and for those numerous rebellions against historical consciousness in general which have marked the literature, social science, and philosophy of the twentieth century. It is hoped that the present study will clarify the reasons for this torpor on the one hand and for those rebellions on the other.

It may not go unnoticed that this book is itself cast in an Ironic mode. But the Irony which informs it is a conscious one, and it therefore represents a turning of the Ironic consciousness against Irony itself. If it succeeds in establishing that the skepticism and pessimism of so much of contemporary historical thinking have their origins in an Ironic frame of mind, and that this frame of mind in turn is merely one of a number of possible postures that one may assume before the historical record, it will have provided some of the grounds for a rejection of Irony itself. And the way will have been partially cleared for the reconstitution of history as a form of intellectual activity which is at once poetic, scientific, and philosophical in its concerns— as it was during history's golden age in the nineteenth century.

Metahistory

INTRODUCTION:

THE POETICS OF HISTORY

This book is a *history* of historical consciousness in nineteenth-century Europe, but it is also meant to contribute to the current discussion of the *problem of historical knowledge*. As such, it represents both an account of the development of historical thinking during a specific period of its evolution and a general theory of the structure of that mode of thought which is called "historical."

What does it mean to *think historically*, and what are the unique characteristics of a specifically *historical method* of inquiry? These questions were debated throughout the nineteenth century by historians, philosophers, and social theorists, but usually within the context of the assumption that unambiguous answers could be provided for them. "History" was considered to be a specific mode of existence, "historical consciousness" a distinctive mode of thought, and "historical knowledge" an autonomous domain in the spectrum of the human and physical sciences.

In the twentieth century, however, considerations of these questions have been undertaken in a somewhat less self-confident mood and in the face of an apprehension that definitive answers to them may not be possible. Continental European thinkers—from Valéry and Heidegger to Sartre, Lévi-Strauss, and Michel Foucault—have cast serious doubts on the value of a specifically "historical" consciousness, stressed the fictive character of historical reconstructions, and challenged history's claims to a place among the sciences.[1] At the same time, Anglo-American philosophers have produced a massive body of literature on the epistemological status and cultural function of historical thinking, a literature which, taken as a whole, justifies serious doubts about history's status as either a rigorous science or a genuine art.[2] The effect of these two lines of inquiry has been to create the impression that the historical consciousness on which Western man has prided himself since the beginning of the nineteenth century may be little more than a theoretical basis for the ideological position from which Western civilization views its relationship not only to cultures and civilizations preceding it but also to those contemporary with it in time and contiguous with it in space.[3] In short, it is possible to view historical consciousness as a specifically Western prejudice by which the presumed superiority of modern, industrial society can be retroactively substantiated.

My own analysis of the deep structure of the historical imagination of nineteenth-century Europe is intended to provide a new perspective on the current debate over the nature and function of historical knowledge. It proceeds on two levels of inquiry. It seeks to analyze, first, the works of the recognized masters of nineteenth-century European historiography and, second, the works of the foremost philosophers of history of that same period. A general purpose is to determine the family characteristics of the different conceptions of the historical process which actually appear in the works of the classic narrators. Another aim is to determine the different possible theories by which historical thinking was justified by the philosophers of history of that time. In order to realize these aims, I will consider the historical work as what it most manifestly is—that is to say, a verbal structure in the form of a narrative prose discourse that purports to be a model, or icon, of past structures and processes in the interest of *explaining what they were by representing* them.[4]

[1] See my "The Burden of History," *History and Theory*, 5, no. 2 (1966): 111–34, for a discussion of the grounds of this revolt against historical consciousness. For the more recent manifestations, see Claude Lévi-Strauss, *The Savage Mind* (London, 1966), pp. 257–62; and *idem*, "Overture to le Cru et le cuit," in *Structuralism*, ed. Jacques Ehrmann (New York, 1966), pp. 47–48. Two works by Michel Foucault also may be consulted: *The Order of Things: An Archeology of the Human Sciences* (New York, 1971), pp. 259ff.; and *L'Archéologie du savoir* (Paris, 1969), pp. 264ff.

[2] The substance of this debate has been ably summarized by Louis O. Mink, "Philosophical Analysis and Historical Understanding," *Review of Metaphysics*, 21, no. 4 (June, 1968): 667–98. Most of the positions taken by the main participants in the debate are represented in William H. Dray, ed., *Philosophical Analysis and History* (New York, 1966).

[3] See Foucault, *The Order of Things*, pp. 367–73.

[4] Here, of course, I verge upon consideration of the most vexed problem in modern (Western) literary criticism, the problem of "realistic" literary representation. For a discussion of this problem, see René Wellek, *Concepts of Criticism* (New Haven and London,

My method, in short, is formalist. I will not try to decide whether a given historian's work is a better, or more correct, account of a specific set of events or segment of the historical process than some other historian's

---

1963), pp. 221–55. In general, my own approach to the problem, as it appears within the context of historiography, follows the example of Erich Auerbach, *Mimesis: The Representation of Reality in Western Literature* (Princeton, 1968). The whole question of the "fictive" representation of "reality" has been handled profoundly, with special reference to the visual arts, in E. H. Gombrich, *Art and Illusion: A Study in the Psychology of Pictorial Representation* (London and New York, 1960). Gombrich himself finds the origin of pictorial realism in Western art in the effort of Greek artists to translate into visual terms the narrative techniques of epic, tragic, and historical writers. Chapter 4 of *Art and Illusion*, on the differences between the conceptual overdetermination of mythically oriented Near Eastern art and the narrative, antimythical art of the Greeks, can be profitably compared with the famous opening chapter of Auerbach's *Mimesis*, which juxtaposes the styles of narrative to be found in the Pentateuch and Homer. Needless to say, the two analyses of the career of "realism" in Western art offered by Auerbach and Gombrich differ considerably. Auerbach's study is Hegelian throughout and Apocalyptic in tone, while Gombrich works within the Neo-Positivist (and anti-Hegelian) tradition represented most prominently by Karl Popper. But the two works address a common problem—that is, the nature of "realistic" representation, which is *the* problem for modern historiography. Neither, however, takes up analysis of the crucial concept of *historical* representation, even though both take what might be called "the historical sense" as a central aspect of "realism" in the arts. I have, in a sense, reversed their formulation. They ask: what are the "historical" components of a "realistic" art? I ask: what are the "artistic" elements of a "realistic" historiography? In seeking to answer the latter question, I have depended heavily on two literary theorists whose works represent virtual philosophical systems: Northrop Frye, *The Anatomy of Criticism: Four Essays* (Princeton, 1957); and Kenneth Burke, *A Grammar of Motives* (Berkeley and Los Angeles, 1969). I have also profited from a reading of the French Structuralist critics: Lucien Goldmann, Roland Barthes, Michel Foucault, and Jacques Derrida. I should like to stress, however, that I regard the latter as being, in general, captives of tropological strategies of interpretation in the same way that their nineteenth-century counterparts were. Foucault, for example, does not seem to be aware that the categories he uses for analyzing the history of the human sciences are little more than formalizations of the tropes. I have pointed this out in my essay, "Foucault Decoded: Notes from Underground," *History and Theory*, 12 no. 1 (1973): 23–54.

In my view, the whole discussion of the nature of "realism" in literature flounders in the failure to assess critically what a genuinely "historical" conception of "reality" consists of. The usual tactic is to set the "historical" over against the "mythical," as if the former were genuinely *empirical* and the latter were nothing but *conceptual*, and then to locate the realm of the "fictive" between the two poles. Literature is then viewed as being more or less *realistic*, depending upon the ratio of empirical to conceptual elements contained within it. Such, for example, is the tactic of Frye, as well as of Auerbach and Gombrich, although it should be noted that Frye has at least conned the problem in a suggestive essay, "New Directions from Old," in *Fables of Identity* (New York, 1963), which deals with the relations among history, myth, and philosophy of history. Of the philosophers who have dealt with the "fictive" element in historical narrative, I have found the following most helpful: W. B. Gallie, *Philosophy and the Historical Understanding* (New York, 1968); Arthur C. Danto, *Analytical Philosophy of History* (Cambridge, 1965); and Louis O. Mink, "The Autonomy of Historical Understanding," in *Philosophical Analysis and History*, ed. Dray, esp. pp. 179–86.

account of them; rather, I will seek to identify the structural components of those accounts.

In my view, this procedure justifies concentration on historians and philosophers of distinctively classic achievement, those who still serve as recognized models of possible ways of conceiving history: historians such as Michelet, Ranke, Tocqueville, and Burckhardt; and philosophers of history such as Hegel, Marx, Nietzsche, and Croce. In the consideration of such thinkers, I will moot the issue of which represents the most correct approach to historical study. Their status as possible models of historical representation or conceptualization does not depend upon the nature of the "data" they used to support their generalizations or the theories they invoked to explain them; it depends rather upon the consistency, coherence, and illuminative power of their respective visions of the historical field. This is why they cannot be "refuted," or their generalizations "disconfirmed," either by appeal to new data that might be turned up in subsequent research or by the elaboration of a new theory for interpreting the sets of events that comprise their objects of representation and analysis. Their status as models of historical narration and conceptualization depends, ultimately, on the preconceptual and specifically poetic nature of their perspectives on history and its processes. All this I assume as a justification of a formalist approach to the study of historical thinking in the nineteenth century.

This being given, however, it is immediately apparent that the works produced by these thinkers represent alternative, and seemingly mutually exclusive, conceptions both of the same segments of the historical process and of the tasks of historical thinking. Considered purely as verbal structures, the works they produced appear to have radically different formal characteristics and to dispose the conceptual apparatus used to explain the same sets of data in fundamentally different ways. On the most superficial level, for example, the work of one historian may be diachronic or processionary in nature (stressing the fact of change and transformation in the historical process), while that of another may be synchronic and static in form (stressing the fact of structural continuity). Again, where one historian may take it as his task to reinvoke, in a lyrical or poetic manner, the "spirit" of a past age, another may take it as his task to penetrate behind the events in order to disclose the "laws" or "principles" of which a particular age's "spirit" is only a manifestation or phenomenal form. Or, to note one other fundamental difference, some historians conceive their work primarily as a contribution to the illumination of current social problems and conflicts, while others are inclined to suppress such presentist concerns and to try to determine the extent to which a given period of the past differs from their own, in what appears to be a predominantly "antiquarian" frame of mind.

In sum, considered purely as formal verbal structures, the histories produced by the master historians of the nineteenth century display radically different conceptions of what "the historical work" *should* consist of. In order, therefore, to identify the family characteristics of the different kinds of historical thinking produced by the nineteenth century, it is first necessary to make clear what the ideal-typical structure of the "historical work" *might* consist of. Once such an ideal-typical structure has been worked out, I will have a criterion for determining which aspects of any given historical work or philosophy of history must be considered in the effort to identify its *unique* structural elements. Then, by tracing transformations in the ways historical thinkers characterize those elements and dispose them in a specific narrative in order to gain an "explanatory affect," I should be able to chart the fundamental changes in the deep structure of the historical imagination for the period under study. This, in turn, will permit one to characterize the different historical thinkers of the period in terms of their shared status as participants in a distinctive universe of discourse within which different "styles" of historical thinking were possible.

✍️ The Theory of the Historical Work

I begin by distinguishing among the following levels of conceptualization in the historical work: (1) chronicle; (2) story; (3) mode of emplotment; (4) mode of argument; and (5) mode of ideological implication. I take "chronicle" and "story" to refer to "primitive elements" in the *historical account,* but both represent processes of selection and arrangement of data from the *unprocessed historical record* in the interest of rendering that record more comprehensible to an *audience* of a particular kind. As thus conceived, the historical work represents an attempt to mediate among what I will call the *historical field,* the unprocessed *historical record, other historical accounts,* and an *audience.*

First the elements in the historical field are organized into a chronicle by the arrangement of the events to be dealt with in the temporal order of their occurrence; then the chronicle is organized into a story by the further arrangement of the events into the components of a "spectacle" or process of happening, which is thought to possess a discernible beginning, middle, and end. This *transformation of chronicle into story* is effected by the characterization of some events in the chronicle in terms of inaugural motifs, of others in terms of terminating motifs, and of yet others in terms of transitional motifs. An event which is simply reported as having happened at a certain time and place is transformed into an inaugurating event by its characterization as such: "The king went to Westminster on June 3, 1321. There the fateful meeting occurred between the king and the man who was ultimately to challenge him for his throne, though at the time the two men appeared to be destined to become the best of friends. . . ." A transitional motif, on the other hand, signals to the reader to hold his expectations about the significance of the events contained in it in abeyance until some terminating motif has been provided: "While the king was journeying to Westminster, he was informed by his advisers that his enemies awaited him there, and that the prospects of a settlement advantageous to the crown were meager." A terminating motif indicates the apparent end or resolution of a process or situation of tension: "On April 6, 1333, the Battle of Balybourne was fought. The forces of the king were victorious, the rebels routed. The resulting Treaty of Howth Castle, June 7, 1333, brought peace to the realm—though it was to be an uneasy peace, consumed in the flames of religious strife seven years later." When a given set of events has been motifically encoded, the reader has been provided with a story; the chronicle of events has been transformed into a *completed* diachronic process, about which one can then ask questions as if he were dealing with a *synchronic structure* of relationships.[5]

Historical *stories* trace the sequences of events that lead from inaugurations to (provisional) terminations of social and cultural processes in a way that *chronicles* are not required to do. Chronicles are, strictly speaking, openended. In principle they have no *inaugurations*; they simply "begin" when the chronicler starts recording events. And they have no culminations or resolutions; they can go on indefinitely. Stories, however, have a discernible form (even when that form is an image of a state of chaos) which marks off the events contained in them from the other events that might appear in a comprehensive chronicle of the years covered in their unfoldings.

It is sometimes said that the aim of the historian is to explain the past by "finding," "identifying," or "uncovering" the "stories" that lie buried in chronicles; and that the difference between "history" and "fiction" resides in the fact that the historian "finds" his stories, whereas the fiction writer "invents" his. This conception of the historian's task, however, obscures the

---

[5] The distinctions among chronicle, story, and plot which I have tried to develop in this section may have more value for the analysis of historical works than for the study of literary fictions. Unlike literary fictions, such as the novel, historical works are made up of events that exist outside the consciousness of the writer. The events reported in a novel can be invented in a way that they cannot be (or are not supposed to be) in a history. This makes it difficult to distinguish between the chronicle of events and the story being told in a literary fiction. In a sense, the "story" being told in a novel such as Mann's *Buddenbrooks* is indistinguishable from the "chronicle" of events reported in the work, even though we can distinguish between the "chronicle-story" and the "plot" (which is that of an Ironic Tragedy). Unlike the novelist, the historian confronts a veritable chaos of events *already constituted*, out of which he must choose the elements of the story he would tell. He makes his story by including some events and excluding others, by stressing some and subordinating others. This process of exclusion, stress, and subordination is carried out in the interest of constituting *a story of a particular kind*. That is to say, he "emplots" his story. On the distinction between story and plot, see the essays by Shklovsky, Eichenbaum, and Tomachevsky, representatives of the Russian School of Formalism, in *Russian Formalist Criticism: Four Essays*, ed. Lee T. Lemon and Marion J. Reis (Lincoln, Neb., 1965); and Frye, *Anatomy*, pp. 52–53, 78–84.

extent to which "invention" also plays a part in the historian's operations. The same event can serve as a different kind of element of many different historical stories, depending on the role it is assigned in a specific motific characterization of the set to which it belongs. The death of the king may be a beginning, an ending, or simply a transitional event in three different stories. In the chronicle, this event is simply "there" as an element of a series; it does not "function" as a story element. The historian arranges the events in the chronicle into a hierarchy of significance by assigning events different functions as story elements in such a way as to disclose the formal coherence of a whole set of events considered as a comprehensible process with a discernible beginning, middle, and end.

The arrangement of selected events of the chronicle into a story raises the kinds of questions the historian must anticipate and answer in the course of constructing his narrative. These questions are of the sort: "What happened next?" "How did that happen?" "Why did things happen this way rather than that?" "How did it all come out in the end?" These questions determine the narrative tactics the historian must use in the construction of his story. But such questions about the connections between events which make of them elements in a *followable* story should be distinguished from questions of another sort: "What does it all add up to?" "What is the point of it all?" These questions have to do with the structure of the *entire set of events* considered as a *completed* story and call for a synoptic judgment of the relationship between a given story and other stories that might be "found," "identified," or "uncovered" in the chronicle. They can be answered in a number of ways. I call these ways (1) explanation by emplotment, (2) explanation by argument, and (3) explanation by ideological implication.

ᴈ§ Explanation by Emplotment

Providing the "meaning" of a story by identifying the *kind of story* that has been told is called explanation by emplotment. If, in the course of narrating his story, the historian provides it with the plot structure of a Tragedy, he has "explained" it in one way; if he has structured it as a Comedy, he has "explained" it in another way. Emplotment is the way by which a sequence of events fashioned into a story is gradually revealed to be a story of a particular kind.

Following the line indicated by Northrop Frye in his *Anatomy of Criticism*, I identify at least four different modes of emplotment: Romance, Tragedy, Comedy, and Satire. There may be others, such as the Epic, and a given historical account is likely to contain stories cast in one mode as aspects or phases of the whole set of stories emplotted in another mode. But a given historian is forced to emplot the whole set of stories making up his narrative in one comprehensive or *archetypal* story form. For example, Michelet cast all of his histories in the Romantic mode, Ranke cast his in the Comic mode, Tocqueville used the Tragic mode, and Burckhardt used Satire. The Epic plot structure would appear to be the implicit form of chronicle itself. The important point is that every history, even the most "synchronic" or "structural" of them, will be emplotted in some way. The Satirical mode provided the formal principles by which the supposedly "non-narrative" historiography of Burckhardt can be identified as a "story" of a particular sort. For, as Frye has shown, stories cast in the Ironic mode, of which Satire is the fictional form, gain their effects precisely by frustrating normal expectations about the kinds of resolutions provided by stories cast in other modes (Romance, Comedy, or Tragedy, as the case may be).[6]

The Romance is fundamentally a drama of self-identification symbolized by the hero's transcendence of the world of experience, his victory over it, and his final liberation from it—the sort of drama associated with the Grail

[6] I am aware that, by using Frye's terminology and classification of plot structures, I throw myself open to criticism by those literary theorists who either oppose his taxonomic efforts or have their own taxonomies to offer in place of his. I do not wish to suggest that Frye's categories are the sole possible ones for classifying genres, modes, *mythoi*, and the like, in literature; but I have found them especially useful for the analysis of historical works. The principal criticism of Frye's literary theory seems to be that, while his method of analysis works well enough on second-order literary genres, such as the fairy tale or the detective story, it is too rigid and abstract to do justice to such richly textured and multi-leveled works as *King Lear*, *The Remembrance of Things Past*, or even *Paradise Lost*. This may be true; it probably is. But Frye's analysis of the principal forms of mythic and fabulous literature serves very well for the explication of the simple forms of emplotment met with in such "restricted" art forms as historiography. Historical "stories" tend to fall into the categories elaborated by Frye precisely because the historian is inclined to resist construction of the complex peripeteias which are the novelist's and dramatist's stock in trade. Precisely because the historian is not (or claims not to be) telling the story "for its own sake," he is inclined to emplot his stories in the most conventional forms—as fairy tale or detective story on the one hand, as Romance, Comedy, Tragedy, or Satire on the other.

It may be recalled that the normally educated historian of the nineteenth century would have been raised on a staple of classical and Christian literature. The *mythoi* contained in this literature would have provided him with a fund of story forms on which he could have drawn for narrative purposes. It would be a mistake, however, to assume that even as subtle a historian as Tocqueville would be able to shape these story forms to the kinds of purposes that a great poet, such as Racine or Shakespeare, would conceive. When historians like Burckhardt, Marx, Michelet, and Ranke spoke of "Tragedy" or "Comedy," they usually had a very simple notion of what these terms signify. It was different with Hegel, Nietzsche, and (to a lesser extent) Croce. As aestheticians, these three philosophers had a much more complex conception of genre, and wrote much more complex histories as a result. Historians in general, however critical they are of their sources, tend to be naive storytellers. For Frye's characterization of the basic plot structures, see *Anatomy*, pp. 158–238. On Frye, see Geoffrey Hartman, "Ghostlier Demarcations: The Sweet Science of Northrop Frye," in *Beyond Formalism: Literary Essays, 1958–1970* (New Haven and London, 1971), pp. 24–41.

legend or the story of the resurrection of Christ in Christian mythology. It is a drama of the triumph of good over evil, of virtue over vice, of light over darkness, and of the ultimate transcendence of man over the world in which he was imprisoned by the Fall. The archetypal theme of Satire is the precise opposite of this Romantic drama of redemption; it is, in fact, a drama of diremption, a drama dominated by the apprehension that man is ultimately a captive of the world rather than its master, and by the recognition that, in the final analysis, human consciousness and will are always inadequate to the task of overcoming definitively the dark force of death, which is man's unremitting enemy.

Comedy and Tragedy, however, suggest the possibility of at least partial liberation from the condition of the Fall and provisional release from the divided state in which men find themselves in this world. But these provisional victories are conceived differently in the mythic archetypes of which the plot structures of Comedy and Tragedy are sublimated forms. In Comedy, hope is held out for the temporary triumph of man over his world by the prospect of occasional *reconciliations* of the forces at play in the social and natural worlds. Such reconciliations are symbolized in the festive occasions which the Comic writer traditionally uses to terminate his dramatic accounts of change and transformation. In Tragedy, there are no festive occasions, except false or illusory ones; rather, there are intimations of states of division among men more terrible than that which incited the tragic agon at the beginning of the drama. Still, the fall of the protagonist and the shaking of the world he inhabits which occur at the end of the Tragic play are not regarded as totally threatening to those who survive the agonic test. There has been a gain in consciousness for the spectators of the contest. And this gain is thought to consist in the epiphany of the law governing human existence which the protagonist's exertions against the world have brought to pass.

The reconciliations which occur at the end of Comedy are reconciliations of men with men, of men with their world and their society; the condition of society is represented as being purer, saner, and healthier as a result of the conflict among seemingly inalterably opposed elements in the world; these elements are revealed to be, in the long run, harmonizable with one another, unified, at one with themselves and the others. The reconciliations that occur at the end of Tragedy are much more somber; they are more in the nature of resignations of men to the conditions under which they must labor in the world. These conditions, in turn, are asserted to be inalterable and eternal, and the implication is that man cannot change them but must work within them. They set the limits on what may be aspired to and what may be legitimately aimed at in the quest for security and sanity in the world.

Romance and Satire would appear to be *mutually exclusive* ways of emplotting the processes of reality. The very notion of a Romantic Satire represents a contradiction in terms. I can legitimately imagine a Satirical

Romance, but what I would mean by that term would be a form of representation intended to expose, from an Ironic standpoint, the fatuity of a Romantic conception of the world. On the other hand, however, I *can* speak of a Comic Satire and a Satirical Comedy, or of a Satirical Tragedy and a Tragic Satire. But here it should be noted that the relation between the genre (Tragedy or Comedy) and the mode in which it is cast (Satirical) is different from that which obtains between the genre of Romance and the modes (Comic and Tragic) in which it may be cast. Comedy and Tragedy represent *qualifications* of the Romantic apprehension of the world, considered as a process, in the interest of taking seriously the forces which *oppose* the effort at human redemption naively held up as a possibility for mankind in Romance. Comedy and Tragedy take conflict seriously, even if the former eventuates in a vision of the ultimate *reconciliation* of opposed forces and the latter in a *revelation* of the nature of the forces opposing man on the other. And it is possible for the Romantic writer to assimilate the truths of human existence revealed in Comedy and Tragedy respectively within the structure of the drama of redemption which he figures in his vision of the ultimate victory of man over the world of experience.

But Satire represents a different kind of qualification of the hopes, possibilities, and truths of human existence revealed in Romance, Comedy, and Tragedy respectively. It views these hopes, possibilities, and truths Ironically, in the atmosphere generated by the apprehension of the ultimate inadequacy of consciousness to live in the world happily or to comprehend it fully. Satire presupposes the *ultimate inadequacy* of the visions of the world dramatically represented in the genres of Romance, Comedy, and Tragedy alike. As a phase in the evolution of an artistic style or literary tradition, the advent of the Satirical mode of representation signals a conviction that the world has grown old. Like philosophy itself, Satire "paints its gray on gray" in the awareness of its *own* inadequacy as an image of reality. It therefore prepares consciousness for its repudiation of all sophisticated conceptualizations of the world and anticipates a return to a mythic apprehension of the world and its processes.

These four archetypal story forms provide us with a means of characterizing the different kinds of explanatory affects a historian can strive for on the level of narrative emplotment. And it allows us to distinguish between *diachronic*, or processionary, narratives of the sort produced by Michelet and Ranke and the *synchronic*, or static, narratives written by Tocqueville and Burckhardt. In the former, the sense of structural transformation is uppermost as the principal guiding representation. In the latter, the sense of structural continuity (especially in Tocqueville) or stasis (in Burckhardt) predominates. But the distinction between a synchronic and diachronic representation of historical reality should not be taken as indicating mutually exclusive ways of emplotting the historical field. This distinction points merely to a difference of emphasis in treating the relationship between continuity and change in a given representation of the historical process as a whole.

Tragedy and Satire are modes of emplotment which are consonant with the interest of those historians who perceive behind or within the welter of events contained in the chronicle an ongoing structure of relationships or an eternal return of the Same in the Different. Romance and Comedy stress the emergence of new forces or conditions out of processes that appear at first glance either to be changeless in their essence or to be changing only in their phenomenal forms. But each of these archetypal plot structures has its implication for the cognitive operations by which the historian seeks to "explain" what was "really happening" during the process of which it provides an image of its true form.

✌§ Explanation by Formal Argument

In addition to the level of conceptualization on which the historian emplots his narrative account of "what happened," there is another level on which he may seek to explicate "the point of it all" or "what it all adds up to" in the end. On this level I can discern an operation which I call explanation by formal, explicit, or discursive argument. Such an argument provides an explanation of what happens in the story by invoking principles of combination which serve as putative laws of historical explanation. On this level of conceptualization, the historian explains the events in the story (or the form of the events which he has imposed upon them through his emplotment of them in a particular mode) by construction of a nomological-deductive argument. This argument can be analyzed into a syllogism, the major premise of which consists of some putatively universal law of causal relationships, the minor premise of the boundary conditions within which the law is applied, and a conclusion in which the events that actually occurred are deduced from the premises by logical necessity. The most famous of such putative laws is probably Marx's so-called law of the relationship between the Superstructure and the Base. This law states that, whenever there is any transformation in the Base (comprised of the means of production and the modes of relationship among them), there will be a transformation in the components of the Superstructure (social and cultural institutions), but that the reverse relationship does not obtain (e.g., changes in consciousness do *not* effect changes in the Base). Other instances of such putative laws (such as "Bad money drives out good," or even such banal observations as "What goes up must come down") are usually at least tacitly invoked during the course of the historian's efforts to explain such a phenomenon as, say, the Great Depression or the Fall of the Roman Empire. The commonsensical or conventional nature of these latter generalizations does not affect their status as the presumed major premises of nomological-deductive arguments by which explanations of events given in the story are provided. The nature of the generalizations only points to the protoscientific character of historical explanation in general, or the inadequacy of the social sciences from which such generalizations, appearing in an appropriately modified and more rigorously stated form, might be borrowed.

The important point is that, insofar as a historian offers explanations by which the configurations of events in his narrative are explained in something like a nomological-deductive argument, such explanations must be distinguished from the explanatory affect gained by his *emplotment* of his story as *a story of a particular kind*. This is not because one might not treat emplotment as a kind of explanation by nomological-deductive means. In fact, a Tragic emplotment might be treated as an application of the laws that govern human nature and societies in certain kinds of situations; and, insofar as such situations have been established as existing at a certain time and place, those situations might be considered to have been explained by the invocation of the principles alluded to, in the same way that natural events are explained by identification of the universal causal laws that are presumed to govern their relationships.

I might want to say that, insofar as a historian provides the "plot" by which the events in the story he tells are given some kind of formal coherence, he is doing the same kind of thing a scientist does when he identifies the elements of the nomological-deductive argument in which his explanation has to be cast. But I distinguish here between the emplotment of the events of a history considered as elements of a story and the characterization of those events as elements in a matrix of causal relationships presumed to have existed in specific provinces of time and space. In short, I am for the moment taking at face value the historian's claim to be doing *both* art and science and the distinction usually drawn between the historian's *investigative operations* on the one hand and his *narrative operation* on the other. We grant that it is one thing to represent "what happened" and "why it happened as it did," and quite another to provide a verbal model, in the form of a narrative, by which to explain the *process of development* leading from one situation to some other situation by appeal to general laws of causation.

But history differs from the sciences precisely because historians disagree, not only over what are the laws of social causation that they might invoke to explain a given sequence of events, but also over the question of the form that a "scientific" explanation ought to take. There is a long history of dispute over whether natural scientific and historical explanations must have the same formal characteristics. This dispute turns on the problem of whether the kinds of laws that might be invoked in scientific explanations have their counterparts in the realm of the so-called human or spiritual sciences, such as sociology and history. The physical sciences appear to progress by virtue of the agreements, reached from time to time among members of the established communities of scientists, regarding what will count as a scientific problem, the form that a scientific explanation must take, and the kinds of data that will be permitted to count as evidence in a properly scientific account of reality. Among historians no such agreement exists, or ever has existed. This may merely reflect the protoscientific nature of the historiographical enterprise, but it is important to bear in mind this congenital disagreement (or lack of agreement) over what counts as a specifically historical explanation of any given set of historical phenomena. For this means that historical explanations are bound to be based on different metahistorical presuppositions about the nature of the historical field, presuppositions that generate different conceptions of the *kind of explanations* that can be used in historiographical analysis.

Historiographical disputes on the level of "interpretation" are in reality disputes over the "true" nature of the historian's enterprise. History remains in the state of conceptual anarchy in which the natural sciences existed during the sixteenth century, when there were as many different conceptions of "the scientific enterprise" as there were metaphysical positions. In the sixteenth century, the different conceptions of what "science" ought to be ultimately reflected different conceptions of "reality" and the different epistemologies generated by them. So, too, disputes over what "history" ought to be reflect similarly varied conceptions of what a proper historical explanation ought to consist of and different conceptions, therefore, of the historian's task.

Needless to say, I am not speaking here of the kinds of disputes which arise on the reviewers' pages of the professional journals, in which the erudition or precision of a given historian may be questioned. I am speaking about the kinds of questions which arise when two or more scholars, of roughly equal erudition and theoretical sophistication, come to alternative, though not necessarily mutually exclusive, interpretations of the same set of historical events, or to different answers to such questions as "What is the true nature of the Renaissance?" What are involved here, on at least one level of conceptualization, are different notions of the nature of historical reality and of the appropriate form that a historical account, considered as a formal argument, ought to take. Following the analysis of Stephen C. Pepper in his *World Hypotheses*, I have differentiated four paradigms of the form that a historical explanation, considered as a discursive argument, may be conceived to take: Formist, Organicist, Mechanistic, and Contextualist.[7]

The Formist theory of truth aims at the identification of the unique

[7] The remarks made with respect to Frye in note 6 apply, *mutatis mutandi*, to Pepper's notion of the basic forms of philosophical reflection. Certainly the greatest philosophers— Plato, Aristotle, Descartes, Hume, Kant, Hegel, Mill—resist reduction to the archetypes provided by Pepper. If anything, their thought represents a mediation between two or more of the kinds of doctrinaire positions which Pepper outlines. Pepper's ideal types do, however, provide a very convenient classification of the more simplistic philosophical systems

characteristics of objects inhabiting the historical field. Accordingly, the Formist considers an explanation to be complete when a given set of objects has been properly identified, its class, generic, and specific attributes assigned, and labels attesting to its particularity attached to it. The objects alluded to may be either individualities or collectivities, particulars or universals, concrete entities or abstractions. As thus envisaged, the task of historical explanation is to dispel the apprehension of those similarities that appear to be shared by all objects in the field. When the historian has established the uniqueness of the particular objects in the field or the variety of the types of phenomena which the field manifests, he has provided a Formist explanation of the field as such.

The Formist mode of explanation is to be found in Herder, Carlyle, Michelet, in the Romantic historians and the great historical narrators, such as Niebuhr, Mommsen, and Trevelyan—in any historiography in which the depiction of the variety, color, and vividness of the historical field is taken as the central aim of the historian's work. To be sure, a Formist historian may be inclined to make generalizations about the nature of the historical process as a whole, as in Carlyle's characterization of it as "the essence of innumerable biographies." But, in Formist conceptions of historical explanation, the uniqueness of the different agents, agencies, and acts which make up the "events" to be explained is central to one's inquiries, not the "ground" or "scene" against which these entities arise.[8]

---

or world views, the kind of general conception of reality which we find in historians *when they speak as philosophers*—that is to say, when they invoke some general notion of being, appeal to some general theory of truth and verification, draw ethical implication from truths putatively established, and so on. Most historians seldom rise above the level of philosophical sophistication represented by, say, Edmund Burke. The great Whig certainly had a world view, though hardly what would be recognized as a "philosophy." So, too, do most historians, Tocqueville not excepted. By contrast, the greatest philosophers of history tend to work out a philosophy as well as elaborate a world view. In this sense they are more "cognitively responsible" than the historians, who for the most part simply *assume* a world view and treat it as if it were a cognitively responsible philosophical position. On the basic "world hypotheses," see Stephen C. Pepper, *World Hypotheses: A Study in Evidence* (Berkeley and Los Angeles, 1966), pt. 2, pp. 141ff.

[8] I have found Kenneth Burke's critical terminology most helpful in my attempts to characterize what I have called the "historical field" prior to its analysis and representation by the historian. Burke maintains that all literary representations of reality can be analyzed in terms of a pentad of hypothesized "grammatical" elements: scene, agent, act, agency, and purpose. The way these elements are characterized and the relative weights given to them as causal forces in the "drama" in which they figure reveal the world view implicit in every representation of reality. For example, a Materialistic writer will be inclined to stress the element of "scene" (the milieu, however conceived) over the elements of "agent," "act," "agency," and "purpose" in such a way as to make the latter set little more than epiphenomena of the former power. By contrast, an Idealist writer will be inclined to see "purpose" everywhere, and will turn "scene" itself into little more than an illusion. See Burke, *A Grammar of Motives*, pp. 3–20, for a general discussion.

While helpful as a device for characterizing a historian's conception of the unprocessed

To use Pepper's terms, Formism is essentially "dispersive" in the analytical operations it carries out on the data, rather than "integrative," as both Organicist and Mechanistic explanations tend to be. Thus, although a Formist explanatory strategy tends to be wide in "scope"—ample in the kinds of particulars it identifies as occupying the historical field—its generalizations about the processes discerned in the field will be inclined to lack conceptual "precision." Romantic historians, and, indeed, "narrative historians" in general, are inclined to construct generalizations about the whole historical field and the meaning of its processes that are so extensive that they bear very little weight as propositions that can be confirmed or disconfirmed by appeal to empirical data. But such historians usually make up for the vacuity of their generalizations by the vividness of their reconstructions of particular agents, agencies, and acts represented in their narratives.

Organicist world hypotheses and their corresponding theories of truth and argument are relatively more "integrative" and hence more reductive in their operations. The Organicist attempts to depict the particulars discerned in the historical field as components of synthetic processes. At the heart of the Organicist strategy is a metaphysical commitment to the paradigm of the microcosmic-macrocosmic relationship; and the Organicist historian will tend to be governed by the desire to see individual entities as components of processes which aggregate into wholes that are greater than, or qualitatively different from, the sum of their parts. Historians who work within this strategy of explanation, such as Ranke and most of the "nationalistic" historians of the middle decades of the nineteenth century (von Sybel, Mommsen, Treitschke, Stubbs, Maitland, etc.), tend to structure their narratives in such a way as to depict the consolidation or crystallization, out of a set of apparently dispersed events, of some integrated entity whose importance is greater than that of any of the individual entities analyzed or described in the course of the narrative.

Idealists in general, and dialectical thinkers such as Hegel specifically,

---

"historical field," Burke's theories are less so for characterizing what the historian might make of the field once it has been "grammatically" encoded. His *Rhetoric of Motives* (Berkeley and Los Angeles, 1965), which is meant to probe the moral dimensions of literary representation, and his *Language as Symbolic Action* (Berkeley and Los Angeles, 1968), which is meant to provide a secularized version of the medieval "anagogical" level of meaning and signification, are disappointingly conventional. Burke is certainly right in holding that all literary representations of reality, however "realistic," are in the last analysis allegorical. But, when he goes on to classify the *kinds* of allegories which might be present within them, he offers little more than a pastiche of Marxist, Freudian, and anthropological symbologies, which are themselves only allegorical representations of the "reality" they purport simply to analyze. Considered as allegories, histories appear to lend themselves to analysis by the methods advanced by Frye. Considered as a form of cognitively responsible discourse, a history seems to be characterizable in Pepper's terminology. And, considered as moral tracts, they seem to be accurately describable in the terms provided by Mannheim's brand of sociology of knowledge, on which see note 11 below.

represent this approach to the problem of explaining the processes discerned in the historical field.

To be sure, as Pepper notes, historians working in this mode will be more interested in characterizing the integrative process than in depicting its individual elements. This is what gives to the historical arguments cast in this mode their "abstract" quality. Moreover, history written in this mode tends to be oriented toward the determination of the *end* or *goal* toward which all the processes found in the historical field are presumed to be tending. A historian such as Ranke, of course, will consciously resist the inclination to specify what the *telos* of the whole historical process might be, and content himself with the effort to determine the nature of certain provisional *teloi*, intermediary integrative structures such as the "folk," the "nation," or the "culture," which he purports to discern in the ongoing historical process. The determination of the *final end* of the whole historical process can be glimpsed, Ranke maintains, only in a religious vision. And therefore Ranke's work may be taken to be an example of a historiography composed in a specifically Formist mode. But, although Ranke excels at the depiction of events in their particularity, his narratives are given their structure and formal coherence as *explanations* of the processes he depicts primarily by their tacit appeal to the Organicist model of what an appropriate historical explanation ought to be, a model embedded within his consciousness as the paradigm of what *any* valid explanation of any process in the world ought to be.

It is a characteristic of Organicist strategies of explanation to eschew the search for the *laws* of historical process, when the term "laws" is construed in the sense of universal and invariant causal relationships, after the manner of Newtonian physics, Lavoisierian chemistry, or Darwinian biology. The Organicist is inclined to talk about the "principles" or "ideas" that inform the individual processes discerned in the field and all the processes taken as a whole. These principles or ideas are seen as imaging or prefiguring the end toward which the process as a whole tends. They do not function as causal agents or agencies, except in historians with a decidedly mystical or theological orientation, in which case they are usually interpreted as manifestations of God's purpose for His creation. In fact, for the Organicist, such principles and ideas function not as restrictions on the human capacity to realize a distinctively human goal in history, as the "laws" of history can be supposed to do in the thought of the Mechanist, but as guarantors of an essential human freedom. Thus, although the Organicist makes sense out of the historical process by displaying the integrative nature of the historical process taken as a whole, he does not draw the kinds of pessimistic conclusions that the strict Mechanist is inclined to draw from his reflections on the nomological nature of historical being.

Mechanistic world hypotheses are similarly integrative in their aim, but they are inclined to be reductive rather than synthetic. To put the matter in Kenneth Burke's terms, Mechanism is inclined to view the "acts" of the "agents" inhabiting the historical field as manifestations of extrahistorical "agencies" that have their origins in the "scene" within which the "action" depicted in the narrative unfolds. The Mechanistic theory of explanation turns upon the search for the causal laws that determine the outcomes of processes discovered in the historical field. The objects that are thought to inhabit the historical field are construed as existing in the modality of part-part relationships, the specific configurations of which are determined by the laws that are presumed to govern their interactions. Thus, a Mechanist such as Buckle, Taine, Marx, or, as I will indicate, even Tocqueville, *studies* history in order to divine the laws that actually govern its operations and *writes* history in order to display in a narrative form the effects of those laws.

The apprehension of the laws that govern history and the determination of their specific nature may be more or less prominent in the representation of "what was happening" in the historical process at a given time and place; but, insofar as the Mechanist's inquiries are carried out in the search for such laws, his account is threatened by the same tendency toward *abstraction* as that of the Organicist. He considers individual entities to be less important as evidence than the classes of phenomena to which they can be shown to belong; but these classes in turn are less important to him than the laws their regularities are presumed to manifest. Ultimately, for the Mechanist, an explanation is considered complete only when he has discovered the laws that are presumed to govern history in the same way that the laws of physics are presumed to govern nature. He then applies these laws to the data in such a way as to make their configurations understandable as functions of those laws. Thus, in a historian such as Tocqueville, the particular attributes of a given institution, custom, law, art form, or the like, are less important as *evidence* than the species, class, and generic typifications which, on analysis, they can be shown to exemplify. And these typifications in turn are regarded by Tocqueville—indeed, by Buckle, Marx, and Taine—as less important than the laws of social structure and process which govern the course of Western history, to whose operations they attest.

Obviously, although they are characterized by conceptual precision, Mechanistic conceptions of truth and explanation are thrown open to the charges of lack of scope and tendency toward abstraction in the same way that their Organicist counterparts are. From a Formist point of view, both Mechanism and Organicism appear to be "reductive" of the variety and color of the individual entities in the historical field. But, in order to restore the desired scope and concreteness, one need not take refuge in so "impressionistic" a conception of historical explanation as that represented by Formism. Rather, one can embrace a *Contextualist* position, which as a theory of truth and explanation represents a "functional" conception of the meaning or significance of events discerned in the historical field.

The informing presupposition of Contextualism is that events can be explained by being set within the "context" of their occurrence. Why they occurred as they did is to be explained by the revelation of the specific relationships they bore to other events occurring in their circumambient historical space. Here, as in Formism, the historical field is apprehended as a "spectacle" or richly textured arras web which on first glance appears to lack coherence and any discernible fundamental structure. But, unlike the Formist, who is inclined simply to consider entities in their particularity and uniqueness—i.e., their similarity to, and difference from, other entities in the field—the Contextualist insists that "what happened" in the field can be accounted for by the specification of the functional interrelationships existing among the agents and agencies occupying the field at a given time.

The determination of this functional interrelationship is carried out by an operation that some modern philosophers, such as W. H. Walsh and Isaiah Berlin, have called "colligation."[9] In this operation the aim of explanation is to identify the "threads" that link the individual or institution under study to its specious sociocultural "present." Examples of this kind of explanatory strategy can be found in any historian worthy of the name, from Herodotus to Huizinga, but it finds expression as a dominant principle of explanation in the nineteenth century in the work of Jacob Burckhardt. As a strategy of explanation, Contextualism seeks to avoid both the radically dispersive tendency of Formism and the abstractive tendencies of Organicism and Mechanism. It strives instead for a *relative integration* of the phenomena discerned in finite provinces of historical occurrence in terms of "trends" or general physiognomies of periods and epochs. Insofar as it tacitly invokes rules of combination for determining the family characteristics of entities occupying finite provinces of historical occurrence, these rules are not construed as equivalent to the universal laws of cause and effect postulated by the Mechanist or the general teleological principles postulated by the Organicist. Rather, they are construed as actual relationships that are presumed to have existed at specific times and places, the first, final, and material causes of which can never be known.

The Contextualist proceeds, Pepper tells us, by isolating some (indeed, *any*) element of the historical field as the subject of study, whether the element be as large as "the French Revolution" or as small as one day in the life of a specific person. He then proceeds to pick out the "threads" that link the event to be explained to different areas of the context. The threads are identified and traced outward, into the circumambient natural and social space within which the event occurred, and both backward in time, in order to determine the "origins" of the event, and forward in time, in order to determine its "impact" and "influence" on subsequent events. This tracing

[9] See W. H. Walsh, *Introduction to the Philosophy of History* (London, 1961), pp. 60–65; Isaiah Berlin, "The Concept of Scientific History," in *Philosophical Analysis and History*, ed. Dray, pp. 40–51. On "colligation" in general, see the remarks of Mink, "Autonomy," pp. 171–72.

operation ends at the point at which the "threads" either disappear into the "context" of some other "event" or "converge" to cause the occurrence of some new "event." The impulse is not to integrate all the events and trends that might be identified in the whole historical field, but rather to link them together in a chain of provisional and restricted characterizations of finite provinces of manifestly "significant" occurrence.

It should be obvious that the Contextualist approach to the problem of historical explanation can be regarded as a *combination* of the dispersive impulses behind Formism on the one hand and the integrative impulses behind Organicism on the other. But, in fact, a Contextualist conception of truth, explanation, and verification appears to be surpassingly modest in what it asks of the historian and demands of the reader. Yet, by virtue of its organization of the historical field into different provinces of significant occurrence, on the basis of which periods and epochs can be distinguished from one another, Contextualism represents an ambiguous solution to the problem of constructing a narrative model of the *processes* discerned in the historical field. The "flow" of historical time is envisaged by the Contextualist as a wavelike motion (this is explicitly indicated by Burckhardt) in which certain phases or culminations are considered to be intrinsically more significant than others. The operation of tracing threads of occurrences in such a way as to permit the discernment of trends in the process suggests the possibility of a narrative in which the images of development and evolution might predominate. But, actually, Contextualist explanatory strategies incline more toward synchronic representations of segments or sections of the process, cuts made across the grain of time as it were. This tendency toward the structuralist or synchronic mode of representation is inherent in a Contextualist world hypothesis. And, if the historian who is inclined toward Contextualism would aggregate the various periods he has studied into a comprehensive view of the whole historical process, he must move outside the Contextualist framework—toward either a Mechanistic reduction of the data in terms of the "timeless" laws that are presumed to govern them or an Organicist synthesis of those data in terms of the "principles" that are presumed to reveal the *telos* toward which the whole process is tending over the long haul.

Now, any of these four models of explanation might be used in a historical work to provide something like a formal argument of the true meaning of the events depicted in the narrative, but they have not enjoyed equal authority among the recognized professional practitioners of the discipline since its academicization in the early nineteenth century. In fact, among academic historians the Formist and Contextualist models have tended to prevail as the main candidates for orthodoxy. Whenever Organicist or Mechanistic tendencies have appeared in recognized masters of the craft, as in Ranke and Tocqueville respectively, these tendencies have been regarded as unfortunate lapses from the proper forms that explanations in history may take. Moreover, when the impulse to explain the historical field in overtly Organicist and Mechanistic terms has come to predominate in a given thinker, such as Hegel on the one hand and Marx on the other, this impulse has been interpreted as the reason for their fall into the nefarious "philosophy of history."

In short, for professional historians, Formism and Contextualism have represented the limits of choice among the possible forms that an explanation of a peculiarly "historical" sort may take. By contrast, Mechanism and Organicism have represented heterodoxies of historical thought, in the opinion of both the main line of professional historians and that of their defenders among philosophers who regard "philosophy of history" as myth, error, or ideology. For example, Karl Popper's influential *The Poverty of Historicism* consists of little more than a sustained indictment of these two modes of explanation in historical thought.[10]

But the grounds for professional historians' hostility to Organicist and Mechanistic modes of explanation remain obscure. Or, rather, the reasons for this hostility would appear to lie in considerations of a specifically extra-epistemological sort. For, given the protoscientific nature of historical studies, there are no apodictic epistemological grounds for the preference of one mode of explanation over another.

It has been argued, of course, that history can be liberated from myth, religion, and metaphysics only by the exclusion of Organicist and Mechanistic modes of explanation from its operations. Admittedly, history cannot thereby be elevated into a rigorous "science," but the contention is that it can at least avoid the dangers of "scientism"—the duplicitous aping of scientific method and illegitimate appropriation of science's authority—by this exclusion. For, by limiting itself to explanation in the modes of Formism and Contextualism, historiography would at least remain "empirical" and resist the fall into the kind of "philosophy of history" practiced by Hegel and Marx.

But, precisely because history is *not* a rigorous science, this hostility toward the Organicist and Mechanistic modes of explanation appears to express only a bias on the part of the professional establishment. If it is granted that Organicism and Mechanism do give insights into any process in the natural and social worlds that cannot be achieved by Formist and Contextualist strategies, then the exclusion of Organicism and Mechanism from the canon of orthodox historical explanations must be based on extra-epistemological considerations. Commitment to the dispersive techniques of Formism and Contextualism reflects only a *decision* on the part of historians not to attempt the kind of integrations of data that Organicism and Mechanism sanction as a matter of course. This decision, in turn, would appear to rest on precritically held opinions about the *form* that a science of man and society

10 Karl R. Popper, *The Poverty of Historicism* (London, 1961), pp. 5–55.

has to *take*. And these opinions, in turn, would seem to be generally ethical, and specifically ideological, in nature.

It is often contended, especially by Radicals, that the professional historian's preference for Contextualist and Formist explanatory strategies is ideologically motivated. For example, Marxists claim that it is in the interests of established social groups to reject Mechanistic modes of historical explanation because the disclosure of the actual laws of historical structure and process would reveal the true nature of the power enjoyed by dominant classes and provide the knowledge necessary to dislodge those classes from their positions of privilege and power. It is in the interest of dominant groups, Radicals maintain, to cultivate a conception of history in which only individual events and their relations to their immediate contexts can be known, or in which, at best, the arrangement of the facts into loose typifications is permitted, because such conceptions of the nature of historical knowledge conform to the "individualist" preconceptions of "Liberals" and the "hierarchical" preconceptions of "Conservatives" respectively.

By contrast, the Radicals' claims to have discovered the "laws" of historical structure and process are regarded by Liberal historians as being similarly motivated ideologically. Such laws, it is maintained, are usually advanced in the interest of promoting some program of social transformation, in either a Radical or a Reactionary direction. This gives to the very search for the laws of historical structure and process a bad odor and renders suspect the scholarship of any historian who claims to be seeking such laws. The same applies to those "principles" by which Idealist philosophers of history purport to explicate the "meaning" of history in its totality. Such "principles," proponents of Contextualist, Formist, and Mechanistic conceptions of explanation insist, are always offered in support of ideological positions that are retrograde or obscurantist in their intentions.

There does, in fact, appear to be an irreducible ideological component in every historical account of reality. That is to say, simply because history is *not* a science, or is at best a protoscience with specifically determinable nonscientific elements in its constitution, the very claim to have discerned some kind of formal coherence in the historical record brings with it theories of the nature of the historical world and of historical knowledge itself which have ideological implications for attempts to understand "the present," however this "present" is defined. To put it another way, the very claim to have distinguished a past from a present world of social thought and praxis, and to have determined the formal coherence of that past world, *implies* a conception of the form that knowledge of the present world also must take, insofar as it is *continuous* with that past world. Commitment to a particular *form* of knowledge predetermines the *kinds* of generalizations one can make about the present world, the kinds of knowledge one can have of it, and hence the kinds of projects one can legitimately conceive for changing that present or for maintaining it in its present form indefinitely.

❧ Explanation by Ideological Implication

The ideological dimensions of a historical account reflect the ethical element in the historian's assumption of a particular position on the question of the nature of historical knowledge and the implications that can be drawn from the study of past events for the understanding of present ones. By the term "ideology" I mean a set of prescriptions for taking a position in the present world of social praxis and acting upon it (either to change the world or to maintain it in its current state); such prescriptions are attended by arguments that claim the authority of "science" or "realism." Following the analysis of Karl Mannheim, in *Ideology and Utopia*, I postulate four basic ideological positions: Anarchism, Conservatism, Radicalism, and Liberalism.[11]

[11] I have simplified Mannheim's classification of the main types of ideologies and the philosophies of history that sustain them. In his essay "Prospects of Scientific Politics," Mannheim lists *five* "representative ideal types" of political consciousness which arose in the nineteenth and twentieth centuries, two of which are species of Conservatism (one "bureauratic," the other "historicist"). I need not make that distinction here, since the "bureaucratic" form can be said to stand over against *all* ideologically inspired efforts at transformation of the social order. I am concerned with the work of intellectuals who seek to transform or sustain the status quo by appeal to specific conceptions of the historical process. As far as I know, no historian or philosopher of history has written in such a way as to promote the attitude of the "bureaucratic Conservative." As I have defined Conservatism, however—that is, as a defense not of an idealized past but of the present social dispensation—"Conservative historicism" as conceived by Mannheim would constitute the natural refuge of the "bureaucratic Conservative." See Mannheim, *Ideology and Utopia: An Introduction to the Sociology of Knowledge* (New York, 1946), pp. 104ff.; and *idem*, "Conservative Thought," in *Essays in Sociology and Social Psychology*, ed. Paul Kecskemeti (New York, 1953), pp. 74–164.

Mannheim also listed "Fascism" among the ideal types of modern political consciousness. I have not used this category, for it would be anachronistic if applied to nineteenth-century thinkers. Instead, I have used the category of "Anarchism," which, in Mannheim's view, is the peculiarly nineteenth-century form that Apocalyptical political thinking takes. It will be recalled that in his essay "The Utopian Mentality" Mannheim listed four ideal types of utopian thinking, each representing a distinctive stage in the evolution of the modern political consciousness. These were Orgiastic Chiliasm (the millenarian tradition represented by the Anabaptists in the sixteenth century), the Liberal-humanitarian idea, the Conservative idea, and the Socialist-Communist utopia. See *Ideology and Utopia*, pp. 190–222. Anarchism was the secularized form that Orgiastic Chiliasm took in the nineteenth century, while Fascism is the form it has taken in the twentieth century. See *ibid.*, p. 233. What makes Anarchism unique in the history of Apocalyptical politics is the fact that, unlike both Chiliasm and Fascism, it seeks to be cognitively responsible—that is to say, it seeks to provide rational justifications for its irrational posture.

In my view, Anarchism is the ideological implication of Romanticism, appeared wherever Romanticism appeared throughout the nineteenth century, and has fed into Fascism in the twentieth century in the same way that Romanticism has. Mannheim tried to link Romanticism with Conservatism in a systematic way when, in reality, in their early nineteenth-century manifestations, they merely happened to be contemporary with each other. The philosophy of history generated by the Romantic *mythos* does not envision that notion of a fully integrated community realizable in historical time which inspires the

There are, of course, other metapolitical positions. Mannheim cites the Apocalypticism of the early modern religious sects, the position of the Reactionary, and that of the Fascist. But these positions are in essence authoritarian in a way that the nineteenth-century forms of the ideologies listed above are not. The Apocalypticist bases his prescriptions for action on the authority of divine revelation, the Reactionary on that of a class or group practice which is seen as an eternally valid system of social organization, and the Fascist on the unquestioned authority of the charismatic leader. And, although spokesmen for these viewpoints may engage in polemics with representatives of other positions, they do not regard it as necessary to establish the authority of their cognitive positions on either rationalist or scientific grounds. Thus, although they may offer specific theories of society and history, these theories are not regarded as being responsible to criticism launched from other positions, to "data" in general, or to control by the logical criteria of consistency and coherence.

The four basic ideological positions identified by Mannheim, however, represent value systems that claim the authority of "reason," "science," or "realism." This claim tacitly commits them to public discussion with other systems that claim a similar authority. It renders them epistemologically self-conscious in a way that the representatives of "authoritarian" systems are not, and it commits them to the effort to make sense out of "data" uncovered by investigators of the social process working from alternative points of view. In short, the nineteenth-century forms of Anarchism, Conservatism, Radicalism, and Liberalism are "cognitively responsible" in a way that their "authoritarian" counterparts are not.[12]

Conservative to hymns of praise to the social status quo. What is unique about Romanticism is its *individualistic* moment, that egoism which inspires belief in the desirability of a perfect Anarchy. This moment may be present in some self-styled Conservative thinkers, but, if they are truly Conservative, it will be there as an ideological ploy, to defend the privileged position of particular groups in the current social dispensation against the demands for programmatic change coming from Radicals, Liberals, or Reactionaries. The Conservative can no more countenance a genuinely Anarchist conception of the world than he can stand a truly Radical conception of it. He defends the status quo by showing it to be the integrated, organic unity that Anarchists and Radicals still dream of achieving.

[12] I got the notion of "cognitive responsibility" from Pepper. He uses it to distinguish between philosophical systems committed to rational defenses of their world hypotheses and those not so committed. Examples of the latter are Mysticism, Animism, and utter Skepticism, all of which, at some point in their arguments, are constrained to fall back on the notions of revelation, authority, or convention. Although specific Mystics, Animists, and Skeptics *might* provide rational justifications of the irrational postures they assume before reality, such justifications are usually set forth as criticisms of the hyper-rationalism of their opponents. The positive content of their doctrines is ultimately indefensible on rational grounds, for they deny the authority of reason itself in the end. See Pepper, *World Hypotheses*, pp. 115–37. The equivalents of such systems in political thinking would be represented by the tradition-bound feudal nobleman; the Reactionary, who denies any worth to either the present or the future; and the Fascist or Nihilist, who rejects both reason and the ideal of consistency in argument with his opponents.

I should stress at this point that the terms "Anarchist," "Conservative," "Radical," and "Liberal" are meant to serve as designators of general ideological preference rather than as emblems of specific political parties. They represent different attitudes with respect to the possibility of reducing the study of society to a science and the desirability of doing so; different notions of the lessons that the human sciences can teach; different conceptions of the desirability of maintaining or changing the social status quo; different conceptions of the direction that changes in the status quo ought to take and the means of effecting such changes; and, finally, different time orientations (an orientation toward past, present, or future as the respository of a paradigm of society's "ideal" form). I should also stress that a given historian's emplotment of the historical process or way of explaining it in a formal argument need not be regarded as a function of his consciously held ideological position. Rather, the form that he gives to his historical account can be said to have ideological implications consonant with one or another of the four positions differentiated above. Just as every ideology is attended by a specific idea of history and its processes, so too, I maintain, is every idea of history attended by specifically determinable ideological implications.

The four ideological positions that concern me can be roughly characterized in the following terms. With respect to the problem of social change, all four recognize its inevitability but represent different views as to both its desirability and the optimum pace of change. Conservatives, of course, are the most suspicious of programmatic transformations of the social status quo, while Liberals, Radicals, and Anarchists are relatively less suspicious of change in general and, correspondingly, are less or more optimistic about the prospects of *rapid* transformations of the social order. As Mannheim notes, Conservatives tend to view social change through the analogy of plantlike gradualizations, while Liberals (at least nineteenth-century Liberals) are inclined to view it through the analogy of adjustments, or "fine tunings," of a mechanism. In both ideologies the fundamental structure of society is conceived to be sound, and some change is seen as inevitable, but change itself is regarded as being most effective when particular parts, rather than *structural relationships*, of the totality are changed. Radicals and Anarchists, however, believe in the necessity of structural transformations, the former in the interest of reconstituting society on new bases, the latter in the interest of abolishing "society" and substituting for it a "community" of individuals held together by a shared sense of their common "humanity."

As for the pace of the changes envisioned, Conservatives insist on a "natural" rhythm, while Liberals favor what might be called the "social" rhythm of the parliamentary debate, or that of the educational process and electoral contests between parties committed to the observance of established laws of governance. By contrast, Radicals and Anarchists envision the possibility of cataclysmic transformations, though the former are inclined to be more aware of the power needed to effect such transformations, more sensitive to the inertial pull of inherited institutions, and therefore more concerned with the provision of the *means* of effecting such changes than are the latter.

This brings us to a consideration of the different time orientations of the various ideologies. According to Mannheim, Conservatives are inclined to imagine historical evolution as a progressive elaboration of the institutional structure that *currently* prevails, which structure they regard as a "utopia"— that is, the best form of society that men can "realistically" hope for, or legitimately aspire to, for the time being. By contrast, Liberals imagine a time in the *future* when this structure will have been improved, but they project this utopian condition into the *remote* future, in such a way as to discourage any effort in the present to realize it precipitately, by "radical" means. Radicals, on the other hand, are inclined to view the utopian condition as *imminent*, which inspires their concern with the provision of the revolutionary means to bring this utopia to pass *now*. Finally, Anarchists are inclined to idealize a *remote past* of natural-human innocence from which men have fallen into the corrupt "social" state in which they currently find themselves. They, in turn, project this utopia onto what is effectively a nontemporal plane, viewing it as a possibility of human achievement *at any time*, if men will only seize control of their own essential humanity, either by an act of will or by an act of consciousness which destroys the socially provided belief in the legitimacy of the current social establishment.

The temporal location of the utopian ideal, on behalf of which the different ideologies labor, permits Mannheim to classify them with respect to their tendency toward "social congruence" on the one hand or "social transcendence" on the other. Conservatism is the most "socially congruent"; Liberalism is relatively so. Anarchism is the most "socially transcendent"; Radicalism is relatively so. Actually, each of the ideologies represents a mixture of elements of social congruence and social transcendence. On this point, their differences from one another are matters more of emphasis than of content. All take the prospect of change seriously. This is what accounts for their shared interest in history and their concern to provide a historical justification for their programs. Similarly, this is what accounts for their willingness to debate with one another, in cognitively responsible terms, such secondary matters as the pace of desirable social change and the means to be used to effect it.

It is the *value* accorded to the current social establishment, however, that accounts for their different conceptions of both the *form* of historical evolution and the *form* that historical knowledge must take. In Mannheim's view, the problem of historical "progress" is construed in different ways by the various ideologies. What is "progress" to one is "decadence" to another, with the "present age" enjoying a different status, as an apex or nadir of development, depending upon the degree of alienation in a given ideology. At the same time, the ideologies honor different paradigms of the form that arguments meant to explain "what happened in history" must take. These different paradigms of explanation reflect the more or less "scientistic" orientations of the different ideologies.

Thus, for example, Radicals share with Liberals a belief in the possibility of studying history "rationally" and "scientifically," but they have different conceptions of what a rational and scientific historiography might consist of. The former seeks the laws of historical structures and processes, the latter the general trends or main drift of development. Like Radicals and Liberals, Conservatives and Anarchists believe, in conformity with a general nineteenth-century conviction, that the "meaning" of history can be discovered and presented in conceptual schemata that are cognitively responsible and not simply authoritarian. But their conception of a distinctively *historical* knowledge requires a faith in "intuition" as the ground on which a putative "science" of history might be constructed. The Anarchist is inclined toward the essentially empathetic techniques of Romanticism in his historical accounts, while the Conservative is inclined to *integrate* his several intuitions of the objects in the historical field into a comprehensive Organicist account of the whole process.

In my view, there are no extra-ideological grounds on which to arbitrate among the conflicting conceptions of the historical process and of historical knowledge appealed to by the different ideologies. For, since these conceptions have their origins in ethical considerations, the assumption of a given epistemological position by which to judge their cognitive adequacy would itself represent only another ethical choice. I cannot claim that one of the conceptions of historical knowledge favored by a given ideology is more "realistic" than the others, for it is precisely over the matter of what constitutes an adequate criterion of "realism" that they disagree. Nor can I claim that one conception of historical knowledge is more "scientific" than another without prejudging the problem of what a specifically *historical* or *social* science ought to be.

To be sure, during the nineteenth century the generally credited conception of science was represented by Mechanism. But social theorists differed from one another over the question of the legitimacy of a Mechanistic science of society and of history. The Formist, Organicist, and Contextualist modes of explanation continued to flourish in the human sciences throughout the nineteenth century because of genuine differences of opinion over the adequacy of Mechanism as a strategy.

I am not concerned, then, with ranking the different conceptions of history produced by the nineteenth century in terms of either their "realism" or their "scienticity." By the same token, my purpose is not to analyze them as *projections* of a given ideological position. I am interested only in indicating how ideological considerations enter into the historian's attempts to explain the historical field and to construct a verbal model of its processes in a narrative. But I will attempt to show that even the works of those historians and philosophers of history whose interests were manifestly nonpolitical, such as Burckhardt and Nietzsche, have specific ideological implications. These works, I maintain, are at least *consonant with* one or another of the ideological positions of the times in which they were written.

I consider the ethical moment of a historical work to be reflected in the mode of ideological implication by which an *aesthetic* perception (the emplotment) and a *cognitive* operation (the argument) can be combined so as to derive prescriptive statements from what may appear to be purely descriptive or analytical ones. A historian may "explain" what happened in the historical field by identifying the law (or laws) governing the set of events emplotted in the story as a drama of essentially Tragic import. Or, conversely, he may find the Tragic import of the story he has emplotted in his discovery of the "law" which governs the sequence of articulation of the plot. In either case, the moral implications of a given historical argument have to be drawn from the relationship which the historian presumes to have existed *within* the set of events under consideration *between* the plot structure of the narrative conceptualization on the one hand and the form of the argument offered as an explicit "scientific" (or "realistic") explanation of the set of events on the other.

A set of events emplotted as a Tragedy may be explained "scientifically" (or "realistically") by appeal to strict laws of causal determination or to putative laws of human freedom, as the case may be. In the former case the implication is that men are indentured to an ineluctable fate by virtue of their participation in history, whereas in the latter case the implication is that they can act in such a way as to control, or at least to affect, their destinies. The ideological thrust of histories fashioned in these alternative ways is generally "Conservative" and "Radical" respectively. These implications need not be formally drawn in the historical account itself, but they will be identifiable by the *tone* or *mood* in which the resolution of the drama and the epiphany of the law that it manifests are cast. The differences between the two kinds of historiography thus distinguished are those which I conceive to be characteristic of the work of a Spengler on the one hand and a Marx on the other. The Mechanistic mode of explanation is used by the former to justify the tone or mood of histories emplotted as Tragedies, but in such a way as to draw ideological implications which are socially accommodationist. In Marx, however, a similarly Mechanistic strategy of explanation is used to sanction a Tragic account of history which is heroic and militant in tone. The differences are precisely similar to those which distinguish Euripidean from Sophoclean Tragedy or, to take the case of a single writer, the tragedy of *King Lear* from that of *Hamlet*.

Specific examples from historiography may be briefly cited for purposes of illustration. Ranke's histories are consistently cast in the mode of Comedy, a plot form that has as its central theme the notion of *reconciliation*. Similarly, the dominant mode of explanation used by him was Organicist, consisting of the uncovering of the *integrative* structures and processes which, he believed, represent the fundamental modes of relationship to be found in history. Ranke dealt not in "laws" but in the discovery of the "Ideas" of the agents and agencies which he viewed as inhabitants of the historical field. And I will argue that the kind of explanation which he believed historical knowledge provides is the epistemological counterpart of an aesthetic perception of the historical field which takes the form of a Comic emplotment in all of Ranke's narratives. The ideological implications of this combination of a Comic mode of emplotment and an Organicist mode of argument are specifically Conservative. Those "forms" which Ranke discerned in the historical field were thought to exist in the kind of harmonious condition which conventionally appears at the end of a Comedy. The reader is left to contemplate the coherence of the historical field, considered as a *completed* structure of "Ideas" (i.e., institutions and values), and with the kind of feeling engendered in the audience of a drama that has achieved a definitive Comic resolution of all the *apparently* tragic conflicts within it. The tone of voice is accommodationist, the mood is optimistic, and the ideological implications are Conservative, inasmuch as one can legitimately conclude from a history thus construed that one inhabits the best of possible historical worlds, or at least the best that one can "realistically" hope for, given the nature of the historical process as revealed in Ranke's accounts of it.

Burckhardt represents another variation on these same possibilities of combination. Burckhardt was a Contextualist; he suggested that historians "explain" a given event by inserting it into the rich fabric of the similarly discriminable individualities that occupy its circumambient historical space. He denied both the possibility of deriving laws from the study of history and the desirability of submitting it to typological analysis. For him, a given area of historical occurrence represented a field of happening which was more or less rich in the brilliance of its "fabric" and more or less susceptible to impressionistic representation. His *Civilization of the Renaissance*, for example, is conventionally regarded as having no "story" or "narrative line" at all. Actually, the narrative mode in which it was cast is that of the Satire, the *satura* (or "medley"), which is the fictional mode of Irony and which achieves some of its principal effects by refusing to provide the kinds of formal coherencies one is conditioned to expect from reading Romance, Comedy, and Tragedy. This narrative form, which is the aesthetic counterpart of a specifically skeptical conception of knowledge and its possibilities, presents itself as the type of all putatively anti-ideological conceptions of history and as an alternative to that "philosophy of history," practiced by Marx, Hegel, and Ranke alike, which Burckhardt personally despised.

But the tone or mood in which a Satirical narrative is cast has specific ideological implications, "Liberal" if cast in an optimistic tone, "Conservative" if cast in a resigned one. For example, Burckhardt's conception of the historical field as a "texture" of individual entities linked together by little more than their status as components of the same domain and the brilliance of their several manifestations, combined with his formal skepticism, is destructive of any effort on the part of his audience to use history as a means of comprehending the present world in anything but Conservative terms. Burckhardt's own pessimism with respect to the future has the effect of promoting in his readers an attitude of *"sauve qui peut"* and "the devil take the hindmost." One *might* promote such attitudes in the interests of either Liberal or Conservative causes, depending upon the actual social situations in which they were advanced; but there is absolutely no possibility of basing Radical arguments on them, and their ultimate ideological implications as Burckhardt used them are strictly Conservative, when they are not simply "Reactionary."

◄§ The Problem of Historiographical Styles

Having distinguished among the three levels on which historians work to gain an explanatory affect in their narratives, I will now consider the problem of historiographical styles. In my view, a historiographical style represents a particular *combination* of modes of emplotment, argument, and ideological implication. But the various modes of emplotment, argument, and ideological implication cannot be indiscriminately combined in a given work. For example, a Comic emplotment is not compatible with a Mechanistic argument, just as a Radical ideology is not compatible with a Satirical emplotment. There are, as it were, elective affinities among the various modes that might be used to gain an explanatory affect on the different levels of composition. And these elective affinities are based on the structural homologies which can be discerned among the possible modes of emplotment, argument, and ideological implication. The affinities can be represented graphically as follows:

Mode of Emplotment	Mode of Argument	Mode of Ideological Implication
Romantic	Formist	Anarchist
Tragic	Mechanistic	Radical
Comic	Organicist	Conservative
Satirical	Contextualist	Liberal

These affinities are not to be taken as *necessary* combinations of the modes in a given historian. On the contrary, the dialectical tension which characterizes the work of every master historian usually arises from an effort to wed a mode of emplotment with a mode of argument or of ideological implication which is inconsonant with it. For example, as I will show, Michelet tried to combine a Romantic emplotment and a Formist argument with an ideology that is explicitly Liberal. So, too, Burckhardt used a Satirical emplotment and a Contextualist argument in the service of an ideological position that is explicitly Conservative and ultimately Reactionary. Hegel emplotted history on two levels—Tragic on the microcosmic, Comic on the macrocosmic—both of which are justified by appeal to a mode of argument that is Organicist, with the result that one can derive either Radical or Conservative ideological implications from a reading of his work.

But, in every case, dialectical tension evolves within the context of a coherent vision or presiding image of the form of the whole historical field. This gives to the individual thinker's conception of that field the aspect of a self-consistent totality. And this coherence and consistency give to his work its distinctive stylistic attributes. The problem here is to determine the grounds of this coherence and consistency. In my view, these grounds are poetic, and specifically linguistic, in nature.

Before the historian can bring to bear upon the data of the historical field the conceptual apparatus he will use to represent and explain it, he must first *pre*figure the field—that is to say, constitute it as an object of mental perception. This poetic act is indistinguishable from the linguistic act in which the field is made ready for interpretation as a domain of a particular kind. That is to say, before a given domain can be interpreted, it must first be construed as a ground inhabited by discernible figures. The figures, in turn, must be conceived to be classifiable as distinctive orders, classes, genera, and species of phenomena. Moreover, they must be conceived to bear certain kinds of relationships to one another, the transformations of which will constitute the "problems" to be solved by the "explanations" provided on the levels of emplotment and argument in the narrative.

In other words, the historian confronts the historical field in much the same way that the grammarian might confront a new language. His first problem is to distinguish among the lexical, grammatical, and syntactical elements of the field. Only then can he undertake to interpret what any given configuration of elements or transformations of their relationships mean. In short, the historian's problem is to construct a linguistic protocol, complete with lexical, grammatical, syntactical, and semantic dimensions, by which to characterize the field and its elements *in his own terms* (rather than in the terms in which they come labeled in the documents themselves), and thus to prepare them for the explanation and representation he will subsequently offer of them in his narrative. This preconceptual linguistic protocol will in turn be—by virtue of its essentially *prefigurative* nature—characterizable in terms of the dominant tropological mode in which it is cast.

Historical accounts purport to be verbal models, or icons, of specific segments of the historical process. But such models are needed because the documentary record does not figure forth an unambiguous image of the structure of events attested in them. In order to figure "what *really* happened" in the past, therefore, the historian must first *pre*figure as a possible object of knowledge the whole set of events reported in the documents. This prefigurative act is *poetic* inasmuch as it is precognitive and precritical in the economy of the historian's own consciousness. It is also poetic insofar as it is constitutive of the structure that will subsequently be imaged in the verbal model offered by the historian as a representation and explanation of "what *really* happened" in the past. But it is constitutive not only of a domain which the historian can treat as a possible object of (mental) perception. It is also constitutive of the *concepts* he will use *to identify the objects* that inhabit that domain and *to characterize the kinds of relationships* they can sustain with one another. In the poetic act which precedes the formal analysis of the field, the historian both creates his object of analysis and predetermines the modality of the conceptual strategies he will use to explain it.

But the number of possible explanatory strategies is not infinite. There are, in fact, four principal types, which correspond to the four principal tropes of poetic language. Accordingly, we find the categories for analyzing the different modes of thought, representation, and explanation met with in such nonscientific fields as historiography in the modalities of poetic language itself. In short, the theory of tropes provides us with a basis for classifying the deep structural forms of the historical imagination in a given period of its evolution.

The Theory of Tropes

Both traditional poetics and modern language theory identify four basic tropes for the analysis of poetic, or figurative, language: Metaphor, Metonymy, Synecodoche, and Irony.[13] These tropes permit the characterization of

[13] The two leading exponents of the tropological conception of nonscientific (mythic, artistic, and oneiric) discourse are the Structuralists Roman Jakobson and Claude Lévi-Strauss. The latter uses the Metaphorical-Metonymical dyad as the basis for his analysis of the naming systems in primitive cultures and as a key to the comprehension of myths. See Claude Lévi-Strauss, *The Savage Mind*, pp. 205–44; and, for an exposition of the method, see Edmund Leach, *Claude Lévi-Strauss* (New York, 1970), pp. 47ff. Jakobson uses the same dyad as the basis for a linguistic theory of poetics. See his brilliant essay "Linguistics and Poetics," in *Style in Language*, ed. Thomas A. Sebeok (New York and London, 1960), pp. 350–77; and the famous chapter 5 of Roman Jakobson and Morris Halle, *Fundamentals of Language* ('s-Gravenhage, 1956), entitled "The Metaphoric and Metonymic Poles," now reprinted in *Critical Theory since Plato*, ed. Hazard Adams (New York, 1971), pp. 1113–16. For a similar application of this dyad to the problem of characterizing the linguistic structure of dreams in psychoanalysis, see Jacques Lacan, "The Insistence of the Letter in the Unconscious," in *Structuralism*, ed. Jacques Ehrmann (New York, 1966), pp. 101–36.

Lévi-Strauss, Jakobson, and Lacan conceive Metaphor and Metonymy as the "poles" of linguistic behavior, representing respectively the continuous (verbal) and discontinuous (nominal) axes of speech acts. In Jakobson's linguistic theory of style, Synecdoche and Irony are treated as species of Metonymy, which in turn is viewed as the fundamental trope of "realistic" prose. Thus, for example, Jakobson writes: "the study of poetic tropes has been directed mainly toward metaphor, and the so-called realistic literature, intimately tied with the metonymic principle, still defies interpretation, although the same linguistic methodology, which poetics uses when analyzing the metaphorical style of romantic poetry, is entirely applicable to the metonymic texture of realistic prose." See Jakobson, "Linguistics and Poetics," p. 375. As a matter of fact, the analysis of the history of realism in the novel in terms of its essentially Metonymical content was carried out by Stephen Ullmann, *Style in the French Novel* (Cambridge, 1967). Ullmann demonstrates the progressive "nominalization" of the essentially "verbal" style of the Romantic novel from Stendhal to Sartre.

Fruitful as the Metaphorical-Metonymical dyad has proven to be for the analysis of *linguistic* phenomenon, however, its use as a framework for characterizing *literary* styles is, in my view, limited. I am inclined to utilize the fourfold conception of the tropes, conventional since the Renaissance, for distinguishing among different stylistic conventions within a single tradition of discourse. As Emile Benveniste has suggested in his penetrating essay on Freud's theory of language: "it is style rather than language that we would take as term of comparison with the properties that Freud has disclosed as indicative of oneiric language. . . . The unconscious uses a veritable 'rhetoric' which, like style, has its 'figures,' and the old catalogue of the tropes would supply an inventory appropriate to the two types of expression [symbolic and significative]." Emile Benveniste, "Remarks on the Function of Language in Freudian Theory," in *Problems of General Linguistics* (Coral Gables, Fla., 1971), p. 75. In this essay, Benveniste collapses the distinction between poetic and prosaic language, between the language of dreams and that of waking consciousness, between the Metaphorical and Metonymical poles. This is consistent with my contention that the similarities between poetic and discursive representations of reality are as important as the differences. For it is with "realistic" fictions as it is with dreams: "The nature of the content makes all the varieties of metaphor appear, for symbols of the unconscious take both their meaning and their difficulty from metaphoric conversion. They also employ what traditional rhetoric calls metonymy (the container for the contents) and synecdoche (the part for the whole) [*sic*], and if the 'syntax' of the symbolic sequences calls forth one device more than any other, it is ellipsis." *Ibid.*

Part of the difficulty in moving from a linguistic to a stylistic characterization of the forms of realistic literature may lie in the failure to exploit the conventional rhetorical distinction between tropes and figures on the one hand and that between tropes and schemes on the other. Sixteenth-century rhetoricians, following Peter Ramus, classified the figures of speech in terms of the four tropes (or modes) of Metaphor, Metonymy, Synecdoche, and Irony, but without stressing their mutual exclusiveness, thereby providing a more supple conception of poetic discourse and a more subtle differentiation of literary styles than that offered by the bipolar system favored by modern linguisticians. While keeping the basic binary distinction between Metaphor and Metonymy, some rhetoricians went on to view Synecdoche as a *kind* of Metaphorical usage and Irony as a *kind* of Metonymical one. This permits the distinction between *integrative* language on the one hand and *dispersive* language on the other, while still allowing further distinctions regarding *degrees* of integration or reduction aimed at in different stylistic conventions. In *The New Science* (1725, 1740), Giambattista Vico utilized the fourfold distinction among the tropes as a basis for differentiating the stages of consciousness through which mankind has passed from primitivism to civilization. Instead of seeing an *opposition* between poetic (mythic) consciousness and prosaic (scientific) consciousness, therefore, Vico saw a *continuity*. See Thomas G. Bergin and Max H. Fisch, trans., *The New Science of Giambattista Vico* (Ithaca, N.Y., 1968), bk. 2, pp. 129ff., on "Poetic Wisdom." On the rhetorical theory of the Renaissance and for a catalog of the standard figures of speech and of the tropes, see Lee A. Sonnino, *A Handbook to Sixteenth Century Rhetoric* (London, 1968), pp. 10–14, 243–46.

The distinction between *schemes* and *figures* is made in conventional rhetoric on the following basis: a *schema* (whether of words [*lexeos*] or of thought [*dianoia*]) is an order of representations involving no "irrational" leaps or substitutions; by contrast, a *figura* involves precisely such an irrational (or at least unexpected) substitution, as, for example, in the phrase "cold passions" when the adjective "hot" might have been expected. But what is rational and what is irrational in linguistic usage? Any figure of speech is rational which produces the effect of communication aimed at by the user. And the same might well be said of schemes, whether of words or of thoughts. The creative use of language admits, indeed demands, departure from what consciousness in the act of reading, thinking, or hearing anticipates on the basis of convention. And this would be as true of "realistic" prose discourse as of poetry, however "Romantic." What formal terminological systems, such as those devised for denoting the data of physics, envisage is the elimination of figurative usage altogether, the construction of perfect "schemata" of words in which nothing "unexpected" appears in the designation of the objects of study. For example, the agreement to use calculus as the terminological system for discussing the physical reality postulated by Newton represents the *schematization* of that area of discourse, though not of the *thought* about its objects of study. Thought about the physical world remains essentially *figurative*, progressing by all sorts of "irrational" leaps and bounds from one theory to another—but always within the Metonymical mode. The problem for the creative physicist is to cast his insights, derived by figurative means, in the schema of words specified for communicating with other physicists committed to the mathematical terminological system provided by Newton.

The fundamental problem of "realistic" representation of those areas of experience not terminologically disciplined in the way that physics is, is to provide an adequate schema of words for representing the schema of thoughts which it takes to be the truth *about* reality. But, when it is a matter of characterizing an area of experience over which there is no fundamental agreement about what it consists of or what its true nature might be, or when it is a matter of challenging a conventional characterization of a phenomenon such as a revolution, the distinction between what is legitimately "expected" and what is not falls away. The thought about the object to be represented and the words to be used in representing either the object or the thought about the object are all consigned to the usages of figurative discourse. It is imperative, therefore, when analyzing putative "realistic" representations of reality to determine the dominant poetic mode in which its discourse is cast. By identifying the dominant mode (or modes) of discourse, one penetrates to that level of consciousness on which a world of experience is *constituted* prior to being analyzed. And, by retaining the fourfold distinction among the "master tropes," as Kenneth Burke calls them, one can specify the different "styles of thought" which might appear, more or less hidden, in any representation of reality, whether manifestly poetic or prosaic. See Burke, *Grammar*, app. D, pp. 503–17. Cf. Paul Henle, ed., *Language, Thought, and Culture* (Ann Arbor, Mich., 1966), pp. 173–95. The literature on the tropes is varied and beset by congenital disagreement. Some of the problems met with in trying to analyze the tropological dimensions of discourse can be seen in the various characterizations of the tropes given in the *Princeton Encyclopedia of Poetry and Poetics*, ed. Alex Preminger *et al.* (Princeton, 1965).

Retention of the fourfold analysis of figurative language has the added advantage of resisting the fall into an essentially *dualistic* conception of styles which the bipolar conception of style-cum-language promotes. In fact, the fourfold classification of the tropes permits the use of the combinatorial possibilities of a dual-binary classification of styles. By its use we are not forced, as Jakobson is, to divide the history of nineteenth-century literature between a romantic-poetic-Metaphorical tradition on the one hand and a realistic-prosaic-Metonymical tradition on the other. Both traditions can be seen as elements in a single convention of discourse in which all of the tropological strategies of linguistic usage are present, but present in different degrees in different writers and thinkers.

objects in different kinds of indirect, or figurative, discourse. They are especially useful for understanding the operations by which the contents of experience which resist description in unambiguous prose representations can be prefiguratively grasped and prepared for conscious apprehension. In Metaphor (literally, "transfer"), for example, phenomena can be characterized in terms of their similarity to, and difference from, one another, in the manner of analogy or simile, as in the phrase "my love, a rose." Through Metonymy (literally, "name change"), the name of a part of a thing may be substituted for the name of the whole, as in the phrase "fifty sail" when what is indicated is "fifty ships." With Synecdoche, which is regarded by some theorists as a form of Metonymy, a phenomenon can be characterized by using the part to symbolize some *quality* presumed to inhere in the totality, as in the expression "He is all heart." Through Irony, finally, entities can be characterized by way of negating on the figurative level what is positively affirmed on the literal level. The figures of the manifestly absurd expression (catachresis), such as "blind mouths," and of explicit paradox (oxymoron), such as "cold passion," can be taken as emblems of this trope.

Irony, Metonymy, and Synecdoche are kinds of Metaphor, but they differ from one another in the kinds of *reductions* or *intergrations* they effect on the literal level of their meanings and by the kinds of illuminations they aim at on the figurative level. Metaphor is essentially *representational*, Metonymy is *reductionist*, Synecdoche is *integrative*, and Irony is *negational*.

For example, the Metaphorical expression "my love, a rose," affirms the adequacy of the rose as a representation of the loved one. It asserts that a similarity exists between two objects in the face of manifest differences between them. But the *identification* of the loved one with the rose is only *literally* asserted. The phrase is meant to be taken *figuratively*, as an indication of the qualities of beauty, preciousness, delicacy, and so on, possessed by the loved one. The term "love" serves as a sign of a particular individual, but the term "rose" is understood to be a "figure" or "symbol" of the qualities ascribed to the loved one. The loved one is identified with the rose, but in such a way as to sustain the particularity of the loved one while suggesting the qualities that she (or he) shares with the rose. The loved one is not *reduced* to a rose, as would be the case if the phrase were read Metonymyically, nor is the essence of the loved one taken to be identical with the essence of the rose, as would be the case if the expression were understood as a Synecdoche. Nor, obviously, is the expression to be taken as an implicit negation of what is explicitly affirmed, as in the case of Irony.

A similar kind of representation is contained in the Metonymical expression "fifty sail" when it is used to mean "fifty ships." But here the term "sail" is substituted for the term "ship" in such a way as to *reduce* the whole to one of its parts. Two different objects are being implicitly compared (as in the phrase "my love, a rose"), but the objects are explicitly conceived to bear a part-whole relationship to each other. The modality of this relationship, however, is not that of a microcosm-macrocosm, as would be true if the term "sail" were intended to symbolize the *quality* shared by both "ships" and "sails," in which case it would be a Synecdoche. Rather, it is suggested that "ships" are in some sense identifiable with that *part* of themselves without which they cannot operate.

In Metonymy, phenomena are implicitly apprehended as bearing relationships to one another in the modality of part-part relationships, on the basis of which one can effect a *reduction* of one of the parts to the status of an aspect or function of the other. To apprehend any given set of phenomena as existing in the modality of part-part relationships (not, as in Metaphor, object-object relationships) is to set thought the task of distinguishing between those parts which are representative of the whole and those which are simply aspects of it. Thus, for example, the expression "the roar of thunder" is Metonymical. In this expression the whole process by which the *sound* of thunder is produced is first divided into two kinds of phenomena: that of a cause on the one hand (the thunder); and that of an effect on the other (the roar). Then, this division having been made, the thunder is related to the roar in the modality of a cause-effect reduction. The sound signified by the term "thunder" is endowed with the aspect of a "roar" (a particular kind of sound), which permits one to speak (Metonymically) of the "thunder causing the roar."

By Metonymy, then, one can simultaneously distinguish between two phenomena and reduce one to the status of a manifestation of the other. This reduction may take the form of an agent-act relationship ("the thunder *roars*") or a cause-effect relationship ("the roar *of* thunder"). And, by such reductions, as Vico, Hegel, and Nietzsche all pointed out, the phenomenal world can be populated with a host of agents and agencies that are presumed to exist *behind* it. Once the world of phenomena is separated into two orders of being (agents and causes on the one hand, acts and effects on the other), the primitive consciousness is endowed, *by purely linguistic means alone*, with the conceptual categories (agents, causes, spirits, essences) necessary for the theology, science, and philosophy of civilized reflection.

But the essentially *extrinsic* relationship that is presumed to characterize the two orders of phenomena in all Metonymical reductions can by Synecdoche be construed in the manner of an *intrinsic* relationship of shared *qualities*. Metonymy asserts a difference between phenomena construed in the manner of part-part relationships. The "part" of experience which is apprehended as an "effect" is related to that "part" which is apprehended as "cause" in the manner of a reduction. By the trope of Synecdoche, however, it is possible to construe the two parts in the manner of an *integration* within a whole that is *qualitatively* different from the sum of the parts and of which the parts are but *microcosmic* replications.

By way of illustrating what is involved in Synecdochic usage, I will analyze the expression "He is all heart." In this expression, there is what appears to be a Metonymy—that is to say, the name of a part of the body is used to characterize the whole body of the individual. But the term "heart" is to be understood figuratively as designating, not a part of the body, but that *quality* of character conventionally *symbolized* by the term "heart" in Western culture. The term "heart" is not meant to be construed as designating a part of the anatomy whose function can be used to characterize the function of the whole body, as in "fifty sail" for "fifty ships." Rather, it is to be construed as a symbol of a quality that is characteristic of the whole individual, considered as a combination of physical and spiritual elements, all of which participate in this quality in the modality of a microcosmic-macrocosmic relationship.

Thus, in the expression "He is all heart," a Synecdoche is superimposed on a Metonymy. If the expression were taken literally, it would be senseless. Read Metonymically, it would be reductive, inasmuch as it would only imply recognition of the centrality of the heart to the functioning of the organism in order to be even figuratively suggestive. But read Synecdochically—that is, as a statement suggesting a qualitative relationship among the elements of a totality—it is integrative rather than reductive. Unlike the Metonymical expression "fifty sail," used as a figure for "fifty ships," it is meant to signal not simply a "name change" but a name change designating a totality ("He") which possesses some quality (generosity, compassion, etc.) that suffuses and constitutes the essential nature of all the parts that make it up. As a Metonymy, it suggests a relationship among the various parts of the body which is to be understood in terms of the central function of the heart among those parts. As a Synecdoche, however, the expression suggests a relationship among the parts of the individual, considered as a combination of physical and spiritual attributes, which is qualitative in nature and in which all of the parts participate.

We consider the three tropes thus far discussed as paradigms, provided by language itself, of the operations by which consciousness can prefigure areas of experience that are cognitively problematic in order subsequently to submit them to analysis and explanation. That is to say, in linguistic usage itself, thought is provided with possible alternative paradigms of explanation. Metaphor is representational in the way that Formism can be seen to be. Metonymy is reductive in a Mechanistic manner, while Synecdoche is integrative in the way that Organicism is. Metaphor sanctions the prefiguration of the world of experience in object-object terms, Metonymy in part-part terms, and Synecdoche in object-whole terms. Each trope also promotes cultivation of a unique linguistic protocol. These linguistic protocols can be called the languages of identity (Metaphor), extrinsicality (Metonymy), and intrinsicality (Synecdoche).

Against these three tropes, which I characterize as "naive" (since they can be deployed only in the belief in language's capacity to grasp the nature of things in figurative terms), the trope of Irony stands as a "sentimental" (in Schiller's sense of "self-conscious") counterpart. It has been suggested that Irony is essentially dialectical, inasmuch as it represents a self-conscious use of Metaphor in the interests of verbal self-negation. The basic figurative tactic of Irony is catachresis (literally "misuse"), the manifestly absurd Metaphor designed to inspire Ironic second thoughts about the nature of the thing characterized or the inadequacy of the characterization itself. The rhetorical figure of *aporia* (literally "doubt"), in which the author signals in advance a real or feigned disbelief in the truth of his own statements, could be considered the favored stylistic device of Ironic language, in both fiction of the more "realistic" sort and histories that are cast in a self-consciously skeptical tone or are "relativizing" in their intention.

The aim of the Ironic statement is to affirm tacitly the negative of what is on the literal level affirmed positively, or the reverse. It presupposes that the reader or auditor already knows, or is capable of recognizing, the absurdity of the characterization of the thing designated in the Metaphor, Metonymy, or Synecdoche used to give form to it. Thus, the expression "He is all heart" becomes Ironic when uttered in a particular tone of voice or in a context in which the person designated manifestly does *not* possess the qualities attributed to him by the use of this Synecdoche.

It can be seen immediately that Irony is in one sense metatropological, for it is deployed in the self-conscious awareness of the possible misuse of figurative language. Irony presupposes the occupation of a "realistic" perspective on reality, from which a nonfigurative representation of the world of experience might be provided. Irony thus represents a stage of consciousness in which the problematical nature of language itself has become recognized. It points to the potential foolishness of all linguistic characterizations of reality as much as to the absurdity of the beliefs it parodies. It is therefore "dialectical," as Kenneth Burke has noted, though not so much in its apprehension of the process of the world as in its apprehension of the capacity of language to obscure more than it clarifies in any act of verbal figuration. In Irony, figurative language folds back upon itself and brings its own potentialities for distorting perception under question. This is why characterizations of the world cast in the Ironic mode are often regarded as *intrinsically* sophisticated and realistic. They appear to signal the ascent of thought in a given area of inquiry to a level of self-consciousness on which a genuinely "enlightened"— that is to say, self-critical—conceptualization of the world and its processes has become possible.

The trope of Irony, then, provides a linguistic paradigm of a mode of thought which is radically self-critical with respect not only to a given characterization of the world of experience but also to the very effort to capture adequately the truth of things in language. It is, in short, a model of the linguistic protocol in which skepticism in thought and relativism in ethics are conventionally expressed. As a paradigm of the form a representation of the world process might take, it is inherently hostile to the "naive" formulations of the Formist, Mechanistic, and Organicist strategies of explanation. And its fictional form, Satire, is intrinsically antagonistic to the archetypes of Romance, Comedy, and Tragedy as modes of representing the forms of significant human development.

Existentially projected into a full-blown world view, Irony would appear to be transideological. Irony can be used *tactically* for defense of either Liberal or Conservative ideological positions, depending on whether the Ironist is speaking against established social forms or against "utopian" reformers seeking to change the status quo. And it can be used offensively by the Anarchist and the Radical, to pillory the ideals of their Liberal and Conservative opponents. But, as the basis of a world view, Irony tends to dissolve all belief in the possibility of positive political actions. In its apprehension of the essential folly or absurdity of the human condition, it tends to engender belief in the "madness" of civilization itself and to inspire a Mandarin-like disdain for those seeking to grasp the nature of social reality in either science or art.

◄§ The Phases of Nineteenth-Century Historical Consciousness

The theory of tropes provides a way of characterizing the dominant modes of historical thinking which took shape in Europe in the nineteenth century. And, as a basis for a general theory of poetic language, it permits me to characterize the deep structure of the historical imagination of that period considered as a closed-cycle development. For each of the modes can be regarded as a phase, or moment, within a tradition of discourse which evolves from Metaphorical, through Metonymical and Synecdochic comprehensions of the historical world, into an Ironic apprehension of the irreducible relativism of all knowledge.

The first phase of nineteenth-century historical consciousness took shape within the context of a crisis in late Enlightenment historical thinking. Thinkers such as Voltaire, Gibbon, Hume, Kant, and Robertson had finally come to view history in essentially Ironic terms. The pre-Romantics— Rousseau, Justus Möser, Edmund Burke, the Swiss nature poets, the *Stürmer und Dränger*, and especially Herder—opposed to this Ironic conception of history a self-consciously "naive" counterpart. The principles of this conception of history were not consistently worked out, nor were they uniformly adhered to by the different critics of the Englightenment, but all of them shared a common antipathy for its rationalism. They believed in "empathy" as a method of historical inquiry, and they cultivated a sympathy for those aspects of both history and humanity which the Enlighteners had viewed with scorn or condescension. As a result of their opposition, there developed a genuine crisis in historical thinking, a deep disagreement over the proper *attitude* with which to approach the study of history. This schism inevitably inspired interest in historical theory, and, by the first decade of the nineteenth century, the "problem of historical knowledge" had moved to the center of concerns of the philosophers of the period.

Hegel was the philosopher who gave this problem its most profound formulation. During the period between his *Phenomenology of Mind* (1806) and his *Philosophy of History* (1830–31), he correctly identified the principal cause of the schism: the irreducible differences between an Ironic and a Metaphorical mode of apprehending the historical field. Moreover, in his own philosophy of history, Hegel offered a reasoned justification for conceiving it in the Synecdochic mode.

During this same period, of course, Enlightenment rationalism was being revised in an Organicist direction by the French Positivists. In the work of Auguste Comte, whose *Cours de la philosophie positive* began to appear in 1830, the Mechanistic theories of explanation of the Enlightenment were wedded with an Organicist conception of the historical process. This permitted Comte to emplot history as a Comedy, thereby dissolving the Satiric *mythos* that had reflected the pessimism of late Enlightenment historiography.

Thus, during the first third of the nineteenth century, three distinct "schools" of historical thought took shape: "Romantic," "Idealist," and "Positivist." And, although they disagreed with one another over the proper method of studying and explaining history, they were one in their repudiation of the Ironic attitude with which late Enlightenment rationalists had approached the study of the past. This shared antipathy to Irony in all its forms accounts in large part for the enthusiasm for historical studies which was characteristic of the time and for the self-confident tone of early nineteenth-century historiography, which prevailed in spite of crucial differences over questions of "methodology."

It also accounts for the particular tone of historical thinking during its second, "mature" or "classic," phase, which lasted from around 1830 to 1870 or thereabout. This period was characterized by sustained debate over historical theory and by the consistent production of massive narrative accounts of past cultures and societies. It was during this phase that the four great "masters" of nineteenth-century historiography—Michelet, Ranke, Tocqueville, and Burckhardt—produced their principal works.

What is most striking about the historiography of this phase is the degree of theoretical self-consciousness in which its representatives carried out their investigations of the past and composed their narrative accounts of it. Almost all of them were inspired by the hope of creating a perspective on the historical process that would be as "objective" as that from which scientists viewed the process of nature and as "realistic" a that from which the statesmen of the period directed the fortunes of nations. During this phase, therefore, debate tended to turn on the question of the criteria by which a genuinely "realistic" conception of history might be judged. Like their contemporaries in the novel, the historians of the time were concerned to produce images of history which were as free from the abstractness of their Enlightenment predecessors as they were devoid of the illusions of their Romantic precursors. But, also like their contemporaries in the novel (Scott, Balzac, Stendhal, Flaubert, and the Goncourts), they succeeded only in producing as many different species of "realism" as there were modalities for construing the world in figurative discourse. Over against the Ironic "realism" of the Enlightenment, they contrived a number of competing "realisms," each a projection of one or another of the modes of Metaphor, Metonymy, and Synecdoche. In fact, as I will show, the "historical realisms" of Michelet, Tocqueville, and Ranke consisted of little more than critical elaborations of perspectives provided by these tropological strategies for processing experience in specifically "poetic" ways. And, in the "realism" of Burckhardt, one witnesses the fall once more into that Ironic condition from which "realism" itself was supposed to liberate the historical consciousness of the age.

The exfoliation of these various modes of historical conceptualization was attended by, and to a large extent caused, further reflection on philosophy of history. During this second phase, philosophy of history tended to take the form of an attack upon Hegel's system, but, in general, it did not succeed in taking thought about historical consciousness beyond the point where he had left it. The exception to this generalization is, of course, Marx, who attempted to combine the Synecdochic strategies of Hegel with the Metonymical strategies of the political economy of his time in order to create a historical vision that was at once "dialectical" and "materialistic"—that is to say, "historical" and "mechanistic" simultaneously.

Marx himself represents the most consistent effort of the nineteenth century to transform historical study into a science. Moreover, his was the most consistent effort to analyze the relationship between historical consciousness on the one hand and the actual forms of historical existence on the other. In his work, the theory and practice of historical reflection are intimately linked to the theory and practice of the society in which they arose. More than any other thinker, Marx was sensitive to the ideological implication of any conception of history which claimed the status of a "realistic" vision of the world. Marx's own conception of history was anything but Ironic, but he did succeed in revealing the ideological implications of every conception of history. And he provided thereby more than ample grounds for the descent into Irony which was to characterize the historical consciousness of the last phase of the historical reflection of the age, the so-called crisis of historicism which developed during the last third of the century.

But historical thought had no need of a Marx to project it into its third, or crisis, phase. The very success of the historians of the second phase was sufficient to plunge historical consciousness into that condition of Irony which is the true content of the "crisis of historicism." The consistent elaboration of a number of equally comprehensive and plausible, yet apparently mutually exclusive, conceptions of the same sets of events was enough to undermine confidence in history's claim to "objectivity," "scientificity," and "realism." This loss of confidence was already perceivable in Burckhardt's work, which is manifestly aestheticist in spirit, skeptical in point of view, cynical in tone, and pessimistic of any effort to know the "real" truth of things.

The philosophical counterpart of the mood represented by Burckhardt in historiography is, of course, Friedrich Nietzsche. But the aestheticism, skepticism, cynicism, and pessimism which were simply *assumed* by Burckhardt as the bases of his peculiar brand of "realism" were self-consciously taken as problems by Nietzsche. Moreover, they were considered manifestations of a condition of spiritual decadence which was to be overcome in part by the freeing of historical consciousness from the impossible ideal of a transcendentally "realist" perspective on the world.

In his early philosophical works, Nietzsche took as his problem the Ironic consciousness of his age and, as a corollary of this, the specific forms of historical conceptualization which sustain it. And, like Hegel before him (though in a different spirit and with a different aim in view), he sought to dissolve this Irony without falling into the illusions of a naive Romanticism. But Nietzsche does represent a return to the Romantic conception of the historical process inasmuch as he attempted to assimilate historical thought to a notion of art that takes the Metaphorical mode as its paradigmatic figurative strategy. Nietzsche spoke of a historiography that is *consciously* metahistorical in its theory and "superhistorical" in its aim. His was, therefore, a defense of a *self-consciously Metaphorical* apperception of the historical field, which is to say that it was only *Metaphorically* Ironic in its intention. In Nietzsche's thought about history, the psychology of historical consciousness is laid open to analysis; moreover, its origins in a specifically poetic apprehension of reality are revealed. As a result, Nietzsche, as much as Marx, provided the grounds for that fall into the "crisis of historicism" to which the historical thought of his age succumbed.

It was in response to the crisis of historicism that Benedetto Croce undertook his monumental investigations into the deep structure of historical consciousness. Like Nietzsche, Croce recognized that the crisis reflected the triumph of an essentially Ironic attitude of mind. And, like him, he hoped to purge historical thinking of this Irony by assimilating it to art. But in the process Croce was driven to contrive a particularly Ironic conception of art itself. In his efforts to assimilate historical thought to art, he succeeded finally only in driving historical consciousness into a deeper awareness of its own Ironic condition. He subsequently attempted to save it from the skepticism which this heightened self-consciousness promoted by assimilating history to philosophy. But, in this effort, he succeeded only in historicizing philosophy, thereby rendering it as Ironically self-conscious of its limitations as historiography itself had become.

As thus envisaged, the evolution of philosophy of history—from Hegel, through Marx and Nietzsche, to Croce—represents the same development as that which can be seen in the evolution of historiography from Michelet, through Ranke and Tocqueville, to Burckhardt. The same basic modalities of conceptualization appear in both philosophy of history and historiography, though they appear in a different sequence in their fully articulated forms. The important point is that, taken as a whole, philosophy of history ends in the same Ironic condition that historiography had come to by the last third of the nineteenth century. This Ironic condition differed from its late Enlightenment counterpart only in the sophistication with which it was expounded in philosophy of history and the breadth of learning which attended its elaboration in the historiography of the time.

ᴄꙬ *One* The Received Tradition:
The Enlightenment and
the Problem of
Historical Consciousness

Chapter 1

THE HISTORICAL IMAGINATION
BETWEEN METAPHOR AND IRONY

≈§ *Introduction*

Nineteenth-century European culture displayed everywhere a rage for a
realistic apprehension of the world. The term "realistic," of course, meant
something other than a "scientific." comprehension of the world, although
certain self-designated "realists," such as the Positivists and Social Darwinists, identified their "realism" with the kind of comprehension of natural
processes which the physical sciences provided. Even here, however, the term
"realism" had connotations which suggested that more was involved than a
simple application of "scientific method" to the data of history, society, and
human nature. For, in spite of their generally "scientistic" orientation, the
"realistic" aspirations of nineteenth-century thinkers and artists were
informed by an awareness that any effort to understand the historical world
offered special problems, difficulties not presented in the human effort to
comprehend the world of merely physical process.

The most important of these problems was created by the fact that the
student of the historical process was enclosed within it or involved in it in a
way that the student of the natural process was not. There was a sense in
which one could legitimately maintain that man was both in nature and
outside it, that he *participated* in the natural process, but that he could also

45

transcend that process in consciousness, assume a position outside it, and *view* the process as manifested in those levels of natural integration which were demonstrably non- or prehuman. But, when it came to reflection on history, only man of all the beings of nature appeared to *have* a history; for all practical purposes, the "historical process" existed only in the form of a generally human process. And, since "humanity" constituted the sole conceivable manifestation of that process which was called "historical," it seemed impossible to make about the process as a whole generalizations of the sort that one could legitimately make about "nature" in its purely physical, chemical, and biological dimensions. "Realism" in the natural sciences could be identified with the "scientific method" developed since Newton at the latest for the analysis of natural processes. But what a "realistic" conception of history might consist of was as much a problem as the definition of such similarly illusive terms as "man," "culture," and "society." Each of the most important cultural movements and ideologies of the nineteenth century—Positivism, Idealism, Naturalism, (literary) Realism, Symbolism, Vitalism, Anarchism, Liberalism, and so on—claimed to provide a more "realistic" comprehension of social reality than its competitors. Even the Symbolist contention that "the world is a forest of symbols" and the Nihilist denial of confidence in *any* possible system of thought were attended by arguments on behalf of the "realistic" nature of their world views.

To be a "realist" meant both to see things clearly, as they *really* were, and to draw appropriate conclusions from this clear apprehension of reality for the living of a possible life on its basis. As thus envisaged, claims to an essential "realism" were at once epistemological and ethical. One might stress the purely analytical or perceptual nature of one's "realism," as the Impressionist painters did, or the moral and prescriptive implications of one's clarity of vision, as did the so-called Neo-Machiavellians in political theory, such as Treitschke. But the claim to represent a "realistic" position on any matter entailed defense of that position on at least two grounds, epistemological and ethical.

From our vantage point in the eighth decade of the twentieth century, we can now see that most of the important theoretical and ideological disputes that developed in Europe between the French Revolution and World War I were in reality disputes over which group might claim the right to determine of what a "realistic" representation of social reality might consist. One man's "reality" was another man's "utopia," and what appeared to be the quintessence of a "realistic" position on one issue might represent the quintessence of "naiveté" from a different perspective of that same issue. What is most interesting about this whole period, considering it as a finished drama of inquiry and expression, is the general authority which the notion "realism" itself commanded. For every age, even the most fideistic, such as the Medieval period, gains its integral consistency from the conviction of its own capacities to know "reality" and to react to its challenges with appropriately "realistic" responses. The express desire to *be* "realistic," then, must reflect a specific conception not so much of what the essence of "realism" is as of what it means to be "unrealistic." The problematics of a "realistic" approach to reality are much the same as those contained in the notions of "sanity" and "health." Such notions are more easily defined by what men of a given time and place recognize as their opposites, "madness" and "sickness." So, too, the specific content of a given age's conception of "realism" is more easily defined by what that age as a whole took to be "unrealism" or "utopianism." And, when it is a matter of trying to characterize the historical thinking of an age in which many different conceptions of "historical realism" were contending for hegemony, it is necessary to ask what it was that these different conceptions of "realism" agreed upon as "unrealism" or "utopianism" in historical thinking in general.

Nineteenth-century historical theorists generally agreed that the principal forms of historical thought of the period which immediately preceded them —that is, those of the Enlightenment—provided models of the dangers confronting any historical theory that claims the authority of a "realistic" world view. This is not to say that they rejected out of hand the entire historiographical productivity of Enlightenment thinkers. In fact, certain of the *philosophes*, and most notably Voltaire, continued to exercise a profound influence during the period of Romanticism, and Voltaire himself was regarded as an ideal worthy of emulation by even as Romantic a historian as Michelet. Nonetheless, in general, what nineteenth-century historical thought aspired to in the way of a "realistic" historiography can best be characterized in terms of what it objected to in its eighteenth-century predecessors. And what it objected to most in Enlightenment historiography was its *essential irony*, just as what it objected to most in its cultural reflection was its *skepticism*.

It did not, be it noted, object to what is usually regarded as the principal characteristic of Enlightenment philosophy of history—that is to say, its presumed "optimism" and the doctrine of progress which usually accompanied it. For historical thinkers during the greater part of the nineteenth century were as interested as their eighteenth-century counterparts had been in providing the bases for belief in the possibility of "progress" on the one hand and some kind of justification for historical "optimism" on the other. For most of them, the concept of "progress" and the feeling of "optimism" were compatible with the "realistic" world view to which they hoped to contribute through their historical writings. For them, the important point was that the concept of progress and its accompanying optimism had *not yet* been provided with adequate cognitive justification. Some of them—most notably, Tocqueville and Burckhardt—feared that such justification could never be provided, and consequently a somewhat soberer tone pervades their work than that which we find in more sanguine spirits such as Michelet (in his early works) and Marx (in all of his).

In general, then, the "realism" of nineteenth-century historical thought consists in its search for adequate grounds for belief in progress and optimism *in the full awareness* of the failure of eighteenth-century historical thinkers to provide those grounds. If one is to understand the specific nature of nineteenth-century historical realism, considered as the matrix of shared beliefs that make of the different schools of historical thought of that time inhabitants of a single universe of discourse, one must specify the nature of the eighteenth century's failure in historical thinking. This failure, I will argue, did not consist in a lack of scholarly achievement—that is to say, a failure of learning—or in an inadequate theory of historical reflection. Rather, it consisted in the Ironic mode in which both scholarly inquiry and theoretical syntheses were cast by the Enlightenment's outstanding historical thinkers.

⁂ The Dialectics of Enlightenment Historiography

Eighteenth-century historical reflection originated in an attempt to apply Metonymical strategies of reduction to the data of history in such a way as to justify belief in the possibility of a human community conceived in the Synecdochic mode. To put it another way, the Enlightenment attempted to justify an Organicist conception of the ideal human community on the basis of an analysis of social process which was essentially Mechanistic in nature. It thus criticized society in the light of an ideal that was moral and valuative, but it pretended to base that criticism on a purely causal analysis of historical processes. As a consequence, the end to which historical representation was meant to contribute was inconsistent with the means actually used in the construction of historical narratives. The result of this conflict between the *means* of historical representation and the *end* to which it was meant to contribute was to drive thought about history into a position that was overtly and militantly Ironic. What started out as a creative tension in early Enlightenment historical thinking, between Comic and Tragic conceptions of the plot of history, between Mechanistic and Organicist conceptions of its processes, and between the Conservative and Radical implications that might be drawn from these, gradually degenerated into an ambiguity, and ultimately an ambivalence, concerning all the principal problems of both historiographical representation and general social goals. By the last quarter of the eighteenth century, this ambivalence had been transformed into Irony, which expressed itself in a historical epistemology that was Skeptical in the extreme and in an ethical attitude, generated by Skepticism, that was manifestly relativistic. By the end of the Enlightenment, such thinkers as Gibbon, Hume, and Kant had effectively dissolved the distinction between history and fiction on which earlier thinkers such as Bayle and Voltaire had based their historiographical enterprises. It was against this "fictionalization" of history, this Ironic stance before the "scientific" tasks which early eighteenth-century historians had set for themselves, that Herder, Burke, and the *Stürmer und Dränger* rebelled. But, before this rebellion can be understood, the tropological dynamics of the historiographical tradition to which it stood opposed must first be revealed.

☙ The Conventional Conceptions of Historiography

In the eighteenth century, thinkers conventionally distinguished among three kinds of historiography: fabulous, true, and satirical. Fabulous historiography was conceived to be a product of pure invention; facts were made up and presented *sub specie historiae*, but in order to entertain or delight by giving to what imagination desired to believe the aspect of an actuality. Needless to say, to thinkers such as Bayle and Voltaire, this kind of *histoire romanesque* was beneath contempt, unfit for a scholar to write or a serious man to read. Truth was what the historian dealt in, and nothing but the truth—so the theory ran. As Bayle said in his *Historical Dictionary*:

History, generally speaking, is the most difficult composition that an author can undertake, or one of the most difficult. It requires a great judgment, a noble, clear and concise style, a good conscience, a perfect probity, many excellent materials, and the art of placing them in good order, and above all things, the power of resisting the instinct of religious zeal, which prompts us to cry down what we think to be true. [I, 170]

I observe that truth being the soul of history, it is an essential thing for a historical composition to be free from lies; so that though it should have all other perfections, it will not be history, but a mere fable or romance, if it want truth. [173]

The historian, then, had to cleave to the truth, insofar as humanly possible, avoiding the "fabulous" at all costs, inventing nothing not justified by the facts, and suppressing his own prejudices and party interests lest he throw himself open to the charge of slander. As Bayle said,

The corruption of manners has been so great, as well among those who have lived in the world, as among those who have lived out of it, that the more a person endeavors to give faithful and true relations, the more he runs the hazard of composing only defamatory libels. ["History and Satire"]

Bayle's cynicism should not go unnoted. Bayle is suggesting that any merely truthful account of mankind is liable to take on the appearance of a slander simply because the usual run of mankind is more likely to be ignoble than noble, and that the *truth itself* is therefore more than likely to take on the aspect of a *calumny*.

Voltaire, writing a generation later, took the same tack: "History," he said, "is the recital of facts represented as true. Fable, on the contrary, is the recital of facts represented as fiction" (*Works*, X, 61). It is all quite symmetrical. Yet Voltaire drew the line between the truthful representation of human errors and folly and histories written to calumniate through falsification. Referring to some "fraudulent memoires" (published under the name of Madame de Maintenon) which had recently appeared, Voltaire remarked:

Almost every page is polluted by false statements and abuse of the royal family and other leading families of the kingdom, without the author's making the smallest probability to give a color to his calumnies. This is not writing history; it is writing slanders which deserve the pillory. [*Phil. dict.*, *Works*, X, 86–87]

In works such as his own *Philosophy of History*, of course, Voltaire was not above slanting the facts or his comments on them in the interest of the cause for which he labored, which was that of truth against untruth, reason against folly, and enlightenment against superstition and ignorance. But here the polemical interest was manifest, and his reflections on world history took on the aspect of a critical essay rather than a scholarly inquiry into what the truth of the facts was. The facts were used merely as occasions for pointing to the more general truths which Voltaire wanted to lay before his readers in an appropriately colored form.

It is quite otherwise with a work like Voltaire's *History of Charles XII*. Here, too, the facts were used to substantiate the proposition that it is "folly" for a ruler, however powerful and talented, to seek "glory" through conquest and battle. As Lionel Gossman has pointed out, this history was written as a "mock epic," which means that in it the events which made up Charles's life were conceived to figure a near-tragedy, a tragedy which misfired because of the essential "folly" of the aims that motivated the protagonist. And Voltaire never missed a chance to comment on the essential folly of what might be called Charles's project or quest, or to figure it in images that suggest as much to the reader without explicitly saying it. Nonetheless, the facts were treated as a structure of objective relationships which the historian may not violate. One may draw a number of different conclusions from the consideration of a given body of facts, Voltaire admitted; but the establishment of the facts, the truth of the facts, he insisted, must be kept quite distinct from the truths—moral, aesthetic, and intellectual—one seeks to derive from reflection on the facts, so that one will not be accused of writing a "fabulous" or a "satirical" history, but praised for writing a "true" one.

There is, of course, an ambiguity contained in the juxtaposition of "truthful" history to "fabulous" history on the one hand and to "satirical" historiography on the other. It seems to suggest that there are three species of the genus "history-writing," two improper and one proper, the differences among which are self-evident. In reality, however, it is obvious that a fourth kind of historical consciousness must be presupposed if the distinctions made

are to be admitted as proper—that is to say, a m\
that stands above, and adjudicates among, the clair.
of historiography (fabulous, satirical, and truthful)\
reader. In short, the very distinction among three k.
conceived not in terms of an *opposition* of the per\
totally invented but as different *mixtures* of truth and .
positive gain in historical consciousness—an advance over
sciousness of the previous age—to which the Enlightenmer.   ...ately
lay claim.

The Enlightenment's own posture vis-à-vis historical writing in general was
Ironic. It not only used historical knowledge for party or polemical purposes
—as all previous ages had done—but did so in full consciousness of the possibility of a choice between so using it and practicing it for its own sake or,
as it is said, for itself alone. This writing of history in the service of truth
itself was practiced by the great antiquarian historians of the eighteenth
century, Ludovico Antonio Muratori and la Curne de Sainte-Palaye, the
outstanding exponents of philological historiography, who were concerned
above all with the editing and critical assessment of documents on scientific principles. But the critical principles on the basis of which moral and
intellectual truths might be derived from the study of chronicles or annals,
themselves established as reliable accounts of "what had happened" in the
past on "scientific" principles, had not been theoretically established by the
great antiquarians.

The rationalists of the Enlightenment—Bayle, Voltaire, Montesquieu,
Hume, Gibbon, and Kant—and that eccentric arationalist, Giambattista
Vico, recognized the need for the critical, which is to say *meta*historical,
principles by which the general truths derived from contemplation of past
facts in their individuality and concreteness could be substantiated *on
rational grounds*. That they failed to provide such principles was not the
result of their method of thinking but of the matter of it. The eighteenth
century lacked an adequate psychological theory. The *philosophes* needed a
theory of human consciousness in which reason was not set over against
imagination as the basis of truth against the basis of error, but in which
the *continuity* between reason and fantasy was recognized, the mode of
their relationship as parts of a more general process of human inquiry into a
world incompletely known might be sought, and the process in which fantasy or imagination contributed as much to the discovery of truth as did
reason itself might be perceived.

The Enlighteners believed that the ground of all truth was reason and its
capacity to judge the products of sensory experience and to extract from
such experience its pure truth content *against* what the imagination wished
that experience to be. Thus, as Voltaire maintained in his *Philosophy of
History*, it appeared to be a simple matter to distinguish between the true and
the false in history. One had only to use common sense and reason to dis-

between the truthful and the fabulous, between the products of
experience as governed by reason and such products as they appeared
under the sway of the imagination, in the historical record. One could
thereby separate the truthful from the fabulous elements, and then write a
history in which only the truthful elements would be treated as the "facts"
from which more general—intellectual, moral, and aesthetic—truths could
be derived.

This meant that whole bodies of data from the past—everything contained
in legend, myth, fable—were excluded as potential evidence for determining
the truth about the past—that is to say, that aspect of the past which such
bodies of data directly represented to the historian trying to reconstruct a
life in its integrity and not merely in terms of its most *rationalistic* manifestations. Because the Enlighteners themselves were devoted to reason and interested in establishing its authority against the superstition, ignorance, and
tyranny of their own age, they were unable to credit as anything more than
testimony to the essential irrationality of past ages those documents in which
those ages represented their truths to themselves, in myths, legends, fables,
and the like. Vico alone in his time perceived that the historical problem
was precisely that of determining the extent to which a purely "fabulous"
or "mythical" apprehension of the world might be adequate, by any criterion
of rationality, as a basis for understanding a specific kind of historical life and
action.

The problem, as Vico saw it, was to uncover the implicit rationality in
even the most irrational of human imaginings, insofar as such imaginings had
actually served as the basis for the construction of social and cultural institutions by which men had been able to live their lives both *with* and *against*
nature itself. The question was: How did rationality (as his own age knew it)
originate in, and grow out of, the greater irrationality by which we must presume ancient man to have been governed and on the basis of which he constructed the original forms of civilized existence? The Enlighteners, because
they viewed the relationship of reason to fantasy in terms of an opposition
rather than as a part-whole relationship, were unable to formulate this question in a historiographically profitable way.

The Enlighteners did not deny the claims of fancy on human consciousness, but they conceived the problem to be the determination of those areas
of human expression in which fancy might be legitimately allowed full play
and those in which it was not permitted to enter. And they tended to think
that the only area in which fantasy could claim full authority was in the
sphere of "art," a sphere which they set over against "life" itself in much the
same relationship of opposition that they conceived "irrationality" to bear
with respect to "rationality." "Life," unlike "art," had to be governed by
reason, and even "art" had to be practiced in the full consciousness of the
distinction between "truth" and "fancy." And, since history was "about life"
primarily and "about art" only secondarily, it had to be written not only

under the direction of reason but also, in its broadest perspective, "about reason," using whatever knowledge history might provide about "unreason" for the promotion of the cause of reason in both life *and* art.

∽§ History, Language, and Plot

In an article on "figurative language" in the *Philosophical Dictionary*, Voltaire wrote:

Ardent imagination, passion, desire—frequently deceived—produce the figurative style. We do not admit it into history, for too many metaphors are hurtful, not only to perspecuity, but also to truth, by saying more or less than the thing itself. [*Works*, IX, 64]

He went on to attack the Church Fathers for their excessive use of figurative language as a means of representing and explaining the processes of the world. He contrasted this misuse of figurative language to its proper uses by Classical pagan poets such as Ovid, who knew how to distinguish between the literally truthful and the fabulous world of his own imaginings, and who, as Voltaire said, used tropes and figures in such a way as to "deceive" no one (*ibid.*, 73). The historian's language, Voltaire suggested, had to be as austere as that reason which directed him in his search for the truth about the past, *literal*, therefore, rather than figurative in its representation of the world before him.

But the same criterion is used to establish the worth, as evidence, of documents that come out of the past clothed in figurative language. Poetry, myth, legend, fable—none of these was conceived to have real value as historical evidence. Once recognized as products of fantasy, they testified only to the superstitious nature of the imagination that had produced them or to the stupidity of those who had taken them for truths. For this reason the historical accounts of remote ages produced by the Enlightenment tended to be little more than condensations of (or commentaries on) the accounts of the historical works actually produced by those ages.

The study of historical documents was of course carried to a high level by the great erudites of the period, but—as Gossman's study of la Curne de Sainte-Palaye and the scholarly circles in which he moved has shown—these men possessed no critical principle by which to synthesize the facts contained in their annals of antiquity into general historical accounts of the processes reflected in the annals themselves. At best, in the historiographers of the age—even in the work produced by the great Edward Gibbon—there is basically only a commentary on the literary remains of the great historians of Classical antiquity, a commentary that is more or less Ironic in accordance with Gibbon's own perception of the rationality of the historian whose work he is paraphrasing and commenting on.

In fact, the Enlighteners' conception of the problem of historical representation, the construction, in a verbal model, of the world of the past, hardly rose above the level of consciousness reflected in their concern over whether any given set of historical events ought to be emplotted as Epic, Comedy, or Tragedy. The problem of choosing the appropriate mode of representation—presented as mutually exclusive alternatives—corresponds to the distinction drawn on the epistemological level between fabulous, satirical, and truthful accounts of the past. The Epic form, it was generally agreed, was not suited to the representation of historical events; and Voltaire's *Henriade*, an epic poem of the career of Henry IV, was generally regarded as a *tour de force*, a poetic triumph, though it was not to be taken seriously as a model to be emulated by either poets or historians in general. The Enlighteners perceived intuitively (and quite correctly) that the Epic form presupposed the cosmology represented in the philosophy of Leibniz, with its doctrine of continuity as its informing ontological principle, its belief in analogical reasoning as an epistemological principle, and its notion that all changes are nothing but transformations by degrees from one state or condition to another of a "nature" whose essence changes not at all. All these ideas stood in apparent opposition to the logic of contradiction and the principle of identity which constituted the principles that rationality was conceived to have to take in the dominant thought of the age.

Yet the choice between Comedy and Tragedy, as the sole alternatives for the writing up of narrative accounts of the past, is itself offered—as in a thinker like Mably, whose *De la manière de l'écrire l'histoire* appeared near the end of the century—Ironically. Most of the Enlighteners could not really conceive that history offered many occasions for emplotment in the Tragic mode, and this because, as Bayle had said earlier, "The corruption of manners has been so great . . . that the more a person endeavors to give faithful and true relations, the more he runs the hazard of composing only defamatory libels." The most likely candidate that Voltaire could conceive as the subject of a Tragic history was Charles XII, but the best he could produce from reflection on the events of that sovereign's life was a prose "mock epic," because the age, as Edmund de Goncourt said of his own, looked everywhere for the "truth" of things, and, having found it, could only despair.

✍ Skepticism and Irony

The skeptical form which rationalism took in its reflection *on its own time* was bound to inspire a purely Ironic attitude with respect to the past when used as the principle of historical reflection. The mode in which all of the *great* historical works of the age were cast is that of Irony, with the result that they all tend toward the form of Satire, the supreme achievement of the literary sensibility of that age. When Hume turned from philosophy to history, because he felt that philosophy had been rendered uninteresting by the skeptical conclusions to which he had been driven, he brought to his study of history the same skeptical sensibility. He found it increasingly difficult, however, to sustain his interest in a process which displayed to him only the eternal return of the same folly in many different forms. He viewed the historical record as little more than the *record* of human folly, which led him finally to become as bored with history as he had become with philosophy.

The seriousness of Hume's great contemporary Gibbon is not, of course, to be doubted, but neither should we dismiss too easily Gibbon's own characterization of his *Decline and Fall of the Roman Empire* as the product of an effort to divert and amuse himself. Gibbon tells us that he was inspired to undertake his project by the irony of the spectacle of ignorant monks celebrating their superstitious ceremonies in a church that stood on the ground where a pagan temple had once stood. This anecdote not only reveals the attitude with which Gibbon approached his task but prefigures the form his narrative account of the decline and fall of Rome ultimately took. His account of the transition from what he regarded as the happiest time for man prior to his own age is not a Tragic account, but rather the greatest achievement of sustained Irony in the history of historical literature. It ends in 1453, with an account of the fall of Byzantium to the fanatical Turk, in the Ironic apprehension, in short, of the triumph of one fanaticism over another. This apprehension, however, is entertained within the context of Gibbon's own knowledge of the rebirth of thought and letters in Western Europe, which brought about the Renaissance and prepared the ground for the Age of Reason, which Gibbon himself represents. The Renaissance itself, however, is conceived to be a product of the ironic fact that it depended upon the triumph of one fanaticism over another in Byzantium, which drove scholars from Constantinople to Italy, there to disseminate the knowledge of Classical antiquity, which would ultimately serve (ironically) to overturn the Christian superstition in whose service it had been (ironically) used by the monks of the Middle Ages.

This irony heaped upon irony, which the image of history produced by Gibbon invokes as its principle of both explanation and representation, could not but generate an Ironic attitude with respect to the values and ideals in the service of which Gibbon himself labored. In the end, it had to lead to the same debilitating skepticism about reason itself which Hume had sought refuge from in historical studies, but which had confronted him even there, in the life of action as well as in the life of thought of all past ages.

One of the more obvious ironies of Kant's intellectual development was his turn, in old age, to a consideration of the moral implications of historical knowledge, a subject to which he denied genuine philosophical interest in the mature phase of his philosophical career. His concern as a philosopher, it will be recalled, was to credit the insights of Hume and Rousseau into the limits of reason on the one hand and into the legitimacy of the emotions' claims against reason on the other. Against Hume, he sought to defend thought against utter skepticism by adducing the grounds on which science's manifest success in mastering the world could be rationally comprehended. Against Rousseau, he sought to make a place in human nature for the emotions and passions, to endow them with authority as the bases for moral and aesthetic judgment without, in the process, overturning the authority of the truths established on scientific and rational grounds. It is interesting to note how these old adversaries returned, in appropriately modified forms, to haunt Kant in his old age, when, under the urgings of Herder's thought about history and the historical events of the Revolution, Kant was forced to reflect on the epistemological bases, the moral value, and the cultural significance of historical knowledge.

The threat of skepticism was present for Kant in the fact that men continued to study history even though it appeared clear that one could learn from history nothing that could not be learned from the study of humanity in its various present incarnations, incarnations which, as objects of study, had the advantage of being directly open to observation in a way that historical events were not. Rousseau's shadow spread itself over Kant's old age in the conviction, growing throughout the period of the Revolution's turn to terror and the broadcast of feelings that the world was falling into ruin, that the whole historical process represented *an inevitable degeneration* under the appearance of progress or the view (promoted by the Ironical insights of late *philosophes*) that, although things might change, there was really nothing new under the sun, that *plus ça change, plus c'est la même chose.*

Like Bayle and Voltaire before him, Kant distinguished among three conceptions of the historical process which are possible for a man to embrace as the *truth about* the process as a whole. He calls these three conceptions the eudaemonistic, the terroristic, and the abderitic. The first conceives that history describes a process of constant progress in both the material and the spiritual conditions of human existence. The second holds that history represents a continual degeneration, or unbroken fall, from an original state of natural or spiritual grace. And the third takes the view ascribed to the ancient Abderitic sect of cynical philosophers, that, although things may *appear* to develop, in reality all movement represents nothing more than a redisposition of primitive elements and not a fundamental alteration in the condition of human existence at all.

I should note that this division corresponds, in its implications for the explaining and writing of history, to that made earlier among the modes of Comedy, Tragedy, and the Epic respectively. The difference in Kant's formulation of the epistemological distinction—among fabulous, Satirical, and truthful historiography—is that Kant regarded all three modes of conceiving the historical process as equally "fabulous" or equally "fictive." They represented to him evidence of the mind's capacity to impose different kinds of formal coherence on the historical process, different possibilities of its emplotment, the products of different *aesthetic* apprehensions of the historical field.

But Kant stressed the moral implications of these aesthetic choices, the effects that the decision to emplot or conceive the historical process in a specific way *might have* on the way one *lived* history, the implications they would have for the way one conceived one's present and projected a future for oneself and other men. Historical knowledge does not make a significant contribution to the problem of *understanding* human nature in general, for it does not show us anything about man that cannot be learned from the study of living men considered as individuals and as groups. But it does provide an occasion for comprehending the problem, the moral problem, of the end or purpose *for which* a life ought to be lived.

Kant's position was something like this: The way I conceive the historical process, apprehended as a process of transition from past to present, the form which I impose upon my perceptions of it, these provide the orientation by which I move into a future with greater hope or despair, in the face of the prospects which that movement is conceived to have as a *movement toward* a desirable (or *away from* an undesirable) goal. If I conceive the historical process as a spectacle of degeneration (and I conceive historical knowledge to be, above all, knowledge of a "spectacle" that passes in review before the historian's eyes), I will live history in such a way as to bring about a degenerate end to the process. And similarly, if I conceive that spectacle as being nothing but "one damned thing after another," I shall act in such a way as to turn the age in which I live into a static age, one in which no progress will be possible. But if, on the other hand, I conceive the spectacle of history, with all its folly, vice, superstition, ignorance, violence, and suffering, as a *process* in which human nature itself is transformed from the capacity to create these evils into the capacity to take up moral cause against them, as a *uniquely human* project, then I will so act as to bring this transformation to pass. Moreover, there are good extrahistorical grounds for taking this view of history as both lived and conceived in thought. Those grounds are provided by philosophy, in which the concept of reason is used as the justification for conceiving nature as that which, in man, attains the powers implicit in it from its origins.

The conception of history thus set forth by Kant is Ironic, but its Irony is moderated by the principles of the philosophical system in which skepticism had been halted short of a rejection of reason itself. Yet, Kant's thought about history remains within the confines of Enlightenment rationalism in a significant sense. The modality of *opposition*, by which things in history are related in thought, has not given place to the modality of *continuity and interchange*, which alone could generate an adequate appreciation of the concreteness, individuality, and vividness of historical events considered for themselves alone. Kant conceived historical data as phenomena, which, like natural phenomena, are considered to be "nature under law" (more specifically, nature under universal and invariant *causal* laws). This means that he construed the historical field Metonymically, as an *opposition* mediated by cause-effect, which is to say extrinsic, relationships. There was no scientific reason, on Kant's terms, for attempting, as Leibniz had done, a Synecdochic identification of the parts of that field in their function as components of the whole. When all is said and done, Kant apprehended the historical process less as a development from one stage to another in the life of humanity than as merely a conflict, an *unresolvable* conflict, between *eternally opposed* principles of human nature: rational on the one hand, irrational on the other. This is why he was forced to conclude, again consistently with the tradition of Enlightenment rationalism represented by Bayle, Voltaire, Hume, and Gibbon, that in the final analysis history must be *apprehended* in an aesthetic, rather than a scientific, way. Only thus can it be converted into a drama, the resolution of which can be envisaged as a Comic consummation rather than as a Tragic defeat or a timeless Epic of conflict with no *specific issue* at all. Kant's reasons for opting for this Comic notion of the meaning of the whole process were ultimately ethical ones. The spectacle of history had to be conceived as a Comic drama or else men would fail to take up those Tragic projects which alone can transform chaos into a *meaningful* field of human endeavor.

The mainstream of Enlightenment rationalist historiography originated in the recognition that history ought not to be written merely to entertain or simply in the interest of advancing a *partis pris* of a confessional or political kind. The rationalists recognized that it was necessary to have a critical principle to guide reflection on the historical record if they were to produce something more than chronicles or annals. They began in conscious opposition to the *historiens romanesques* or *galants* of the previous century, the kind of "amusing" history written by the Abbé de Saint-Réal or Charles de Saint-Évremond, the foremost exponent of "libertine" historical theory and the prototype of the "aestheticist" historiography later represented by Walter Pater and Egon Friedell. History—the *philosophes* recognized—had to be "truthful" or it could make no claim to "instruct and enlighten" the reader in the process of "entertaining and delighting" him. What was at issue, then, was the criterion by which the truth was to be recognized. In short, what was the *form* the truth had to take? What was the *paradigm* of truth in general, by comparison to which a truthful account of things could be recognized?

In order to understand the answers the rationalists gave to these questions it is not enough merely to point to the distinction they drew between "fabulous" and "satirical" history on the one hand and "truthful" history on the other. Nor is it enough merely to point to the general idea of truth

signaled by their formal dedication to the principles of empirical establishment of the data, rational criticism of the evidence, and narrative representation of the "meaning" of the evidence in a story well told. We can understand what they had in mind only by considering the kinds of historical
thinking they rejected or did not take seriously as possible alternatives to their
own Ironic preconceptions and skeptical proclivities.

⌁§ The Main Forms of Pre-Enlightenment Historiography

In his classic account of the history of historical writing, *Geschichte der
neuren Historiographie,* Eduard Fueter identified four major strands in the
historical tradition of seventeenth-century Europe on the basis of which, and
against which, what he called the "Reflective" or "critical" historiography
of the Enlighteners developed. These were Ecclesiastical (and largely "confessional") history; the Ethnographic history produced by missionaries to,
and students of, the new worlds which the Age of Exploration and Discovery
had opened up to scientific and historical scrutiny; the Antiquarian historiography of the great erudites of the period, largely philological in its approach
and dedicated to the construction of accurate chronicles and annals of the
remote and near past; and, finally, the *historiographie galante* or *romanesque,*
based upon the *"romans* of intrigues and affairs" and written in an openly
belletristic spirit (Fueter, 413). This last, which Fueter in his seriousness as a
German *Gelehrter* of Positivistic persuasion was inclined to dismiss much
too quickly, is characterized as bearing the same relation to the humanistic
historiography of the Renaissance that "the *salon* mythology of the Rococo
poets" bore to "the robust paganism of the great poets of the Renaissance"
(*ibid.,* 412). It was, Fueter said, the historiographical equivalent of the
"galant style" in the music of the time (*ibid.*).

What is striking about the four strands of seventeenth-century historical
thinking identified by Fueter is the extent to which the first two of them—
Ecclesiastical history and Ethnographic history—are inspired by an oppressive
sense of fatal *schism* in the human community, religious *division* in the case
of confessional history, and racial and spatial *separation* in the case of
Ethnographic history (of the sort written by Las Casas, Oviedo, Herrera,
and so on). Here history is written in the apprehension of divisions which
give every evidence of fatally hindering the march of civilization itself.

The annalistic form which history-writing tended to assume in the hands
of the great antiquarian erudites of that same century—Mabillon, Tille-
mont, and, a bit later, Muratori—represents a specifically historiographical
effort at the apprehension of the *kind of continuity* which might be conceived to make of this severed reality a whole, a comprehensible totality. In
the annals form of historical writing I discern not only a rage for *order of*

some kind but the implicit suggestion that the order of temporal occurrence may be the only ordering principle that might be used to make some *slight sense* out of them. The desire for "the truth and nothing but the truth" and a compulsive need to deal with events only in their extrinsic aspects, their aspects as functions of a serial order, constituted the basis of the erudites' critical principles; and it set the limits on their conception of historical understanding. As a form of historical representation, the annals represented an advance in critical consciousness over the work of the great confessional historians (such as Foxe) and the great ethnographers (such as Las Casas). The annalists sought to rise above the prejudices and party biases of a historiography written with religious disputes and racial conflicts in mind. To the Manichean nature of the latter, they opposed the order of temporal seriality as a mode of representation which at least left the historian free of the taint of subjectivity and special pleading. They tried to be as cold and remote as the confessionalists and ethnographers were involved in the histories they wrote. But, in the end, they were able to provide only the materials out of which a true history might be written, not true histories themselves. And the same can be said of their successors—even of la Curne de Sainte-Palaye—in the next century.

When measured against the moral passion of the confessionalists and the coldness of the annalists, the cultivation of a purely aestheticist historiography of the sort provided by the *historiens galants* appears less retrograde than Fueter would have us believe. If Saint-Réal did little more than "divert" his readers by depicting "nouvelles amusantes and emouvantes," his histories, such as *Don Carlos* (1672) and *Conjuration des Espagnols contre la république de Venise en 1618* (1674), at least signaled a desire to achieve a critical perspective that would at once distance the phenomena to be represented and unite them in a comprehensible whole, even if the whole were little more than an exciting story. Yet, because the only unity which Saint-Réal's histories have is that of story, story conceived as little more than a device for achieving rhetorical effects, the histories he actually wrote are flawed by the fact that, on his own terms, they represent not a "truth" about the past but only a "fiction" of how the facts *might have been*. They might well have been otherwise, and they might well be represented as parts of a story (or number of stories) of a completely different kind.

✃§ Leibniz and the Enlightenment

Actually, the annalistic form of historical representation had been implicitly provided with a sophisticated theoretical basis in the philosophy of Leibniz. Fueter maintained that Leibniz merely applied the method of the annalists to the writing of history, but unlike them, failed to conceive of an "annals of Imperial Germany," limiting himself to the construction of genealogies and chronologies of such petty houses and sovereignties as that of Bruns-wick. "In sum," Fueter said, "he collected the materials, but he did not work them" (*ibid.*, 393). But Fueter failed to do justice to the vision which informs Leibniz's work. The annalistic form of historiography was consistent with his notions of continuity, of transition by infinitesimal degrees, of the harmony of the whole in the face of the dispersion in time and space of the elements or parts. Leibniz, perhaps alone among all the major figures of his time, had adequate grounds for believing that annalistic historiography was a philosophically justified mode of historical representation. His *Monad-ology* (1714), with its doctrine of continuity, theory of evolution by degrees, and conception of the particular event as a microcosm of the macrocosm, represented a formal defense of that mode of comprehension which we have called Synecdoche. This mode of comprehension appeals to the microcosmic-macrocosmic relationship as a paradigm of all explanation and representation of reality. In Leibniz's historical thought it appears as the belief that the representation of an event in its total context, the context itself being con-strued as a plenum of individual events that are *united in their difference* from one another, is an adequate way of figuring that event's meaning and relation to the whole.

The cosmos, as Leibniz conceived it, is a plenum of individual monads, each perfect in itself, the unity of which consists in the autonomy of the whole considered as a process of infinite creativity. The perfect harmony of the whole, which overrides and destroys the impression of conflict and extrinsic causality which *appears* to make impossible any intrinsic relation-ship between the various parts, is confirmed by the goodness of the Creator, whose beneficence is such that He is all but indistinguishable from His crea-tion. This manner of conceiving the world and the relation of the parts of it to the totality justifies an annalistic representation of the processes of history, no less than of nature, considered in their individual concrete reality and as moments of a total process which only *appear* to be dispersed in time and space. Leibniz could write history in an annalistic form because he believed that the dispersiveness of phenomena was only apparent; in his view, the world was one and continuous among its parts. Accordingly, his conception of the historical process, in which transition by infinitesimal degrees can be figured in annalistic accounts of finite provinces of occurrence, did not require that he distinguish between larger and smaller provinces. The same process of transition-in-unity and unity-in-transition is at work in all the parts, whether the individual part be construed as a person, a ruling family, a principality, a nation, an empire, or the whole human race.

But it was precisely this vision of the essential unity of the human race which the Enlighteners took to be the ideal *yet to be realized* in historical time. They could not take it as a *presupposition* of their historical writing, not merely because the data did not bear it out, but because it did not accord with their own experience of their own social worlds. For them the unity of humanity was an *ideal* which they could *project* into the future, but they could not use this ideal as a paradigm for either historical explanation or historical representation, because it was in the interest of that ideal that they were studying and writing history to begin with, as part of their effort to bring about such a unification. The world they knew as a fact of experience required them to invoke a paradigm of representation and explanation which took the fact of schism and severance, of conflict and suffering, as given realities. The *opposition* of forces, of which schism and conflict are manifestations, determined the modalities of their experience of history conceived as a process of transition from past to present. The past to them *was* unreason, the present was a conflict of reason and unreason, and the future alone was the time which they could envision as that of the triumph of reason over unreason, perfect unity, redemption.

☙ The Historical Field

When Leibniz surveyed the remote past he saw there precisely the same powers at play which he saw all around him in the present, and in the same proportions. These forces were neither those of reason exactly nor those of unreason exclusively, but rather the harmony of opposites—which makes reason and unreason merely different manifestations of the same unified force or power, which is ultimately God's. When the Enlighteners surveyed the remote past, they were obsessed by the differences between it and the world they themselves occupied, so much so that they were almost inclined to idealize their own age, and to set it over against the remote past as an antithetical opposite. They were saved from the inclination to idealize their own age—though certain of them (notably, Turgot and Condorcet) submitted to the temptation to do so—by the skepticism which guided their use of reason in criticism of the evils of their time. But the sense of opposition was strong enough to prohibit the lavishing of any great tolerance or sympathy on archaic man, except in those rare instances when, like Gibbon, they thought they perceived in the past some prototype of the kind of men they conceived themselves to be or wished they could become. Since their relationship to the remote past was conceived under the auspices of a Metonymical paradigm—that is, in the mode of severance or extrinsic opposition—and since the explanatory mode which Metonymy suggests for explicating the relationship between opposed aspects of the whole is that of cause-effect, the Enlighteners comprehended the spectacle of the almost total ignorance, superstition, and violence of those past ages as all but completely *causally determined*.

They had no need to give very great care to the representation of events in the remote past (such as that of the ancient Hebrews as reported in the Old Testament) since all of those events figured the single truth of the absolute determinateness of the humanity of that time. Everything was conceived to be a manifestation of an essential and unalloyed passion, ignorance, or irrationality (often simply dismissed by Voltaire as insanity). Special care might have been given to the representation of some prototype of rational man honored as an ideal in his own time, but they could no more account for the appearance of such rational men in the midst of unrelieved irrationality than they could account for the growth of reason out of unreason itself. Both were equally "miraculous," though the latter was seen as a "Providential" gift, inasmuch as the present age and the future could be conceived as positive beneficiaries of the rise of the Age of Reason.

But note: the growth of reason out of a state of unreason is ultimately "irrational," inasmuch as the original irrationality of man cannot be accounted for on the theory of the essentially rational nature of nature itself. For, if nature is ruled by reason and is itself intrinsically orderly and harmonious in its operations, why then are not the first men of whom we have record, men living in a state of nature, themselves presumed to have been rational? As immediate products of a rational system of invariant causal processes, the first men must be supposed to have been as rational in their mode of existence as nature itself. But not only are they apparently irrational; they are—as they appear in the records of remote antiquity—especially irrational. How can one account for this?

The tactic of the Enlighteners was to postulate the existence of a condition, prior to the primitive ages of which we have record, in which men were as rational as nature itself, but from which they fell as a result of their ignorance and the condition of scarcity caused by the multiplication of their numbers, itself caused by the beneficence and bounty of nature. The condition of scarcity caused a struggle among men for the goods of nature which an inadequate technology could not efficiently augment. This, in turn, led to the "creation" of society, which regulated human conflict by force and sustained its authority over men by the aid of religion, itself also a product of the combination of want and ignorance. Thus, the state of society itself became identified as at once the cause and the manifestation of unreason in the world. And progress was conceived as the gradual unmasking of the irrational nature of the social state by the small group of rational men capable of recognizing its intrinsically tyrannical nature. Thus, the meaning of the historical process was to be found, not in the growth of reason *out of* unreason, but in purely quantitative terms, as the *expansion* of an originally limited reason into areas of experience formally occupied by the passions, emotions, ignorance, and superstition. It was not a process of *transition* at all.

But this meant that—in accordance with the Mechanistic principles being invoked—the growth of reason had to be conceived to occur at the expense of something else. This something else was the past itself, as it existed in the present, as tradition, custom, and anything else—institutions, laws, cultural artifacts—that claimed authority or respect merely because it was old. The Enlighteners, therefore, wrote history against history itself, or at least against that segment of history which they experienced as "past." Their sympathy for the past was extendable finally, as Voltaire noted, only to the near past, where they could find things to admire and respect because these so nearly resembled themselves. This search into the near past for objects for sympathetic historical representation permitted the *philosophes* their few excursions into Synecdochic (Organicist and sympathetic typological) representation.

But even here their capacities for sympathy and tolerance were marred by their ongoing apprehension of the flaw, the element of unreason still present in every putatively rational man. This was especially the case in their consideration of men of action, such as Charles XII. In Voltaire's picture of him, Charles was represented as the most highly gifted, talented, and best-endowed ruler known to world history; but he was still fatally flawed by his irrational passion for "glory by conquest," considered by Voltaire to be a residuum of a barbaric past that stupidly saw in war a virtue in itself. This flaw was not a tragic flaw at all, not a function of Charles's excellence; it was a taint, a corruption in the heart of an otherwise superbly healthy organism. Charles's fall, therefore, was not tragic; it was pathetic. Hence, his history was only an occasion for lamenting the power of unreason to penetrate into, and to overturn, even the strongest of men.

What Voltaire might have concluded from his consideration of Charles's career was that unreason is a part of the world and of man, as ineluctable and as irreducible as reason itself, and a power which is not to be eliminated in time so much as it is to be tamed, sublimated, and directed into creative and humanly useful channels. He was incapable of considering this possibility because he shared with his age a purely Mechanistic conception of the human psyche, a conception which required that it be considered a battle ground on which opposed, and mutually alternative, forms of consciousness, reason and unreason, met in eternal strife until one had totally broken the power of the other. The closest that either Voltaire or the other historical geniuses of the age—Hume and Gibbon—came to understanding unreason's creative potentialities was in their Ironic criticism of themselves and in their own efforts to make sense out of history. This, at least, led them to view themselves as being as potentially flawed as the cripples they conceived to be acting out the spectacle of history.

✍ The Historiographical Achievement of the Enlightenment

Having indicated the nature of the advance that the rationalist historiography of the Enlightenment represents over the major conventions of historical reflection which came before it, and having noted the flaws or limitations of

that historical vision, I will now specify the precise content of its achievement. The historiography of the seventeenth century began with an apprehension of the historical field as a chaos of *contending* forces, among which
the historian had to choose and in the service of one or more of which he
had to write his history. This was the case with both the confessional historiography of the seventeenth century and the Ethnographic historiography
of the missionaries and *conquistadores*. This *historiography of essential
schism* was succeeded by, or called up, two alternatives to it. One of these,
the tradition of the erudite antiquarians, developed out of a desire for
perfect objectivity, which resulted in the creation of the annalistic mode of
explanation and representation, the characteristic of which was the conception of order and unity as mere seriality, or succession in time. Leibniz's
tacit defense of this mode of historical writing, contained in his *Monadology*
and in the doctrine of continuity which is expounded there, was intrinsically
hostile to the *philosophes'* conception of social reality as inherently severed
and atomized and in contrast to which Leibniz's own doctrine of the essential
harmony of opposites appeared to be as naive as it was "Idealistic." The
other reaction to the historiography of essential schism was a purely aesthetic one, represented by the *historiens galants*, who, even if they did represent a desire to rise above party history, felt able to do so only by denying
that the historiographical enterprise was a part of the more general search
for the "truth" which motivated the science and philosophical thought of the
age.

The alternative to all of these historiographical conventions was the
Ironic mode of conceiving history, developed by the *philosophes*, which at
once strove for objectivity and disengagement and, at least tacitly, recognized the impossibility of attaining these goals. Dominated by a conception
of rationalism derived from the (Newtonian) physical sciences, the *philosophes* approached the historical field as a ground of cause-effect relationships,
the causes in question being generally conceived to be the forces of reason
and unreason, the effects of which were generally conceived to be enlightened men on the one hand and superstitious or ignorant men on the other.

The "lexical" elements of this system were men, acting as individuals
and as groups, who were "grammatically" classifiable into the major categories of carriers of superstitious or irrational values and carriers of enlightened or rational ones. The "syntax" of relationships by which these two
classes of historical phenomena were bound together was that of the unremitting conflict of opposites; and the (semantic) meaning of this conflict was
nothing but the triumph of the latter over the former, or the reverse. But
neither the evidence offered by reflection on the times nor that provided by
reflection on history was really capable of definitively confirming or denying
this conception of history's meaning. As a result, the historical thought of the
main tradition of the Enlightenment was progressively driven back from its
original Metonymical apprehension of the world into the Ironic comprehen-

sion of it which the evidence demanded, given the terms in which the inquiry was conceived in the first place. For, if I *begin* with an apprehension of the field of human history as an area of happening dominated by cause-effect relationships, then I am bound ultimately to regard anything in this field, any man, institution, value, or idea, as nothing but an "effect" of some casual nexus—that is to say, as a contingent (hence determined) reality, and thus as *irrational* in its essence.

In the face of this inevitability, Enlightenment thought was driven, as the historical thought of the previous century had been driven, to consider historical writing as a kind of art. But, since the Enlighteners' conception of art was Neo-Classical—that is, an art which set causation and law at the center of its apprehension of the world in the same way that science did—the historiography of the age was necessarily impelled toward a purely Satirical mode of representation, in the same way that the literature of the age in general was. This age produced no great Tragic historiography, and for the same reason that it produced no great Tragic theater. The bases for believing in the heroic Tragic flaw, conceived as an excessive degree of virtue, were lacking in it. Since all effects had to be presumed to have both the necessary and sufficient causes required for their production, the notion of an existential paradox, a dialectical contradiction that was lived rather than merely thought, could hardly be conceived by the thinkers or artists of this age. This is why the Comedy produced by the age, even that of Molière, tends to correspond to that of the New, rather than the Old, Attic Comedy; it is in the line of the farce of Menander, rather than in that of the high-mimetic seriousness of Aristophanes, which is a Comedy based upon an acceptance of the *truths of tragedy* rather than the flight from, or derogation of, those truths, as Menander's—and Molière's—tend to be.

Verlaine is supposed to have remarked that the beautiful ladies painted by Reynolds and Gainsborough had the appearance of goddesses who did not believe in their own happiness. The same may be said of the writers, historians, and philosophers of the Age of Enlightenment; but this was not because they did not believe in happiness, but rather because they could not believe themselves to be gods—or even heroes. Neither a Comic nor a Tragic vision of history was plausible to them, and so they fell back upon Satirical and Ironic representations of the world they inhabited and of the processes by which it had been constituted. This should not, however, be taken as an ignoble choice on their part. Having precritically decided by their prefiguration of the world as a severed field, of causes on the one hand and effects on the other, that no unity was possible, they progressively gave up the ideal on behalf of the reality. This reality presented itself to them as an irreducible mixture of reason and unreason, as tainted beauty, and finally as a dark fate that was as incomprehensible as it was ineluctable.

I can now characterize the general aspect of the historical thought of the Enlightenment as a whole. In the main line, I perceive the establishment of a paradigm of historical consciousness in the mode of Metonymy, or of cause-effect relationships, in the service of which both Metaphorical identifications (the naming of the objects in the historical field) and Synecdochic characterization of individuals in terms of species and genera were used to yield a meaning that was finally Ironic in its specific content. And I can say that, in this case, an Ironic *comprehension* was the fruit of a Metaphorical and Synecdochic investigation of a field that had been precritically apprehended, and therefore construed in the mode of Metonymy. Put as a rule, this might yield a generalization: He who approaches history as a field of cause-effect relationships is driven, by the logic of the linguistic operation itself, to the comprehension of that field in Ironic terms.

This means that Enlightenment historical thought moved in its explanatory mode from nomological apprehensions to typological comprehensions, which is to say that the best it offered to historical understanding was a succession of "types" of humanity, which tended to fall apart into positive or negative classes, in this case, reason and unreason respectively. The mode of representation began in an Epic prefiguration of the historical field, which is to say in the apprehension of a great contest between the powers of reason and unreason, a contest inspired by the hope that history would show the triumph of the heroic powers over the blocking figures that were needed for the tension leading to the movement in the whole. But historians soon began to recognize that, when it is a matter of divine contests, something must be lost or gained *absolutely* in the conflict, that it is not a matter simply of redisposing the forces at play on the field, that, in short, neither life nor history is a *game*. This, in turn, led to the investigation of the possible Comic or Tragic meanings that the whole historical process might yield to investigation. But it was finally recognized that a Comic representation of historical occurrence can be sustained only on dogmatic grounds, as Turgot and Condorcet tried to sustain it, and never on empirical ones, as Bayle and Voltaire had hoped to do.

The result of this perception was to drive thought to the consideration of the feasibility of a Tragic emplotment of the historical process. This, however, was undermined from the beginning by the conception of human nature as nothing but a field of causal determinations, which makes of every potentially Tragic flaw in a protagonist a genuine *corruption* rather than a virtue which has been transformed by excess into a vice. The result was that historical thought, like the philosophical and literary sensibility of the age, was carried into the mode of Satire, which is the "fictional" form that Irony takes.

Satire can be used—and here I move into the area of ideological implications—for either Conservative or Liberal purposes, depending upon whether the object satirized is an established or an emerging social force. The historical thought of the Enlightenment, that produced by its best representatives, could have been used for either Liberal or Conservative purposes, but to no very high effect in the service of either, because, in its Irony, it recognized that the specific truths it established were ambiguous and taught no general truths at all, only that, *plus ça change, plus c'est la même chose*. In the end, the forces of democracy that were emerging during the time appeared as reprehensible and as frightening to the *philosophes* as did the forces of aristocracy and privilege which they had originally opposed, because, in the very way they construed reality, they could not believe in the possibility of a genuine *transformation* of anything—society, culture, or themselves.

Kant's decision to treat historical comprehension as a fiction having distinct moral implications represented the coming to consciousness of the age's Ironic predisposition. And, just as in Kant's philosophy his Ironic defense of science paved the way for Idealism, so too did his Ironic analysis of historical thought pave the way for the rebirth of that Organicist conception of reality taught by Leibniz. Kant disliked Fichte's Idealism, which was an eccentric development of his own system, because it made of science nothing but a projection of the subjective will. What he disliked about the Organicism of Herder, who revived Leibniz's doctrine of continuity and turned it into the basis of a new philosophy of history, was that it made of change and transformation the very bases of life, the nature of which now required that one not even raise the question of whether or not history was progressing.

In a work that I will consider later, as another example of an Ironic approach to historical knowledge (Nietzsche's *Use and Abuse of History*), a distinction is drawn between three kinds of historical sensibility—the Antiquarian, the Monumental, and the Critical—on the basis of what might be called the dominant form of the "temporal yearning" which characterizes each. Antiquarian history, Nietzsche said, places an absolute value on anything old, just because it is old, and succors man's need for a feeling of having roots in a prior world and his capacities for reverence, without which he could not live. Monumental history, by contrast, seeks not the old but the manifestly great, the heroic, and holds it up as an example of man's creative power to change or transform his world; hence it is future-oriented and destructive of Antiquarian pieties and present practical concerns. Critical history, on the other hand, judges both inherited pieties and utopian dreams of the future, working in the service of present felt needs and desires, preparing the way for that creative forgetting, the cultivation of the faculty of "oblivion" without which action in the present is not possible at all.

The eighteenth century produced representatives of all three types of history-writing, but it was weakest in the promotion of the monumental, the hero-serving, form. The conception of history as the story of heroes, of the historical process as "the essence of innumerable biographies," as Carlyle would later conceive it, was the special achievement of the Romantic age of the early nineteenth century. But the Enlightenment produced nothing of this sort, because the Enlightenment did not really have very much confidence in individual men—in humanity, yes; in individual men, no. The reason for this lay in the perspective from which the Enlighteners viewed their own attempts to write history, whether in the Antiquarian, the Monumental, or the Critical form.

The Enlighteners came to their study of history from the fourth level of awareness that Nietzsche himself sought to promote, a *meta*historical awareness—an Ironic awareness—of the limitation which nature places on every human action and the restriction which human finitude places on every effort to comprehend the world in either thought or imagination. But they did not fully exploit their ascent to this level of awareness. They did not believe in their own prodigious powers of dreaming, which their Ironic self-consciousness should have set free. For them, the imagination was a threat to reason and could be deployed in the world only under the most rigorous rational constraints.

The difference between the Enlighteners and Nietzsche was that the latter was aware of the "fictive" nature of his own Ironic perceptions, and turned his own oneiric powers against them, using the "unhistorical" position, from which he could survey the efforts of historians to "make sense" of the historical process in Antiquarian, Monumental, and Critical terms, as a base from which to ascend to the "super historical" position, on which new and life-serving, rather than death-serving, "myths" of history could be generated.

By contrast, the Enlighteners never rose to full awareness of the creative possibilities contained in their own Ironic apprehension of the "fictive" nature of historical reflection. This is one reason why they never succeeded in understanding the "fictive" representations of truth given in the myths, legends, and fables of earlier times. They did not see that fables may be the forms given to truths that are incompletely grasped just as often as they may be the contents of falsehoods that are incompletely recognized. Thus, they never freed themselves for that mythic immersion in the historical process conceived as the *divine* mystery, which Herder celebrated in his philosophy, or for that poetic immersion in history conceived as a *human* mystery, which Vico celebrated in his "New Science."

❧ Herder's Rebellion against Enlightenment Historiography

Herder's thought is "mythical" because it seeks escape from Metonymy and its Ironic consequence by recourse to the most basic kind of explanation and representation, the basis of mythic comprehension itself, naive Metaphor. But Herder's thought is not "naive"; it is *consciously* directed to the recovery of the individuality of the event in its particularity, uniqueness, and concreteness in discrete sets of Metaphorical identifications. Thus, Herder's thought may be said to have begun in an apprehension of the historical field as an effectively infinite set of particulars, the origins or causes of which were presumed to be utterly unknowable to reason, hence miraculous, and the whole of which appeared to him as a heaving, tossing ocean of *apparently* casual happening. But Herder could not rest with the mere entertainment of this randomness as the ultimate reality. He insisted—for religious or metaphysical reasons—that this field of happening has an ontologically prior and spiritually superior ground or purpose, a purpose which assured *him* of the ultimate unity, integration, and harmonization of the parts in the whole.

Herder's thought strained for the principle in virtue of which this intimation of harmony and integration can be justified, but in such a way as to avoid its specification in merely physical or causal (that is to say, Metonymical) terms, so as to avoid the descent into Irony which such specification inevitably entails when fully thought through to its ultimate conclusion. He contented himself with discoveries of limited formal coherencies among the individualities he conceived to inhabit the historical field as immediately given—that is to say, with the apprehension of what might be called putatively concrete universals, which are nothing other than the species and genera of events found in the historical field but treated as *concrete* individualities in themselves: nations, peoples, cultures. This is why his conception of history can be seen as both individualistic and typological, and why Herder's whole system of thought can be legitimately linked to Romanticism on the one hand and to Idealism on the other.

As a philosophical system which took shape after—and in reaction to—Enlightenment Mechanism, Herder's Organicist philosophy asserted at one and the same time the primacy and irreducibility of the individual human being as well as of the typifications of individuals' modes of relationship with one another. Herder felt no need to decide whether the concrete individual or the type which it represents is ontologically more primary, for he conceived the individual and the type to be equally "real." Both are equally expressive of the spiritual force or power God, which is ultimately responsible for the integrity of the individual and of the type, and for their harmonization within a larger, cosmic totality over the course of time. For the same reasons, the coming into being and passing away of both the individual and the species and genera they represent were not problems for him, because he presumed that this process of coming into being and passing away is not to be defined as either a natural or a spiritual process, but as a process which is both natural and spiritual, at one and the same time. Coming into being and passing away were equally precious to him as the *means* by which the unified organic force accomplishes its task of ultimately integrating being with itself.

Thus, not even death was a termination for Herder; it is not real, but is rather a *transition point* from one *state of integration* to another. In the

Ideen zur Philosophie der Geschichte des Menschheits (1784–91), for example, he said:

Everything in nature is connected: one state strives towards and prepares for the next. *If, then, man be the last and highest link,* closing as it were the chain of terrestrial organization, *he must also begin the chain of a higher order of creatures* as its lowest link. He is, therefore, *the middle ring* between two adjoining systems of Creation. . . . This view of things . . . alone gives us a key to the wonderful phenomenon of man and hence also to a possible *philosophy of human history.*
   For if we bear this view in mind, it helps us to throw light on the peculiar *contradiction* that is *inherent in the human condition.* Man considered as an animal is a child of the earth and is attached to it as his habitation; but considered as a human being; as a creature of *Humanität, he has the seeds of immortality within* him, *and these require planting in another soil.* As an animal he can satisfy his wants; there are men who wish for no more and hence can be perfectly happy here below. But *those who seek a nobler goal find everything around them imperfect and incomplete,* since *the most noble has never been accomplished* and the *most pure has rarely endured on this earth.* This is amply illustrated by the history of our species, by the many attempts and enterprises that man has undertaken, and by the events and revolutions that have overtaken him. Now and then a wise man, a good man, emerged to scatter ideas, precepts and deeds onto the flood of time. They caused but ripples on the waters. . . . Fools overpowered the counsels of the wise and spendthrifts inherited the treasures of wisdom collected by their forefathers. . . . An animal lives out its life, and even if its years be too few to attain higher ends, its innermost purpose is accomplished; its skills are what they are and it is what it is meant to be. Man *alone of all creatures is in conflict with himself* and with *the world. Though the most perfect among them,* in terms of potentialities, *he is also the least successful* in developing them to their fullest extent, even at the end of a long and active life. *He is the representative of two worlds at once,* and from this derives the *apparent bipolarity* of his nature. . . . This much is certain: in each of man's powers dwells an infinity which cannot be developed in his present state where it is repressed by other powers, by animal drives and appetites, and weighed down, as it were, by the pulls and pressures of our daily chores. . . . The expression of Leibniz, that the mind is the mirror of the universe, contains a more profound truth than is commonly realized. For the *powers of the universe* that *seem to lie concealed* in the mind require only *an organization,* or a *series of organizations,* to set them in action. . . . To the mind, even in its present fetters, *space* and *time are empty concepts.* They *only measure* and denote *relations of the body* and *do not bear upon the eternal capacity of the mind which transcends space and time.* [Herder, *Ideen,* 146–49 (Barnard trans., 280–81); italics added]

   In this passage we can see how Herder managed to enclose within an apprehension of the nobility and harmony of the whole—and to neutralize it —that Ironic conclusion which a merely Metonymical apprehension of the world must be driven to if it be consistently developed and thought through to its ultimate implications. The "contradiction" of the human condition, the *paradox* that man is the highest of creatures and is *at the same time* in constant conflict with himself, that he is possessed of the highest faculties and is *at the same time* the only animal organism that is at constant war with his environment, the irony of the fact that the *noblest exemplars* of the race are *most discontented* with their lot and are the *least effective* in their efforts to ennoble their fellow men—all of this is taken to account for the "apparent bipolarity" of human nature, which is, in turn, transformed into a basis for belief in man's *inhabitance of two realms*, natural and spiritual, between which he forms the link and bridge, and from which his aspirations as a man impel him to a higher order of *integration* beyond time and space. All of this is what justifies the twofold path which Herder's thought followed in his consideration of the historical process: his *apprehension* of the structure of the historical field in the mode of Metaphorical identification of the individual entities—human beings and groups—which constitute it in its immediacy; and his *comprehension* of this field as a process, as a structure in process of articulation in the direction of the *integration of all the parts into a spiritual whole*.

Herder removed the necessity of Metonymical characterization of the historical field, dissolved it as a field of causal happening, and made a *datum* out of what, in Mechanistic philosophies of history, must be entertained as the crucial *problem*—that is, the problem of *change*. At the same time, he did not deny the justification of the Ironic conclusion to which a Metonymical analysis is driven—that is, the apparently "contradictory" nature of human history. He simply took that "contradiction" as an "apparent" reality, a thing which is not so much to be explained as simply to be *explained away* by appeal to the presumed harmonization of the parts in the whole over the long run. Hence his thought oscillated between his apprehension of the individual in its concreteness and integrity as a particularity characterized by purpose and movement toward a goal, which made him precious to the Romantics who followed him, and the comprehension of the whole as a plenum of typifications suggesting the progressive idealization of the totality, which made him dear to the Idealists. What made him anathema to the Positivist philosophers of his own time (such as Kant, who in his scientific philosophy constituted the beginning of a philosophically secure Positivism) and those who come after him (such as the Comteans) was that the category of causality had been drained of all efficacy for the analysis of human phenomena, or rather had had its competence limited to that of analyzing physical and animal nature and those aspects of mankind which fall under the (now epistemologically insignificant) laws of material causation.

But, if this insight into the different spheres over which different kinds of sciences (the physical sciences on the one side, the human sciences on the other) presided endeared him to the Idealists and the Neo-Kantians of the end of the nineteenth century and our own time, it was received with something less than wholehearted enthusiasm by Hegel. The great critical Idealist Hegel recognized that Herder and others like him had correctly perceived that *change* was a fundamental category of historical analysis, but he also perceived that neither Herder, nor the Absolute Idealists (Fichte and Schelling), nor the Positivists had provided a *rational* theory adequate to the determination of what this change imported for human life in general, what the meaning of this change, its direction and ultimate purpose, might be.

Herder not only saw the plan of the whole historical drama as a Comic plan, he saw every act of that drama as a Comic play in miniature, a small, self-enclosed world in which things are always precisely what they *ought to be* as well as what they manifestly *are*. Yet this very characterization of historical existence as a "contradiction" and a paradox denies implicitly what he consistently reiterated as an established truth. And this reveals the moral limitation of Herder's conception of history, the formalism toward which it strove as the highest kind of knowledge one can aspire to in historical comprehension itself. This formalism, which was Herder's response to the Irony of the historiography of late (skeptical) rationalism, this willingness to halt with the apprehension of formal coherence in the historical process, signaled Herder's will to reconstitute *mythically* the grounds on which historical explanation and representation can be carried out, his desire for a new paradigm of historical comprehension.

Herder shared this desire for a new paradigm for conceiving the historical field with the generation of writers and thinkers which appeared all over Europe in his time (the "Pre-Romantics" and *Stürmer und Dränger*), a generation which sought to break with all the presuppositions of Enlightenment rationalism in philosophy and science and with Neo-Classicism in art. Their desire to break with rationalism (at least in its Mechanistic form) and materialism (at least in its non-evolutionary concept) betokened the imminent crystallization of a new paradigm, on the basis of which explanation, representation, and ideological implication were to be carried out on such "chaotic" fields of occurrence as that represented by history. Because he made change immediately categorial in his system and only proximately or finally derivative from a higher, changeless power, Herder served well the felt need of his generation to reinvestigate the phenomena of historical change in general. And, since he refused to specify what the higher governing agency might be, those who shared his apprehension of the historical field—as a congeries of concrete individualities differently engaged in the process of their own self-articulation—could utilize his mode of apprehending the historical field in the interests of contemplating either the individualities met with on that field or the higher unity to whose existence their capacities for self-articulation testified.

Here is Herder's real significance as a historical methodologist. If the historian's interest turns primarily upon interest in the individualities occupying the field, he will tend to write history in the Romantic mode, the mythical nature of which was immediately manifest to such hard-headed "realists" of the next generation as Wilhelm von Humboldt, Ranke, and Hegel. If the historian wants to study the individualities in the field in order to determine the nature of the mysterious "spirit" to whose existence *their* existence is supposed to testify, as Fichte, Schelling, and Wilhelm von Schlegel did, he will write Idealist history, the "mythic" nature of which was equally obvious to those self-same "realists" of the next generation. If, however, the historian detaches Herder's technique of investigation from the more general spiritualist interests which, in his mind, it was conceived to serve, and makes the simultaneous apprehension of things in their individuality and formal coherence the object of his study of the historical field, in such a way as to define a specifically "historical" explanation as a *description* of the formal coherence displayed by an individuality, whether as a particular or a congeries of particulars, he will write history in the mode which has come to be called "historism"—which has lately come to be viewed as a distinctive world view, with ideological implications that are as ineluctable as those of the "mythic" systems against which it was originally proposed as an antidote.

⮑ Herder's Idea of History

Before proceeding to a discussion of the origins of historism and the characterization of its paradigm and various modalities of articulation, I will note, for purposes of clarification, the ways in which Herder's world view functions as a ground for a potential methodology for historical study. I will begin by noting the usual characterization of Herder's achievement as a historical thinker. A late Herderian and an exponent of the same Synecdochic intelligence which Herder represented in his own time (and, moreover, one who advanced his philosophy in a similar spirit—that is, as a way of transcending the Irony of his own age), Ernst Cassirer, said that Herder "broke the spell of analytical thinking and the principle of identity which had held Enlightenment thinking in thrall to causal analysis in historical thinking." History, as Herder conceived it, Cassirer wrote, "dispells the illusion of identity; it knows nothing really identical, nothing that ever recurs in the same form. History brings forth new creatures in uninterrupted succession, and on each she bestows as its birthright a unique shape and an independent mode of existence. Every abstract generalization is, therefore, powerless with respect to history, and neither a generic nor any universal norm can comprehend its wealth. Every human condition has its peculiar value; every individual phase of history has its immanent validity and necessity" (Cassirer, 231). Yet, *at the same time*, Cassirer continued, for Herder, "These phases are not separated from one another, they exist only in and by virtue of the whole. But each phase is equally indispensable. It is from such complete heterogeneity that real unity emerges, which is conceivable only as the unity of a process not as a sameness among existing things" (*ibid.*).

Herder's feeling for the diversity of life forms, his sense of unity in diversity, and his substitution of process for structure as the mode of comprehending history in its totality constitute his distinctive contributions to the historical sense of the nineteenth century. But, as he presented his system in *Ideen zur Philosophie der Geschichte des Menschheits*, he attempted too much. He sought to unite the spheres of the natural and the historical within the same complex of causes. Consider, for example, the following remarks, which come at the end of his reflections on the causes of Rome's decline and fall.

The law that sustained the mundane system, and formed each crystal, each worm, each flake of snow, formed and sustained also the human species: it made its own nature the basis of its continuance and progressive action, as long as men shall exist. All the works of God have their stability in themselves, and in their beautiful consistency: for they all repose, within their determinate limits, on the equilibrium of contending powers, by their intrinsic energy, which reduces these to order. Guided by this clue, I wander through the labyrinth of history and everywhere perceive divine harmonious order: for what can anywhere occur, does occur; what can operate, operates. But reason and justice alone endure: madness and folly destroy the Earth and themselves. [Herder, *Ideen*, 419 (Manuel ed., 116–17)]

The immediate appeal of this passage turns upon the image which it evokes of a system that is both growing and orderly, energic and stable, active yet reposed, developing but systematic, infinite yet limited, and so on, all of which is summed up in the idea of equilibrium. The implication of the passage is that everything that has ever existed was adequate to the conditions of its existence. Herder delighted in the fact that "what can anywhere occur, does occur; what can operate, operates." And on the basis of this insight he cautioned his readers against any impulse to perplex themselves with any "concern" of a "provident or retrospective" sort. (39) Things are always what they must be, but the necessity of their being what they are is nothing but the relationship between themselves and their milieux: "All that can be, is; all that can come to be, will be; if not today, then tomorrow." The spectacle of coming into being and passing away which the historical record displays to consciousness was no occasion for despair to Herder. Time did not threaten him, because he did not take time seriously. Things pass away when *their* time has come, not when Time requires it of them. Time is internalized in the individual; it exercises no hegemony over organic nature: "Everything has come to bloom upon the earth which could do so, each in its own time and in its own milieu; it has faded away, and it will bloom again, when *its* time comes."

Herder did not presume to place himself above anything he encountered in the historical record. Even the slovenly natives of the far off land of California, reports of whom he had from a missionary, excited in him more wonder than the disgust they would have inspired in Voltaire. Although they changed their habitation "perhaps a hundred times a year," slept wherever the urge seized them, "without paying the least regard to the filthiness of the soil, or endeavoring to secure themselves from noxious vermin," and fed on seeds which, "when pressed by want, they pick . . . out of their own excrement," he still found redeeming qualities in them. For they were "always cheerful; forever jesting and laughing; well made, straight, and active"; they lifted stones and other things from the ground "with their two foremost toes"; and when they awoke from sleep, they "laugh[ed], talk[ed], and jest[ed]," going on, "till worn out by old age, when they [met] death with calm indifference" (181 [9]).

Herder *judged* nothing. Those things that appeared to be evil, suffering, wrongdoing, were seen by him always to judge themselves; their perishing was their judgment—they simply *did not endure*. And, according to Herder, it was the same with the great agents of history as it was with the small, with the Romans as with Californians. "The Romans," Herder wrote, "were precisely what they were capable of becoming: everything perishable belonging to them perished, and what was suspectible of permanence remained" (394 [267–68]). Nothing existed *for* anything else, but everything was an indispensable part of the whole; the law of the whole was the rule of the part: "Natural history has reaped no advantage from the philosophy of final causes, the sectaries of which have been inclined to satisfy themselves with probable conjecture, instead of patient inquiry: how much less the history of mankind, with its endlessly complicated machinery of *causes mutually acting upon each other*" (393 [266–67]; italics added). In history, as in nature, Herder concluded, "all, or nothing, is fortuitous; all, or nothing, is arbitrary. . . . This is the only philosophical method of contemplating history, and it has been even unconsciously practiced by all thinking minds" (392 [264–65]).

Of course, to Herder nothing was fortuitous, nothing was arbitrary. He believed that the governing agency which gives to everything the form it ought to have is not extrinsic to the historical process; in the process itself, through a mutual interaction among the elements of the process, things are made into what they ought to be. All agencies in history carry within them the rule of their own articulation, the operation of which is testified to in the *formal coherencies* which individual things actually succeed in attaining. Humility in the presence of the multiplicity of these forms is the historian's, as it is the philosopher's, and, indeed, in Herder's conception, as it is the scientist's, rule of procedure. Viewed from within the process itself, rather than from outside it in the light of generic preconceptions, the historical world is a plethora of unique forms, concrete universals, no one of which is

like any other, but every one of which testifies to the presence of an informing principle within the whole.

The limitation of this conception of history is easily discernible. Lovejoy
has pointed out that Herder lacked any principle that might permit him to
explain why, if everything was always adequate to what nature required of
it, things had to change at all (Lovejoy, *Essays*, 181). Unable to relate the
fact of change to the fact of duration in any theoretically convincing way,
Herder was compelled, Lovejoy says, to elevate both change and duration
into *sacramenta*, and to consider manifestations of either as epiphanies of a
mysterious power, "the unified organic force" before which he was alternately reduced to pious silence or inspired to hymns of praise. In his review
of the *Ideen*, Kant, that relentless detector of metaphysics, laconically
exposed the unscientific character of Herder's reflections on both nature and
history. The notion of a unified organic force as "self-constituting with
respect to the manifold of all organic creatures and as subsequently acting
upon organs according to their differences so as to establish the many genera
and species" lay "wholly outside the field of empirical natural science," Kant
maintained. Such an "idea" belonged "solely to speculative philosophy,"
Kant held, and he went on to argue that, "if it were to gain entry even there,
it would cause great havoc among accepted conceptions" (Kant, *On History*,
38). The desire to relate everything to everything else was denied to science,
Kant said; and, in a witty passage on Herder's attempt to deduce the functions of the parts of the body from its general physiognomy, Kant laid bare
the metaphysical thrust of Herder's entire system:

To want to determine the arrangement of the head, externally with respect to its
shape and internally with respect to its brain, as necessarily connected with a pro-
pensity toward an upright posture; still more, to want to determine how a simple
organization directed solely to this end could contain the ability to reason (a pursuit therefore in which the beast participates)—that patently exceeds all human
reason. For reason, thus conceived, totters on the top rung of the physiological
ladder and is on the point of taking metaphysical wing. [38–39]

What Kant discerned in Herder's system as an error, however, was precisely what appealed to the historians and philosophers of history who
followed him. In the first place, the fact that Herder's system was metaphysical rather than scientific was less important than the mode of conceiving history which it promoted. The metaphysical aspects of the system were
the results of an abstraction from the root metaphor which underlay it and
sanctioned a particular *posture* before the facts of existence on the one hand
and a particular *mode of representing* natural and historical processes on
the other. The posture before the facts which it encouraged was especially
attractive to men who had lived through the period of the Revolution and
its aftermath and who ardently desired some principle on the basis of which
they could affirm the adequacy of their own lived reality against the extrem-

ist criticisms of it which emanated from Reactionaries on the one hand and from Radicals on the other. Herder's acceptance of every reality as inherently possessing its own rule of articulation could be extended to a contemporary society, as well as to past social orders, in a spirit acceptable to both the Conservative and Liberal ranges of the spectrum of political ideology. The attitude which served as the basis of historism when directed toward the past was the same as that which served as the basis of realism when turned upon the present. The same "catholicity of appreciation and understanding" which Herder lavished on every aspect of nature and past history became in spirits as diverse as Hegel, Balzac, Tocqueville, and Ranke the basis of a distinctively realistic historical self-consciousness. Once drained of its excessive claims as a form of scientific explanation and entertained as an attitude, Organicism generated a whole set of perspectives on both the past and the present that were especially satisfying to spokesmen for established classes in the social order, whether those spokesmen thought of themselves as Liberals or Conservatives.

In characterising Herder's conception of history, then, I should distinguish among the *point of view* from which he regarded historical agents and agencies, the *voice* with which he addressed his audience, the formal *theory* of Organicism which he offered as an explanation of the events of history, the *story* he told about history, and the *plot structure* which underlay this story and made of it a story of a particular kind. If I make such distinctions, I can see that, although Kant was no doubt right in his proscription of Herder's Organicism as a metaphysical theory, he had really undermined only one of five different aspects of Herder's whole system. As a storyteller, Herder provided a model for a way of depicting history that can be disengaged from its formal theoretical basis and judged on its own terms as a methodological protocol which can be shared by romantics, realists, and historists alike, and the sharing of which makes of the historical thinkers who followed him, whether romantic, realist, or historist, representatives of a single family of attitudes.

First of all, the *voice* in which Herder presented his conception of history was that of the priestly celebrant of a divine mystery, not that of the prophet admonishing his people for their fall from grace and recalling them to participation in the law. Herder spoke for rather than against humanity's detractors, but not only for humanity in general; he also spoke for, or on behalf of, his contemporary audience, which he addressed directly and whose attitudes and values he shared. Second, the *point of view* assumed by Herder with respect to his materials was that of one who is neither below nor above them in dignity. Herder did not credit the idea that he and his own age were demented coinage of a nobler age or incomplete anticipations of an age yet to come. Although his attitude toward the past was that of a celebrant of its inherent virtue, he extended this same attitude toward his own time, so that the virtue that was presumed to have existed in prior times and would exist in future times was also presumed to be present in his time as well. Third, the *story* he told was that of the coming into being and passing-away of things *in their own time*; it was a story organized around the motifs of change and duration and the themes of generation, growth, and fulfillment, motifs and themes which depend for their plausibility on the acceptance of the analogy between human life and plant life, the root metaphorical identification at the heart of the work. It was the abstraction from this metaphor that gave Herder the specifically Organicist philosophy, with its attendant strategy of explanation and criterion of truth, criticized by Kant in his review as unscientific and metaphysical. And, finally, the *plot structure* or underlying myth which permitted Herder to bind together the themes and motifs of his story into a comprehensible story of a particular sort was that which has its archetype in Comedy, the myth of Providence, which permitted Herder to assert that, when properly understood, all the evidence of disjunctions and conflict displayed in the historical record adds up to a drama of divine, human, and natural *reconciliation* of the sort figured in the drama of redemption in the Bible.

In Herder's whole system, then, distinctions can be made between the way he approached the data of history and worked it up into evidence on the one hand and the way he explained and represented it on the other. His approach to the data was that of the pious celebrant of its variety and vitality, and he worked it up in such a way as to make of it a story in which this variety and vitality are stressed rather than explained away. Variety and vitality were not, for him, secondary, but rather primary categories, and the kind of events he depicted in the story of world history which he wrote was intended to present these characteristics as the data to be accounted for. They were accounted for by being set within a double order of explanatory strategies, theoretical and metaphysical on the one hand and poetic and Metaphorical on the other. Thus, in Herder's *Ideen* the reader experiences a twofold explanatory effect: the metaphysical theory, which conflicts with the formal philosophizing, and especially the Kantian criticism, of his time; and the Metaphorical identification of the doctrine of Providence with the life of the plant, which permits the ordering of the story material into a typical Comedy.

✍§ From Herder to Romanticism and Idealism

In my characterization of eighteenth-century historiography I have distinguished between four modalities of historical conceptualization. The main tradition of rationalism I have characterized as Metonymical and Ironic in its apprehension and comprehension, respectively, of the historical process, and I have shown how this approach to history justified an essentially Satirical mode of representation, the Absurdist implications of which accorded perfectly with the Skepticism in thought and relativism in ethics which a consistently Mechanistic apprehension of the world must in the end lead to. Over against this tradition I have set, as a subdominant convention of historical thought which persisted throughout the century, from Leibniz to Herder, a Metaphorical-Synecdochic mode of historical conceptualization which promotes an Organicist notion of explanation and a Comic mode of representation, which has distinctively optimistic implications, but which is also essentially ambiguous in its moral and political, which is to say its ideological, implications. Both of these conventions arose in opposition to the "confessional" historiography of the preceding century, which was conceived to want in objectivity; to the annalistic mode of representation, which was (correctly) perceived to want in color, conceptualization, and interpretive power; and to the belletristic conception of the historian's task as promoted by the *historiens galants* or *romanesques* of the Rococo Age. I have suggested that the full development of Mechanism into Irony on the one hand and of Organicism into spiritual self-certitude on the other created a schism in the historical consciousness of the age which exposed it to the threat of mythification, a threat which Kant at once warned against and exemplified in his suggestion that the *form* of the historical process must be provided on aesthetic grounds for moral reasons.

This tendency toward the mythification of historical consciousness was carried out in the interest of defending the individual against the collectivity in Romanticism and in the interest of defending the collectivity against the individual in Idealism. Both of these movements represented reactions to the moral Irony into which rationalist historiography had been driven from Bayle to Gibbon and the ideological ambiguity into which the Synecdochic presuppositions of Herder's Organicist thought had led him by the early 1790s.

Romanticist historical thought can be conceived as an attempt to rethink the problem of historical knowledge in the mode of Metaphor and the problem of the historical process in terms of the will of the individual conceived as the sole agent of causal efficacy in that process. Idealism may be viewed in a similar light. It, too, represents an attempt to conceive historical knowledge and historical process in the mode of Metaphor; however, it conceives the sole agent of the historical process to be mind, not in its individuality, but in its generic essence, as the World Mind, in which all historical events are seen as effects of remote, first and final, "spiritual" causes.

Chapter 2 HEGEL: THE POETICS OF HISTORY
AND THE WAY BEYOND IRONY

⁂§ *Introduction*

Hegel's thought about history began in Irony. He presupposed history as a prime fact of both consciousness (as paradox) and human existence (as contradiction) and then proceeded to a consideration of what the Metonymical and Synecdochic modes of comprehension could make of a world so apprehended. In the process he relegated Metonymical comprehension to the status of a base for physical scientific explanations of the world, and further limited it to the explanation of those occurrences that can legitimately be described in terms of cause-effect (mechanical) relationships. He conceived Synecdochic consciousness to have a more general applicability—that is, to the data of both nature and history—inasmuch as both the physical and the human world *can* be legitimately comprehended in terms of hierarchies of species, genera, and classes, the relationships among which suggested to Hegel the possibility of a synchronic representation of reality in general, which is itself hierarchical in nature, even though he denied that this hierarchy could be conceived to have unfolded in time in the physical world. This position was consistent with the science of Hegel's time, which did not permit the attribution of the capacity to evolve to either physical or organic nature; in general, it taught the fixity of species.

Hence, Hegel was forced to conclude that the formal coherence which man perceives in physical objects is only that—that is, formal—and that the appearance of an evolutionary connection between them that man thinks he discerns is a function of the mind's effort to comprehend the world of purely spatial relationships under the aspect of time. This means that, insofar as Hegel was driven toward the doctrine of natural evolution, he was so driven by *logical considerations* alone. The mind properly organizes the natural world, conceived as a hierarchy of ever more comprehensive forms—from individual and species to genus and class—and is driven by speculation to imagine the possibility of the class of all classes, which would be the formal aspect of the whole of Being. But man has no grounds for imputing to this hierarchy of forms an *evolution* from lower to higher or higher to lower in time. Each apprehended formal coherence is only a *logical presupposition* of that above it, just as it is the logical consequence of that below it. But none is the *actual precedent* of the other, for in nature the species themselves do not change or evolve; only individuals do, and they change or evolve in the movement of straight lines (as in gravitational fall) or cycles (as in organic processes of reproduction, birth, growth, decay, and death), which is to say that they develop *within* the limits of a specific form, not *across* species.

For Hegel, every instance of cross-species fertilization represented a degeneration, a corruption of species, rather than in improvement or higher form of life. Nature, therefore, exists for man in the modes of Metonymy and Synecdoche; and man's consciousness is adequate to the full comprehension of its modes of existence when he deploys causal concepts to explain changes in nature and typological systems to characterize the formal coherence and levels of integration or dispersion which nature offers to perception guided by reason and aesthetic sense. It is, however, quite otherwise with history, for which causal explanations and typological characterizations of its data represent *possible* modes of conceiving its more primitive levels of occurrence, but which, if they alone are employed for its comprehension, expose understanding to the dangers of mechanism on the one hand and formalism on the other.

Hegel took the limitations of a purely mechanistic approach to history to be manifest, since the very primacy which such an approach conceded to concepts of causal explanation led inevitably to the conclusion not only that the whole of history was totally determined but also that no change of any genuine significance could ever occur in history, the apparent development of human culture perceived there having to be construed as nothing but the rearrangement of primitive elements in different combinations. Such a view did as little justice to the obvious evolution of religious, artistic, scientific, and philosophical consciousness as it did to the evolution of society itself. Such an approach had to lead to the conclusion that, in fact, there had been no qualitative progress of mankind, no essential advancement of culture and society, from the time of savagery to Hegel's time, a conclusion that was absurd on the face of it.

Formalism was another matter. It made sense of the historical process on the basis of a distinction between higher and lower forms of life, in both natural and historical existence. But, since it took the formal coherencies in terms of which this distinction was specified to be timeless in essence, formalism possessed no principle by which to account for their evolution from lower to higher forms of integration and no criterion by which to assess the moral significance of the evolution that could actually be seen to have occurred in the historical sphere. Like the mechanistic approach to history, the formalist approach was forced to choose between the conclusion that the formal coherencies it discerned in history appeared and disappeared at random or represented the eternal recurrence of the same set of formal coherencies throughout all time. No genuine evolutionary development could be derived from consideration of them.

Thus, formalism and mechanism alike forced a choice between the ultimate total incoherence of all historical processes (pure contingency) and their ultimate total coherence (pure determination).

But formalism was more dangerous than mechanism, in Hegel's view, because the spiritual atmosphere of the age promoted allegiance to its different modes of deployment, as an apprehension of total incoherence or of total coherence in the two dominant cultural movements of the time, Romanticism and Subjective Idealism, both of which Hegel despised.

In his introduction to *Philosophy of History* Hegel characterized one type of reasoning which utilizes merely formalist procedures in the following terms:

A . . . process of reasoning is adopted, in reference to the *correct* assertion that genius, talent, moral virtues, and sentiments, and piety, may be found in every zone, under all political constitutions and conditions; in confirmation of which examples are forthcoming in abundance. [65]

This is the sort of apprehension from which Herder derived his Organicist conclusions about the nature of the historical process. But, Hegel went on to note,

If in this assertion, the *accompanying distinctions* are intended to be repudiated as unimportant or non-essential, reflection evidently limits itself to abstract categories; and ignores the [specific attributes] of the object in question, which certainly fall under no principle recognized by such categories. [65–66]

And he then pointed out,

That intellectual position which adopts such merely formal points of view, presents a vast field for ingenious questions, erudite views, and striking comparisons. [66]

But, he maintained, such "reflections" are "brilliant" only

in proportion as the subject they refer to is indefinite, and are susceptible of new and varied forms in inverse proportion to the importance of the results that can be gained from them, and the certainty and rationality of their issues. [*Ibid.*]

On such grounds, Hegel insisted, there can be no certainty regarding the question of whether or not humanity has progressed over the course of time and in the movement from one form of civilization to another. Moreover, such formalism remains prey to the moral relativism of which it is the epistemological counterpart.

It is similar with respect to that other kind of formalism, fostered by Romanticism, which takes the individual in its concreteness and uniqueness as a formal coherence, as against the species, genus, and class to which the individual belongs. Hegel pointed to the inherently amoral—or immoral— implications of this point of view also. This "is something merely formal, inasmuch as it aims at nothing more than the analysis of the subject, what- ever it may be, into its constituent parts, and the comprehension of these in their logical definitions and forms" (68). Thus, he said, in those (Romantic) philosophers who claim to find "genius, poetry, and even philosophy" every- where in equal abundance (or equal scarcity), there is a failure to distin- guish between form and content and to identify the latter as a unique particularity along with the identification of the form as a precious evidence of the spirit's equal dispersion throughout the world (67). It is true, Hegel said, that we find "among all world historical peoples, poetry, plastic art, science, even philosophy"; but, he insisted,

not only is there a diversity in style and bearing generally, but still more remark- ably in subject-matter; and this is a diversity of the most important kind, affecting the rationality of that subject-matter. [69]

It is therefore "useless" for a "pretentious aesthetic criticism to demand that our good pleasure should not be made the rule for the matter—the substantial parts of their contents—and to maintain that it is the beautiful form as such, the grandeur of the fancy, and so forth, which fine art aims at, and which must be considered and enjoyed by a liberal taste and cultivated mind" (*ibid.*). The healthy intellect cannot, Hegel maintained, "tolerate such abstractions," because "there is not only a classical *form*, but a classical order of *subject-matter*; and in the work of art, form and subject matter are so closely united that the former can only be classical to the extent to which the latter is so" (70).

All of this adds up to a condemnation of what is now called the "compara- tive method" of historical analysis, which is the form that Metaphorical consciousness takes when it is projected theoretically into a method. Hegel's objections to the Metaphorical mode of representing history were even more virulent than his objections to the Metonymical mode, for the effects of the formalist explanations it provides and the Epic plot structures it uses to characterize the stories it tells are morally more dangerous. Mechanistic theories of explanation, and the Absurdist emplotments of history which they encourage, at least do not seek to clothe the meaninglessness of the processes they explicate behind distracting chatter about the "beauty" of it all. They may even serve as the basis for a particular kind of Tragic apprehension of the world—the kind of tragedy produced by the Greeks, in which destiny is apprehended as "blind fate"—which in turn can serve as the basis for a Stoic resolve. Yet, in the end, mechanism and the kind of Absurdist Tragedy conceived on its basis as a principle of artistic representation can, as they did in ancient Greece, promote an Epicurean, as well as a Stoic, moral response. Unless there is some principle by virtue of which the whole spectacle of human chance and determinancy, freedom and restraint, can be transformed into a *drama*, with a specifically rational, and at the same time moral, significance, the Ironic consciousness in which the thought of Hegel's own age began its reflection is bound to end in despair—or in the kind of egoistic self-indulgence which would bring about the end of civilization itself.

◆§ Language, Art, and Historical Consciousness

It is frequently not noted that Hegel dealt with historical writing and the whole problem of historiography (as against philosophy of history) more fully in his *Encyclopedia* and his *Lectures on Aesthetics* than in his *Lectures on the Philosophy of History*. The "science" of history which it was his purpose to establish in *Philosophy of History* was, in his conceptualization of it, the product of a *post*historical consciousness, of *philosophical* reflection on the works actually produced by "Reflective" historians. In *Aesthetics*, however, Hegel elaborated his theory of historical writing itself, which he saw as one of the verbal *arts* and hence conceived to fall under the imperatives of the aesthetic consciousness. It is profitable, therefore, to consider what Hegel had to say about historical writing and historical consciousness in this context, as a way of rendering clear the specific content of his "theory of the historical work."

In Part III of his *Lectures on Aesthetics*, Hegel dealt with the verbal arts. He began with a characterization of poetic expression in general and then proceeded to draw a distinction between poetry and prose. Poetry, he said, is of greater antiquity than speech modelled in the artistic form of elaborate prose. It is the *original imaginative grasp of truth*, a form of *knowledge* which [1] *fails as yet to separate the universal from its living existence in the particular* object, which [2] *does not as yet contrast law and phenomena, end and means*, or [3] *relate the one to the other in subordination to the process of human reason*, but [4] *comprehends the one exclusively in the other and by virtue of the other*. [IV, 22 (German ed., 240); italics added]

This characterization of poetry as a form of knowledge is precisely the same as Vico's, which is to say that it conceives poetry as a *Metaphorical apprehension* of the world, containing within itself the potential of generating the other modes of tropological reduction and inflation, Metonymy, Synecdoche, and Irony respectively. Later on Hegel said, "The character of this mode of apprehending, reclothing, and expressing fact is throughout purely theoretical [*rein theoretisch*]. It is not the fact itself and its contemplative existence, but construction [*Bilden*] and speech [*Reden*] which are the object of poetry" (*ibid.* [241]). In poetry, he continued, what is expressed is simply made use of to attain the ideal of verbal "self-expression." And he took as an example of the poetization of a fact the distich recorded by Herodotus in which the Greeks commemorated the slain in the Battle of Thermopylae, a historical event. The inscription reads:

> Four thousand here from Pelops' land
> Against three million once did stand.
> [Herodotus, *The Histories*, bk. VII, chap. 228, p. 494]

Hegel pointed out that the *content* of this distich is simply the *fact* that 4,000 Peloponnesians fought against three million at a certain time and place. The main interest of the distich, however, is the "composition" of an inscription which "communicates to contemporary life and posterity the historical fact, and is there exclusively to do so" (*Aesthetics*, 23 [241]). The mode of expression is "poetical," Hegel said, because the inscription "testifies to itself as a deed [a *poiein*, ποιεῖν]" which conveys the content in its simplicity and at the same time expresses that content "with a definite purpose." The language in which the idea is embodied, he went on to say, is "of such increased value" that "an attempt is made to distinguish it from ordinary speech," and therefore "we have a distich in place of a sentence." (*Ibid.*) The content of the sentence, then, was rendered more vivid, more immediately self-projective, than it would have been had it been expressed as a simple prose report of an event which occurred at a given time and place. A "prosaic" statement of the same fact would leave the content unaltered, but would not *figure itself forth* as that intimate union of content with form which is recognized as a specifically poetic utterance.

Prosaic speech, Hegel argued, presupposes a "prosaic" mode of life, which it must be assumed developed *after* that stage of human consciousness in which speech was "poetical without [conscious] intention" (*ibid.*). Prosaic language presupposes the evolution of a post-Metaphorical consciousness, one which "deals with finite conditions and the objective world generally, that is, the limited categories of science or the understanding" (24 [242]). The world in which prosaic utterance developed must be supposed to have been one in which experience had become atomized and denuded of its ideality and immediately apprehended significance, and voided of its richness and vitality. Against this threat of atomicity and causal determination, consciousness erected a third way of apprehending the world, "speculative thought," which "does not rest satisfied with the differentiations and external relations proper to the conceptions and deductions of the understanding," but "unites them in a free totality" (25 [243]). Thus, Synecdoche projects—over against, and as an antithesis to, the world apprehended in Metonymical terms—a "new world." But, because this new world exists only in consciousness and not in actuality (or at least is not *felt* to exist there), the problem of consciousness is to relate this new world to that of concrete things. It is the poet's task, Hegel concluded, to reconcile the world existing in thought with that of concrete things by figuring the universal in terms of the particular, and the abstract in terms of the concrete.

Poetic expression thus seeks to restore to a prosaic world the consciousness of its inherent ideality. In earlier times, when the distinction between poetry and prose was not so well developed as it has since become with the advance of science and philosophy, the poet had an easier task—that is, simply to deepen all that is "significant and transparent in the forms of ordinary consciousness." After the advent of higher civilization, however, in which "the prose of life has already appropriated within its mode of vision the entire content of conscious life, setting its seal on all and every part of it, the art of poetry is forced to undertake the task of melting all down again and re-coining the same anew." (26 [244]) This means that it must not only

wrest itself from the adherence of ordinary consciousness to all that is indifferent and contingent, and . . . raise the scientific apprehension of the cosmos of fact to the level of reason's profounder penetration, or . . . translate speculative thought into terms of the imagination, give a body to the same in the sphere of intelligence itself; it has further to convert in many ways the *mode of expression* common to the ordinary consciousness into that appropriate to poetry; and, despite all deliberate intention enforced by such a contrast and such a process, to make it appear as though all such purpose was absent, preserving the original freedom essential to all art. [*Ibid.* (244–45)]

And, having designated the content and form of poetic consciousness, Hegel then proceeded to "historicize" poetic consciousness itself, setting its various periods of brilliance and decline within the general framework of the history of consciousness explicated in the *Phenomenology of Mind,* the *Philosophy of Right,* and the *Philosophy of History.*

Poetry is born, then, of the separation of consciousness from its object and the need (and attempt) to effect a union with it once more. This essential distinction generates the two principal classes of poetry: Classical and Romantic, which emphasize the universal and the particular, objective and subjective expression, respectively. And, in turn, the tension between these two classes of poetry generates the three basic species of poetic composition: Epic, Lyric, and Dramatic, the first two representing externality and internality as effectively stable perspectives on the world, the last representing the effort of poetic imagination to envisage the *movement* by which this tension is resolved and the unity of the subject with the object is achieved.

The Epic, Hegel said, "gives us a more extensive picture of the external world; it even lingers by the way in episodical events and deeds, whereby the unity of the whole, owing to this increased isolation of the parts, appears to suffer diminution." The Lyric "changes conformably to the fluctuation of its types, adapts itself to a mode of presentment of the great variety: at one time it is bare narration, at another exclusive expression of emotion or contemplation; at another it restricts its vision," and so on. By contrast to both Epic and Lyric, the Drama "requires a more strenuous conjunction" of external and internal reality, even though it may, in a specific incarnation, adopt either the Classic or the Romantic *point of view* as its constitutive principle. (37 [256–57])

Thus, Hegel's discussion of poetry began with a discussion of speech as the instrument of man's mediation between his consciousness and the world he inhabits; proceeded to a distinction among the different modes in which the world can be apprehended, thence to a distinction between poetry and prose, between Classical and Romantic forms of both, and between Epic and Lyric forms of these; and ended in a discussion of Drama as the art form in which is imaged the modality of the movement by which this severed condition is healed. It is significant that, having done this, Hegel immediately launched into a discussion of *history* as the prose form closest in its immediacy to poetry in general and to the Drama in particular. In fact, Hegel not only historicized poetry and the Drama, he poeticized and dramatized history itself.

⌐§ *History, Poetry, and Rhetoric*

Hegel's formal discussion of history-writing as an art form is placed between his discussions of poetry and oratory. Its location between these two forms— one concerned with the expression of ideality in the real, the other concerned with the pragmatic uses of linguistic tools—suggests its resemblance to the Drama, which (as noted above) is the *form of mediation* taken in art between the Epic and Lyric sensibilities. History is the prose representation of a dialectical interchange between externality and internality, as that interchange is *lived*, in precisely the same way that Drama is the poetic representation of that interchange as it is *imagined*. And, in fact, Hegel left very little doubt that, in his mind, the formal aspects of both historical and dramatic representation are the same.

"As regards history," he said, "there can be no doubt that we find ample opportunity here for one aspect of genuine artistic activity," for

The evolution of Human life in religion and civil society, the events and destinies of the most famous individuals and peoples who have given emphasis to life in either field [that is, in religion or civil life] by their activity, all this presupposes great ends in the compilation of such a work or the complete failure of what it implies. The historical representation of subjects and contents such as these admits of real distinction, thoroughness, and interest; and however much our historian must endeavor to reproduce actual historical fact, it is nonetheless incumbent upon him to bring before our imaginative vision this motley content of events and characters, to create anew and make vivid the same to our intelligence with his own genius. [38 (257)]

This means, above all, that the historian cannot "rest satisfied with the bare letter of particular fact," but must rather strive to "bring this material into a coordinated whole; he must conceive and embrace single traits, occurrences and actions under the unifying concept" (*ibid.*). The wedding of such contents with the form of representation under which they are appropriately gathered will permit the historian to construct a narrative, the action of which is carried forward by tension between two concrete manifestations of a specifically human life. These manifestations are both particular and general.

Great historical narrative—of the sort produced by Herodotus, Thucydides, Xenophon, Tacitus, "and a few others"—images "a clear picture of nationality, epoch of time, external condition, and the spiritual greatness or weakness of the individuals concerned in the very life and characterization which belonged to them"; at the same time, it asserts from such concrete entities the "bond of association" in which the "various parts of [the] picture" are transformed into a comprehensible totality of "ideal historical significance" (*ibid.* [258]). This implies that historical analysis proceeds both Metonymically and Synecdochically, simultaneously breaking down the subject into concrete manifestations of the causal forces of which they must be presumed to be effects and seeking the coherencies which bind these entities together into a hierarchy of progressively spiritualized unities. Yet the historian cannot proceed with either the "freedom" that the pure poet may claim or with the purposefulness of the orator. The former is free to invent "facts" as he sees fit, the latter to use his facts selectively for the specific purposes of the oration he is composing. History stands somewhere between poetry and oratory because, although its form is poetic, its content is prosaic. Hegel put it thus: "It is not exclusively the manner in which history is written, but the nature of its *content*, which makes it prose" (39 [258]).

History deals with the "prose of life," the materials of a specifically "common life" (*Gemeinwesen*), whether considered from the side of shared religious beliefs or from the side of polity, with its laws, institutions, and instruments for enforcing the adherence of the subject to the values of the commonwealth (*ibid.*). Out of such a common life, Hegel said, are generated those forces which lead to "either the preservation or change" of the same, and for which we must assume the existence of individuals fitted for both tasks. In short, the historical process is pre-eminently a product of a conflict within the context of a shared life style and across a whole set of such shared life styles, the conflict of achieved form with a force which seeks to transform it or of an established power with some individual who opposes it in the interest of its own sensed autonomy and freedom. Here, in short, is the classical situation of the classical tragedy *and* the classical comedy.

The social life of man is not merely an Epic life which, for all the movement, color, and violence of action, remains substantially what it was all along. Great individuals come to the fore, against the background of a common life shared by ordinary men, and transform this *Epic situation* into a *Tragic conflict* in which neither mere beauty nor mere strength triumphs, but in which two contending rights, two equally justifiable moral principles, become locked in combat in order to determine what the *form* of human life in a specific social incarnation *may* be. For this reason Hegel envisioned three basic categories of actors in the historical drama: great, small, and depraved (heroes, ordinary men, and criminals).

These individuals are great and eminent insofar as they show themselves, through their effective personality, [to be] in cooperation with the common end which underlies the ideal notion of the conditions which confront them; they are little when they fail to rise in stature to the demand made on their energy; they are depraved when, instead of facing as combatants of the practical needs of the times, they are content merely to give free rein to an individual force which is, with its implied caprice, foreign to all such common ends. [40 (259)]

In this catalog of types of "historical" personalities is a recapitulation of the categories of analysis of poetry itself, but under the mode of Metonymy —that is, causal efficacy. But, as Hegel indicated in the *Philosophy of Right*, the historical field is not to be conceived as merely a field of brute force. For, where such force predominates, where it is not in conflict with a more general principle—that is, the "common life" of the group—there is no genuinely historical conflict and consequently no specifically "historical event." Hegel made this quite clear in a passage following that quoted above. Where any of the three conditions listed obtains as the *general condition*, where we have the tyranny of one man, the tyranny of custom (which is the tyranny of the ordinary man), or the tyranny of chaos, "we do not have either a genuine [historical] content or a condition of the world such as we established in the first part of our inquiry as essential to the art of poetry," which is the condition of all specifically human creativity (*ibid.*), because:

> Even in the case of personal greatness the substantive aim of its devotion is to a large or less extent something given, presupposed, and enforced upon it, and to that extent the unity of individuality is excluded, wherein the universal, that is the entire personality should be self-identical, an end exclusively for itself, an independent whole in short. For however much these individuals discover their aims in their own resources, it is for all that not the freedom or lack of it in their souls and intelligence, but the accomplished end, and its result as operative upon the actual world already there, and essentially independent of such individuality which constitutes the object [of study] of history. [*Ibid.*]

Moreover, Hegel added, in history we find a much greater variety, more contingencies, more subjectivity displayed in the expression of passions, opinions, and fortunes, "which in this prosaic mode of life present far more eccentricity and variation than do the wonders of poetry, which through all diversity must remain constant to what is valid in all times and places" (*ibid.* [259–60]).

Finally, history has to do with the carrying out of projects and aims by specific individuals and groups, which requires the dreary work of finding means adequate to the task, itself a prosaic, because utilitarian, activity; and evidences of this activity must be depicted in the historian's account. This attention to the details of practical activity, which must be derived from study of the historical record and not merely presupposed by the historian, in either a poetic or a speculative mood, makes his work so much more prosaic than either that of the poet or that of the philosopher.

It therefore follows, according to Hegel, that the historian has no right to "expunge these prosaic characteristics of his content or to convert them into others more *poetical*; his narrative must embrace what lies actually before him and in the shape he finds it without amplification [*ohne umzudeuten*] or at least poetical transformation" (41 [260]). However much his thought may strain to grasp the ideal significance of the form of the myriad events he perceives, he is not permitted to make "either the conditions presented him, the characters or events, wholly subordinate to such a purpose," even though he may "remove from his survey what is wholly contingent and without serious significance" (*ibid.*). The historian "must, in short, permit them to appear in all their objective contingency, dependence, and mysterious caprice" (*ibid.*). This means that the historian's imagination must strain in two directions simultaneously: *critically*, in such a way as to permit him to decide what can be left out of an account (though he cannot invent or add to the facts known); and *poetically*, in such a way as to depict, in its vitality and individuality, the medley of events as if they were present to the sight of the reader. In its critical function, historical consciousness is operative only as an excluding agency. In its synthetic function, it operates only in an inclusive capacity. For, even if the historian may add to his accounts his private reflections as a philosopher, "attempting thereby to grasp the absolute grounds for such events, . . . he is nonetheless debarred, in reference to the actual conformation of events, from that exclusive right of poetry, namely, to accept this substantive resolution as the fact of most importance" (42). The historian may not fall into metahistory, even though he may speculatively apprehend the grounds by which a metahistorical synthesizing vision might be possible, because:

To poetry alone is the liberty permitted to dispose without restriction of the material submitted in such a way that it becomes, even regarded on the side of external condition, conformable with ideal truth. [Ibid.]

In this respect, oratory has a greater freedom than history, for, since the orator's art is developed as a means to the achievement of practical ends, just as the poet's is developed for the achievement of ideal ones, the orator is permitted to use historical facts as he wishes, selectively and in response to the end envisaged (43).

Thus, Hegel again invoked the distinction, made at the beginning of his introduction to Philosophy of History, between "Original" and "Reflective" historiography, on the basis of the essentially poetic nature of the former and the increasingly prosaic nature of the latter, and within Reflective historiography, among the Universal, Pragmatic, and Critical types. Universal history is, as he noted, the most poetic, taking as its subject the whole known historical world and fashioning it, in response to apprehended ideal forms, by metaphor, into a coherent poetic whole. Pragmatic historiography, written under the impulse to serve some cause, some practical end, rises above the universal variety inasmuch as it moves from a poetic to an oratorical mode of conceiving its task, from the vision of the ideality of the whole to an awareness of the uses to which a vision of the whole can be put. The manufacture of a number of such conflicting visions of the historical process inspires a "Critical" reflection on historical writing itself, which in turn permits the rise in consciousness of the possible ideality of the whole through reflection in the mode of Synecdoche. This paved the way for Hegel's own Philosophical history, which was meant to explicate the presuppositions and forms of thought by which the essentially poetic insights of the historian can be gathered into consciousness and transformed into a Comic vision of the whole process. But this is the philosopher of history's task, not the historian's; like Thucydides, the historian must remain closer to the poetic mode of apprehension, closer to Metaphorical identification with his object, but at the same time be more self-critical, more aware of the modalities of comprehension used to transform a poetic insight into the content of a more rational knowledge.

⁓§ The Possible Plot Structures

This brings me to Hegel's theory of historical emplotment. When I deal with this subject, I move from the consideration of history as an object, a content, the form of which is to be perceived by the historian and converted into a narrative, to that in which the form provided, the narrative actually produced, becomes a content, an object of reflection on the basis of which a truth about history-in-general can be asserted on rational grounds. And this raises the problem of the possible content of that truth and the form its affirmation must take. Hegel's solution to this problem can be formulated in the following way. The truths figured in historical narratives of the highest sort are the truths of Tragedy, but these truths are only poetically figured there as the forms of historical representations whose contents are the actual life dramas lived by individuals and peoples at specific times and places. Hence, it requires philosophical reflection to extract the truth contained in the form in which historical accounts are presented. Just as the philosopher of art takes as his objects of study the various forms of works of art which have appeared in world history, so the philosopher of history takes as his objects the various forms of the histories actually written by historians in the course of history itself. He apprehends these histories as formal systems which may work up an account of a life in any of four modes: Epic, Comedy, Tragedy, Satire, or in any combination of these.

But the Epic is not an appropriate form of historiography, according to Hegel, because it does not presuppose substantial change. And the same can be said of Satire, because, although it admits change, it perceives no substantial base against which the changes perceived can be measured. For the Epic, all is change conceived against a basic apprehension of substantial changelessness; for Satire, all is changelessness conceived in the light of the perception of a substantial mutability. (Cf. Hegel's remarks on Voltaire's *Henriade*, 131–32) So it is in the mixed genre of the (modern) Romantic Tragicomedy, which seeks to mediate between the Comic and Tragic visions of the world, but does so only formally—that is, by representing within the same action the representatives of each view, never combining or unifying them, but leaving the world as sundered as it originally found it, with no higher principle of unity being given which consciousness might turn into an object of contemplation for the promotion of wisdom about a world thus severed within itself. Only Comedy and Tragedy, therefore, are left as appropriate modes of emplotment of historical processes, and the problem is to work out their interrelations as different stages of self-conscious reflection on consciousness' relation to the world.

Hegel maintained that philosophical wisdom, when turned upon history, bears the same relationship to historical wisdom, when turned upon the facts of history, that the Comic vision does to the Tragic vision. That is to say, philosophy mediates between the concrete embodiments of human historical existence represented in specific histories as a content for which it seeks to find an adequate form of representation and mode of emplotment. And it finds such in the Comic vision itself. Comedy is the form which reflection takes after it has assimilated the truths of Tragedy to itself.

◄§ Tragedy and Comedy as Generic Plot Structures

"Dramatic action," Hegel wrote, "is not confined to the simple and undisturbed execution of a definite purpose, but depends throughout on conditions of collision, human passion and characters, and leads therefore to actions and reactions, which in their turn call for some further resolution of conflict and disruption" (249). Dramatic action, then, has precisely the same formal characteristics as historical action:

What we have . . . before us are definite ends individualized in living personalities and situations pregnant with conflict; we see these as they are asserted and maintained, as they work in cooperation or opposition—all in a momentary and kaleidoscopic interchange of expression—and along with this, too, the final result presupposed and issuing from the entirety of this interthreading and conflicting skein of human life, movement, and accomplishment, which has nonetheless to work out its tranquil resolution. [249–50 (475–76)]

Thus, Dramatic action rises above and comprehends the Epic or objective, and the Lyric or subjective, points of view; the Drama as such adopts as its standpoint neither one nor the other, but moves between them in such a way as to keep both present to consciousness. It can be said, then, that the Drama moves in the mode of Irony itself, the dialectical exchange of point of view being nothing but this Ironic perspective. (251–52; cf. Burke, *Grammar*, 511–17)

According to Hegel, Drama begins in the apprehension of the one-sidedness of all perspectives on reality, and strives for the "resolution of the one-sided aspect of these powers, which discover their self-stability in the dramatic character" (*Aesthetics*, IV, 255). "And," Hegel added,

this is so whether, as in tragedy, they are opposed to such in hostility, or, as in comedy, they are displayed within these characters themselves, without further mediation, in a condition of resolution. [256]

This last passage is significant, for it suggests that Hegel regards Tragedy and Comedy, not as opposed ways of looking at reality, but as perceptions of situations of conflict from different sides of the action. Tragedy approaches the culmination of an action, carried out with a specific intention, from the standpoint of the agent who sees deployed before him a world which is at once a means and an impediment to the realization of his purpose. Comedy looks back upon the effects of that collision from beyond the condition of resolution through which the Tragic action has carried the spectators, even if the action has not carried the protagonist there but has consumed him in the process. Thus, like historical situations, Dramatic situations begin in the apprehension of a conflict between a world already formed and fashioned in both its material and social aspects (the world displayed immediately in Epic) and a consciousness differentiated from it and individuated as a self intent upon realizing its own aims, satisfying its needs, and gratifying its desires (the interior world expressed in Lyric). But, instead of halting at the contemplation of this condition of severance, the Dramatic artist goes on to contemplate the modality of the conflicts which result from this asymtotic relationship between the individual consciousness and its object. The mode of resolution and the depth of wisdom reflected in it will produce the actions of three kinds of post-Epical and non-Lyrical forms of Drama: Tragedy, Comedy, and (the counterpart of Satire) the Social Play, which is a mixed genre that seeks to mediate between the insights of Tragedy and those of Comedy.

The content of Tragic action, Hegel wrote, is the same as that of history: we *apprehend* it immediately in the aims of Tragic characters, but *comprehend* it fully only as "the world of those forces which carry in themselves their own justification, and are realized substantively in the volitional activity of mankind" (295). This substantive world is that of the family, the social, political, and religious life of civilized society, a world which at least implicitly recognizes the legitimacy both of individual aspiration to selfhood on the one hand and of the laws and morality of the collectivity on the other. Family, society, religion, and politics provide the grounds of such actions as those we call "heroic": "It is of a soundness and thoroughness consonant with these that the really tragic *characters* consist. They are throughout that which the essential notion of their character enables and compels them to be. They are not merely a varied totality laid out in the series of views of it proper to the epic manner." They are not unmediated individualities, but personalities, possessing a unity of character which permits them to stand as representatives of different aspects of "the common life" or as free agents seeking their own self-reliance. (295–96) And in Tragic conflict, as in historically significant conflict, either the common life or the personality seeking its own self-reliance causes the conflict itself.

Tragic Drama, however, takes not conflict itself as its object (as the Epic tends to do), but rather that condition of resolution, in which both the hero and the common life are transformed, which lies on the other side of this conflict.

In tragedy individuals are thrown into confusion in virtue of the abstract nature of their sterling volition and character, or they are forced to accept that with resignation, to which they have been themselves essentially opposed. [301]

Comedy, however, attains to a vision of that reconciliation as a "victory of the wholly personal soul-life, the laughter of which resolves everything, through the medium and into the medium of such life" (*ibid.*). In short, the general basis of Comedy is "a world in which man has made himself, in his conscious activity, complete master of all that otherwise passes as the essential content of his knowledge and achievement; a world whose ends are consequently thrown awry on account of their own lack of substance" (*ibid.*).

One could hardly ask for a better characterization of the world that is viewed, in *Philosophy of History*, from the standpoint of philosophical reflection on the tragedy of individual historical lives. The essence of the Comic vision is to be found not in Satirical reflection on the contrast between what is and what ought to be, that contrast which is the basis of moral conflict within the heroic subject, but rather in an "infinite geniality and confidence capable of rising superior to its own contradiction and experiencing therein no taint of bitterness or sense of misfortune whatever" (302).

The Comic frame of mind is "a hale condition of soul which, fully aware of itself, can suffer the dissolution of its aims and realization" (*ibid.*). This is why, Hegel suggested, the action of Comedy requires a "resolution" even more stringently than Tragedy does (304). "In other words," Hegel said, "in the action of comedy the contradiction between that which is essentially true and its specific realization is more fundamentally reasserted" (*ibid.*). And the reason for this, he continued, lies in the fact that, "viewed as a genuine art," Comedy "has not the task set before it to display through its presentation what is essentially rational as that which is intrinsically perverse and comes to naught, but on the contrary as that which neither bestows the victory, nor ultimately allows any standing ground to folly and absurdity, that is to say the false contradictions and oppositions which also form part of reality" (*ibid.*). This is the kind of consciousness which is earned by the agon of Aristophanes' comedy, which never caluminiates anything of genuinely ethical significance "in the social life of Athens," but only exposes to ridicule the "spurious growth of the democracy, in which the ancient faith and former morality have disappeared" (*ibid.*). This is also the consciousness that informs philosophy of history, in which the "mode of actual appearance adequate to what is, so to speak, substantive, has vanished out of it; and, if what is essentially without fundamental subsistence comes to naught with its mere pretence of being that which it is not, the individual asserts himself as master over such a dissolution, and remains at bottom unbroken and in good heart to the end" (305).

That this is the mode of a specifically *philosophical comprehension* of history, is that to which the responsible consciousness must come under the guidance of reason, and that it is the antithesis of Irony, are shown by Hegel's virtual denial to the Satirical form of Dramatic representation the status of a genuine Dramatic genre. Satirical Drama, in his view, is a result of a failure to bring the opposing sides of human existence, the subjective and the objective, into any resolution. The best that ancient Satire, and, in Hegel's view, modern (Romantic) Tragicomedy can provide is not "the juxtaposition or alternation of these contradictory points of view" but a "mutual accommodation, which blunts the force of such opposition" (306). There is a tendency in such Drama, as in that "valet's historiography" which belongs to the same genre, to look for purely personal, "psychological" analyses of character or to make the "material conditions" the deciding factor in the action, so that nothing noble can be finally either asserted or denied of noble men (307). And so it is with that historiography of the modern, Romantic age. The Romantic historian seeks refuge from the reality of personality and that "fate" which is nothing but the "common life" into which it is born by sentimental contemplation of the psychological motives of the protagonist on the one side hand or the materiality of his condition on the other.

ᴥᔱ History in Itself and History for Itself

At the beginning of the Introduction to his *Philosophy of History*, Hegel distinguished among three classes of historical consciousness (Original, Reflective, and Philosophical), to the second of which his objections to the limitations of both mechanism and formalism equally apply. These three classes of historical consciousness represent different stages of historical self-consciousness. The first corresponds to what might be called *mere* historical consciousness (historical consciousness *in itself*), the second to a historical consciousness which recognizes itself as such (historical consciousness *for itself*), and the third to a historical consciousness which not only knows itself as such but which reflects upon both the conditions of its knowing— that is, its relation to its object (the past)—and the general conclusions about the nature of the whole historical process that can be derived from rational reflection on its various products, specific historical works (historical consciousness *in and for itself*).

Mere historical consciousness, the product of which is "Original" (*ursprünglich*) historiography, develops out of the simple *awareness* of the historical process itself, a sense of the passage of time and an awareness of the possibility of the development of human nature. It is found in thinkers like Herodotus and Thucydides, "whose descriptions are for the most part limited to deeds, events, and states of society, which they had before their eyes, and whose spirit they shared. They simply transferred what was passing in the world around them, to the realm of re-presentative intellect." According to Hegel, such historians work like poets who operate on material "supplied by [the] emotions, projecting it into an *image* for the conceptual faculty [*für die Vorstellung*]" (*Phil. of Hist.*, 1 [German ed., 11]). To be sure, these historians may have used accounts of deeds written by other men, but they made use of them in the same way that one makes use of a "language already fashioned"—that is to say, only as an *ingredient*. For them, there is no distinction between the history they live and the history they write (*ibid.* [12]).

What Hegel was suggesting here is that "Original historians" work primarily in the mode of Metaphorical characterization: they "bind together *the fleeting elements of story*, and lay them up as treasures in the Temple of Mnemosyne" (*ibid.*, 2 [12]). Their mode of explanation *is* poetic representation, though with this difference: the Original historian takes as his content "the domain of reality—actually seen or capable [in principle] of being seen," not the domain of dreams, fantasies, and illusions (*ibid.*). These "poetic" historians actually "create" (*schaffen*) the "events, the deeds, and the states of society" as an object (*ein Werk*) for the conceptual faculty (*Vorstellung*) (*ibid.*). Hence, their narratives are both restricted in range and limited in time. Their principal aim is to make a lifelike "image" of the events that they know at first hand or on adequate authority. "Reflections" are not for them, for they live "in the spirit of [their] subject" (*ibid.*). And, since they share the same spirit as that which informs the events they depict, they are able, with perfect impunity to criticism, to interpolate the details of the narrative—such as the speeches which Thucydides put in the mouths of his protagonists—as they see fit, as long as these details cohere with the spirit of the whole (*ibid.*).

Such poetic historiography is as rare among modern historians, Hegel said, as it was among the ancients. It can be produced only by spirits who combine a talent for practical affairs on the grand scale, participation in events, and poetic talent, as was the case with Cardinal de Retz or Frederick the Great. To penetrate to the essential truths of the works produced by such "Original historians" requires long study and patient reflection, Hegel concluded, for their works represent a form of historiography that is both a history and an original document of the times in which they were written. Here the identification of the soul of the historian and the events about which he writes (and in which he has participated) is all but complete, and if we would know any of these—the poetry, the events, or the works of the historian—we must seek to know them all. We can read them for poetic inspiration or intellectual sustenance, it might be added; but to subject them to the criteria we use for the assessment of modern "reflective" historiography, the historiography of the professional scholar, is, Hegel implied, as much an indication of bad taste as of the misunderstanding of scientific criticism.

Certain kinds of "Original histories," such as the works of the monks of the Middle Ages, may be criticized for their abstractness or formalism; but these limitations result from the remoteness of the lives of those who wrote them from the events about which they wrote. We have no reason to try either to empathize with or to criticize such works; we need only plunder them for whatever factual data they contain and use them for the construction of our own historical accounts of the past.

The second class of historical works, "Reflective" histories—histories for themselves—are written not only out of an apprehension of the passage of time but also in the full awareness of the distance between the historian and his object of study, which distance the historian consciously tries to close. This effort to close the distance between present and past is conceived to exist as a distinct problem. The spirit of reflective history therefore "transcends the [historian's own] present," Hegel wrote; and the various theoretical devices that different historians use to close the gap which separates them from the past, to enter into that past, and to grasp its essence or content, account for the various species of reflective history which this kind of historian produces.

Hegel distinguished four species of Reflective history: Universal, Pragmatic, Critical, and Conceptual (*Begriffsgeschichte*). All four species display the attributes—in his characterizations of them—of either the Metonymical or the Synecdochic mode of comprehension. Universal history deals, by the very necessity of having to *reduce* its materials, with abstractions and foreshortenings; it is arbitrary and fragmentary—not only because of the scope of its subject, but also because of the need to ascribe causes without sufficient reasons and to construct typologies on the bases of inadequate evidence. Pragmatic histories produce the same kind of pictures of the past, but, rather than do so in the interest of *knowing* the whole past (which predominates in Universal history), they strive to *serve* the present, to illuminate the present by adducing to it analogies from the past, and to derive moral lessons for the edification and instruction of living men. Such histories may, like their Universalist counterparts, be great works of art or, as in the case of Montesquieu's *L'Esprit des lois*, be genuinely enlightening; but their authority is limited, not only because the truths on which they base their lessons for the present are as fragmentary and abstract as those found in Universal history, but also because "what experience and history teach is this—that peoples and governments have never learned anything from history, or acted on principles deduced from it" (6). Hegel thought this because:

Each period is involved in such peculiar circumstances, exhibits a condition of things so strictly idiosyncratic, that its conduct must be regulated by considerations connected with itself, and itself alone. Amid the pressure of great events, a general principle gives no help. It is useless to revert to similar circumstances in the past. [*Ibid.*]

And thus he was led to articulate one of his most famous apothegms:

The pallid shades of memory struggle in vain with the life and freedom of the present. [*Ibid.*]

History, Paul Valéry asserted much more bitterly nearly a century later, "teaches precisely nothing." Hegel, however, would have emphasized the "precisely" rather than, as Valéry did, the "nothing." The reader of both Universal and Pragmatic histories, then, is likely to grow "disgusted" with them, in reaction either to their "arbitrariness" or to their inutility, and to take refuge in the entertainment provided by the simple "narrative," which adopts "no particular point of view."

What I have noted from Hegel's writings thus far adds up to this: we can neither learn about history in toto from the historians nor learn very much from them that is useful for the solutions of our own problems. What, then, is the point of writing history at all, other than the aesthetic enjoyment of the poetic creativity which attends the writing of "Original" history or the moral sense of serving a cause which the writer of Pragmatic history may delight in?

From his characterization of the other two forms of "Reflective" history, it would seem that, for Hegel, the reason for writing history is to be sought in the transformations of consciousness which the attempt to do so effects in the minds of historians themselves.

"Critical history" attains to a higher level of historical consciousness than is manifested in the other two species of Reflective historiography, for here the problem of bridging the gap between past and present is apprehended as a problem in itself, which is to say a problem whose solution is not to be provided by general or practical considerations (as in Universal and Pragmatic historiography), but by theoretical intelligence alone. For, in Critical history, the historian criticizes both the sources and other historical accounts of the subject he is studying, in an effort to extract their actual truth content from them, so as to avoid the pitfalls of arbitrariness, fragmentariness, and subjective interest which mar the preceding types of historiography. According to Hegel, Critical history-writing might be more properly called "a History of History." But, Hegel noted, this form of historical reflection has been cultivated in the absence of any agreed upon criterion by which to establish the relationship between the histories actually written and the objects they represent. It tends to expend all of the historian's energy on the Critical operation, so that, instead of the history of the subject, one gets a history of various historians' histories of the subject. The inherently formalist nature of this enterprise is shown by the fact that the so-called "higher criticism" of Hegel's own time in Germany manifestly substituted all sorts of subjective fancies for the conceptual apparatus that a genuinely critical history would not only display but also defend in rational arguments: "fancies whose merit is measured by their boldness, that is, in the scantiness of the particulars on which they are based, and the peremptoriness with which they contravene the best established facts of history." (7)

Thus, when we arrive at the last species of reflective history, Conceptual history (the histories of art, religion, law, and the like), we have no reason to be surprised by the fact that it "announces its fragmentary character on the very face of it" (*ibid.*). Conceptual history adopts an "abstract position," but it also "takes a general point of view." It thereby provides the basis for a transition to Philosophical history, the third class of historical reflection for which Hegel's own work is supposed to provide the principles (7–8), because such branches of a nation's or a people's life as its art, laws, and religion stand in the most intimate relation to the "entire complex of its annals" that is, the realm of social and cultural praxis in general. Hence Conceptual history necessarily raises the question of "the connection of the whole" (*der Zusammenhang des Ganzen*), which a nation's history represents as an actuality and not merely as an idea yet to be actualized, or not merely grasped as an abstraction but actually lived. (9 [19]). The articulation of the principles by which the content of a people's history as well as its own ideal apprehension of its way of life are to be extracted from its "annals," and the ways in which the relationships among all these are to be explicated —these form the aim of the third class of historical reflection, the Philosophical, which is "the object of [Hegel's] present undertaking" (8).

History in and for Itself

Now, it is obvious that the four species of Reflective history provide a typically Hegelian characterization of the stages of historical consciousness which are possible *within* the class of historical consciousness *for itself*. Original history is a product of historical consciousness *in itself*, and Philosophical history is a product of that same consciousness *in and for itself*. Reflective history can be broken down into the categories of the in-itself (Universal history), the for-itself (Pragmatic history), and the in-and-for-itself (Critical history), with the fourth type (*Begriffsgeschichte*) serving as the transition to, and basis of, the new class, Philosophical history. This is so because the fourth species begins in the (Ironic) apprehension of the *necessarily* arbitrary and fragmentary character of all *genuinely historical* knowledge of particular parts of history.

As Hegel said later on, historians *must* deal with events and subjects in their concreteness and particularity; they betray their calling when they fail to do so. But this means that their perspective is *always* limited and restricted. This limitation is the price they pay for trying to re-present a past life in all its ideality *and* concreteness; they serve their purpose best when they do not seek to rise above the mere reconstruction of the past and try to adduce from their knowledge of the concrete event the universal principles which link a specific past life to its total context.

Philosophical history, however, asks what principles are necessary to make sense out of representations of the parts of the historical world provided by different Reflective histories. Philosophical history, Hegel said, can be defined as simply "the thoughtful consideration" (*die denkende Betrachtung*) of history (*ibid.* [20]). That is to say, it is not the bringing to bear of reason upon the individual facts of history in the interest of adducing new facts from those known, or of correcting the accounts given by "Reflective" historians in the execution of their legitimate, though limited, tasks; it is "thoughtful reflection" on the works produced by historians. Hegel supposed that, if the works produced by historians cannot be synthesized in the light of the general principles of reason, in the way that the works of physicists or chemists can be, history cannot claim the status of a science at all. For, if the historian were to say that he has added to our knowledge of humanity, culture, or society in the history he has written, but then deny that thought can legitimately generalize about the significance of the structures and processes truthfully (though incompletely) represented in those histories, this would be to set a restriction on both history and thought which neither science nor philosophy could sanction.

It should be noted that, in stressing the fragmentary and arbitrary character of every historical work actually produced by historians, Hegel took his stand *within* the Ironic position to which Enlightenment thinking had been pushed by its apprehension of the arbitrary nature of its own historical reflection. But, instead of concluding, as the Romantics did, that one could then make of history what one would, Hegel insisted that reason alone must claim the authority to extract the truth (however partial) from these imperfect accounts of the past and to weld them together into the basis for a genuine science of history—not, mind you, into a science of history, but into the *theoretical basis for* a science of history. As he put it, "The only thought which philosophy brings to the contemplation of history, is the simple conception of *reason*, that reason might be the sovereign of the world, and the history of the world therefore might present to us [the aspect of] a rational process" (*ibid.*). This conviction, he warns, "is a hypothesis in the domain of history as such" (*ibid.*). It is not such in philosophy, for, without absolutely presupposing it, philosophy itself would not be possible. If *Begriffsgeschichte* serves as the transition stage between Reflective and Philosophical history, it must be construed in the mode of simple self-consciousness—that is, as Philosophical history in itself. Hegel's problem was to articulate the principles that would inform such historical self-consciousness *for itself*—that is, in the mode of *Begriffsgeschichte* reflecting upon its own operations and its relationship to its subject.

To conceive the problem thus is to move from the naive Irony of a mode of historical reflection which simply assumes the arbitrariness and fragmentary nature of its findings to that which strives to grasp that inner connectedness by which events are endowed with a specific historicity. This effort will necessarily carry thought through the consideration of the Metaphorical, the Metonymical, and the Synecdochic characterizations of the objects occupying the historical field and of the relations among them (both causal and typological), to a higher stage of Ironic *self*-reflection, on which the essential meanings of both historical consciousness and historical being are exposed to philosophical reflection on their essential natures. As thus conceived, the aim of philosophy of history is to determine the adequacy of historical consciousness to its object in such a way that the "meaning of history" is perceived as both a fact of consciousness and a lived reality. Only then will historical consciousness have been raised to a level beyond Irony, to a level of reflection on which it will not only be in itself and for itself but also by, in, and for itself—that is, at one with its object.

Of course, all these anticipations of the level beyond Irony to which historical consciousness might ascend were articulated in Hegel in the full consciousness of the impossibility of ever arriving at such a state of integration of subject and object within historical time. The higher truth of historical consciousness and historical being, which must be supposed ultimately to be the same truth, the truth of reason's rule over history and of the rational aspect which history bears to the consciousness sufficiently reflective to grasp its essence, is, finally, a truth of philosophy. Though art may grasp this truth in its concreteness and formal coherence, and religion may name it as the truth of God's governance of His world, philosophy itself can never name it, because, as Hegel said, philosophy knows that "the Truth is the Whole," and "the Absolute is Life."

But all these considerations are inconsequential for the more modest aim of working out the bases on which the imperfect and fragmentary truths provided by individual historians can be legitimately considered as the subject matter of a possible science of history. And they are outweighed by the fact that the historical process alone provides us with a necessary part of the materials on the basis of which we can envisage a science of human nature. Philosophy, Hegel wrote, is nothing but the attempt to satisfy "the wish for rational insight" (10). It is not "the ambition to amass a mere heap of acquirements"—that is to say, the data that have to be "presupposed" as the possession of every practitioner of a specific discipline (*ibid.*). "If the clear idea of Reason is not already developed in our minds, in beginning the study of Universal history, we should at least have the firm, unconquerable faith that Reason *does* exist there; and that the world of intelligence and conscious volition is not abandoned to chance, but must show itself in the light of the self-cognisant [*sich wissenden*] idea" (10[22]).

Yet, Hegel insisted, he was "not obliged to make any such preliminary demand upon [the reader's] faith," for "What I have said thus provisionally

. . . is to be regarded . . . as a summary view of the whole; the result of the investigation we are about to pursue . . . the ultimate result" of an investigation that will "proceed historically—empirically" (*ibid.*). This means that one must "faithfully adopt all that is historical" as material for reflection, even though the terms "faithfully" and "adopt" are ambiguous in the extreme (11). That hypotheses regarding the ultimate rationality of the world process are to be applied to the data supplied by the historians in the various "modes" in which historians reflect (*ibid.*), Hegel viewed as no cause for alarm, for, in history as in science, even the most "impartial" historian, "who believes and professes that he maintains a simply receptive attitude, surrendering himself to the data supplied him, is by no means passive as regards the exercise of his thinking powers. He brings his categories with him, and sees the phenomena presented to his mental sight exclusively through these media" (*ibid.*). The philosopher reflecting on history must only be sure to keep his reason alive and in full play throughout his investigation. Given the nature of reason itself, the result must be a rational account of history as a rationally comprehensible process, for, "To him who looks upon the world rationally, the world in turn presents a rational aspect. The relation is mutual" (*ibid.*). The important point is that this rational aspect should not be entertained as a *merely* formal coherence. The laws that govern history must be apprehended as inhering in the historical process itself, as it unfolds in time, in the same way that, in science, the actual operations of nature are grasped rationally in the form of the laws that are used to conceptualize it. (12)

The way beyond Irony leads, by a path which circumvents the simply naive or religious *conviction* that history is ruled by Providence, to the scientific—that is, rational and empirical—*demonstration* of the providential nature of history, not insofar as the life of an individual man or group is concerned, but rather in respect of the life of the species. The appeal to *belief* in Providence is forbidden, according to Hegel, "because the science of which we have to treat proposes itself to furnish the proof (not indeed the abstract Truth of the doctrine, but) of its correctness as compared with the facts." And this "correctness as compared with the facts" requires that we begin with the recognition that, considered empirically, as merely a field of happening simply perceived, mankind is, above all, ruled by passions. This means that any explanation of history must "depict the passions of mankind, the genius, the active powers that play their part on the great stage," and show, by a demonstration that is both rational and empirical, that this chaos of facts can be conceived not only to have a *form* but that it also actually manifests a *plan* (*Endzweck*). (13) To disclose the general aspect of this plan, to purport to reveal "the ultimate design of the world," implies the "abstract definition" of the "meaning" (*Inhalt*) of this design and the provision of the evidence of its actualization (*Verwirklichung*) in time (16 [29]).

Now, in the paragraphs that follow, I will point out Hegel's dilation on the nature of that "spirit" which he conceived to be the agency by which the Ironies of thought, feeling, and existence experienced by man are finally transcended in the apprehension of a possible integration of consciousness with being. I will give only a summary sketch of his doctrine of spirit here, since it appears in detail elsewhere—that is, in his *Phenomenology, Logic,* and *Philosophy of Right.* The important point is that he began his discussion of spirit with an apprehension of a radical antithesis between spirit and matter. The term "World," he said, "includes both physical and psychical nature." He admitted that physical nature plays a part in world history, and he also granted that an account of its mechanical operations would have to be provided where it bore upon his subject. But his subject was the spirit, the "nature" of which can be characterized in terms of its "abstract characteristics": the "means" it uses to realize its idea or to actualize itself in time; and the "shape" which the perfect embodiment of spirit would assume.

Spirit, Hegel said, can be understood as the opposite of matter, the nature of which is to be determined by something extrinsic to itself. Spirit is "self-contained existence" (*bei-sich-selbst-sein*), which is to say "freedom," for freedom is nothing but independence or autonomy, the absence of all dependence upon, or determination by, anything outside itself. Self-contained existence, he continued, is also self-consciousness—consciousness of one's own being, which is to say, consciousness of that which one is potentially capable of becoming. Hegel took this abstract definition of self-consciousness to be the analogue of the very idea of history: "it may be said of Universal History that it is the exhibition of spirit in the process of working out the knowledge of that which it potentially is" (17–18). And, insofar as history is process, actualization in time, this working out of the knowledge of what spirit potentially is, is also the actualization, or realization, of what it is potentially able to become. Since self-consciousness is nothing but freedom, it must be supposed that the actualization of spirit in time figures the growth of the principle of freedom. Thus, Hegel wrote, "The history of the world is none other than the progress of the consciousness of freedom." And this insight, he said, provided him with "the natural division of universal history and suggests the mode of its discussion." (19)

◄§ The Historical Field as Structure

There are two crucial passages in the Introduction to *Philosophy of History* in which Hegel characterizes the historical field as a problem to be solved in its aspect as a set of phenomena from which the critical intelligence must be expected to extract a meaning. These two characterizations are quite different in nature, and they will reward close study for the determination of their individual characteristics.

In his first characterization of the historical field, Hegel considered it as a synchronic structure, apprehended as a *chaos of passions,* self-interest, violence, dashed hopes, and frustrated plans and projects. In his second characterization of the historical field, he considered it as a diachronic process, as a field which appears to be characterized by *mere* change. The first characterization was meant to serve as a basis for the generation of the concepts by which the field, considered as a chaos of passions, could be comprehended as a spectacle of *purpose.* The second characterization was meant to serve as a basis for the generation of the concepts by which the field, considered as a chaos of changes, could be comprehended as a process of *development.*

The first characterization of the historical field, as a field of phenomena, was given in the Metaphorical mode, which is to say, not as *mere* phenomena but as phenomena *named.* Hegel characterized the historical field which offers itself to "external and phenomenal" intuition in terms of its aesthetic form, the moral implications of the form offered, and the philosophical question which the combination of these necessarily raises. Thus, he said,

The first glance at history convinces us that the actions of men proceed from their needs, their passions, their characters and talents, and impresses us with the belief that such needs, passions, and interest are the sole springs of action—the efficient agents in this scene of activity. [20]

True, Hegel noted, even on this level of comprehension we may very well discern actions and projects undertaken out of devotion to "aims of a liberal or universal kind," such as "benevolence" or "noble patriotism," but such "virtues and general views are but insignificant as compared with the world and its doings." Reason itself may display its effects to the understanding, but, on the basis of the data themselves, we have no reason to deny that the "most effective springs of human action" are "passions, private aims, and the satisfaction of selfish desires." (*Ibid.*)

When we reflect on this "spectacle of passions" (*Schauspiel der Leidenschaften*) and perceive the essential irrationality both of evil and of "good designs and righteous aims," when we "see the evil, the vice, the ruin that has befallen the most flourishing kingdoms which the mind of man ever created," we can scarcely avoid being hurled into an essentially Absurdist conception of the drama there displayed. The whole of history thus viewed appears to bear the mark of "corruption," and, since this "decay is not the work of mere nature, but of the human will" itself, "a moral embitterment" (*einer moralische Betrübnis*) and "a revolt of the good spirit, if it have a place within us," may well arise within us. (20–21) A merely aesthetic or, what amounts to the same thing, "simply truthful combination of the miseries that have overwhelmed the noblest of nations and polities and the finest exemplars of human virtue" forms a "picture of such a horrifying aspect" (*furchtbarsten Gemälde*), and inspires emotions of such profound sadness, that we are inclined to take refuge in fatalism and to withdraw in disgust "into the more agreeable environment of our individual life, the present formed by our private aims and interests" (21).

But this *moral* response to an *aesthetic* perception itself inspires reflection on a question which "involuntarily arises" within any consciousness in which reason has play. The question is: "to what principle, to what final aim have these enormous sacrifices been offered?" (*ibid.*).

When we reach this point, Hegel said, the usual procedure is to undertake the kind of investigation which he characterized as "Reflective history"—that is, causal and typological reductions, by which the field can be "arbitrarily" and "fragmentarily" ordered. On the other hand, Hegel purported to resist such reductive strategies by taking "these phenomena which [make] up a picture so suggestive of gloomy emotions and thoughtful reflections as *the very field*" [Hegel's italics] which exhibits the "*means* [italics added] for realizing . . . the essential destiny . . . or . . . the true result of the world's history" (*ibid.*). Moral reflection, he insisted, cannot serve as a method of historical understanding. The causal and typological reductions of the historical field inspired by such moral reflection, even though attempted in the interest of dissipating depression by understanding, can at best only *explain away* the phenomena they are intended to explain and at worst only confirm our fears regarding the essential absurdity of the picture of the whole. History *is* a "panorama of sin and suffering," and any view of history which requires denial of this fact of perception is untrue to the principles of art, science, and morality alike. Hegel thus fully credited the immediate perception of the historical field as "a panorama of sin and suffering." But he set his perception of this panorama within the means-ends question which he insisted is raised in the consciousness by moral reflection on it ("to what principle, to what final aim these enormous sacrifices have been offered").

In short, "sin and suffering" must be viewed as the *means* for the realization of some principle that is superior to them. This superior principle is not given to sense perception but is considered to be knowable *in principle* by a transcendental deduction of the categories by which it can be inferred—the kind of deduction that Kant carried out with respect to natural phenomena and science. Hegel characterized the end of the whole process as "Principle–Plan of Existence–Law," which, he admitted, is a "hidden, undeveloped essence, which *as such*, however true in itself, is not completely real [*wirklich*]" (22 [36]). The conceivable final cause, or principle yet to be realized in concrete existence, must be recognized as ultimately unknowable to science inasmuch as it is still in the process of actualization in history. Thought must therefore begin with the data there before it and the apprehension of them as a *means* to some greater end.

Hegel thus accepted as a truth that insight into history which had driven the *philosophes* to despair and the Romantics to heights of buoyancy and exhilaration—namely, the fact that "passion" alone is the immediate cause of all historical events. "We may affirm absolutely," he said, "that nothing great has been accomplished in the world without passion [*nichts Grosses in der Welt ohne Leidenschaft vollbracht worden ist*]" (23 [38]). The historian thus has as his object of study precisely what appears before him: a panorama of sin and suffering. But he also has his "concept" (*Begriff*), which is the means-ends relationship, and its "idea" (*Idee*), which is the full realization, by concrete actualization, of all the beings that appear in history as recognizably historical (as against merely natural) entities, by which to extract meaning from this panorama. Both Metonymical reduction and Irony are to be avoided by bracketing the data (the panorama of sin and suffering) within the concept adequate to their apprehension as a means to some end:

Two elements, therefore, enter into the object of our investigation; the first, the idea, the second the complex of human passions; the one the warp, the other the woof of the vast arras-web of history. [*Ibid.*]

Thus, passion, "which is [conventionally] regarded as a thing of sinister aspect" and as "more or less immoral," is not only recognized as a fact of human existence but is elevated as a necessary and desirable condition for the achievement of ends greater than any which an individual man or group, governed by private interests or traits of character, can possibly imagine. The severance of passion from the higher human ends which individuals and groups actually realize in time is thus overcome. The dualism of reason and passion which the Enlighteners had failed to overcome (by Metonymical analysis) is transcended along with the (Romantics') false monism of passion's hegemony over reason and the (Subjective Idealists') false monism of reason's absolute hegemony over passion. The instrument of mediation between passion and reason was conceived by Hegel to be the state—not the *state mechanism*, which is only a means of such mediation in concrete existence, but the state in its ideal essence, the state as *objectified* morality. The "concrete mean" and "union" of the idea and passion is "liberty, under the conditions of morality in a state." (*Ibid.*).

❧ The State, the Individual, and the Tragic View of History

The ideal state, Hegel noted, would be that in which the private interests of its citizens are in perfect harmony with the common interest, "when the one finds its gratification and realization in the other" (24). But every actual state, precisely because it is a concrete mechanism, an actualization rather than merely a potentiality or a realization of the ideal state, fails to attain this harmonious reconciliation of individual interests, desires, and needs with the common good. This failure of any given state to incarnate the ideal, however, is to be experienced as a cause for jubilation rather than despair, for it is precisely this *imbalance of private with public (or public with private) interests* which provides the space for the exercise of a specifically *human* freedom. If any given state were perfect, there would be no legitimate basis for that dissatisfaction which men feel with their received social and political endowments, justification for the moral indignation which stems from the disparity between what men desire for themselves and feel, because it is the only criterion of right they *immediately* feel, to be a *morally justifiable* desire, and what the community into which they are born and are asked to live out their lives insists that they *should desire.* Human freedom, which is a specifically moral freedom, arises in the circumstance that no "present" is ever adequately "adapted to the realization of aims which [men] hold to be right and just." There is always an unfavorable contrast between "things as they *are* and things as they *ought* to be." (35) But this precondition of freedom is also a limitation on the exercise of it; every attempt to correct or improve the state, by reform or revolution, succeeds only in establishing some new mechanism which, however superior it may be to what came before, is similarly limited in its capacity to reconcile private interests and desires with the common good and needs.

The aim, Hegel suggested, is to retain awareness of the Ironic (that is, paradoxical and contradictory) nature of this uniquely human condition; which is a product of the very distinction between private and public interests. For this alone permits consciousness to believe in the *possibility* of its own exercise of freedom and the legitimacy of the feelings of dissatisfaction which impel it to the further perfection of the forms of human community in which all private interests and the public good *may* be identified.

Nothing was more common in his own time, Hegel remarked, than "the complaint that the *ideals* which imagination sets up are not realized, that these glorious dreams are destroyed in cold actuality" (*ibid.*). Such complaints, however, are, he insisted, products of a merely sentimental character, if those who make them condemn the social condition as such simply because *their* ideals have not been realized *in their own time.* It is easier, Hegel said, to find deficiencies in individuals, states, and the whole historical process than to "discern their real import and value" (36). "For in this merely negative fault-finding a proud position is taken," and the positive aspect of every historical situation, its provision of the conditions for realizing a limited freedom, is overlooked (*ibid.*). Hegel's own perspective was meant to reveal that "the real world," with its contradictoriness and conflict, its limited freedom and suffering, "is as it ought to be" for the achievement of human ends by means adequate to the task (*ibid.*). The spirit of this assertion accords with the saying of Seneca with which Vico (misquoting) ends Book V of *The New Science*: "Pusilla res hic mundus est, nisi id, quod quaerit, omnis mundus habeat" (1096: 415).

This does not mean that the individual is exempted from a Tragic fate in the pursuit of *his* aims. On the contrary, it means that those who pursue their own aims with a passion, a will and intelligence adequate to their immediate realization—that is, the actual transformation of their societies

in the light of their privately held conceptions of what a good life might be
—will be Tragic figures. The ordinary man, Hegel said, holds fast to what his
society insists must be the limits within which he may realize his desires and
private interests. The criminal seeks to evade the laws and the limits set by
public morality by subterfuge, in such a way as to realize his private desire
for material satisfaction, but without effecting any substantial changes in the
canons of public morality and law in the process. (*Phil. of Hist.*, 28–29) By
contrast, the heroes of history are precisely those whose passionate belief in
the legitimacy of their own private aims and interests is such that they cannot
abide *any* disparity between what they desire for themselves and what the
public morality and legal system demand of men in general. Caesar, for
example, in seeking the realization of his own ideal self-conception, succeeded in completely reconstituting Roman society. Great men, Hegel noted,
form "purposes to satisfy themselves, not others," and they are those who do
not learn from others but from whom others learn (30). The great conflicts
between an individual will, adequately endowed for its task, and the received
social order, whose devotees seek to sustain its achieved form, constitute the
axial events of world history; and it is with the "comprehensive relations"
which are figured in such encounters that world history has to do (29).

For this reason, the spectacle of history, when viewed from *within* the
process of its own unfolding, from the vantage point of the individuals who
succeeded in actually changing the form of life of a people or of many peoples—or, it might be added, in resisting heroic efforts to effect such transformations—is conceivable as a specifically Tragic Drama. On the ground of
historical consciousness alone, without the superaddition of the hypothesis
which philosophical reflection brings to history—that is to say, on the basis of
a combination of aesthetic and moral sensibility alone—one is able to transform the history of the world from an Absurdist Epic of senseless conflict
and strife into a Tragic Drama with a specifically ethical import. Thus,
Hegel wrote:

If we go on to cast a look at the fate of world historical personalities . . . we shall
find it to have been no happy one. They attained no calm enjoyment; their whole
life was labor and trouble; their whole nature was nothing but their master passion. When their object is attained they fall off like empty hulls from the kernel.
They die early, like Alexander; they are murdered, like Caesar; transported to St.
Helena, like Napoleon. [31]

In short, they lived their lives like the heroes of a Shakespearean Tragedy.
And the danger of a merely moral reflection upon their lives is that it might
lead to the conclusion, similar to that which "any simply truthful account" of
the historical field inspires, that *their* lives had been as meaningless, as inconsequential, as the lives of those ordinary men who rested content with the
roles in which fate had cast them.

Such a view, however, is possible only on the grounds provided by the

Metonymical mode of comprehension, which, being based on a false analogy between nature and history, sees every action only as the effect of some prior, Mechanical, cause. Thus, the subjective impulse behind the act—the will, reason, or emotions of the individual who strives for something great—is reduced to the same essential nature as that of the ordinary man, who strives for nothing great at all and, as a result, leaves no mark on history except in his function as a unit of an aggregate. It is small wonder, Hegel remarked later on, that those who begin with the assumption that history is only nature in a different guise are led by the logic of the mode of explanation suitable for comprehending nature alone to the conclusion that history has no meaning, for

The state of nature is [in fact] predominantly that of injustice and violence, of untamed natural impulses, of inhuman deeds and feelings. [41]

If man were "mere nature," we would be as unable to account for the domestication of the ordinary run of mankind as we are unable to account for the origination of that "social state" which is the instrument of that domestication. Moreover, we would be forced to conclude that the highest achievements of individual geniuses in art, science, religion, and philosophy were products of a consciousness that was not essentially different from that which characterizes man in his savage condition; that they reflect merely rearrangements, rather than progressive perfections, of a finite number of elements, all of which must be presumed to have been present in the savage state.

But the truth is that savage man does not create anything of specifically high cultural significance except religion and a rudimentary (customary) form of society. This permits us to conclude that the "form of religion" determines the form of the state that arises on the principles of consciousness which inform it (51) and gives to the culture of a people *its* distinctive aspect (50). But to presume that the same *form* of consciousness which characterizes the savage mind also characterizes the civilized mind is to weight the scales of analysis in favor of the discovery of similarities alone when what is needed is an assessment and an explanation of the differences between the two states of consciousness and their products. Such a search for similarities at the expense of differences lies at the basis of all those myths of Arcadia, myths of the happy state of nature, which tantalized Enlightenment thinkers and inspired the Romantics to seek escape from the pains of present existence in a nowhere land where nothing but happiness prevails.

The problem, then, is to explicate the principles by which the *development* of mankind through history can be comprehended. This development, considered in its diachronic aspect, will appear as a *transition* from a lower condition to a higher one, and, in its aspect as a synchronic structure, will appear as a coherent system of exchange between the principle of savagery and that of civilization.

✑ The Historical Field as Process

This carries us to the level of comprehension on which Synecdochic consciousness replaces causal explanation by typological explanation and on which the image of mere chaos is replaced by that of a *succession of forms or types* of cultural achievement, the immediate apprehension of which is given under the aspect of Tragedy. It is here that Hegel made the remark which has so often been misinterpreted as evidence of the essentially formalist nature of his own philosophy of history. He wrote:

The investigator must be familiar *a priori* (if we like to call it so), with the whole *circle of conceptions* to which *the principles* in question belong—just as Kepler (to name the most illustrious example of this mode of philosophizing) must have been familiar *a priori* with ellipses, with cubes and squares, and with ideas of their relations, before he could discover, from the empirical data, those immortal "Laws" of his, which are none other than *forms of thought* pertaining to those *classes of concepts.* He who is unfamiliar with the science that embraces these abstract elementary conceptions is as little capable—though he may have gazed on the firmament and the motions of the celestial bodies for a lifetime—of *understanding* those Laws, as of *discovering* them. [64; italics added]

Here Hegel distinguished between the "circle of conceptions" and the "principles" of characterization, and between the "forms of thought" and the "classes of concepts" which the forms of thought utilize in the explanation of data of different sorts. Principles and classes of concepts which are permissible in the characterization of the historical process derive from the circle of conceptions by which various forms of thought are, simultaneously, differentiated from, and related, to one another. If a merely a priori method, by which a preconception inspired by a prejudice is simply *imposed* upon the historical record as an explanation of it, is to be avoided, there must be some principle by which a given form of thought can be directed to the articulation of the classes of concepts necessary for the distinction between what is "essential" and what is not in a given aspect of the world process. In the circle of conceptions, determinancy and freedom are conceived to generate the principles, forms of thought, and classes of concepts adequate for the characterization and understanding of the natural and historical processes respectively. It is here that thought about history is exposed to the dangers of mechanism, by confusion of a historical with a merely natural process, and to the threat of formalism, by the *simple recognition* of a succession of formal coherencies in the historical process.

The concepts which the consideration of history as a process of development requires are beginning, middle, and end, but not conceived in the mode by which such processes are apprehended in physical nature—that is, as merely inauguration, extension and expansion, and termination. Historical processes must be regarded as analogous to the kinds of *completed* moral actions which we enjoy in the contemplation of the highest products of art and religion—that is, as processes which originate as a "commencement," proceed through a "dialectical" transformation of the contents and forms of the original disposition, and culminate in a "consummation or resolution" that figures more than a mere termination.

Physical nature as such has no beginning, middle, or end; it is always and eternally what it *has to be*. We can *imagine* it coming into existence at a given time and ending at a given time, but it does not *develop* in its passage from one instant to another, which is why we say that it exists only in space (72). Organic nature, it is true, does represent a kind of development which can be conceived as a realization of the potential for growth contained in the seed; but the individual may or may not realize this potential. If it does, it comes to an end that is preordained by natural law—in such a way that every growth process carried to its termination is precisely like every other, there being *no development from one individual to another*, and no development in the whole of organic life from one species to another. Here, insofar as there is movement at all, there is no development, only cyclical recurrence.

Significant transitions in history, however, display the kind of gain which we often intuit to be present, even when we cannot specify its content, at the end of a Tragic play or a philosophical dialogue carried out in the dialectical mode. In it, when something dies, something else is born; but that which is born is not merely the same thing in its essence as that which has died, as it is in plant and animal life. It is something new in which the earlier form of life—the action of the play, the argument of the dialogue—is contained within the later form of life as its material or content, which is to say it is turned from an end in itself into a means for the attainment of a higher end only dimly apprehended in the afterglow of the resolution.

This insight into the nature of the historical process is built upon the Synecdochic inflation of the Metaphorically apprehended and Metonymically comprehended field of historical happening originally perceived as "a panorama of sin and suffering." The dynamics of this Synecdochic inflation are signaled in Hegel's second major characterization of the whole historical field, now conceived not merely as *chaos* but as *change* as well.

Hegel's second characterization of the historical field begins with the famous apothegm,

History in general is therefore the development of spirit in *time*, as nature is the development of the idea in *space*. [*Ibid.*]

The word which is conventionally rendered in English as "development" in this context is the German *Auslegung*, literally a "laying out, spreading out, or display" with secondary associations of "explanation" or "explication"— from the Latin roots *ex* and *plicare*, which, combined, convey the notion of a "smoothing out" of wrinkles, as in a crumpled piece of paper or cloth. The connotation is that of an unfolding or clarification of latent contents.

But the apprehension of this process for what it truly is cannot be provided by Synecdochic inflations alone. This is pointed out in the passage which follows. Here the same transition of consciousness from an aesthetic, through a moral, to an intellectual perception which we encountered in Hegel's original characterization of the historical field in the modes of Metaphor and Metonymy are recaptitulated:

If then we cast a glance over world-history in general, we see a vast picture of changes and deeds [*Taten*], of infinitely manifold *forms* of peoples, states, individuals, in unresting succession [*Aufeinanderfolge*]. [*Ibid.*]

This *spectacle of the succession of forms* arouses an emotional state which is quite different from that which the *spectacle of chaos* originally described arouses:

Everything that can enter into and interest the soul of man—all our sensibility to *goodness, beauty, and greatness*—is called into play. [*Ibid.*]

We still see "human action and suffering predominant," but we also see something akin to ourselves that "excites *our* interest for or against," whether that "something" attracts our attention by its "beauty, freedom, and rich variety" or by its "energy" alone (*ibid.*).

Sometimes we see the more comprehensive mass of some general interest advancing with comparative slowness, and subsequently sacrificed to an infinite complication of trifling circumstances, and so dissipated into atoms. Then again with a vast expenditure of power a trivial result is produced; while from what appears unimportant a tremendous issue proceeds. On every hand there is the motliest throng of events drawing us within the circle of its interest, and when one combination vanishes another immediately appears in its place. [*Ibid.*]

The first *general* thought that arises in response *to* the spectacle thus apprehended, "the category which first presents itself in this restless mutation of individuals and peoples, existing for a time and then vanishing," is that of "change in general" (*die Veränderung überhaupt*). This apprehension is then quickly transmuted into a feeling of "sadness," such as that which we might feel in the presence of the ruins of some mighty sovereignty, such as Rome, Persepolis, or Carthage. But the "next consideration, which allies itself" with that of mere change and which arises from the recognition of the formal coherences to be seen *in* the spectacle, is this: "that while change imports dissolution, it involves at the same time the rise of a *new life*

—that while death is the issue of life, life is also the issue of death." (72–73)

The problem which immediately suggested itself to Hegel was that of the modality by which this *succession of formal coherences* is to be comprehended—that is to say, *how the sequence of forms is to be emplotted*. And in the paragraphs which follow can be seen his differentiation among three different plot structures that might be used to characterize this process conceived as a succession of forms, as distinguished from the Epic plot structure, which might be used to emplot the spectacle of *mere change* in the original apprehension of the historical field as chaos.

Reverting to nature (that is, to the Metonymical mode of characterizing changes as such) for an analogue, this succession of forms might be conceived in one of two ways, both of which might be called Tragic inasmuch as they credit the apprehension of the fact that, in human nature at least, "while death is the issue of life, life is *also* the issue of death" (italics added). For example, the succession of forms might be emplotted as a *transfer* of a content to a new form, as in the Oriental doctrine of metempsychosis; or it might be conceived, not as a transfer, but as a ceaseless *re*-creation of a new life out of the ashes of the old, as in the Phoenix myth. (73) Hegel called the insight contained in the Oriental conceptions of the world process "grand," but denied them status as *earned* philosophical truths for two reasons. First, this insight ("that while death is the issue of life, life is also the issue of death") is only *generally* true of nature, rather than specifically true of natural individualities. Second, the simple notions of transfer and of successive recurrence do not do justice to the variety of life forms which the historical process, unlike the natural process, displays to perception. As Hegel put it:

Spirit—consuming the envelope of its existence—does not merely pass into another envelope, nor rise rejuvenescent from the ashes of its previous form; it comes forth exalted [*erhoben*], glorified [*verklärt*], a purer spirit [*ein reinerer Geist*]. It certainly makes war upon itself—consumes its own existence; but in this very destruction it works up that existence into a new form, and each successive phase becomes in its turn a material on which it exalts itself [*erhebt*] into a new grade [*Bildung*]. [*Ibid.*]

And this suggests another reason why this whole process cannot *yet* be credited as prefiguring a Comic resolution. The principles in virtue of which apprehension of the plot of the succession of forms might be permitted still remain unexplicated. The explication of these principles requires a view from a perspective within the process, so that it will not be apprehended as merely a succession of formally equal coherences, but rather as a kind of autonomous process of self-manipulation, exertions "in different modes and directions," in which the prior form serves as the material for, and stimulus to, the creation of its successor (*ibid.*). From this perspective,

The abstract concept of mere change gives place to the thought of spirit *manifesting, developing*, and *perfecting* its powers in every direction which its manifold nature can follow. [*Ibid.*; italics added]

The *powers* that the spirit which must be presumed to govern this process *inherently* possesses can be learned only "from the variety of products and formulations which it originates" (*ibid.*). This means that the historical process must be viewed, not as mere movement, change, or succession, but as "activity": "Der Geist *handelt* wesentlich, er macht sich zu dem, was er an sich ist, zu einer Tat, zu seinem Werk; so wird er sich Gegenstand, so hat er sich als ein Dasein vor sich" (72 [99]). Thus it was with historical individualities, those Tragic heroes who succeeded in leaving their societies at least significantly *transformed* as a result of their exertions; and so it is with whole peoples and nations, who are at once beneficiaries and captives of the spiritual forms in which their exertions against the world and for the world manifest themselves. This implies that the life of every people or nation is, like the life of every heroic individual in history, a Tragedy. And the appropriate mode of its emplotment, the apprehension of it as a historical reality, is that of the Tragic Drama. In fact, Hegel emplotted the histories of all the civilizational forms that he discerned in world history in Tragic terms. And in his *Encyclopedia of the Philosophical Sciences* and the *Lectures on Aesthetics*, he provided the justification for this mode of emplotment as the highest kind of reflective historiography.

In his *Philosophy of History*, however, he simply *applied* this mode of figuring the process of origination, rise, dissolution, and death to individual civilizations. He did not try to justify the Tragic mode of emplotment but simply presupposed it as the appropriate mode for characterizing the processes of development which can be discerned in the life cycles of a specific civilization, such as the Greek or the Roman. This mode can be presupposed because it is that in which any comprehensive history of a civilization whose term has run out is conventionally emplotted by professional historians. The philosophically unselfconscious historian might draw erroneous conclusions from his reflection on the pattern of rise and fall, with its aspect of fate and inevitability. He might conclude that this pattern could not have been otherwise and that, because of what it is, it can be comprehended only as a Tragedy *en gros*.

Contemplation of the historical process does yield the apprehension of it as a sequence of Tragedies. What originally appeared as an Epic "spectacle of passions" is transmutted into a sequence of Tragic defeats. Each of these Tragic defeats, however, is an epiphany of the *law* that governs the whole sequence. Yet this law of historical development is not conceived to be analogous to the kinds of laws which determine the evolution or interaction or physical bodies; it is not natural law. It is, rather, the law of history, which is the law of freedom that is figured in every human project culminating in a Tragic resolution. And this law figures the ultimately Comic outcome of the whole succession of forms which is immediately apprehended under the aspect of Tragedy.

Hegel's purpose is to justify the transition from *the comprehension of the Tragic nature of every specific civilization* to *the Comic apprehension of the unfolding drama of the whole of history*. In the same way that, in *Phenomenology of Spirit*, he suggested that the Comic vision of Aristophanes was superior to the moral insight contained in the Tragic vision of Euripides, in his consideration of world history he sought to endow the whole of history with a Comic import which is based upon, responsible to, yet transcends, the implications of a merely Tragic conception of the course of historical *life in general*.

✑ *From Tragedy to Comedy*

In the cycle of moral attitudes, Comedy is logically posterior to Tragedy, for it represents an affirmation of the needs of life and its rights against the Tragic insight that all things existing in time are doomed to destruction. The death of a civilization is not strictly analogous to the death of an individual, even to that of a heroic individual. For, just as the heroic individual finds a kind of immortality in the changes he effects in the life forms of the people he molds to his will, so, too, a heroic people finds a kind of immortality in the changes it effects on the life forms of the race. A great people does not die a "simply natural death," Hegel wrote, for a people "is not a mere single individual, but a spiritual, generic life." The deaths of whole civilizations are more like suicides than natural deaths, he continued, because *as genera* they carry within themselves *their own negations*—"in the very generality which characterizes" them. (75)

A people sets for itself a task, which, generally considered, is simply to be *something* rather than nothing. Its whole life is bound up with, and its distinctive formal coherence is expressed in, its dedication (both conscious and unconscious) to this task. But, as a task, this effort to be some*thing* requires means, the specificity of which is implied in the concreteness of their application to specific rather than general problems. General tasks, such as merely keeping body and soul together, reproducing, caring for children, protecting oneself from the elements, the activities of precivilized peoples, are carried out in response to general human inclinations and instincts represented by custom, "a merely external sensuous existence which has ceased to throw itself enthusiastically into its object" (74–75). But, in order to carry out the task of becoming something particular and unlike the general run of mankind, a people must set itself both an ideal task and certain practical ones, for the "highest point in the development of a people is this—to have gained a conception of its [own] life and condition—to have reduced its laws, its ideas of justice and morality to a science" (76). Here the unity of ideal and real is achieved as completely as the nature of the human spirit itself permits. It is never fully achieved, and in this asymmetry between the general intention and the specific means and activities used to effect its realization lies the Tragic flaw at the heart of every form of civilized existence. This flaw is perceived for what it really is in the late stages of a civilization's cycle; or, rather, when this flaw becomes perceptible for what it really is, the civilization evidences a form of life grown stale and becomes imminently moribund. When this flaw is perceived for what it really is—that is, as a contradiction between the specific ideal which the civilization embodies and the specific actualizations of that ideal in customary, institutional, social, political, and cultural life, the cement that holds society together in devotion to the ideal, the sense of piety, duty, morality, begins to crumble. And

At the same time the isolation of individuals from one another and from the whole makes its appearance. [*Ibid.*]

People begin to talk about virtue instead of practicing it; they demand reasons why they should do their duties and find reasons not to do them; they begin to live Ironically: speaking of virtue publicly, practicing vice privately, but ever more openly (76–77).

By the transformation of practice into vice, however, this separation of the ideal from the real is itself a purification of the ideal, a release of it from the trammels of actualized existence, an opportunity for concrete minds to grasp the ideal in its essence, to conceptualize and image it. Thus they prepare the ideal for its release from the time and place in which it has achieved its actualization and for transmission across time and space to other peoples, who in turn can use it as the material out of which to further specify the nature of human ideality in its essential purity.

Thus, Hegel said, if we wish a specific idea of what the Greeks *were*, we will have to go to those records in which they naively revealed the modes of their practical relationships in society. If we wish to know this idea in its generality, its pure ideality, however, we shall "find it in Sophocles and Aristophanes, in Thucydides and Plato" (76). The choice of these witnesses of the ideal is not casual; they represent the late forms of Greek consciousness in tragedy, comedy, historiography, and philosophy, respectively, and are to be distinguished quite clearly from their "naive" predecessors (Aeschylus, Herodotus, the pre-Socratic philosophers). The grasping of the ideality of a people or civilization by consciousness is an act that at once "preserves" and "dignifies" it. While the people falls into nullity and casual catastrophe, surviving perhaps as a folk but declining as a power (in both the political and cultural sense), the spirit of that people is thus saved through consciousness in thought and art as an ideal form.

While then, on the one side, spirit annuls the reality, the permanence of that which it *is*, it gains on the other side, the essence, the thought, the universal element of that which *it only was*. [77]

This grasping, by consciousness, of the inner essence of a finite mode of actualization of the spirit in a heroic people must be seen, not as merely a preservation, or mummification, of the ideal it represents, but rather as the alteration of the spirit of the people itself—the raising of its principle to a "another and in fact higher principle." It is this elevation, by consciousness and in consciousness, of the ideal to another and higher principle that provides justification for belief in the ultimately *Comic* nature, the providential nature, of the "panorama of sin and suffering" which perception immediately finds in the data of history as a "simply truthful combination" of the facts. And it is of the "highest importance," Hegel noted, that we understand "the thought involved in this transition [*dieses Übergangs*]." The "thought" alluded to is that contained in the contradiction of human growth and development, which is that, although *the individual remains a unity* throughout the grades of his development, he does *rise to a higher consciousness of himself* and does in fact *pass* from a lower and restricted stage of consciousness to a higher, more comprehensive one. So, too, Hegel said, does a people develop, at once remaining what it was in its essential being as a specific people and at the same time developing until "it reaches the grade of universality." In this point, Hegel concluded, "lies the fundamental, the ideal necessity of change [*Veränderung*]," which is "the soul, the essential consideration, of the philosophical comprehension of history." (78)

This "comprehension," then, is founded on an apprehension of the historical process as a development toward the grade of universality, whereupon the spirit in general "elevates and completes itself to a self-comprehending *totality*" (*ibid.*). *The necessity of every civilization's ultimate destruction* by its own hand is sublimated into an apprehension of that civilization's institutions and modes of life as only means, abstract modes of organization, by which its ideal ends are realized. They are not eternal realities, and ought not be considered as such. Their passing, therefore, should be of less retrospective "concern" than the death of a friend or even the death of those Tragic heroes whose excellence can be identified with to such an extent that we may experience *their* death as an intimation of our own.

Hegel presented his perception of the dissolution of institutions and modes of life in the following metaphor:

The life of a people ripens to a certain fruit; its activity aims at the complete manifestation of the principle which it embodies. But this fruit does not fall back into the bosom of the people that produced and matured it; on the contrary, it becomes a poison-draught to it. That poison-draught it cannot let alone, for it has an insatiable thirst for it: the taste of the draught is its annihilation, though at the same time the rise of a new principle. [*Ibid.*]

Comparison of this passage with those in which Hegel depicted and reflected on the meaning of Socrates' life and death for Athenian culture as a whole illuminates the use of the metaphor of the "poison-draught" which, once consumed, ends an old life and establishes the principle of a higher one. Socrates' death was Tragic as a spectacle of the death of a virtuous man and as a revelation of the contradiction of his relationship to the Athenian people, to whom he taught a new principle of morality. Socrates, Hegel wrote, was the "inventor of morality," and his death was necessitated as one of the acts by which that principle was confirmed as a practical rule of life and not merely affirmed as an ideal (269). His death was at once the death of the teacher Socrates and the elevation of the principle by which he lived and died into a concrete model of moral activity. His death showed not only that men can live by a moral principle but that, when they die on behalf of it, they transform it into an ideal by which others can live. The recognition that this "death" is also the means to the transformation of human life and morality itself onto a level of self-consciousness greater than the "life" which led up to it, was, for Hegel, the informing insight of the Comic vision and the highest comprehension of the historical process to which the finite mind can aspire.

The Comic vision, Hegel wrote in *Phenomenology*, transcends the fear of "fate." It is

the return of everything universal into certainty of self, a certainty which, in consequence, is this complete loss of fear of everything strange and alien, and complete loss of substantial reality on the part of what is alien and external. Such certainty is a state of spiritual good health and of self-abandonment thereto, on the part of consciousness, in a way that, outside this kind of [Aristophanean] comedy, is not to be found anywhere. [748–49]

This last remark, that the state of "spiritual good health and of self-abandonment thereto . . . is not to be found anywhere" outside a certain Comic vision, suggests that the Comic nature of the historical process itself can be apprehended (never comprehended except in abstract terms) only as a *possibility* which enjoys the authority, on the basis of historical evidence rationally processed, of *high probability*, because, as Hegel said in the introduction to his *Philosophy of History*, history has to do only with the *past and the present*; of the future it can make no pronouncements. Yet, on the basis of our comprehension of the historical process as a progressive development which, beginning in remote times, has come down to our own present, the twofold nature of history as a cycle and a progression is rendered clear to consciousness. We can now see that the life of the ever present spirit is a circle of progressive embodiments, which looked at in one aspect still exist beside one another, and only as looked at from another point of view appear as past. [*Phil. of Hist.*, 79]

And this means that the "grades which spirit seems to have left behind it" are not lost and abandoned but are still alive and retrievable "in the depths of the present" (*ibid.*). These words and this hope, with which Hegel closed the Introduction to *Philosophy of History*, echo the closing paragraph of *Phenomenology of Spirit*, with which he had opened the mature phase of his own philosophical career:

The goal, which is Absolute Knowledge or Spirit knowing itself as Spirit, finds its pathway in the recollection of spiritual forms (*Geister*) as they are in themselves and as they accomplish the organization of their spiritual kingdom. Their conservation, looked at from the side of their free existence appearing in the form of contingency, is *History*; looked at from the side of their intellectually comprehended organization, it is the *Science* of the ways in which knowledge appears. Both together, or History (intellectually) comprehend (*begriffen*), form at once the recollection and the Golgotha of Absolute Spirit, the reality, the truth, the certainty of its throne, without which it were lifeless, solitary, and alone. Only

> The chalice of this realm of spirits
> Foams forth to God His own Infinitude.

I can now chart the dimensions and power of Hegel's conception of historical knowledge as a mode of explanation, representation, and ideological implication. I begin by noting that the whole of it is a sustained effort to hold the essential Irony of the human condition in consciousness without surrendering to the skepticism and moral relativism into which Enlightenment rationalism had been led on the one hand or the solypsism into which Romantic intuitionism had to be led on the other. This aim is achieved by the transformation of Irony itself into a method of analysis, a basis for the representation of the historical process, and a means of asserting the essential ambiguity of all real knowledge. What Hegel did was to bracket the Metonymical (causal) and Metaphorical (formalist) strategies for reducing phenomena to order within the modalities of Synecdochic characterizations on the one hand and the self-dissolving certitudes of Irony on the other. The principal certitude which is dissolved, however, is intellectual certitude, the kind of certitude which breeds pride in the possession of a putatively absolute truth about the whole. The only "absolute" truths that are permitted to the finite intelligence are such "general" truths as "The truth is the whole" and "The Absolute is life," both of which are liberating rather than repressive truths, inasmuch as they tacitly assert that absolute truth is possessed by no single individual. But this kind of certitude is dissolved in such a way as to promote that other kind of certitude, moral self-certitude, which is required for the living of an effectively "free" life, the existential truth that everything is precisely as it ought to be, including one's desire regarding what "ought to be," which means that one is justified in affirming those desires as his right against the social whole as long as he has the will, the energy, and the means to do so. At the same time, it means that the will of the group, the collectivity's conception of "what ought to be," which is usually identical with "what is," is equally justified, so that the conflict of finite individualities on the ground of history cannot be prejudged as to its intellectual or moral worth prior to the conflict in which their claims to authority and the allegiance of the mass of men are finally arbitrated. In the end, then, it can be seen that Hegel's whole philosophy of history *led from* an original Metaphorical characterization of the world-process *through* a Metonymical reduction and Synecdochic inflation of the process in which its various possible modes of relationship are explicated, *to* an Ironic comprehension of the ambiguity of the "meaning" of the process—until it came to rest, finally, in the more general Synecdochic identification of the whole process as a Drama of essentially Comic significance.

Thus, the mode of explanation of all historical events is *immediately* Metonymical and Synecdochic, which justifies the characterization of any specific whole act of the Drama as a sequence of formal coherences governed by causal laws (though the laws of causality invoked must be those of spirit, or freedom, rather than those of nature, or determinancy). Accordingly, the emplotment of any given segment of the whole process must be in the Tragic mode, which is the mode in which the conflict between being and consciousness is resolved as an elevation of consciousness itself to a higher awareness of its own nature and, simultaneously, of the nature of being, an epiphany of law. But the ideological implications of history so construed and so emplotted remain ambiguous, because in a causal system there is neither right nor wrong, but simply cause and effect, and in a formal system there is neither better nor worse, but simply the end of formal coherence and the means of realizing it.

In this interplay of causes and effects and means and ends, however, the Ironic consciousness perceives the effects of which the whole interplay of these elements is a cause and the end of which it is the means—that is to say, the progressive elevation of humanity itself through the attainment of higher forms of self-consciousness, the recognition of its differences from nature, and the progressive clarification of the end of rational enlightenment, liberation, and human integration which the process from past to present manifests as an undeniable trend. Thus, the whole series of Pathetic, Epic, and Tragic Dramas contained in the historical record are sublated into a Drama of essentially Comic significance, a human Comedy, a theodicy which is a justification not so much of the ways of God to man as of man's own ways to himself.

Thus is suggested the essentially Comic issue, the ultimately integrative and reconciliatory condition, toward which the whole process is tending. The aesthetic sense affirms this as the form that the historical process assumes in consciousness; the moral sense confirms it as what human self-certitude requires to be the case; and the intellectual sense, represented by reason, explicates the principles in virtue of which both the perception and the desire are rendered plausible. In the final analysis, the most that consciousness can extract from reflection on history is only an aesthetic apprehension for which there are good moral and rational grounds. The laws that govern the whole, as well as the form which the whole will finally take, can be specified by thought only in their most general terms.

> The chalice of this realm of spirits
> Foams forth to God His own Infinitude.

But the "owl of Minerva" takes its *final* flight only at the close of the cosmic day. Until that time, thought can deliver itself of the truth of history only within finite provinces of meaning and in anticipation of the time when the truth of the whole will be *lived* rather than simply *thought*.

ᴥᔫ *The Plot of World History*

It should by now be a relatively simple matter to explicate the specific principles of explanation and emplotment which Hegel utilized in his *Philosophy of History* proper. These are of interest in themselves, as the products of a profound and well-informed historical intelligence, the wit as well as the learning of which justify their study for themselves alone. But their real worth lies in the texture of the narrative as Hegel illuminated a point here, addumbrated a context there, threw in a speculative aside that later generations would have to labor for years to earn, and generally dominated the historical record with an arrogance that is justified only by its profundity. Yet, we can profitably linger on one or two points of the text, not only in order to clarify Hegel's views on the nature of historical explanation and representation in general, but also in order to demonstrate the consistency with which he applied his own explicit principles of historical analysis.

It is a commonplace that Hegel broke down the history of any given civilization and of civilization as a whole into four phases: the period of birth and original growth, that of maturity, that of "old age," and that of dissolution and death. Thus, for example, the history of Rome is conceived to extend in its first phase from its foundation down to the Second Punic War; in its second phase from the Second Punic War to the consolidation of the Principate by Caesar; in its third phase from this consolidation to the triumph of Christianity; and in its last phase from the third century A.D. to the fall of Byzantium. This movement through four phases represents four levels of civilizational self-consciousness: the phases of the in itself, the for itself, the in and for itself, and the by, in, and for itself. These phases can also be taken as marking out the elements of a Classical Drama, with its phases of *pathos*, *agon*, *sparagmos*, and *anagnorisis*, which have their spatial counterparts in the consolidation and dissolution of the elements of the Roman spirit: conflict with foreign foes, expansion outward in the creation of an empire, a turning back upon itself, and a dissolution which prepared the ground for the advent of a new power, Germanic culture, for which Rome itself was a subject and victim.

It is noteworthy that these phases can be regarded as indicating existential relationships, as ways of explaining those relationships, as ways of representing them, or as ways of symbolizing their "meaning" within the whole process of Roman historical development. The important point is that, to Hegel, what Rome *was* at any given stage of its evolution was not considered to be reducible to *what it did*, to an effect of an exhaustive set of causes, to merely a formal coherence (that is, generic case), or to a self-enclosed totality of relationships. In other words, the identification of a historical state of affairs as constituting a phase, the explanation of why it is what it is, the characterization of its formal attributes, and the relations which it sustains with other phases of the whole process are all conceived to have equal worth as elements of the total characterization of both the phases and the whole process in which they appear. Of course, to those who regard Hegel as nothing but a practitioner of the a priori method of historical representation, all these ways of characterizing a phase in the history of a civilization appear as nothing but *projections* of the categories of the dialectic: the in itself (thesis), the for itself (antithesis), and the in and for itself (synthesis), followed by a negation of the synthesis, which itself implies a new thesis (which is nothing but a new in itself), and so on, without end.

It is true that one could effect such a conceptual reduction of Hegel's method of analysis, and in a way that might not have offended Hegel himself, since he regarded these categories as fundamental to both logic and ontology and as the key to the comprehension of any process, whether of being or of consciousness.

But, in accordance with my way of characterizing his thought, in terms of the linguistic modes utilized in his characterizations, not only of the stages of being and logic, but also of history, I prefer to view these phases as conceptualizations of different modes of relationship in general as generated by Hegel's insight into the levels on which language, and therefore consciousness itself, had to operate.

It will be remembered that Hegel characterized Rome as "the *prose* of life," as against the "primeval wild poetry" of the East and "the harmonious poetry" of the Greek way of life (*Phil. of Hist.*, 288 [350]). This characterization is reminiscent of Vico's distinction among the ages of gods, of heroes, and of men. The Romans lived not a "natural" but a "formal" way of life, which is to say a life of extrinsicality and of relationships mediated by force and ritual, a severed life which was held together only by the most arduous exertions in the practical spheres of politics, positive law, and war, but which left little energy or will to create either a high art or a high religion or philosophy, such as the Greeks created. In short, the Romans *apprehended* the world in the mode of Metonymy (that is, in terms of contiguities) and strove for a *comprehension* of it in a purely Synecdochic system of relationships. The Roman "reality" was nothing but a field of force, its ideality a world of formally ordered relationships—in time (ancestor worship; possession of sons, wives, and daughters as property by the *paterfamilias*; laws of inheritance, and so on) and in space (roads, armies, proconsuls, walls, and so on). Ironically, it fell victim to a world view and a spirit which apprehended both its reality and its ideal in precisely opposed terms. Christianity represents the denial of the efficacy of force for the conquest of both space and time and of the value of any merely formal relationships. The Christian apprehends the world as one term of a Metaphor, the other and dominant term of which, that by which the world is given its meaning and identity, is conceived to exist in another world. And, far from recognizing the claims of a Metonymical or Ironic comprehension of the world, the Christian strives for the transcendence of all the tensions between the ideal and reality which these very modes of comprehension imply.

Once we have grasped the dynamics of the system by which Hegel characterized a given phase of the world historical process, we can understand more clearly in present-day terms how he arrived at his notions of the origin and evolution of world history and why he divided it into four major periods. This division corresponds to the four modes of consciousness represented by the modalities of tropological projection itself. For example, the condition of savagery can be likened to that stage in which human consciousness lives in the apprehension of no essential difference between itself and the world of nature; in which custom dictates life without any recognition of the inner tensions that might be generated in society by the right of the individual to aspire to something other than what custom dictates as a possible aspiration; in ignorance, superstition, and fear, without any sense of a specific goal for the folk as a totality; with no notion of history, but in an endless present; with no sense of any abstract notion that might generate religious (as against mythic), artistic (as against craft), and philosophical (as against concrete) reflection; in a state of repression rather than of morality, which implies the capacity to choose; and without any law other than the rule of the strongest.

The transition from savagery to the great civilizations of the Orient and Near East, the archaic cultures as they are called, can be likened to the awakening of consciousness to the possibility of Metaphorical apprehension, which is itself inspired by the sense of difference between that with which one is familiar and that which is unfamiliar. Metaphor is the mode of bridging the gap between these two orders of apprehended reality, and in the civilizations of the ancient Orient are examples of what is essentially a Metaphorical mode of life and consciousness. The East, Hegel wrote, is "unreflected consciousness—substantial, objective, spiritual existence . . . to which the subject will sustain a relation in the form of faith, confidence, obedience" (105). Thus, when Hegel likened the Orient to the period of childhood in history, he was suggesting—as Vico had earlier—that the mode of comprehending the world which emerges in that place at a certain time is that of simple Metaphorical identification of the subject with the object.

The transition from the childhood of history to its adolescence goes by way of Central Asia, where the individuality of the subject expressed itself in the "boisterousness" and "turbulence" of the tribes which arose there and which challenged the monolithic order imposed by the ruler on the subject, on the basis of a unity that is sensed to exist but does not yet have its basis in mutual self-consciousness (ibid., 106). The transition to the Greek world, the adolescent phase, proceeded from the *apprehension of the isolation of the individual within* the *Metaphorical identification of the unity to the affirmation of the ideal as individuality*—that is, as self-contained cause— which is to say, Metonymical reduction. As Hegel expressed it: "That which in the East is divided into two extremes—the substantial as such, and the individuality absorbed in it—meets here. But these distinct principles are only *immediately* in unity; and consequently involve the highest degree of contradiction" (107). This is why, in Hegel's view, Greek civilization only *appeared* to be a concrete unity, why it blossomed very quickly, only to fade and die as quickly as it had arisen. It lacked the principle in virtue of which the very mode of conceiving the unity of part with whole was possible. Rome conceived this mode of relationship, which was that of Synecdoche, but only formally, abstractly, as duty, power, or might. Its "seriousness" represented history's transition to manhood: "For true manhood acts neither in accord- ance with the caprice of a despot, nor in obedience to a graceful caprice of its own; but works for the general aim, one in which the individual perishes and realizes his own private object only in that general aim" (ibid.).

Thus far I have characterized the first three phases of a Classical Tragic plot, with the first phase representing the *pathos*, or general state of feeling, which opens the action; the second representing the *agon*, or conflict, which carries it forth; and the third representing the tearing apart of the subject, the *sparagmos*, which creates the conditions of the *dénouement* and carries the action forward to a resolution (*anagnorisis*). The three phases of this Drama are not, however, to be *resolved* in the mode of Tragedy, even though each phase describes a pattern of Tragic rise and fall. The phase of reconciliation (*anagnorisis*) into which the action is carried by the essential contradiction in Roman civilization and its spirit is marked, not by the epiphany of the iron law of fate or justice which Classical Greek Tragedy demanded as its resolution, but rather by the enclosure of what appears to be such a law within the Christian (Comic) vision of the ultimate liberation of man from his world and his ultimate reconciliation with God. The Tragic vision is annulled in the vision of the whole, which transcends the Irony implicit in the resolution of Classical Tragedy, in which, while something new is revealed to the consciousness, this something new is always set against the background of a still greater mystery, which is Fate itself.

Although the phase of history represented by the crystallization of a new civilization in Western Europe might appear to be the entrance of humanity into its "old age," this conclusion would be justified only if the proper analogue of history were that of natural process. But, Hegel argued, history is, above all, "spirit," which means that in history, as against nature, "maturity" is the kind of "strength" and "unity" glimpsed in the Christian vision of the "Reconciliation" of the Creation with the Creator (109). The Tragic vision is thus transcended in the apprehension of the whole world process on the analogy, not of nature or Classical Tragedy or even Classical Comedy (which only asserts the right of life against the vision of fate given in Tragedy), but of the Christian "Divine Comedy," in which, in the end, as in Dante's epic expression of its informing idea, everything finally comes to rest in its appropriate place in the hierarchy of being. But the Christian vision is itself only a *Metaphorical apprehension* of the truth of the whole. Its articulation must be carried out through the *agon* and *sparagmos* of *its* relationship with the world, which carries Western civilization through the conflict of church and state in the Middle Ages and the conflict of the nations in the early modern period to that point at which the whole process of history is finally comprehended in principle as the drama of the unification of man with his own essence, which is to say freedom and reason, and points to the time in which perfect freedom will be perfect reason and reason freedom, the truth of the whole, which is the Absolute, which is, as Hegel said, nothing but *life* itself in the full comprehension of what it *is*.

This means that Hegel could "place" his own time within a perspective which was manifestly providentialist in nature but which, by his lights, made no appeal to naive faith or conventional belief, but rather had its grounds in both empirical evidence and the rational apprehension of what that evidence signifies. The Period of the Revolution represented for him the culmination of an agonistic period in which the nations had fallen apart into their otherness, but carried within themselves the principles of their own inner coherence and intrinsic relationships with one another. These principles respresented, in the Synecdochically comprehended forms in which Hegel arranged them as parts to the whole, the bases for belief in the ultimate unification of the world in a new form of state, the form of which can be specified only conjecturally. America and Russia are envisioned as possibilities for the development of new kinds of states in the future, but historical knowledge and the philosophical comprehension of it are forced to halt with the consideration of only that which has already occurred and that which is currently the case. At most, they can speak of possibilities of future development by logical extension of the trends already discerned in the whole process and can suggest the forms through which future development must pass in the transition from the concrete embodiment of the human spirit in the nation-state to the world-state which their actualized integrations augur.

That these forms will possess, viewed from the context of a higher level of integration of consciousness and being, the same modal relationships as those through which the individual phases of the whole historical process have passed and through which the whole historical process has passed *across* these phases, Hegel suggested must be the case since these forms are the forms of consciousness itself. World history can be comprehended only in such terms, for these are the modalities of consciousness in its dimensions of intelligence, emotion, and will. The internal dynamics of a single phase in the process figure the dynamics of the whole.

For example, the "plot" of Oriental history is itself analyzable into four phases. Hegel characterized its inauguration as a break with the purely organic processes of savage existence in which the diffusion of language and the formation of the races occurred. Historical consciousness as such does not and cannot know this primitive existence. Man knows it only as myth and can (Hegel implied) comprehend it only in the mode of myth—that is, intuitively, Metaphorically. However, once the union of man with nature, as mediated by mere custom, is broken, and consciousness falls out of mythic (or naively poetic) apprehensions of the world into an apprehension of the distance between consciousness and its object (which is the presupposition of naive prosaic existence), history proper can be said to have begun, because historical development, as against primitive change and evolution, is possible only within the context of a sensed contradiction between consciousness and its object. Human consciousness experiences this tension as a *lack* which it tries to overcome by the imposition of order, the four forms of which appear as the subphases of Oriental historical development: Chinese, Indian, Persian, and Egyptian successively.

The succession of these four phases of Oriental civilization can itself be comprehended both as a Tragic Drama in four acts and as a process in which consciousness passes from merely Metaphorical apprehension of its civilizational projects, through Metonymy and Synecdoche, to Ironic division and dissolution. The whole process is to be conceived, according to Hegel, in its aspect as the achievement of order through the imposition of an arbitrary will on human materials (111). China is thus characterized as a "theocratic despotism" operating in the mode of (Metaphorical) identification of the (political) subject with the sovereign. No formal *distinction* is made in Chinese civilization between the private and public spheres, between morality and legality, between past and present, or between inner and outer worlds. The Chinese emperors claimed sovereignty over the world in principle, though they were unable to exercise such. It is a world of pure subjectivity, though this subjectivity is concentrated, not in the individuals who make up the Chinese empire, but in the "supreme head of the state," who alone is free (112–13).

But, Hegel said, in the "second realm—the Indian realm—we see the unity of political organization . . . broken up. The several powers of society appear as dissevered and free in relation to each other." The castes are fixed, but "in view of the religious doctrine that established them, they were the aspect of *natural* distinctions." They exist in the mode of causally determined separation—that is, Metonymy—and in constant *agonic* tension, in contrast to the *pathos* which formally united the ruler and the ruled, the subject and the object, in the Metaphorically oriented Chinese realm. Thus, too, in India, theocratic *despotism* gave place to theocratic *aristocracy*, with a corresponding loss of order and direction. Since *separation* is presumed to inhere in the very nature of the cosmos, there can be no order and common direction in the totality. The principle of this civilization *"posits the harshest antithesis*—the conception of the purely abstract unity of God, and of the purely sensual powers of nature. The *connection* of the two is only a constant change—a restless hurrying from one extreme to the other—a wild chaos of fruitless variation, which must appear as madness to a duly regulated, intelligent consciousness." (113)

The principle in virtue of which this separation can be overcome and the unity of human being can be asserted on grounds more adequate to its translation into social and political principles—that is, the (Synecdochic) apprehension of the spiritual nature of all being—appeared in Persia, where, however, this "spirit" was still envisaged in terms of its material analogue, pure light. Thus, Hegel wrote,

China is quite peculiarly Oriental; India we might compare with Greece; Persia on the other hand with Rome. [*Ibid.*]

For, not only did the theocratic power appear in Persia as monarchy, but the principle by appeal to which it exercised its rule, the *spiritual* principle, was *materially construed* and therefore possessed no means by which to conceive its conscious ideal, the rule by law, in terms which would actually permit the recognition of the dignity of the subject. Persia's unity was conceived in terms of the "beneficial sun" which shines equally on all, binding the parts into a whole in a purely extrinsic relationship which is, however, conceived and experienced by the subject as a beneficent one (114). As in any merely formal coherence in which the principle of the relation of part to whole is grasped as fundamental, the Persian Empire permitted the crystallization and development of individual peoples, such as the Jews, in the misapprehension that such parts can be permitted to develop without fracturing or rupturing the putatively spiritual unity of the whole (*ibid.*).

That the development of the part in such a way as not to threaten the unity of the whole at all is impossible, however, is shown by two facts: the rebellion of the Greeks of Ionia, who asserted the absolute worth of individuality against a specious universality; and that of the Egyptians, who reasserted the claims of materiality against a specious spirituality.

In Egypt, Hegel said, the "antitheses in their abstract form are broken through; a breakthrough which effects their nullification" (115). The Egyptians apprehended the world Ironically, as a schismatic condition in which the separation of spirit and matter is experienced as profound pain and anxiety. Hence, Egyptian culture presented the aspect of the "most contradictory principles, which are not yet capable of harmonizing themselves, but, *setting up the birth of this harmony as the problem to be solved*," turn themselves into a "riddle" for themselves and for others. This riddle was to be solved finally—and with its solution the principle for the transition to a new world was provided—in Greece. The solution to the "riddle" was, of course, the solution which Oedipus gave to the riddle of the Sphinx which he met at the convergence of the three roads on his way to Thebes. (220– 21) The riddle which the Egyptians could not solve was "man," but the fact that the solution was found, not in the Orient, but in the West (in the Oedipus myth, the Sphinx traveled to Greece), suggests that the gain made in human consciousness by the Tragic rise and fall of one or another a humanity's incarnations in a specific culture is given, not to the culture itself, but to the culture which comes *after* it, the culture which succeeds in solving the "riddle" created by Ironic consciousness of the law in its own constitution. The characterization of the enigma of human existence as a riddle is yet another way of indicating the essentially Comic nature of the whole historical quest.

It is not necessary here to deal with the full articulation of the drama of human history which Hegel provided in the *Philosophy of History*. The important point is that Hegel asked us to regard ourselves as actors in a drama which, although its actual end is unknowable, displays the order and continuity of a well-wrought play or a dialectical argument, and which therefore gives us good reasons for believing that the resolution of this drama not only will not be meaningless but will not even be Tragic. The Tragic vision is given its due as a means of illuminating a certain aspect of our existence and a certain phase of both the evolution of a specific culture and the evolution of civilization in general. But it is enclosed within the higher perspective of the Comic nature of the whole. So, too, the various modes in which we apprehend the world and comprehend it in consciousness—the modes of Metaphor, Metonymy, and Synecdoche—are given their due as means to the attainment of that higher consciousness of the imperfect and fragmentary nature of any given comprehension of the world which is Irony.

Beyond this Ironic posture we cannot go in science, because, since we exist *in* history, we can never know the final truth *about* history. We can glimpse the *form* which that truth will take, however—its form as harmony, reason, freedom, the unity of consciousness and being which is intuited in religion, Metaphorically imaged in art, Metonymically characterized in science, Synecdochically comprehended in philosophy, and, Ironically distanced and made the object of greater efforts of comprehension in historical consciousness itself. The justification of these ever greater efforts at comprehension, in the face of the Ironic awareness of their inevitable limitation, is provided by art itself, in the Comic vision of the chaos of forms which becomes a revel, a joyous affirmation of the whole.

The movement from perception of the world through religious, artistic, scientific, philosophical, and historical comprehensions of it (each comprehension taking the preceding one as simply an apprehension) reflects the essential movement of being in its actualization, and consciousness in its realization, in history. Historical consciousness in itself is born at the same time as a specifically historical mode of existence in the history of humanity. From the Greeks to Hegel's own time this historical consciousness became "for itself," separating out from other forms of consciousness, and was used by individual historians for the production of the various kinds of "reflective" histories they actually wrote. The actual writing of history creates the occasion for a third kind of historical reflection—that is to say, reflection on the nature of historical consciousness itself and on its relation to historical being —and promotes what are effectively the preconditions for a higher kind of consciousness in general within religious, artistic, scientific, and philosophical consciousness alike.

Religion, art, science, and philosophy themselves reflect the different stages in a given civilization's (and in consciousness-in-general's) closure with its object (which, in the case of consciousness in general, is pure being). These can be used to characterize the *quality* of a culture's apprehension and comprehension of itself and its world as they develop in time in the modalities of the in-, for-, in-and-for, and in-for-and-by itself, which in turn provide the modes of characterizing the four stages through which all civilizations pass from birth to death. But the apprehension of the nature of these four stages by philosophical history, of the sort proposed by Hegel in his work, reflects the rise of a yet higher order of consciousness which provides the ground for transcending the "Ironic" nature of consciousness' relation to being in general as well as of civilization's relationship with its various incarnations in world history. This new mode of consciousness represents the rise to consciousness of the Comic vision of the world process, which now not only asserts the primacy of life over death in the face of any given Tragic situation, but also knows the reasons for that assertion.

𝒆𝓈 *Two* FOUR KINDS OF "REALISM" IN
NINETEENTH-CENTURY HISTORICAL
WRITING

Chapter *3* MICHELET: HISTORICAL REALISM
AS ROMANCE

✌§ *Introduction*

Hegel, the critic of every historian that preceded him, was the historical conscience of the age that followed him. No one came near to achieving the
insight and depth of his inquiry into the problem of historical consciousness,
not even Croce, the philosopher who resembled him most in temperament
and breadth of interests. But, then, few historical thinkers desired to penetrate to the interior of their own preconceptions about history and the kind
of knowledge to be derived from its study. Those who studied history as a
profession were too busy writing history to inquire very closely into the
theoretical bases of their activity. The justification of historical knowledge
which Hegel had sought. to provide seemed both unnecessary and unneces-
sarily prolix. The study of history was professionalized during the very years
that Hegel pondered the problem of its theoretical justification as a special
form of consciousness and tried to define its relationship to art, science,
philosophy, and religious sensibility. And this transformation of history from
a general area of study, cultivated by amateurs, dilettantes, and antiquarians,
into a professional discipline seemed sufficient justification for the severance
of historiography from the endless speculations of the "philosophers of history."

Chairs of history were founded at the University of Berlin in 1810 and at the Sorbonne in 1812. Societies for the editing and publication of historical documents were established soon after: the society for the *Monumenta Germaniae Historica* in 1819, the *École des Chartes* in 1821. Government subsidies of these societies—inspired by the nationalist sympathies of the time —were forthcoming in due course, in the 1830s. After mid-century, the great national journals of historical studies were set up: the *Historische Zeitschrift* in 1859, the *Révue historique* in 1876, the *Rivista storica italiana* in 1884, and the *English Historical Review* in 1886. The profession became progressively academicized. The professorate formed a clerisy for the promotion and cultivation of a socially responsible historiography; it trained and licensed apprentices, maintained standards of excellence, ran the organs of intraprofessional communication, and in general enjoyed a privileged place in the humanistic and social scientific sectors of the universities. In this disciplinization of the field of history, England lagged behind the Continental nations. Oxford established the Regius Professorship of History, first held by Stubbs, only in 1866; Cambridge followed thereafter, in 1869. But English undergraduates could not specialize in historical studies as a distinct field until 1875.

Yet, if historical studies were professionalized during this period, the theoretical basis of its disciplinization remained unclear. The transformation of historical thinking from an amateur activity into a professional one was not attended by the sort of conceptual revolution that has accompanied such transformations of other fields, such as physics, chemistry, and biology. Instruction in the "historical method" consisted essentially of an injunction to use the most refined philological techniques for the criticism of historical documents, combined with a set of statements about what the historian ought *not* to attempt on the basis of the documents thus criticized. For example, it soon became a cliché that history was not a branch of metaphysics or religion, the mixtures of which with historical knowledge were what caused the "fall" of historical consciousness into the heresies of "philosophy of history." Instead, it was maintained, history was to be viewed as a combination of "science" and "art." But the meanings of the terms "science" and "art" were unclear. To be sure, it was clear that the historian should try to be "scientific" in his investigation of the documents and in his efforts to determine "what actually happened" in the past, and that he ought to represent the past "artistically" to his readers. But it was generally agreed that history was not a "rigorous" science (a law-using or a law-discovering discipline), in the way that physics and chemistry were. That is to say, history was not a Positivist science, and the historian should remain content with a Baconian, empirical and inductivist, conception of the scientist's task, which meant that historiography should remain a pre-Newtonian science. And the same was said with respect to the "artistic" component in historical representation.

Though an art, historical writing was not to be regarded as what was called at the beginning of the nineteenth century a "free art"—that is, a creative art of the sort that the Romantic poets and novelists cultivated. As an art form, historical writing might be "lively" and stimulating, even "entertaining," so long as the artist-historian did not presume to utilize anything other than the techniques and devices of traditional storytelling. As the prefatory note of the first issue of the *English Historical Review* (*EHR*) put it: "So far from holding that true history is dull, we believe that dull history is usually bad history, and shall value those contributors most highly who can present their researches in a lucid and effective form."

The general idea was that, given the breach which had opened up between the "rigorous" (Positivist) sciences and the "free" (Romantic) arts during the first half of the nineteenth century, history might legitimately claim to occupy a neutral middle ground on the basis of which the "two cultures" might be brought together and reunited in common service to the goals of civilized society. As the *EHR*'s prefatory note put it:

We believe that history, in an even greater degree than its votaries have as yet generally recognized, is the central study among human studies, capable of illuminating and enriching all the rest. [Stern, *Varieties*, 177]

But, in order to achieve this goal of illumination and enrichment, history had to be cultivated in a spirit beyond party interests and confessional allegiances. This meant that historical researches and generalizations had to be kept within the bounds of an essential modesty, skirting the dangers of narrowness on one side and of vagueness on the other. As the *EHR* pointed out, two views of history's function prevailed by mid-century: one, that it was merely another form of political commentary, and, another, that it was commentary on everything that had ever happened in human time. The *EHR* proposed to avoid both extremes by encouraging contributions from "students of each special department" (175) of historical studies and, above all, "refusing contributions which argue . . . questions with reference to present controversy" (176).

In this proposal the *EHR* followed the line indicated by the *Révue historique*—that is, "to avoid contemporary controversies, to treat the subjects . . . with the methodological rigidity and absence of partisanship which science demands, and not to seek arguments for or against doctrines which are only indirectly involved" (173). But this appeal to methodological "rigidity" and nonpartisanship was made in the absence of any but the most general notions of what they might consist of. Actually, the aim was, as the preface to the first issue of the *Historische Zeitschrift* made quite clear, to remove historical study from the uses to which it was being put by Radicals and Reactionaries on the political scene, and to serve—by the disciplinization of historical studies—the interests and values of the new social orders and classes which had come to power after the Revolutionary Age.

The *Historische Zeitschrift* insisted that it would be a "scientific" periodical, the aim of which was to "represent the true method of historical research and to point out the deviations therefrom." Still, it also insisted that its interests were not to be conceived as narrowly antiquarian nor as intimately political. "It is not our aim," the Preface to its first issue read, "to discuss unresolved questions of current politics, nor to commit ourselves to one particular political party." It did not seem "contradictory," however, to rule out as legitimate approaches to historical study the points of view represented by "feudalism, which imposes lifeless elements on the progressive life; radicalism, which substitutes subjective arbitrariness for organic development; [and] ultramontanism, which subjects the national spiritual evolution to the authority of an extraneous Church." (171–72) All of this meant that the professionalization of historical studies did have specific political implications and that the "theory" on which its scientization was ultimately based was nothing other than the ideology of the middle sectors of the social spectrum, represented by Conservatives on the one hand and Liberals on the other.

As a matter of fact, in both France and Germany the academic fortunes of leftwing historians and philosophers of history waxed and waned with the fortunes of Radicalism itself. This meant that they mostly waned. In 1818, both Victor Cousin and Guizot were fired from the Sorbonne for teaching "ideas" rather than "facts" (Liard, II, 157–59). Feuerbach and D. F. Strauss were denied careers in the German academy for their "radical" ideas. In 1850, freedom of instruction was rescinded in the French universities in the interests of protecting "society" from the threat of "atheism and socialism" (234). Michelet and Quinet and the Polish poet Mickiewicz were fired, "dangerous books" were proscribed, and historians were specifically prohibited from departing from the chronological order in the presentation of their materials (246). And this time Cousin and Thiers, themselves formerly victims of political discrimination, supported the repressive actions (234). Small wonder that the poet-revolutionary Heine reserved some of his sharpest barbs for professional historians and the cultivators of academic humanism.

Writing in exile in Paris, Heine lashed out at the professorate, which hid its support of repressive regimes behind the mask of objectivity and the disinterested study of the past, and thus opened an offensive against academic scholarship which would be continued by Marx and Nietzsche, from the Left and Right respectively, and which would culminate in the last decade of the century in a full-scale revolt among both artists and social scientists against the burden of historical consciousness in general.

> Zu fragmentarisch ist Welt und Leben!
> Ich will mich zum deutschen Professor begeben.
> Der weiss das Leben zusammenzusetzen,

Und er macht ein verständlich System daraus;
Mit seinen Nachtmützen und Schlafrockfetzen
Stopft er die Lücken des Weltenbaus. [Stössinger

The philosophers of history, the philosophers of nature, the Goeth   ..ᴄes,
and the "wiseacres" of the Historical School were all engaged, Heine maintained, in a conspiracy to dampen "the three day fever for freedom in the
German people." The historians especially were "creepers and intriguers"
(*Ranken and Ränken*) (98), who cultivated a "convenient soothing fatalism" as an antidote to political concern. Not even the Romantic poets were
exempted from the charge. While the historians deflected consciousness to a
consideration of the past, the poets projected it into an indefinite future,
turning the present into nothing more than a vague anticipation of what
might have been or might yet be, but in either case suggesting that living
men were not ends in themselves but rather only the means for attaining a
dimly perceived "*Humanität*." Neither "scientific" history nor "aesthetic"
poetry, Heine said,

harmonizes fully with our own vivid sense of life. On the one hand, we do not
wish to be inspired uselessly and stake the best we possess on a futile past. On the
other hand, we also demand that the living present be valued as it deserves, and
not merely serve as a means to some distant end. As a matter of fact, we consider
ourselves more important than merely means to an end. We believe that means
and ends are only conventional concepts, which brooding man has read into
nature and history, and of which the Creator knows nothing. For every creation
is self-purposed, and every event is self-conditioned, and everything—the whole
world itself—is here, in its own right. [Ewen ed., 810]

And he concluded with a challenge to both the antiseptic concepts of history
cultivated by the professional historians on the one hand and the hospital
philosophy of the Romantic poets on the other:

Life is neither means nor end. Life is a right. Life desires to validate this right
against the claims of petrifying death, against the past. This justification of life is
Revolution. The elegaic indifference of historians and poets must not paralyze our
energies when we are engaged in this enterprise. Nor must the romantic visions of
those who promise us happiness in the future seduce us into sacrificing the interests of the present, the immediate struggle for the rights of man, the right to life
itself. [809–10]

In his juxtaposition of the rights of life against the claims of the dead past
and the future yet unborn, Heine anticipated Nietzsche's attack, in the
1870s, on all forms of academic historiography, an attack which threatened to
become a cliché in the literature of the 1880s (Ibsen), the 1890s (Gide,
Mann), and the early 1900s (Valéry, Proust, Joyce, D. H. Lawrence).

⤳ The Classics of Nineteenth-Century Historiography

Yet the period between 1821 (the year of Wilhelm von Humboldt's "On the Historian's Task") and 1868 (the year of Droysen's *Historik*) produced the works which still serve as the models of modern historical accomplishment, for professionals and amateurs alike. A simple chronological listing of the works of four undisputed masters of nineteenth-century historiography will suffice to indicate both the scope and the profundity of this effort to comprehend the past in ways that illuminated contemporary problems. The masters in question are Jules Michelet (1798–1877), the presiding genius of the Romantic School of historiography; Leopold von Ranke (1795–1886), the founder of the Historical School, the historist *par excellence*, and the paradigm of academic historiography; Alexis de Tocqueville (1806–59), the virtual founder of social history and the prototype of the modern historical sociologists, Émile Durkheim and Max Weber; and, finally, Jacob Burckhardt (1818–97), the archetypal cultural historian, cultivator of an aesthetic historiography and exponent of the Impressionistic style of historical representation. The works in question are:

1824, Ranke, *Histories of the Latin and Germanic Peoples*
1827, Michelet, translation of Vico's *The New Science*
1828, Michelet, *Précis of Modern History*
1829, Ranke, *History of the Serbian Revolution*
1831, Michelet, *Introduction to Universal History*
1833–44, Michelet, *History of France*, 6 volumes on the Middle Ages
1834–36, Ranke, *History of the Popes*
1835–40, Tocqueville, *Democracy in America*
1839–47, Ranke, *German History in the Age of the Reformation*
1846, Michelet, *The People*
1847, Ranke, *Nine Books of Prussian History*
1847–53, Michelet, *History of the French Revolution*
1852–61, Ranke, *History of France in the Sixteenth and Seventeenth Centuries*
1853, Burckhardt, *The Age of Constantine the Great*
1856, Tocqueville, *The Old Regime and the Revolution*
1859–68, Ranke, *History of England in the Seventeenth Century*
1860, Burckhardt, *Civilization of the Renaissance in Italy*
1872–73, Michelet, *History of the Nineteenth Century*

The works of a host of other historians, almost as distinguished, might be added to this list: those of the great Classical historians Grote, Droysen, Mommsen, and Fustel de Coulanges; of the Medievalists Stubbs and Maitland; of the nationalists Sybel and Treitschke; of the so-called doctrinaires Thierry and Guizot; or of the philosophers of history, Comte, Spencer,

Buckle, Gobineau, Hegel, Feuerbach, Marx and Engels, Nietzsche, and Taine. But none of these, except possibly those listed among the philosophers of history, can claim the authority and prestige of the four masters, Michelet, Ranke, Tocqueville, and Burckhardt. For, while the others created whole fields of study and can be seen as representing different fashions in nineteenth-century historical thinking, only these four—Michelet, Ranke, Tocqueville, and Burckhardt—still serve as paradigms of a distinctively modern historical consciousness. Michelet, Ranke, Tocqueville, and Burckhardt represent not only original achievements in the writing of history but also alternative models of what a "realistic" historiography might be.

✑§ Historiography against Philosophy of History

In his Philosophy of History, Hegel attempted to provide theoretical justification for a type of historical reflection that he regarded as unique to the modern age. What he called "Original history" had existed from the time of the Greeks. Each of the four species of Reflective history that had appeared in the development of historical thinking since the Greeks, had represented a higher form of historical self-consciousness. Philosophy of history itself, as Hegel conceived it, was nothing but the explication of the principles underlying "Reflective history" and their systematic application to the problem of writing universal history in a higher, more self-consciously "Reflective" manner. He did not suggest that historians themselves attempt to write such universal history, but insisted that they leave its composition to the philosophers, because the philosophers alone were capable of comprehending what was implied in the achievement of reflective historiography, of raising its epistemological, aesthetic, and ethical principles to consciousness, and then of applying them to the problem of the history of humanity in general.

This way of distinguishing between historiography and philosophy of history was not generally understood or, when it was understood, granted, by the historians of the nineteenth century. For most of them, "philosophy of history" represented the effort to write history on the basis of philosophical preconceptions which required the bending of the evidence to the schema arrived at by a prioristic reasoning. The "historical method"—as the classic historiographers of the nineteenth century understood the term—consisted of a willingness to go to the archives without any preconceptions whatsoever, to study the documents found there, and then to write a story about the events attested by the documents in such a way as to make the story itself the explanation of "what had happened" in the past. The idea was to let the explanation emerge naturally from the documents themselves, and then to figure its meaning in story form.

The notion that the historian himself emplotted the events found in the documents was only vaguely glimpsed by thinkers sensitive to the poetic element in every effort at narrative description—by a historian like J. G. Droysen, for example, and by philosophers like Hegel and Nietzsche, but by few others. To have suggested that the historian emplotted his stories would have offended most nineteenth-century historians. That different "points of view" might be brought to bear upon the past was not denied, but these "points of view" were regarded more as biases to be suppressed than as poetic perspectives that might illuminate as much as they obscured. The idea was to "tell the story" about "what had happened" without significant conceptual residue or ideological preformation of the materials. If the story were rightly told, the explanation of what had happened would figure itself forth from the narrative, in the same way that the structure of a landscape would be figured by a properly drawn map.

A history might have an explanatory component, like the "legend" of a map, but this component had to be relegated to a place on the periphery of the narrative itself, in the same way that the legend of the map was. The "legend" of a history was to be put in a special box, as it were, contained in the "general remarks" with which one prefaced one's histories or concluded them. The true explanation lay in the telling of a story that was as accurate in its details as it was compelling in its meaning. But accuracy in the details was often confused with the truth of the meaning of the story. It was not seen that the meaning of the story was given by the mode of emplotment chosen to make of the story told a *story of a particular kind*. It was not understood that the choice of a mode of emplotment itself reflected commitment to a philosophy of history, and that Hegel had been pointing this out in his discussion of history as a form of literary art in his *Aesthetics*.

What, then, was the difference between "history" and "philosophy of history"? The four master historians of the nineteenth century gave different answers to this question, but all agreed that a true history should be written without preconceptions, objectively, out of an interest in the facts of the past for themselves alone, and with no aprioristic inclination to fashion the facts into a formal system. Yet, the most striking attribute of the histories written by these masters was their formal coherence, their conceptual *domination* of the historical field. Of the four, Burckhardt managed best to convey the impression of one who simply let the facts "speak for themselves" and kept the conceptual principles of his narratives most completely buried in the texture of his works. But even Burckhardt's impressionistic histories have a formal coherence of their own, the coherence of "Satire," the form in which the hypersensitive soul figures the folly of the world.

With the exception of Tocqueville, none of these historians thrust the formal explanatory argument into the foreground of the narrative. One has to extract the principles being appealed to by drawing implications from what is said in the story line of the histories they wrote. This means, how-ever, that the weight of explanatory effect is thrown upon the mode of emplotment. And, in fact, that "historism" of which Michelet, Ranke, Toc-queville, and Burckhardt are now recognized to have been equally represen-tative can be characterized in one way as simply the substitution of emplot-ment for argument as an explanatory strategy. When, in the manner of Ranke, they purported to be simply "telling what actually happened" and to be explaining the past by telling its "story," they were all explicitly embracing the conception of explanation by description but were actually practicing the art of explanation by emplotment. Each told a different *kind of story*—Romance, Comedy, Tragedy, or Satire—or at least presupposed one or another of these story forms as the general framework for the segment of history that he was depicting in detail. The "philosophies of history" that they represented must be characterized, then, not only in terms of the formal explanatory strategies they embraced, but also in terms of the modes of emplotment they chose for framing or informing the story they told.

But even more important than the mode of emplotment they chose to give the form to the stories they told is the mode of consciousness in which they prefigured the historical field as a domain, the posture they assumed before this structure, and the linguistic protocol in which they characterized it. The four master historians of the nineteenth century represent different solutions to the problem of how to write history, having chosen the modes of Romance, Comedy, Tragedy, and Satire to emplot it. But they assumed different ideo-logical postures before the historical field—Anarchist, Conservative, Liberal, and Reactionary respectively. None of them was a Radical. The linguistic protocols in which they prefigured this field were similarly diverse: Meta-phorical, Synecdochic, Metonymical, and Ironic.

ᴥᔄ *Romantic Historiography as "Realism" in the Metaphorical Mode*

In the introduction to my chapter on eighteenth-century historical thought, I suggested that the "realism" of its nineteenth-century counterpart con-sisted primarily in the attempt to justify belief in progress and optimism while avoiding the Irony into which the *philosophes* had been driven. Romantic historiography, I now suggest, represents a return to the Meta-phorical mode for the characterization of the historical field and its processes, but without the adoption of the Organicist explanatory strategy with which Herder had burdened it. The Romantics repudiated all formal systems of explanation and tried to gain an explanatory effect by utilizing the Meta-phorical mode to describe the historical field and the *mythos* of Romance to represent its processes.

✑ *The Historical Field as a Chaos of Being*

This repudiation of all formal systems of explanation should not be taken at face value, however, for most of the Romantics presupposed a theory of knowledge adequate to their characterization of the historical field as what Carlyle called a "Chaos of Being," with respect to which the historian could assume a posture as both observer and agent of its processes. In such Romantics as Constant, Novalis, and Carlyle, to take three examples, this "Chaos of Being" notion of history inspired three distinct attitudes, each of which implied a different notion of the historian's task. Constant's position represents a Romantic variant on the Ironic viewpoint inherited from the late eighteenth century, but made more Nihilistic by the color of his response to the events of the Revolution and the Reaction. One of his characterizations of the historical world may be taken as representative of the feeling of apprehension which the historical thinking of his age was meant to transcend. In a passage which appears in the essay "On Religion," Constant wrote:

Man, victor of the fights he has engaged in, looks at a world depopulated by protective powers, and is astonished at his victory. . . . His imagination, idle now and solitary, turns upon itself. He finds himself alone on an earth which may swallow him up. On this earth the generations follow each other, transitory, fortuitous, isolated; they appear, they suffer, they die. . . . No voice of the races that are no more is prolonged into the life of the races still living, and the voice of the living races must soon be engulfed by the same eternal silence. What shall man do, without memory, without hope, between the past which abandons him and the future which is closed before him? His invocations are no longer heard, his prayers receive no answer. He has spurned all the supports with which his predecessors had surrounded him; he is reduced to his own forces. [Quoted in Poulet, *Studies*, 212]

The passage is manifestly Ironic. Its essential Irony is signaled by the opening sentence, in which a seemingly "victorious" humanity is depicted as being "astonished" by the attainment of that for which it had long and at last successfully struggled. This victory, however, has been turned back upon man himself, for now man "finds himself alone," occupant of a world "which may swallow him up." The threat to which men now stand exposed is identified by Constant as arising from the discovery of the meaninglessness of history, apprehension of the senseless succession of the generations, which "follow each other, transitory, fortuitous, isolated; they appear, they suffer, they die." Nothing consoling can be adduced from reflection on the relations between the generations: the "voices" of past generations provide no aid or counsel for the living; and the living must face a world in which they, too, will soon be consumed and relegated to "the same eternal silence." Living men are thus placed between a "past" which "abandons" them and a "future" which is "closed"; they are forced to live "without memory, without hope." All the customary "supports" of communal life have disintegrated, and man is reduced "to his own forces"; but these forces, the passage clearly implies, are inadequate to the prosecution of the tasks which all previous societies and civilizations set for themselves. Human consciousness is thus depicted as inadequate to both the comprehension of reality and the exercise of any effective control over it. Men are awash in a historical sea more threatening than that natural world which primitive savages confronted in their ignorance and debility at the dawn of human time.

It was precisely this Ironic posture before history which the dominant philosophical systems of the early nineteenth century were meant to overcome and to supplant with a theoretically more justified conception of man's abilities to control his own destiny and to give meaning and direction to history. The metaphysical tendencies of the age, reflected in the great systems of Idealism, Positivism, and Romanticism, sought to dissolve the kind of Ironic stance which thinkers like Constant, in their despair, had taken to be the sole form that "realism" could take in the post-Revolutionary Age.

The Romantic response to this mood of *angoisse* took two forms, one predominantly religious, the other aesthetic. An example of the religious response is Novalis, who, in the face of the skepticism and nihilism of the late Enlightenment and immediate post-Revolutionary period, simply affirmed—in much the same way that Herder had done—the redemptive nature of the historical process itself. For the dogmatism of the utter skeptic, Novalis substituted the dogmatism of the fideist. In "Christendom or Europe," he stated that the anxiety of his age stemmed from its failure to recognize the inadequacy of *any* purely secular, or purely human, solution to social problems:

Let the true beholder contemplate calmly and dispassionately the new state-toppling era. . . . All your props are too weak if your state retains its tendency towards the earth. But link it by a higher yearning to the heights of heaven, give it a relevancy to the universe, and you will have in it a never wearying spring, and you will see your efforts richly rewarded. [56]

Novalis hoped for a new form of Christianity, neither Catholic nor Protestant, but cosmopolitan and unifying. And he believed that a justification for his hope was to be found in the study of history. "I refer you to history," he said. "Search amid its instructive coherency for parallel points of time and learn to use the magic wand of analogy" (*ibid.*). Thus could man at last discover the spirit of the Christian word and get beyond the endless substitution of one "letter" for another. "Shall the letter make way for the letter?" he asked. "Are you seeking the seed germ of deterioration in the old order too, in the old spirit? And do you imagine yourselves on a better tack toward the understanding of a better spirit?" (*ibid.*). Salvation, Novalis insisted, lay neither in a sentimental return to the old order nor in a doctrinaire adherence to the "letter" of a new one, but rather in a faith which took the "spirit" of history itself as a model.

O would that the spirit of spirits filled you and you would desist from this foolish effort to mold history and mankind and to give it your direction! Is it not independent, not self-empowered, as well as infinitely lovable and prophetic? To study it, to follow after it, to learn from it, to keep step with it, to follow in faith its promises and hints—of these no one thinks. [*Ibid.*]

Novalis's ideas are as "mythical" as those of Constant, which is to say that they represent a mood, a state of soul, that has been elevated to the status of a truth. The historical mysticism of the one stands in direct contrast to the historical pyrrhonism of the other, but they are equally dogmatic. The latter proposed to solve the problem of life by affirming the meaninglessness of history, the former by asserting that the only meaning life can have must come from uncritical faith in history's power to provide its own meaning and the belief that men must "follow" history in the same way that they had, in the past, followed religion. The same condition that Constant experienced as a nightmare, Novalis apprehended as the material for a dream of deliverance.

It should be noted, however, that the two positions thus outlined would generate the same kind of historiography. In both cases the individual event would take on a value which it could not claim in a historiography governed by some critical standard in which the historian was asked to distinguish between the insignificant and significant events in the historical record. For Constant, every event was equally insignificant as a contribution to man's quest for meaning; for Novalis, all events were equally significant as contributions to man's self-knowledge and discovery of the meaningfulness of human life.

A similarly aestheticist, but ethically more responsible, form of Romanticism appeared in Carlyle's essay on *Boswell's Life of Johnson*. Here Carlyle defined the purpose of history as the attempt to revoke "the Edict of Destiny, so that Time shall not utterly, not so soon by several centuries have dominion over us." The historian's purpose, in Carlyle's view, was to transmute the voices of the great men of the past into admonitions of, and inspirations for, the living. In great historical writing, he said, "they who are gone are still here; though hidden they are revealed; though dead they yet speak." Here the historian's task is conceived as palingenesis, the pious reconstruction of the past in its integrity, the spirit of which has continued to dominate nostalgic historiography down to the present. It is inspired by the feeling that G. B. Niebuhr expressed when he wrote: "There is one thing which gives happiness—to restore forgotten and overlooked greatness to a position where it can be recognized. He to whom fortune grants this enters into a relation of the heart with spirits long departed, and he feels himself blessed, when similarity of deeds and sentiments unites with the feeling of them, that feeling with which he loves a great man as a friend" (quoted in Neff, *Poetry of Hist.*, 104–5).

But Carlyle's conception of history, like his conception of philosophy, was more activist than contemplative, ethically more vigorous and assertive, and, surprisingly, more resistant to nostalgic self-indulgence than the historical philosophies of the early Romantics. In the essay "On History" he argued that

it is not in acted, as it is in written History: actual events are nowise so simply related to each other as parent and offspring are; every single event is the offspring not of one, but of all other events, prior or contemporaneous, and it will in its turn combine with others to give birth to new: it is an ever-living, ever-working Chaos of Being, wherein shape after shape bodies itself forth from innumerable elements. [59–60]

This "Chaos of Being"—Carlyle said in his essay "On Biography"—must be faced by the historian in a spirit which he characterized as both scientific and poetic:

Scientific: because every mortal has a Problem of Existence set before him, which, were it only, what for the most part it is, the Problem of keeping soul and body together, must be to a certain extent original, unlike every other; and yet, at the same time, so *like* every other; like our own therefore; instructive, moreover, since we also are indentured to *live*. A Poetic interest still more: for precisely this same struggle of human Free-will against material Necessity, which every man's Life, by the mere circumstance that the man continues alive, will more or less victoriously exhibit—is that which above all else, or rather inclusive of all else, calls the Sympathy of mortal hearts into action; and whether as acted, or as presented and written of, not only is Poetry, but is the sole Poetry possible. [52–53]

Unlike Novalis and the religious Romantics, Carlyle's rebellion against skepticism included a rejection of any effort to find the meaning of human life outside humanity itself. Human life in its individual incarnations was a supreme value for him; and the task of the historian, therefore, was not simply to celebrate the historical process itself, *à la* Novalis, but rather to give human life an awareness of its potentially heroic nature.

But Carlyle excluded any possibility of advancing beyond the (Metaphorical) insight that every life is both "like every other" and at the same time "utterly unique." He excluded the possibility of what we would recognize as a distinctively historical "explanation" of the world. If "every single event is the offspring . . . of all other events, prior or contemporaneous," and the historical field is a "Chaos of Being, wherein shape after shape bodies itself forth from innumerable elements," it appears impossible to conceive any way of reducing this "Chaos" to order. In Carlyle's view, however, the comprehension of the historical field is provided by a twofold movement of thought and imagination, or "science" and "poetry," by which things are first apprehended in their *similarity* to other things *and then* grasped in their uniqueness, or *difference*, from everything else. What Carlyle did was to enclose the scientific and poetic apprehensions of the world *within the mode of Metaphor* in such a way as to conceive the relationship between them as a natural "transfer" of concepts. The Metaphorical mode of construing the historical field, prefigured as a "Chaos of Being," requires that the historian simply position himself before that field in a posture of waiting and of anticipating the riches that *it* will reveal *to him*, in the firm conviction that, since every individual life is like every other, it is "like our own therefore" and is, therefore, immediately present to consciousness in both its integrity and its relationship to everything else.

This notion of history, however, differs from Herder's, to which it bears many resemblances, by virtue of the fact that the field is regarded literally as a Chaos; it is not viewed as an *apparent* chaos which is presumed to be working *ultimately* toward a total integration of its infinitely numerous components. As a matter of fact, Carlyle, like most of the later Romantics, saw this Chaos as ultimately divisible into two orders of being, the natures of which are provided by the categories of similarity and difference which he used to distinguish scientific from poetic comprehension in the passage cited. History as a process represents an endless struggle of the mob against the exceptional man, the hero. For Carlyle, then, historical knowledge is gained by simply inquiring into the "Chaos of Being" in order to determine the points at which certain exceptional individuals appeared and imposed their will upon an indolent and recalcitrant mob. The appearance of a hero represents a "victory" of "human Free-will over Necessity." The historian's task, at this point, is to contrive a paean in honor of the hero, not, *à la* Novalis, to sing a hymn of praise to "history-in-general."

Carlyle, in short, possessed a critical principle, one that singled out the individual hero, the man who accomplishes something *against* history, as the proper object of a humanly responsible historiography. The "Chaos of Being," which Constant apprehended as a horrifying void and which Novalis viewed as an undifferentiated plenum of vital force, was conceived by Carlyle to be the *situation* the heroic individual faces as a field to be dominated, if only temporarily and in the full knowledge of the ultimate victory this "Chaos" will enjoy over the man who seeks to dominate it. "History," in Carlyle's thought, was endowed with greater inherent meaning than it possessed in Constant's apprehension of it. And human life is endowed with greater value precisely in the degree to which the individual takes it upon himself to impose form upon this "Chaos," to give to history the mark of man's own aspiration to be something more than *mere* chaos.

The "Chaos of Being" notion of history, however, at least had the advantage of releasing historical consciousness from the kind of determinism which had driven the historical thought of Enlightenment rationalism into Irony and Satire; it made of the historical field and the historical process a panorama of happening in which the stress is on the novel and emergent, rather than on the achieved and inherited, aspects of cultural life. It made of history an arena in which new things can be seen to appear, rather than one in which old elements simply rearrange themselves endlessly in a finite set of possible combinations. But it provided no rule by which the individual elements appearing in the field can be brought together in such a way as to encourage any confidence that *the whole process* has a comprehensible meaning. It simply constituted the historical field as a "revel of forms" to which the poet may go for inspiration, to test his capacities for sympathy, for understanding, and for appreciation.

&§ *Michelet: Historiography Explained as Metaphor and*
Emplotted as Romance

Constant, Novalis, and Carlyle were all manifestly "Romantic" thinkers, and their reflections on history turned upon their apprehension of the historical field as a "Chaos of Being" which they then proceeded to comprehend respectively as simply a chaos, a plenum of creative force, and a field of struggle between heroic men and history itself. These comprehensions, however, were not so much earned as merely asserted as truths, to be accepted on faith in the poetic sensibilities of their different advocates. The French historian and philosopher of history Jules Michelet represented a different position *within* the Romantic movement apropos of its conception of the historical process. In the first place, Michelet purported to have discovered the means by which to raise the Romantic apprehension of the world to the status of a scientific insight. For him, a poetic sensibility, critically self-conscious, provided the accesses to a specifically "realistic" apprehension of the world.

Michelet specifically denied that he was a Romantic. The "Romantic movement," he said in his letters, had passed him by; while it had flourished, he had been busy in the archives, fusing his knowledge and his thought together into a new historical method, of which Vico's *The New Science* could be regarded as a prototype. He characterized this new "method" as that of "concentration and reverberation." In his view, it provided him with "a flame sufficiently intense to melt down all the apparent diversities, to restore to them in history the unity they had in life." As will be seen, however, this new method was nothing but a working out of the implications of the mode of Metaphor, conceived as a way of permitting the historian actually to identify with, resurrect, and relive the life of the past *in its totality*.

Michelet began the effort to escape Irony by abandoning the tactics of Metonymy and Synecdoche alike, and by taking a stand immediately on a faith in the adequacy of Metaphorical characterization of the historical field and its processes. Michelet denied all worth to Mechanistic (causal) reductions and to Formalist (typological) integrations of the historical field. The Metaphorical apprehension of the essential *sameness* of things overrides every other consideration in his writing and distinguishes him absolutely from Carlyle and other Romantic devotees of individualism. It was this apprehension of sameness which permitted him to claim for his perfervid characterizations of history the status of scientific truths, in the same way that Vico had claimed scientific status for his essentially "poetic" conception of history. Michelet strove for a *symbolic fusion* of the different entities occupying the historical field, rather than for a means for characterizing them as individual symbols. Whatever uniqueness there is in history was conceived by Michelet to be the uniqueness of the whole, not of the parts that comprise the whole. The individuality of the parts is only apparent. Their significance derives from their status as symbols of the *unity* that everything—in history as in nature—is *striving to become*.

But the mere fact that there is *striving* in the world suggests that this unity is a goal to be reached, rather than a condition to be described. And this has two implications for Michelet. One of them is that the historian must write his histories in such a way as to promote the realization of the unity that everything is striving to become. And the other is that everything appearing in history must be assessed finally in terms of the contribution it makes to the realization of the goal or the extent to which it impedes its realization. Michelet therefore fell back upon the mode of emplotment of the Romance as the narrative form to be used to make sense out of the historical process conceived as a struggle of essential virtue against a virulent, but ultimately transitory, vice.

As a narrator, Michelet used the tactics of the dualist. For him, there were really only two categories into which the individual entities inhabiting the historical field could be put. And, as in all dualistic systems of thought, there was no way in his historiographical theory for conceiving of the historical process as a dialectical or even incremental progress toward the desired goal. There was merely an interchange between the forces of vice and those of virtue—between tyranny and justice, hate and love, with occasional moments of conjunction, such as the first year of the French Revolution—to sustain his faith that a final unity of man with man, with nature, and with God is possible. At the extreme limits of human aspiration, Michelet envisioned the discovery of the ultimate symbol, the Metaphor of Metaphors, which may be precritically apprehended as Nature, God, History, the Individual, or Mankind in general.

How the mode of Metaphor and the myth of Romance function in Michelet's historiography can be seen in his *History of the French Revolu-*

tion. His description of the spirit of France in the first year of the Revolution is a sequence of Metaphorical identifications that moves from its characterization as the emergence of light from darkness, to description of it as the triumph of the "natural" impulse toward fraternity over the "artificial" forces which had long opposed it, and ends, finally, in the contemplation of it as a symbol of pure symbolization. France, he wrote, "advances courageously through that dark winter [of 1789–90], towards the wished-for spring which promises a new light to the world." But, Michelet asked, what is this "light"? It is no longer, he answered, that of "the vague love of liberty," but rather that of "the unity of the native land." (440) The people, "like children gone astray, . . . have at length found a mother" (441). With the breakup of the provincial estates in November, 1789, he averred, all *divisions* between man and man, man and woman, parent and child, rich and poor, aristocrat and commoner, are broken down. And what remains? "Fraternity has removed every obstacle, all the federations are about to confederate together, and union tends to unity.—No more federations! They are useless, only one now is necessary,—France; and it appears transfigured in the glory of July" (441–42).

Michelet then asked: "Is all this a miracle?" And his answer, of course, was "Yes, and the greatest and most simple of miracles, a return [of man] to nature." For, since "the fundamental basis of human nature is sociability," it had "required a whole world of inventions against nature to prevent men from living together." (442) The whole *Ancien Régime* was seen as an *artificial barrier* to the *natural impulse* of men to *unite* with one another. The whole burdensome structure of customs, duties, tolls, laws, regulations, weights, measures, and money, the whole rotten system of "carefully encouraged and maintained" rivalries between "cities, countries, and corporations— all these obstacles, these old ramparts, crumble and fall in a day" (*ibid.*). And, when they crumble, "Men then behold one another, perceive they are alike, are astonished to have been able to remain so long ignorant of one another, regret the senseless animosity which had separated them for so many centuries, and expiate it by advancing to meet and embrace one another with a mutual effusion of the heart" (*ibid.*). There is nothing, Michelet said,

but what breathes the pure love of unity. . . . *geography* itself is *annihilated*. There are no longer any mountains, rivers, or barriers between men. . . . Such is the power of love. . . . *Time and space*, those material conditions to which life is subject, *are no more.* A strange *vita nuova*, one eminently spiritual, and making her whole Revolution a sort of dream, at one time delightful, at another terrible, is now beginning for France. *It knew neither time nor space.* . . . All the old emblems grow pale, and the new ones that are tried have little significance. Whether people swear on the old altar, before the Holy Sacrament, or take the oath before the cold image of abstract liberty, the true symbol is elsewhere.

The beauty, the grandeur, the eternal charm of those festivals, is that the symbol is a living one.

This symbol for man is man. [444-45]

And then, switching to a voice which was at once his own and that of the people who believed in the Revolution on that day, Michelet wrote:

We, worshippers of the future, who put our faith in hope, and look towards the east; we, whom the disfigured and perverted past, daily becoming more impossible, has banished from every temple; we who, by its monopoly, are deprived of temple and altar, and often feel sad in the isolated communion of our thoughts, we had a temple on that day—such a temple as had never existed before! No artificial church, but the universal church; from the Vosges to the Cévennes, and from the Alps to the Pyrenees.

No conventional symbol! All nature, all mind, all truth! [450-51]

It was all, he said, "the greatest diversity . . . in the most perfect unity" (452).

Michelet *emplotted* his histories as dramas of disclosure, of the liberation of a spiritual power fighting to free itself from the forces of darkness, a redemption. And his conception of his task as a historian was to serve as the preserver of what is redeemed. In his book *The People*, written in 1846, he said of his conception of historical representation: "Let it be my part in the future to have not attained, but marked, the aim of history, to have called it by a name that nobody had given it. Thierry called it *narration*, and M. Guizot *analysis*. I have named it *resurrection*, and this name will remain" (quoted in Stern, *Varieties*, 117). This conception of history as "resurrection" applies both to the plot structure which the various histories that Michelet wrote were intended to figure and to the explanatory strategies used in them. It determines both the contents of Michelet's histories and their form. It is their "meaning" as both explanation and representation. But because Michelet located the macrohistorical point of resolution at the moment when, during the Revolution, perfect freedom and perfect unity are attained by "the people," through the dissolution of all the inhibiting forces ranged against it, the *tone* of his historical work was bound to grow more melancholic, more elegiac, as the ideals of the Revolution in its heroic phase receded into the background among the social classes and political elites which had originally fostered them.

Michelet dominated the field of historiography in France during the July Monarchy; his *Précis d'histoire moderne* (1827) was the standard survey of European history in the French schools until 1850, when a new wave of Reaction swept Liberalism into its own Conservative phase and destroyed Michelet's career in the university in its wake. His *History of the French Revolution* (in seven volumes, published in the heat of passions which the years 1847–53 generated among Frenchmen of all parties) is prefaced by a note in which the elegiac tone is associated with Michelet's memories of the death of his father, which occurred while he was painfully watching the slow death of the ideals of the Revolution. His historical reflections, he wrote, had been carried out in "the most awful circumstances, that can attend human life, between death and the grave,—when the survivor, himself partly dead, has been sitting in judgment between two worlds" (Michelet, *Rev.*, 14). Michelet's Romantic emplotment of the history of France up to the Revolution was thus set within a larger Tragic awareness of its subsequent dissipation. This realization of the Tragic nature of his own time gave to Michelet another reason to claim the title of a realist. He conceived this condition to be precisely the same as that which had existed in France in the 1780s.

The *Précis* ends on the eve of the Revolution, with a characterization of the fractured condition into which the whole of French society had fallen by that time. As Michelet described it:

All the world was interested in the people, loved the people, wrote for the people; *la Bienfaisance était de bon ton, on faisait de petites aumones et de grandes fêtes.* [395]

But, while "high society" sincerely played out a "*comédie sentimentale,*" the "great movement of the world" continued in a direction that would shortly transform everything.

The true confidante of the public, the Figaro of Beaumarchais became more bitter each day; it turned from comedy to satire, from satire to tragic drama. Royalty, Parlement, nobility, all staggered from weakness; the world was drunken [*comme ivre*]. [395–96]

Philosophy itself had become ill from the "sting" of Rousseau and Gilbert. "No one believed any longer in either religion or irreligion; everyone, however, would have liked to believe; the hardier spirits went incognito to seek belief in the illusions of Cagliostro and the tub of Mesmer." However, France, like the rest of Europe, was caught up in "the endless dialogue of rational skepticism: against the nihilism of Hume arose the apparent dogmatism of Kant; and everywhere one heard the great poetic voice of Goethe, harmonious, immoral and indifferent. France, distracted and anxiety-ridden, understood nothing of this. Germany played out the epic of science; France produced the social drama." (396) The comic sadness (*le triste comique*) of these last days of the old society was a result of the contrast between great promises and the complete impotency of those who made them: "L'impuissance est le trait commun de tous les ministères d'alors. Tous promettent, et ne peuvent rien" (*ibid.*).

The Comic resolution which succeeded this severed condition was the

Revolution itself. The contest which precipitated the Revolution is laid out as a struggle "between two principles, two spirits—the old and the new" (Michelet, *Rev.*, 22). And the "new" spirit, the spirit of justice, comes "to fulfill, not to abolish" (*ibid.*). The old spirit, the spirit of injustice, existed merely to oppose the fulfillment of the new. And this principle of radical opposition gave to Michelet the basis for his characterization of the Revolution in a single phrase: "The Revolution is nothing but the tardy reaction of justice against the government of favor and the religion of grace" (27). The Revolution was a reversal, a substitution of perfect justice for absolute tyranny. But this reversal was not so much accounted for as simply characterized as such. It was the "redemption" of the people in whose history Michelet had been vicariously participating all along.

Another image used by Michelet to characterize the Revolution was that of a birth process. But the birth envisaged was more Caesarean than natural. During his travels, he wrote, he went for a walk in the mountains. Reflecting on a mountain peak that had thrust itself up "from the deep bowels of the earth," Michelet said, he was driven to muse:

What were then the subterraneous revolutions of the earth, what incalculable powers combated in its bosom, for that mass, disturbing mountains, piercing through rocks, shattering beds of marble, to burst forth to the surface? What convulsions, what agony forced from the entrails of the globe that prodigious groan! [28]

These musings, he said, produced a desperate anguish in his heart, for "Nature had but too well reminded me of history." And "history" in turn had reminded him of "justice" and its burial for years in the prisons of darkness:

That justice should have borne for a thousand years that mountain of [Christian] dogma upon her heart, and, crushed beneath its weight, have counted the hours, the days, the years, so many losing years—is, for him who knows it, a source of eternal tears. He who through the medium of history has participated in that long torture, will never entirely recover from it; whatever may happen he will be sad; the sun, the joy of the world, will never more afford him comfort; he has lived too long in sorrow and in darkness; and my very heart bled in contemplating the long resignation, the meekness, the patience, and the efforts of humanity to love that world of hate and malediction under which it was crushed. [*Ibid.*]

An essential difference between Herder's and Michelet's approach to history should be noted here. On the one hand, Michelet certainly did not refuse to judge the various figures which he discerned in the historical landscape. Moreover, he did not perceive the historical process as an essential harmony which manifests its goodness and beneficence to mankind in all its operations. Like Ranke, Michelet took struggle and conflict seriously, as ineluctable aspects of historical existence. This is another earnest of his "realism." But, since he located the resolution of that drama in a period and a set of events which were progressively being shorn of their status as ideal incarnations of human community—that is to say, in the Revolution in its popular (and, to him, Anarchist) phase—Michelet's essentially Romantic apprehension of the historical process was progressively colored by a doleful apprehension of its growing meaninglessness as a principle around which history-in-general can be organized. He continued to assert his belief in the ideals of the Revolution and in the social vision which justified both the belief and the ideal, but his tone became increasingly desperate as the events of 1789 receded in time.

The historical situation from which he looked back upon the period of the Revolution, a situation in which the forces of tyranny had once more gained control of the national and international life, forced upon him an increasingly Ironic apprehension of the historical process, a sense of the eternal return of evil and division in human life. But he resolutely interpreted this eternal return of evil and division as a temporary condition for mankind over the long run. The doubt which the recognition of his own condition inspired within him was transformed by an act of will into the precondition for hope—in fact, was *identified with hope*. He could say to himself, as he said of "the people" on the eve of the Revolution, when life must have looked darkest to them:

Be not alarmed by thy doubt. That doubt is already faith. Believe, hope! Right, though postponed, will have its advent; it will come to sit in judgment, on the dogma and on the world. And *that day* of Judgment will be called the Revolution. [30]

Thus, the Romantic plot structure of the *whole* historical process remained intact. The conditions of Tragedy and Irony could be set within it as *phases* of the total process, to be annulled in the fire of Revolution which his own histories were meant to keep alive.

Unlike Herder, who conceived history as a *gradual* transformation of humanity from one unique set of particulars to another, Michelet conceived it as a series of cataclysmic reversals caused by long-growing tensions which force humanity into *opposed* camps. In these reversals, false justice is replaced by true justice, inconstant love replaced by true love, and the false religion of love, Christianity, the tyrant which "covered the world with [a] sea of blood," by its true antithesis, the spirit of the Revolution (31). And his purpose, Michelet said, was to bear true witness against the flatterers of kings and priests, "to drown false history and the hired flatterers of murder, to fill their lying mouths" (33).

The emblem of the old monarchy was, in Michelet's account, the Bastille; it was the symbol of the Ironic condition in which a "government of grace" showed its "good nature" by granting *lettres de cachet* to favorites on a whim and to the enemies of justice for money. The most horrible crime of the old regime was to condemn men to an existence that was neither life nor death, but "a middle term between life and death: a lifeless, buried life," a world organized "expressly for oblivion," the Bastille. It was this "buried" life which the Revolution exhumed and called to sit in judgment. The Revolution was the political and moral *resurrection* of everything good and human "buried" by the old regime.

As thus envisaged, the Revolution represented the revenge which memory —that is to say, "history"—takes on the selective immolation of living men and the annullment of the rights of the dead. In the Bastille, men were not simply killed, Michelet wrote; instead, they were—more horribly in Michelet's mind—simply "forgotten."

Forgotten! O terrible word! That a soul should perish among souls! Had not he whom God created for life the right to live at least in the mind? What mortal shall dare inflict, even on the most guilty, this worst of deaths—to be eternally forgotten? [73]

But, in a passage which reveals his own conception of the sanctity of the historian's task. Michelet insisted:

No, do not believe it. Nothing is forgotten—neither man nor thing. What once has been, cannot be thus annihilated. The very walls do not forget, the pavement will become accomplice, and convey signs and noises; the air will not forget. [*Ibid.*]

Rather than fall into the Ironic contemplation of life itself as a prison, Michelet took it upon himself to "remember" the living dead and the ideals of the Revolution, which had aimed to restore the living dead to their rightful place among the living.

On the eve of the Revolution—as in the world which Michelet was forced to inhabit after the renewed immolation of the Revolutionary ideal by Napoleon III—"The world [was] covered with prisons, from Spielberg to Siberia, from Spandau to Mont-St.-Michel. The world [was] a prison!" (*ibid.*). And, writing the history of the Revolution's advent, Michelet sympathetically entered into and relived the popular movement that would soon explode in violence against this offense to memory and life alike:

From the priest to the king, from the Inquisition to the Bastille, the road is straight, but long. Holy, holy Revolution, how slowly dost thou come!—I, who have been waiting for thee for a thousand years in the furrows of the Middle Ages,—what! must I wait still longer?—Oh! how slowly time passes! Oh! how I have counted the hours! Wilt thou never arrive? [79]

And when the women and children descended upon the Bastille to liberate their husbands, sons, lovers, and brothers imprisoned there, Michelet broke out in a cry of joy: "O France, you are saved! O world, you are saved!"

This salvation resulted in a dissolution of all differences among men, between men and women, young and old, rich and poor, which finally transformed the nation into a people. This condition of perfect integration was symbolized by the image of Joan of Arc: "Again do I behold in the heavens my youthful star in which so long I placed my hope—Joan of Arc." But then, in another of those lyrical effusions, in which he offended both reason and science, but not Metaphor, Michelet remarked: "What matter, if the maid, changing her sex, has become a youth, Hoche, Marceau, Joubert, or Kleber." (*Ibid.*)

In his enthusiasm for the events he was depicting, Michelet dissolved all sense of difference among men, institutions, and values. His Metaphorical *identification of things* that appear to be different utterly overrode any sense of the *differences among things*, which is the occasion for Metaphorical usage to begin with. All difference was dissolved in his apprehension of the unity of the whole. Thus, Michelet wrote, "the most warlike of men" become the "harbingers of peace"; and "Grace, in whose name Tyranny has crushed us, is found to be consonant, identical with Justice." Conceived as a process, the Revolution, he said, is nothing but the "reaction of equity, the tardy advent of Eternal Justice"; in its essence it is "truly Love, and identical with Grace." (80)

These conflations of one abstraction with another were not dialectically earned; they were merely asserted. But they were experienced neither as abstractions nor as conflations by Michelet, but as *identifications* of the one essence which is both the substance of history and the cause in whose name Michelet worked as a historian. "Love" and "Grace" were for him "Justice," which he called his "mother," and "Right," which he called his "father." But even justice and right were too distinct for him, and so he finally identified both with God ("ye who are but one with God!"). (*Ibid.*)

Thus, finally, God sustained Michelet in his service to history, and insured his objectivity, which was but another form of "Justice" and "Grace." At the close of the Introduction to his *History of the French Revolution*, Michelet addressed God directly, as he had earlier addressed the "Revolution":

And as thou art Justice, thou wilt support me in this book, where my path has been marked out by the emotions of my heart and not by private interest, nor by any thought of this sublunar world. Thou wilt be just towards me, and I will be so towards all. For whom then have I written this, but for thee, Eternal Justice? [*Ibid.*]

Now, there is no denying that the tone and point of view of Michelet's work stand in the starkest of contrasts to those of his more "realistic" counterpart in Germany, the judicious Ranke, who steadfastly insisted on his unwillingness either to "judge" the past or to legislate for the future. But, on the matter of "objectivity," the principal differences between Michelet and Ranke are more superficial than real. They reside in the fact that the principles of love, grace, and justice, which informed Michelet's approach to the study of history, were worn on his sleeve and explicitly incarnated in the principles of "the nation, the people, and the Revolution" rather than implicitly honored and identified with "the state, the church, and established society" as in Ranke. Michelet was no less interested in the truthful representation of the past, in all its particularity and unity, than was Ranke; but he believed one could write history, not out of any "private interest" nor governed "by any thought of this sublunar world," but simply by following the "path marked out by the emotions of [his] heart." That Ranke professed to be governed by the desire to rise above such "emotions" should not obscure the fact that his own histories are no less marked by evidences of personal preference and party biases than are Michelet's. The important point is that both historians acted as custodians of the memory of the race, against any tyranny which might have offended that memory by systematic suppression of the truth.

Michelet conceived the historian's task to be precisely similar to that of those women who descended upon the Bastille to restore the claims of its "forgotten" prisoners. The historian, Michelet said in one of his most self-critical moments, is "neither Caesar nor Claudius, but often in his dreams he sees a crowd which weeps and laments its condition, the crowd of those who have not yet died, who would like to live again [*qui voudraient revivre*] (a fragment written by Michelet in 1842, cited by Barthes, 92). These dead do not ask only for an "urn and tears," and it is not enough merely to repeat their "sighs." What they require, Michelet said, is:

an Oedipus who will solve for them their own riddle, which made no sense to them, one who will explain to them the meaning of their words, their own actions which they did not understand. [*Ibid.*]

This seems to suggest that the historian, writing on behalf of the dead, is also writing *for* the dead, not to some living audience in the present or the future.

But then Michelet changed the image once more, and substituted the figure of Prometheus for that of Oedipus. As Prometheus the historian will bring to the dead a fire sufficiently intense to melt the ice in which their "voices" have been "frozen," so that the dead will be able "to speak once more" for themselves.

But even this is not enough. The historian must be able to hear and to understand "words that were never spoken, words which remained in the abysses of [the dead's] hearts." The task of the historian, finally, is "to make the silences of history speak, those terrible organ notes [*points d'orgue*] which will never sound again, and which are exactly its most tragic tones." Only when the voices of the dead, and their silences, have been restored to life will

> the dead rest easily in their graves. [Then] they begin to comprehend their fate, modulate their dissonances into a softer harmony, to say to themselves and very softly the last words of Oedipus: "Be fortunate for all the time to come." The shades are saluted and are appeased. They permit their urns to be closed. . . . Precious urn of forgotten times, the priests of history carry it and transmit it with what piety, what tender care! . . . as they might carry the ashes of their father or their son. Their son? But is it not themselves? [*Ibid.*]

Again, in 1872, at the end of his life, in the preface to his *Histoire du XIXe siècle* (II, 11), Michelet spoke of the historian's role as essentially a custodian of the "memory" of the dead.

> Yes, each dead person leaves a little goods, his memory, and demands that someone take care of it. For him who has no friends, a magistrate must care for it. For the law, justice is more certain than all our forgetful tendernesses, our tears so quickly dried.
>
> This magistrate is History. . . . Never have I in my whole career lost sight of this, the Historian's duty. I have given to many of the dead too soon forgotten the aid of which I myself will have need.
>
> I have exhumed them for a second life. [Cited by Barthes, 91]

This conception of the historian's duty in no way conflicted with Michelet's notion of the necessity of the historian's "frank and vigorous partiality for the right and the truth." False partiality entered into history only when historians wrote in fear, or in the hope of currying the favor of established authority. The most honorable historian, Michelet insisted in 1856, at the conclusion of his *History of France,* had to lose all "respect" for certain things and certain men in order to serve as the judge and redeemer of the world. But this loss of respect would permit the historian to see the extent to which, "*dans l'ensemble des siècles et l'harmonie totale de la vie de l'humanité,*" "*fact and the right coincide* over the long run, and never contradict one another." But, he warned,

> to locate in the details, in the conflict, this fatal opium of the philosophy of history, these *ménagements* of a false peace, is to insert death into life, to kill history and morality, to have to say, in the manner of the indifferent soul: "What is evil? what is good?" [90]

Michelet frankly admitted the "moral" orientation of his work, but his research, he insisted, had permitted him to see the true "physiognomy" of the centuries he had studied; and he had at least given *"une impression vraie"* of it (*ibid.*).

Michelet cited Vico as the thinker who had provided the theory of the interaction of consciousness with society by which the fact of mere succession of social forms could be entertained as a providential process of a purely secular nature. Vico's theory permitted Michelet to dissolve all apparent formal collectivities into particularities and, after that, to characterize in purely Metaphorical terms the essential natures of both the particularities and the larger process in which they have a place. Ranke's suspicion of large-scale theories of any kind inclined him to halt his search for meaning and order in history with the apprehension of the finished forms of society and culture that had taken shape in his own time and to use these forms as the standard for whatever meaning history in the large might have. Thus, these two historians, who had so much in common in the way they prefigured the historical field and its processes, tended toward alternative modes of characterization which gave them escape from the threat of Irony.

Michelet came to rest in the mode of Metaphor, and emplotted history as Romance, because his sense of the coherence of the whole process was sustained by a belief in the unitary nature of the parts. Michelet grasped the essential point that Vico had made about any specifically historical conception of human reality—namely, that the forces which are overcome in any advance in society or consciousness themselves serve as the materials out of which the new society and consciousness will be fashioned. As Michelet commented in the introduction to his translation of *The New Science*, "Principes de la philosophie de l'histoire," faith in the providential nature of the historical process is secured, not by belief alone, but by society itself:

The miracle of [society's] constitution lies in the fact that in each of its revolutions, it finds in the very corruption of the preceding state the elements of the new form which is able to redeem it. It is thus eminently necessary that there be ascribed to it a wisdom greater than man . . . [*au-dessus de l'homme*]. [xiv]

This "wisdom" does not govern us by "positive laws," he continued, but serves itself by regulating those "usages which we freely follow." Thus, Michelet concluded, the central principle of historical understanding lies in the ideas which Vico set forth in *The New Science*:

men themselves have made the social world what it is [*tel qu'il est*]; but this world is not less the product of an intelligence, often contrary and always superior, to the particular ends which men have set for themselves. [xlv]

He then repeated the list of public goods (issuing from privately projected interests) that mark the course of human advancement from savagery to civilization and concluded with the remark that, "even when nations try to destroy themselves, they are dispersed into solitude . . . and the phoenix of society is reborn from the ashes" (xlvi).

This phoenix image is important because its suggestion of an eternal return points to the inherently antiprogressivist tendency contained in any system of tropological characterization not informed by a firm dialectical sense. The Metaphorical mode promotes the degeneration of the conception of the historical process into a "chaos of forms" when a presumption of history's Metaphorical integrity begins to fade. Once Michelet's faith in the triumph of right and justice began to dissipate, as the antirevolutionary forces gained the ascendancy, there was nothing left but a fall into melancholic reflection on the defeat of the ideal whose original triumph he had chronicled in his early histories.

The principal differences between Michelet's conception of history and that of Herder may now be specified. Herder characterized the objects occupying the historical field in the mode of Metaphor, and then proceeded to a Synecdochic integration of the field by the explanatory strategies of Organicism and the emplotting strategies of Comedy. Michelet began in the same way, but the patterns of integration which he discerned in that field were represented from a perspective given to him by his Ironic awareness of their evanescent and transitory nature. The "Romance" of the French people's struggle against tyranny and division and their attainment of a perfect unity during the first year of the Revolution is progressively distanced by the growing awareness in Michelet of the resurgence and (at least temporary) victory of the blocking forces. Michelet continued to write history as the defender of the innocent and just, but his devotion to them was progressively hardened, rendered more "realistic," by his awareness of the fact that the desired outcome was still yet to be attained. Unlike Herder, who was capable of believing that every resolution of a historical conflict was desirable simply because it was a resolution, Michelet recognized that the historian must take up a position pro or contra the forces at play in different acts of the historical drama. His own perspective on the agents and agencies in the historical process was Ironic; he distinguished between those that were good and those that were evil, even though he was governed by the hope that the conflict between their representatives would have the kind of triumphant outcome for the forces of good which he thought had been achieved in France in 1789. The supposed "realism" of his method consisted in his willingness to characterize in a language heavily freighted with Metaphor the representatives of both types of forces in the historical process. Unlike his eighteenth-century predecessors, Michelet conceived his task as a historian to be that of the custodian of the dead, whether they be conceived as good or evil by him, though in the interest finally of serving that justice in which the good are finally liberated from the "prison" of human forgetfulness by the historian himself.

Although Michelet thought of himself as a Liberal, and wrote history in such a way as to serve the Liberal cause as he understood it, in reality the ideological implications of his conception of history are Anarchist. As can be seen in the way he characterized the condition to which the French people attained in 1789 in his *History of the French Revolution*, he conceived the ideal condition to be one in which all men are naturally and spontaneously united in communities of shared emotion and activities that require no formal (or artificial) direction. In the ideal condition of mankind distinctions between things, and between things and their significations, are dissolved—in pure symbol, as he puts it, in unity, perfect grace. Any division of man from man is viewed as a condition of oppression, which the just and virtuous will strive to dissolve. The various intermediary unities represented by states, nations, churches, and the like, regarded by Herder as manifestations of essential human community and viewed by Ranke as the means to unification, were regarded by Michelet as impediments to the desired state of anarchy, which, for him, would alone signal the achievement of a true humanity.

Given Michelet's conception of the sole possible ideal form of human community, it seems unlikely that he would have been able to accredit any specific form of social organization actually met with in history as even a remote approximation to the ideal. Whereas Herder was compelled, by the logic of his conception of history, to accept everything, to criticize nothing, and to praise anything simply for having come to be, Michelet was unable, by the logic of his conception of history, to find virtue in anything except the one moment of pure conjunction that he thought he had seen in the history of France during a single year, 1789. In the end, he could praise those individuals he identified as soldiers in the service of the ideal, and he could dedicate his life to telling *their* story in a tone and mood that would promote the ideal in the future. But the ideal itself could never be realized in time, in history, for it was an evanescent as the condition of anarchy which it presupposed for its realization.

Chapter **4**   Ranke: Historical Realism
              as Comedy

◈§ *Introduction*

In a passage that has become canonical in the historiographical profession's credo of orthodoxy, the Prussian historian Leopold von Ranke characterizes the historical method of which he was the founder in terms of its opposition to the principles of representation found in Sir Walter Scott's novels of romance. Ranke had been enchanted with the pictures Scott had drawn of the Age of Chivalry. They had inspired in him a desire to know that age more fully, to experience it more immediately. And so he had gone to the sources of medieval history, documents and contemporary accounts of life in that time. He was shocked to discover not only that Scott's pictures were largely products of fancy but that the actual life of the Middle Ages was more fascinating than any novelistic account of it could ever be. Ranke had discovered that truth was stranger than fiction and infinitely more satisfying to him. He resolved, therefore, to limit himself in the future to the representation of only those facts that were attested by documentary evidence, to suppress the "Romantic" impulses in his own sentimental nature, and to write history in such a way as to relate only what had actually happened in the past. This repudiation of Romanticism was the basis of Ranke's brand of realistic historiography, a brand which, since Meinecke's popularization of the term, has come to be called "historism" and which still serves as the model of what an appropriately realistic and professionally responsible historiography ought to aspire to.

But Ranke's conception of history was based on more than a rejection of Romanticism. It was hedged about by a number of other rejections as well: the a priori philosophizing of Hegel, the Mechanistic principles of explanation which prevailed in the physical sciences and in the Positivist schools of social theory of the time, and the dogmatism of the official religious creeds. In short, Ranke rejected anything that prevented the historian from seeing the historical field in its immediacy, its particularity, and its vividness. What he regarded as an appropriately realistic historical method was what was left for consciousness to perform after it had rejected the methods of the Romantic art, Positivist science, and Idealistic philosophy of his own time.

This did not mean, as some of Ranke's interpreters have concluded, that his conception of objectivity approximated that of the naive empiricist. Much more was involved in the world view which has since come to be called historism. This world view is undergirded by a number of preconceptions peculiar to specific sectors of the academic community of Ranke's time. In order to distinguish the peculiar conception of "realism" which it promoted in that time, and to differentiate it from the Romantic, Idealist, and Positivist conceptions of "realism" against which it was launched, I will call it "doctrinal realism"; for it takes realism to be a point of view which is derived from no specific preconceptions about the nature of the world and its processes, but which presumes that reality can be known "realistically" by a conscious and consistent repudiation of the forms in which a distinctively *modern* art, science, and philosophy appear.

✍§ *The Epistemological Bases of Ranke's Historical Method*

It is often remarked that Ranke's conception of historical explanation and representation was pretty well fixed by 1850 or thereabout, and that it did not significantly change or develop (in fact, it tended to degenerate into a mechanically applied system) in the next thirty years or so. The revolutions of 1848–51 and 1870–71 had no real effect on him; they did not suggest to him the weaknesses or essential flaws in the system of social and cultural organization which Europe had forged, in the 1830s and 1840s, out of nearly two millenia of struggle. The Comic vision remained undimmed, as Droysen saw quite clearly in his appreciation of Ranke of 1868.

In the preface to his *Histories of the Latin and Germanic Nations from 1495 to 1514,* which appeared in 1824, Ranke stated that his purpose had been to relate the histories of the nations "in their unity" (Stern, 56–57). But the comprehension of that unity could come, he maintained, only through a consideration of particulars. He admitted that his concentration on "particulars" might give a "harsh, disconnected, colorless, and tiring" aspect to his narrative. But the "sublime ideal" to which his work aspired, "the event in its human intelligibility, its unity, and its diversity," could be attained only by a movement from the particular to the general, never by the reverse procedure. (57) Later on, in a fragment written in the 1830s, he dilated on the only "two ways of acquiring knowledge about human affairs" available to a purely secular human consciousness: that which went "through the perception of the particular" and that which proceeded "through abstraction." The first was, he said, the "method" of history; the second was that of philosophy. (58–59) In addition, he indicated what he conceived to be the two "qualities" without which no one could aspire to the office of the historian: a love for "the particular for itself" and a resistance to the authority of "preconceived ideas" (59). Only by "reflection on the particular" would the course of "the development of the world in general . . . become apparent" (*ibid.*).

This course of development could not, however, be characterized in terms of those "universal concepts" in which the philosopher legitimately traded: "The task of history is the observation of this life which cannot be characterized through One thought or One word" (60). At the same time, it could not be denied that the world presented evidence of its governance by a spiritual power in which the particulars of history must ultimately find their unity as parts of a whole (*ibid.*). The presence of this "spirit" justified the belief that history was more than a spectacle of "brute force." And the nature of this spirit could be glimpsed only by a religious consciousness, which could not be appealed to for the solution of specific historical problems. But a sublimated form of this religious apprehension of the world was necessary to a proper appreciation of the parts and of the relation of the parts to the whole. As Ranke wrote in another fragment during the 1860s, "the study of particulars, even of a single detail, has its value, if it is done well. . . . But . . . specialized study, too, will always be related to a larger context. . . . The final goal—not yet attained—always remains the conception and composition of a history of mankind" (61).

Specialized studies might, of course, obscure the unity of the whole historical process, but there was no need, Ranke insisted, "to fear that we may end up in the vague generalities with which former generations were satisfied." In fact:

After the success and effectiveness of the diligently and effectively pursued studies which have been everywhere undertaken, these generalities could no longer be advanced. Nor can we return to those abstract categories which people used to entertain at various times. An accumulation of historical notes, with a superficial judgment of human character and morality, is just as unlikely to lead to thorough and satisfactory knowledge. [62]

Thus, historical work had to proceed on two levels simultaneously: "the investigation of the effective factors in historical events and the understanding of their universal relationship." Comprehending "the whole" while "obeying the dictates of exact research" would always remain the "ideal goal, for it would comprise a solidly rooted understanding of the entire history of man." Historical research would not suffer, he concluded, "from its connection with the universal," for, without "this link," research would become "enfeebled." At the same time, "without exact research, the conception of the universal would degenerate into a phantasm." (*Ibid.*)

Remarks such as these are frequently quoted to indicate the extent to which the ideal envisioned by Ranke violated the methodological principles that guided him in his research. For example, Von Laue distinguished between the "larger conclusions of Ranke's historiography, his religious overtones and his philosophical ambition to grasp the divine intentions of history," and his "method," the latter of which has survived while the former have been rejected. The fact is, Von Laue said, Ranke "left a large school of historians who are in fundamental agreement on common standards of objectivity. Academic historians everywhere still insist upon the need for critically studying the most original sources, of penetrating all details, of arriving at generalizations and synthesis from the primary facts. They still cling to the ideals of objectivity and subordination of the historian to his materials" (138).

All this is true, but it does not adequately indicate the extent to which the notions of "objectivity," "critical study," the "penetration of details," and the production of generalizations out of consideration of "the primary facts" all *presuppose* conceptions of the nature of truth and reality on which the kind of "larger conclusions," which Ranke *claimed to derive* from his study of the materials, can be justified. Ranke's massive productivity (his collected works run well over sixty volumes), reflecting a uniformly high standard of research and talent for narrative representation, is understandable only in terms of the certitude he brought to his consideration of the materials and his confidence in the adequacy of the criterion he used to distinguish between significant and insignificant historical evidence among the data. It was his confidence in his criterion, the nature of which he conceived to distinguish his approach to history from that of Positivists, Romantics, and Idealists alike, which caught the fancy of the historians—Conservative and Liberal, professional and amateur alike—of his age, and in such a way as to make him the model of what a "realistic" historical consciousness ought to be.

Ranke intuitively grasped that the historiography of the new age, if it was to serve the purposes his values required that it serve, had to begin with a preliminary repudiation of the Metonymical mode, with its Mechanistic conception of causation and its Ironic implications for values and sublime ideals. This repudiation did not have to be formally defended, for Herder had already justified it. Moreover, the Revolution and Reaction had confirmed the bankruptcy of any abstract approach to social reality, and Romanticism had demonstrated the justification of the irrational impulses of man in its poetry and art. But neither could historical thought revert to a merely Metaphorical mode of characterizing the historical field and still claim that title of a "science" with which Ranke recognized it must be endowed if it was to be permitted to claim an authority greater than that of subjective opinion. At the same time, it could not be pushed too precipitately into the Synecdochic mode of comprehension, which sanctioned the search for formal coherences in the historical system, without having to sustain the charge of Idealism, which would have been as fatal to it as the charge of Romanticism itself. So Ranke prefigured the historical field in the mode of Metaphor, which sanctioned a primary interest in events in their particularity and uniqueness, their vividness, color, and variety, and then suggested the Synecdochic comprehension of it as a field of formal coherences, the ultimate or final unity of which could be suggested by analogy to the nature of the parts. This not only relieved Ranke of having to look for universal causal and relational laws in history, whether of a synchronic (Positivist) or a dialectical (Hegelian) sort, but it allowed him to believe that the highest kind of explanation to which history might aspire was that of a *narrative description* of the historical process. What Ranke did not see was that one might well reject a Romantic approach to history in the name of objectivity, but that, as long as history was conceived to be *explanation by narration,* one was required to bring to the task of narration the archetypal myth, or plot structure, by which alone that narrative could be given a form.

◄§ The Historical Process as Comedy

The Comic mythos served as the plot structure for most of Ranke's historical works and as the framework within which each of these works can be envisaged as an individual act of a macrocosmic drama. This mythos permitted Ranke to concentrate on the individual details of the scenes that he narrated, but to proceed with unwavering self-confidence through the flood of documents to the sure selection of those that were significant and those that were insignificant as evidence. His objectivity, critical principles, tolerance, and sympathy for all sides of the conflicts he encountered throughout the historical record were deployed within the sustaining atmosphere of a metahistorical prefiguration of the historical field as a set of conflicts that must necessarily end in harmonious resolutions, resolutions in which "nature" is finally supplanted by a "society" that is as just as it is stable. Thus, in his essay "The Great Powers," Ranke wrote:

World history does not present such a chaotic tumult, warring, and planless succession of states and peoples as appear at first sight. Nor is the often dubious advancement of civilization its only significance. There are forces and indeed spiritual, life-giving, creative forces, nay life itself, and there are moral energies, whose development we see. They cannot be defined or put in abstract terms, but one can behold them and observe them. One can develop a sympathy for their existence. They unfold, capture the world, appear in manifold expressions, dispute with and check and overpower one another. In their interaction and succession, in their life, in their decline and rejuvenation, which then encompasses an ever greater fullness, higher importance, and wider extent, lies the secret of world history. [Von Laue ed., 217]

Here the sanctioning Metaphor is manifestly Organicist, the emphasis is on process itself; but the process indicated is not a simple coming into being and passing away of things in time, in their own time. Time itself is endowed with value by virtue of the perception of a progression toward a goal, even though the goal itself remains unspecified and is characterized only as the achievement of formal coherence in general.

The end or goal toward which the whole development points is, however, specified in Ranke's "Dialogue on Politics." Pointing to the individual nation-states which have taken shape over the long passage from late medieval times to the Restoration, Ranke invoked a Metaphor of a celestial system to characterize the *outcome* of the historical process in Europe.

These many separate, earthly-spiritual communities called forth by moral energy, growing irresistibly, progressing amidst all the turmoil of the world towards the ideal, each in its own way! Behold them, these celestial bodies, in their cycles, their mutual gravitation, their systems! [180]

Here the Organicist insight used to characterize the process of growth and development gives place to a Mechanical one more adequate to the characterization of a system in balance. The image of the solar system has the advantage of suggesting continued movement within the system. History is not conceived to come to an end in Ranke's own time, but the movement is now rule-governed, orderly. It is movement within the confines of an achieved *system* of relationships which itself is no longer conceived to change.

Ranke perceived the period before the French Revolution as one in which the forces at play were striving toward their own proper place in a system; the system itself was being constituted, or was constituting itself by a process of conflict and mediation. Ranke envisaged his own time, the postrevolutionary age, as the time in which the constitution of the system was at last achieved; in which the system became a self-balancing mechanism, the appropriate general form of which was completed. Movement, growth, and development were conceived to continue, but on a basis quite different from what had been the case *before* the elements in the system had been fully constituted. Society finally replaced nature as the medium within which history must operate for the realization of its immanent goal, the achievement of a full humanity.

◄§ The "Grammar" of Historical Analysis

For Ranke the *historical* process per se, as distinct from the *total* world process, was a perfectly stable field (its stability was guaranteed by God) populated by discrete objects (human beings, each one individually constituted by God) which come together and combine into distinct entities (peoples, also individually constituted by God), which in turn contrive specific institutions (churches and states) for the realization of their destinies as nations. Human beings, as both individuals and as peoples, were conceived to be governed by natural, or animal, passion and to be, as a consequence, naturally disorderly and destructive. But, according to Ranke, in two institutions, the church and the state, instruments are provided by which the directionless energies of peoples can be channeled into humanly beneficial projects.

Ranke did not concern himself with useless speculations on the origins of churches and states or the manner in which they were constituted at the beginning. The *generally* beneficial character of these two institutions he took to be a *fact* of history, a truth established not only by historical reflection but also by quotidian experience. He was privately convinced that these institutions had been founded by God to impose order on a disorderly humanity; and he thought that a dispassionate study of history would confirm the generally beneficent role played by these two institutions in human life, which might suggest to the pious their divine origin. But it was not necessary to believe in their divinity to appreciate their ordering function in the lives of peoples. They constitute the sole ordering principles in historical time; it is through them that a "people" can direct its spiritual and physical energies toward the constitution of itself as a "nation."

As thus envisaged, the forces of order and disorder which constitute the primary terms in the world process find their historical forms in *churches and states* on the one hand and in *peoples* on the other. These categories are not mutually exclusive, because churches and states are manned by human beings just as peoples are made up of human beings sharing a common dwelling place and a common cultural endowment in language, specific sets of customs, mores, and the like. The consequence of this fact is that churches and states do not always militate on behalf of the principles of order and peaceful progress, but from time to time seek to exceed their natural spheres of authority. For example, the churchmen may attempt to usurp the authority of the state, with the result that the political strength of a people will decline; or statesmen may seek to usurp all spiritual authority, with the result that the spiritual energy of the people will be diminished and the private lives of the citizens and morality in general will degenerate. At such times, the nation will be racked with civil strife and will invite conquest by neighboring nations which, because they have struck a more adequate balance of political and ecclesiastical authority within the terms of their specific national "ideas," will be able to give unitary form and direction to their inherent impulse to growth and expansion at the weakened nation's expense. And, unless a nation so threatened can call upon reserves of spiritual or physical strength in such periods of crisis, unless it can institute reforms and re-establish the relationship between ecclesiastical and political institutions which is required by its informing "idea," disaster will result, and that nation's people will disappear from history to reappear no more.

Again, a specific conception of the state or church may gain excessive power over the imaginations of men everywhere and may expand its power beyond the confines of the people for whom it alone is suitable, constituting itself as a "universal church" (such as the Roman Catholic) or a "universal state" (such as the *Sacrum Imperium* of the German people). This, in fact, is what happened in the Middle Ages, Ranke believed, with the result that— as he put it—"peaceful progress" was slowed down, the development of peoples into nations was hindered, and culture languished in a Gothic gloom of indecision, anxiety, and fear. But, in the end, reformers appeared among all the various peoples which together constituted European civilization and attacked both the idea of a *universal church* and that of a *universal state*. Moreover, while holding firm to the *essential* truth of the Christian religion and the *essential* unity of European culture, these reformers worked out forms of ecclesiastical and political organization, and of the relations between them, that were adequate to the expression of the specific needs of the various peoples themselves, in accordance with the national "ideas" that informed them.

This was the true significance of the Renaissance and Reformation and of the era of religious wars which followed. During this period, the "idea" of the nation emerged as the self-consciously governing principle of the various peoples of Europe, which constituted themselves as distinct nations with unique historical destinies and founded churches and states adequate to the direction of their energies in orderly and humanly beneficial ways.

The "Syntax" of Historical Happening

Once the peoples of Europe had constituted themselves as nations, with churches and states uniquely suited to their specific spiritual and physical needs, and within the general European context of certain shared religious and cultural attributes, European civilization entered a qualitatively new phase of historical development. The constitution of the peoples of Europe as distinct nation-states created the conditions for the emergence of a completely autonomous, progressive, and self-regulating system of cultural organization. Once the various "ideas" of the various nations had emerged to consciousness in the various peoples of Europe, controls were *automatically established* for regulating relations among people, church, and state *within* the nations on the one hand and *among* the various nations thus constituted on the other. The system was not completely worked out for nearly three centuries, and, before it was finished, it had to withstand attacks by the secular equivalents of the older, medieval, universalist concept of social organization, the attempts at European and even world hegemony by such political leaders as Charles V, Philip II, Louis XIV, the Jacobins, and Napoleon. But these bids for political hegemony were frustrated by the operations of the principle of diversity-in-unity which Ranke took to be the distinct mode of social organization of the European system of nation-states. This mode found its overt expression in the emergence of the principle of *balance of power* as the corollary of national differentiation.

Just as a nation found in its "idea" the mechanism for adjusting relations internally, among people, church, and state, so the "idea" of Europe functioned as the governing mechanism for adjusting relations externally, among the various "nations" which had taken shape out of the amorphous and heterogeneous world of the Middle Ages. Unlike many of the Archaist Conservatives who saw nothing but evil in the French Revolution, Ranke granted that much good had resulted from it. For example, as a result of the Revolution, the nations had come into a final stage of self-consciousness, the great powers had found a common purpose in the maintenance of each by all the others, and European civilization had finally entered upon its millennium, in which "peaceful progress" could proceed indefinitely without real fear of revolution from below or of wars of total annihilation from without. Thus, in the Introduction to his essay "The Great Powers," Ranke wrote: "If the main event of the hundred years before the French Revolution was the rise of the great powers in defense of European independence, so the main event of the period since then is the fact that nationalities were rejuvenated, revived, and developed anew" (215). His own age, he said, had "achieved a great liberation, not wholly in the sense of dissolution but rather in a creative, unifying sense. It is not enough to say that it called the great powers into being. It has also renewed the fundamental principle of all states, that is, religion and law, and given new life to the principle of each individual state" (216).

It would seem that, to Ranke, the constitution of self-regulating nation-states united in a larger community of self-regulating power relationships represented an end to history *as men had known it up to that time*. In short, history ended in the present for him; with the constitution of Europe at mid-nineteenth century, the basic form of all future development was fixed. The system was in near-perfect balance; adjustments might be called for from time to time, just as Newton's system required the occasional intervention of the divine watchmaker to set it right, and these adjustments would take the form of occasional civil disturbances or limited wars among the states.

It is obvious that Ranke's conception of European historical development can be dissociated from the enabling postulates of his total world view and judged on its own merits as an interpretation or as a schema for organizing the study of European history. And, by employing his own method of source criticism and objective determination of the facts, another historian could take issue with him over what constituted the components of the historical field and the possible modes of relationship among them. Ranke himself was generous with critics of his work, who directed his attention not only to "facts" that he had overlooked in his characterization of specific periods, states, individuals, ideas, and so on, but also to whole categories of facts, such as economic ones, which his system did not originally accommodate. But it is important to recognize that one element in his system of *historical inter-pretation* functioned as more than a purely historical datum: this was his notion of the "idea of the nation."

⤙ The "Semantics" of Historical Interpretation

The redundancy of my characterization of the "notion" of the "idea of the nation" is required by the function which this notion serves in Ranke's system, for the "idea of the nation" is not merely one idea among many which men may have of the ways of organizing human society; it is the sole possible principle of organizing them for the achievement of "peaceful progress." In short, the "idea of the nation" was for Ranke not only a datum but also a value; more, it was the principle in virtue of which everything in history could be assigned a positive or a negative significance. Ranke revealed as much when he characterized the "idea of the nation" as eternal, change-less, a thought of God. He admitted that peoples may come and go, churches may form and disappear, and states may arise and perish; and that it is the historian's task to chronicle their passage or, in later times, to reconstruct them in their individuality and uniqueness. But to grasp their essence, to perceive their individuality and uniqueness, is to seize the "idea" which informed them, which gave them their being as specific historical existents, and to find the unitary principle which made them a something rather than an anything. And this is possible only because the "idea" of a nation is time-less and eternal.

But in principle this "idea" is knowable only as it is actualized in a specific historical form—that is, only insofar as a people actually succeeds in becoming a specific nation. This suggests that all peoples and all civilizations which have not yet arrived at the stage of self-realization represented by the nation-state exist in a kind of protohistorical night before the truly historical dawn of modern European history in the sixteenth century. And, to carry this diurnal Metaphor to its logical conclusion, it follows that the noontime of history is located in Ranke's own present, when, out of the trauma of the Revolution, the self-regulating system of fully constituted European nation-states achieved a final form. In short, Ranke made of the *reality of his own time* the *ideal for all time.* He admitted the possibility of genuine transformation, revolution, convulsion, only for ages prior to his own; but the future for him was merely an indefinite extension of his own present.

Because the creation of a system of self-regulating nation-states was for Ranke the goal toward which everything tends, the final stasis toward which all movement points, he necessarily required that every other form of social organization be regarded as an imperfect attempt to realize what he conceived actually to have been achieved in his own present. And he was consequently forced to maintain that, once this present has taken shape, no further forms of social organization can emerge. Like Hegel, Tocqueville, and Marx, the only alternative form of social organization that he could conceive was international, or transnational, based on some cosmopolitan or universal principle. But he ruled out this possibility on the basis of an appeal to history itself: such universal forms had been tried in the Middle Ages—in the universal church and the *Sacrum Imperium*—and found wanting; they had therefore been permanently superseded. Ranke admitted the possibility of attempts to revive these universalist forms of community in the future; and he saw such attempts in Liberalism, Democracy, Socialism, and Communism. But he regarded such movements as being, like war itself, merely occasions for the strengthening and further articulation of the eternally viable national "idea."

✑ The Conservative Implications of Ranke's Idea of History

In the *Politische Gespräche* Ranke argued that wars do not determine "the forms of internal political organization" but only "their modifications." In "The Great Powers" he likened his own age to that of the Hellenistic period. The Hellenistic period, he wrote,

provides many similarities to our own, a highly developed common culture, military science, and action and interaction of complicated foreign relations, also the great importance of the trading interests and of finance, rivalry of industries, and a flowering of the exact sciences based on mathematics. But those [Hellenistic] states, produced by the enterprise of a conqueror and the dissension among his successors, had neither possessed nor been able to attain any individual principles of existence. They were based upon soldiers and money alone. It was for that very reason that they were so soon dissolved and at last entirely disappeared. [217]

By contrast, Ranke's own age had been enlivened to the creative power of "moral strength" and "the principle of nationality." "What would have become of our states," he asked, "if they had not received new life from the national principle on which they were based? It is inconceivable that any state could exist without it." (*Ibid.*) It was thus conceivable, Ranke implied, that, as long as the principle of national self-identity could be maintained, the system of self-regulating nation-states would also continue to exist.

Ranke made it plain that he considered it the task of the historian to write history in such a way as to re-enforce the principle of nationality as the sole safeguard against a fall into barbarism. And, in a passage which he subsequently omitted from his own edition of his *Collected Works*, he made it plain that for him a system of nation-states could, like a conversation among the gods, last forever. To the question of whether the system of nation-states might not hinder the development of a world community, he replied that civilization itself depended upon diversity and division.

There would be only a disagreeable monotony if the different literatures should let their individual characters be blended and melted together. No, the union of all must rest upon the independence of each single one. Then they can stimulate one another in lively fashion and forever, without one dominating or injuring the others.

It is the same with states and nations. Decided, positive prevalence of one would bring ruin to the others. A mixture of them all would destroy the essence of each one. Out of separation and independent development will emerge the true harmony. [218]

In short, Ranke did not entertain the possibility of new forms of community in which men might be politically united and freed of the restrictions placed upon them by national states and churches. This is at once the measure and the form of his Conservatism. Because the "idea of the nation" functions as an absolute value in his theory of history, the very notions of universality and individual freedom are seen as *alternatives to history itself*. These are identified—as in Camus later—with the principles of totalitarianism on the one hand and anarchy on the other. And, similarly, the "idea of the nation" functions to discourage any (social scientific) search for universal laws of human association and comportment. Such a search would necessarily bring into question the value of nationally provided characteristics, would in short reveal the *purely historical nature* of national characteristics, and would require the "idea of the nation" itself to be treated as *merely* an idea. That is, it would require that the "idea of the nation" be treated as what, in fact, it is, a concept of association which took shape during a particular period of world history, in a particular time and place; which assumed a specific institutional and cultural form between the sixteenth and nineteenth centuries; and which, therefore, might conceivably give place to some other concept of human association, such as class, race, or merely human capacities for creative sublimation of man's destructive energies in the future.

Ranke regarded human problems as soluble *only within* the context of the nation and the institutions formed in the nation for those restraining impulses which he took to be inevitably destructive in their immediate forms of expression. He regarded anything that threatened the authority of the church (such as materialism and rationalism), of the state (such as capitalism, imperialism, racism, or Liberalism), or of the nation (such as Socialism, Communism, or ecumenical religion) as a threat to civilization itself. He saw any movement which vested faith in a liberated human nature as little more than sentimental humanitarianism. And, insofar as any such movements sought to establish themselves by revolutionary means, he saw them as the forces which the state and the church had been established to suppress.

Thus, insofar as Ranke took the church and the state, on the one hand, and the people, on the other, as *givens* in his system, as discrete entities with observable and determinable characteristics, and charged the historian to reconstruct the *ways* in which these entities came together to form national communities with individual national "ideas" as their informing principles, his ideal of "objective" historical investigation was perfectly satisfactory. But, at any place in the historical record where such entities as states, churches, peoples, and nations constituted "problems" rather than "data," his empirical method could not possibly work. Historical investigation could proceed on the basis of the Rankean method where social establishments were already solidly enough established as to be able to offer their conception of what constituted the real nature of man, the state, and the church as a precritically affirmed rule for directing the historian's research. Where such social establishments had not yet taken shape or were beginning to weaken or totter, and the principles of social organization ceased to be self-evidently provided to the professional establishment, and the problem of what constituted the *best* form of human community was raised, other methods of investigating both the present and the past, other conceptual categories for characterizing the historical process, were called for. The search for these other methods and these other conceptual categories generated the new social sciences which took shape in the last three decades of the nineteenth century. These new social sciences were, as a rule, concerned with historical problems, but they were uniformly hostile to what had by that time come to be called the historical method. For, by this time, the historical method was the Rankean method, not merely with its naive inductionism, but above all with its presupposition that the nation was the sole possible unit of social organization (and the sole desirable one) and its conviction that, *therefore*, national groups constituted the sole viable units of historical investigation.

History Emplotted as Comedy

It will be noted that in one sense Ranke lends himself to general characterization more easily than does Michelet, and yet, in another sense, less easily. This is because the plot structure of history written in the Comic mode is formally more coherent on the story level of the narrative than Romantic history is likely to be. The plot of Michelet's history of France describes the gradual rise of the protagonist (the French people) to a full sense of its own essential nature and to a full, though momentary, achievement of its inherent unity against the blocking figures, institutions, and traditions seeking to frustrate its growth and self-realization. But the purity of this line of ascent is obscured by the Metaphorical characterizations of its component points, each of which must be more dazzling, more extreme, more comprehensive and intense, in order to image the higher stage at which the protagonist arrives with each of its successive triumphs. Moreover, since Michelet wrote the history of this process of ascent from the far side of its culmination, in the awareness of a subsequent fall from the apex attained, by the betrayal of the ideals of the Revolution, the effort to capture the purity, brilliance, and sanctity of the climactic moment could be sustained only by the most tortuous poetic projections onto a receding shore where the events themselves occurred.

Like Ranke, Michelet was a historian of the Restoration, though he experienced that period of history in which he wrote in a way precisely opposed to Ranke's experience of it. What Michelet suffered as a fall away from the ideal, a postcoital depression, as it were, Ranke enjoyed as a consummation, but a consummation in the literal sense of the term. It was not, as in Michelet's conception of the revolutionary moment, a point at which unity was achieved by the elimination of the barriers which had been artificially erected to prohibit the people's union with itself, but was rather a genuine integration of elements formerly at odds with themselves and with one another within a higher form of community, the nation-state and the international system in which each nation-state had its place and functioned as a necessary part of the whole.

The Organicist apprehension of the historical process offered by Herder was still present in Ranke's work as the Metaphor by which the process as a whole was to be comprehended. But it had been sublimated into the Comic plot structure by which the story told about European history was to be comprehended as a story figuring a specific meaning. This plot structure was itself more complex than that which informed and gave a secondary meaning to the Romantic histories of Michelet.

Michelet emplotted history as a Manichean conflict in which protagonist and antagonist are locked in mortal combat and in which one or the other must be eliminated in order for the story to find its culmination, as an epiphany either of redemption or of damnation. But Ranke set the spectacle of conflict within an apprehension of the larger unities which struggles between protagonists and antagonists bring about, and he stressed what was to be gained by the social order in general by the fact of struggle itself. The image of the final unity of humanity was displaced to a point at the end of historical time to serve as the envisioned goal that faith or imagination may conceive the process to be moving toward; and primary significance was accorded to the forms of social unity already achieved in the institutions and nations created out of the process of millennial conflict which extended from the High Middle Ages to the Restoration itself.

The ternary movement of Comedy, from a condition of apparent peace, through the revelation of conflict, to the resolution of the conflict in the establishment of a genuinely peaceful social order, permitted Ranke to delineate, self-confidently and convincingly, the main units of time into which the gross historical process can be divided. The fact that the temporal process can be so surely emplotted inspires confidence in Ranke's acceptance of the political and social forms of his own time as the "natural" units of historical analysis by which to map the historical field considered as a spatial, or synchronic, structure.

Western European civilization is divided into its Latinate and Germanic cultural substrata, and these are further divided into the families of languages found in each. These families of languages serve as the basis of the symbiotic relationship, between culture and nature at different places in Europe, by which the peoples are constituted. Then, within the nations, specific forms of political and ecclesiastical organization, adequate to the organization and expression of the different peoples' peculiar virtues and powers, are postulated. Then, among the nations themselves a particular modality of relationship— expressed in the notion of the balance of power—is invoked as the end toward which all of the conflicts among the nations have been pointing. Parts are analyzed out of wholes, and then wholes are reconstituted out of the parts in the course of the narrative actually written, so that the gradual revelation of the relationship which parts bear to wholes is experienced as the *explanation of why things happened as they did*.

The mode of tropological characterization which sanctions these strategies of explanation is Synecdoche. The "methodological projection" of this trope is that Organicism which modern historians of historical thought have identified as "Historism." Ranke's explanations of why things happened as they did thus resemble Michelet's on one level, that on which the event to be explained is set within its context by the identification of all the strands that give to the event the "texture" of a particularity. But the characterization of a given context—such as that of "the Middle Ages," or "the Reformation," or "the seventeenth century," and so on—provides the reader with the sense of a succession of formal coherencies through which the action moves in such a way as to suggest the *integration* of the parts with a larger historical whole, which is the form of European civilization itself in its latest phase.

Just as the narrative has story elements that provide answers to the questions "What happened next?" and "How did it all come out in the end?" as well as plot elements that provide the answer to the question "What's the point of it all?" so, too, the explanation moves on two levels. On one level the question "What happened?" is answered by the insertion of an event or set of events within a context by the discrimination of the strands that link the event to other events, providing thereby an impression of a rich texture of occurrence which is not susceptible to any nomological explanation. On another level the question "Why did it happen as it did?" is answered by the movement from one context, considered as an achieved form, to another in such a way as to show the higher integration of phenomena with one another in each successive stage—in the mode of Organicism. Denial that the Form of Forms can be known to the historian has the effect of endowing the latest stage of the process, that in which the achieved formal coherence of the historian's own time is postulated, with the status of putative *telos*, end, or purpose of all preceding stages. In short, the historical field is first surveyed as a complex of dispersed events related to one another only by the strands and threads that make them an arras web of event-context relationships; the field is then enmapped as a pattern of integrated totalities that bear the relationship of microcosm-macrocosm, or part-whole, to one another—and always in such a way as to suggest that the latest formal coherence discernible in history is the supreme form of social and cultural organization that can be legitimately perceived in the process at large.

Ranke conceived history, then, in the mode of Synecdoche. Translated into a method, this permitted him to emplot it in the mode of Comedy and to explain it in the manner of Organicism. If, however, we desire a formal defense of both the mode of emplotment and the mode of explanation which give to Ranke's historiography its distinctive characteristics as a putatively "realistic" science, we must look elsewhere than to Ranke's works. This defense was provided as early as 1821, by the statesman, philosopher, and scientist Wilhelm von Humboldt, in an essay (originally delivered as a lecture in Berlin) entitled "On the Tasks of the Historian."

The Formal Defense of Organicism as Historical Method

Momigliano named Ranke, along with Boeckh and Droysen, as an "ideal pupil" of Humboldt (105). And, recently, George Iggers explicated the similarities of their views on such subjects as the nature of historical thought, the state, society, and the future of European culture (chaps. III–IV). Humboldt's essay, however, will reward further scrutiny as a formal defense of the explanatory principles which Ranke combined with his Comic emplotment of history in order to derive specifically Conservative ideological principles from the "objective" consideration of the "data" of history.

Humboldt began with an explicit denial that the historian can aspire to a nomological comprehension of history; instead, he argued, the most the historian can hope for is "a simple presentation" of "what actually happened" (57). This does not mean, of course, that the historian is "merely receptive and reproductive." On the contrary, he must be "himself active and creative" because: events are only "partially visible in the world of the senses; the rest has to be added by intuition, inference, and guesswork"; the "manifestations of an event are scattered, disjointed, isolated"; and the essential "unity" of this "patchwork" of events "remains removed from direct observation." (57–58) Observation alone, Humboldt stressed, can give only "the circumstances which either accompany or follow one another"; it cannot penetrate to the "inner causal nexus" on which the "inner truth" of a set of events "is solely dependent" (58). What observation reveals is a field of objects incompletely perceived and a complex of relationships that are apparently ambiguous, the individual clusters of events appearing, "as it were, rather like the clouds which take shape for the eye only at a distance" (*ibid.*).

The "inner truth" of these clusters of events is the "shape" which the historian, utilizing a faculty rather like that of the poet, gives to them. As Humboldt said, the historian must use his "imagination" to "reveal the truth of an event by presentation, by filling in and connecting the disjointed fragments of direct observation." But, unlike the poet, the historian may not use "pure fantasy." He must instead call upon a uniquely historical mode of comprehension, which Humboldt called the "connective ability." (58–59) This connective ability is a product, Humboldt suggested, of the historian's application of "the laws of necessity" to serve as a brake on the operations of the "intuitive faculty" (*ibid.*), which means that the historian must follow "two methods . . . simultaneously in the approach to historical truth: . . . the exact, impartial, critical investigation of events . . . [and] the connecting of the events explored" (59).

But the connective ability must not be extended to the *whole* historical process, because the historical field is a

vast, serried turmoil of the affairs of this world, in part arising out of the nature of the soil, human nature, and the character of nations and individuals, in part springing up out of nowhere as if planted by a miracle, dependent on powers dimly perceived and visibly activated by eternal ideas rooted deeply in the soul of man—all [of which] composes an infinitude which the mind can never press into a single form. [60]

And the historian's willingness to halt short of the imposition of a single form upon the whole historical field, contenting himself with the imposition of provisional, middle-range formal coherencies on finite provinces of the field, makes his calling a specifically "realistic" one.

The historian must strive, Humboldt said, "to awaken and to stimulate a sensibility for reality." In fact, he maintained, "the essential element" in which historians operate is "the sense of reality," which is defined as "the awareness of the transience of existence in time and of dependence upon past and present causes" and, *at the same time*, "the consciousness of spiritual freedom and the recognition of reason." Only this dual awareness of temporal transience and causality on the one hand and consciousness of spiritual freedom on the other permits the historian to "compose the narrative of events in such a way that the reader's emotions will be stirred by it as if by reality itself." (*Ibid.*)

The most interesting aspect of this conception of historical realism is that on the face of it it hardly differs from the Romantic "Chaos of Being" notion of history advanced by Carlyle. The realism of historical knowledge appears to consist in the historian's maintaining in the mind of the reader the paradox that human life is both free and determined. In fact, Humboldt specifically denied that historical knowledge might be used to instruct the present as to "what to do and what to avoid." But, at the same time, he refused to accept the notion that historical knowledge consists only of that "sympathy" which the Romantics' "poetic" conception of it put at its center. History, Humboldt said, is useful by virtue of "its power to enliven and refine our sense of acting on reality," but this power is manifested more in its provision of "the form attached to events" than in the simple apprehension of the events themselves. (61) And here the Synecdochic presuppositions of his conception of historical explanation become manifest. A historical explanation, he argued, is the representation of the form to be discerned in a set of events, a representation in which "every event" is shown to be a "part of a whole," or in which "every event described" is shown to reveal the "form of history per se" (*ibid.*).

Although Humboldt conceived historical representation to consist in the revelation of "the true form of events" and the "inner structure" of the whole set of events contained in a narrative, it is obvious that what he intended was a Synecdochic operation in which all events are conceived to bear a relationship to the whole which is that of microcosm to macrocosm. But he saw that, in this view, a historical representation, or *mimesis*, must be a reproduction, not of the events themselves in their particularity, but of the formal coherence of the total fabric of events, which, if fully carried out, would result in "philosophy of history." This is why he distinguished between two kinds of *mimesis*: the mere copying of the external shape of a thing and the figuring of its "inner form." The former operation merely *reproduces the contours* of an object, as a draftsman might do, while the latter *provides a model* of the proportion and symmetry of it, as the true artist does. (61–62) The latter operation requires that the artist himself provide "the idea" which can transform a body of data into a specific formal coherence. It was this "idea" which per-

mitted Humboldt to distinguish between the truth of a photographic reproduction on the one hand and the "truth of form" on the other (63). When applied
to historical representation, of course, this distinction throws the historian
open to the kind of subjectivity and relativism which Romantics like Michelet
invoked to justify their notions of "sympathy" as a proper guide to historical
understanding. But Humboldt resisted this fall into subjectivity by raising the
question of "whether there are ideas capable of guiding the historian and, if
so, of what kind" (*ibid.*).

In the passages immediately following those just cited, Humboldt revealed
the essentially Classical, and ultimately Aristotelian, bases of his conception
of historical knowledge by distinguishing between "ideas" in an aesthetic, a
philosophical, and a historical sense. And he did this in such a way as to permit
the identification of historical knowledge with the kind of knowledge which
Aristotle specifically consigned to poetry. The kind of understanding which the
historian has of reality, he argued, is not the kind claimed by the Romantic
artist, which is a purely subjective knowledge, or an expression of a subjective
emotional state, but rather an apprehension of the world which *might* have
existed at the interior of the events that appear in the historical record.

Historians, Humboldt said, seek the truth of an event "in a way similar to
the artist," who seeks "the truth of form" (64). In history, "understanding" is
"the combined product of [the event's] constitution and the sensibility
applied by the beholder" (*ibid.*). There is, he suggested, an elective affinity
between the nature of historical events and the modes of comprehension
which the historian brings to bear upon such events. Historical events are
manifestations of the tensions which exist between achieved forms of life and
tendencies conducing to the transformations of those forms; historical comprehension consists of the twofold apprehension of those "forces" which conduce
to the production of novelties in society and culture and those "trends" which
bind individualities into larger unities of thought, feeling, and will (*ibid.*).
This is why "historical truth" is, "generally speaking, much more threatened
by philosophical than by artistic handling" (*ibid.*).

Philosophy, in Humboldt's view, always seeks to reduce the totality to the
status of a consummation of an integrative process that is teleological in
nature. The historian, on the other hand, must deal not with ultimate ends or
consummations but rather with trends and processes. And, in his handling
of these trends and processes, he must not impose his notions of what they
might *ultimately* import upon them, but rather should permit the "ideas"
which give to them their formal coherence to "emerge from the mass of the
events themselves, or, to be more precise, originate in the mind through contemplation of these events undertaken in the true historical spirit" (*ibid.*).
The historian must therefore at once "bring" the forms of "ideas" to his
"observations" of the events of world history and "abstract" that "form from
the events themselves" (*ibid.*). This may seem like a "contradiction," Humboldt admitted, but actually, he said, all "understanding" presupposes an "orig-

inal, antecedent congruity between subject and object"; it always consists of "the application of a pre-existent general idea to something new and specific" (65). And, in the case of historical understanding, that pre-existent general idea consists of the operations of the "human heart," which provide at once the bases of historical existence and those of the consciousness necessary for its comprehension (*ibid.*).

Only the most generous critic could concede to this argument any claim to the rigor that a genuine philosophical analysis ought to display. Actually, it repeatedly raises the possibility of a scientific conception of historical explanation only to dissolve that possibility in the denial of the adequacy of any causal, or nomological, explanation to the attainment of historical truth. This was the main thrust of Humboldt's desire to sever historical reflection from philosophy and to bring it closer to his conception of art as a strictly mimetic activity. He located historical knowledge between the chaos of data which the unprocessed record presents to perception and the ideal of a science of laws by which that chaos might be submitted to order and comprehension, and then denied to the historian the possibility of aspiring to any nomological comprehension of the forces dominating the historical process. He fell back upon an analogy between art and historiography, but invoked a conception of art which assumes the adequacy of the ideas of form contained in the imagination to the representation of the forms of things met with in individuated being. The resultant theory of historical knowledge was Formist in nature and typological in implication, but the mystery of historical being was left undissolved and its chaos was reduced to a general formal coherence of the sort envisaged by Neo-Classical art as the highest goal it might aspire to. The Romantic and Subjective Idealist conception of the extent to which the mind *imposes* form upon perception and, in that distortion of reality, achieves its humanization, was ignored. Humboldt reasserted the fiction of the perfect consonance of consciousness and being, promoted by Leibniz and Herder, but in a much less metaphysical and less angular form.

Thus, Humboldt argued, the historian "conceives for himself a general picture of the *form* of the *connection* of all *events*" from which he can derive a picture of the *essential connection* of the events that make up the historical process (*ibid.*; italics added). But he excluded three conceptions of connectedness in history as inadequate to the proper comprehension of its subject of study. These were the mechanistic, the physiological, and the psychological approaches to history, which, in his view, concentrate on causal connection to explain what actually happens in the historical process (66–67). Humboldt's objections to these three approaches turned upon their inability to achieve a point of view "outside the compass of the finite," from which "every part of world history" can be comprehended and dominated (67). Here he offered his own doctrine of ideas, based on the notion of the adequacy of generalizations derived from reflection on the totality of the human heart's operations to the totality of events contained in world history, as a basis for a distinctively "historical" apprehension of reality.

The parts of world history must be—Humboldt said—integrated into a vision of the whole, conceived on the basis of a notion of "world governance" or the idea that the whole historical process manifests the operations of a higher principle of unity, *the precise nature of which cannot be specified* but the *existence of which can be inferred* from evidence that is historically understood.

It would appear, then, that the historian can aspire no more to the identification of the necessary conditions of emergent novelty than to the determination of their sufficient conditions. In principle it is asserted that the circumstances themselves can never account for the appearance of new forms in the historical process. And, since it is the purpose of science to determine both the necessary and sufficient conditions for an event's occurrence, it would appear that the historian's search for such conditions is ruled out from the beginning. What the historian is left with in the presence of such novelties is wonder and the task of "representing" them in terms of the formal coherence they offer to a consciousness historically conditioned to their apprehension.

But, if this method is well suited to the appreciation of the coming into being of such novelties in history, it has no way—any more than Herder had—of accounting for their dissolution.

Humboldt gave as examples of "the creation of energies, of phenomena for the explanation of which attendant circumstances are insufficient," the eruption of art "in its pure form" in Egypt and the sudden development of a "freer art" among the Greeks (68). Humboldt conceived the Greek achievement especially as miraculous; there can be no "explanation" of it, for it represents a purely "individual" achievement of "individuality." The historian's task, in the presence of this miracle, is not to explain it, then, but simply to represent it for what it is—that is, a manifestation of an essential human freedom. (*Ibid.*) At the same time, the historian must admit that the effect of this miracle did not last, that Greek culture degenerated and passed away. Its dissolution is attributed to the involvement of its idea in the forms of phenomenal existence, and so a material and causal explanation of its dissolution is tacitly sanctioned by Humboldt. (*Ibid.*)

The notion is a curious one, inasmuch as phenomena are conceived to be governed by one rule in their process of actualization and by another in their process of dissolution, by a uniquely "spiritual" force in the first case and by specifically material, physiological, and psychological forces in the second. This has the effect of endowing the process of germination, birth, and growth with greater value than that granted maturation, degeneration, and dissolution, a strange asymmetry which is explicable only by the presumption of a need to overbalance historical consciousness in a specifically optimistic and sanguine direction. "The taking of the first step, the first flashing of the spark"—that is to say, the emergent reality—is "miraculous" in Greek history, not that which passes into obscurity at the same time the new makes its appearance. Without this "taking of the first step," Humboldt said, "favorable circumstances could not become operative, and no amount of practice or of gradual improvement, even for centuries, would lead to any fulfillment." (*Ibid.*)

The value attached to emergent novelty leads to the conception of the historical process as one in which the spirit can be set over against matter as form to content, the interchange of which is governed by the anomalous power of the former. Humboldt wanted to throw the "weight-of-meaning feeling" backward onto the early stages of the process. But this desire was not fully justified by his characterization of the process of birth, growth, and decay in historical time.

The "idea" of a thing, he said, must be entrusted to an *"individual* spiritual force." Its individuation, however, is the occasion for its dissolution, since by its very individuation the spiritual force falls under the sway of the laws that govern phenomenal existence. Its eternal value is transmitted into a temporal finitude and indentured to a degenerative process. But, he insisted, its passing away in time must be conceived, not as evidence of the determinate nature of historical existence, but rather as an epiphany of the spirit's capacity to seek its articulation in the phenomenal sphere; its articulation and dissolution are seen as evidence of the spirit's "independence" of phenomenal causality, not as evidence of the operations of causal laws in it. (69) The movement of the idea to its full articulation in time and space is conceived, not as a development *in* time and space, but as a movement *from* "inner" *to* "outer" being.

Humboldt wanted to establish this movement from inner to outer as the *form* of historical development without specifying the end toward which the whole development tends and falling thereby into Idealism and a "philosophical" conception of historical knowledge. What he seemed to say was that thought permits us to *conceive* history in an "Idealistic" manner but not to *comprehend* the various forms of historical existence under the terms of an Idealistic vision of the whole. Here we are met with that "Formalism" in historical thought which Hegel condemned for the intellectual and moral ambiguity it fostered. This ambiguity became manifest in Humboldt's thought when, at the end of his essay, he granted that we may perceive, *across* the trends and emergent energies appearing in history, "ideal forms which, although they do not constitute human individuality, are related to it, if only indirectly." He professed to perceive such ideal forms in language itself, which "reflects" both "the spirit of its people" and "an earlier, more independent base," which is "more influential than influenced," so that "every important language appears as a unique vehicle for the creation and communication of ideas." (70) And from this analogy Humboldt went on to remark on the manner in which "original and eternal ideas of everything that can be thought to achieve existence and power" do so "in a manner even more pure and complete: they achieve beauty in *all* spiritual and corporeal shapes, truth in the ineluctable working of every force *according to its innate law,* and justice in the inexorable process of events which eternally *judge and punish themselves"* (*Ibid.*; italics added).

But he denied the capacity of *human* judgement to perceive the "plans of the governance of the world directly." It can at most, he said, "divine them in the ideas through which they manifest themselves." (*Ibid.*) This permitted him to conclude that "the goal of history" must be "the actualization of the idea which is to be realized by mankind *in every way* and *in all shapes* in which the finite form may enter into union with the idea." The whole process can end only at the point where "the finite form" and "the idea" are united and "where both are no longer capable of further mutual integration." (*Ibid.*; italics added)

Returning, then, to his original comparison of the historian to the artist, Humboldt asserted that "what knowledge of nature and . . . of organic structures are to the latter, research into the forces appearing in life as active and guiding [principles] is to the former." What the artist perceives as "proportion, symmetry, and the concept of pure form," the historian perceives as "the ideas which unfold themselves . . . in the nexus of world events without, however, being part of [those events]." (*Ibid.*) And this gave Humboldt the basis for his "final, yet simplest solution to the [problem of the] historian's task," which is "the presentation of the struggle of an idea to realize itself in actuality" (*ibid.*).

The emphasis should be placed on the word "struggle," for, as Humboldt said, the idea will not always succeed on its first attempt to realize itself; it may become "perverted" by its failure to master completely the "actively resisting matter" in which it seeks its actualization (*ibid.*). But that the series of tragedies which the failure of the idea to actualize itself may go through must be conceived as an ultimately Comic process was a foregone conclusion with him because "no event is separated completely from the general nexus of things"; the whole is governed by a freedom which the part only dimly figures in its process of actualization. Thus, the emphasis is shifted to the freedom contained in the whole—that is, to the phenomena of change and emergence—and provides all the more reason for resisting interest in any "search for the coherent pattern of the whole." To search for the pattern of the whole would be to impute determinancy to it.

We can see from this consideration of Humboldt's conception of history the relationship which Ranke and the academic historiography he represents bear to the Organicist approach of Herder. There has been a shift of emphasis. This shift consists of a diminution of the impulse to seek evidences of a *total integration* of the historical world which was still predominant in Herder's thinking. A Formist conception of explanation has been substituted for the Organicist conception which Herder openly advocated. Consequently, there is a loosening of the texture of the historical field and a dimming of the impulse to seek general understanding of the processes which characterize it as a total field of happening or occurrence. But the general framework, the mythic significance, the *essentially Comic nature of the mode* by which those processes are to be *emplotted*, remains intact. The transition can be characterized as a modification in which *the impulse to explanation* is sublimated to a desire simply to *describe* the process as it unfolds before the historian's gaze. The *meaning* of the process remains the same. It is conceived as a Comic drama, the resolution of which is *yet to be realized*. But the maintenance of the Comic frame, which is now presupposed, permits the events that occur within the frame to be apprehended in a specifically optimistic mood. By leaving the ending of the drama unspecified, while at the same time affirming the necessity of believing that the whole process imports a drama of specifically Comic resolution, struggle and conflict can be entertained as genuine elements of historical reality without in any way attributing to those elements the possibility of their triumph in history in the long run. Every defeat of an aspiration is regarded as only an occasion for the further working up of the idea contained in it so that its ultimate triumph in reality will be assured.

Evil, pain, and suffering can be entertained merely as *occasions* for the spirit to achieve its many possible actualizations in time. The blocking characters in the historical drama are real enough, but their function is now seen to be that of providing the occasions on which the spirit succeeds in overcoming the conditions of its own actualization. Every past conflict between man and man, nation and nation, or class and class can be distanced and contemplated in the full self-certitude of the triumph of beauty, truth, and justice *in the long run*. The Comic import of the whole drama is *not* made an object of reflection, as it is in Hegel's thought, but *is simply presupposed* as an end which we can apprehend from our position within history, the actual comprehension of which must await the "integration" of "finite shapes" and "form" in the last scene of the last act. *How* the whole process works is only generally known and only generally knowable. The best the historian can aspire to is the narrative representation of the processes in which a transient formal coherence is achieved at different times and places in the world. The appearance of new forms remains a "miracle," an object of perception but not of comprehension.

The dissolution of achieved forms is referred to the involvement of their governing ideas in the conditions of their specification—that is to say, to laws of physical change and dissolution. But Humboldt's system could not account for the rise and triumph of what he called "abnormal states of life, as in types of disease," for it was unthinkable to him that evil, error, and injustice might have their "ideal" forms in the way that goodness, truth, and justice do. Undoubtedly, he said, there is some kind of analogy between "abnormal" and "normal" states of life, an analogy of trends "which arise suddenly or gradually without explicable causes, seem to follow their own laws, and refer to a hidden connection of all things." But he was at a loss to imagine how these trends might be made a part of the historical drama as he conceived it. This dark side of the historical process remained mysterious to him, and, Humboldt averred, "it may take a very long time before [its principles] can be made useful to history." (69)

By conceiving the transition from Herder through Humboldt to Ranke in terms of a shift from an Organicist to a Formist explanatory strategy, with the essentially Comic mode of emplotment remaining intact, I am permitted to dispense with the usual terminology, now become cliché, in which the historiographical disputes of the early nineteenth century are conventionally discussed. It can be seen that the issues do not turn so much on the problem of the opposition of the individual to the general, or of the concrete to the abstract, or even on the matter of whether history must be philosophically conceived or empirically derived, or whether it is more a science than an art. The issue in all the discussions in which such terms are used is what is meant by the terms themselves, the ways in which art, science, and philosophy are conceived on the one hand and the nature of the *relationship* between the individual event and its context on the other.

As a matter of fact, Humboldt, like Ranke, held that history is the knowledge of the individual event in its concrete actualization and that the problem the historian faces is to relate the individual to the context in which it appears and achieves its destiny. Moreover, he and Ranke held that history is ultimately an art form, and specifically a classical art form, which is to say a *mimetic* art form concerned with the representation of reality as it "actually" appears in a given time and place. In addition, he maintained that the purpose of historical study, finally, is to divine the meaning of the whole historical process, not merely to produce a set of discrete pictures of the past, but rather to ascend to a higher conceptualization of the relationships figured in the process of which these pictures represent only parts or fragments. Historical reflection, Humboldt said, is prompted by specifically moral concerns, by man's need to know in some way what his nature is so that he can act for the construction of a future better than his own present life affords him. What is at issue is how the context within which historical events occur, the frame or ground on which they take place, is to be conceived, and whether the process figured by the concatenation of events in time is to be conceived as elevating or depressing in its moral implications.

✒§ Conclusion

In Ranke's thought about the historical process we encounter ideas which mark a definitive break with some of the principal presuppositions of literary Romanticism. The Romantic impulses behind Ranke's historiographical exercises cannot, of course, be denied; he himself testified to their power over his thinking during his young manhood. They are present in his interest in the individual event in its uniqueness and concreteness, in his conception of historical explanation as narration, and in his concern to enter into the interior of the consciousness of the actors of the historical drama, to see them as they saw themselves and to reconstruct the worlds which they faced in their time and their place. At the same time, however, Ranke steadfastly fought the impulse to glory in the "revel of forms" which the historical record appears to represent to the uncritical eye. In his view, history—for all its apparently chaotic nature—does display to the properly conditioned historical consciousness a meaning and comprehensibility that fall somewhere short of the total certitude about its ultimate meaning which the religious sensibility is capable of deriving from reflection on it. This "meaning" consists in the apprehension of the formal coherence of finite segments of the historical process, the apprehension of the structures which succeed one another as ever more comprehensive integrations of human life and society. In short, for Ranke, the meaning which history displays to consciousness is a purely Organicist one. It is not, however, the holistic Organicism which Novalis purported to see in the entire process, but that of the part-whole relationship which permits the observer to see in the microcosm an *intimation* of the larger coherence contained in the totality. Ranke consigned the proper apprehension of the nature of this larger coherence to a specifically religious sensibility and denied it to historical consciousness properly construed. But to the historian he granted a kind of insight that yields a meaning, or number of meanings, which can overcome the despair suffered by Constant on the one hand and the kind of naive faith advocated by Novalis on the other. To find the forms in which historical reality disposes itself in different times and places, in the efforts of the race to realize a human community—this was Ranke's conception of the historian's task. And this Organicist doctrine constituted Ranke's principal contribution to the theory by which history was constituted as an autonomous discipline in the second quarter of the nineteenth century.

It is true that disputes such as those entered into between Ranke and Hegel's disciple Heinrich Leo turn upon such matters as whether understanding is to proceed from the particular to the general or from the general to the particular; but these disputes are entered into from *within* the shared assumption that the historical field is the place where the general and the particular, the universal and the individual, meet and are fused in the historical process at large. The real issue has to do with the demand for rigor in conceptualization on the one hand (the position represented by Hegel) and the possibility of resisting a rigorous conceptualization of the bases of historical knowledge on the other (the position represented by Humboldt and Ranke). In the Organicist conception of explanation, *obscurity at some point in the analysis is an unquestioned value,* is required by the apprehension of the historical field as a place where essential novelty intrudes itself under conditions and impulses which are *intrinsically unknowable*. This is the real content of the claim to an "empirical" method in the historical research of Ranke and his followers. But this "empiricism" stems less from a rigorous observation of particulars than from a decision to treat certain kinds of processes as inherently resistant to analysis—and certain kinds of comprehension as inherently limited.

This apprehension of the ultimately mysterious (or miraculous, if it is preferred) nature of historical happening is saved from the obscurantism to which it is naturally inclined by virtue of the belief which attends it in the essentially Comic plot structure figured in every story that might be told about the historical process in its macroscopic dimensions. This apprehension of the ultimately Comic nature of the process underlies the so-called optimism of the historist world picture. What designations of Rankean historism's "optimistic" preconceptions obscure is the extent to which a *merely* optimistic 'attitude is experienced as a puerile notion when it is unattended by a rationale by which belief in its truth is justified. In the Synecdochic consciousness of Humboldt and Ranke, this rationale is a *pre*conception, itself critically unanalyzed and unjustified, but simply affirmed as the attitude with which men are morally compelled to view history if they are not to fall into despair. But the justification for believing in it is provided by the actual *representation* of the world process in which a Comic emplotment of the total process passes the test of plausibility.

The threat to which historism lay exposed was not theoretical, since an Organicist conception of explanation cannot be attacked from outside the range of its own enabling postulates. What was needed to undermine these postulates was not a demonstration that the historical record can be comprehended by Mechanistic, Formist, or Contextualist modes of explanation, but rather a demonstration that the same process that is represented as a Comic Drama by one historian can be represented as a Tragic Drama or Absurd process by another. When such alternative emplotments are offered to a public which has already lost faith in its own ability to provide the Comic resolution of the Drama in which it plays the role of major protagonist, interest in Organicist explanations of history may give way to a desire for Mechanistic or Contextualist explanatory techniques. And this is what occurred in large sections of the scholarly world in the last quarter of the nineteenth century, with the advent of Positivism and Marxism on the one hand and Aestheticism on the other.

But, under such circumstances, Organicism *need not be* abandoned; it is necessary only to shift from representation of the historical process as a Comic Drama to representation of it as an Absurdist Drama to reflect the loss of nerve of dominant classes of a society when belief in their own capacities for scientifically comprehending reality have dissipated. And this is what Burckhardt accomplished.

The significance of Humboldt's essay lay, not in his conception of historical explanation, which was less than adequate on both logical and scientific grounds, but rather in the confidence that it displayed in the adequacy of an Organicist approach to historical study. What it suggested was that, if historical representation were undergirded by the conviction of the ultimate formal coherence of the whole historical process, historical thought could be saved from the "Chaos of Being" notion of the Romantics on the one hand and the notion of its perfect comprehensibility suggested by the Idealists and Positivists on the other. In short, it represented a *commitment* to the Synecdochic mode of comprehension.

The *mythos* of Synecdoche is the dream of Comedy, the apprehension of a world in which all struggle, strife, and conflict are dissolved in the realization of a perfect harmony, in the attainment of a condition in which all crime, vice, and folly are finally revealed as the *means* to the establishment of the social order which is finally achieved at the end of the play. But the Comic resolution may take two forms: the triumph of the protagonist over the society which blocks his progression to his goal, or the reassertion of the rights of the collectivity over the individual who has risen up to challenge it as the definitive form of community. The first kind of Comic emplotment may be called the Comedy of Desire, the second kind the Comedy of Duty and Obligation. Michelet wrote his histories of France up to the Revolution in the first mode; Ranke wrote his histories of all the nations of Europe in the second. What linked them together as representatives of the new, or "realistic," historiography of the second quarter of the nineteenth century was the conviction which they shared: that the simple description of the historical process in all its particularity and variety will figure forth a drama of consummation, fulfillment, and ideal order in such a way as to make the telling of the tale an explanation of why it happened as it did. Behind their willingness to immerse themselves in the chaos of data and events which the historical record contains was their conviction that an accurate description of the events in their particularity will result, not in an image of chaos, but in a vision of a formal coherence which neither science nor philosophy is capable of apprehending, much less of capturing in a verbal representation. Both sought to grasp the essence of an "idea" at the heart of the process of development which it was their purpose first to ensnare in narrative prose.

Chapter 5 Tocqueville: Historical Realism as Tragedy

~§ Introduction

The consistency of Michelet's historical thought derived from the constancy with which he applied his capacities for Metaphorical characterization of both the individuals and the processes he discerned in the historical field. Michelet's Formist apprehension of the objects occupying the historical field was buttressed by the myth of Romance which he used to emplot the sequence of events culminating in the Revolution of 1789. A principal inconsistency in his thought lay in his effort to derive specifically Liberal ideological implications from a conception of the historical process which was essentially Anarchist in nature. No such inconsistency marred the thought and work of Ranke. His theory of knowledge was Organicist, his mode of emplotment Comic, his ideological position Conservative. As a result, when we read Ranke, however much we are impressed with his learning and his powers as a narrator, we are aware of an absence in everything he wrote of the kind of tension we associate with great poetry, great literature, great philosophy—and even great historiography. This may be one reason why it is possible, from time to time, to revive interest in a historian like Michelet in a way that is all but impossible with respect to a historian like Ranke. We admire the *achievement* of the latter, but we respond directly and sympathetically to the *agon* of the former.

When it comes to charting the history of man and society on the grand scale, no one can be permitted the kind of certitude which appears to inform Ranke's work. Knowledge is a product of a wrestling not only with the "facts" but with one's self. Where alternative visions of reality are not entertained as genuine possibilities, the product of thought tends toward blandness and unearned self-confidence. We respond to Ranke rather as we are inclined to respond to Goethe; neither thinker was driven to attempt anything that he did not already know in his heart he could accomplish. The calm we intuit at the center of Ranke's consciousness was a function of the coherence between his vision and his application of that vision to his work as a historian. That coherence was lacking to Michelet on the level at which he sought to move from his vision of history to the ideological position to which he was consciously committed but which was inconsistent with the vision itself. His work is therefore much more turbulent, more passionate, and more immediate to us who live in an age in which moral self-certitude, if not impossible, at least appears as dangerous as it is desirable.

A turbulence similar to that which we apprehend in Michelet resides at the heart of the work of his great contemporary and fellow countryman, Alexis de Tocqueville. This turbulence has its source in two emotions that Tocqueville shared with Michelet: an overriding capacity for sympathy for men different from himself, and a fear of the destruction of those things he valued most in both the past and the present. We have noted how Michelet tended toward an increasingly Ironic conception of history-in-general as French political life moved farther away from the conditions under which an ideal union of the nation had been achieved, by Michelet's lights at least, in the euphoria of 1789. As the culminating point of French history receded into the past, the Romantic myth which Michelet used to give shape and form to the history of France *up to* 1789 became progressively sublimated, suppressed, treated as an intimation of *what might yet be* the outcome of French history, if the historian could but successfully carry out his work of reconstruction and resurrection of the past in its integrity, color, vividness, and life. In the evolution of the historical thought of Tocqueville, we witness a similar drift into Irony as we trace the development of his thought about history, and about French history in general, from the *Democracy in America* (1835) to the *Souvenirs* (written in the years before his death in 1859). But the point from which Tocqueville began this descent is different from that from which Michelet began his. Whereas Michelet began in Romance, moved through a Tragic apprehension of the fates that betray the ideals for which he labored as a historian, and came to rest in that mixture of sublimated Romanticism and overt Irony with which he viewed French history after 1789, Tocqueville began in an effort to sustain a specifically Tragic vision of history and then gradually subsided into an Ironic resignation to a condition from which he perceived little prospect of liberation, soon or late.

Recent Tocqueville scholarship has disclosed fully the intellectual and emotional bases of his thought; the "influences" working on him, from both previous and contemporary thinkers; and his position in the social and political world of Orleanist France. His stature as a major precursor of modern sociological thinking is well established, and his contributions to the ideologies of both Liberalism and Conservatism are now taken for granted. It is not my purpose to add to the understanding of these aspects of Tocqueville's thought, work, and life. I am much more interested in analyzing his thought about history as a model of a specific style of historical reflection.

This style is not exhaustively describable in terms of a given ideological label (such as Liberal or Conservative) or a specifically disciplinary one (such as "sociological"). In fact, it is my contention that the actual logical implication of Tocqueville's work as a historian is Radical. Inasmuch as he studied history in order to determine the causal laws that govern its operations as a process, he was implicitly committed to a conception regarding the manipulation of the social process of the sort that we associate with Radicalism in its modern, materialistic form. This implicit Radicalism is reflected in the Tragic *mythos* that underlies and provides the macrohistorical context of both of Tocqueville's major works, *Democracy in America* and *The Old Regime and the Revolution*.

In these two works, the manifest form which knowledge of social reality takes is typological, which might suggest that, ultimately, it was Tocqueville's purpose to effect either a Formist dispersion or an Organicist unification of the processes and forces identified in terms of the types actually constructed. But, unlike Michelet on the one hand and unlike Ranke on the other, neither a revel of forms nor a synthesis of contending forces was entertained by Tocqueville as a genuine possibility for Europe's future. For him, the future held little prospect for the reconciliation of man with man *in society*. The forces at play in history, which make it an arena of irremissible conflict, are not reconcilable, either in society or in the heart of man himself. Man remains, as Tocqueville put it, "on the verge between two abysses," the one comprised of that social order without which he cannot be a man, the other comprised of that demonic nature within him which prevents his ever becoming fully human. It is to the consciousness of this existence "on the verge between two abysses" that man constantly returns at the end of every effort to raise himself above the animal and to make thrive the "angel" which resides within him, suppressed, tethered, and unable to gain ascendancy in the species.

Underlying all of Tocqueville's thought is an apprehension of a primordial chaos which makes of the order found in history, society, and culture as much of an enigma as a blessing. Like his great contemporary, the novelist Balzac, Tocqueville exulted in the mystery of the fact that man "has" a history; but his conception of the dark abysses out of which man arises, and against which he throws up "society" as a barrier to total chaos, did not permit him to hope for anything other than modest gains, from time to time, in his knowledge of the forces that ultimately govern the world process. Because, for him (unlike Marx), being itself was a mystery, Tocqueville could not push his thought to the contemplation of the genuine *science* of history which his typological organization of historical phenomena seemed to sanction. This indigestible residue of mystery prohibited his conceptualization of *the laws of process* that might have permitted him to account for the fact that history itself appears to fall apart into mutually exclusive, but recurrent, *types* of social phenomena.

But, unlike the pure Ironists who preceded him in the Enlightenment and who followed him at the end of the nineteenth century, Tocqueville did not permit himself to believe that history has no general meaning at all. What the tragic *agon* reveals, again and again, is that the secret of history is nothing but man's eternal contest with, and return to, himself. The mystery of history is thus conceived now in an Aeschylean way, now in a Sophoclean way, first as an aid to self-confident action in the present on behalf of a better future, then as a reminder of the dangers of a premature foreclosure of possibilities or a precipitate commitment to incompletely comprehended social or personal programs. And this dual perspective on history was the basis of Tocqueville's Liberalism. Only near the end of his life did the tone and mood of his reflections on history lapse into the Ironic conviction of Euripides or of the late Shakespeare, the conviction that life may have no meaning at all. When this conviction arose, Tocqueville suppressed it, for moral reasons, out of fear of its debilitating effect upon men who must labor, as best they can, to make a life of some kind out of the paltry materials given them by fate. And he even attacked his friend Gobineau for presuming, in the name of truth, to broadcast a conception of history that would contribute to the promotion of a fear which it is the responsibility of the philosopher and historian to dissipate.

If Tocqueville had asserted either that history has no meaning at all and therefore offers no basis for hope, or, conversely, that it has a meaning and that this meaning can be fully known to man, he would have been impelled toward either the Reactionary position of his successor Burckhardt or the Radical position of his contemporary Marx. But he wanted to believe both that history has a meaning and that this meaning is to be found in the *mysterious* nature of man himself. It was the value that Tocqueville placed on this mystery that made him the spokesman for the ideological position that has been called Liberal, in spite of the fact that his notion of the nomological nature of the historical process might have led him to adopt a Radical position on most of the important social issues of the day.

Tocqueville's "scientific" study of history eventuated in the arrangement of historical events into *types*, classes, genera, species, and the like. Data were transformed into knowledge when their emplacement in a finite set of types of social, political, and cultural phenomena had been effected. For example, Tocqueville analyzed two types of society: democratic and aristocratic. And his conception of the history of modern Western civilization, from the late Middle Ages to his own time, turned on the problem of how these two kinds of society had arisen within that civilization, the nature of the relationship and interaction between them, and the assessment of the prospects for the future of each. The question which Tocqueville had to answer was the following: What is the nature of the *process* within which these two essentially change-less types of society arise, interact, and conflict with each other?

Tocqueville did not actually deal with this question directly. He purported to discern long-range trends, of a political, social, and cultural-historical nature, which indicated by his lights the decline of one of the types of society (the aristocratic) and the rise of the other (the democratic). And he suggested that the decline of the aristocratic type is a function of the rise of the democratic type, which means that he viewed the whole historical process as a closed system, containing a finite amount of usable energy, in which whatever is gained in any process of growth must be paid for by some loss in another part of the system. The system as a whole, viewed as a process, was thus Mechanistically conceived, and the relationships between the parts were conceived in mechanical-causal terms.

If Tocqueville had been an Idealist (or Organicist) thinker, he would have been impelled to see in this exchange of energy the occasion for a positive growth in human consciousness in general, a growth which would have been perceivable in the increased sophistication of thought and expression in his own age over that of all previous times—in the manner of Hegel or for that matter Ranke. But the growth which Tocqueville discerned in the process is not to be found in the progress of consciousness in general so much as in the *power* of the forces which alone benefit from the decline of aristocracy and the rise of democracy: the power of the centralized state on the one hand and the power of the masses on the other. And, in his view, these two forces aggregate and combine in such a way as to offer a critical threat, not only to civilization and culture as he conceived them, but also to humanity itself. Moreover, the growth of these forces was viewed by him, not as a sporadic or casual process, but as a sustained and constant erosion of precious human resources—intellectual, moral, and emotional.

The whole process has the inevitability of a Tragic Drama, and Tocqueville's early reflections on history and historical knowledge explicitly envisioned the task of the historian as that of a mediator between the new, conquering forces appearing on his own temporal horizons and the older, languishing cultural ideals which they threaten by their ascent. Tocqueville inhabited a severed world. His purpose was to minister to it as best he could, so that the rents and tears in its structure could be patched over, if not completely healed.

Tocqueville took for the broader context of his reflection the whole history of Western civilization, in which he placed his analyses of its European and

American species variations as examples of relatively pure types of potentialities contained in the totality as possible *futures* for his own generation. Consequently, both the point of view from which he surveyed the histories of the two types and the tone of voice in which he narrated the histories differ significantly. The point of view assumed for the survey of American democracy is that of the observer who is *superior* to the agents and agencies that make up that type of society. The mood is one of benign Irony, at least in the first volume of *Democracy in America*, inasmuch as Tocqueville wrote in the interest of alerting his European readers to both the strengths and the weaknesses of this potentiality which European society contained within itself as a possible future. In *The Old Regime*, by contrast, both the tone and the point of view changed, in the direction signaled by the second volume of *Democracy in America*, which is more sharply analytical of American institutions, customs, and beliefs and more directly critical of the threat they represent to timelessly valuable components in European cultural life. The point of view is much more that of a participant in a process who must strive mightily to get outside it, in order to divine its general drift or tendency, to anticipate its end or direction, and to warn those involved in it wherein dangers to them reside. The tone has changed correspondingly, to match the shift in point of view. The mood is more somber; the Tragic *mythos* dictates the form of the narrative closer to the surface. The language is predominantly Metonymical, as it is in the second volume of the *Democracy in America*, but the images of process are much more prominent, and the flow of time and the sense of development are more pressingly invoked.

Between the first volume of *Democracy in America* and *The Old Regime*, there was an important shift of emphasis from the consideration of structure to the consideration of process, with the result that the weight-of-meaning feeling was thrown more openly onto the narrative level of the representation in the latter work. The process of Western European history from the Reformation to around 1830 was simply assumed as a context for the analysis of the structure of American democracy that was carried out in the former work. *Within* that process, American democracy appears as a rigid structure whose only movement or growth is in the articulation of its component elements and their relationships. In *The Old Regime*, by contrast, the distinction between process and structure is all but dissolved. The effect is correspondingly more literary, the ideological affect correspondingly more overtly striven for. But the implications of the two works converge on a single image of stasis, determination, frustration, oppression, and dehumanization. The presiding impulse behind the whole of Tocqueville's work was the vision of puzzled defeat and despair which inspires the Ironic *mythos* wherever it appears. Tocqueville was kept from falling into this despair only by an act of will, the kind of act which permitted him to continue to speak like a Liberal to the end, when everything he wrote about history should have driven him to either Radical rebellion on the one hand or Reactionary Nihilism on the other.

◆§ Antidialectic

In Tocqueville's work, unlike Ranke's, there is very little sense of a dialectical transformation of the historical field; the dominant sense is that of a sustained fall from a position of eminence and a failure to exploit given possibilities. The dualism of historical forces which Ranke saw as the precondition of the social compromise actually achieved in his own time Tocqueville saw as a principal threat to civilization itself. In fact, Tocqueville's whole historiographical achievement was a product of his effort to determine if something short of total disaster could be salvaged from the conflict of forces which, as he saw them, appeared to be irreconcilable.

The dualism which for Tocqueville characterized the historical process was mirrored in (or projected from) his conception of human nature itself. As he wrote to a friend in 1836:

Whatever we do, we cannot prevent men from having a body as well as a soul. . . . You know that the animal is not more subdued in me than in most people, [but] I adore the angel and would give anything to make it predominate. I am, therefore, continually at work to discover the middle course which men may follow without becoming disciples either of Heliogabulus or of Saint Jerome; for I am convinced that the great majority will never be persuaded to imitate either, and less the saint then the emperor. [*Memoir*, I, 318]

The same dualism was carried over into Tocqueville's politics and resulted in a quest for a similar "middle course" there as well. Of his political position he once remarked:

They ascribe to me alternately aristocratic and democratic prejudices. . . . But my birth, as it happened, made it easy to me to guard against both. . . . When I entered life, aristocracy was dead and democracy was yet unborn. My instinct, therefore, could not lead me blindly to one or to the other. . . . Balanced between the past and the future, with no natural instinctive attractions towards either, I could without effort look quietly on each side of the question. [*Ibid.*, II, 91]

Tocqueville resembled Machiavelli in his conviction that his own age was suffering from an incapacity to choose between *alternative* social systems and cultural ideals. Since the fall of Napoleon, he believed, Europe had been suspended between the older aristocratic system and the newer democratic one; it had neither fully abandoned the former nor completely embraced the latter, and, while it suffered from the shortcomings of both, it enjoyed the benefits of neither. The main problem, as Tocqueville saw it, was to weigh the advantages and disadvantages of both systems, evaluate the prospects of each for the future, and encourage the choice of whatever seemed unavoidable in a way that would best promote the cause of human freedom and creativity. Part of this inquest had to be historical, but no conventional historical examination could serve the needs of the age adequately. The age required a historical vision that was neither "aristocratic" nor "democratic" per se, but that was capable of judging both systems objectively, and of salvaging whatever was useful in them for the future.

Similarly, the culture of his own age, Tocqueville believed, vacillated between the Idealism of the older aristocratic period and the Materialism of the emerging democratic epoch. The Enlightenment had criticized aristocratic Idealism and turned the attention of men to "the real and visible world" as a proper object of study. At first, both thought and art had concentrated exclusively on the physical world, the world "external to man." But this fascination with nature was neither the sole possible interest of the age nor really appropriate to it; it belonged, Tocqueville said, "only to a period of transition." In the coming age, he predicted in *Democracy in America*, thought and imagination would become fixed on "man alone" and more specifically on the *future* of mankind (II, 76–77).

Unlike aristocracies, which tend to idolize the past, democracies "are haunted by visions of what will be; in this direction their unbounded imagination grows and dilates beyond all measure" (78). Thus, although the Materialistic and Utilitarian nature of democratic culture inevitably promoted the despiritualization of man, at the same time, it at least encouraged hope for the future. For example, "Among a democratic people poetry will not be fed with legends or the memorials of old traditions. The poet will not attempt to people the universe with supernatural beings, in whom his readers and his own fancy have ceased to believe, nor will he coldly personify virtues and vices, which are better received under their own features" (80). The vast range of possible subjects for poetry which had been offered by the febrile aristocratic imagination is suddenly contracted, the imagination is driven back upon itself and into itself, and the poet finds in human nature his sole proper object. "All these resources fail him; but Man remains, and the poet needs no more" (80–81).

If man himself could be made the object and measure of all thought and art, it would be possible, Tocqueville believed, to create a new cultural vision that was neither Idealistic nor Materialistic, but a combination of the two, heroic and realistic at the same time. Thus he wrote:

I need not traverse the earth and sky to discover wondrous objects woven of contrasts, of infinite greatness and littleness, of intense gloom and amazing brightness, capable at once of exciting pity, admiration, terror, contempt. I have only to look at myself. Man springs out of nothing, crosses time and disappears forever in the bosom of God; he is seen but for a moment, wandering on the verge of two abysses, and there he is lost. [80]

This existence "on the verge of two abysses" produces a sense of a uniquely human suffering, or despair, but it also generates a uniquely human aspiration, an impulse to know and to create.

If man were totally ignorant of himself, he would have no poetry in him; for it is impossible to describe what the mind does not conceive. If man clearly discerned his own nature, his imagination would remain idle and would have nothing to add to the picture. But the nature of man is sufficiently disclosed for him to know something of himself, and sufficiently obscure for all the rest to be plunged in thick darkness, in which he gropes forever, and forever in vain, to lay hold on some completer notion of his being. [*Ibid.*]

It was necessary, Tocqueville felt, to keep both the despair and the aspiration alive to human consciousness, to keep men's minds directed toward the future, but at the same time to remind them that a better, more human future could be won only against the harshest suffering and with the most painful labor. For the coming age, therefore, he envisioned an art which had moved from the Epic mode of the aristocratic age, through the Lyrical mode of the period of transition, to a new Tragic perception of the human condition. And he envisioned philosophy moving from the older Idealism, through the Materialism of the age of transition, to a new, more realistic Humanism. The social system proper to this new vision of man was not exclusively either aristocratic or democratic, but a combination of the two: egalitarian, Materialistic, and utilitarian in accordance with the principles of democracy; individualistic, Idealistic, and heroic in accordance with the principles of aristocracy. The task of the historian was to aid in the creation of this new social system by showing how the principles of both aristocracy and democracy were functions of the single abiding impulse in European civilization, the desire for freedom which had characterized Western culture since its beginnings.

I should stress at this point that Tocqueville's conception of the mediative role of the historian presaged the Ironic frame of mind into which he progressively fell during the course of his subsequent historical reflections. At the beginning of his career as a historian, he aimed at the attainment of a Tragic vision of history, which presupposes a perception of the laws governing human nature in its contest with fate and, a fortiori, of the laws governing social processes in general. If, in fact, these laws are discoverable by historical inquiry, then in principle they should be applicable to the effort to bring to pass the situations and circumstances that are inevitable in human development with minimum pain and suffering—as Thucydides suggested in the famous opening section of *The Peloponnesian Wars*. But the optimism which the possibility of discovering such laws of historical process ought to foster is crucially limited by the conception of that *human nature* in whose behalf they are meant to be applied. If man himself is conceived to be crucially flawed, for example, by the presence in him of irrational forces that might preclude his acting in his own best interests as rationally conceived, the discovery of the laws that govern his actions as a social being must be seen as illuminative, not of an essential freedom, but of a fatal determinancy. And it is this conception of a fatally flawed human nature, of a humanity which is never with itself but always, in some way, *beside* itself, that prohibited Tocqueville from moving into the Radical ideological position toward which his search for the laws of history originally impelled him.

In point of fact, Tocqueville suppressed the Radical implications of his nomological conception of history and moved progressively from the search for laws to the construction of typologies. This movement on the epistemological level was mirrored on the aesthetic level by a similar shift from a plot structure that was implicitly Tragic to one that was increasingly Satirical. In the later stages of his thought, Tocqueville was driven to reflect on the extent to which men are *bound* by the conditions under which they must labor to win their kingdom on earth and on the impossibility of their ever truly winning it. And the increasing press to the fore of this Ironic perception confirms his essential Liberalism as an ideologist.

Tocqueville's loyalties were—and remained—aristocratic ones, which justifies the labeling of his *forma mentis* as essentially Conservative by those who have studied him in this light. But Tocqueville resisted the Conservative's typical satisfaction with things as they are. In some ways, as I will note shortly, his dissatisfactions with his own age were similar to those of the Reactionary Count de Gobineau. But, unlike Gobineau, Tocqueville did not yield to the temptation to assert what his respect for the virtues of aristocratic culture urged upon him—namely, the conviction that his own time represented an *absolute decline* from an earlier ideal age. Like Croce later, Tocqueville insisted on seeing the flaws in every past ideal or social reality that *required* its passing away and supplanting by another, more vigorous form of historical life. This meant that he had to view both aristocracy and democracy *Ironically* in the last analysis. But he even refused to assert *publicly* the implications of his own Ironic sensibility. He remained formally committed to a Tragic view of history, but betrayed that viewpoint in his unwillingness to specify the laws of history which were implicitly presupposed by his emplotment of the course of European history as a Tragic Drama and in his reluctance to draw the Radical conclusions which his nomological conception of history demanded that he draw.

◁§ Poetry and History in Two Modes

That Tocqueville envisaged a historiography capable of yielding the laws of social process—*à la* Marx—is shown by his discussion in *Democracy in America* of the relation between history and poetry and by his conception of the modalities of historical consciousness set forth in the second volume of that work.

As he noted, whereas poetry is "the search after, the delineation of, the Ideal" (75), history has to tell the truth about the world of human affairs, display the *real* forces met with in any attempt to realize the Ideal, and chart the *real* possibilities for the future of society. But, Tocqueville argued, neither an aristocratic nor a democratic idea of history alone can provide a completely true and full vision of the real, because the aristocratic and the democratic historian necessarily look for, and see, different things when they survey the historical record. For example:

When the historian of aristocratic ages surveys the theatre of the world, he at once perceives a very small number of prominent actors who manage the whole piece. These great personages, who occupy the front of the stage, arrest attention and fix it upon themselves; and while the historian is bent on penetrating the secret motives which make these persons speak and act, the others escape his memory. [90]

Aristocratic historians are inclined "to refer all occurrences to the particular will and character of certain individuals; and they are apt to attribute the most important revolutions to slight accidents" (*ibid.*). The result is that, while they are frequently able "to trace out the smallest causes with sagacity," they just as often "leave the greatest unperceived" (*ibid.*). It is quite otherwise with democratic historians. In fact, they exhibit "precisely opposite characteristics." They tend to "attribute hardly any influence to the individual over the destiny of the race, or to citizens over the fate of a people; but, on the other hand, they assign great general causes to all petty incidents." (*Ibid.*) The aristocratic historian, even though he idealizes less than the poet, still excels only at describing the extent to which individuals control their own destinies; he is insensitive to the force which general causes exert upon the individual, how they frustrate him and bend him to their will. By contrast, the democratic historian seeks to discover some larger meaning in the mass of petty details which he discerns on the historical stage. He is driven to refer everything, not to individuals at all, but only to great, abstract, and general forces. He therefore tends to view history as a depressing story of man's inability to control his future, and inspires either a depressing cynicism or a groundless hope that things will take care of themselves.

These two ideas of history I would call Formist and Mechanistic and would view as functions of two modes of consciousness, Metaphorical and Metonymical. Tocqueville "Ironically" distanced these two modes of historical consciousness, pointing out (correctly) that, as he conceived them, neither could account for the fact of historical development, the evolution of one state or condition out of another, *different* one. The aristocratic brand sees *nothing but* movement, color, agitation in the historical field, and therefore cannot credit duration and continuity. The democratic brand sees the *same thing behind* all apparent movement and change, and therefore cannot perceive any essential development at all.

What Tocqueville proposed as an alternative to these conflicting and inadequate forms of historical consciousness was not a third form but rather a *combination* of the aristocratic and democratic forms. Each is valid in a way, he suggested, but each has to be employed for the analysis of a specific *kind* of society. There is a kind of elective affinity between the mode of historical consciousness to be used in the study of a given society and the social structure of the age or culture under analysis. In fact, Tocqueville suggested that there *are* two orders of causation at work in the historical process, one endemic to aristocratic, the other to democratic, societies. Thus, he wrote:

> I am of the opinion that, at all times, one great portion of events of this world are attributable to very general facts and another to special influences. These two kinds of causes are always in operation; only their proportion varies. General facts serve to explain more things in democratic than in aristocratic ages, and fewer things are then assignable to individual influences. During periods of aristocracy the reverse takes place: special influences are stronger, general causes weaker; unless, indeed, we consider as a general cause the fact itself of the inequality of condition, which allows some individuals to baffle the natural tendencies of all the rest. [91]

This suggests that Tocqueville regarded it as unnecessary to choose between the individualist and the deterministic, the chaotic and the providential, conceptions of the historical process that were then vying for authority. It was merely a matter of finding the dominant causal principle in operation in the kind of society being studied. Thus, "Historians who seek to describe what occurs in democratic societies are right . . . in assigning much to general causes and in devoting their attention to discover them; but they are wrong wholly in denying the special influence of individuals because they cannot trace or follow it" (91–92).

But the problem that arises in trying to apply this principle of interpretation to historical studies is that it takes as a solution to a problem what is in reality the problem itself. If I want to explain the decline of an aristocratic society, I will not be enlightened very significantly by the application of that society's own conception of the true nature of historical reality to the phenomena to be analyzed. This would be to accept at face value the heuristic utility of the ideology of a dominant class of a given society. After all, Tocqueville's problem was to explain to a displaced aristocratic class *why* it had been displaced, a problem which the spokesmen for that class had been unable to solve satisfactorily by the application of the mode of historical consciousness that was "natural" to it by virtue of its "aristocratic" nature.

And so it was with the problem of the advent of "democracy" in the modern age. If Tocqueville's purpose was to reveal—to democrats and aristocrats alike —the true nature of this new form of society and to account for its triumph in postrevolutionary times, the invocation of a mode of historical consciousness endemic to societies that had *already* been democratized could not serve *as an explanation* for those members of the aristocracy for whom both the society under analysis and the mode of consciousness produced by it were regarded as unalloyed disasters.

What Tocqueville was looking for was some way of *translating* perceptions given from within one social system into terms comprehensible to men who were inclined to view the world process from the perspective offered by loyalties to another social system. This meant that his task was to mediate between two modes of consciousness, Metaphorical and Metonymical, in such a way that the claims to a kind of "realism" of each could be sustained. Given Tocqueville's own intellectual proclivities, the ground on which this mediation had to be effected was Irony. But he was prohibited from moving *directly* to the assumption of an Ironic conception of history by *moral* considerations. The Comic conception of history, with its sanctioning Synecdochic consciousness, he could not accept at all, because *he* did not inhabit a world of putatively reconciled social forces. The Comic vision was not even considered as a possible option by him, and, as his remarks on Fichte and Hegel suggest, to him it would have been immoral to foist such an idea of history onto an age as distracted as his own.

But this was also true of the "democratic" idea of history and its sustaining Metonymical consciousness. Although Tocqueville was formally committed to the search for the causes by which the specific form of his age could be explained, he regarded the search for *general* causes to be both limited as a program of study and morally debilitating in its effects on those who onesidedly pursued it. Thus, he pointed out:

When the traces of individual action upon nations are lost, it often happens that you see the world move without the impelling force being evident. As it becomes extremely difficult to discern and analyze the reasons that, acting separately on the will of each member of the community, concur in the end to produce the movement in the whole mass, men are led to believe that this movement is involuntary and that societies unconsciously obey some superior force ruling over them. But even when the general fact that governs the private volition of all individuals is supposed to be discovered upon the earth, the principle of human free-will is not made certain. A cause sufficiently extensive to affect millions of men at once and sufficiently strong to bend them altogether in the same direction may well seem irresistible; having seen that mankind do yield to it, the mind is close upon the inference that mankind cannot resist it. [92]

The historical thought of his own age, Tocqueville (wrongly) believed, had succeeded only in producing a history which denied "that the few have any power of acting upon the destiny of a people" and that the people themselves have any "power of modifying their own condition" (*ibid.*). Historians everywhere had succumbed to the belief that history was governed either by an "inflexible Providence" or by "some blind necessity" (93). Tocqueville feared that if this doctrine passed from the historians to their readers it could "infect the mass of the community" and "even paralyze the activity of modern society" (*ibid.*).

Tocqueville's purpose, then, was to credit the operation of "general causes" in history, but in such a way as to limit the efficacity of such causes to specific kinds of societies on the one hand and therefore to specific times and places on the other. In a democratic society, such as that which had taken shape in America in his own time, the search for general causes was justified because the society itself was a product of such general causes. In Europe, by contrast, the search for such general causes was not only intellectually but also morally questionable, because European society was—or at least appeared to be in the 1830s—a *mixture* of democratic and aristocratic elements. To Tocqueville, this meant that it was possible to analyze its processes in terms of two sets of laws, general and specific, or rather in terms of two kinds of causal agencies, generally cultural on the one hand and individually human on the other. The sense of conflict between these two kinds of causal agencies, each of which is regarded as being equally legitimate in moral authority and all but equally autonomous within the historical process, gave to Tocqueville's earlier reflections on history the aspect of a Tragic vision.

Tocqueville viewed the task of the historian as essentially similar to that which Aeschylus conceived to be the task of the Tragic poet—that is, therapeutic. A chaste historical consciousness would help to exorcise the residual fear of old gods and prepare men to assume responsibility for their own destinies by the construction of institutions and laws adequate to the cultivation of their own noblest capacities. The cultivation of such a historical consciousness, however, specifically required the salvation of the aristocratic point of view, not so much as a basis of social organization, but as a possible perspective on reality, as an antidote to the morally debilitating effects of a "democratic" idea of history.

The aristocratic idea of history, which taught that, "to be a master of his lot and to govern his fellow creatures, a man requires only to be master of himself," had to be set over against the democratic idea, which held that "man is utterly powerless over himself and all around him." Was it possible, Tocqueville asked, to combine the aristocratic historiography, which instructed men "only how to command," and the democratic, which promoted the instinct "only to obey?" He concluded that it was possible not only to combine these two conceptions of history in a new kind of historiography but to go beyond them both, to frame history in such a way as to merge it with poetry, the real with the ideal, the truthful with the beautiful and the good. Only thus, he said, could thought "raise the faculties of man" rather than "complete their prostration." (*Ibid.*) Tocqueville therefore offered *Democracy in America* as a book which professed to favor "no particular views, and . . . entertained no design of serving or attacking any party." He had not, he said, "undertaken to see differently from others, but to look further." He claimed to have added a new dimension to history; for, while other historians had been "busied for the morrow only," he had turned his thoughts "to the whole future." (I, 17) He had, in fact, attempted to treat the *future* as *history*.

✍§ The Liberal Mask

It should be noted that Tocqueville's characterization of the interests of contemporary historians "for the morrow only" as against his own interest in "the *whole* future" was on the face of it wrong, or was at least an egregious exaggeration. As a matter of fact, most of the significant historiography of his time, apart from the specialized work of antiquarian academics, was set forth in an effort to explain the present and to prepare contemporary society for a "realistic" movement into the future. But the distinction between a historiography of the immediate future and a historiography which addresses the "whole future" is one of the bases on which a Liberal ideology in its postrevolutionary phase can be constructed. It permits the historian to claim for his own reflections on the possibilities of that future a scientific, or objective, character which is denied to the utilitarian and pragmatic observations of his more immediately socially involved counterparts. Mill recognized this bias in Tocqueville—and the essentially antilibertarian implications of it—in his review of *Democracy in America* in 1836.

Tocqueville professed not to doubt at all that a future different from anything known in either the past or the present was possible; that was how he distinguished himself from the Conservatives, with whom he is sometimes grouped by commentators who see only his desire to salvage what was commendable in the *ancien régime*. However, that the future would be a *historical* future, that it would be continuous with, though differentiated from, both past and present—these were the convictions that placed him solidly in the Liberal tradition. He participated in this tradition by refusing to predict the precise form the future would take, by his inclination to move from his study of the past to the delination of all of the *possible* futures facing the present, and then to return to the present to stress the necessity of human choice for the determination of the *specific* future that would actually come to pass. Tocqueville used historical thought to ground living men in a situation of choice, to enliven them to the possibilities of choosing, and to inform them of the difficulties attending any choice they might make. This constant movement, from a celebration of man's capacities to make his own future, to the remembrance that every action carries with it certain dangers and certain sufferings, and back again to the celebration of struggle and labor, made Tocqueville both a Liberal and a Tragic "realist."

✐ The Historiography of Social Mediation

Tocqueville saw it as his task, then, to mediate not only between alternative concepts of society and between the past and the present, but between the present and the future as well. Between the poles of aristocracy and democracy, a number of possibilities offered themselves for consideration, ranging from the tyranny of the elite to the tyranny of the mob. The task of the historian was to show how these *possibilities* had crystalized as *distinct alternatives* for the future and to inspire by an articulation of the Tragic nature of historical existence a proper mixture of seriousness and hope in the face of those choices. Tocqueville did not doubt for a moment that democracy in one form or another was inevitable for Europe; but *how* men would fashion their existence in that democratic future remained an open question. Or so he believed in 1835, when he wrote to a reviewer of *Democracy in America* that he had "endeavored to make [his readers] bend to an irresistible future; so that the impulse in one quarter and the resistance in the other being less violent, society may march on peaceably towards the fulfillment of its destiny. This is the dominant idea of the book—an idea which embraces all others" (*Memoir*, I, 398). This "destiny," he hoped, would be neither aristocratic nor democratic as such, but a combination of the two which conserved that independence of spirit of the old order and that respect for the rights of all of the new.

Tocqueville's *impulse*, then, was at this time dialectical; he sought some way of justifying belief in the possibility of a synthesis between antithetical elements in history. But the *method* of analysis which he used precluded any possibility of a synthesis; he proposed a typological method of analysis, but constructed a reductive, dualistic typology. Therefore, the more perfectly his analysis was carried out, the more remote the possibility of any synthesis of the conflicting elements became. Since he conceived history in Metonymical terms, his thought was driven necessarily to the perception of the impossibility of uniting the principal components discerned in the analysis in an imaginable system of either thought or praxis.

Looked at in the most superficial manner, Tocqueville's *Democracy in America* does not qualify as a historical narrative. The chronological framework is simply presupposed; knowledge of it in detail is not required for comprehension of the categories of analysis used in the explication of the phenomena of democratic society. The development, or evolution, of democracy in America is simply taken for granted; the idea of *evolution* is not, therefore, an organizing principle of the exposition. Everything that happened in America, from the time of the original settlement by the first European colonizers to the Jacksonian era, represents simply a purification or articulation of changeless elements in the system, so that what is finally produced at the end of the process—Tocqueville's own time—can hardly be conceived as anything more than a monstrosity, a monolithic system in which all the elements that might have served as checks and balances within it have been expunged.

Tocqueville said in the Introduction to *Democracy in America* that he had written the work "under the influence of a kind of religious awe" produced by reflection on the "great democratic revolution" which "has advanced for centuries in spite of every obstacle and which is still advancing in the midst of the ruins it has caused" (I, 3, 7). The growth of democracy, he said, had the appearance of "a providential fact. . . It is universal, it is lasting, it constantly eludes all human interference, and all events as well as all men contribute to its progress" (6). It was in the nature of a Tragic destiny. European society had already felt the first shocks of this democratic revolution, but "without that concomitant change in the laws, ideas, customs, and morals which was necessary to render such a revolution beneficial" (8). Europe had cleared the way to a new society, but now hesitated to enter upon it: "we have destroyed an aristocracy, and we seem inclined to survey the ruins with complacency and to accept them" (11).

It was natural, Tocqueville pointed out, for men to cling to idealized memories of the past after the first revolutionary enthusiasm had cooled: "placed in the middle of a rapid stream, we obstinately fix our eyes on the ruins that may still be descried upon the shore we have left, while the current hurries us away and drags us backwards towards the abyss" (7). But it was not possible to turn back: "I am persuaded that all who attempt, in the ages upon which we are entering, to base freedom upon aristocratic privilege will fail; that all who attempt to draw and to retain authority within a single class will fail" (II, 340). It followed therefore that the problem confronting the age was, "not how to reconstruct aristocratic society, but how to make liberty proceed out of that democratic state of society in which God has placed us" (*ibid.*).

Tocqueville was not, however, an advocate of what appeared to be the inevitable. He believed that the "principle of equality" was fraught with dangers to "the independence of mankind"; indeed, "these dangers are the most formidable as well as the least foreseen of all those which futurity holds in store" (348). But these dangers were not, he hoped, insurmountable. Men in democratic societies would be "impatient of regulation" and "wearied by the permanence even of the condition they themselves prefer"; they would be fond of power, prone to hate those who wielded it, and able easily to elude the grasp of those who had it (*ibid.*). Yet he tried to believe that there was nothing intrinsically horrifying about this. "These propensities" he argued, "will always manifest themselves; . . . they originate in the groundwork of society, *which will undergo no change*; for a long time they will prevent the establishment of any despotism, and they will furnish fresh weapons to each succeeding generation that struggles in favor of the liberty of mankind" (*ibid.*). It was important, then, to maintain a proper historical perspective on what was happening in the present age and not to judge the state of society that is now coming into existence by notions derived from a state of society that no longer exists; for as these states of society are exceedingly different in their structure, they cannot be submitted to a just or fair comparison. It would scarcely be more reasonable to require of our contemporaries the peculiar virtues which originated in the social conditions of their forefathers, since that social condition is itself fallen and has drawn into one promiscuous ruin the good and evil that belonged to it. [351]

It was impossible to determine in advance whether the emerging state of the world would be better or worse than the former one; virtues and vices alike were present in both. The men of the new age and the men of the old were like "two distinct orders of human beings, each of which has its own merits and defects, its own advantages and its own evils" (ibid.). In his own time, Tocqueville noted, some men could "perceive nothing in the principle of equality but the anarchical tendencies that it engenders." These "dread their own free agency, they fear themselves." Others took the opposite view: "beside that track which starts from the principle of equality to terminate in anarchy, they have at last discovered the road that seems to lead men to inevitable servitude. They shape their souls beforehand to this necessary condition; and, despairing of remaining free, they already do obeisance in their hearts to the master who is soon to appear. The former abandon freedom because they think it dangerous; the latter, because they think it impossible." (348) Tocqueville sought grounds for rejecting both alternatives. A correct and sufficiently extensive vision of history could show the folly of a naive faith in the principle of equality as well as of the thoughtless fear of it. Tocqueville closed Democracy in America with an injunction to the public to "look forward to the future with that salutary fear which makes men keep watch and ward for freedom, not with that faint and idle terror which depresses and enervates the heart" (ibid.).

◆§ The "Syntax" of Significant Historical Processes

Tocqueville did not, he said, enter upon his study of democracy in America "merely to satisfy a curiosity," but rather, first, to contrive an "image of democracy itself, with its inclinations, its character, its prejudices, in order to learn what we have to fear or to hope from its progress" (I, 14, 17), and, second, to provide a basis for the "new science of politics" that would be "needed for a new world" (7). His true subject was the ideal of freedom which had informed European cultural life from the beginning and to which both aristocracy and democracy, each in its own way, had contributed.

Yet Tocqueville's conception of democracy in America was that of a kind of monstrosity. To him, American democracy represented a rent, a schism, in the fabric of Western civilization, the one-sided and extreme development of a tendency which had existed in Europe since the breakup of the feudal community in the sixteenth century. America offered an example of the *pure type* of democracy; there, "for the first time, . . . theories hitherto unknown, or deemed impracticable, were to exhibit a spectacle for which the world had not been prepared by the history of the past" (26). The vast natural wealth of America and the absence of any pre-existing social order made it possible for a tradition of thought and action which had remained recessive in Europe to grow and flower and to manifest all its potential for both creativity and destructiveness in the ideal of freedom. Thus, America offered a kind of hothouse environment for the full development of a social system that was only beginning to take shape in a Europe "still encumbered by the remains of the world that is waning in decay" (II, 349). But it was precisely the existence of these historical remains of an older society which provided the possibility of creating in Europe a better social system than that which had taken shape in America.

By the time the second volume of *Democracy in America* was being written, American society had begun to manifest certain potentially fatal flaws to Tocqueville. The most apparent of these was its tendency *to change without developing*. Tocqueville found a depressing stasis in American social and cultural life, a resistance to innovation, an inability *to turn change into progress*. Thus, he said, the American people offer themselves to the contemporary observer in *essentially the same condition* as that in which they had arrived from Europe two centuries earlier (7). He was also depressed by the endemic Materialism of American life, and in a number of places he expressed the fear that a plutocracy might take shape in America which, while undermining the ideal of equality, would fail to substitute the healthy independence of thought and action that had characterized aristocracy in Europe during its early, creative phase.

That Europe was potentially threatened by similar dangers was indicated by Tocqueville's claim that there is nothing essentially "American" in American democracy. Every aspect of American life had its origins, he claimed, in Europe. Thus he wrote, "If we carefully examine the social and political state of America, after having studied its history, we shall remain perfectly convinced that not an opinion, not a custom, not a law, I may even say not an event is on record which the [European] origin of that people will not explain" (I, 29). And he attributed the static quality of American life in large part to the want of a tradition of "democratic revolution" by which the established social system could be subjected to periodic criticism and evaluation and the impulse to progressive transformation of it could be husbanded (7).

It was this want of a revolutionary tradition which really distinguished American from European social life. Whereas in America the democratic ideal was merely *established*, in Europe that ideal had to *establish itself against the opposition of the aristocracy* and *against a centralized state*, which was the enemy of aristocracy and democracy alike. This opposition forced certain segments of aristocratic culture to embrace the democratic ideal, which led to the fusion of the principle of equality with the revolutionary impulse, and created thereby that tradition of democratic revolution by which Europe was endowed with a potential for progressive transformation which was lacking in American democracy. Thus, whereas only two factors had to be considered for the comprehension of American history (the informing social ideal and the natural environment in which it develops), in the comprehension of European history four factors had to be studied. These were the aristocratic social ideal, the democratic social ideal, the centralized state, and the tradition of revolution. And, whereas the drama of America showed itself to be, in the final analysis, a struggle of men against nature solely for the establishment of the principle of equality, and hence a pathetic one, the European drama was essentially a sociopolitical one, involving conflicting ideas of society, a state power which transcended and opposed these ideas and used them to its own advantage, and the revolutionary tradition which in turn opposed the principle of state power and periodically dissolved it in the service of the ideal of liberty. That is to say, the European, as against the American, drama had all the ingredients of a real Tragedy.

✠§ The "Semantics" of American History

All of this is sketched in the opening chapters of the second volume of *Democracy in America*. Here Tocqueville traced the main principles of democratic thought in both America and Europe back to the religious reformers of the sixteenth century. But he pointed out that, whereas the spirit of independent judgment and criticism continued to develop in Europe—from Luther through Descartes to Voltaire—in America this spirit degenerated into an acceptance of common opinion. Thus, in Europe there was a democratic *philosophical* tradition, which fed and succored the revolutionary tradition in culture, politics, and religion, while in America there was scarcely a philosophical tradition at all or even an interest in philosophy. American society, born of religious convictions, had accepted those convictions "without inquiry" and was "obliged to accept in like manner a great number of moral truths originating in it and connected with it" (II, 7). In Europe, by contrast, the development of both philosophy and revolution was fostered by resistance to the principle of equality in both the aristocratic classes and the centralized state. Accordingly, both the tradition of speculative self-criticism and the tradition of criticism by revolutionary *action* had been kept alive there. And they offered the possibility of creating a new society which, while egalitarian in principle, still promoted an individuality in thought and action that was lacking in America.

In the end, therefore, America represented a kind of grotesque development of only *one-half* of the European tradition of freedom. European civilization developed out of the conflict of two social ideals (aristocratic and democratic) and two political tendencies (state centralization and revolution). By contrast, American civilization lacked the aristocratic social ideal to serve as a counterbalance to democratic ideals, and the tradition of revolution to serve as a counterbalance to state centralization. The main danger to the future of freedom in America thus lay in the possible union of the principle of state centralization with the democratic social ideal, which would create a tyranny of the majority. (13) In Europe the tradition of aristocratic independence and that of revolution offered checks on the development of the democratic ideal which could be harmful or beneficial, depending on how they were applied. Thus, Tocqueville pointed out to his contemporaries in Europe, "The nations of our time cannot prevent the conditions of men from becoming equal," but it still depends "upon themselves whether the principle of equality is to lead them to servitude or freedom, to knowledge or barbarism, to prosperity or wretchedness" (352).

In Tocqueville's reflections on America, then, there is very little that can be taken as unqualified praise and much that can be taken as criticism. His attitude toward it was Ironic in the extreme. He both stood above it and judged it in all its aspects and viewed it as a complex of conditions and processes that offered very little reason to hope that it could produce anything worthwhile to humanity in general. Tocqueville emplotted American history, not as any Romantic ascent, or even as a Tragic rise and fall in which the protagonist gains in consciousness by the suffering he endures. Democracy *in its American form*—which is to say, without any restraints upon its inherent impulses toward tyranny—could come only to a pathetic issue in the long run.

To be sure, Tocqueville reminded us that nations are never entirely governed by "some insurmountable and unintelligent power arising from anterior events, from their race, or from soil and climate of their countries." Tocqueville excoriated belief in such deterministic principles as "false and cowardly"; it could produce only "feeble men and pusillanimous nations." While Providence had not created mankind completely independent or perfectly free, it was possible to imagine an *area of freedom* in which every man was his own master. The task of the historian was to show that, although "around every man a fatal circle is traced beyond which he cannot pass," nonetheless "within the wide verge of that circle he is powerful and free." And, "as it is with men, so with communities." (*Ibid.*) But Tocqueville gave very little reason for anyone to invest much hope in America's future, or that of democracy, which probably accounts for the lack of interest in his work in the country throughout the second half of the nineteenth century. Mill recognized this implicit hostility to democracy in Tocqueville's thought; and, though he praised him for the profundity of his historical insights and his sociological observations, he denied the legitimacy of the implications drawn by the French aristocrat for the future of democracy in both America and Europe.

⋙ The Drama of European History

With respect to the drama of European civilization, Tocqueville believed that he was living through the last scene of the first, or aristocratic, act, and that he had seen in America one possible outcome of the dawning second, or democratic, act. His purpose was to show how that act might be played out in Europe with a Comic rather than a Tragic resolution. His study of democracy in America was meant to be not merely a hypothetical description of the next European age but a contribution to Europe's avoidance of a monolithically democratic fate.

Western civilization, as he saw it in his time, existed in a severed, a schismatic, condition: on one side of the Atlantic, the American monster; on the other, Europe torn by conflicting ideals and unable to choose between them, uncertain of its own powers, mindless of its own resources for renewal, vacillating, indecisive, unsure. Having completed his diagnosis of American society and his prognosis of its imminent degeneration into the tyranny of the mob, Tocqueville turned to his analysis of European society, to an assessment of what was living and what was dead of its millennial traditions, and to the determination of its prospects for the future. His *The Old Regime and the Revolution*, the first of a projected multivolume study of the impact of the Revolution on European society, was intended as a vindication of aristocratic cultural ideals. The strategy of the book was the same as that of *Democracy in America*, but the tactics were somewhat different. The study of American democracy had been injected into the static world of Orleanist France as an antidote to the fear of democracy on the one hand and to the thoughtless devotion to democracy on the other. It was meant to assuage the fears of Reactionaries by showing the extent to which democracy was endemic to European history, and at the same time to temper the enthusiasm of Radicals by revealing the flaws in the pure democracy which had developed in the New World. *The Old Regime* had a similar twofold purpose. On the one hand it modulated the enthusiasm of democrats by showing how their own precious revolutionary tradition was itself a creation of an aristocratic society and how (Ironically) the Revolution had been a product of the very social system it had tried to overthrow. On the other hand, however, it emphasized (Ironically) the elements of continuity between the old regime and the new, especially in the growth of the centralized state, which threatened the principle of liberty on behalf of which the revolutionaries had fought. The conviction that the clock of history can never be turned back to an earlier time was maintained throughout, and the desire to turn it back was suppressed whenever it cropped up in Tocqueville's own mind. But the price that men must pay for egalitarianism was coldly assessed, and the losses to human culture which gains in social progress through egalitarianism demand were pressed home to consciousness.

Liberal Point of View, Conservative Tone

In the introduction to *The Old Regime* Tocqueville wrote that his book was intended "to make clear in what respects [the present social system] resembles and in what it differs from the social system that preceded it; and to determine what was lost and what was gained by that vast upheaval" (xi). Thus, he noted,

Whenever I found in our forefathers any of those virtues so vital to a nation but now well-nigh exinct—a spirit of healthy independence, high ambitions, faith in oneself and in a cause—I have thrown them into relief. Similarly, whenever I found traces of any of those vices which after destroying the old order still affect the body politic, I have emphasized them; for it is in the light of evils to which they formerly gave rise that we can gauge the harm they yet may do. [xii]

Here again, then, the study of the old regime was not meant to be merely an exercise in historical reconstruction as an end in itself; its purpose was to help Tocqueville's age liberate itself from a sterile rage over what had already happened in the past and an equally sterile, uncritical satisfaction with its own achievement in the present. The point of view was manifestly Liberal, but the tone was Conservative. The mood, though ostensibly objective and impartial, was modulated from a Tragic acceptance of the inevitable to an Ironic admonition of the devotees of the old order to look to their own best interests and to act accordingly.

The Revolution was presented by Tocqueville not as a product of some ineluctable metahistorical process nor as a monolithically determining possibility for the future. On the contrary, it was, he insisted, a product of *human choices* in the fact of alternatives offered by nature and specific social conditions. The Revolution, like the old regime itself, was a historical event; it was a *distinct past* with a characteristic physiognomy and life style, with vices to be deplored and virtues to be husbanded. Like the old regime, the Revolution had its reasons for happening, its reasons for coming to an end or taking the form it had assumed in the minds of living men. But Tocqueville sought to show how the transition from the old regime to the new had taken place, not dialectically, but rather cataclysmically, in a process by which human consciousness becomes reconciled with the conditions of its social existence, and *in spite of* the specific intentions of the various actors who took part in that drama of transition.

The Old Regime, then, was an essay in conservation. Tocqueville's purpose was not to turn Europe back to an earlier time or to halt it in the present, but to make of the democratic future a freer, more human one. But this more human future was conceived in primarily aristocratic terms. In a notable comment on Burke, Tocqueville made this purpose explicit:

"You wish to correct the abuses of your government," [Burke] said to the French, "but why invent novelties? Why not return to your old traditions?" . . . Burke did not see that what was taking place before his eyes was a revolution whose aim was precisely to abolish that "ancient common law of Europe," and that there could be no question of putting the clock back. [21]

The Revolution had called the "entire social system" into doubt; it was an attempt on the part of the French people to "break with the past, to make, as it were, a scission in their life and to create an unbridgeable gulf between all they had hitherto been and all they aspired to be" (vii). But the important point was that this attempt was not realized, and study would show that, "Radical though it may have been, the Revolution made far fewer changes than is generally supposed" (20). At the same time, the failure of the attempt to break completely with the past could not be construed as an argument against the Revolution. For, even if the Revolution had not occurred, Tocqueville said,

the old social structure would nonetheless have been shattered everywhere sooner or later. The only difference would have been that instead of collapsing with such brutal suddenness, it would have crumbled bit by bit. At one fell swoop, without warning, without transition, and without compunction, the Revolution effected what in any case was bound to happen, if by slow degrees. [*Ibid.*]

To Tocqueville the Revolution was comprehensible as a manifestation of a higher logic in history, but in French history in particular: "It was the inevitable outcome of a long period of gestation, the abrupt and violent conclusion of a process in which six generations had played an intermittent part." Tocqueville thus presented the Revolution as "an immanent reality" in the old regime, a "presence on the threshold." (*Ibid.*) Far from being the radical break with the past that its leaders intended it to be—and that its enemies believed it to be—the Revolution was actually "the *natural* outcome of the very social order it made such haste to destroy." Thus envisaged, the Revolution was neither a divine nor a diabolic, but quintessentially a *historical*, event —that is to say, a product of the past, a present in its own right, and a necessary element in the disposition of any future for Europe. Thus, while most of his contemporaries, both Liberal and Conservative, were beginning to arrive at a consensus over the uniformly vicious effects of any "unleashing" of the masses, and especially of their unleashing during the Revolution, Tocqueville continued to cultivate the realist's respect for both the Revolution and the masses, above all because they existed (and therefore had to be dealt with), and, second, because of what they revealed about men in general and about the relations among individuals of all classes and the social systems created to serve their needs.

৵§ Tragic Conflict from the Ironic Perspective

The protagonist of *The Old Regime* was the old regime itself, caught between the dead weight of its own past and its awareness of the changes necessary for its continued survival. It is too strong to say that Tocqueville actually personified the old regime and made of it the Tragic hero of his story, but there is a certain Lear-like quality about its dilemma. Tocqueville portrayed the monarchy and its sustaining institutions as impaled on the horns of a dilemma created by the logic of state centralization on the one hand and the logic of human aspiration on the other. He showed how the old regime attempted a number of reforms for bettering the conditions under which people of all classes had to live, but how, time after time, the proposed reforms ran afoul of contradictory commitments of the regime to particular parts of the social order; and how, when a given reform was undertaken, it merely promoted the demand for other reforms rather than satisfied the class or group in whose interest it had been undertaken. On the eve of the Revolution, France was a web of contradictions and paradoxes which promoted in the people a uniform feeling of hostility to the social system that nothing short of an attempt at total renovation could possibly assuage.

On the one hand was a nation in which the love of wealth and luxury was daily spreading; on the other a government that while constantly fomenting this passion, at the same time frustrated it—and by this fatal inconsistency was sealing its own doom. [179]

For many centuries, Tocqueville wrote, the French people had felt

a desire, inveterate and uncontrollable, utterly to destroy all such institutions as had survived from the Middle Ages and, having cleared the ground, to build up a new society in which men were as much alike and their status as equal as possible, allowing for the innate differences between individuals. The other ruling passion, more recent and less deeply rooted, was a desire to live not only on an equal footing but also as free men.

Toward the close of the Old Regime these two passions were equally sincerely felt and seemed equally operative. When the Revolution started, they came in contact, joined forces, coalesced, and reinforced each other, fanning the revolutionary ardor of the nation to a blaze. [208]

As thus presented, the Revolution was a product of the conflict between human consciousness and the social system; and, in its most general nature, it was an expression of a justified attempt to re-establish harmony between thought and feeling on the one hand and legal and political institutions on the other. It was a product neither of purely spiritual nor of purely material factors; nor was it a manifestation of some autonomous and determining metahistorical power. The main cause of the Revolution was a *sudden perception* on the part of Frenchmen that their ideal aspirations were no longer consonant with the social system that had served them adequately for the past two centuries.

In large part, this severance of consciousness from society was the result, Tocqueville wrote, of the intellectuals' criticism of the old regime. Their utopian visions had the effect of alienating the masses from the social order that purported to serve them best. Thus:

alongside the traditional and confused, not to say chaotic, social system of the day there was gradually built up in men's minds an imaginary ideal society in which all was simple, uniform, coherent, equitable, and rational in the fullest sense of the term. It was this vision of the perfect State that fired the imagination of the masses and little by little estranged them from the here-and-now. Turning away from the real world around them, they indulged in dreams of a far better one and ended up by living, spiritually, in the ideal world thought up by the writers. [146]

This utopianism was not justified, Tocqueville suggested, not because the old regime was not chaotic (for it was), but because the objective condition of the French people had been better in the years before the Revolution than it was for many decades after the Revolution. "A study of comparative statistics," Tocqueville wrote, "makes it clear that in none of the decades immediately following the Revolution did our national prosperity make such rapid forward strides as in the two preceding it" (174). The "paradox" in the situation was that this very increase in prosperity worked to the disadvantage of the regime that fostered it. Thus, in a characteristic passage Tocqueville remarked:

The belief that the greatness and power of a nation are products of its administrative machinery alone is, to say the least, shortsighted; however perfect that machinery, the driving force behind it is what counts. We have only to look at England, where the constitutional system is vastly more complicated, unwieldly, and erratic than that of France today. Yet is there any other European country whose national wealth is greater; where private ownership is more extensive, takes so many forms, and is so secure; where individual prosperity and a stable social system are so well allied? This is not due to the merits of any special laws but to the spirit animating the English constitution as a whole. That certain organs may be faulty matters little when the life force of the body politic has such vigor. [175]

He went on to indicate the effect on the populace of the "steadily increasing prosperity" of France immediately before the Revolution. This increasing prosperity "everywhere promoted a spirit of unrest," he argued. "The general public became more and more hostile to every ancient institution, more and more discontented; indeed, it was increasingly obvious that the nation was heading for a revolution." (*Ibid.*)

Tocqueville then turned to a consideration of the social situation in specific regions, contrasting the Ile-de-France, where the old order was most quickly uprooted by the demands for reform, and those areas of France where the methods of the past were maintained most rigidly, and pointing out that "it was precisely in those parts of France where there had been most improvement that popular discontent ran highest" (176). Continuing, he commented:

This may seem illogical—but history is full of such paradoxes. For it is not always when things are going from bad to worse that revolutions break out. On the contrary, it oftener happens that when a people which has put up with an oppressive rule over a long period without protest suddenly finds the government relaxing its pressure, it takes up arms against it. Thus the social order overthrown by a revolution is almost always better than the one immediately preceding it, and experience teaches us that, generally speaking, the most perilous moment for a bad government is one when it seeks to mend its ways. Only consummate statecraft can enable a King to save his throne when after a long spell of oppressive rule he sets to improving the lot of his subjects. Patiently endured so long as it seemed beyond redress, a grievance comes to appear intolerable once the possibility of removing it crosses men's minds. For the mere fact that certain abuses have been remedied draws attention to the others and they now appear more galling; people may suffer less, but their sensibility is exacerbated. At the height of its power feudalism did not inspire so much hatred as it did on the eve of its eclipse. In the reign of Louis XVI the most trivial pinpricks of arbitrary power caused more resentment than the thoroughgoing despotism of Louis XIV. The brief imprisonment of Beaumarchais shocked Paris more than the *dragonnades* of 1685.

In 1780 there could no longer be any talk of France's being on the downgrade; on the contrary, it seemed that no limit could be set to her advance. And it was now that theories of the perfectibility of man and continuous progress came into fashion. Twenty years earlier there had been no hope for the future; in 1789 no anxiety was felt about it. Dazzled by the prospect of a felicity undreamed of hitherto and now within their grasp, people were blind to the very real improvement that had taken place and eager to precipitate events. [177]

What these passages suggest is a conception of the laws of social change similar to those met with in Greek Tragedy, the laws by which those whose condition of life is improving should look to the advent of some calamity, usually a product of the overextension of their own limited capacities for understanding the world or for looking at it and themselves "realistically." At the same time, Tocqueville invoked an Organicist metaphor to characterize the powers of the old regime and the forces which failed it in its time of trial.

It would seem that in all human institutions, as in the human body, there is a hidden source of energy, the life principle itself, independent of the organs which perform the various functions needed for survival; once this vital flame burns low, the whole organism languishes and wastes away, and though the organs seem to function as before, they serve no useful purpose. [79]

Once this "hidden source of energy" dried up, the old regime was propelled upon a path leading to its own self-destruction; no matter what it did, it could only contribute to its own demise. Its very efforts to improve its position created that social condition of atomization against which men were naturally inclined to rebel.

Once the bourgeois had been completely severed from the noble, and the peasant from both alike, and when a similar differentiation had taken place within each of these three classes, with the result that each was split up into a number of small groups almost completely shut off from each other, the inevitable consequence was that although the nation came to seem a homogeneous whole, its parts no longer held together. Nothing had been left that could obstruct the central government, but, by the same token, nothing could shore it up. This is why the grandiose edifice built up by our Kings was doomed to collapse like a card castle once disturbances arose within the social order on which it was based. [136–37]

And, from these generalizations, Tocqueville went on to remark Ironically on the failure of his own generation to learn anything from these experiences:

In the event this nation, which alone seems to have learned wisdom from the errors and failings of its former rulers, has been unable, though it so effectively shook off their domination, to rid itself of the false notions, bad habits, and pernicious tendencies which they had given it or allowed it to acquire. Sometimes, indeed, we find it displaying a slave mentality in the very exercise of its freedom, and as incapable of governing itself as it was once intractable vis à vis its masters. [137]

These passages reveal Tocqueville's ability to move with serene assurance from economic, to social, to political, to psychological factors, considering them all as different aspects of the single historical process, giving to each its proper weight, and, on principle, ruling out none as an active force. They contain, however, a number of assumptions about the actions of individuals as functions of class membership alone, signs of methodologically limiting preconceptions about a static human nature, and hints of class loyalty and ideological preference. Tocqueville purported to stand above the battle, and so he did. But he was by no means the sympathetic observer of all the forces engaged in it. He was, rather, the impartial judge of persons caught in the operations of forces and situations of which they had not the slightest understanding.

ᴥᔥ *The Ironic Resolution of the Revolutionary Drama*

At the same time, however, Tocqueville presented the transition from old to new as a process in which the *worst* elements of the past would be saved as aspects of the achieved present. Like Michelet and Ranke, Tocqueville discovered the lines of continuity which linked his own age to that of the old regime. But this continuity constituted a dubious legacy; it was made up of the tendency toward state centralization and the love of equality. Unfortunately, he pointed out, these two factors are *not* antithetical. The French nation, he maintained, was inclined to suffer, in any government, "practices and principles that are, in fact, the tools of despotism" so long as that government "favors and flatters its desire for equality" (210).

Another, more tenuous thread was conceived to link the present with the past, a thread made up of what Tocqueville called "the desire for freedom" (*ibid.*). While the impulse toward state centralization and the love of equality had been continuous and growing, the desire for freedom had waxed and waned: "On several occasions during the period extending from the outbreak of the Revolution up to our own time we find the desire for freedom reviving, succumbing, then returning, only to die out once more and presently blaze up again" (*ibid.*). Neither state centralization nor the love of equality was the necessary carrier of the desire for freedom, the former for obvious reasons, the latter because its devotees tended to be zealous, obstinate, and "often blind, ready to make every concession to those who give it satisfaction" (*ibid.*).

Wherein, then, lay the hope for freedom in the future? Tocqueville purported to find it in the *anomalous* character of the French people themselves, a character which had given birth to and succored the tradition of revolution.

It hardly seems possible that there can ever have existed any other people so full of contrasts and so extreme in all their doings, so much guided by their emotions and so little by fixed principles, always behaving better, or worse, than one expected of them. At one time they rank above, at another below, the norm of humanity; . . . So long as no one thinks of resisting, you can lead [the Frenchman] on a thread, but once a revolutionary movement is afoot, nothing can restrain him from taking part in it. . . . Thus the French are at once the most brilliant and the most dangerous of all European nations, and the best qualified to become, in the eyes of other peoples, an object of admiration, of hatred, of compassion, or alarm—never of indifference. [210–11]

In their unpredictability, their infinite variety, and their extremism, the French constitute a veritable antitype to the American people, and Tocqueville left no doubt that he found much to commend in them. But he did not endow the French people with the characteristics of a divine mystery, as did Michelet. The anomalous nature of the French people had its origins in discernible historical causes, some of which Tocqueville set forth in *The Old Regime*. But he viewed the French as the custodians *par excellence* of the *revolutionary tradition* which might save Europe from anarchy and tyranny. This tradition was the solvent to the vices of egalitarianism in its extreme form, a counter-poise to the excesses of political centralization, an antidote to any impulse to return to the past or remain content with the present, and the best guarantor of the continued growth of human freedom in the future.

~§ The Attempt to Resist the Ideological Implications of the Ironic Viewpoint

Tocqueville valued order more than he valued freedom, but he never allowed his love of order to appear as a significant argument for resisting social change, as Burke had done earlier and the Hegelian Right did in Tocqueville's own time. In fact, Tocqueville's personal admiration for Hegel's moral philosophy was seriously undermined, when, during a visit to Germany in 1854, he saw the uses to which Hegel's thought had been put by the "ruling powers" in Prussia. In a letter written during that year, he pointed out that Hegelianism, as currently interpreted, "asserted that, in a political sense, all established facts ought to be submitted to as legitimate; and that the very circumstance of their existence was sufficient to make obedience to them a duty" (*Memoir*, II, 270). In short, Hegelianism, as Tocqueville encountered it a quarter of a century after Hegel's death, seemed to make of the status quo a deity. And this offended Tocqueville's conviction of the essential historicity of everything, of the right of men to render judgment on anything received from the past and to revise it in the light of changing circumstances and human needs. He was equally repelled by the racist doctrines of his friend Gobineau, but for a different reason. Gobineau made of a remote, mythic past a deity every bit as tyrannical as the "Hegelianized" present of Prussia.

The Ironic historiography of the late Enlightenment did not die out with the transition to the period of *Stürm und Dräng* and Romanticism; it was simply pushed into the background. An Ironic conception of history underlies de Maistre's antirevolutionary jeremiads, Chateaubriand's doleful reflections on Europe's fall from Christian faith, Kierkegaard's neo-orthodoxy, Stirner's nihilism, and Schopenhauer's philosophy, which, in large part, is little more than the Ironic answer to Hegel's Comic emplotment of the whole world process. But the Ironic approach to history did not succeed in establishing itself as a serious alternative to the Romantic and Comic approaches until after mid-century, when, like Schopenhauer's philosophy itself, it took hold as an alternative to the "naiveté" of historians like Michelet and Ranke and the conceptually overdetermined "philosophy of history" of Marx and Engels. In the atmosphere of "realism" which characterized European academic scholarship, art, and literature after the revolutions of 1848–51, the Ironic perspective on history everywhere succeeded both the Romantic and Comic perspectives as the dominant mode of thought and expression. And this perspective sanctioned the "*Staatsraison*" school of nationalist historiography represented by Treitschke and Von Sybel; the "Positivist" school represented by Taine, Buckle, and the Social Darwinists; and the "Aestheticist" school represented by Renan, Burckhardt, and Pater.

Tocqueville fully recognized the appeal of an Ironic conception of history, and foresaw its advent. In the early 1850s, he discerned it in the work of his friend, Arthur de Gobineau, and he tried to contrive an alternative, Tragic conception of history which, while granting the justification of the Ironic insight, would transcend it and provide the grounds for a modest hope for his own generation at least.

✌️ Criticism of Gobineau

In his now famous *Essai sur l'inégalité des races humaines,* Gobineau unqualifiedly rejected the myths of progress which sustained the Romantic and Comic conceptions of history alike. Far from viewing either the immediate (revolutionary) past or his own present as a *culmination* of a long drama of human liberation, Gobineau viewed the whole of history as one long "fall" from a presumed age of racial purity into the degenerate condition of universal racial corruption and "mongrelization." The voice in which Gobineau spoke was that of the pure Ironist, with its insistence upon the writer's own hard realism and unflinching recognition of "the facts" of life and history. In response to criticisms of the "corruptive" nature of his book, Gobineau wrote:

If I am corrupting at all, I corrupt with acids and not with perfumes. Believe me that this is not at all the purpose of my book. I am not telling people: "You are acquitted" or "You are condemned"; I tell them: "You are dying." . . . What I say is that you have spent your youth and that you have now reached the age of decline. Your autumn is more vigorous, undoubtedly, than has been the decrepitude of the rest of the world, but it is autumn nonetheless; the winter will come and you will have no children. [Gobineau to Tocqueville, 1856, in Tocqueville, ER, 284–85]

The contrast between the mood of this passage and that of Constant, cited earlier as an example of the Nihilism of postrevolutionary despair, is manifest. Constant's tone was melancholy, that of Gobineau perversely cold and objectivist. Whereas the former reported an impression, the latter asserted a scientific truth. Gobineau, like many other historians of the 1850s and afterward, claimed to be acting only as a diagnostician of social processes, not as a poet or a prophet:

By telling you what is happening and what is going to happen, am I taking something away from you? I am not a murderer; neither is the doctor who announces the coming of the end. If I am wrong, nothing will remain of my four volumes. If I am right, the facts will not be subdued by the desire of those who do not want to face them. [285]

Tocqueville's principal objections to Gobineau's theories were ethical; he feared the effect they would have on the spirit of his own age. In 1853,

Tocqueville wrote to Gobineau: "Don't you see how inherent in your doctrine are all the evils produced by permanent inequality: pride, violence scorn of one's fellow men, tyranny and abjection in every one of its forms?" (229). Gobineau's doctrines, Tocqueville argued, were merely a modern, Materialistic version of Calvinist fatalism (227). "Do you really believe," Tocqueville asked Gobineau, "that by tracing the destiny of peoples along these lines you can truly clarify history? And that our knowledge about humans becomes more certain as we abandon the practice followed since the beginning of time by the many great minds who have searched to find the cause of human events in the influence of certain men, of certain emotions, of certain thoughts, and of certain beliefs?" (228). The difference between Tocqueville's own approach to history and that of Gobineau was the difference, Tocqueville insisted, between a method which depended on "facts" and one which depended on "theories" alone (Letter of 1855, 268). The former yielded the truth, the latter only opinion, an opinion, moreover, which was characteristic of generations having to adjust to postrevolutionary conditions that inspired feelings of depression and pessimism without any prodding from historians (Letter of 1853, 231).

To these objections, Gobineau responded that, on the contrary, it was he who dealt in "facts" rather than in the moral implications of the truths revealed through his discovery of the facts. In a letter dated 1856, he wrote: "My book is research, exposition, presentation of facts. These facts exist or they do not. There is nothing else to say" (Gobineau to Tocqueville, 1856, 286). To this Tocqueville responded:

You profoundly distrust mankind, at least *our* kind; you believe that it is not only decadent but incapable of ever lifting itself up again. Our very physical constitution, according to you, condemns us to servitude. It is, then, very logical that, to maintain at least some order in such a mob, government of the sword and even of the whip seems to have some merit in your eyes. . . . For myself, I do not think that I have either the right or the inclination to entertain such opinions about my race and my country. I believe that one should not despair of them. To me, human societies, like persons, become something worth while only through their use of liberty. I have always said that it is more difficult to stabilize and to maintain liberty in our new democratic societies than in certain aristocratic societies of the past. But I shall never dare to think it impossible. And I pray to God lest He inspire me with the idea that one might as well despair of trying. No, I shall not believe that this human race, which is at the head of all visible creation, has become that bastardized flock of sheep which you say it is, and that nothing remains but to deliver it without future and without hope to a small number of shepherds who, after all, are not better animals than are we, the human sheep, and who indeed are often worse. [Tocqueville to Gobineau, 1857, 309–10]

This last passage points to the essentially ethical bases of Tocqueville's own conception of historical knowledge, which, far from being a disinterested inquiry into the facts "for themselves alone," was *nothing but* that search for the superhistorical standpoint which the writer of Tragedy seeks to gain for himself and his readers and from consideration of which the representatives of the different parties in the political arena might be reconciled to the *limited* character of all human knowledge and the *provisional* nature of all solutions to the problem of social construction.

If the Comic conception of history produces the historiography of social accommodation, the Tragic conception is the basis of what might be called the historiography of social mediation. The Ironic perspective has a mediative aspect, when it is written in the spirit of benign Satire, which is the point of view which begins beyond the Comic resolution. But, in general, Ironic historiography begins on the other side of Tragedy, with that second look which the writer takes *after* the truths of Tragedy have been registered and even *their* inadequacy has been perceived. Tocqueville sought to resist the fall, out of a condition of Tragic reconciliation with the harsh truths revealed by reflection on the history of the modern age, into that resentment which was on the basis of Gobineau's Ironic historiography and that spirit of accommodation to "things as they are" which inspired Ranke's Comic historiography.

The Fall into Irony

In his *Souvenirs*, written in 1850, Tocqueville looked back upon the history of his country from 1789 to 1830. This history appeared to him, he said, *"comme le tableau d'une lutte acharnée qui s'était livrée pendant quarante et un ans entre l'ancien régime, les traditions, ses souvenirs, ses espérances et ses hommes représentés par l'aristocratie, et la France nouvelle conduite par la classe moyenne."* By 1830, Tocqueville remarked, the triumph of the *"classe moyenne"* over the *"aristocratie"* was "definitive." All that had remained of the *ancien régime*, of both its vices and its virtues, had been dissolved. Such was the *"physionomie générale de cette époque."* (30)

The mood of *Souvenirs* is different from that which pervades *Democracy in America*, published some fifteen years earlier. And it is different from that which pervades the correspondence with Gobineau. For, in *Souvenirs*, the Ironic perspective replaced the Tragic standpoint from which *Democracy in America* was composed. In *Souvenirs* Tocqueville gave full vent to the despair which he forbade himself to show to Gobineau and to which he refused to give full expression in his public reflections on French history. His *Souvenirs*, Tocqueville noted, were not meant to be *"une peinture que je destine au public,"* but rather *"un délassement de mon esprit et non point une oeuvre de littérature."* The work on the Revolution which the historian planned to put before the public had to assay "objectively" what had been gained and what had been lost by the Revolution itself.

In *Democracy in America* (1835–40), Tocqueville had insisted that though much had been lost by the growth of "the democratic principle" in both Europe and America, much had been gained also; and, on balance, he argued, the gain had been worth the loss. Thus, the turmoil of the years 1789–1830 in Europe might be seen as bringing into being not only a new social order but also a kind of social wisdom capable of guiding men to the realization of a new and better life. But, by the time Tocqueville had begun plans for the second volume of his history of the fall of the *ancien régime* and the advent of the Revolution, his earlier hope and the Stoic resignation which had succeeded it had given place to a despair not unlike that which pervades Gobineau's reflections on history in general.

By 1856, the year of the publication of the first volume of *The Old Regime and the Revolution*, the mediative tone had been diminished considerably. The stated purpose of this work was "to make clear in what respects [the present social system] resembles and in what it differs from the social system that preceded it; and to determine what was lost and what was gained by that vast upheaval" (xi). The social context that had seemed to justify the qualified optimism of the 1830s had by the 1850s changed so much, in Tocqueville's view, that he now had difficulty justifying little more than a *cautious* pessimism. Yet the faith of the Tragic writer was still alive. He was convinced that the fall of the old regime, the Revolution, and its aftermath reflected the operations of social processes which, if objectively determined, could still be instructive and moderating of the passions and prejudices which they engendered. There was still an *acceptance* of the Revolution and its ideals as manifestations of social processes which could not be ignored and which it would be madness to resent and folly to try to circumvent. The hope of the first book had given way to resignation in the second.

In his notes on the Revolution, however, Tocqueville wrote: "A new and terrible thing has come into the world, an immense new sort of revolution whose toughest agents are the least literate and the most vulgar classes, while they are incited and their laws written by intellectuals" (*ER*, 161). Something new had been born, but not the self-adjusting and self-regulating social system which Ranke discerned, from his secure position in Berlin, on the far side of the Revolution—a "new and terrible thing" with potentialities for good and evil. To determine the nature of this "new and terrible thing" and the laws which governed it, so as to be able to divine its likely future development, remained the aim of Tocqueville's work as a historian throughout his career. The tone and mood of his work tended consistently toward Irony and pessimism, but the point of view remained Tragic. The law which the spectacle displayed to historical consciousness was not contemplated in the perverse mood of Gobineau, who delighted in the havoc it portended for Europe and the world, but in the constant effort to bring it to consciousness so that it could be turned to social good.

Tocqueville tried to resist, to the end, the impulse to make of a specific age in the historical record the criterion by which all others might be judged and condemned. And he tried to maintain the same open-mindedness with respect to all social classes. But, even though he professed to have "hope" for the lower orders, he had no faith in them. In 1848, in what can only be called a mood of benign skepticism, he wrote:

Our condition is indeed very serious; still the good sense and feeling of the masses leave some room for hope. Till now, their conduct has been above all praise; and if they had only leaders capable of turning these good dispositions to account, and of directing them, we soon should get rid of all these dangerous and impracticable theories, and place the Republic on the only durable foundation, that of liberty and right. [*Memoir*, II, 91]

Because he was a Liberal in his personal political convictions (and hence *welcomed change on principle*) and an aristocrat who had lived through many revolutions (and hence knew from experience that there could be no change without suffering), Tocqueville brought to his reflections on history a more "realistic" attitude than did Michelet. But, as in Michelet, the tone of his work became more melancholy near the end of his life and more Reactionary for being so. And the reason why Tocqueville was not appreciated fully by the generation which followed is not difficult to seek. The Tragic realism which he had cultivated from the beginning was too ambiguous to be appreciated by an age in which ambiguity had no place. The revolutions of 1848 destroyed the middle ground upon which Liberalism had flourished since the eighteenth century. In the following age historians, like everyone else, had to take a stand for or against revolution and to decide to read history with either a Conservative or a Radical eye. The vision of Tocqueville, like that of Hegel, seemed far too flexible, too ambivalent, too tolerant, to thinkers who felt the necessity to choose in philosophy between Schopenhauer and Spencer, in literature between Baudelaire and Zola, and in historical thought between Ranke and Marx.

ᴥ§ Conclusion

I have praised Tocqueville as an exponent of a tragic-realist conception of history and as the heir of that synthetic-analytic historicism which found its highest theoretical expression in Hegel. Like Hegel, Tocqueville turned his vision on the social nexus as the prime phenomenon of historical process; but he found in it primarily the point where human consciousness and external exigencies meet, conflict, and *fail* to find their resolution in an essentially progressive unfolding of human freedom. All thought of supernatural or transcendental cause was exorcised from his historical reflections, but at the same time Tocqueville resisted the temptation to explain human actions by reference to physicochemical impulse. For him, nature played a role in history, but as stage, means, passive restriction on social possibilities, rather than as determinant. According to Tocqueville, human consciousness, reason as well as will, operate as the main forces of history, working always against the social fabric inherited from past ages, seeking to transform it in the light of an imperfect human knowledge to future advantage. Although an individualist in his ethical ideals, Tocqueville resisted both the Promethean and the Sisyphean conceptions of human possibilities which informed Romantic thought in its two main phases. In Tocqueville's conception of history, as in that of his great counterpart in the novel, Balzac, man springs from nature, creates a society adequate to his immediate needs out of his reason and will, and then engages in a fatal combat with this, his own creation, to provide the drama of historical change. Historical knowledge serves, as it did for Hegel, as a factor in the issue of this combat at specific times and places. By placing man in his own present and informing him of the forces with which and against which he must militate in the winning of his kingdom here on earth, historical knowledge moves from the contemplation of the past as dead to the past as living in the present, turns man's attention to this demon in his midst, and tries to exorcise his fear of it, showing it to be his own creation and thus potentially subject to his will. But, in the end, Tocqueville was forced to admit that the drama of human history was neither a Tragic nor a Comic one, but a drama of *degeneration*, the very kind of drama which he had criticized Gobineau for presenting to public view.

Tocqueville is often denied the title of historian and is either relegated or elevated to the position of a sociologist, largely because his interest in historical details is continually dissolved in a more intense interest in typologies, or because he *seemed* more interested in structure and continuity than in process or diachronic variation. But, while such distinctions as those between historians and sociologists may be helpful in the effort to locate the point of emergence of new disciplines in the history of the human sciences, they are potentially invidious, and almost always destructive of a proper appreciation of an individual thinker's contribution to human thought. In Tocqueville's case, the attempt to locate him definitively among the historians or the sociologists is really anachronistic, since *in his own time* there was nothing inconsistent in a historian's attempt to rise above a mere interest in the past to a theoretical analysis of the forces which made of individual events elements of general processes. This attempt was in the best tradition of pre-Romantic historiography and was perfectly consistent with Hegel's analysis of what historians actually did in the construction of their narratives. More important, it *was* Hegelian in its refusal to remain content with a mere contemplation of how *this* grew out of *that*, in its desire to discover the general principles which linked the lived present with the known past and to *name* those principles in terms of classical principles derived from the Tragic awareness of man's struggle with inherited social forms.

Before Tocqueville, many Liberal, Conservative, and Radical historians were content to take the fact of revolution as a datum and to give themselves over, all unconsciously, to the construction of alternative—doctrinaire Liberal, Conservative, Radical, or Reactionary—accounts of *how* the Revolution had happened, and, in the best cases, *why* it happened as it did. Tocqueville moved the debate back one step, to the prior question of *whether* the Revolution had in fact happened or not—that is to say, to the question of whether or not a revolution had *actually occurred*. And he raised this question not as a semantic exercise but as a genuine inquiry into the ultimate nature of things in the historical world, as an inquiry into the ways in which things ought to be *named*. This denaming of complex events like the Revolution or American democracy, this attempt to lay bare the complexities obscured by premature or imperfect linguistic usage, was much more Radical than any doctrinaire approach to "what actually happened" in different times and places could be. For, whereas the latter exercise leaves untouched the ideological bases of disagreement over "what actually happened," and merely serves a confirming function for the parties for which and in whose behalf it is written, Tocqueville's questioning of traditional linguistic usage in the characterization of complex historical events drives thought to the margins of human choice, deprives the individual of the comforts of familiar usage, and forces the reader to decide for himself "what actually happened" in terms of what he desires to happen in his own future, asking him to choose between a comfortable drifting on history's stream and a struggle against its currents.

Tocqueville's historical analyses are, contrary to the commonly held view that he sociologized history, actually de-reifying of language in their effect. Such is the effect of any genuinely Ironic conception of history. For, in the interplay of the components of its fractured vision of the present, Irony invites the reader who is sensitive to its appeal to give his own name to the past by choosing a future in the interest of his own immediately felt present needs, desires, and aspirations. Nothing could be more liberating than Tocqueville's mediating historicism, for it places the "meaning" of historical events such as the Revolution and the rise of democracy, not in the past or the present, but in the future, in the future chosen by the individual who has been purified by the revelation of the past's inherent ambiguity.

Tocqueville's intuited conception of historical writing as a creative denaming, in the interests of moral ambiguity, ultimately made him a Liberal—and one with his great British contemporary J. S. Mill. In his essay "Nature," Mill wrote:

The only admissible moral theory of Creation is that the Principle of God cannot at once and altogether subdue the powers of evil, either physical or moral; could not place mankind in a world free from the necessity of an incessant struggle with the malificent powers, or make them always victorious in that struggle, but could and did make them capable of carrying on the fight with vigor and with progressively increasing success. [386]

Such a theory, Mill held, "seems much better adapted to nerving [the individual] to exertion than a vague and inconsistent reliance on an Author of Good who is supposed to be also the author of Evil" (387). And, in his essay "The Utility of Religion," Mill suggested that there is "only one form of belief in the supernatural" which

stands wholly clear of intellectual contradictions and of moral obliquity. It is that which, resigning irrevocably the idea of an omnipotent creator, regards Nature and Life not as the expression throughout of a moral character and purpose of the Diety, but as the product of a struggle between contriving goodness and an intractable material, as was believed by Plato, or a Principle of Evil, as was the doctrine of the Manichaeans. [428]

In such a dualistic conception of the world process, Mill claimed,

a virtuous human being assumes . . . the exalted character of a fellow laborer with the Highest, a fellow combatant in the great strife, contributing his little, which by the aggregation of men like himself becomes much, toward that progressive ascendancy and ultimately complete triumph of good over evil which history points to, and which this doctrine teaches us to regard as planned by the Being to whom we owe all the benevolent contrivance we behold in nature. [*Ibid.*]

I have quoted these passages from Mill because, in spite of their impeccable credentials as Liberal sources, they might well have been written by Tocqueville. Tocqueville found a place in the Liberal pantheon by virtue of his addition of a historical dimension to this typically Liberal ethical Manicheanism. Tocqueville's idea of history suggests a dualism whose constituent terms are dialectically related but in which there is no possibility of a specifiable final synthesis. The human advantages of such a dualism are manifest, for, as Mill said of the Manichean creed, the evidence for it is shadowy and unsubstantial (that is to say, nondogmatic) and the promises of reward which it holds out to men are distant and uncertain (and hence make little appeal to simple self-interest).

One can question neither the motives nor the aims of the ethical Manichean. Suspended between conflicting forces, deprived of any hope of an easy victory, the believer in this creed turns whatever talent he has and whatever power his profession or vocation gives him to the service of the good *as he sees it*. At the same time, he recognizes the legitimacy and truth of what *appears to him* as evil. Suspended between two abysses, he *may* indulge himself in the unprovable hypothesis of life after death; but he regards this as a possibility as much open to his enemies as to himself. And, if the Manichean succeeds in becoming a Liberal, he gives up this hypothesis, and contents himself with service to a humanity that has neither a known origin nor a perceivable goal, but only a set of tasks immediately before it, generation by generation. By his choices, the Liberal constitutes this humanity as an essence. By self-criticism and criticism of others, he seeks to assure the *gradual* development of a complex human inheritance. By progressive denaming, by successive revelations of the complex reality that underlies familiar names, inherited with the institutional baggage they specify, the Liberial historicist succors a tragic-realist vision of the world, and, by dissolving the impulse to *absolute* commitment, Ironically labors for a minimal but hopeful freedom for his heirs.

Chapter 6   BURCKHARDT: HISTORICAL REALISM AS SATIRE

⤶§ Introduction

As we move from the Romantic and Comic, to the Tragic and Ironic, representations of history, and from processionary, or diachronic, history to structural, or synchronic, history, the element of theme tends to override the element of plot, at least insofar as plot may be conceived to be the strategy by which an *unfolding* story is articulated. Michelet and Ranke confronted history as a *story that develops*. Tocqueville conceived it as an exchange between irreconcilable elements in human nature and society; to him, history moved toward the collision of great forces in the historian's present or immediate future. Burckhardt, however, saw nothing developing; for him, things coalesced to form a fabric of greater or lesser brilliance and intensity, greater or lesser freedom or oppression, more or less movement. From time to time conditions conspired with genius to produce a brilliant spectacle of creativity, in which even politics and religion took on the aspect of "arts." But, in Burckhardt's estimation, there was no *progressive* evolution in artistic sensibility, and in the end nothing but oppression stemmed from political and religious impulses. The truths taught by history were melancholy ones. They led neither to hope nor to action. They did not even suggest that humanity itself would *endure*.

"Irony," Vico said in his discussion of the tropes, "could not have begun until the period of reflection, because it is fashioned of falsehood by dint of a reflection which wears the mask of truth" (*NS*, 408: 131). In his theory of the cycles (*corsi*) through which civilizations pass from their beginnings to their ends (the ages of gods, of heroes, and of men), Irony is the mode of consciousness which signals the final dissolution. Thus, Vico said in the Conclusion of *The New Science*, speaking of times such as the late Roman Empire:

> As the popular states became corrupt, so also did the philosophies. They descended into scepticism. Learned fools fell to calumniating the truth. There arose a false eloquence, ready to uphold either of the opposed sides of a case indifferently. Thus it came about that, by abuse of eloquence like that of the tribunes of the plebs at Rome, when the citizens were no longer content with making wealth the basis of rank, they strove to make it an instrument of power. And as the furious south winds whip up the sea, so these citizens provoked civil wars in their commonwealths and drove them to total disorder. Thus they caused the commonwealths to fall from a perfect liberty into the perfect tyranny of anarchy or the unchecked liberty of the free peoples, which is the worst of all tyrannies. [1102: 423]

It should be noted that Vico listed Irony among the four master tropes by which a specific *kind* of linguistic protocol can be constituted, that in which it has become customary "to say one thing and mean another." Irony is fashioned, he stressed, "of falsehood" by dint of "a reflection which wears the mask of truth." Evidences of the crystallization of an Ironic language are the rise of skepticism in philosophy, of the sophistic in public speaking, and of the kind of argument that Plato called "eristic" in political discourse. Underlying this mode of speech is a recognition of the fractured nature of social being, of the duplicity and self-serving of politicians, of an egotism which governs all professions of interest in the common good, of naked power (*dratos*) ruling where law and morality (*ethos*) are being invoked to justify actions. Ironic language, as Hegel remarked later, is an expression of the "unhappy consciousness," of the man who acts as if he is free but knows that he is bound to a power outside himself, this power being a tyrant which is as little interested in the freedom of the subject as it is in the health of the *res publica* in general.

A central theme of Ironic literature, Frye remarks, is the disappearance of the heroic (*Anatomy*, 228). There is an element of Irony in every literary style or mode—in Tragedy and Comedy by virtue of the "double vision" that informs them, to be sure, but also in Romance to a certain extent, at least insofar as the Romantic writer takes the fact of struggle seriously enough to allow his readers to entertain the *possibility* of the triumph of the blocking forces in the end. But in Ironic literature in general, this double vision degenerates (or is elevated) into a debilitating second nature, which looks for the worm in the fruit of virtue everywhere—and finds it.

"Irony is the non-heroic residue of tragedy," Frye continues, which centers on "a theme of puzzled defeat" (224). In its benign form, as met with in the early Hume, it entertains the spectacle of human frustration and inadequacy within the framework of a general satisfaction with the current social establishment. And in this form, it *tends* toward the Comic mode, concentrating on the "unmasking" of folly wherever it appears and contenting itself with the general truth that, even in the most heroic personality, one can find evidence of at least a minimal folly. In its most extreme form, however, when Irony arises in an atmosphere of social breakdown or cultural demise, it tends toward an Absurdist view of the world. Nothing is more Ironic than the early Existentialist philosophy of Sartre, in which the emphasis is everywhere placed on man's capacities for "bad faith," for betrayal of himself and others; in which the world is entertained as a spectacle of brutal self-servitude, and commitment to "others" is regarded as a form of death.

Ironic styles have generally predominated during periods of wars against superstition, whether the superstitions in question be identified as naive religious faith, the power of the monarchy, the privileges of aristocracy, or the self-satisfaction of the bourgeoisie. Irony represents the passage of the age of heroes and of the capacity to believe in heroism. This anti-heroism is what makes it the "antithesis" of Romanticism. When it begins, however, on the other side of a Tragic apprehension of the world, with a survey of what has been left *after* the hero's *agon* with the gods, fate, or his fellowmen, it tends to stress the dark underside of life, the view "from below." From this perspective, Frye notes, Irony stresses the "human, all-too human" aspect of what was formerly seen as heroic and the destructive aspect of all seemingly epic encounters. This is Irony in its "realistic" phase (237). Tocqueville represented this phase of the Ironic attitude in his last work—in his *Souvenirs* and in the notes on the Revolution written just before his death.

When the implications of Irony "on the other side of Tragedy" are pushed to their logical conclusions, and the fatalistic element in human life is raised to the status of a metaphysical belief, thought tends to revert to and to see the world in the imagery of the *wheel*, eternal recurrence, closed cycles from which there is no escape. Frye calls this apprehension of the world the Irony of Bondage; this is the nightmare of social tyranny rather than the dream of redemption, a "demonic epiphany" (238–39). Consciousness turns itself to the contemplation of the "city of dreadful night" and Ironically destroys all belief in both the ideal goal of man and any quest for a substitute for the lost ideal. This is why we may say, with Frye, that "*sparagmos,* or the sense that heroism and effective action are absent, disorganized or foredoomed to defeat, and that confusion and anarchy reign over the world, is the archetypal theme of irony and satire" (192).

The linguistic mode of the Ironic consciousness reflects a doubt in the capacity of language itself to render adequately what perception gives and thought constructs about the nature of reality. It develops in the context of an awareness of a fatal asymmetry between the processes of reality and *any* verbal characterization of those processes. Thus, as Frye indicates, it tends toward a *kind* of symbolism, in the same way that Romanticism does. But unlike Romanticism, Irony does not seek the ultimate metaphor, the metaphor of metaphors, by which to signify the essence of life. For, since it is stripped of all "illusions," it has lost all belief in "essences" themselves. Thus Irony tends in the end to turn upon word play, to become a language about language, so as to dissolve the bewitchment of consciousness caused by language itself. It is suspicious of *all* formulas, and it delights in exposing the paradoxes contained in every attempt to capture experience in language. It tends to dispose the fruits of consciousness in aphorisms, apothegms, gnomic utterances which turn back upon themselves and dissolve their own apparent truth and adequacy. In the end, it conceives the world as trapped within a prison made of language, the world as a "forest of symbols." It sees no way out of this forest, and so it contents itself with the explosion of all formulas, all myths, in the interest of pure "contemplation" and resignation to the world of "things as they are."

✑ Burckhardt: The Ironic Vision

The German philosopher and historian of ideas Karl Löwith argued that it was only with Burckhardt that the "idea of history" was finally liberated from myth, and from that nefarious "philosophy of history" spawned by the confusion of myth with historical knowledge which had dominated historical thought from the early Middle Ages to the middle of the nineteenth century (*Meaning*, 26). Löwith did not see that the urbanity, the wit, the "realism," the desire to see "things as they are," and the Reactionary implications of knowledge as pure "seeing" which Burckhardt promoted were themselves elements of a specific kind of mythic consciousness. Burckhardt liberated historical thinking not from myth but only from the myths of history which had captured the imaginations of his age, the myths of Romance, Comedy, and Tragedy. But in the process of liberating thought from these myths, he consigned it to the care of another, the *mythos* of Satire, in which historical knowledge is definitively separated from any relevance to the social and cultural problems of its own time and place. In Satire, history becomes a "work of art," but the concept of art which is presupposed in this formula is a purely "contemplative" one—Sisyphean rather than Promethean, passive rather than active, resigned rather than heroically turned to the illumination of current human life.

In general, there are two views on Burckhardt as historian. One sees him as a sensitive commentator on the degeneration of culture as a result of the nationalization, industrialization, and massification of society. The other sees him as a fine intelligence possessed of an inadequate vision of history as *developmental process* and *causal analysis* resulting from a not very deeply buried Schopenhauerian conception of human nature, the world, and knowledge. The first view is inclined to overlook Burckhardt's shortcomings as a theorist in the interest of praising his "perception," and it makes of his doctrine of "seeing" (*Anschauen*) a historical method of timeless value. The second view homes in on Burckhardt's inadequacies as a philosopher and social theorist, criticizes the one-sidedness of his historical, as well as his ethical, ideas, and tends to relegate him to the status of a representative of his times, rather than to take seriously his ideas about the nature of the historical process.

The truth does not lie "between" these two views but beneath both of them. For the former, laudatory conception of Burckhardt's achievement obscures the ethical and ideological implications of the epistemological position that yields to Burckhardt both the originality of his conception of history and the authenticity of his way of writing it. And the second, derogatory conception of his achievement obscures the aesthetic justification of the ethical principles that it correctly exposes as evidence of Burckhardt's essential nihilism, egotism, and reactionary ideological position.

Burckhardt's historical vision began in that condition of Irony in which Tocqueville's ended. The enthusiasm of Romance, the optimism of Comedy, and the resignation of a Tragic apprehension of the world were not for him. Burckhardt surveyed a world in which virtue was usually betrayed, talent perverted, and power turned to service of the baser cause. He found very little virtue in his own time, and nothing to which he could give unqualified allegiance. His only devotion was to "the culture of *old* Europe." But he contemplated this culture of old Europe as a ruin. It was to him like one of those crumbling Roman monuments which stand in the midst of a Poussin landscape, all covered over with vines and grasses, resisting its reconfiscation by the "nature" against which it had been erected. He had no hope of restoring this ruin. He was satisfied simply to remember it.

But Burckhardt's attitude toward the past was not uncritical. Unlike Herder (whom he cited often, and approvingly), he was no uncritical advocate of everything old. Unlike Ranke, he entertained no illusions about things always working out for the best in the long run and in such a way as to translate private vice into public benefit. Unlike Tocqueville, he did not suppress his privately held worst fears, in the hope that reason and judicious language could contribute to the salvaging of something valuable from present conflicts. And—needless to say—unlike Michelet, he felt no *enthusiasm* for anything, for either the struggle or the prize. Burckhardt was ironic about everything, even himself. He did not really believe in his own seriousness.

In his youth Burckhardt flirted with Liberal causes. He lost the Protestant faith of his fathers, and at an early age he came to regard the Liberal heritage as a fitting substitute for religion. But his new Liberalism was—as his old religious convictions had been—an intellectual, rather than an existential, commitment. He looked down on politics as unsuited to the tastes of a gentleman; like business, politics distracted one from that assiduous cultivation of style in life which he admired in the ancient Greeks and the Italians of the Renaissance. "I should never," he wrote in 1842, "think of becoming an agitator or a revolutionary" (*Letters*, 71). So throughout the 1840s, the time of the "liberal euphoria" as it has been called, Burckhardt diverted himself with the study of art history, music, drawing, and the *bel monde* of Paris, Rome, and Berlin, all the while styling himself a Liberal and regarding "the spirit of freedom" as "the highest conception of the history of mankind" and his own "leading conviction" (74).

The revolutions which closed the 1840s shook his faith to its roots. His own beloved Basel, where he had gone to teach at the university, was racked by civil strife, and he saw all that he valued in the culture of old Europe tottering or being swept aside by "radicals." He wrote of those events somewhat petulantly: "You simply cannot conceive how utterly this sort of business devastates one's mind and puts one out of humour. One cannot even work, not to mention better things" (93). And after the events had run their course, he bitterly observed: "The word freedom sounds rich and beautiful, but no one should talk about it who has not seen and experienced slavery under the loud-mouthed masses, called 'the people,' seen it with his own eyes and endured civil unrest. . . . I know too much about history to expect anything from the despotism of the masses but a future tyranny, which will mean the end of history" (*ibid.*).

Like many of his cultivated Liberal contemporaries, Burckhardt had been abruptly torn from the quiet of his study and exposed to the crude realities of the marketplace where naked power ruled, and the spectacle was too much for him. "I want to get away from them all," he wrote, "from the radicals, the communists, the industrialists, the intellectuals, the pretentious, the reasoners, the abstract, the absolute, the philosophers, the sophists, the State, the fanatics, the idealists, the 'ists' and the 'isms' of every kind" (96). And so he took once more the vow that he had made as a young man: "I mean to be a good private individual, an affectionate friend, a good spirit; . . . I can do nothing with society as a whole" (*ibid.*). And he added to that vow: "We may all perish; but at least I want to discover the interest for which I am to perish, namely the old culture of Europe" (97).

In effect, Burckhardt went underground. He secluded himself in Basel, taught the few students who came to the struggling university, lectured to the citizens of the town, severed all relations with learned societies, and even refused to publish after 1860. By that time, however, his fame was already high. Offers of more prestigious posts continually came to him, but he refused them all. From his vantage point on the Upper Rhine he looked down upon Europe rushing to its doom, surveyed the failure of Liberalism, diagnosed its causes, and predicted its results as Nihilism. But he refused to enter the struggle himself. Out of his disillusionment he forged a theory of society and history which was as accurate in predicting the crises of the future as it was symptomatic of the illnesses that would bring them on. Burckhardt regarded his own withdrawal from the world as an act which absolved him from any further responsibility for the coming chaos. Actually it merely reflected that failure of nerve in the European man of culture which in the end left unopposed the forces that would ultimately plunge European civilization into the abyss of totalitarian terror.

Burchkardt's major historical works are *The Age of Constantine the Great* (1852) and *The Civilization of the Renaissance in Italy* (1860), both of which were published during his own lifetime, and *The Cultural History of Greece* and *Reflections on World History*, published posthumously from lecture notes. The *Constantine*, a study of cultural decline, consciously evoked a comparison of the fall of the Roman Empire with the coming end of European civilization. The *Renaissance* was a *tour de force* in which Burckhardt all but single-handedly created the picture of that age of cultural flowering known to modern scholarship. But both books, the one of decline, the other of rebirth, dealt with a single problem: the fate of culture in times of crisis, its subjugation to, and liberation from, the great compulsive forces (*Potenzen*) of world history, conceived by Burckhardt to be religion and the state. The *Constantine* showed culture freed from the grip of the absolute state of the ancient world but tied by the constricting bonds of religion in the Middle Ages. The *Renaissance* dealt with the breakdown of the religious spirit and the flowering of the individualistic culture of the Renaissance prior to the foundation of the modern power state in the eighteenth century.

In his books Burckhardt's heroes, the representatives of culture, are always those dynamic personalities who are governed by their own inner vision of the world and who rise above the mundane conception of virtue. They either (like himself) withdraw from the world and cultivate their own autonomous personalities in secret or they rise above the ordinary human condition by supreme acts of will and submit the world to the domination of their own creative egos. Burckhardt found the former type represented in the Pythagoreans of ancient Greece and the anchorites of the Middle Ages; the latter type was represented by the artists and princes of the Renaissance. In short, Burckhardt's general theme was the interplay of great personalities and the compulsive forces of society, a theme which received full theoretical treatment in his *Reflections on World History*.

Burckhardt always denied that he had a "philosophy of history," and he spoke with open contempt of Hegel, who had presumed to deliver a *Weltplan* that explained everything and placed everything within a prearranged intellectual frame. Yet in his letters Burckhardt praised Taine, whose general purpose was much the same as Hegel's and whose "philosophy of history" was much less subtle and elastic. For Burckhardt the essential difference between Hegel and Taine lay in the fact that the former's philosophy of history was susceptible to, indeed invited, Radical conclusions, whereas that of the latter discouraged them. Actually, as Burckhardt well knew from the example of Ranke, to deny the possibility of a philosophy of history is in effect to affirm another philosophy of a particularly Conservative sort. For to deny the possibility of a philosophy of history is to deny either reason's capacity to find a pattern in events or the right of the will to impose a pattern on them. Like his master Ranke, Burckhardt wanted to remove history from the political squabbles of the time or at least to show that the study of history precluded every chance of deriving political doctrines from it—which would be a boon to the Conservative cause. So Burckhardt called his "philosophy of history" a "theory" of history, and presented it as nothing more than an "arbitrary" arrangement of the materials for purposes of presentation and analysis. He could not attempt to give the "real nature" of the events, because his pessimism denied him the luxury of assuming that events had any "nature" at all. This pessimism found its intellectual justification in Burckhardt's mind in the philosophy of Schopenhauer. What Feuerbach was to Marx and the political Left, Schopenhauer was to Burckhardt and the political Right.

⮡ Pessimism as a World View: Schopenhauer's Philosophy

Although it appeared in a preliminary form as early as 1818, Schopenhauer's philosophy received very little attention until the 1840s. After 1850, however, it moved to the very center of European intellectual life, not so much among professional philosophers as among artists, writers, historians, and publicists: among intellectuals whose interests verged on the philosophical or who felt that what they were doing required some kind of grounding in a formal philosophical system. Schopenhauer's conception of the world was especially well suited to the needs of intellectuals of the third quarter of the century. It was materialistic but not deterministic; it allowed one to use the terminology of Romantic art and to speak of the "spirit," the "beautiful," and the like, but it did not require that these ideas be granted supernatural status. Moreover, it was morally cynical to the ultimate degree. It permitted whatever pleasure one received from one's present situation to be justified as a necessary balm for a distracted soul, but it allowed the pain and suffering of others to appear as both necessary and desirable so that one need not give special care or attention to them. It reconciled one to the *ennui* of upper-middle-class existence and to the suffering of the lower classes as well. It was egoistic in the extreme.

Schopenhauer's philosophy constituted, therefore, both the starting point and the barrier to be overcome by many young writers and thinkers of the last quarter of the century. Nietzsche, Wagner, Freud, Mann, and Burckhardt all learned from it and found in Schopenhauer a teacher who explained the dissatisfaction with life which each of them as creative artists and students of human suffering felt. Of the five, two remained Schopenhauer's devotees to the end: Wagner and Burckhardt.

Schopenhauer had no social theory or philosophy of history. Yet his whole system was a sustained attempt to show why social concerns and historical interests are unnecessary. Thus he had a negative theory of both. He provided an alternative to historicism in any form. Georg Lukács sees Schopenhauer as the ideologue of the German bourgeoisie after 1848, when the liberal, humanistic naturalism of Feuerbach was definitively abandoned and a reactionary, pessimistic, and egoistic world-view was required by the times and the situation in which the German middle class found itself. Schopenhauer was no simple ideologue, however, as was Spencer in England and Prévost-Paradol in France. According to Lukács, Schopenhauer was an *indirect apologist* for the style of life of a class which, in the face of its own affirmed ideals, had to find some reason for justifying its failure to act, and for denying, in the face of its prior talk of progress and enlightenment, the possibility of further reform (*Hist. Novel*, 178–81).

In one sense, of course, Schopenhauer was the ruthless critic of bourgeois values—that is, of interest in practical activity, the passion for security, and the merely formal adherence to Christian morality. He denied all the shibboleths of laissez-faire capitalist theory and of Ranke's pious historism, the notion that a hidden hand directs society to the realization of a general good, that competition under law is really productive of cooperation, and the like. Instead, he professed to reveal life as it *really* is: a terrible, senseless striving after immortality, an awful isolation of man from man, a horrible subjection to desire, without end, purpose, or any real chance of success. But in the end, Schopenhauer's general world view leaves whatever happens to be the case at any particular time completely untouched, undermining any impulse *to act* out of any motives whatsoever, either selfish or unselfish.

One attraction of Schopenhauer's system to late nineteenth-century intellectuals lay in the extent to which it could be accommodated to the Darwinian picture of nature. Darwin's nature was purposeless, and so was Schopenhauer's. By extension, man was purposeless too. Schopenhauer's social world was an aggregate of atomic individuals, each imprisoned within his own desires, individuals bumping against one another in random movement, each appearing merely as a possible *means* of egoistic gratification for every other. Marx recognized this alienation of man from nature, of man from man, and of man from himself, but he saw it as something that could be ultimately *lived through* to the attainment of a genuine reunion with nature, other men, and the self. And Marx's theory of social change in history allowed him to believe that certain provisional communities of endeavor, thought, and belief could be achieved in certain restricted cases.

Schopenhauer denied all this: all apparent communities are delusions; all pretense of love is a fraud; all apparent progress in the creation of manifestly more human understanding is sheer myth. Marx grounded man's alienation in a specific relationship with nature at a specific time and place, and envisioned the transcendence of this alienation and the attainment of universal human community in time. Schopenhauer, however, asserted that man's separation from man is grounded in the ontological bases of nature itself, and is therefore intrinsic to society; he also asserted that this separation can be transcended only in a few isolated geniuses, who commune not with other men but with themselves in a state of consciousness characterized by the destruction of the will to any action whatsoever.

Schopenhauer agreed with Feuerbach that reality and sensuality are the same thing. And he agreed with Feuerbach that man is that phase of nature in which life attains to consciousness. But for Schopenhauer, consciousness was as much a burden as a liberation, for to him it was the source of the distinction between present and future, hence of expectation and remorse, and ultimately, therefore, of the basic human feeling of suffering.

Man not only feels pain, like all animals, but he also knows that he is feeling pain—that is, he suffers—and he is thus the victim of a double pain, the pain itself and the knowledge that he *might not* be suffering that pain. It is the impulse to relieve pain through action which leads to specifically human effort in the world. But the effort to relieve pain or to gratify desire is revealed in the end to be utterly self-defeating. For an effort is either successful or unsuccessful. If it is unsuccessful, it heightens the original pain; if it is successful, it supplants the original pain, felt as want, with another pain, felt as satiety and its consequent, boredom—thereby instituting another cycle characterized by a search for something to desire to relieve the boredom felt from having obtained what one originally wanted.

Thus, all human effort is grounded in a cycle of will-acts which is utterly without purpose or meaning, unsatisfactory, yet compelling until death releases the individual to the common natural ground out of which all individuated wills crystallize. Schopenhauer discovered that the sense of *Streben*, of aspiration, which had been triumphantly held up to man by Feuerbach as constituting his humanity and the justification of his pride, was both the fundamental fact and the fundamental burden of human existence. Human reason and knowledge were not construed by him as instruments for mediating the process of human growth through cooperative action or acts of love. Reason only informs you of your determinate quality; it locates the will in time and space, the sphere of complete determinateness, and thereby destroys in the individual any feeling that he can act as will at all. Reason allows man to survey his condition in the abstract, but it does not permit hope that any attempt to relieve suffering and pain will be successful.

On the strength of this argument, Schopenhauer had to consider the possibility of self-destruction as a way out of a life that was nothing but frustrated desire. He ruled this alternative out, however, insofar as, for him, it was less a solution to the problem of human existence than evidence that one was taking life too seriously. The suicide loves life but cannot bear the conditions under which life must be lived. He does not surrender the will to live; he surrenders only life. "The suicide denies only the individual, not the species" (Schopenhauer, 325).

Schopenhauer's aim was to "deny the species." And he saw man's power of imagistic representation as the means by which this could be accomplished. Man's true freedom lies in his image-making capacities. The will finds its freedom in its capacity to fashion a world out of perceptions as it chooses. It experiences its determinate nature only when it seeks to act on the basis of these fantasies. It follows, then, that the highest aim of the individual will is to experience its freedom, and that, if the only way it can do so is through the exercise of its fictive capability, the best life is that which uses phenomena only as material for fictive recreation.

Historical thought is bound to occupy a secondary position in such a schema, because it assumes that there is such a thing as real time, that human events have an objective reality apart from the consciousness which perceives them, and that the imagination is restricted to the use of causal categories when it seeks to make sense out of these events. As lived, historical existence is a changeless game of desire, the effort to satiate desire, the success or failure to do so, and the consequent impulsion to new desire when it is successful, to pain when it is not. It is a chaos of conflicting actions, all of which are masked behind motives, statements, and forms that can be shown, on analysis, to be nothing but blind, egoistic will.

The outer limits of the cycle are set by pain and boredom. This implies that great social events, such as wars, revolutions, and the like, have their real causes in some dissatisfaction felt by individual wills, and that the slogans under which they offer themselves for consideration are mere façades (152–55). But in its quintessential nature genius is not involvement in the historical process but the capacity to remain a pure spectator. The aim of genius is to complete in the mind's eye the form being striven for in the phenomenon. With respect to history, this means doing what one wants to with historical materials, accepting or rejecting them as one likes, in order to make of them a pleasing image for contemplation.

Thus envisaged, historical knowledge is a second-order form of knowing, for, since it directs its attention to things in their detailed existence, it prohibits moving easily from the phenomenon to the contemplation of its immanent idea. Historical reflection is thus greater in the degree to which it approximates poetry—that is, abandons the detail which forces upon one an apprehension of the flaw in everything and rises to the contemplation of the "inner truth" of the details.

Thus, those ancient historians who, like Thucydides, invented the speeches of the historical agents in accordance with what they *ought* to have said on the occasion rather than relate what they actually said, were more enlightened then those Rankeans who halted where the documents ended or limited themselves to the reconstruction of what really happened. Knowledge is dignifying and liberating only in the extent to which it is itself liberated from the facts on the one hand, and consideration of the categories that link things together in their mutual determination in the world of time and space on the other.

Thus, Schopenhauer ranked the arts in terms of the extent to which they both abandoned the attempt to copy reality and actually transcended spatial and temporal limitations.

Fantasy is superior to fact, which means that poetry is superior to history. Within a given art form the same ranking can be made; thus tragedy is superior to comedy, comedy to epic, and so on. The same is true in the plastic and visual arts. Architecture is inferior to sculpture, since the practical interests of the former inhibit its aspiration to formal consistency. And sculpture is inferior to painting, since in sculpture the spatial determination is greater. Similarly, poetry is superior to paintng, since words can be more freely arranged than visual images. But poetry is inferior to music, since the latter liberates itself from words altogether and aspires to the contemplation of pure form beyond the limits of time. And so it continues, to the highest art form of all, which is never translated into spatial terms or even uttered, but remains pure and inviolate in the mind of the artist as a felt union with the underlying forms of all things, which it is the world's purpose, as will, to reunite with itself.

It is obvious that, to Schopenhauer, any prospect of salvation offered to the individual could be only an individual, never a communal, one. We are irredeemably cut off from other individuals, whom we are able to contemplate only as contending wills that view us as objects in *their* visual fields. All social institutions are thus denuded of their intrinsic worth, and all general social impulses are regarded as errors and flaws. But Schopenhauer refused to believe that any general theory, either physical or psychological, could mediate between what we are and what we might like to be. Science is merely a provisional, and essentially inferior, way of ordering reality under the modalities of time and space and the categories of determination for the achievement of immediate practical ends necessary to the survival of the organism. The antithesis of science, art, is not unifying but isolating, since the artistic vision is a vision the worth of which is purely private, known and knowable only to the mind that entertains it. Thus, both art and science are by their very nature alienating—the former by heightening our desire to withdraw from action, the latter by treating the world as made up of *things* in order to manipulate them for practical ends. History breeds a certain species consciousness by encouraging the search for variations on the human idea which every failure to attain a goal suggests to consciousness. Insofar as it tells us about these variations, however, history is the story of unrelieved disaster. It gives a sense of species consciousness only insofar as we are capable of completing *in our imaginations* the forms of which the individual events are evidences of misfires. Thus, we attain to genuine humanity by our transcendence, not only of history, but of time itself.

All of this means that the usual distinctions used by historians to organize their materials, chronological and causal, are themselves quite useless except as steps in the attainment of the truth taught by the Tragic poets, which, according to Schopenhauer, is: "The greatest crime of man is that he was ever born." It is pointless to talk about mankind as evolving or developing; in fact, it is pointless to talk about change at all. It is all the more pointless to talk about men as having projects which they undertake in common in order to build a shared society of greater or lesser scope. Schopenhauer's vision of history was constructed out of purely personal needs and resources. For him, the only history that counted was that which heightened in his own mind the necessity of ignoring history altogether.

Thus, Schopenhauer rose above the dispute between Hegel and Ranke over such matters as the "historically significant" class and the "historically significant" age. For, according to him, all men are basically alike; some have an ability to withdraw from action, and these are the blessed. Those who act, fail. So do those who refuse to act, but the latter at least can aspire to the pleasure of contemplating pure form.

Similarly, any distinctions among past, present, and future dissolve in Schopenhauer's thought. There is only present. Past and future are merely the modes of organizing an anticipation of change in one's own mind. And Schopenhauer's message to the present is the same for all: train yourselves to want only what you can have and what you can enjoy for as long as you live. This want must be directed toward the nonmaterial, for material things change. It must be purely personal, since, if it is dependent on anything else, it can be withdrawn. Thus, Schopenhauer's philosophy ends by being perfectly narcissistic. In the contemplation of one's own conception of the form manifested by the phenomenon, one attains to that state aspired to by the Buddhist sage—Nirvana. In the unalloyed pleasure provided by the contemplation of the changeless realm of personally projected form, one awaits one's final return to the blind nature that spewed one forth into painful individuation. Schopenhauer thus transcended the pains of historical and social existence lamented by Rousseau. For him the tensions set up by the realists in their conception of a threefold world made up of nature, consciousness, and society were completely transcended. The whole was dispersed into a chaos. Schopenhauer thus dissolved history by denying not only humanity but nature as well.

Schopenhauer's world view was perfectly suited to the needs of those parts of society which wanted to ignore social questions altogether. For anyone who found the tensions between the classes on the one hand and between the imperatives of tradition and innovation on the other too painful to contemplate, Schopenhauer's philosophy allowed them to believe that it was futile to contemplate them at all. At the same time, it allowed those still burdened by the necessity of having to study mankind as a way of defining their own humanity—as a way of avoiding solipsism—to study only those parts of history which gave them pleasure; or, better still, to study only those aspects of a given age which reinforced their pleasure in their own conception of themselves. Burckhardt wrote his one-sided and distorted picture of fifteenth-century Italy under the sway of these preconceptions; Neitzsche's study of Greek Tragedy was a product of it; Wagner's "total art form" was composed under its aegis; and Thomas Mann's *Buddenbrooks* was justified by it.

What was typical of all of these thinkers was a manifest disgust with the society in which they lived, but a refusal to countenance the notion that any public or private action could possibly change the society for the better. All of them showed an impulse to flee reality into artistic experience conceived not as something that unifies man with man in shared apprehensions of a minimal humanity but as something that isolates him within his own communings and prohibits any communication with society. Nietzsche and Mann later repudiated their early Schopenhauerian conception of art, correctly seeing that it was escapist and inconsistent with the notion of art as a human activity. Wagner remained true to the Schopenhauerian vision to the end, investigating its capacities for self-delusionment with consummate artistry and skill. And so did Jacob Burckhardt, perhaps the most talented historian of the second half of the nineteenth century.

◆§ *Pessimism as a Basis of Historical Consciousness*

Like Schopenhauer, Burckhardt was not much appreciated in his own time. Most historians felt that he was too irresponsible, too subjective, to merit their attention. It was only near the end of the century, when it became apparent that the Rankean approach left too many questions unanswered, and historically engaged thinkers began to realize that they would have to choose between the attitudes of Marx and those of Schopenhauer, that Burckhardt's star began to rise. It tells us something about both Burckhardt and late nineteenth-century scholarship that this Schopenhauerian pessimist who saw history as an egoistic artistic exercise came into his own at this time.

It was an age characterized by a sense of breakdown and decline but an age unwilling to admit it, an age which took refuge in a conception of art as an opiate, which Burckhardt finally won to his view of history. By that time Nietzsche had already discovered the worm in the core of Schopenhauerian philosophy and had exposed it for all to see as merely a fear of living. He had tried to warn Burckhardt of the dangers contained in it and had suggested that, although Burckhardt's history pointed the way to a new conception of society which might oppose the leveling tendencies of both Marx and

Ranke, it was not enough. Burckhardt refused to respond to Nietzsche's criticism. This has often been put down to a commendable unwillingness to become embroiled in fruitless philosophical disputes, but there was nothing commendable about it. Burckhardt refused to become embroiled in intellectual disputes because he disliked disputes of any kind. Schopenhauer had shown him that exertion was futile and that a man lived well who did only that which pleased him, in thought as well as in action.

The Satirical Style

Burckhardt opened his most famous work, *The Civilization of the Renaissance in Italy*, with the following introduction:

This work bears the title of an essay in the strictest sense of the word. . . . To each eye, perhaps, the outlines of a given civilization present a different picture; and in treating of a civilization which is the mother of our own, and whose influence is still at work among us, it is unavoidable that individual judgment and feeling should tell every moment both on the writer and the reader. In the wide ocean on which we venture, the possible ways and directions are many; and the same studies which have served for this work might easily, in other hands, not only receive a wholly different treatment and application, but lead also to essentially different conclusions. [1–2]

He then signaled his original intention to have included a special section on the "Art of the Renaissance" and his failure to have provided it. And then, without further introduction, he launched into the history of Italy in the twelfth and thirteenth centuries, as a prelude to his analysis of Renaissance culture and learning.

What followed was a brilliant survey, in the nature of one of those drawings of an Impressionist master, in which the main lines of the political development of Italy were sketched out. The general outlines of the histories of the various Italian city-states were given, the nature of international policy was indicated, and the unique quality of the political life of the time was breathlessly summarized. This was the content of the famous opening section, "The State as a Work of Art." After a brief discussion of the nature of war in the Renaissance and the position of the papacy in Italian political life, the section concluded with a short characterization of the nature of the patriotism of the time. The central idea was that the nature of Italian political life was such as to "excite in the better spirits of the time a patriotic disgust and opposition" (79). Burckhardt contrasted the Italian political situation with that of Germany, France, and Spain. Each of these nations had an *external* enemy with which to do battle and against which a monarchy could unite its people and fashion a unity out of the feudal chaos. In Italy, the situation was different. There the existence of the papacy, an "ecclesiastical state," remained a "permanent obstacle to national unity" (80). Thus, Italian political life missed its chance for unity and integration. By the time the idea of national unity really took hold in Italy, it was too late. The country had been inundated with Frenchmen and Spaniards. The "sense of local patriotism" may be said to have taken the place of a genuine national feeling, but, as Burckhardt wrote, "it was but a poor equivalent for it" (*ibid.*). The section thus ended on a note of melancholy, a sense of opportunities lost, of national purposes betrayed, of tides missed and noble tasks ignored.

The section of the book entitled "The State as a Work of Art" was one of six parts, each of which consisted of an analysis of a different aspect of the culture of Italy during the Renaissance, culture conceived in its broadest sense, of course—that is to say, as manners, social customs, law, religion, literature, drama, festivals, ceremonies, and so on—and always with an eye to the broad-gauged characterizations of the categories under which the wealth of data were organized: "The Development of the Individual," "The Revival of Antiquity," "The Discovery of the World and of Man," "Society and Festivals," and "Morality and Religion." The book was thus organized under a rubric later analyzed by Burckhardt in his *Reflections on World History*, the worlds of politics and religion as "determined" by "culture." The Renaissance, in Burckhardt's view, was a period in which the "cultural" moment cut itself free of subordination to both politics and religion, to float above, to dominate, and to determine the forms they would take. Everything that mattered in the more mundane spheres of human existence was transformed into an art, which is to say that it was indentured to strive for its own intrinsic sublime *form*, the perfect combination of practical and aesthetic concerns. All that mattered in the life of society had been released from service to practicality on the one hand and from transcendental aspiration on the other. Everything sought to be what it was "in itself," not to be perverted by considerations that would destroy the perfection of its own essential outline. Things came to be seen *clearly*, and life was lived for the achievement of formal consistency alone.

Yet Burckhardt's account of each of the themes that he dealt with—individualism, the revival of antiquity, humanism, social intercourse, and religion—ended on the same melancholy note with which the section on politics ended. This melancholy note was like a vesper bell that called the faithful to a remembrance of piety at the close of the day. The theme was introduced and carried to its full realization in some representative figure or crucial event, but only to be modulated by the reminder that all things human pass into nothingness. The section on the development of the individual ended with a consideration of the cunning and "ironic" Aretino. Of him Burckhardt remarked:

It is a good sign for the present spirit of Italy that such a character and such a career have become a thousand times impossible. But historical criticism will always find in Aretino an important study. [103]

The section on "The Revival of Antiquity" ended with a notice of the humanists' loss of control over the academies and the banalization of culture which resulted from it. The short concluding paragraph ended with the cryptic remark: "The fate of the Italian stage, and afterwards of the opera, was long in the hands of these [provincial] associations" (170). The sections "Society and Festivals" and "Morality and Religion" ended with no comment at all, except an oblique one, suggested by quotations from the sources. The former ended with a passage from Pico della Mirandola's famous "Oration on the Dignity of Man," which, in the place assigned it, can only suggest the extent to which his sublime conception of human nature was *not* honored in the world that followed him. The latter, by contrast, ended with a verse of Lorenzo the Magnificent:

> Youth is beautiful,
> But it flies away!
> Who would be cheerful, let him be;
> Of the morrow, there is no certainty. [260]

Finally, the section "Morality and Religion," which ended the book, concluded with no general summation of the thesis of the whole work, but with only a discussion of the "General Spirit of Doubt" and a consideration of the Platonism of Ficino and the Academy of Florence:

Echoes of medieval mysticism here flow into one current with Platonic doctrines and with a characteristically modern spirit. One of the precious fruits of the knowledge of the world and of man here comes to maturity, on whose account alone the Italian Renaissance must be called the leader of modern ages. [341]

Thus Burckhardt's "essay" on the Renaissance ended. The essay had no proper beginning and no end, at least no end that was a consummation or resolution of a drama. It was all *transition*. And as such it really said much more about what came before it (the Middle Ages) and what came after it than about its ostensible subject, the "Renaissance" itself. Not that it did not say a lot about the Renaissance in Italy; for this "essay" was full of information, insights, brilliant *aperçus*, and shrewd assessments of the gap between ideals and realities in this period of cultural flowering and activity. But there was no "story" of the Renaissance, no integrated *development* that would permit a summary characterization of its essence. In fact, as Burckhardt made quite clear in his *Judgements on History and Historians*, his lecture notes for his course in the Age of Revolutions, the Renaissance represented an interlude, an *entracte* between two great periods of oppression—the Middle Ages, in which culture and politics were subordinated to the imperatives of religion; and the Modern Age, in which both culture and religion gradually became subordinated to the state and the imperatives of political power.

As thus conceived, the Renaissance was nothing but the "free play" of the cultural moment in the intermission between two tyrannies. Since it was free play, it could not be submitted to the same kind of analysis as either the Middle Ages or the Modern Age. Its products could only be caught on the wing, as it were, contemplated in their individuality and gathered under certain very broad and general categories, solely for representational—though not narrative—purposes. Where it began and where it ended were not easily discernible. Its products were like the crestings of the surf as it flows between two obdurate cliffs. It did not so much end as simply subside. Its late, weak pulsations (muted, but not halted completely) resembled the lapping of waves against a stone breakwater, erected almost perversely by willful men of power who appeared to be unable to live with its vibrant variety, brilliance, and fecundity. This breakwater, in Burckhardt's view, was the French Revolution, and it was made of the Materialism, philistinism, and banality of "the Modern Age."

Burckhardt's picture of the Renaissance reminds one of a combination of the themes of a painting by Piero di Cosimo and Raphael, a painting bathed in the tired light of Burne-Jones and Rossetti. The tone is elegiac, but the subjects of the picture are both savage and sublime. The "realism" of the subject-matter stems from the refusal to hide anything crude or violent, yet all the while the reader is reminded of the flowers that grew on this compost heap of human imperfection. But the purpose is Ironic. Throughout the work, the unspoken antithesis of this age of achievement and brilliance is the gray world of the historian himself, European society in the second half of the nineteenth century. By comparison not even the Middle Ages suffered in the same way that the Modern Age does. The Renaissance was everything that the modern world is *not*. Or, rather, the Modern Age represents the one-sided development of all those traits of human nature which were sublimated into a great cultural achievement during the Age of the Renaissance. The Modern Age is a product of human *losses*. Something was misplaced during the period between 1600 and 1815, and this "something" is "culture."

✑ The "Syntax" of Historical Process

In his lectures on modern history, delivered at the University of Basel from 1865 to 1885, Burckhardt considered the sixteenth century to be a period of inauguration. It was followed, he said, by a set of "metastases," which is to say, sudden irrational displacements of powers and symptoms from one organ or part of the body social to another (*Judgements*, 66). This concept of "metastasis" was a central Metaphor in Burckhardt's thinking about history. He did not purport to be able to account for these transfers, or shifts; they were mysterious. Their causes could not be specified, but their effects were manifest. This is why, even though one can offer no definitive explanation of why history develops as it does, one can at least break up the chronological record into discrete segments or provinces of occurrence. For example, just as in the fourteenth century, something new and mysterious made its appearance in the Italian city-states, so, too, in "the last decades before the French Revolution, events and personalities are of a specifically new kind" (163). This means that the period between the Renaissance and the French Revolution had, in principle, the same kind of perceivable, though ultimately undefinable, coherence as the Renaissance itself. "In relation to the great beginnings of the modern world epoch after 1450 it is a continuation; in relation to the age of revolution it is only the termination of an earlier age and a preparation for the coming one" (165). It, too, is an "entracte, or, rather, an interlude" (*ibid.*).

But the Age of Revolution was for Burckhardt, as it had been for Tocqueville, a "new and terrible thing." The Revolution, he wrote, "unfettered, first, all ideals and aspirations, then all passions and selfishness. It inherited and practiced a despotism which will serve as a model for all despotism for all eternity." (219) There was none of Tocqueville's attempt to assay "what has been gained, and what lost" as a result of the birth of this new and terrible thing. For Burckhardt it was all loss. Looking back upon the period in which Tocqueville wrote, he said:

To be sure, in the three decades in which we were born and grew up it was possible to believe that the revolution was something completed, which therefore might be described objectively.

At that time there appeared those books, well written and even classic, which tried to present a general view of the years 1789–1815, as of a completed age— not impartial, to be sure, but trying to be fair and quietly convincing. *Now*, however, we know that the very same tempest which has shaken humanity since 1789 bears us onward, too. We can asseverate our impartiality in good faith and yet unconsciously be caught up in extreme partiality. [225]

For "the decisive new thing that has come into the world through the French Revolution is the permission and the will to change things, with public welfare as the goal." And the result has been to elevate politics to the highest position, but without any principle to guide it, except anarchy on the one side and tyranny on the other—"constantly endangered by the desire for revision, or as a despotic reaction with a breaking down of political forms." (229)

The driving force behind this "demonry" was the "illusion" of "the good-ness of human nature" (230). "Idealistic minds" had let their "desires and fantasies batten upon a radiant vision of the future in which the spiritual world will be reconciled with nature, thought and life would be one," and so on (231). But all of this is the product of "illusion," Burckhardt said. A realist knows better, and a historian at least knows that "wishing" makes nothing so. Burckhardt's aim was to dissolve these illusions and to return human consciousness to the recognition of its own limitations, its finitude, and its incapacity ever to find happiness in this world (*ibid.*). "Our task," he said, "in lieu of all wishing, is to free ourselves as much as possible from foolish joys and fears and to apply ourselves above all to the under-standing of historical development" (231–32). He recognized the difficulty of this task, for objectivity is the most difficult of all perspectives in history, "the most unscientific of all the sciences" (*Force and Freedom*, 199), the more so since, "as soon as we become aware of our position" in our own times, "we find ourselves on a more or less defective ship which is drifting along on one wave among millions." And, he reminded his auditors, "one could also say that we ourselves are, in part, this wave" (*Judgements*, 232). The best we can hope for, then, is certainly not prophecy, but the location of our *place* within a segment of history which began with the Revolution; the form that our understanding of history must take is nothing more than the identification of "which wave of the great storm-tossed sea we are drifting on" (252).

Wave and metastasis—these two images sum up Burckhardt's conception of the historical process. The former image suggests the notion of constant change, the latter the lack of continuity between the impulses. His concep-tion is not cyclical; there are no *necessary* rejuvenations after a fall (27). But the *falls* are necessary, or at least *inevitable* at some time. What have to be explained in history are the moments of cultural brilliance and achieve-ment; *they* are the problem.

The will to power (the basis of political achievement) and the desire for redemption (the basis of religious commitment) need no explanation; they are the *fundamental* bases of human nature. And they ebb and flow con-stantly, both as to quantity and quality in a given civilization. By contrast, culture, Burckhardt asserted, is both discontinuous in its moments and incre-mental. That is to say, it produces qualitatively equal moments of brilliance and clarity of vision, but an infinite number of these, and with an effect which constantly enlarges the human spirit. Culture can flourish, however, only when the "compulsive" powers, the state and religion, are so weakened that they cannot frustrate its innermost impulses, and only when the mate-rial conditions are right for its flowering (*Force and Freedom*, 127).

✑§ The "Semantics" of History

This is what appears to have happened, in Burckhardt's estimation, during the Renaissance in Italy. No formal explanation of this period of cultural flowering is offered except the general notion of culture as an eternal moment in human nature which flowers when the compulsive powers are weak. That is to say, only a negative condition is postulated: because the church and the state were weak in Italy at the same time, and as a result of a millennial contest which had exhausted both, culture found room to grow, expand, and blossom. But the flowering itself is a mystery, or so it appears. For the springs of culture have their origins in the innermost vibrations of the human soul, and this is especially true of the arts:

They arise from mysterious vibrations communicated to the soul. What is released by those vibrations has ceased to be individual and temporal and has become symbolically significant and immortal. [*Ibid.*]

Alongside the practical life represented by the state and the illusory life represented by religion, culture raises a "second, ideal creation, the only perdurable thing on earth, exempt from the limitations of individual temporality, an earthly immortality, a language for all the nations" (128). The outward form of this "ideal creation" is material and hence is subject to the ravages of time, but only a fragment is needed to suggest "the freedom, inspiration, and spiritual unity" of the images that originally inspired them. In fact, Burckhardt said, the fragment is "particularly poignant," for art is still art, "even in the excerpt, the outline, the mere allusion." And we can, "with the assistance of analogy," perceive the "whole from fragments." (*Ibid.*)

The language in which Burckhardt dealt was the language of Irony, both in the form in which it was presented and in the content that it directed attention to as that which is to be most highly valued. And Burckhardt's manner of representing the Renaissance was that of the connoisseur beholding a heap of fragments assembled from an archeological dig, the context of which he divines "by analogy" from the part. But the form of the context can only be pointed to, not specified. It is like those "things in themselves" which Kant maintained we must postulate in order to account for our science, but about which we cannot *say* anything. The voice with which Burckhardt *addressed* his audience was that of the Ironist, the possessor of a higher, sadder wisdom than the audience itself possessed. He *viewed* his object of study, the historical field, Ironically, as a field whose meaning is elusive, unspecifiable, perceivable only to the refined intelligence, too subtle, to be taken by storm and too sublime to be ignored. He *apprehended* the world of historical objects as a literal "satura," stew or medley, fragments of objects detached from their original contexts or whose contexts are unknowable, capable of being put together in a number of different ways, of figuring a host of different possible, and equally valid, meanings. "After all," he said in *Force and Freedom*, "our historical pictures are, for the most part, pure constructions" (74). We can put the fragments together in a number of ways, though we ought not to put them together in such a way as either to foster illusions or to divert attention from the here and now. The *story* he told was Ironic, with its aphoristic style, anecdote, witticism, and throwaway (the revolutions of 1848 were caused by "ennuie," Napoleon was defeated by his own "impatience," and so on). The *plot structure* of this story was Ironic; that is to say, "the point of it all" was that there is no "point" toward which things in general tend, no epiphanies of law, no ultimate reconciliations, no transcendence. In his epistemology he was a skeptic; in his psychology he was a pessimist. He took a dour delight in his own resistance to the forces that prevailed in his own time and to the direction in which he saw them tending. He had no respect for "mere narration," as he called it (*Judgements*, 29), because he not only refused to prophesy how "things will come out in the end," but did not even see any ultimately significant provisional terminations in the ambiguous meantime between unknowable beginning and unforeseeable end.

Yet, if anything was constant in Burckhardt's thought, it was the enemies he opposed. These enemies were for him, as for all Ironists, "illusions," and they came in two principal forms: metaphorical reduction, which gives birth to allegory; and excessive symbolization, which gives birth to metaphysics. In fact, his formal theory of history, with its conception of the threefold interaction of culture, religion, and the state, was really a reflection of his theory of culture, which consisted, in his view, of a threefold action of allegorical, symbolical, and historical sensibilities. This theory of culture, which was the very quintessence of Burckhardt's brand of realism, was not set forth in any of his formally theoretical works, and was probably not even admitted by him to be a theory. But it was present, and was presented quite clearly, in the section on Italian painting in his *Cicerone*, a guidebook to the "enjoyment" of the artworks of Italy, published in 1855.

◄§ The "Satura" Plot Structure

Burckhardt spoke most directly, least self-consciously, as a historian in his capacity as an appreciator of art, and especially of Italian art. This was the subject closest to his heart, and in his guidebook to the art of Italy, *The Cicerone*, subtitled *A Guide to the Enjoyment of the Artworks of Italy* (*Eine Anleitung zum Genuss der Kunstwerke Italiens*) (1855), composed in the year following publication of his first major historical production, *The*

Age of Constantine the Great (1852), Burckhardt revealed himself at his best—and most *engagé*. *The Cicerone* offered Burckhardt the opportunity to indulge himself in direct and highly personal reflections on historical objects in a way that reflections on the *life* of the past did not. The whole universe of artistic products was *directly* present to him as objects of perception; their contents or meanings were not mediated by language, at least not by verbal language. One did not have to divine what the medium was saying before proceeding to the consideration of its meaning. For Burckhardt, insofar as art objects were concerned, the medium and the message were—or ought to be—literally indistinguishable. One had only to confront the art object in its integrity and extract from it its formal coherence. A similar operation on history-in-general was not possible, Burckhardt thought, because the documents themselves might be formally coherent without bearing any essential relationship at all to the nature of the events they purported to represent. Art objects were self-referential, and, although the quality, mood, style, of an age might be reflected in them, in order to enjoy them one did not have to consider the problem of the artifact's relationship to the milieux in which it arose. In fact, Burckhardt's decision to exclude a consideration of the visual arts from his *Civilization of the Renaissance in Italy* may well have been a product of his desire to discourage the notion that high art was dependent in any significant way on the external circumstances in which it was produced.

In his discussions of the artists of the Renaissance Burckhardt was always concerned to determine the extent to which either the content or the form of a given artistic work was produced by the interests and pressures of the patrons. And his discussions of medieval art were carried out under the notion that, while a great artist may rise above it, art produced under extra-artistic pressures, such as religion or politics, is almost invariably flawed art.

It is interesting to observe that this least "historical" of Burckhardt's works is the one that is superficially organized most completely on chronological principles. *The Cicerone* is divided into three parts, architecture, sculpture, and painting, which, in accordance with Schopenhauer's aesthetics, describe a hierarchy of ascending "spirituality" (see the Preface to the 1st ed.). Each of the separate sections proceeds from a discussion of the classical and paleo-Christian period to the period of the Baroque, which for Burckhardt extended into the eighteenth century. The story told is one of gradual rise, to the condition of excellence represented by the High Renaissance, and of the subsequent fall or dissolution of the harmony and balance achieved there in all three fields. The terminal periods, however, are characterized in pathetic, more than in Tragic, terms. The tone or mood of the concluding passages of each of the three parts is elegiac, melancholy. The section on architecture ends with a description of "villas and gardens" (specifically, with a brief description of the villas on Lake Como); that on sculpture ends with a discussion of Canova (specifically, the funeral monument of Clement XIV);

and the section on painting ends with reflections on the landscapes of Poussin and Claude Lorraine (specifically, their landscapes of the Roman Campagna).

The section on architecture had the most immediate impact on Burckhardt's public, but the section on painting is the most revealing of the principles of historical sensibility and narration which Burckhardt himself brought to bear upon the data of history-in-general. The paleo-Christian and Byzantine phases of Western art were regarded as inferior by virtue of the tendencies toward "mere mechanical repetition" which dogma and authority enforced upon the artists of the time. The art of the Romanesque period was viewed primarily as mythical and symbolical, though evidences of an essential healthiness were contained, in Burckhardt's estimate, in the appearance of a "simple narrative" style (*The Cicerone*, Clough ed., 18). The Gothic period in Italian art (as distinguished from its northern counterpart) was presented as signaling the birth of that naturalism which flowered in the Renaissance. Painting was liberated from service to architecture; and, though it remained in the service of religion, it was released to the development of its own unique potentialities of representation, especially in Giotto, who was seen by Burckhardt as the base on which the high achievements of Michelangelo and Raphael would finally take shape.

Giotto's achievement was not defined primarily in terms of an aim "to express ideal beauty" or in terms of his "power of realistic execution," in both of which he was surpassed by both contemporary and modern artists (32). It lay, rather, in his capacities as a "narrator," a teller of stories. Giotto "gave what was needed to make the story clear, simply and beautifully" (33). Giotto thus showed himself to Burckhardt as a master of the *historical* scene, narrator of those events in the life of Christ, Saint Francis, and the Church which the people of his time took to be actual historical occurrences. The figures in the great frescoes and panels of Padua, Assisi, and elsewhere all exist for the sole purpose of illuminating a *story* (35); they do not function primarily as icons. They do not *point* or allude to something outside themselves. Everything in them exists for the sake of the story being told, to contribute to the explanation of the *action in the picture* (*ibid.*). To be sure, the *allegorical* element is not completely eliminated in Giotto's art, any more than it is in Dante's; and precisely to this extent it remained, in Burckhardt's view, enfeebled, exposed to the dangers of allegory from which it had only barely managed to escape. This element of allegory, with its tendency toward metaphorical corruption of the subject, remained, in Burckhardt's account, the threat to the art of the Renaissance. Raphael was the supreme representative of the Renaissance because he dominated the element of allegory in his art, and used it to his own purposes rather than fall prey to its mastery. For Burckhardt, allegory represented submission to the element of "mystery" (39), which is, in turn, a failure of "vision"—that is, of perception (*Anschauen*).

❧§ Anti-Metaphor

The mark of the triumph of the mysterious over the effort to perceive reality clearly and to render it whole is metaphor, which in Burckhardt's estimation, always destroys art and truth. Thus, he said in his remarks on Giotto:

> To represent the obligation to poverty as a marriage with her is a metaphor, and a work of art ought never be founded on a metaphor, that is, an idea transferred to a new fictitious reality, which gives a necessarily false result in a picture. . . . As soon as the allegorical figures are to be put into action, nothing can be done without metaphor, and with it arise simple absurdities. [*Ibid.*]

Burckhardt suggested a short while later that the whole triumph of the Renaissance could be characterized in terms of its insight into the dangers of Metaphorical characterizations of the world.

> The insufficiency of all Allegory could not fail to be felt in art. As a complement were produced the representations of abstract ideas mostly derived from antiquity, and used singly in connection with allegories. . . . (Dante also makes the greatest use of this mode of representation.) Such figures . . . remain mere curiosities; they give the measure of the naive historical knowledge of the age. [39–40]

In short, he set the naiveté of the historical knowledge of the age over against its tendencies toward a Metaphorical characterization of the world. And he showed the measure of its impulse to escape the trap of Metaphor in Giotto's development of a specifically "narrative" style of representation.

The allegorical element in a work of art is not, however, to be confused with the symbolic element. Symbolism is necessary, Burckhardt indicated, for the expression of "sublime ideas" which "cannot be embodied in any merely historical composition, and yet look to art for their highest rendering." Artwork which attempts to render these "sublime ideas" will therefore be "more impressive in proportion as it contains less allegory and more living distinct action." (40)

These sublime ideas have to do with "everything connected with the world beyond the grave" and, he added, beyond the "prophecies" of the Gospel and the Apocalypse, the kinds of considerations that inform Dante's *Commedia*. But, Burckhardt warned, this interest in sublime ideas must be mediated by an interest in the "artistic representation of single incidents." "The symbolic meaning of the *Divina Commedia* . . . is only valuable as literature and history, not as poetry. The poetical value rests entirely on the lofty artistic representation of single incidents, on the measured grand style through which Dante became the father of Western poetry." (*Ibid.*).

The history of Western art, then, is seen to develop within a threefold tension generated by the tendencies toward allegorical, historical, and symbolic representation. And the Renaissance style, in the end, is seen as a product of the gradual dissolution of the allegorical, or metaphorical, impulse in its tradition, an impulse which was sustained by "the theological tendency" of medieval civilization. Once this theological tendency had been expunged, the high art of the Renaissance could be consigned to the creative tension between two kinds of representation, sublime ideas on the one hand (a symbolic activity) and narration (a "historical" activity) on the other.

✀§ Realism as Irony

Eliminating metaphor, while remaining true to the twofold task of historical narration and symbolization of "sublime ideas," constituted the essence of Renaissance "realism." Burckhardt introduced his discussion of Quattrocento art with an analysis of this realistic element, expressed in the desire to render details of the human form (as against the effort to render the type), the flow and movement of the human figure in action, and the discovery of the rules of perspective (57–58). All this was a result, not of dependency upon antique models, but rather of the study of nature (58). But this interest in external reality was not carried forward in a vacuum; it developed within the full consciousness of those "sublime ideas" which permit "tact" to set limits on "fancifulness":

[The Renaissance] possessed, as an original gift from heaven, the tact to follow out external reality not into every detail, but only so far as that the higher poetic truth might not suffer from it. Where it is too rich in details it is superabundant in architecture and decoration, and in beautiful draperies, not in the prosaic accidents of external life. The impression, therefore, is not of weariness, but of splendour. Few give the essential parts grandly and nobly; many lose themselves in fancifulness, which is the general tendency of the fifteenth century, yet the general grandeur of the forms give to their fancies a tasteful and even pleasing character. [59]

Here is Burckhardt's definition of the most desirable kind of "realism," the kind of realism which he would have liked to claim for his own historical studies, conceived as works of art in the Renaissance manner. This realism stood in starkest contrast to its nineteenth-century counterparts, which, in his view, consisted of nothing more than a vulgar interest in the photographic reproduction of details and was not governed by a general rule of devotion to "sublime ideas." Thus, contrary to his protestations against "philosophy of history," his own conception of realistic historiography required a distinct, even though suppressed, *general conception* of the nature of reality, quite apart from any knowledge of concrete details and, however sublimated, by which to give a historical work a desirable formal coherence.

Though he refused to render this general conception as a formal theory, except of the most vague kind, it nonetheless formed the limit on his apprehension of the facts of historical existence, so that a "tactful" realism, a realism that would not degenerate into "fancifulness," could be realized. Like Renaissance art itself, Burckhardt's historiography developed in the middle ground between symbolism and narration. Its principal enemy was metaphor and the form that metaphor takes in the representation of reality, allegory.

The Renaissance, Burckhardt said, "suddenly springs forth" in the Cinquecento, "like a flash of lightning, . . . like a gift from heaven. The time had come. . . . The great masters now gather eternal truths for imperishable works of art. Each has his way, so that one beauty does not exclude another, but all together form a multiform revelation of the highest." To be sure, as with all things fine, "the time of full bloom is indeed but short. . . . We may say that the short lifetime of Raphael [1483–1520] witnessed the rise of all that was most perfect, and that immediately after him, even with the greatest who outlived him, the decline began." (111)

This decline had already been signaled in the work of Raphael's two great contemporaries, Leonardo and Michelangelo. The former was given to an excessive dependency upon "the help of landscape," which produced that "dreamy effect" of the Giaconda (disturbing to Burckhardt) and reflected a reversion to allegory (114). In Michelangelo, by contrast, the "historical" element tended to give place to the symbolic. Everything was too sublime; there was no counterbalance to it, no concrete detail "of all that makes life dear to us," with the result that, in his work, "the simply sublime and beautiful in nature" were "exaggerated" (123).

What Michelangelo's paintings lacked, Burckhardt made clear in his discussion of the Sistine Chapel frescoes, was "history" (125). This at once gave them their "grandeur" and marked the appearance of the imminent decline from the perfection of Raphael's art. Michelangelo's want of tact was shown in his *Last Judgment*, which, Burckhardt suggested, was not a fit subject of representation, either as to possibility or desirability (*ibid.*). "Michelangelo reveals in the Promethean pleasure of calling into existence all the capabilities of movement, position, foreshortening, grouping of the pure human form" (126). This was the tendency which showed itself, as a defect, in mannerism (128). And, in the end, Burckhardt's judgment on Michelangelo was, for all the praise he accorded him as a genius, a negative one. "After his death, all principle in all the different arts was overthrown; everyone strove to reach the absolute, because they did not understand that what in him appeared uncontrolled, in fact, took shape from his inmost personality" (*ibid.*).

It would appear, then, that Leonardo's genius erred (if at all) in the direction of fancifulness, while that of Michelangelo erred in the direction of symbolism. In Raphael, by contrast, the fancifulness was eliminated, and perfect balance was struck between symbolism and history: "In Raphael the detail strikes so powerfully that one thinks it is the essential part; yet the charm of the whole is infinitely the most distinctive point" (139). But the sense of the whole was a formal perfection, not a *crude* symbolism. In the early Florentine portraits, Burckhardt said, Raphael already showed himself to be a "great historical painter" (*ibid.*). Even in his pictures of the Virgin, Burckhardt maintained, Raphael "always uses as little symbolism as possible; his art does not depend on associations which are beyond the sphere of form, thoroughly as he had mastered the expression of the symbolical in its proper place, as is shown by the frescoes in the Vatican" (143). Even in *The Vision of Ezekiel*, Raphael took a subject long conventionalized in medieval art and "transformed it in the spirit of the greatest beauty as far as it was possible with the coarse symbol" (144). In the frescoes of the *Camera della Segnatura* in the Vatican, finally, Raphael took allegorical and historical subjects dictated to him by tradition and authority, separated them for individual handling—so as not to permit their mixture in the eye of the beholder —and then represented the historical scenes in ways that conformed to his peculiarly balanced genius.

The figures in the *Disputa*, for example, are "treated according to purely pictorial motives. They are almost entirely figures belonging to a past, more or less removed, which already had ceased to live except in idealizing remembrance" (150). The *School of Athens* is utterly "without mystery," the background being a "consciously intended symbol of the healthy harmony between the powers of the soul and the mind," and the arrangement of the figures being a "complete harmony of the picturesque and dramatic motives" (151). The *Camera of the Segnatura*, Burckhardt concluded, "is the first extensive work of art entirely harmonious in form and idea" (152). And in his general characterization of Raphael in this period, Burckhardt revealed his definitive idea of artistic perfection.

Raphael is the first in whom the form is entirely beautiful, noble, and at the same time intellectually alive, without injury to the whole effect. No detail comes forward, is too prominent; the artist understands exactly the delicate life of his great symbolical subjects, and knows how easily the special interest overweights the whole. And nevertheless, his single figures have become the most valuable study of all after-painting. [152–53]

In the great cycles of the *Stanza d'Eliodoro*, the *Stanza del incendio*, and the *Sala di Costantino*, in the *Loggie* of the Vatican and the cartoons for the tapestries, Burckhardt continued, Raphael's powers as a historian and dramatist were consolidated and deepened. Above all, in his rendition of the *Battle of Constantine*, what Burckhardt called "an ideal historical moment" was captured with perfect vividness and ideality (157). Working under instructions from the pope, pressed by demands for specific handlings of themes and figures, Raphael successfully turned all internal and external requirements to the uses of his genius. Remaining true to history and art simultaneously, he created works of beauty and eternal interest to the eye. "The soul of the modern man has, in the region of the beautiful form no higher master and guardian then he is," Burckhardt concluded, "for the antique has only come down to us as a ruin, and its spirit is never our spirit" (164). It was Raphael's power to remain true to the historical sense and the aesthetic sense simultaneously, Burckhardt insisted, that made him a quintessentially "moral," rather than a merely "aesthetic," genius. And the assessment of this ideal artist ended, characteristically for Burckhardt, on an elegiac note.

This moral quality would have remained with him even to his old age, had he lived longer. If we think over the colossal power of creation of his very last years, we shall feel what has been lost for ever by his early death. [*Ibid.*]

After this tribute to Raphael, Burckhardt's story of Italian art is one of sustained decline. Titian and Tintoretto represented high excellences, each in his own way, but the descent to mediocrity and vulgarity was unrelenting. Burckhardt found a number of other examples of high craftsmanship, talent in one line or another, but nothing finally to halt the drift into decay which ended in what he called the "modern school."

The dominant attribute of the modern school, in his view, was its tendency toward vulgar realism.

In all undertakings of an ideal kind this modern painting fails in the highest aims, because it attempts too much direct representation and illusion, while yet, as the product of a late period of culture, it cannot be sublime by simple ingenuousness. It aims at making all that exists and occurs real; it regards this as the first condition of all effect, without counting on the inner sense of the spectator, who is accustomed to look for emotions of quite a different kind. [235]

Burckhardt analyzed the specific faults of the modern school without sympathy or tolerance. In narrative pictures, anything "impressive" is included (237), and usually ends in little more than "vulgarity," as in Guercino's *St. Thomas* (240). In historical painting, Burckhardt said, everything gives way before a gory interest in martyrdoms, and the more "naturalistic" the better. Speaking of Caravaggio's *Medusa*, Burckhardt said that the element of horror is such as to arouse disgust rather than deep emotion (241). Sacred subjects have been represented in the "good style and measured forms of contemporary society" (242). Expression alone, rather than form, is used to represent the emotions (243); swooning females predominate in the representations of ecstasies and glories, and the most sacred and profane subjects are run together, swamped in a common supersensual naturalism (249). For Burckhardt, genre painting, created by Caravaggio, tended to be "repulsively humorous or horribly dramatic" (252). Only in landscape did genius express itself fully and directly, though the Italian landscape immortalized in the modern style was for the most part a creation of non-Italian artists. In Poussin and those who followed him, Burckhardt said, is seen "a virgin nature, in which the traces of human work only appear as architecture, chiefly as ruins of old times, also as simple huts. The human race which we imagine or find represented there belongs either to the old fabulous world, or to sacred history, or to pastoral life; so that the whole impression is heroic pastoral" (257). Claude Lorraine, finally, depicted a nature which spoke in a voice suited to "console the human race." And, Burckhardt concluded his guide to the enjoyment of Italian art, "for him who buries himself in his works . . . no further words are necessary" (*ibid.*).

~§ *History and Poetry*

"The rivalry between history and poetry," Burckhardt said in *Force and Freedom*, "has been finally settled by Schopenhauer. Poetry achieves more for the knowledge of human nature . . . [and] history is indebted to poetry for insight into the nature of mankind as a whole." Moreover, the "end to which [poetry] is created is much sublimer than history." (136) But this clearly means that poetry provides the principles by which historical visions of events in their particularity are related to one another to form a construction which is more or less adequate to the representation of those events' inner content or essential form. And Burckhardt left no doubt that the most informative documents of any civilization, the documents in which its true inner nature is most clearly revealed, are poetic ones: "history finds in poetry not only one of its most important but also one of its purest and finest sources" (*ibid.*).

But the threat to pure poetic expression is the same as that to tactful "realism." For, although poetry, in Burckhardt's estimation, originally appeared "as the *voice of religion*," it soon became the vehicle for the expression of the poet's own "personality" (139). This splitting off of poetry from religion represented, for Burckhardt, an aspiration of the human will to the sublime, the high point of which was reached in the Attic drama of Aeschylus and Sophocles, the aim of which "was to make ideal figures speak with the voice of all mankind" (142). By contrast, the poetry of the Middle Ages remained "part of the liturgy and bound to a definite story," while that of the Modern Age was shot through with the impulses of an "allegorical and satirical 'morality' " (143).

Burckhardt's historiography "lays no claim to system"; his historical pictures, he candidly admitted, were "mere reflections of ourselves" (74-75). But it is quite apparent that he regarded the insights that historical narration can yield to consciousness to be of essentially the same nature as those of poetry properly written. History, like poetry, and moreover like the visual poetry of Raphael, avoids the dangers of excessive allegorization on the one hand and of excessive symbolism on the other. What this reduces to is an attack upon all forms of Metaphorical characterization of the objects that occupy the historical field and of the relationships presumed to obtain among those objects. And this anti-Metaphorical attitude is the quintessence of Burckhardt's Irony, as it is the quintessence of every Ironist's attitude. Hence we see the apparent "purity" of Burckhardt's style. It abounds in simple declarative sentences, and the verb form most often chosen, almost to the point of expunging the active voice from Burckhardt's characterizations of events and process, is the simple copulative. His paragraphs represent virtuoso variations on the simple notion of *being*. A passage chosen at random, from the section on "The Discovery of the World and of Man," in *The Civilization of the Renaissance* book, illustrates what I have in mind.

The second great age of Italian poetry, which followed at the end of the fifteenth and beginning of the sixteenth centuries, as well as the Latin poetry of the same period, is rich in proofs of the powerful effect of nature on the human mind. The first glance at the lyric poets of that time will suffice to convince us. Elaborate descriptions of natural scenery, it is true, are very rare, for the reason that, in this energetic age, the novels, and the lyric and epic poetry had something else to deal with. Boiardo and Ariosto paint nature vigorously, but as briefly as possible, and with no effort to appeal by their descriptions to the feelings of the reader, which they endeavour to reach solely by their narrative and characters. Letter-writers and the authors of philosophical dialogues are, in fact, better evidence of the growing love of nature than the poets. [183]

The rapid delineation of a field and the figures occupying it is reminiscent of the deft strokes of the Impressionist painters, in which the impression is given of nothing but a report of separate perceptions which add up to a theme, not a thesis (184). The structure of the whole paragraph, like the structure of the sections that make up the parts, and of the parts themselves, is paratactical. There appears to be a conscious suppression of any impulse toward hypotactical construction of the events so as to suggest an argument. The section which follows, on the theme of "The Discovery of Man," does have an explicit thesis, and was labeled as such by Burckhardt (185), but he engagingly admitted that the "facts which we shall quote in evidence of our thesis will be few in number." Here, he said,

The author is conscious that he is treading on the perilous ground of conjecture, and . . . that what seems to him a clear, if delicate and gradual, transition in the intellectual movement of the fourteenth and fifteenth centuries, may not be equally plain to others. The gradual awakening of the soul of a people is a phenomenon which may produce a different impression on each spectator. Time will judge which impression is the most faithful. [*Ibid.*]

Then, after a number of examples of the new spirit expressed in poetry, Burckhardt summarized the impression of the whole: "Thus, the world of Italian sentiment comes before us in a series of pictures, clear, concise, and most effective in their brevity" (187). It is obvious that Burckhardt was matching not merely his "impressions" against others' impressions, but his sense of the sublime against other, more defective ones. But none of this was argued for so much as it was simply asserted. Its force as an explanation of what was happening in the historical field to which it directed our attention was a function of the poetic sensibility of Burckhardt himself, a sensibility which, in his own estimation, had been definitively liberated from Metaphor as a device of both description and explanation. It was the antithesis of the Romantic conception of poetry and of history, and in its purest expressions it resisted the temptations to indulge, not only in Metonymy, but in Synecdoche as well.

Burckhardt's theory of the rise and fall of Renaissance art provides crucial insights into his conception of history-writing as a work of art. The twin threats to the art of history were to him the same as those which threatened the art of the Renaissance: allegory and symbolization—the drawing of moral implications from historical facts on the one hand and the sublimation of concrete reality into intimations of timeless spiritual forces on the other. St. Augustine's *City of God* represented the first threat, the reduction of historical events to the status of manifestations of moral forces presumed to direct the universe. Augustine's book represented the enthralldom of historical consciousness to one of the "compulsive powers," in this case religion, though history written in the service of a specific ideology would qualify just as well as an example of "allegorical" historiography. On the other hand, Hegel represented the dangers of excessive symbolization, the dissolution of concrete historical events in the interest of promoting some formal system, metaphysical in nature, by which *all* events would be deprived of their particularity and translated into members of classes, genera, and species. Genuine historiography, like the art of Raphael, represented a subordination of the allegorical and symbolizing impulses in the historian's consciousness to the needs of "realistic" representation. This "realism," in turn, was conceived to have two components: the apprehension of the historical field as a set of discrete events, no two of which are precisely alike; and the comprehension of it as a fabric of relationships. The sense of structure should appear like that stage on which Raphael positioned his figures in the *School of Athens* or the *Battle of Constantine* or the *Miracle of Bolsena*. Even those periods in which brute force prevailed, when culture was enslaved to politics, have a certain formal coherence when narrated by the master historian, like the sense of form that arises from the contemplation of Raphael's *Fire of the Borgo*, which is all apparent movement and excitement, but is actually a masterpiece of formal coherence, in its parts as well as in the whole. But the different periods of the historical process are as detachable from one another as the various pictures that Raphael painted. Each picture is different, both as to content and as to the formal problem which its composition solved. The criteria are strictly aesthetic. The elements of a historical picture can be as varied as the elements of any given "historical" painting. There are no rules to determine what must go into the picture as its content, though the historian may not, of course, invent the characters any more than Raphael was permitted to do in the *Battle of Constantine*. What the historian "invents" are the formal relationships which obtain among the elements in the picture. These elements are related as event to context, rather than as microcosm to macrocosm. It is no more possible to distinguish between an event and its context with precise accuracy than it is possible to distinguish between the *Fire of the Borgo* and the elements depicted in Raphael's rendition of it. And, needless to say, the "causes" of an event's being what it is are hardly considered at all.

◆§ Conclusion

Whatever formal theory of historical explanation Burckhardt offered us is only a theory of the "framework" within which historical events develop. It is not a theory of the relationship between events and the framework itself. Or, rather, the theory of relationship is founded upon the apprehension of the impossibility of distinguishing finally between an event and the larger historical framework in which it occurs. This theory is Contextualist, for it supposes that an explanation of historical events is provided when the various strands that make up the tapestry of a historical era are discriminated and the linkages among the events, which make a "fabric" of the historical field, are displayed. The relationship between an event and its context is not, however, a Synecdochic one, that of the part's relation to the whole conceived as a microcosmic-macrocosmic relationship. It is true that Burckhardt used this language often in his historical works, but it was usually reserved for the characterization of the great moments of culture's hegemony over the compulsive powers of state and church, or politics and religion. There is an internal consistency and coherence among the parts of a whole work of art —and an individual life lived as a work of art—which stands in direct opposition to the mode of relationship of culture itself to politics and religion. *This* relationship is conceived Metonymically, as a fractured condition, a condition of schism and conflict of interests, an unremissible struggle of forces that have their origins in the depths of human nature and are ultimately mysterious in their operations. One can deal with the products of this conflict only "phenomenologically," as it might be put today. One can write the "history" of these products in the form of a "narrative," but this narrative will not describe a line of development leading to a redemption, a reconciliation, or an epiphany of law which is healing by virtue of its revelation.

The story that Burckhardt told of the past was always the story of a "fall" from high achievement to bondage. All that is left for the historian to consider, after this "fall" occurs, is the historical artifact, conceived as "fragments" and "ruins," the pathos of which derives from the cry contained within them for the "remembrance of things past." This remembrance of things past is the sole obligation of the historian. He is required not to impose upon the fragments fables that might inspire to heroism in the present. He is not permitted to "dramatize" them in such a way as to induce faith in the healing capacities of cooperative social action. And he is specifically enjoined from seeking the general laws of historical, and cosmic, process which might give to living generations a confidence in their own capacities to revive their flagging powers and to press on to the struggle for a proper humanity.

Burckhardt professed to find in history an intimation of the truths of Tragedy, but his conception of Tragedy was that of Schopenhauer. The only moral he could draw was the depressing conclusion that "it were better not to have been born at all." Or at least he made of the joy of life a possibility only for men of past ages, and only a few past ages at that. He looked forward to the possibility of a rebirth of culture in the future, but he held out no hope that men might contribute to that rebirth by any positive action they might take in the present. He consigned the immediate future to a series of wars between the various representatives of the current political reality, wars from which he expected nothing positive to result. His view of the future was precisely the same as Spengler's, though arrived at by different means. The only action that the sensitive soul could take was to go underground, cultivate his own garden, remember things past, and wait for the current madness to dissipate itself by its own resources. Then, possibly, on the far side of the holocaust, culture again *might be* revived. In the meantime there was only withdrawal from the city to the countryside, waiting, cultivated conversation with a few chosen kindred spirits, and a consistent disdain for the activities of "practical" men.

Burckhardt's pessimism concealed a germ of faith in the ultimate creative potential of humanity. He loved life too much to deny completely the ideal of culture which had come to him from the Enlightenment. As Croce observed, Burckhardt's was a moral, not an intellectual, failing. "Like all pessimists," Croce wrote, "he had in him a streak of unsatisfiable hedonism" (*History as the Story of Liberty*, 96). And it was this that made him want to flee the world rather than face it and work in it to save those parts of it which he valued most highly. This is perhaps why both his books and his life were conceived as "works of art" in defense of "works of art." Yet, for all of his aestheticism, Burckhardt was much more than a mere dilettante. His sensi-

tivity to the tensions and pressures of his age made him a superb analyst of
the phenomena of cultural decline. He differed from the aesthete in his
desire to justify his flight from the world in world-historical terms. He
thought that he saw the way the world was tending, but he lacked the will
to oppose that tendency in any active way. In this failure of will, he differed
essentially from his friend and colleague Nietzsche.

Three The Repudiation of "Realism" in Late Nineteenth-Century Philosophy of History

Chapter 7 HISTORICAL CONSCIOUSNESS AND THE REBIRTH OF PHILOSOPHY OF HISTORY

The eighteenth century had conventionally distinguished among three types of historiography: true, fabulous, and satirical, with philosophy of history being regarded as merely the serious reflection on the implications for mankind of the facts provided by the first, or true, variety of historical representation. The nineteenth century tended to stress the differences between "true" historiography on the one hand and "philosophy of history" on the other. In order to count as such, it was maintained, historiography had to be a *true* account of what had happened in the past, without any interest in the fanciful per se, and it had to be offered in a spirit of objectivity and from a vantage point above all contemporary party strife, without the distortions and abstractness which a genuinely "philosophical" reflection on their meaning might produce. Hegel maintained the distinction between historiography and philosophy of history, though he was more interested in determining the extent to which the former could be submitted to analysis on the basis of the latter than in stressing the gap which separated them as different departments of inquiry. At the same time, however, his analysis of the various forms that a strictly historical representation of past reality might take appeared to condemn historiography to the status of only a protoscience, if philosophy were not invoked to bring order out of the chaos of the conflicting accounts of the past which historiography necessarily engendered.

Hegel's distinction between the different forms of historiography—universal, pragmatic, critical, and conceptual—was not, however, taken up as a principle by which to distinguish among the different kinds of historiography that the nineteenth century subsequently produced. Historians did distinguish among the principles on which national and local histories had to be written and those on which a survey of "universal" or world history might be attempted. And they did distinguish among original accounts of a given set of historical events, the documents and observations of the events under study, and the historian's reconstruction of what "actually" happened at the time of the events' occurrences as these appeared in his narratives. But a more important distinction was that which turned upon the differences between a "true" account of the past on the one hand and those accounts of the past produced out of commitment to apriori conceptions of what "had to have happened" in the past—that is, "philosophy of history"—and notions of what "should have happened"—that is, ideological or, as it was called, "doctrinaire" history—on the other.

Aside from this distinction between "true" history and "philosophical" history, historians of the nineteenth century stressed the notion that, whatever a true historical account might consist of, it could not be constructed out of purely "artistic" principles on the one hand or in the interest of producing the kind of laws in which the physical sciences dealt on the other. This was not to say that "true" history did not have scientific, philosophical, and artistic elements in it; in fact, the main line of historiographical work in the nineteenth century stressed the historian's dependence upon principles that were scientific, philosophical, and artistic, all at the same time. But history's claim to the status of an autonomous discipline, with its own aims, methods, and subject matter, depended in large part upon the conviction that the scientific, philosophical, and artistic elements within it were *not* those of the science, philosophy, and art of the early nineteenth century, the period in which a "true" historiography was presumed to have first taken shape. That is to say, the science in historiography was not to be Positivistic, the philosophy in it was not to be Idealistic, and the art in it was not to be Romantic. All of this meant, in the end, that historians' efforts to give a true account of what had happened in the past had to be carried out on the bases of a science, a philosophy, and an art that were essentially commonsensical and conventionalist in nature. It would not be too much to say that, insofar as history in the main line of nineteenth-century thought contained scientific, philosophical, and artistic elements, it remained locked in older, pre-Newtonian and pre-Hegelian, more specifically Aristotelian, conceptions of what these consisted of. Its science was "empirical" and "inductive," its philosophy was "realistic," and its art was "mimetic," or imitative, rather than expressive or projective.

This is not to say, of course, that Positivistic, Idealistic, and Romantic historiography was not written, for all three varieties of historiography flourished throughout the century—as the names of Comte, Buckle, and Taine; Heinrich Leo, Strauss, and Feuerbach; Chateaubriand, Carlyle, Froude, and Trevelyan are enough to suggest. But insofar as the historiography actually written could be identified as being either Positivistic, Idealistic, or Romantic, it was regarded by the main line of professional historiographers as being a deviation from the principles of "true" history, a fall into the ground of that "philosophy of history" from which history had been delivered by its professionalization.

Within the main line, different "schools" of historiography took shape, carrying either "national" designations (the Prussian school, the Kleindeutsche school, the French school, the English school, and so on) or labels of a more particularly political sort, labels indicative of the ideological coloration of the historians (Conservative, Liberal, Radical, Socialist, and so on). These "schools" of historiography were intended, however, to signal interests in specific fields of inquiry or subject matter, or to indicate different conceptions of the immediacy of historiographical work to the most pressing concerns of the societies in and for which the historians wrote. They were not considered to threaten seriously the effort to write "true" histories of the past in the way that "philosophy of history" did. Thus, when, during the first decade of the twentieth century, three major surveys of the historiography of the preceding hundred years appeared—those of Fueter, Gooch, and Croce —the distinction between historiography and philosophy of history was taken to be a self-evident principle for discriminating between legitimate and illegitimate historiography by all three.

Fueter, in his *Geschichte der neuren Historiographie* (1911), discerned four major strains or phases in the historical thought of the post–French Revolution period. These were the Romantic, the Liberal, the Realist, and the Scientific—the last beginning sometime after 1870 and in the spirit of which Fueter himself purported to write. Croce, in *Teoria e storia della storiografia* (1912–13), distinguished between Romantic, Idealist, and Positivist historiography, all of which were presumed by him to be flawed by the residues in them of the "philosophies of history" which these names indicated, and the New (or correct) historiography, in which the proper relationship between philosophy, science, and art to history had at last been established and of which he himself was the foremost exponent. And, in *History and Historians in the Nineteenth Century* (1913) Gooch used the "natural" system of classification of historians by "national" school and subject matter, but also assigned to his own age the task of finally synthesizing, in appropriately "historical-scientific" terms, the achievement of the preceding century.

What is most striking about these three surveys of historical writing is the extent to which all of them succeeded in ignoring the reflections on history and historical writing of two of the most profound critics of its academic or professional forms: Marx and Nietzsche. In Fueter's book, Marx was mentioned once as the critic of Proudhon, and Nietzsche was mentioned only to stress the differences between him and Burckhardt. Gooch mentioned both thinkers only in asides. And Croce, while ignoring Nietzsche altogether, disposed of Marx by identifying him as a member of the Romantic school of historiography. Yet all three lamented—or pretended to lament—the extent to which philosophy of history (or, in Croce's case, "theory of history") had lagged behind the actual writing of history by its failure to provide something resembling general laws of the historical process or rules of historical method and analysis. Fueter looked forward hopefully to the appearance of someone who might do for historical study what Darwin's work had done for biology and ethnology, while Gooch stressed the work yet to be done in drawing the different traditions of historiographical work together, so that general scientific principles of historical analysis might be constructed. Croce, of course, with a characteristic disdain for false modesty, suggested that his own work consisted of precisely such a construction. But among the three, only Croce recognized that, if philosophy of history was unable to serve as the general science or theory of historiography, the principles of historical synthesis, for which the thought of the age longed, had to be derived from the different traditions of historiography which the nineteenth century's hostility to modern science, philosophy, and art had produced.

In 1868, of course, an effort to do just that had been made by the Prussian historian J. G. Droysen (1808–84). In his *Historik: Vorlesungen über Enzyklopädie und Methodologie der Geschichte*, Droysen tried to characterize the main forms that historical interpretation might take and the forms of representation which were appropriate for each of them. The intention of the book was to do for historical studies what Aristotle had done in his *Topic* for dialectic, in his *Logic* for demonstration, in his *Rhetoric* for oratory, and in his *Poetic* for literary art. Hence came his title, "Historic," and subtitle, which might best be rendered as "Lectures on the Anatomy and Methodology of History." Like Hegel, Droysen distinguished among four kinds of historical interpretation: the Biographical, the Pragmatic, the Conditional, and what he calls "The Interpretation of Ideas." These four modes of interpretation correspond to what today might be called the Psychological, the Causal, the Teleological, and the Ethical approaches to history respectively. What is remarkable about Droysen's work—and about the abstract of it, the *Grundriss der Historik*, published in 1868, though circulated in manuscript for more than ten years previously—is the extent to which it anticipated the "crisis of historicism" into which historical thinking would be plunged by the very success of nineteenth-century historiography and the kinds of second thoughts about history's claims to the status of a science advanced by thinkers like Fueter, Croce, and Gooch in the decade preceding World War I.

Like Wilhelm von Humboldt and Leopold von Ranke in the first half of the nineteenth century, Droysen began with the assumption that historiography must be considered an autonomous field of study and a discipline with its own particular aims, methods, and subject matter, and hence must be distinguished from Positivistic science, Idealistic philosophy, and Romantic art. But he wrote in a different intellectual and spiritual atmosphere. Philosophy was no longer identified, even in Germany, with Idealism alone. Positivism could no longer be considered as merely a residue of an outmoded enthusiasm for rationalism and mechanistic modes of explanation, appropriate to the analysis of physicochemical matter but inadequate to the characterization of biological and human processes. Darwinism had given the Positivist movement new life, and the prospects for a genuine science of man and society were never brighter than they appeared to be in the 1860s. Moreover, the Romantic movement in literature had given place, at least by the late 1840s, to realism in the novel, so that the threat to the historian's objectivity, which originally appeared to come from the novelist and the poet, was now moderated, or at least limited to those circles of poetic expression occupied by the Symbolists. It thus made sense for Droysen to see in the demand for the scientization of history—coming from Positivists, Marxists, and Social Darwinists alike—the principal threat to history's precious autonomy. And it made more sense for him to suppose that, in the admission of history's similarity to art, a way might be found by which to assert at once the *objectivity* of historiography and its difference from the *science of his own time*. Thus he could account for the different interpretations of the same set of events which a half-century of "objective" historiography had produced, while at the same time asserting their status as real contributions to human knowledge. What Droysen suggested was that historians necessarily give partial and fragmentary accounts of the past, depending on the way they cut into the historical field, but that the ways they might legitimately cut into that field were limited to four general types, each of which illuminated a different area of historical existence, the representation of which inevitably led to contrasting (though not necessarily conflicting) accounts of the same set of events.

Droysen brought to his consideration of the scientific, philosophical, and artistic aspects of the historical field a distinctively *Aristotelian* conception of what science, philosophy, and art, as they are used in historiography, ought to be. His discussion of historiography was divided into three main parts: Method of Investigation (*Methodik*), Systematic Analysis of the Materials Turned up in Investigation (*Systematik*), and Techniques of Representation (*Topik*), which corresponded to the scientific, the philosophical, and the artistic dimensions of the historian's enterprise. The problem of interpretation arises at the very outset, when the historian is forced to choose a way of looking at the documents, monuments, and literary artifacts that he must constitute as evidence. If he looks for information regarding the human agents of the events that interest him, he will be inclined toward Biographical interpretation. If he looks for the causes of events, considers events as functions of sets of causal nexuses, he will be inclined toward a Pragmatic interpretation. If he considers the circumstances or conditions that made a general course of events likely or necessary, in terms of the social, cultural, and natural factors that predominated in the milieux in which the events occurred, he will work toward a Conditional interpretation. And, if he views the events as parts of a larger, ongoing moral or ideational process, he will be inclined toward an Ethical interpretation.

What the historian actually makes out of the materials thus ordered in a preliminary form will depend on four factors: the contents of the materials themselves, the forms in which they appear, the means of historical articulation, and the end or purpose of such articulation. Here, too, the personal or subjective orientation of the historian is at play, and the danger of distortion is ever present; but at the same time the occasion is given, by the very openness of the problem of understanding, for the historian's highest moral, scientific, and philosophical talents to be engaged. The payoff of the whole enterprise comes, however, only in the third phase of the historian's work, when he must choose the mode of representation by which to give his readers the opportunity to re-experience both the reality of the original course of events, as set forth in the narrative, and the operations by which the historian himself has come to understand them.

Droysen distinguished four modes of representation: Interrogative, Didactic, and Discussive, all of which intrude the historian between the reader and his subject matter and seek to lead the reader to some general conclusion or achieve some affect which the historian himself requires, and (the form which Droysen obviously believed to be the most appropriate to true historiography) the Recitative (*die erzählende Darstellung*). In Recitative representation, he noted, the attempt is made to "set forth the results of investigation as a course of events in imitation [*Mimesis*] of its actual development. It takes the results [of investigation] and shapes them into an image of the genesis of the historical facts upon which the investigation has been at work" (English ed., 91: 52). But this mimesis is not to be regarded as either a photographic reproduction of the events or as an operation in which the events are allowed to "speak for themselves." For, Droysen insisted, "Without the narrator to make them speak, they would be dumb." And, far from seeking to be objective, he added, it is not "objectivity which is the historian's best glory. His justness consists in seeking to understand." (*Ibid.*)

"Understanding" can manifest itself in four distinct forms, corresponding to the modes of interpretation outlined in the first section of Droysen's book. In this crucial section, the distinctions drawn among the Biographical, the Monographic, the Catastrophic, and the Pragmatic modes point to the possibility of different positions from which to view the events within the narrative itself and accounts for tendencies to emplot the events in different ways, as different kinds of stories.

Droysen specifically denied that the "forms of representation" have been "determined after the analogy of epic, lyric, or dramatic composition," in the way that Georg Gottfried Gervinus, in his *Grundzüge der Historik* (1837) had proposed (*ibid.*). But it is quite obvious, from his discussion of the four forms of Recitative exposition, that they are abstractions from the basic plot structures of the Western literary tradition. Thus, the Biographical mode of exposition, stressing personality as the decisive causal force in history, can be identified with the story form of the Romance. The Monographic mode, which is teleological in principle, stressing the conditions that permitted the unfolding of a destiny and an epiphany of law, corresponds to Tragedy. The Catastrophic mode, which illuminates the "right" of all parties in the contest and which figures the birth of a new society out of the old, corresponds to the Comic mode in literary art. And the Pragmatic mode, which stresses the rule of law, and in such a way as to imply that events are fated to take the courses they actually take, corresponds to the mode of Satire. These modes of exposition thus comprise the appropriate literary forms for the representation of processes conceived to be governed by the forces identified, in the interpretative phase of the historian's operations, as different kinds of causal agencies: Individual, Moral, Social, and Natural.

Droysen's fourfold schema for classifying the different modes of explanation and representation in historiography is reminiscent of other such schemata. We have already encountered the fourfold classification in Hegel's characterization of the species of Reflective history (Universal, Pragmatic, Critical, and Conceptual). We recall Croce's characterizations of the main forms of nineteenth-century historical thought (Romantic, Idealistic, Positivistic, and "New") and Fueter's categories (Romantic, Liberal, Realistic, and Scientific). A similar kind of classificatory scheme was worked out by Wilhelm Dilthey during the first decade of the twentieth century. In his *Der Aufbau der geschichtlichen Welt in den Geisteswissenchaften*, Dilthey identified the three principal contributors to the historiographical tradition of the early nineteenth century as Ranke, Carlyle, and Tocqueville, and suggested that his own *Einleitung in die Geisteswissenschaften* (1883) represented, in the tradition of "philosophy of history," the beginning of a serious effort to provide a *"Kritik der historischen Vernunft"* of the sort that historians had seriously needed since the establishment of their field as an autonomous discipline (117–118). And one is reminded, finally, of Nietzsche's fourfold classification of the forms of historical consciousness in his "Use and Abuse of History": Antiquarian, Monumental, Critical, and his own "Superhistorical" vision of these.

The recurrence of a fourfold schema for classifying historical thinking is not in itself remarkable, since the cultural history of the nineteenth century can be broken down into four major movements—Romanticism, Idealism, Naturalism, and Symbolism—and the different conceptions of history could be seen as nothing more than abstractions of the different world views represented by these movements projected onto the problem of historical knowledge and extended to the historical field so as to produce the four conflicting conceptions of history which the analysts of the age attempted to characterize in their various schemata of classification. Each movement brought with it its own unique conceptions of what "science," "philosophy," and "art" ought to be; and it is not surprising that theorists of history should build into their conceptualizations of the problem of history's relationship to these other fields their predilections for one or another of the different notions of those fields sanctioned by the different cultural movements to which they belonged. The problem is to get behind these preconceptions and to seek yet another mode of characterization that will identify their *shared* preconceptions, so as to show them to be members of a single family of values and attitudes toward history, and at the same time to illuminate the differences of stress and subordination among them that make them different phases of, or variations on, the single tradition of thought which they represent.

Here I revert to my original formulation of the basic problem of historical thought, which is to construct a verbal model of the historical process, or some part of it, which, by virtue of its status as a linguistic artifact, can be broken down into the levels of lexicon, grammar, syntax, and semantic. If I proceed in this way, I am permitted to assert that different historians stress different aspects of the same historical field, the same set or sequence of events, because they actually *see* different objects in that field, provisionally group them into different classes and species of historical existence, conceive the relationships among them in different terms, and explicate the transformations of those relationships in different ways, in order to figure different meanings for them by the structure of the narratives they write about them. Thus conceived, histories are attempts to use language (ordinary or technical language, but usually the former) in such a way as to constitute different universes of discourse in which statements about the meaning of history in general or of different segments of the whole historical process can be made.

The different levels of linguistic integration—from the simple naming operation, through the synchronic classificatory scheme on the one hand and the diachronic scheme on the other, by which the classes of historical phenomena and the relations they bear to one another as parts of a process can be established, to the "meaning" they have for the understanding of the whole historical process—would themselves generate different conceptions of the historian's task, according to the importance the individual historian conceded to one or another of the different operations necessary for the constituting of a comprehensive "language of historical discourse." The historian who concentrated on the lexical level would represent one extreme and would produce what were essentially chronicles—though much "fuller" ones than those produced by his medieval counterparts—while the historian who pushed too rapidly through to the detection of the ultimate meaning (semantics) of the whole historical field would produce "philosophies of history."

If I considered lexical operations as one pole of historiographical activity and semantic operations as the other, I could then see that what the academic historians of the nineteenth century meant by "true" history would have to be located somewhere between these two extremes, on the *grammatical level,* where general classificatory operations predominate and representation of the synchronic structure of the historical field is aimed at, or on the *syntactical level,* where the dynamics of the field considered as a process would be the principal object of analysis and representation of the diachronic dimensions of historical being would be apprehended. Of course, every historical work, simply because it aims at the construction of an adequate universe of discourse within which the historical process in general can be talked about meaningfully, would operate on all four levels. And different kinds of historiography would be produced more by the stress given to one or another of the levels of linguistic constitution than by the elimination of any of the levels of meaning.

If historiographical discourse remains too rigidly limited to the simple naming of the objects that occupy the historical field and merely arranges them on a time line in the order of those objects' appearance in the field, the historical work degenerates into chronicle. If, however, it thins out the factual detail in the interest of clarifying the relations that are presumed to exist among all historical objects of all classes, the result is what Danto called "conceptual narrative" or "philosophy of history." That is to say, a "true" historical account of what actually happened in history would be one which remained on the levels of synchronic classification of the data on the one hand and of diachronic representation of them on the other. This would explain the tendency of historiographers within the main line of the professional convention of the nineteenth century to regard *formalistic characterizations of the historical field* and *narrative representations of its process* as the appropriate way to write "history." And it would provide a way of characterizing their own characterization of "historiography" as a kind of discourse which falls between the emptiness of mere chronicle on the one hand and the nefarious "philosophy of history" on the other.

As thus conceived, a "historical account" would be any account of the past in which the events that occupied the historical field were properly named, grouped into species and classes of a distinctively "historical" sort, and further related by general conceptions of causation by which changes in their relationships could be accounted for. These operations would *presuppose* a general conception of historical meaning, an idea or notion of the nature of the historical field and its processes; in short, they would imply a "philosophy of history." But this "philosophy of history" would be present in a given "historiographical" account of the past only as "displaced," sublimated, or sublated. It would appear only in the mode of explanation actually used to account for "what happened" in the historical field and in the plot structure used to transform the *story actually told* in the narrative into *a story of a particular kind*. This displaced "philosophy of history," presupposed in any moderately comprehensive account of the past or present, would be the "ideological" element identified by critics of any given "interpretation" of the past or present, or of any set of events of special interest to the groups engaged in the political arena of any given period. But, since there would be no way of arbitrating among the different modes of explanation that might be chosen by a given historian (Organicism, Contextualism, Mechanism, Formism) on the one hand or the different modes of emplotment he might use to structure his narrative (Romance, Comedy, Tragedy, Satire) on the other, the field of historiography would appear to be rich and creative precisely in the degree to which it generated many different possible accounts of the same set of events and many different ways of figuring their multiple meanings. At the same time, historiography would derive whatever integrity it was supposed to have from its resistance to any impulse either to move to the level of outright conceptualization of the historical field, as the philosopher of history was inclined to do, or to fall into apprehensions of chaos, as the chronicler did.

Philosophy of history, then, would be a threat to historiography inasmuch as the philosopher of history is impelled to make explicit the explanatory and narrative strategies that remain implicit in the work of the professional historiographer. But the philosopher of history represents a greater threat also, because philosophy of history is characteristically a product of *a desire to change the professionally sanctioned strategies by which meaning is conferred on history*. The virulence of the nineteenth-century professional historian's opposition to philosophy of history and the contempt with which the philosophers of history of the time viewed professional historiographers had to do in large part with the philosophers of history's insistence that professional historiography is just as value laden and just as conceptually determined as "philosophy of history" itself. The most adamant critics of academic or professional historiography discerned that history's "disciplinization" consisted for the most part in the exclusion of certain kinds of explanatory concepts on the one hand and the use of certain modes of emplotment on the other. Nietzsche's charges of the "banality" of professional historians is really, in the final analysis, a criticism of their philistinic conception of art, just as Marx's charges of the "servility" of those same historians is, in the final analysis, a criticism of their bourgeois conception of science.

These charges make the achievements of Marx and Nietzsche "radical" indictments of academic historical thinking. For, whereas other philosophers of history—such as Comte and Buckle—had sought to import ideas and techniques of representation from the fields of art and science into history, and apply them mechanically to the same data that the professionals had presented in their "narratives," Marx and Nietzsche challenged the very conceptions of art and science from which the entire high culture of the nineteenth century received its form and on the basis of which it preconceived the problem of relating science *to* art. This suggests that historical studies, in becoming professionalized, also become a rule-governed activity, in much the same way that language itself becomes rule-governed when lexicographers and grammarians reflect on the usages of current speech in order to explicate the rules of that speech and then define proper usage as speech which follows *those* rules. Within the concept of proper usage thus enshrined as an orthodoxy, a number of different stylistic strategies become possible, all of which may conform more or less to the "rules" thus given.

In the historical thinking of the nineteenth century, the different stylistic protocols that were given the status of orthodoxy were represented by Michelet, Ranke, Tocqueville, and Burckhardt respectively. Each prided himself on his "realism" and on his discovery of the most appropriate way of characterizing a field of historical happening inside the limits set by the concept of "correct" usage honored by the historiographically "literate" society of his time.

But the very diversity of interpretations of the same set of historical events, which this notion of historiography as a kind of natural-language universe of discourse permitted, could not fail to suggest to the most philosophically acute observers that the "rules of the game" might well be construed differently, and that a different universe of discourse for the characterization of the historical field might well be conceivable. And in Marx and Nietzsche this conceptualization of the nature of historical knowledge was pushed to its logical conclusions. Both sought to change the linguistic rules of the historiographical game, Marx on the basis of a critique of the scientific component in historical thinking, Nietzsche by a critique of the artistic component. To put the matter in Hegelian terms, then, what Marx and Nietzsche tried to do, each in his own way, was to carry out the (Hegelian) injunction to transform the insights of the different kinds of Reflective history into a basis for a genuinely Philosophical history, a history which not only *knows* something about the historical process but knows *how* it knows it, and is able to *defend* its way of knowing in philosophically justifiable terms.

The principal forms of philosophy of history that appeared between Hegel and Croce represented efforts to avoid (or to transcend) the Ironic implications of a historiography conceived as an exercise in explanation by description. The two most profound representatives of philosophy of history during this period, Karl Marx and Friedrich Nietzsche, both began their reflections on historical knowledge in the full recognition of the Ironic implications of the official professional orthodoxy in historical thinking (as represented by

Ranke and his followers) and the acceptable forms of deviationism from the orthodox norms (as represented by Michelet, Tocqeuville, and Burckhardt). Of course, for neither Marx nor Nietzsche was recourse to a Romantic historiography possible, any more than it was for Ranke, Tocqueville, or Burckhardt. Like their counterparts in historiography, Marx and Nietzsche conceived their "realism" to consist in the effort to rise above the subjectivism of the Romantic approach to history on the one hand and the naive mechanism of its late Enlightenment, rationalistic predecessor on the other. In this conception of "realism" they followed the path marked by Hegel.

But, like Hegel also, they conceived of historical knowledge as a problem of consciousness, and not merely one of "methodology." Moreover, like him, both Marx and Nietzsche insisted on the necessity of turning historical knowledge to the needs of the *present* social and cultural life. Neither of them desired a "contemplative" knowledge of the past. Both were aware of the debilitating, not to say tragic, effects to which a purely contemplative historiography would contribute. They saw clearly, in a way that Michelet, Ranke, Tocqueville, and Burckhardt only glimpsed, that the way one thought about the past had serious implications about the way one thought about one's own present and future. And they put the problem of historical consciousness directly in the center of their philosophies. No two thinkers in the nineteenth century, with the exception of Hegel himself, were so obsessed with the problem of history, or rather with the problem of the "problem" of history. And the achievements of both as philosophers can be understood, in large part, in terms of their quest for the grounds on which the problem of the "problem" of history could be dissolved.

What they actually achieved, however, was little more than a theoretical justification for the alternative modes of historical reflection worked out by Michelet, Ranke, Tocqueville, and Burckhardt considered as members of a single tradition of linguistic practice. Marx spoke in the idiom of Metonymy for his analysis of history and his criticism of the academic historians and the dilettantes whom he despised as "ideologists." But his ultimate purpose was to show how the divisions and conflicts of history can be sublated in such a way that the next stage of human development can be realistically conceived as a field of Synecdochic unities. In short, Marx's purpose was to translate Irony into Tragedy and, ultimately, Tragedy into Comedy.

By contrast, Nietzsche viewed both Tragedy and Comedy "Ironically," seeing both visions as constructions of human consciousness itself rather than as residues of a "realistic" perception of reality. At the same time, he asserted the fictional nature of all putative laws of history and the subordination of human knowledge to some system of values anterior to them. By unmasking the mythic nature of both Tragedy and Comedy on the one hand and all forms of science on the other, Nietzsche sought to return consciousness to its own origins in the human will. He sought to heal this will of whatever doubts it entertained about its own capacities, both for conceiving reality in life-giving ways and for acting upon it in its own best interests. Thus, although Nietzsche began his discussions of the historical process with a preliminary characterization of it as an essentially Ironic condition—that is to say, as utterly chaotic and governed by no rule except the so-called will to power—he was ultimately concerned to emplot the history of man as a Romantic Drama, a drama of human self-transcendence and individual redemption, though the redemption was not *from* an iron-bound "nature" or *to* a terrifying transcendental deity, but *from man himself*, man as he has been in history, *to* man *as he might be* in his self-reconciled condition. Like Marx, then, Nietzsche envisioned a liberation from history that was simultaneously a liberation from society. But the form that this liberation would take, in his presentation of it, was not that of a revivified human community; it was, rather, a purely individual one, possible for the Superman but denied to the herd, which he once more consigned to *both* nature and history.

Marx and Nietzsche asked how it was possible to conceive the birth of a healthy historical life out of a condition of suffering and conflict. Both were supreme optimists, in a way that none of their counterparts in historiography was. Ranke's optimism was not defended on theoretical grounds by which the *possible* transformation of private vice into public benefits could be accounted for. Michelet's optimism was not defended at all; it simply represented a mood, a need which he profoundly felt and which dictated everything he attempted in the way of historical justification. There were no grounds for optimism in either Tocqueville or Burckhardt. Marx and Nietzsche criticized the optimism both of the Romantics and of the self-styled realists of the academy, as well as the pessimism of their dilettantish counterparts. They sought to return historical thought to the consideration of the categories by which it alone can lay claim to the status of either a science (in Marx) or an art (in Nietzsche). The rebellion of Marx against Hegel (which was primarily a revision rather than a revolution) and that of Nietzsche against Schopenhauer (which also was more in the nature of a revision rather than a repudiation) had similar goals. Both sought synthetic thought about the historical field and its processes, what might be called the construction of a grammar and a syntax of historical analysis by which the "meaning" of history could be given a clear scientific formulation on the one hand or a clear artistic representation on the other.

In the thought of Marx the problem of history turned upon the problem of the *mode of explanation* to be used in characterizing its structures and processes. This conformed with his conception of history as a science. In the thought of Nietzsche, by contrast, the problem turned on the *mode of emplotment* to be chosen for the creative explication of a phenomenal field that appeared not to be governed by any law whatsoever. Each recognized that the choice between the different modes of explanation and emplotment open to the historical thinker must be governed by appeal to some extrahistorical principle or rule. For neither of them was there anything like a value-

free ground on which the choice between the different strategies of explanation and emplotment could be objectively justified. As a result of all this the
question of what is meant by "objectivity" was raised.

The contributions of Marx and Nietzsche to the "crisis of historicism" of
the late nineteenth century, then, consisted in their historicization of the
very concept of objectivity itself. For them, historical thought was not the
result of a criterion of objectivity that one could simply "apply" to the data
of the historical field. It was the nature of objectivity itself which they brought
under question.

Chapter 8   Marx: The Philosophical Defense of History in the Metonymical Mode

❧ Introduction

Marx apprehended the historical field in the Metonymical mode. His categories of prefiguration were the categories of schism, division, and alienation. The historical process, therefore, appeared to him as that "panorama of sin and suffering" which Tocqueville and Burckhardt asserted to be history's true meaning *once their analyses of it were complete.* Marx began where they ended. Their Irony was his point of departure. His purpose was to determine the extent to which one can *realistically* hope for the ultimate integration of the forces and objects that occupy the historical field. Marx regarded the kinds of integrative trends which Michelet and Ranke purportedly found in the historical process as illusory, false integrations or only partial ones, the benefits of which were shared by only a fragment of the whole human species. And he was interested in determining whether this fragmentation of humanity must be considered the *ineluctable* condition of the human animal.

Hegel's Comic conception of history was based ultimately on his belief in the right of life over death; "life" guaranteed to Hegel the possibility of an ever more adequate form of social life throughout the historical future. Marx carried this Comic conception even further; he envisioned nothing less than the dissolution of that "society" in which the contradiction between consciousness and being had to be entertained as a fatality for all men in all times. It would not, then, be unjust to characterize the final vision of history which inspired Marx in his historical and social theorizing as a Romantic one. But his conception did not envisage humanity's redemption as a deliverance from time itself. Rather, his redemption took the form of a reconciliation of man with a nature denuded of its fantastic and terrifying powers, submitted to the rule of technics, and turned to the creation of a genuine community, to the end of creating individuals who are free because they no longer have to struggle with one another for their own selfhood, but only with themselves. As thus conceived, Marx's idea of history represented a perfect Synecdoche: the parts merged into a whole which is qualitatively superior to any of the entities that comprise it.

In Marx's thought the problem which had been raised by Vico, worried by Rousseau, skirted by Burke, and formulated as a major philosophical problem by Hegel—that is, the "problem of society," or the "problematical nature of social existence"—was moved to the center of historical investigation. For Marx, society was no longer either the sole protective barrier between a beleaguered humanity and a chaotic nature (as it was for Burke) or the obstructive barrier between individual men and their true "inner natures" (as it was for Rousseau and the Romantics). For Marx, as for Hegel, society was both these things—that is, the instrument of man's liberation from nature and the cause of men's estrangement from one another. Society both unified and divided, liberated and oppressed, at one and the same time. The purpose of historical investigation, as Marx conceived it, was, first to show how society functions in this twofold manner in the life of man and, then, to demonstrate how the paradox represented by this condition *must* be resolved in time.

The Problem of Marxian Scholarship

It is conventional today to study Marx's writings in order to determine (1) the continuity or discontinuity between his early work, represented above all by the *Economic and Philosophical Manuscripts* (1844) and such tracts as *The German Ideology* (1845), and the mature work, represented by the *Communist Manifesto*, the *Contribution to a Critique of Political Economy*, *The Eighteenth Brumaire of Louis Bonaparte*, and *Capital*; (2) the extent to which Marx's thought may be characterized as "humanistic" or, conversely, "totalitarian" in its social implications; and (3) the degree to which Marx's theories, taken as a whole and however interpreted, qualify as a positive contribution to the social sciences. A number of modern critics have made an industry out of reflection on problems such as these, and we must be grateful to them for their clarification of Marx's relationship to the principal figures in the thought world in which, and against which, his mature system took shape.

Central to the concerns of these critics are such issues as the consistency of Marx's work as a philosopher, the relevance of his thought to the analysis of contemporary social problems, and the validity of his vision of the course that history must take in the future. To contemporary Marxist ideologists, as well as to their opponents, it is imperative to determine whether Marxism is or is not the scientific system of social analysis that it claims to be, whether the Marxist analysis of social crises is applicable to contemporary crises, and whether Marxist economic theory represents the best possible way of explaining the systems of exchange developed in the wake of modern industrial capitalism.

My own approach to the study of Marx's thought moves many of these questions to the periphery of discussion. My aim is to specify the dominant style of Marx's thought about the structures and processes of history-in-general. I am interested in Marx primarily as a representative of a specific modality of historical consciousness, a representative who must be regarded as neither more nor less "true" than the best representatives of other modalities with which it contended for hegemony in the consciousness of nineteenth-century European man. In my view, "history," as a plenum of documents that attest to the occurrence of events, can be put together in a number of different and equally plausible narrative accounts of "what happened in the past," accounts from which the reader, or the historian himself, may draw different conclusions about "what must be done" in the present. With the Marxist philosophy of history, one can do neither more nor less than what one can do with other philosophies of history, such as those of Hegel, Nietzsche, and Croce, even though one may be inclined to do different *kinds* of things on the basis of a belief in one philosophy's truth.

That is to say, one can either adopt Marx's philosophy of history as providing the perspective from which one *wills* to view one's own place in the stream of historical becoming or one can reject it on similarly voluntaristic grounds. We apprehend the past and the whole spectacle of history-in-general in terms of felt needs and aspirations that are ultimately personal, having to do with the ways we view our own positions in the ongoing social establishment, our hopes and fears for the future, and the image of the kind of humanity we would like to believe we represent. As these felt needs and aspirations change, we adjust our conception of history-in-general accordingly. It is not with history as it is with nature. We have no choice with respect to the principles of knowledge we must adopt for effecting transformations in, or for exercising control over, the physical world. We either employ scientific principles of analysis and understanding of the operations of nature or we fail in our efforts to control nature.

It is different with history. There are different possible ways of comprehending historical phenomena because there are different, and equally plausible, ways of organizing the social world which we create and which provides one of the bases of our experience of history itself. As Lucien Goldmann pointed out, it is in the interest of every modern class, and indeed of every individual, to promote the growth of objective physical sciences, for it is in the interest of all classes of contemporary society to extend man's control over the "nature" that lies before him as the resources out of which a "society" is to be constructed. But, as social beings, we have different stakes in the different kinds of society we can imagine to be potentially realizable as a result of our scientific exploitation of nature. This means that the kind of social science we will be inclined to promote will be characterized by certain crucial limitations on what we can envisage as that science's capacities for promoting or frustrating the growth of a particular kind of society.

Thus, there are bound to be alternative and even radically incompatible ways of conceiving the form that an adequate social science must take. Among these ways we recognize the legitimacy of a specifically Radical conception of social analysis, of which Marx was undoubtedly the outstanding nineteenth-century exponent, but alongside this we must set Anarchist, Liberal, and Conservative varieties. Each of these notions of social analysis is attended by, or generates, a *specific conception* of the historical process and of its most significant structures, to which a given individual may be drawn by epistemological, aesthetic, or ethical considerations. It is fruitless, then, in my view at least, to try to arbitrate among contending conceptions of the nature of the historical process on cognitive grounds which purport to be value-neutral in essence, as both Marxist and non-Marxist social theorists attempt to do. The best reasons for being a Marxist are moral ones, just as the best reasons for being a Liberal, Conservative, or Anarchist are moral ones. The Marxist view of history is neither confirmable nor disconfirmable by appeal to "historical evidence," for what is at issue between a Marxist and a non-Marxist view of history is the question of precisely what counts as evidence and what does not, how data are to be constituted as evidence, and what implications for the comprehension of the present social reality are to be drawn from the evidence thus constituted.

Marx wrote history neither for purposes of social mediation (á la Tocqueville) nor for purposes of social accommodation (á la Ranke). He was a prophet of social innovation, and he conceived historical consciousness as an instrument of human liberation in a way that no other nineteeth-century thinker of similar stature ever tried to do. When he wrote in his "Theses on Feuerbach" that "the philosophers have only *interpreted* the world in different ways; the point, however, is to *change* it" (69), he meant to imply not that men should not try to understand the world but that the sole test of their understanding of it was their capacity to change it. Thus he laid siege to every plan for creating a merely *contemplative* historiography such as that which, under Ranke's name, had been established as orthodoxy in the academies all over Europe. Science for Marx was *transforming* knowledge, the transforming of nature in the physical sphere, the transforming of human consciousness and praxis in the social sphere. And he envisaged his theory of history as a means of liberating men from the infinite series of infinitesimal approximations to a genuine humanity, conceived to extend indefinitely into the future by thinkers like Hegel and Tocqueville, so that they might finally realize their humanity fully. For Marx, *history properly comprehended* not only provided an image of man come into his kingdom on earth; it was also one of the instruments by which that kingdom was finally to be won.

Within the context of considerations such as these I will consider the problem of the continuity between Marx's early and late works. It is my contention that, as far as Marx's general theory of history is concerned, this is a pseudo problem. It may be interesting to speculate on the effects that contemporary events and Marx's encounter with specific thinkers during the 1840s had on the constitution of his system as represented by *The Eighteenth Brumaire* or *Capital*. But these are hagiographical, not theoretical, concerns. It is my contention that, considered as a representative of a distinctive style of historical philosophizing, Marx's thought displays a consistent recourse to a set of tropological structures that give his thought its unique attributes, from *The German Ideology* (1845) through *Capital* (1867).

✎§ The Essence of Marx's Thought about History

The essence of Marx's thought about history, its structures and processes, consists less in an attempt to *combine* what he thought was valid in the thought of Hegel, Feuerbach, the British Political Economists, and the Utopian Socialists than in his effort to synthesize the tropological strategies of Metonomy and Synecdoche in a comprehensive image of the historical world. This way of characterizing Marx's work permits me to specify the relationship that exists in his thought between the Mechanistic-Materialistic elements on the one hand and the Organicist-Idealistic elements on the other, the Positivism he is supposed to have derived from his study of the British Political Economists, and the dialectical method he is supposed to have borrowed from Hegel. It also permits me to distinguish between the *tactics* Marx used for criticizing opponents and those he used for setting forth the truths of history which he purported to find in the historical record.

Marx's thought moved between Metonymical apprehensions of the severed condition of mankind in its social state and Synecdochic intimations of the unity he spied at the end of the whole historical process. How can man be both immediately determined and potentially free; how can he be both severed and fragmented in his becoming, yet whole and one in his being? These are the questions that concerned Marx. He needed two kinds of language to characterize these different states or conditions. And he effectively divided the historical record into two orders of phenomena, horizontally, as it were, one order of which was related integrally by Metonymical, the other of which was related by Synecdochic, strategies of characterization. Marx's problem, then, was to relate the two orders thus distinguished.

He related them, in fact, Metonymically, in a cause-effect relationship; and this is the mark as well as the measure of Marx's ultimately Materialistic conception of history. When Marx said that his conception of history was "dialectical-materialistic," what he meant was that he conceived the processes of the Base of society mechanistically and the processes of the Superstructure Organicistically. This combination alone permitted him to believe that, over the long run, a structure of human relationships that is essentially extrinsic and mechanical in nature can eventuate in a qualitatively different structure, intrinsic and organismic in the way it relates parts to wholes.

Marx thus emplotted the historical process on two levels, that of the Base and that of the Superstructure. On the level of the Base, there is nothing but a succession of distinctive means of production and of the modes of their relationships, a succession that is governed by strict causal laws similar to those that obtain in nature. On the level of the Superstructure, however, there is a genuine *progressus*, an evolution of modalities of relating man to man. On the level of the Base, where the modes of production take shape, there is a *progressus*, to be sure—that of man's every more certain understanding of, and control over, the physical world and its processes. On the Superstructural level, by contrast, the *progressus* consists of a deepening of human consciousness' perception of man's alienation from himself and from his fellow man and a corresponding development of the social conditions within which that alienation can be transcended.

Thus, as Marx conceived it, the history of mankind in general represents a twofold evolution: an ascent, insofar as man gains ever greater control over nature and its resources through the development of science and technology; and a descent, insofar as man grows ever more alienated from himself and from his fellow man. This twofold movement permitted Marx to believe that the whole of history was heading toward a decisive *crisis*, a conflict in which man would either come into his kingdom on earth or destroy himself—and the nature that he both arose from and opposed in the struggle for his own humanity.

This means that Marx's philosophy of history comprises both a *synchronic* analysis of a basic structure of relationships which remains constant throughout history and a *diachronic* analysis of the significant movement by which this structure is transcended and a new modality of relating man to man is constituted. And this implies that, for Marx, history had to be emplotted in two ways simultaneously: in the mode of Tragedy and in the mode of

Comedy. For, although man *lives* Tragically, inasmuch as his attempts to construct a viable human community are continually frustrated by the laws that govern history while he remains in the social state, he also lives Comically, insofar as this interaction between man and society progressively moves man toward a condition in which society itself will be dissolved and a genuine community, a communistic mode of existence, will be constituted as his true historic destiny.

⌑§ The Basic Model of Analysis

The model of the analytical strategy that Marx used for comprehending all historical phenomena received one of its clearest formulations in Chapter I of *Capital*, where he set forth the labor theory of value in order to earn a distinction between the "content" and the "form" of value of all commodities produced by man. This chapter, entitled "Commodities," is divided into four parts, the first two of which have to do with the *content* of the value of commodities, and the second two of which have to do with the *forms* that value assumes in different systems of exchange.

Commodities, Marx said, are the "elementary units" of the "wealth of societies in which the capitalist method of production prevails" (*Capital*, Paul ed., 3). And he went on to distinguish, on the basis of the labor theory of value, between the use value of a commodity and its exchange value, in terms of the distinction between the *content* and the phenomenal *form* of any commodity offered for exchange in any economic system, whether primitive or advanced. The use value of a commodity, Marx argued, is provided by the "abstract human labor that has been embodied or materialized in it." Man can measure this value, Marx asserted, in terms of "the quantity of the 'value-creating' substance it contains—the quantity of labor." (7) This means that, "as values, commodities are nothing but particular masses of congealed labor time" (8).

Marx pointed out, however, that the exchange value of a commodity is not the same as the value *assigned to it in a given system of exchange.* In any actual system of exchange, commodities will have values that appear to bear no relation to the amounts of labor required for their production. Men exchange commodities *within systems* that endow them with an exchange value different from that by which their use values might be accurately determined. This means that the *forms* of the values that commodities represent in a given system of exchange are different from their actual use values, or value contents. Commodities have different values for purposes of exchange than they have for purposes of use. And the problem, as Marx saw it, is to account for this differential between the form (the exchange value) and the content (the use value) of commodities. If we can account for the differential, we can provide a method of distinguishing between the changing phenomenal forms of value on the one hand and the changeless value content of commodities on the other. Marx's notion was that, while the use value of a commodity is constant, given by the amount of socially necessary labor required for its production, the exchange value is variable and changing, given by the actual relationships that obtain within different historical situations, or systems of exchange, at different times and in different places.

What interests me here is Marx's analysis of the different *forms* that the phenomenal aspect of the value of a commodity assumes and the relationship between these forms and the actual, or real, value of any commodity which, by his lights, remains constant throughout whatever changes the phenomenal form undergoes. For these two kinds of relationships, *between the forms of value* on the one hand and *between the forms and the constant content of value* on the other, are precisely analogous to the relationships he took to exist between the phenomenal forms of historical (social) being on the one hand and its constant (human) content on the other.

In the first place, Marx insisted that, although the actual value of any commodity is fixed by the amount of socially necessary labor expended in its production, the phenomenal form of the value of any commodity, its exchange value, varies and may assume any one of four forms: the Elementary (Isolated, or Accidental) form of value, the Total (or Extended) form, the Generalized form, and the Money form (*Geldform*). In the first form, the value of a commodity is *equated* with the value presumed to exist in some other commodity. In the second, the value of a commodity is, as Marx put it, "expressed in terms of *numberless* other elements in the world of commodities" (34), such that the value of a commodity can be expressed in an "interminable series" of different commodities. In the third form, the value of *all* commodities may be expressed in terms of *one commodity* in the series, as when a coat, specific amounts of tea, coffee, wheat, gold, iron, and so on, are considered to be "worth" a certain amount of some other commodity, such as linen, so that the common value of all, the amount of labor necessary for their production, can be equated in terms of *only one other commodity*. And, in the fourth form, value comes into being when the specific commodity, gold, is hit upon as the standard by which the presumed value of every other commodity can be set and specified.

In Marx's view, this fourth form of value, the Money form, represents the point of departure from which all analyses of the actual value of commodities must set forth. The Money form of value is the "mystery" to be solved in economic analysis, a mystery which consists of the fact that men, who by their labor create the value that inheres in commodities as use value, insist on interpreting the value of commodities in terms of their exchange value, and specifically in terms of their exchange value in gold. As Marx put it:

Man's thought about the forms of social life, his scientific analysis of these forms, runs counter to the actual course of social evolution. He begins by an examination of the finished product, the extant result of the evolutionary process. The characters which stamp labor products as commodities, the characters which they must possess before they can circulate as commodities, have already acquired the fixity of natural forms of social life, when economists begin to study, not indeed their history . . . , but their meaning. Thus, it was only the analysis of prices of commodities which led to the determination of the magnitude of values, it was only the common expression of all commodities in money which led to their being recognized as "values." But this finished form of the world of commodities, this money form, is the very thing which *veils* instead of disclosing the social character of private and individual labor, and therewith *hides* the social relations between the individual producers. When I say that coats or boots or what not are related to linen as the general embodiment of abstract human labor, the statement seems manifestly absurd. Yet when the producers of coats, boots, etc., bring these commodities into relation with linen as the general equivalent (or with gold or silver as the general equivalent, for the nature of the case is the same), it is precisely in this *absurd form* [*Verrückten Form*] that the relation between their own private labor and the collective labor of society discloses itself to them. [49 (German ed., 89–90); italics added]

It should be noted that Marx characterized the Money form of value as "absurd." It is absurd because men, in the bourgeois world at least, insist upon characterizing the value of the commodities they produce and exchange in terms of their exchange value *for gold*, the least useful of all the metals in Marx's view. The whole burden of Marx's analysis of both the content and the form of value of commodities was to reveal the absurdity of this impulse to equate the value of a commodity with its gold equivalent. This is what Marx meant when he characterized bourgeois society as having been founded upon the "mystery" of the fetishism of commodities. In bourgeois society, men insist upon obscuring the extent to which the value of commodities resides in the amount of socially necessary labor expended in their production, and in equating that value with its exchange value for gold. The constitution of a socially useless commodity, such as gold, as the criterion for determining the value of commodities produced by human labor, is, according to Marx, evidence of the madness of the kind of society that is organized along bourgeois lines, in response to the imperatives of the capitalist mode of production.

In Marx's view, commodities exist *in reality* as a set of individual entities, the actual value of which is determinable by the specific amounts of socially necessary labor expended in their production. But they exist in the consciousness of men only insofar as they have an exchange value for other commodities, and specifically for the commodity of gold. How can this strange fact be accounted for?

In Chapter I, Part 3, of *Capital*, Marx dilated on the *form* of value—that is to say, the exchange value of commodities—in order to explain the development of the Money form of value on the one hand and to prepare his readers for his solution of the "mystery of the fetishistic character of commodities" on the other. As he put it in the introduction to this section of his work:

We have to discover the origin of the money form; to trace the development of the expression of value contained in the value ratio of commodities to follow up from its simplest and most inconspicuous configuration to the glaringly obvious money form. Then the enigma of money will cease to be an enigma. [17 (62)]

He then proceeded to distinguish among the four forms of value: the Elementary (or Accidental) form, the Total (or Extended) form, the Generalized form, and the Money form.

What interests me in Marx's analysis is the strategy he used to derive the alleged fact of the fetishism of gold from the fact of an ordinary, and natural, *equation* of relative use values in the original form of exchange. For this strategy can serve as a model of Marx's method of analyzing the transformations that occur on the phenomenal level of all processes of development which are specifically social and historical (rather than natural).

The strategy may be thought of as dialectical in essence, in the Hegelian sense of that term; and the four forms of value may be thought of, if one wishes, as value in itself, value for itself, value in and for itself, and value by, in, and for itself. But it is obvious—as Michel Foucault has observed—that Marx's dialectical analysis of the phenomenal form of value represents little more than an extended exegesis of the word "value" (Foucault, 298), and that what Marx carried out was a tropological analysis of the way the concept "value" is apprehended by men in different stages of their social evolution.

For example, Marx's model of the Elementary (or Accidental) form of value is that of an equation construed as a Metaphorical relationship between any two commodities. He said:

We write x commodity $A = y$ commodity B; or we say that x commodity A "are worth" y commodity B. In the concrete, we write, 20 yards of linen $= 1$ coat; or we say that 20 yards of linen "are worth" one coat. [*Capital*, Paul ed., 18]

But this kind of equation is not the simple statement of an arithmetical equivalent. A deeper, more profound relationship lies hidden within its *apparently* arithmetical form. Marx argued that "the whole mystery of the form of value lies hidden in this elementary form" (*ibid.*). For, as he said, in the statement of the equivalency of A and B:

A and B, two different kinds of commodity (linen and coat in our concrete instance), obviously play different parts. The linen *expresses* the value of the coat; the coat *serves as the means* for the expression of this value. The former commodity plays an *active* role; the latter, a *passive* one. The value of the former commodity is presented as *relative* or comparative, or appears in a relative form. The latter commodity *functions as an equivalent* or appears in an equivalent form. [*Ibid.*; italics added]

In short, the copula which links A and B in a relationship of *apparent* equivalency is *transitive*, active, and more specifically, anaclastically appropriative.

In the expression "A = B," the value of the commodity signified by A is "presented as relative or comparative," while that of the commodity signified by B is "equivalent." The copula establishes a *Metaphorical* relationship between the things compared. It expresses at one and the same time a difference and a similarity, or a "relative value form" and an "equivalent form," which, in Marx's words, "are reciprocally dependent factors, mutually determining one another, and inseparable: but at the same time they are mutually exclusive or contrasted extremes, polar opposites of the same expression of value." (*Ibid.*). As Marx concluded:

Whether a commodity is in the relative value form, or in the opposed equivalent form, *depends solely upon what happens to be its position in the expression of value*—upon whether it is the commodtiy whose value is expressed, or the commodity in terms of which the value of some other commodity is expressed. [*Ibid.*; italics added]

In short, in the language of valuation, whether a commodity is endowed with relative or equivalent value depends upon its placement on one or the other side of a Metaphorical expression. The Metaphor that resides at the heart of any expression assigns a value to a commodity in terms of some other commodity, which is the key to the "whole mystery of the form of value" itself. The Metaphor provides the key to the understanding of how purely material or quantitative entities come to be endowed with spiritual or qualitative attributes. And the understanding of Metaphor provided Marx with the method by which the false spirituality of all commodities, and especially of gold, is disclosed.

That the different *forms* of value (as against the true content of the value of any given commodity, the amount of socially necessary labor expended in its production) are products of modes of consciousness is evident from what Marx said in his analysis of the Relative value form. If we wish to discover how the elementary expression of the value of a commodity "lies hidden in the value ratio between the two commodities," Marx said, we must "begin by contemplating the ratio independently of its quantitative aspect." He criticized those who "take the opposite course, seeing in a value ratio nothing more than the proportion in which specified quantities of two different kinds of commodities can be equated." In Marx's view, such an analysis obscures the fact that "magnitudes of different things cannot be *qualitatively compared* until they have been expressed in terms of the same unit." (19; italics added) In Metaphorical expressions this presupposed *same unit* is hidden, and attention is directed solely to the external attributes of the objects compared in the equation. But what is this hidden same unit?

We may put the matter thus. As values, commodities are mere jellies [*Gallerten*] of human labor, and for this reason our analysis reduces them to value in the abstract, but does not give them any value form differing from their bodily form. It is otherwise when we are concerned with the value relation between one commodity and another. Then the character of the value of the former commodity is disclosed in virtue of its relation to the latter. [20 (65)]

Commodity A and commodity B are, in reality, Marx argued, "concreted" forms of a "jelly of human labor," which is the hidden content of every human product. When a coat is equated with a commodity of linen, in an expression of a value form, "the tailoring is in actual fact reduced to that which is identical in the two kinds of labor" required for the production of both commodities—that is to say, "is reduced to their common quality as human labor." In this "roundabout way," Marx was, in fact, "saying that weaving, insofar as it weaves value, cannot be differentiated from tailoring, for it is abstract human labor." This abstract human labor is expressed in the assertion of an equivalency between any two given commodities. And this assertion reduces "the different kinds of labor embodied in the different commodities to that which is common to them all, to human labor in the abstract." (20–21)

By linguistic means, then, men obliquely pay tribute to their own labors as that which *gives* value to all commodities. Hence, to grasp the nature of linguistic reduction is to grasp the nature of what Marx called "the language of commodities" (*dei Warensprache*) (22[66]), and therewith to understand the phenomenal forms that value assumes in different systems of exchange. This language of commodities is a language of *extrinsic relationships*, masking what is in reality an *intrinsic relationship* (the common element of labor inherent in all commodities) between any two commodities that might be compared with each other as a basis for any act of exchange. Thus, Marx wrote:

In the production of the coat, human labor has been expended in the form of tailoring. Human labor has, therefore, been stored up in it. In this aspect the coat is a "depository of value," although its quality as such a depository remains hidden even though it be worn threadbare. Tightly buttoned up though the coat may be, the linen looks within and recognizes in the coat the beautiful soul of value akin to linen's own. But the coat cannot express value in relation to the linen, unless, from the outlook of the linen, this value assumes the form of a coat. In like manner, A cannot assume the aspect of a king's majesty for B unless, in B's eyes, the idea of "majesty" becomes associated with the bodily form of A—this meaning that "majesty" will have to change features, hair, and other bodily characteristics, when a new king ascends the throne. . . . As a use-value, the linen is something which to our senses is obviously different from the coat; as a value it is the equivalent of the coat, and therefore looks like a coat. In this way it acquires a value form different from its bodily form. The essence of its value is manifest in its likeness to the coat, just as the sheep nature of the Christian is manifest in his resemblance to the Lamb of God. [*Ibid.*]

The fancifulness of Marx's language in these passages should not be dismissed as irrelevant to the aim of his analysis of the forms of value. This fancifulness is necessary for conveying his conception of the way consciousness functions to endow things, processes, and events with (false) meaning. The world of things, in Marx's view, is a world of isolated individualities, particulars which appear to bear no essential relationship to one another. The value actually ascribed to a given commodity as a basis for an act of exchange is a product of consciousness. Marx suggested that men give *meanings* to things, just as, by their labor, they create commodities and endow them with value. In fact, in a footnote Marx said that,

after a fashion, it is with the human being as with the commodity. Since the human being does not come into the world bringing a mirror with him, nor yet as a Fichtean philosopher able to say "I am myself," he first recognizes himself as reflected in other men. The man Peter grasps his relation to himself as a human being through becoming aware of his relation to the man Paul as a being of like kind with himself. Thereupon Paul, with flesh and bone, with all his Pauline corporeality, becomes for Peter the phenomenal form of the human kind. [23, n. 1]

The *relationships* between things interested Marx, those relationships by which things are capable of taking on a phenomenal aspect different from what they are "in themselves." Men enjoy no specific "humanity" except in their relationships to one another. So, too, a clue to the understanding of the value of commodities is found in the placement of any given commodity in a Metaphorical relationship to some other commodity in the minds of men. As Marx said:

We see that everything which our analysis of the value of commodities has told us, is disclosed by the linen itself as soon as it comes into relation with another commodity. It conveys its thoughts in the only language it knows—the language of commodities. In order to tell us that its own value is created by labor in the abstract form of human labor, it says that the coat, so far as equivalent to itself, is likewise value, consisting of the same labor as linen. In order to tell us that its sublimated reality as value differs from its buckram body, it says that *value looks like a coat*, and that consequently, so far as linen is a value, it and the coat are as like as two peas. Let me say in passing that the language of commodities has many other more or less correct dialects over and above Hebrew. The German "werth-sein," for instance, expresses (though less forcibly than the Romance verb "valere," "valer," "valoir") the fact that the equating of commodity B to commodity A is A's own way of expressing its value. "Paris vaut bien une messe." [22–23]

By means, then, of the "value ratio" expressed in the Metaphorical expression "A = B," the "bodily form of commodity B thus becomes the value form of commodity A, or the body of commodity B acts as a mirror to the value of commodity A." And, inasmuch as "commodity A becomes related to commodity B as the embodiment of value, as materialized human labor, it makes the use-value B serve as material for the expression of its own value. The value of commodity A, as thus expressed in the use-value of commodity B, has taken the form of relative value." (23)

I have stressed Marx's distinction between the "form" and the "content" of the value contained in any given commodity because it is precisely analogous to the distinction he wanted to establish in his philosophy of history between the "phenomena" of the historical process and their inner, or hidden, "meaning." The phenomenal form of history is the succession of different kinds of society testified to by the historical record in its unanalyzed form. The forms of society change in the same way that the forms of value do, but their meaning, the significance of these changes, remains as constant as does the "jelly" of labor which endows all commodities with their *true*, or essential, value. This means that the *forms of society produced by the historical process* are to the *forms of value* as the *modes of production* which determine those forms of society are to the *value content of commodities*. The *forms* of historical existence are given in the Superstructure; the *content* of historical existence is given in the Base (the modes of production). And the forms of historical existence, the fundamental forms of society, are the same in number as the forms of value.

There are four basic forms, both of value and of society. The forms of value are Elementary, Total, Generalized, and Money. The forms of Society are Primitive Communist, Slave, Feudal, and Capitalist. And the question which arises is this: Are the forms of society and the modes of transition from one form of society to another analogous to the forms of value and the modes of transition from one form of value to another (offered in *Capital* as the solution to the "enigma" of the fetishism of gold)? If they are, in fact, analogous, we have discovered a clue to the proper understanding of Marx's theory of history and, at the same time, have established the conceptual continuity between his earlier and later works.

Let me be more specific. For Marx, writing in *Capital*, the forms of value were conceived to be generated out of the primitive, original, or Metaphorical expression of equivalence in such a way as to explain the fetishism of gold which characterizes advanced systems of exchange. But the true value content of all commodities remains *essentially* the same: the labor expended in the production of the commodities. So it is with the history of societies. Their forms change, but the content that underlies these changes in form remains constant. This content is comprised of the modes of production by which man relates himself to nature. The components of these systems may change, thereby dictating transformations in the social relations created on their basis. But the true meaning of these changes is not to be found in the contemplation of the phenomenal form of the society under study; it lies in the hidden transformations that occur in the modes of production.

It should be stressed that, once Marx analyzed the Elementary form of value and disclosed its essentially Metaphorical nature, he proceeded to explicate the natures of the other three forms of value, culminating in the fetishism of gold, in purely *tropological* terms. The Total, or Extended, form of value is nothing but the conceptualization of the value of commodities in the modality of Metonymy. Here the relationships among commodities are conceived on the basis of the apprehension of their placement in a *series* that is infinitely extendable, such that commodities are related to all other commodities in the form of the set: "A = B," "B = C," "C = D," "D = E," . . . n, the value of any given commodity being apprehended as equivalent to a specific *quantity* of *any other commodity* in the system of exchange. But this apprehension of the existence of commodities within an extended series suggests, by the very extensiveness of the set, the possibility of a value that is shared commonly by all of them. In short, the possibility of the *Generalized* form of value is suggested by the very fact that commodities can be arranged in such a way as to be parts of a *total system* of purely extrinsic relationships. Thus, by Synecdoche, the Metonymically provided series of commodities can be endowed with the attributes of parts of a whole. In Marx's view, this value of the whole set is really nothing but the "congealed" labor expended in the production of the individual commodities. But, because of the inclination of men involved in specific systems of exchange to obscure from themselves the true content of the value they perceive to inhere in all commodities, the shared value that inheres in the whole set of commodities is Synecdochically unified as the quantity in gold which commodities can command in the exchange system. And this "absurd" ascription to gold of the power to *represent* the value of all commodities in any system of exchange accounts for the "fetishism of gold" which characterizes advanced systems of exchange.

Thus, the course or evolution of the forms of value, leading from the original (Metaphorical) characterization of the value of a commodity in terms of its equivalence to some other commodity to the (Ironic) characterization of the value of a commodity in terms of the quantity of gold (or money) which it brings in the system of exchange, proceeds by way of the two tropological strategies of reduction and integration that we would expect: by Metonymy on the one hand and by Synecdoche on the other. The last form of value analyzed by Marx in this section of *Capital*, that of the Money form, is Ironic precisely inasmuch as, in his account of it, the necessary labor expended in its production, is hidden from view by the ascription to it of a value conceived in the form of a money (or gold) equivalent. It is Ironic also inasmuch as the characterization of the value of a commodity in terms of its money equivalent contains both a truth and an error. The truth contained in it is reflected in the impulse to view all commodities in terms of a universal standard of valuation; the error consists in the identification of this standard as the money equivalent a commodity might command within a given system of exchange. The fetishistic nature of the identification of the value of *all* commodities with their gold equivalent is at once the condition of self-delusionment of the most advanced systems of exchange and the precondition for the liberation of consciousness to the apprehension of the true basis for ascribing value to any commodity, the labor theory of value which Marx used as the basis of his analysis of both the strengths and the weaknesses of the system of exchange known as Capitalism.

The second half of the first chapter of *Capital*, then, is an exercise in Irony, consisting as it does of the exposure of the purely fictional nature of all conceptions of the value of commodities which do not begin from the apprehension of the truth of the labor theory of value. In short, the labor theory of value serves as the base line from which all erroneous conceptions of value can be transcended.

It should be stressed, however, that Marx did not insist that the various forms of value provided by the tropological reductions are totally erroneous. Each contains an important insight into the nature of value in general. These insights derive from a legitimate impulse to discover the true nature of the value that commodities have in any system of exchange. But the true basis of all value is obscured and remains hidden to perception in any analysis that begins from a consideration of form rather than content. Thus, the history of thought about the forms of value describes a sustained descent of consciousness into the depths of its own capacities for self-deception and alienation. The nadir of this descent is the situation in which men deny to themselves the worth of their own labor, which is concealed as the true content of the values of all commodities, in order to endow a worthless metal, gold, with the virtues of their own unique power to create value itself.

But what is the nature of the relationship between the labor theory of value, on the basis of which Marx criticized all other conceptions of the value of commodities, and those other false, or illusory, forms of value that he analyzed? It would appear to be a Metonymical relationship and inevitably, therefore, a reductive one. For Marx insisted that the phenomena of commodity exchange be divided into two orders of being: their *form* on the one hand and their true *content* on the other—in short, into phenomenal and noumenal orders of being. Once this distinction is admitted, it is necessary to inquire into the grounds on which they are conceived to be related in practice. Why is the true content of the value of all commodities suppressed by consciousness in favor of the various phenomenal forms analyzed by Marx? This problem is at once psychological, sociological, and historical; and, in order to comprehend Marx's solution to it, we must turn to an analysis of his theory of consciousness on the one hand and his philosophy of history on the other.

⊷§ *The "Grammar" of Historical Existence*

Marx laid out the broad lines of his theory of history in the late 1840s, while he was trying to come to terms with the main schools of social thought of the previous generation: German Idealism, French Socialism, and English Political Economy. Basic to his position at this time—a position which he and Engels would regard as scientifically confirmed by Darwin later on—was the conviction that consciousness in man is merely a more efficient, rather than a qualitatively different, capacity for regulating relations between the human animal and its environment for the satisfaction of primary (physical) and secondary (emotional) needs. And he followed Feuerbach by putting at the very center of his thinking the fact that while nature can exist without consciousness, consciousness cannot exist without nature. Thus, in *The German Ideology*, Marx wrote: "we must begin by stating the first presupposition of all human existence, and therefore of all history, namely, that men must be in a position to live in order to 'make history.' But life involves before everything else eating and drinking, a habitation, clothing and many other things" (Bottomore ed., 62). From this postulate he went on to argue that the first historical act is not a spiritual, but a purely animal, one: "the production of material life itself." This allowed Marx to criticize every prior attempt to discover an "essential" distinction between a generally animal, and a specifically human, nature. Thus, he wrote: "Men can be distinguished from animals by consciousness, by religion, or by anything one likes. They themselves begin to distinguish themselves from animals as soon as they begin to produce their means of subsistence" (53). The nature of this production, Marx argued, is "determined" by men's physical constitution. In producing their means of subsistence, men indirectly produce "their actual material life." As thus envisaged, human consciousness is merely the peculiar means which man has at his disposal, as part of his natural endowment, to exploit his environment and live off it. Later on, in *Capital* (1867), Marx expanded on this idea:

Labour is, in the first place, a process in which both man and Nature participate, and in which man of his own accord starts, regulates, and controls the material relations between himself and Nature. *He opposes himself to Nature as one of her own forces, setting in motion arms and legs, head and hands, the natural forces of his body, in order to appropriate Nature's productions in a form adapted to his own wants.* By thus acting on the external world and changing it, he at the same time changes his own nature. He develops his slumbering powers and compels them to act in obedience to his sway. We are not now dealing with those primitive instinctive forms of labour that remind us of the mere animal. An immeasurable interval of time separates the state of things in which a man brings his labour-power to market for sale as a commodity, from that state in which *human labour was still in its first instinctive stage.* [Bottomore ed., 88 (192); italics added]

In the dynamics of human exertion, therefore, a specifically human nature is potentially present. Thus, Marx wrote:

We *presuppose* labour in a form that stamps it as exclusively human. A spider conducts operations that resemble those of a weaver, and a bee puts to shame many an architect in the construction of her cells. But what distinguishes the worst architect from the best of bees is his, that the archiect raises his structure in imagination before he erects it in reality. At the end of every labour-process, we get a result that already existed in the imagination of the labourer at its com-mencement. He not only effects a change of form in the material on which he works, but he also realizes a purpose of his own that gives the law to his *modus operandi*, and to which he must subordinate his will. And this subordination is no mere momentary act. Besides the exertion of the bodily organs, the process de-mands that, during the whole operation, *the workman's will* be steadily in con-sonance with his purpose. This means close attention. The less he is attracted by the nature of the work, and by the mode in which it is carried on, and the less, therefore, he enjoys it as something which give play to his bodily and mental powers, the more close his attention is forced to be. [88–89 (192–93)]

And thus it followed, as Marx had already noted in *The German Ideology*, that

the way in which men produce their means of subsistence depends in the first place on the nature of the existing means which they have to reproduce. This mode of production should not be regarded simply as the reproduction of the physical existence of individuals. It is already a definite form of activity of these individuals, a definite *mode of life*. As individuals express their life, so they are. What they are, therefore, coincides with their production, with what they produce and with how they produce it. What individuals are, therefore, depends on the material conditions of their production. [Bottomore ed., 53–54]

This reduction permitted Marx to deduce the three presuppositions (or, as he called them in an ironic reference to the practice of German philosophers of the time, the "moments") of human consciousness. They are: first, the impulse to satisfy needs (primary and secondary); next, the capacity to reproduce other men and maintain the life of the species, from which derives the first social group, the family; and, finally, the constitution of the modes of production adequate to the maintenance of human life in different environments. Thus, he concluded, in order for us even to conceive the existence of human consciousness, we must postulate a *natural connection* between the human animal and his environment and a *social connection* by which men enter into cooperative activity with other men, within and between families. This postulate allowed Marx to combine in his theory of history his materialistic metaphysics on the one hand with his dialectical theory of social development on the other.

Marx looked for the intimate relation which exists in every society among human consciousness, the material world, and the current modes of production. Thus, he wrote:

It follows from this, that a determinate mode of production, or industrial stage, is always bound up with a determinate mode of cooperation, or social stage, and this mode of cooperation is itself a "productive force." It also follows, that the mass of productive forces accessible to men determines the condition of society, and that the "history of humanity" must therefore always be studied and treated in *relation to* the history of industry and exchange. [62]

Marx stressed that the "moments" he had analytically shown to underlie any conception of a distinctively human consciousness are to be regarded as only *logically prior* to that consciousness, not existentially differentiated from it; they have existed contemporaneously with consciousness "since the dawn of history and since the first men," and they "still assert themselves in history today" (*ibid.*).

Even so, he continued, man's consciousness is not "an original, 'pure' consciousness." From the very beginning " 'spirit' is cursed with the 'burden' of matter." At first, consciousness is "merely an awareness of the immediate sensible environment and of the limited connection with other persons and things outside the individual who is becoming self-conscious. At the same time, it is a consciousness of Nature, which first appears to men as a completely alien, all-powerful and unassailable force, with which men's relations are purely animal and by which they are overawed like beasts; it is thus a purely animal consciousness of Nature (natural religion)." (70–71)

Just as the Elementary (or Accidental) form of Value contains "the whole mystery of the form of value" in general, so too the elementary form of society and its attendant form of consciousness contain the mystery of the form of society in general. In *The Communist Manifesto*, to be sure, Marx spoke of three principal forms of social organization (Slave, Feudal, and Capitalist); and it was only in a note added by Engels that a fourth form, that of Primitive Communism, was alluded to. But, already in *The German Ideology*, Marx had characterized the mode of consciousness of this primitive form of social organization as *Metaphorical*. Thus, he wrote:

Here, as everywhere, the *identity* of nature and man appears in such a way that the restricted relation to one another determines men's restricted relation to nature, just because nature is as yet hardly modified historically; and, on the other hand, man's consciousness of the necessity of associating with the individuals around him is the beginning of the consciousness that he is living in society at all. This beginning is as *animal* as social life itself at this stage. It is mere herd-consciousness, and at this point man is only distinguished from sheep by the fact that with him consciousness takes the place of instinct or that his instinct is a conscious one. [71]

Marx thus postulated as the precondition of all genuinely historical development an original stage in human development in which men live in a condition of consciousness which is strictly Metaphorical in its modality. Men exist in the simultaneous apprehension of their similarity to, and difference from, nature. And the consciousness of humanity at this stage resembles an "animal" consciousness, a "sheep-like" or "herd" consciousness, which serves to consolidate human existence in the first form of society, which is tribal, and in which a kind of Primitive Communism must be supposed, by Marx's light, to have existed as the dominant form of economic organization. During this stage, men live parasitically off nature, as hunters and food-gatherers, which is to say that they participate in a form of production and consumption which is the same as that of other animals endowed with similar instincts and physical capacities.

But Marx appeared to believe that a factor in human life works to transform this Metaphorical modality of relationship between human consciousness and nature and between men and other men, an economic factor which originally was nothing but a function of sexual differentiation; and this factor is the division of labor. The division of labor, working Mechanistically, as we would say, upon the forms of social relationship, brings about a change in the way men relate to nature and, as a result, to other men. Thus, Marx wrote:

This sheeplike or tribal consciousness receives its further development and extension *through increased productivity*, the increase of needs, and, what is fundamental to both of these, the increase of population. With these there develops the division of labor in the sexual act, then that division of labor which develops spontaneously or "naturally" by virtue of natural predisposition (e.g., physical strength), needs, accidents, etc., etc. [72–73; italics added]

In short, the division of humanity is brought about by purely *physical* factors, differences of sex on the one hand and of power on the other. These kinds of division within the species dissolve the original identification of man with nature and with his own kind, which produced the original tribal union. This original division of the species on the basis of physical, or genetically provided, attributes then gives place, Marx suggested, to another and much more fundamental schism within the species, that which is expressed in the distinction between "material and mental labor."

"Division of labor," Marx said, "becomes truly such" only when this distinction appears in society. "From this moment onward consciousness *can* really flatter itself that it is something other than consciousness of existing practice, that it is *really* conceiving something without conceiving something *real*; from now on consciousness is in a position to emancipate itself from the world and to proceed to the formation of a 'pure' theory, theology, philosophy, ethics, etc." (Feuer ed., 252–53) In other words, *as a result* of a division of labor, caused by purely mechanical factors in the distribution of physical attributes and powers, mankind is set upon the path of its own alienation from itself and from its own creative powers, and is impelled toward the attribution of these powers to imaginary "spirits" of the sort postulated by " 'pure' theory, theology, philosophy, ethics, etc."

Men now begin to *exist contiguously* with one another, as separate and as separated beings, as members of different classes, and in such a way as to preclude belief in the possibility of an ultimate reconciliation of the parts within the whole which is a single species. Thus, Marx wrote:

it is quite immaterial what consciousness starts out to do on its own [that is, as individual consciousness]: out of all such muck we get only the one inference that these three moments, the forces of production, the state of society and consciousness, *can and must come into contradiction with one another*, because the division of labor implies the possibility—nay, the fact—that intellectual and material activity—enjoyment and labor, production and consumption—*devolve on different individuals* and that the only possibility of their not coming into contradiction lies in the negation in its turn of the division of labor. [253; italics added]

With the division of labor, then, the *Metaphorical* relationship between man and man on the one hand and between man and nature on the other is dissolved, a *Metonymical* relationship is established, and, instead of existing with one another in the modality of *identity*, as was the case in primitive society, men come to exist in the modality of *contiguity*. Or, as Marx put it:

With the division of labor . . . and the separation of society into individual families opposed to one another, is given simultaneously the distribution, and indeed the unequal distribution (both quantitative and qualitative), of labor and its products, hence property; the nucleus, the first form, of which lies in the family, where wife and children are the slaves of the husband [*ibid.*].

This means, in Marx's view, that the social expression of this condition of severance within the species is slavery.

This latent slavery in the family, though still very crude, is the first property, but even at this early stage it corresponds perfectly to the definition of modern economists who call it the power of disposing the labor power of others. Division of labor and private property are, moreover, identical expressions: in the one the same thing is affirmed with reference to activity as is affirmed in the other with reference to the product of the activity. [253–54]

Thus, the primal unity, expressed in the social modality of Primitive Communism, gives place to a severed condition. What had before been unified, in both consciousness and praxis, is now divided; and mankind, formerly unified within itself against nature, is now severed within itself into two kinds of producers, and therefore into two kinds of consumers, and, as a result, into two kinds of humanity, two classes. Therewith begins the history of human *society*, which in its various phases exists in the modality of opposition of part to part, in conflict, struggle, and exploitation of man by man. Men now exist in a mode of relationship with one another as master and slave, in consciousness as well as in fact, a condition in which the *differences* between one segment of humanity and another are apprehended as being much more basic and important than any *similarities* which their possession of common species attributes might suggest.

But this transformation of both consciousness and the modes of social relationship is not seen as having been caused by a *dialectical* transformation of consciousness itself. The shift from the Primitive Tribal stage to the ancient Slave stage of social organization is caused by purely material factors, a genetic factor on the one hand (sexual differentiation) and a functional differentiation on the other (a division of labor). And the division of labor, the cause of social differentiation among men, serves as the basis for the "ennoblement" of the consciousness of man himself, the "elevation" of man in his own consciousness *above* nature.

Following upon the division of function in the sexual act is the division of labor in primitive society between those who do manual labor and those whose work is primarily mental, between workers and priests. From this moment on, Marx said, "consciousness *can* really flatter itself that it is something other than consciousness of existing practice . . . ; from now on consciousness is in a position to emancipate itself from the world" (252–53), because it can turn its attention on itself, hypostatize its fancies about itself in its uniquely human—that is, mental—aspects, and treat those fancies as if they were real, and even deify and worship images of them. But, by this very process of hypostatization, thought prepares itself for the discovery and the reintegration of that which makes man a potentially unifiable species. Thought is prepared for the *Synecdochic* unification of the fragments of humanity as elements of a whole which is greater than the sum of the parts. Thus is born all of that "pure" theology, philosophy, and theory on which man has prided himself since the dawn of civilization, and to which he has looked for the determination of his own properly *human* ends and purposes in life ever since.

⇜§ The "Syntax" of Historical Process

It may be noted that, as early as *The German Ideology*, Marx had prefigured the grammar and syntax of the theory of history that would serve him to the end of his days as a thinker. He could from that point on divide all historical phenomena coming under his gaze into the categories of Base and Superstructure. The Base is comprised of (1) the *means* of production (defined by Marx as [a] the natural resources available to a given human group at a given time and place, [b] the labor force or population potentially capable of performing productive labor, and [c] the available technological endowment) and (2) the *modes* of production—that is, the actual ratios of humanly usable power given by the means at a specific time and place. The Superstructure is comprised of the actual class divisions generated by the struggle for control of the means of production in a condition of material scarcity, the institutions, laws, forms of state organizations, and so on, which the division of labor necessitates. To the Superstructure also belongs the whole body of customs, mores, and folkways which sanction the actual social forms on the one hand and the realm of high culture—religion, science, philosophy, art, and the like—which provides rationalizations of the ongoing social structure on the other. The data of history, in the form of atomic facts or documentary attestations to the occurrences of certain kinds of events—the lexical elements of the historical record, as it were—are rendered comprehensible, in Marx's view, solely by their susceptibility to inclusion in the two categories of historically significant happening provided by the concepts of the Base and the Superstructure.

Once this grammatical classification of historical phenomena has been carried out, it becomes possible to apply syntactical principles to "explain" why changes occur in the areas of human praxis which these categories conceptually represent. These syntactical principles are nothing less than the laws of *mechanical causation* which govern relations between the Base and the Superstructure raised upon it. The central syntactical principle in Marx's system of historical analysis, by which the "meaning" or "significance" of the whole historical process is to be provided, simply states that, although changes in the Base determine changes in the Superstructure, the reverse is not the case—that is, changes in social and cultural dimensions of historical existence do not cause changes in the Base.

To be sure, human ingenuity or action may cause changes in the means of production. Wars deplete the labor force, as do famine and pestilence; inventions change the nature of the technological endowment; natural resources become exhausted by use, and so on. But the changes caused in the means of production are not functions of alterations of the social order or the officially credited cultural endowment (the philosophy, religion, art, and so on) of a given society. The relationship between the Base and the Superstructure is therefore not only unidirectional but also strictly Mechanistic. There is nothing dialectical about this relationship at all.

The fundamental forms of the Superstructure, however, display the same categorical characteristics as the forms of value in Marx's analysis of commodities in *Capital*. They are four in number, they are similarly tropological in his characterizations of them, and they succeed one another in the same way that the forms of value are conceived to do in *Capital*. These four forms of society (Primitive Communist, Slave, Feudal, and Capitalist) thus comprise the basic categories into which the phenomena of history considered as a diachronic process are to be grouped. And their succession constitutes the acts of the drama of significant historical occurrence for which Marx purported to provide the underlying plot structure (in which the meaning of the whole process can be disclosed) in his historical works.

It should be stressed at this point that Marx did not argue that the external world determines the specific content of *individual* mental processes. Like the similarly materialistic Hobbes before him, Marx granted that individual fancy can throw up an infinite number of possible images of the world which may have no relation to the external world at all but merely express the inner longings of the human heart. But he denied that such creations of individual fancy can become significant social forces, except in the degree to which they conform to the modes of production and their corresponding social products.

More important, *changes* in publicly authenticated forms of human consciousness follow only upon changes in the fundament of every form of human society, the modes of production. These cause changes in the dependent social and cultural Superstructure. When the necessity for changes in the social order becomes apparent, individual products of "pure" consciousness become possible candidates for admission to the publicly authenticating group consciousness. This was the basis of Marx's fundamental law of historical change in all its dimensions, the law which he set forth in the preface to his *Contribution to a Critique of Political Economy* in 1859, the approximate midpoint between his earliest philosophizing in the 1840s and his death in 1883.

In the social production which men carry on they enter into definite relations that are indispensable and independent of their will; these relations of production correspond to a definite stage of development of their material powers of production. The totality of these relations of production constitutes the economic structure of society—*the real foundation*, on which legal and political superstructures arise and to which definite forms of social consciousness correspond. The mode of production of material life *determines* the general character of the social, political and spiritual processes of life. It is not the consciousness of men that determines their being, but, on the contrary, their social being determines their consciousness.

At a certain stage of their development, the material forces of production in society come in conflict with the existing relations of production, or—what is but a legal expression of the same thing—with the property relations within which they had been at work before. From forms of development of the forces of production these relations turn into their fetters. Then occurs a period of social revolution. With the change of the economic foundation, the entire immense superstructure is more or less rapidly transformed. In considering such transformations the distinction should always be made between the material transformation of the economic conditions of production which can be determined with the precision of natural science, and the legal, political, religious, aesthetic or philosophical—in short ideological, forms in which men become conscious of this conflict and fight it out. Just as our opinion of an individual is not based on what he thinks of himself, so can we not judge of such a period of transformation by its own consciousness; on the contrary, this consciousness must rather be explained from the contradictions of material life, from the existing conflict between the social forces of production and the modes of production. No social order ever disappears before all the productive forces for which there is room in it have been developed; and new, higher relations of production never appear before the material conditions of their existence have matured in the womb of the old society. [51–52; italics added]

As can be seen from this passage, for Marx, significant causal efficacity proceeds from the Base to the Superstructure by a *direct*, not a dialectical, path. There is a lag between the causal forces that promote social transformations and between social transformations and cultural changes; but this lag is *inertial*, caused by the incapacity of human consciousness in situations of fundamental transformations in the Base to relinquish the modes of conceiving reality inherited from, because they are based upon, earlier modes of productivity. Only after a new mode of production has been established as the dominant one in a given society can the publicly sanctioned forms of both consciousness and praxis themselves be established, in new laws, a new form of state organization, a new religion, a new art, and so on.

What *is* dialectical in all this—and here is the measure of Marx's debt to German Idealism—is the *mode of transition* from one *form* of *publicly sanctioned consciousness* to another. The adjustment in human consciousness and in the Superstructure to the transformations caused by changes in the Base *is* a dialectical process and is precisely analogous to the kind of tropological change that occurs when Primitive consciousness falls *out of* a Metaphorical relation to nature and to mankind in general and *into* a Metonymical apprehension of those relationships. From Metaphorical, to Metonymical, to Synecdochic consciousness—these are the phases through which humanity passes by dialectical transformation of the ways it relates itself to its contexts (natural and social) in its passage from savage to advanced civilized consciousness.

But precisely because these transformations of consciousness are dialectically engendered, by principles governing the operations of consciousness itself, we cannot, as Marx put it, judge a period of transformation by its own consciousness of itself—as conventional historians, seeking to reconstruct the consciousness of an age in its own terms, are inclined to do. The consciousness of an age is always more or less than what pure perception, were it not clouded by inherited preconceptions about what reality *must be*, would reveal to be the actual social reality of that age.

As a theory of consciousness' transformations in history, Hegel's *Phenomenology of Mind* had value for Marx as a model of analytical method. States of consciousness (*publicly sanctioned* forms of consciousness) are related to one another dialectically, by affirmation, negation, and negation of the negation, and so on; but these states of consciousness represent only the *phenomenal forms* of historical being. The true *content* of historical being, that which makes it subject to scientific analysis—that is, nomological causal analysis—is to be found in the modes of production of which the phenomenal forms are mere reflections.

Men relate themselves in their own minds to nature and to other men *dialectically*, but they are *really* related to nature, Marx insisted, in the modality of *mechanical* causality. Their *apprehension* of the world is mediated by consciousness, but their *existence* in the world is determined by the actual relationships they sustain to the natural and social worlds; and these actual relationships, in turn, are strictly causal and deterministic in nature. This is the meaning of Marx's oft-quoted aphorism "Life is not determined by consciousness, but consciousness by life" (*German Ideology*, Feuer ed., 247).

Changes that occur in the Base are not, then, products of a dialectical interaction of the modes of production and the natural world; on the contrary, changes in the modes of production are occasioned by strict mechanical laws. Soil exhaustion, population depletion, inventions of new techniques for exploiting nature—all of these changes in the *means* of production result from changes that are explainable by natural scientific concepts of causal relationships. The invention of a new machine such as the steam engine, which might transform the relationship between the technological endowment and the labor force, is conceived as a function of intelligence dedicated to the solution of *practical* problems; and it represents not a *dialectical* process but rather the application of a mode of thought, Mechanism, to the solution of a specific problem suggested by the need to increase productivity for consumption or exchange.

Moreover, the transformation of the Base is strictly *mechanical* and incremental, not dialectical. Its effect on the Superstructure is such as to set up a dialectical interaction between inherited social forms and their attendant modes of consciousness and new ones called for by the transformations occurring in the Base. But even this effect on the Superstructure is *mechanical* in nature, not dialectical. For, as Marx pointed out in his *Contribution*, the forms of consciousness that will gain public accreditation, in response to the changes called for in society by the changes in the Base, are *predetermined* by those changes. "Therefore," he said,

mankind always sets itself only such problems as it can solve; since, on closer examination, it will always be found that the problem itself arises only when the *material conditions* necessary for its solution already exist or are at least in the process of formation. [52; italics added]

In short, all publicly significant social "problems" are not problems at all but "puzzles," inasmuch as, in Marx's view, such "problems" can always be presumed to be soluble and to make available to those trying to solve them the means for their solution in the time and place in which they arise. There is nothing "dialectical" about the process that generates the crucial problems with which mankind must deal at different stages of the historical process. And there is nothing "dialectical" about the means to be employed by men in different historical situations in their efforts to solve those problems. What is "dialectical" is the succession of the "forms" of society and culture which consciousness constructs in the wake of its solutions to the social problems caused by transformations in the Base. And Marx used the "dialectical" method for analyzing the true content of the forms of social and cultural existence which appear in history, in the same way that he used this method to disclose the true content of the forms of value in the opening chapter of *Capital*.

The concept of the division of labor served as the organizing idea of Marx's social theory in the same way that the labor theory of value served as the organizing idea of his economic theories. It is the division of labor which hurls mankind into that condition of schism and self-alienation to which the historical record testifies as man's seemingly *natural* condition of existence. Thus, Marx wrote in *The German Ideology*: "With the division of labor . . . is given simultaneously the distribution and indeed the unequal distribution (both quantitative and qualitative) of labor and its products, hence property: the nucleus, the first form, of which lies in the family, where wife and children are slaves of the husband." He went on to call this slavery the "first property" and defined property, in accordance with the conventions of contemporary political economy, as "the power of disposing the labor-power of others." And he concluded that "division of labor and private property are . . . identical expressions: in the one the same thing is affirmed with reference to activity as is affirmed in the other with reference to the product of the activity." (253–54)

In the division of labor, too, Marx found the origins of that *schism* in social life between private and public, individual and general, interests. To be sure, he admitted that the very *nature* of human life generates the distinction. The communal interest, he said, exists "first of all in reality, as the mutual interdependence of the individuals among whom the labor is divided." But as soon as labor is divided, he insisted, "each man has a particular, exclusive sphere of activity, which is forced upon him and from which he cannot escape. He is a hunter, a fisherman, a shepherd, or a critical critic, and must remain so if he does not want to lose his livelihood." (254) Thus, men become slaves to their own creation, instruments of the very power which had given *the species in general* control over nature. Mankind becomes fragmented and atomized; and individuals become torn between their desire to be whole men and the necessity of functioning as specialized instruments of production. "This crystallization of social activity" into functionally differentiated spheres had been, Marx believed, "one of the chief factors in historical development up till now" (*ibid.*). And in the conflict within individual men between their human aspirations and their socially provided roles, and in society in general between individual and communal interests, Marx found the driving force behind the creation of the state. Thus, he said, although the state is always "based on real ties existing in every family and tribal conglomeration . . . and especially . . . on the classes already determined by the division of labor, which in every such mass of men separate out, and of which one dominates all the others" (255), a particular form of state is really an expression of the *specific* interests of a specific class which offers itself as a *definitive* expression of the *general* interests of mankind as a whole.

This is why, in the end, every putative "general interest" is always experienced by both dominant and subordinant classes as something outside, beyond, or alien to men—alien but benign in the case of dominant classes (since it establishes the "natural" quality of their power and privileges), alien but maleficent in the case of subordinant classes (since it frustrates their impulse to realize their individual and class interests fully). "Just because individuals seek *only* their particular interest, i.e., that not coinciding with their communal interest . . . , the latter will be imposed on them, as in its turn a particular, peculiar 'general interest' " (*ibid.*). On the other hand, "the *practical* struggle of these particular interests, which constantly *really* run counter to the communal and illusory communal interests, makes *practical* intervention and control necessary through the illusory 'general-interest' in the form of the State" (*ibid.*). Thus, "social power, i.e., the multiplied productive force, which arises through the cooperation of different individuals as it is determined within the division of labor, appears to these individuals, since their cooperation is not voluntary but natural, not as their own united power but as an alien force existing outside them" (*ibid.*), as an abstract force which "lives" them, rather than as what it truly is, their *own force*, objectified and reified and turned to communal ends.

This reification generates that "terror" which man has experienced in every prior attempt to make sense of history. Since social force is perceived as natural force, of the "origin and end of which (men) are ignorant, which they thus cannot control, which on the contrary passes through a peculiar series of phases and stages independent of the will and action of man, nay even being the prime governor of these," man is inclined to see himself as history's victim instead of its governor. Thus originate all of those *deterministic theories* of history which reduce man to the status of servant of forces greater than himself, contributing thereby to the degradation of *most* men while simultaneously justifying the elevation of the *few*: the theological determinism of St. Augustine, the metaphysical determinism of Hegel, the traditionalistic determination of Burke, the crude materialistic determinism of British political economy, and even, in principle, the sociological determinism of Tocqueville. This is also the origin of all those naive rebellions of well-meaning humanitarians, humanists, aesthetes, Romantics, and Utopian Socialists who affirm the freedom of the individual will and the capacity of man to change his world through the transformation of the sensibility with which he apprehends it.

None of these conceptions of the historical process, however, comes to grips with the essential truth: the *simultaneous* necessity and transience, the constraining and liberating power, of the social order itself. None, in short, comprehends the dynamics of society and the developmental pattern of the whole historical process. One explains away man's freedom in the face of a lived necessity which governs him at the beginning and requires the iron subordination of the interests of the individual to the group; another merely laments this necessity and takes refuge in puerile dreams of a freedom which will be realizable only when, and if, society itself is dissolved.

꧁ *The "Semantics" of History*

Marx, by contrast, claimed to have found in the Mechanistic relationship obtaining between the Base and the Superstructure the conceptual basis of a dynamic science of history and the instrument for predicting the outcome of history in its *transient* social phase. "Dialectical Materialism," the combination of Hegel's logic with the Feuerbachian conviction that all knowledge must begin with sense experience, Marx's "New Science," provides scientific justification for the conviction that "social" life, as known to every phase of history since primitive times, *must disappear*. More, it finds in bourgeois society, the superstructural form of the Capitalist mode of organizing the means of production, both the last phase and the agency of destruction of this social life. If all previous history is the history of class struggle, as the *Communist Manifesto* proclaims, "bourgeois relations of production are the last antagonistic form of the social process of production. . . . At the same time the productive forces developing in the womb of bourgeois society create the material conditions for the solution of that antagonism. With this social formation, therefore, the prehistory of human society comes to an end" (*Contribution*, 52–53).

The dynamics of this process of transformation, in which society itself is transcended, is set forth most clearly in *The Manifesto of the Communist Party* (1848). In *A Grammar of Motives*, Kenneth Burke has analyzed the *Manifesto* in "dramatistic" terms, stressing the extent to which, in Marx's presentation of history in this work, the element of "scene" determines and provides understanding of the "agents, acts, and agencies" that appear to make up the gross matter of the historical process. In Burke's view, this elevation of "scene" over "agent" reveals Marx's essentially *materialistic* conception of history, reveals him as a *deterministic* philosopher in the tradition of Hobbes, and sets him apart from genuinely dialectical thinkers such as Hegel, for whom "agency" and "purpose" play greater roles in the comprehension of history's true significance.

Burke's analysis is true enough as far as it goes, but it obscures the extent to which, in the *Manifesto* as elsewhere, Marx's thought moved simultaneously on two levels, by appeal to *both* Mechanistic and Organicist conceptions of reality, and utilized two fundamentally different linguistic protocols, Metonymical on the one hand and Synecdochic on the other. So, too, Marx emplotted the historical process in two modes, Tragic and Comic, simultaneously, but in such a way as to make the former emplotment a *phase* within the latter, and so as to permit himself to claim the title of a "realist" while sustaining his dream of a utopian reconciliation of man with man *beyond* the social state. The sublation of the Tragic condition, which has prevailed in history since the fall of man into society through the division of labor, constituted, in Marx's thought, the scientific justification of the *Radical* political position he purported to derive from his study of history.

A brief analysis of the theory of history set forth in the first part of the *Manifesto* will illustrate what I had in mind when I characterized Marx's idea of history in the foregoing terms.

The *Manifesto* opens with a characterization of the specific nature of the structure of *all* previous periods of history: "The history of all hitherto existing society is the history of class struggles." The various classes of all previous societies "stood in constant opposition to one another" and "carried on an uninterrupted, now hidden, now open fight." (7) This uninterrupted fight, Marx argued, resulted in the eruption, from time to time, of crucial revolutionary reconstitutions of the whole social order. But no peace resulted from any of these reconstitutions; each simply substituted "new classes, new conditions of oppression, new forms of struggle in place of the old ones" (8). Nonetheless, the process resulted in the "simplification" of "the class antagonisms." Society was progressively split into two camps, with two great classes facing each other: bourgeoisie and proletariat.

The essential structural relationship in history is *opposition*, but the relationship between the *phases* of the developmental process is *dialectical*. Thus, Marx said of the succession of the classes:

From the serfs of the Middle Ages *sprang* [*hervorspringen*] the chartered burghers of the earliest towns. *From these burgesses* the first elements of the bourgeoisie *developed* [*entwickelten*]. [*Ibid*.; italics added]

The images of development are Organicist; the mode of relationship is Synecdochic. The modality of the relationships among the different *phases* in the evolution of the Base, however, is characterized in different terms.

The feudal system of industry . . . now no longer sufficed for the growing wants of new markets. The manufacturing system *took its place* [*antreten*]. The guild masters were *pushed to one side* [*verdrängt*]; division of labor between the corporate guilds *vanished* in the face of division of labor in each single workshop. [*Ibid*.; italics added]

Here the imagery is Mechanistic, the mode of the relationship of the parts is Metonymical, and the conditions for the further transformation of the social order are described in what is essentially the language of mechanical causality:

Meantime the markets kept *ever growing* [*immer wuchsen*]; the demand *ever rising* [*immer steigt*]. Even manufacture no longer sufficed. The *place* of manufacture *was taken* [*antreten*] by the giant, modern industry, the place of the industrial middle class by industrial millionaires, the leaders of whole industrial armies, the modern bourgeois. [*Ibid*.; italics added]

And Marx concluded this overture to his essay, his delineation of the elements of the historical field and his classification of them into types in terms of their historical *functions*, in the following way:

We see, therefore, how the modern bourgeoisie is itself the product of a long course of development, of a series of revolutions in the modes of production and of exchange. [*Ibid*., 9]

He then went on to characterize the development of the modern bourgeoisie, and in such a way as to depict it as a form of social organization which bears the seeds of its own dissolution and autotransformation within it. Ironically he depicted the ways in which the modern middle class, in its pursuit of profits, effectively succeeds in overturning, dementing, and depleting its own ideological resources, its own most highly cherished *conscious* beliefs and allegiances. This development, he argued, not only puts "an end to all feudal, patriarchal, idyllic relations" and "drown[s] the most heavenly ecstasies of religious fervor, of chivalrous enthusiasm, of Philistine sentimentalism in the icy water of egotistical calculation," but also "resolve[s] personal worth into exchange value," and, "for exploitation, veiled by religious and political illusions, . . . substitute[s] naked, shameless, direct, brutal exploitation" (9–10). In short, the bourgeoisie produces the conditions in which man must at last face the depraved condition of his millennial existence in "society" with a clear and unclouded eye. It thereby constitutes the mode of consciousness in which a "realism" with respect to the true nature of the social order can take shape, a realism as powerful in its capacity to transform "reality" itself as that which permitted the constitution of modern science for the exploitation of the material world.

The irony of bourgeois society, Marx suggested, is that it cannot exist "without constantly revolutionizing the instruments of production, and thereby the relations of production, and with them the whole relations of society" (10). This revolutionary impulse is inspired by the "need of a constantly expanding market" (*ibid.*). The achievement of the bourgeoisie is truly heroic, truly Promethean, in Marx's account of its rise and development, but its present situation is one of internal contradiction: the need for ever-expanding markets causes the bourgeoisie to revolt against "the property relations that are the conditions for the existence of the bourgeoisie and of its rule" (13). From this paradoxical state arise the "crises" that periodically break out in the most highly developed capitalist economic systems.

The internal contradictions of bourgeois life generate "epidemics," and especially one kind of epidemic, which "would have seemed an absurdity in all earlier epochs—the epidemic of overproduction" (*ibid.*). And, ironically, the cures provided by the bourgeoisie for these epidemics promote even more virulent outbreaks of them in the future:

And how does the bourgeoisie get over these crises? On the one hand, by enforced destruction of a mass of productive forces; on the other, by the conquest of new markets, and by the more thorough exploitation of old ones. That is to say, by paving the way for more extensive and more destructive crises, and by diminishing the means whereby crises are prevented. [*Ibid.*]

The result of all this is that the very weapons with which the bourgeoisie "felled" the older feudal order are "turned against the bourgeoisie itself" (*ibid.*). But the agency forged by the bourgeoisie, the agency by which its own destruction is to be brought about, does not arise *ex nihilo*, as an *effect of some cause operating mechanically* in its environment, in the way that new systems of production are created. The agency which will bring about the destruction of the bourgeoisie is to be made up of all the alienated of all the classes which have been reduced to the status of mere "commodities"—that is, to a purely nonhuman or natural status, by the exploitative operations of the most efficient members of the bourgeois class itself. This new class of radically alienated "refuse" of the capitalist system is the proletariat, "recruited from all classes of the population."

The origins of the proletariat, then, are the most diverse imaginable. It exists originally in the condition of total dispersion, without even any consciousness of its status as "refuse." In the process of its development, however, this refuse is transformed into gold; from the wretched of the earth is fashioned the instrument of human liberation.

Thus, while Marx emplotted the history of the bourgeoisie as a Tragedy, that of the proletariat is set within the larger framework of a Comedy, the resolution of which consists of the dissolution of all classes and the transformation of humanity into an organic whole. It is not surprising that Marx emplotted this Comedy as a drama in four acts that correspond to the stages of the Classical drama: *pathos, agon, sparagmos,* and *anagnorisis* successively.

The action of the drama is carried forward by the struggle with the bourgeoisie, but in the opening act the "contest is carried on by individual laborers" who "form an incoherent mass" and who do not even know their real enemy, the bourgeoisie, but fight instead against "the enemies of their enemies, the remnants of absolute monarchy" (15). At this stage, the consciousness of the proletariat is only a mood (*pathos*). The proletariat simply exists in itself, neither for itself nor in the consciousness of others. With the advent of industry, however, "the proletariat not only increases in number; it becomes concentrated in greater masses, its strength grows, and it feels its strength more." Workers begin to form "combinations (trade unions) against the bourgeoisie" and to engage their exploiters in open contests with their own interests in mind. (16) These contests consolidate the workers into political parties, groups organized for struggle in the political arena. This is the agonic stage; here the proletariat exists in conscious *opposition* to the bourgeoisie. It exists for itself, therefore, inhabits a world which it knows to be severed and in which raw power is recognized as the means to the only end that the masses can envisage, betterment of their own material condition *against* the threat of others. (*Ibid.*)

This "organization of the proletarians into a class, and consequently into a political party," is, however, constantly upset "by competition between the workers themselves." The agonic stage is thus followed by *sparagmos,* the falling apart of the proletariat into its several elements. This falling apart, however, is necessary (in Hegelian terms) for the proletariat's coming to consciousness of its own potential unification. The proletariat, Marx said, "ever rises up again, stronger, firmer, mightier." (17) This recurrent rise of the proletariat from the condition of dispersion into which it falls as a result of its *agon* is aided by divisions which occur within the bourgeoisie itself.

The bourgeoisie, put upon by the remnants of the older aristocratic order and by elements of itself which have become antagonistic to it, is forced to call upon the proletariat from time to time to aid it in its struggle against its enemies. The political education of the proletariat follows as a matter of course. Those elements of the aristocracy and bourgeoisie which are the victims of the stronger elements within the bourgeois order sink into the condition of the proletariat, unite with it, make its cause their own, and "supply the proletariat with fresh elements of enlightenment and progress" (*ibid.*). Thus, the proletariat is gradually transformed, not only into the repository of the refuse of all other classes, but into the class which *knows itself to be* this repository, and hence is rendered cosmopolitan and classless in its own aspirations. It becomes a class which is not only in itself and for itself but in and for itself simultaneously, and hence is a genuinely revolutionary class, the class that solves the "riddle of history." This process of transformation was described by Marx in the following terms:

Finally, in times when the class struggle nears the decisive hour, the process of dissolution going on within the ruling class, in fact within the whole range of old society, assumes such a violent, glaring character that a small section of the ruling class cuts itself adrift and joins the revolutionary class, the class that holds the future in its hands. Just as, therefore, at an earlier period, a section of the nobility went over to the bourgeoisie, so now a portion of the bourgeoisie goes over to the proletariat, and in particular a portion of the bourgeois ideologists, who have raised themselves to the level of comprehending theoretically the historical movement as a whole. [*Ibid.*]

And the result of this growth and transformation of consciousness is that the proletariat becomes the only "really revolutionary class," a superclass, the class of all classes, so that, while the "other classes decay and finally disappear in the face of modern industry," the proletariat becomes the "special and essential product" of this industry (*ibid.*). The "special and essential" nature of this revolutionary class will be manifested, Marx wrote, in the fact that the proletariat will occupy a position in society and history in which it will be unable to "fortify [its] already acquired status by subjecting society at large to [its] powers of appropriation" (18).

The proletarians cannot become masters of the productive forces of society, except by abolishing their own previous mode of appropriation, and thereby also every other previous mode of appropriation. [*Ibid.*]

This is because the proletariat, ironically, "[has] nothing of [its] own to secure and to fortify; [its] mission is to destroy all previous securities for, and insurances of, individual property" (*ibid.*). And, when the proletariat comes into its own, the result will be Communism, that condition of society in which "the free development of each is the condition for the free development of all" (29).

It is obvious that this fourfold movement of the proletariat is a *historical description* not of the actual stages through which the proletariat had *already* passed but of the stages through which Marx conceived that it *must* pass if the kind of society which he envisioned as the end of all historical development *is to come to pass.* What were the grounds, apart from the manifestly polemical purposes of the essay, for Marx's characterization of these four stages in the way he has in fact characterized them?

What I have laid out in the above passages is the plot structure, in embryo, of all significant processes in history, cast in terms that would allow Marx to postulate the final stage of proletarian development as a Synecdochic union of parts in the whole. The analysis is cast in the Metonymical mode—that is, in manifestly mechanical, or causal, terms. But what is being described is the transformation of a condition characterized originally in the Metaphorical mode, through a description of it in its Metonymically reduced state, to that of a Synecdochic union of parts into a whole. Marx wrote history from the standpoint of a thinker who was consciously committed to the Metonymical strategies of reducing a field of occurrences to the matrix of Mechanistic causal agencies which effect its transformations in strictly deterministic terms. But he exempted the social order from complete determination by causal forces as a way of comprehending the dynamics of its internal structural attributes. Although the whole social order follows, and is determined in its gross configuration by, the causes operating mechanically in the Base (the modes of production), the internal dynamics of the Superstructure are to be comprehended in the mode of Synecdochic relationships. And Communism, in Marx's mind, was nothing but the social order conceived in the mode of a perfect Synecdochic integration.

The structural similarities between Marx's method of analyzing history and his method of analyzing commodities (in Chapter I of *Capital*) should be obvious. The historical record is divided into a manifest and a hidden level of meaning, which are related to each other as phenomenal form to true content. The content of history changes incrementally—that is, quantitatively—through changes in the means of production which require transformation in the modes of production. But the primacy of the modes of production as a causal agency, determining the forms that appear in the Superstructure, remains constant throughout all changes. The different ways in which men relate to the natural world, in their efforts to provide for species needs, determine the forms that their social relationships must take. Fundamental alterations in the modes of production, such as the shift from Primitive Communism to an agrarian system exploiting Slave labor, or from the latter to a Feudal organization of the labor force, or from this to modern commercial Capitalism, provide the criteria for delineating the various "acts" of the historical drama as viewed from a macrocosmic level of conceptualization. The path which consciousness follows in response to these fundamental alterations in the modes of production is that from Metaphorical consciousness, through Metonymical and Synecdochic consciousness, to an Ironic apprehension of the essentially paradoxical nature of a social organization which breeds poverty in the midst of plenty, war in a situation in which peace is possible, scarcity (both material and psychic) in the midst of affluence. And this Ironic awareness of the condition of modern man prepares the ground for a transition of human consciousness to a new and higher (because it is a more self-conscious) form of Metaphorical union of man with nature, with other men, and with himself—the condition of consciousness in which Communism becomes a *realistic* possibility for men in the next stage of their development.

In short, the Ironic condition in which modern men find themselves is precisely similar to that which becomes possible, in Marx's view, once the fetishism of gold is recognized for what it truly is after one has followed the analysis carried out in the opening chapter of *Capital*. A dialectical analysis of the forms of value is possible because Marx distinguished between form and content on the basis of a belief in the labor theory of value. So, too, a dialectical analysis of the forms of the historical process is possible because Marx distinguished between history's form and content on the basis of his belief in the primacy of the Base as the agency of *significant* historical change. This dialectical analysis constitutes the formal argument in defense of his unique explanation of the true meaning of history, and it justifies the emplotment of the historical process given in the *Manifesto* as an image of the form of history-in-general.

But in the drama of history, as Marx actually conceived it, different actors dominate the various acts: first master and slave, then nobleman and serf, then bourgeoisie and proletariat. But the proletariat is endowed with a role and a being such as to make it the true protagonist of the whole drama, as that which the whole historical process from its beginning has been straining to become. As Marx characterized the proletariat, it is obvious that for him it is the whole of humanity which the different parts of humanity in the historical process have been (unsuccessfully) striving to become in their various incarnations. And because of the special place given to the proletariat, Marx was forced to endow the bourgeoisie itself with a special role in the historical drama.

The bourgeoisie becomes, in Marx's emplotment of history, the Tragic hero through whose fall the proletariat is raised to consciousness of its uniquely Comic destiny in world history. That is to say, by virtue of the fact that the proletariat is not only the victim, but also the spectator, of the bourgeoisie's rise and fall, the whole historical process can be provided with a Comic resolution as its preordained end. Just as, in *Capital*, the explication of the forms of value was carried out in the interest of justifying the labor theory of value, so, too, in the *Manifesto*, the explication of the forms of society was carried out in the interest of justifying the imminent triumph of the proletariat over both society and history itself. This is what lay behind

Marx's relegation of what was conventionally called "history" to the status of "prehistory." Man's true history, he predicted, will begin only with the triumph of the proletariat over its bourgeois oppressors, the dissolution of class differences, the withering away of the state, and the establishment of Socialism as the system of exchange based upon the acceptance of the labor theory of value.

✑§ Marx's Method Applied to Concrete Historical Events

Thus far, I have analyzed parts of *The German Ideology*, the *Manifesto*, and *Capital* with a view toward identifying the fundamental structures of Marx's analytical method. In the course of my analysis of his thought, I have stressed the tropological nature of what is commonly thought of as his "dialectical" method. No matter what Marx undertook to analyze, I have suggested, whether it was stages in the evolution of society, forms of value, or forms of socialism itself, he was inclined to break down the phenomenon under study into four categories or classes, corresponding to the tropes of Metaphor, Metonymy, Synecdoche, and Irony. Thus, to give yet another example, at the end of the *Manifesto*, when he classified the different forms of Socialist consciousness, he spoke of four major types: Reactionary, Conservative (or Bourgeois), Utopian, and (his own "Scientific") Communist. The evolution of Socialist consciousness proceeds by way of an original Metaphorical (Reactionary) type, through Metonymical (Bourgeois) and Synecdochic (Utopian) varieties, to the crystallization of that Scientific brand of Socialist consciousness (his own) by which all previous forms can be identified as fragmentary, incomplete, or flawed. Thus, Marx said, while Utopian Socialists still "endeavor . . . to deaden the class struggle and to reconcile class antagonisms . . . ," Communists "fight for the attainment of the *momentary* interests of the working class . . . [and] everywhere support *every* revolutionary movement against the existing social and political order of things" (*Manifesto*, 41). This passage suggests that, even in the enthusiasm of 1848, Marx was under no illusion that the revolution of the proletariat could possibly be realized *at that time*.

Communists "Ironically" join every revolutionary movement in the interest of promoting the *ultimate* victory of the proletariat. This Ironic stance, not only with respect to the bourgeoisie, but also with respect to revolutionary movements directed against it, protected Marx from any optimistic illusion that *the* time had come for the ultimate victory. The *Manifesto*, with its call to arms to the proletariat, is itself an Ironic document, inasmuch as Marx himself at the time of its composition entertained few hopes for the consummation of the revolution that it enthusiastically proclaimed.

Marx knew that the revolution could not be consummated, because he knew that the Synecdochic stage of consciousness, presupposed by the aims it envisioned, had not yet been attained by the proletariat of Europe. In fact, in *The Holy Family* (1845), Marx had defined Communism as "the *positive* abolition of *private property*, of *human self-alienation*, and thus, the real *appropriation of human* nature, through and for man. It is therefore the return of man himself as a social, that is, really human, being; a complete and conscious return which assimilates all the wealth of previous development" (243–44; italics added). The whole assimilates to itself and transforms into a unity the totality of the parts. That such an assimilation and transformation were hardly in the offing in the eruptions of 1848 was signaled by Marx's own characterization of Communist consciousness in that year as encompassing only *limited* aims. It was further signaled in his analysis of *The Class Struggles in France, 1849 to 1850*, written in the latter year as a series of articles commenting on the events as they evolved before him.

In his 1891 introduction to Marx's *The Civil War in France* (1871), Engels remarked on Marx's ability to grasp "clearly the character, the import, and the necessary consequences of great historical events, at a time when these events are still in progress before our eyes or have only just taken place" (349). In *The Class Struggles in France*, Marx had characterized the revolutionary movement of 1848 as a "tragicomedy," which served the interests of the proletariat only insofar as it brought into being a "powerful united counterrevolution" and created thereby "an opponent in combat with whom, only, the party of revolt ripened into a really revolutionary party" (281). In short, here the revolution was depicted as serving primarily as a means of developing the consciousness of the proletariat itself, by way of negation, opposition, or antithesis. The creation of a counterrevolutionary party alone permitted the revolutionary party to define itself, in both its similarity to, and difference from, the counterrevolutionary party.

Marx argued, in fact, that the nature of the proletariat's consciousness and its actual historical condition *required* its defeat. For since the

proletarians rightly regarded themselves as the victors of February, . . . They had to be vanquished in the streets, they had to be shown that they were worsted as soon as they did not fight *with* the bourgeoisie, but *against* the bourgeoisie. . . . Arms in hand, the bourgeoisie had to refute the demands of the proletariat. And the real birthplace of the bourgeois republic is not the *February victory*; it is the *June defeat*. [303]

This uncovering of the events of June as the true birthplace of the bourgeois republic, as the defeat of its "true" enemy, the proletariat, which had fought with it in February to depose Louis Philippe, is rather like that dialectical analysis of the Money form of value given in *Capital*. That is to say, it is at once a reduction and a clarification through a reduction. The false equivalence stated in the explicit form of the Metaphor "the revolution = the February uprising" is corrected by the Ironic negation "the revolution = the triumph of the bourgeoisie." Thus, Marx said,

The February revolution was the *beautiful* revolution, the revolution of universal sympathy, because the antagonisms which had flared up in it against the monarchy slumbered peacefully side by side, still *undeveloped*, because the social struggle which formed its background had won only an airy existence, an existence of phrases, or words. [305]

By contrast,

The *June revolution* is the *ugly* revolution, the repulsive revolution, because deeds have taken the place of phrases, because the republic uncovered the head of the monster itself by striking off the crown that shielded and concealed it. [*Ibid.*]

The true beneficiary, then, of the June uprising was the bourgeoisie, which, because it had triumphed in Paris, now had its "self-assurance" raised all over Europe. Accordingly, Marx argued, the triumph of the bourgeoisie in June 1848 laid the groundwork for the overthrow of the bourgeoisie itself precisely because it revealed it for what it was, a monster. Its monstrous character was displayed in the contradictions contained in the new constitution which the Constituent National Assembly had put together.

The "most comprehensive contradiction of this constitution" consisted, according to Marx, in the way it disposed political power among the various classes of France.

The classes whose social slavery the constitution is to perpetuate, proletariat, peasantry, petty bourgeoisie, it puts in possession of political power through universal suffrage. And from the class whose old social power it sanctions, the bourgeoisie, it withdraws the political guarantees of this power. It forces the political rule of the bourgeoisie into democratic conditions, which at every moment help the hostile classes to victory and jeopardize the very foundations of bourgeois society. From the former classes it demands that they should not go forward from political to social emancipation; from the others that they should not go back from social to political restoration. [313]

In such a contradictory situation, only a nonentity such as Louis Bonaparte could possibly have appealed to the broad sectors of the French electorate. Thus, ironically, it happened

that the most simple-minded man in France acquired the most multifarious significance. Just because he was nothing he could signify everything save himself. [315]

Thus, the condition of France under the rule of Louis Bonaparte was precisely the same as that of modern capitalist society under the sway of the "fetishism of gold." A totally worthless entity was identified with the interests of all groups precisely because the specific interest of every group had been negated by constitutional maneuvering. French society was relegated to that "farcical" condition which would become the subject of a more comprehensive analysis in Marx's classic, *The Eighteenth Brumaire of Louis Bonaparte*.

⤪ History as Farce

The Eighteenth Brumaire opens with a famous apothegm:

Hegel remarks somewhere that all facts and personages of great importance in world history occur, as it were, twice. He forgot to add: the first time as tragedy, the second as farce. [320]

The coup of Louis Bonaparte is thus prefigured in the first paragraph of Marx's work as an Ironic anaclasis to the genuinely Tragic events that had brought Napoleon I to power in the great bourgeois revolution in 1789. Although French society in 1848 thought that it was carrying out the revolutionary program of 1789, in reality, in Marx's view, it was regressing to a point "behind its point of departure" (323). The whole set of events which occurred from February 24, 1848, to December 1851 Marx characterized, as he had in *The Class Struggles in France*, as a "tragicomedy," a charade of revolution, which left the French nation in a state of bondage more oppressive than that from which it had been liberated in 1789.

Moreover, Marx denied that one can legitimately say, "as the French do, that their nation was taken unawares. . . . The riddle is not solved by such turns of speech, but merely formulated differently." The real problem, he maintained, is to explain "how a nation of thirty-six million can be surprised and delivered into unresisting captivity by three swindlers" (325)

Of course, this was not really a problem for Marx. At least, it was not an analytical problem, for he already knew the answer to that problem. Marx's problem was a literary one; he had to present "what really happened" in a convincing narrative.

Marx's formal answer to the question "what really happened" must be distinguished from the analytical method he used to arrive at an answer to that question. Formally, Marx simply argued that Louis Bonaparte's victory was a result of bourgeois fear of the proletariat, combined with peasant resentment of both the bourgeoisie and the proletariat (see 332, 339). The causes of this fear on the one hand and of the resentment on the other are referred to as the "material conditions" which underlay and informed relationships among the bourgeoisie, proletariat, peasantry, and the Bonapartist *form* of government in 1850. Here, as in the analysis of value in *Capital*, it was a matter of distinguishing between the form and the content of the phenomenon to be analyzed.

But the question of *how* these various factors coalesced to provide the specific form of their relationship under the Second Empire required that Marx reveal the "true story" behind the events that made up the chronicle of significant historical occurrences in France between 1848 and 1851. And, in turn, the disclosure of this true story required the emplotment of the events as a story of a particular kind. This story had already been characterized as a "farce" in Marx's opening remarks, which means that he had cast the story in the mode of Satire. There was, in short, nothing Tragic about the events of 1848–51, in which France delivered itself into the care of "three swindlers." The events that Marx depicted as leading from the February revolution to the establishment of the Second Empire describe a sustained fall into a condiction of bondage unrelieved by any evidence of the kind of noble aspiration that would have permitted their characterization as a genuine Tragedy.

This differs from Marx's characterization of the events of 1789, the activities of the bourgeoisie during the course of the French Revolution. Referring to the revolution of 1789, Marx wrote:

But unheroic as bourgeois society is, it nevertheless took heroism, sacrifice, terror, civil war, and battles of peoples to bring it into being. And in the classically austere traditions of the Roman Republic its gladiators found the *ideals* and the art *forms*, the *self-deceptions* that they needed in order to conceal from themselves the bourgeois limitations of the *content* of their struggles and to keep their enthusiasm on the high plane of the great historical tragedy. [321–22; italics added]

The bourgeois revolution of 1789 was Tragic *because* the disparity between ideals and realities was obscured. The revolution of 1848–51 was another matter. It was "farcical" precisely *because* the ideals were subordinated to realities. As a result,

Instead of *society* having conquered a new content for itself, it seems that the *state* only returned to its oldest form, to the shamelessly simple domination of the saber and cowl. This is the answer to the *coup de main* of February 1848, given by the *coup de tête* of December 1851. Easy come, easy go. [323]

The establishment of the Second Empire, then, represented the final phase of a course of events which had begun in the uprising of February 1848. It was the datum to be explained, and Marx explained it by dividing its "history" into four phases of development: the February period; the period of the Constituent National Assembly, May 4, 1848–May 28, 1849; the period of the Legislative National Assembly, May 28, 1849–December 2,

1851; and, finally, the Second Empire itself, which lasted from December 2, 1851, to its overthrow in the days of the Paris Commune in 1871.

Marx's characterization of these phases corresponds to that offered in the analysis of the four forms of value in *Capital*. Thus, he described the February period as a "prologue to the revolution" (326) since, during this time, everyone involved in the uprising was inspired only by "general," not by specific, revolutionary aims.

In no period do we . . . find a more confused mixture of high-flown phrases and actual uncertainty and clumsiness, of more enthusiastic striving for innovation and more deeply rooted domination of the old routine, of more apparent harmony of the whole society and more profound estrangement of its elements. [326–27]

The appearances and the realities of the revolutionary situation *existed* in the strongest contrast to one another, but were not *perceived* to be such—in the same way that, in the Elementary form of value, the disparity between content and form is obscured, to the detriment of the former. Thus, all of the "elements that had prepared or determined the revolution . . . provisionally found their place in the February *government*" (326). "Every party construed [the revolution] in its own way." The proletariat, having secured arms at last, "impressed its stamp upon it and proclaimed it to be a *social republic*," thereby indicating the "general content of the modern revolution," but one which, in the circumstances, "was in most singular contradiction to everything that . . . could be immediately realized in practice" (*ibid.*). Meanwhile, the old powers of society regrouped themselves, "assembled, reflected, and found unexpected support in the mass of the nation, the peasants and the petty bourgeois, who all at once stormed onto the political stage" (327).

This contrast between the ideal of the revolution and what "could be immediately realized in practice" corresponds to the "form" of value and its true "content" as set forth in *Capital*. The true content of the situation in February 1848 is masked by a general condition of consciousness which might be called Metaphorical in a strict sense. What is hidden is also present, but present in a distorted form. The true content of the revolution is to be found in the material conditions which made the February uprising possible, but this content exists in contradiction to the *forms* of social action present on the scene in 1848. That this was implicitly recognized by the parties of the revolution is shown by the fact that the February regime was designated as "provisional." "Nothing and nobody," Marx said, "ventured to lay claim to the right of existence and of real action" (326). The condition of stasis into which the nation fell after the success of the coup against Louis Philippe was evidence enough for Marx of the existence of a practical contradiction which could be resolved only by force.

And it was resolved, according to Marx, during the second phase, the period of the Constituent National Assembly, which lasted from May 4, 1848, to May 28, 1849, the period of the "bourgeois republic . . . , a living protest against the pretensions of the February days" (327). The function of the National Assembly, Marx said, was "to *reduce* the result of the revolution to the bourgeois scale" (*ibid.*; italics added). In short, the purpose of the second phase was to resolve the contradictions contained in the first phase by reducing the general content of the revolution to a particular content, the general rule to that of the bourgeoisie.

The demands of the Paris proletariat are utopian nonsense, to which an end must be put. To this declaration of the Constituent National Assembly the Paris proletariat replied with the June insurrection, the most colossal event in the history of European civil wars. [*Ibid.*]

But, ironically, this most "colossal event in the history of European civil wars" was historically significant, in Marx's estimation, primarily because of its failure. Only by the defeat of the proletariat would the proletariat prevail.

The bourgeois republic triumphed. On its side, stood the aristocracy of finance, the industrial bourgeoisie, the middle class, the petty bourgeois, the army, the lumpen-proletariat organised as the Mobile Guard, the intellectual lights, the clergy, and the rural population. On the side of the Paris proletariat stood none but itself. More than three thousand insurgents were butchered after the victory, and fifteen thousand were transported without trial. With this defeat the proletariat passes into the background of the revolutionary stage. [327–28]

The defeat of the June insurgents was thus characterized as a lamentable, but hardly Tragic, event, inasmuch as their resistance to the bourgeoisie was not informed by a clear notion of their aims or by any realistic assessment of their prospects for victory. Little wonder, in Marx's view, that attempts to revive the proletarian cause were consistently frustrated. The proletariat "seems unable either to rediscover revolutionary greatness in itself or to win new energy from the connections [with other groups] newly entered into, until *all classes* with which it contended in June themselves lie prostrate beside it" (328)—until, in short, all classes have become *one with it*. The fact that the proletariat "at least . . . succumbs with the honors of the great world-historical struggle" cannot obscure the more important fact that its defeat "leveled the ground on which the bourgeois republic could be founded and built up" (*ibid.*). The reductive nature of the bourgeois order is revealed in the fact that, for it, "Society is saved just as often as the circle of its rulers contracts, as a more exclusive interest is maintained against a wider one" (329).

The evolution of bourgeois society was marked by the systematic *betrayal of the ideals* on behalf of which it had prosecuted the revolution of 1789. These very ideals, when appealed to by spokesmen for the proletariat, seeking to gain for their constituency the same "liberties" and "organs of progress" that had brought the bourgeoisie to power, were now branded as "socialistic." Its own *ideals* were rejected as a threat to the "class rule" which the bourgeoisie sought to establish. But, ironically, Marx pointed out, the bourgeoisie did not realize that "its own parliamentary regime, that its political rule in general," would be regarded as "socialistic" by those elements in its own ranks which now desired "tranquility" above all (332). The bourgeoisie, once the champion of competition, discussion, debate, rule by majority, and so on, could no longer countenance these processes insofar as they were demanded by others. It therefore necessarily rejected these along with its commitment to the ideals of "liberty, equality, and fraternity" and to the principle of parliamentary democracy. Ironically,

by now stigmatizing as "socialistic" what it had previously extolled as "liberal," the bourgeoisie confesses that its own interests dictate that it should be delivered from the danger of its *own rule*; that *in order to restore tranquility* in the country *its bourgeois Parliament must*, first of all, *be given its quietus*; that *in order to preserve its social power* intact *its social power must be broken*; that the individual bourgeois can continue to exploit the other classes, . . . only on condition that this class be condemned . . . to . . . political nullity; that in order to save its purse it must forfeit the crown, and the sword that is to safeguard it must be at the same time hung over its own head as a sword of Damocles. [333]

This series of ironic inversions provided the dramatic principle by which Marx "dialectically" explicated the self-destructive operations of both the bourgeoisie and the proletariat which serve the "cunning of history." The transition from the first to the second phase of the revolution is a transition from a Metaphorical to a Metonymical mode of existence. In the second, or bourgeois, phase, "society" is Metonymically identified with the "bourgeoisie"; the part has taken the place of the whole. "The parliamentary republic, together with the bourgeoisie, takes possession of the entire stage; it enjoys its existence to the full (*ibid.*). But on December 2, 1851, this republic was buried, "to the accompaniment of the anguished cry of the royalists in coalition: 'Long live the republic!' " (333–34) And it was buried by Louis Bonaparte, who provided the transition from the Metonymical to the Synecdochic (Generalized) phase of the revolution. Marx described the transition thus:

In Parliament the nation made its general will the law, that is, it made the law of the ruling classes its general will. Before the executive power it renounces all will of its own and submits to the superior command of an alien will, to authority. The executive power, in contrast to the legislative power, expresses the heteronomy of the nation, in contrast to its autonomy. [336]

This "executive power" (Bonaparte) stood with respect to the French nation, with its various classes, as linen did to all other commodities in Marx's analysis of the Generalized form of value in Capital. Thus, Marx wrote:

France, therefore, seems to have escaped the *despotism of a class* only to fall back beneath the *despotism of an individual*. [*Ibid*.]

But, ironically, it had fallen back beneath the authority of "an individual without authority. The struggle seems to be settled in such a way that all classes, equally impotent and equally mute, fall on their knees before a rifle butt" (*ibid*.). Thus, the "total," or "Extended," condition of class conflict, characteristic of the bourgeois republic, now gave place to the "Generalized" condition of the bourgeois dictatorship, and in such a way that, while coming to the fore as the dominant class of society, the bourgeoisie was stripped of that very *political* power to which it had aspired in 1789. All political power was vested in a single individual, Bonaparte: "As against civil society, the state machine has consolidated itself so thoroughly that [Bonaparte] suffices for its head" (337).

Marx argued that Bonaparte's success depended upon support of the smallholding peasants of France, but he noted that this success was not attended by the ascent of this class to political power. In much the same way that, in the analysis of the forms of value, the fetishism of gold succeeded the Generalized form of value, in the succession of political forms, the fetishism of Bonaparte succeeded the Generalized form of political power represented by the presidential office occupied by Bonaparte. Bonaparte, "an adventurer blown in from abroad, raised on the shield of a drunken soldiery, which he has bought with liquor and sausages" (*ibid*.), not only betrayed the peasantry but all other orders as well. Looking upon himself "as the representative of the middle class, . . . he is somebody solely due to the fact that he has broken the political power of the middle class and daily breaks it anew" (345). Looking upon himself as "the representative of the peasants" and of the "lumpen-proletariat," he betrayed them also, insisting that they must learn to be happy "within the frame of bourgeois society" (346).

Bonaparte's program was a masterpiece of duplicity and contradiction. The French bourgeoisie were right, then, when they proclaimed (as Marx has them say): "Only the chief of the Society of December 10 can still save bourgeois society! Only theft can still save property; only perjury, religion; only bastardy, the family; disorder, order!" (345). The same "absurdidity" which Marx subsequently ascribed to the "fetishism of gold" was here ascribed to a whole society. Thus, for example, he wrote with reference to Bonaparte's contradictory relationship to the various classes of society:

The contradictory task of the man explains the contradictions of his government, the confused groping about which seeks now to win, now to humiliate first one class and then another and arrays all of them uniformly against him, whose practical uncertainty forms a highly comical contrast to the imperious, categorical style of the governmental decrees, a style which is faithfully copied from his uncle. [346]

The contradictions of Bonaparte's regime are precisely analogous to the contradictions which inform, and render congenitally unstable, the Money form of value. And this is what permitted Marx to predict, with perfect self-confidence, the regime's ultimate dissolution. Marx ended *The Eighteenth Brumaire* with a characterization of the regime which presaged the judgment he would render on it retrospectively in his *Civil Wars in France* in 1871. *The Eighteenth Brumaire* ends thus:

Driven by the contradictory demands of his situation and being at the same time, like a conjurer, under the necessity of keeping the public gaze fixed on himself, . . . by springing constant surprises, that is to say, under the necessity of executing a *coup d'état en miniature* every day, Bonaparte throws the entire bourgeois economy into confusion, violates everything that seemed involable to the Revolution of 1848, makes some tolerant of revolution, others desirous of revolution, and produces actual anarchy in the name of order, while at the same time stripping its halo from the entire state mechanism, profanes it and makes it at once loathsome and ridiculous. [348]

In 1871, then, all that was needed to lay bare the "rottenness" both of the regime and of the society which it pretended to serve was the prick of the Prussian bayonet (*The Civil Wars in France*, 365). The disintegration of this "farcical" form of government was inevitably followed by its "direct antithesis"—that is to say, the Paris Commune—which launched French society on a new cycle of development.

The Commune also launched the proletariat on a new cycle of consciousness. Thus, Marx wrote in *The Civil Wars in France*:

The cry of "social republic," with which the revolution of February was ushered in by the Paris proletariat, did not express a vague aspiration after a republic that was not only to supersede the monarchical form of class rule, but class rule itself. The Commune was [thus] the positive form of that republic. [*Ibid.*]

The positiveness of the called-for "social republic" was reflected, Marx argued, in its attempts to construct a social order greater than the sum of the parts which made it up. Thus, for example, the Commune was "emphatically international" (373), admitting "all foreigners to the honor of dying for its immortal cause" (374). Marx even went so far as to assert that crime was virtually unknown in Paris during its heyday: "No more corpses in the morgue, no nocturnal burglaries, scarcely any robberies" (376). In contrast to the decadent remnants of the former regime, now gathered at Versailles and endeavoring to subvert the Commune, Paris was a virtual paradise: "Opposed to the new world at Paris behold the old world at Versailles. . . . Paris all truth, Versailles all lie; and that lie vented through the mouth of Thiers" (377). In Paris during the Commune, a group of men succeeded for a moment in creating, according to Marx, a model of what the Communist society of the future would look like. As Engels wrote in 1891: "Well and good, gentlemen: do you want to know what [the dictatorship of the proletariat] looks like? Look at the Paris Commune. That was the dictatorship of the proletariat" (362).

Yet, here, as in 1848, the revolution was predestined to defeat, not only because the material conditions were not yet right for the establishment of a Communist society, but also because "the majority of the Commune was in no wise socialist, nor could it be" (Marx to F. Domela-Nieuwenhuis, 1881, 391). The cry for a "social republic" was only a Metaphor, containing within it an unspecified content, which was "socialism," but which appeared under the vague designation of "class rule." The idea of the Commune would have to undergo the *agon* of Metonymical reduction before it could emerge purified and self-consciously Socialist in its next incarnation. The Third Republic, established by the force of Prussian arms, was the social form that this reduction took. Its contradictions were not less glaring than those of the Second Empire, which it supplanted. And it was not more stable. If anything, it was even more morbid, existing as it did as an uneasy compromise between a frightened bourgeoisie and a proletariat grown more self-conscious of itself as a revolutionary class, for having the historical experience of the Commune to draw upon for inspiration. That it would become more "absurd" in the course of time, Marx did not doubt at all. It was as fated to absurdity as that economic system which confused value with gold.

⇜§ Conclusion

I can now summarize Marx's idea of history, conceived as both a method of analysis and a strategy of representation. I have indicated that, in my view, Marx's view of history has two dimensions, or two axes of conceptualization: one Synchronic, having to do with the timeless relationships presumed to exist between the Base and the Superstructure; the other diachronic, having to do with the transformations that occur over time in both of these. Marx broke with Hegel in his insistence that the fundamental ground of historical being is nature, rather than consciousness, and in his conviction that the publicly sanctioned forms of consciousness are *determined* in a Mechanistic way by the modes of production of which they are reflections. This causal relationship is unilinear and is conceived to be irremissible throughout history. He remained one with Hegel, however, in his use of the "dialectical" method to analyze the succession of forms appearing in the Superstructure. Here his categories are the same as Hegel's, and his conception of the relationships among the entities classified under their rubrics is identical. Hegelian "logic" is thus remanded to the task of analyzing the fundamental forms of human self-conceptualization and the social matrices within which these forms of self-conceptualization gain public accreditation. Moreover, both the categories used to characterize the forms and matrices and those used to characterize relations among them were derived from Marx's perception of the essentially tropological nature of the categories of Hegel's *Logic*. The types of human self-conceptualization and the social projections of such conceptualizations are given in, and are ultimately limited to, the modes of characterizing reality provided by language in general, as are the modalities of transformation of these types and projections. Metaphor, Metonymy, Synecdoche, and Irony offer not only the means of human self-conceptualization but also the categories of analysis by which such self-conceptualizations are to be comprehended as *stages* in the history of any aspect of the Superstructure. Whether Marx was analyzing a micro-event, such as the revolution of 1848–51 in France, or a macro-event, such as the whole evolution of humanity, he always fell back upon tropology as the basis for his categorization of classes of events and the stages through which they pass in their evolution from an inaugural to a terminal condition.

So, too, as in Hegel, the tropes provided the basis for Marx's fourfold analysis, in dramatistic terms, of sets of historically significant phenomena. The plot structure of every historically significant sequence of events—from *pathos*, through *agon* and *sparagmos*, to *anagnorisis*—represents a movement either toward liberation or toward bondage, *toward* a "Romantic" transcendence of the world of experience or *toward* an "Ironic" condition of bondage. But Marx denied both extremes; mankind is indentured neither to total bondage nor to perfect transcendence. His historical vision, like that of Hegel, oscillated between apprehensions of the Tragic outcome of every act of the historical drama and comprehensions of the Comic outcome of the process as a whole. For Marx, as for Hegel, humanity achieves the condition of a Comic reconciliation, with itself and with nature, *by means* of Tragic conflicts which, in themselves, appear to offer nothing more than the consolations of a philosophical comprehension of their nobility. Thus, just as in his "explanations" of history Marx moved between a Mechanistic and an Organicist mode of argument, so, in his "representations" of it, he moved between a Tragic and a Comic conception of its fundamental form.

This twofold movement distinguishes the Radical from the Conservative historian (it distinguishes both Hegel and Marx from Ranke), even though both kinds of historian end with a Comic conception of the whole historical process. Hegel and Marx took conflict seriously in a way that Ranke did not. Both Hegel and Marx knew that things are never for the best in the best of all possible worlds, that mankind sustains genuine losses and mutilations in its efforts to realize itself against a cosmos that is as intractable as it is, at different times and places, unknowable. But that cosmos can, in their estimation, *be known*; the laws which govern it can be progressively discerned. But the laws governing the cosmos can be known only through practice, through action, through heroic—not to say Promethean—assertions of will. Such assertions are as dangerous to individuals and groups as they are problematical. They carry with them the possibility of genuinely Tragic failure and defeat. But, if they are truly heroic in their aspiration, men can contribute through their failures and defeats to the human knowledge of the laws that govern both nature and history. And their knowledge of such laws provides the basis for the human transcendence of the limitations they lay upon humanity.

The charge conventionally leveled against Marx by Liberal and Conservative historians, that of being crudely reductionist, can thus be seen to be not even half true. On the contrary, Marx was anything but reductionist in his method, even though his conception of history was governed by a vision of the *integrative* trends discernible in its macrocosmic dimensions. If anything, Ranke was much more reductionist than Marx, much more the captive of a myth, even though his work *appears to have been* directed to the appreciation of historical phenomena in their particularity and uniqueness. As a matter of fact, it should by now be obvious that the penchant for *dispersive* strategies of representation, as against *integrative* ones, represents an ideological bias neither less nor more conceptually overdetermined than that which inspired Marx in his quest for the solution to "the riddle of history." To conclude, as Burckhardt did, that history is not susceptible to rational analysis, except in terms of the most general categories, and that its processes can never be comprehended as anything more than a sequence of "metastatic" transformations, is neither more nor less mythopoeic than the conclusions to which Marx was led by his reflections on history. The belief that the meaning of history is that it has no meaning, or that it is illegitimate to conceptualize it in such a way as to give a specific meaning to it, is not merely a cognitive judgment; it is also an ideological one. What Marx sought to do was to provide an analytical method and a strategy of representation which would permit him to write about history in the active, rather than the passive, voice. The active voice is the voice of Radicalism. But Marx's Radicalism was that of the Left, and was distinguishable from its rightwing counterpart by its insistence that history is no more a mystery in principle than is nature itself, that the study of history yields laws by which one can comprehend both its meaning and its general direction of development. It thereby positions the reader in a situation of choice between possible alternatives without specifying what his decision in a given situaton *has to be*. More important, it places the reader in a position in which, whatever choice he makes, he is forced to make it in a condition of self-consciousness more profound than if he had made his decision in the Rankean apprehension of things working out for the best no matter what one does or the Burckhardtian belief that, whatever one does, it does not matter.

Chapter 9 Nietzsche: The Poetic Defense of History in the Metaphorical Mode

Introduction

In historical thought, as in almost everything else in nineteenth-century cultural activity, Friedrich Nietzsche marked a turning point, for he rejected the categories of historical analysis which historians had used since the 1830s and denied the reality of any such thing as *a* historical process upon which those categories could be turned. This is not to say that Nietzsche had no interest in historical questions. On the contrary, most of his philosophical works are based in the consideration of historical problems, and most of them could even be considered historical in their methods. For example, *The Birth of Tragedy out of the Spirit of Music* (1871) is not only an essay on the aesthetics of Tragedy but—perhaps more important—also a history of the rise and fall of the Tragic spirit in Classical Greece; and *The Genealogy of Morals* (1887) is not only a prolegomenon to a nihilistic ethics but also—and again more important—a bold and original essay on the history of the ideas of good and evil in Western civilization. Moreover, most of Nietzsche's works contain a discourse on, or extensive references to, historical consciousness, criticisms of conventional historical thought, and suggestions for turning historical ideas to creative purposes. Thus, there was more than just a grain of truth in the remark that Burckhardt made to Nietzsche in 1882: "fundamentally of course you are always teaching history" (Burckhardt, *Briefe*, 427).

Yet Nietzsche's idea of history was as little appreciated by professional historians as Hegel's, not because his reflections on history were clouded by a technical language of the sort used by Hegel, but because his meaning was all too clear and all too obviously threatening to professional conceptions of history's competence. Nietzsche's purpose was to destroy belief in a historical past from which men might learn any single, substantial truth. For Nietzsche—as for Burckhardt—there were as many "truths" about the past as there were individual perspectives on it. In his view, the study of history ought never to be merely an end in itself but should always serve as a means to some *vital* end or purpose. Men looked at the world in ways that conformed to the purposes which motivated them; and they required different visions of history to justify the various projects which they had to undertake in order to realize their humanity fully. Basically, therefore, Nietzsche divided the ways in which men looked at history into two kinds: a life-denying kind, which pretended to find the single eternally true, or "proper," way of regarding the past; and a life-affirming kind, which encouraged as many different visions of history as there were projects for winning a sense of self in individual human beings. The desire to believe that there was one, eternally true, or "proper," idea of history was, in Nietzsche's opinion, another vestige of the Christian need to believe in the one, true God—or of Christianity's secular counterpart, Positivist science, with its need to believe in a single, complete, and completely true body of natural laws. To both of these essentially constrictive conceptions of truth and to their equivalents in art—Romanticism and Naturalism—Nietzsche opposed his own conception of the *relativity* of every vision of the real.

Nietzsche was not, however, cut off from the art and science of his time. From the very beginning he accepted the *nihilistic* implications of both. He celebrated Positivist science's establishment of the essential meaninglessness of the natural process and Symbolist art's conception of the ultimately constructivist nature of any form, meaning, or content which men seemed to have found in the world. To Nietzsche the form, meaning, and content of all science and all religion were aesthetic in origin, products of a human need to flee from reality into a dream, to *impose* order on experience in the absence of any substantive meaning or content. He held all "truths" to be perversions of the original aesthetic impulse, perversions insofar as they took the dream for the formless reality and tried to freeze life in the form provided by the dream. The aesthetic impulse was dynamic in nature—I would say dialectical—moving restlessly between the dream and the reality, constantly dissolving atrophied dreams through renewed contacts with the primal chaos and generating new dreams to sustain the will to life. The highest kind of art, Tragedy, effected this dialectical movement from dream to reality and back to dream self-consciously, keeping the accesses to the life force open, but allowing the release of those forces in humanly assimilable quanta of energy.

When Nietzsche reflected on history, therefore, he was always concerned to determine how history itself could be transformed into a similarly creative form of dreaming, how, in short, it could be transmuted into a kind of Tragic art. He shared this concern with Hegel; but ultimately Nietzsche differed from Hegel in his conception of what Tragedy teaches. For Nietzsche, Tragedy offers no "superior point of view," as Hegel thought, but is characterized by the impulse to dissolve all such points of view before they harden into life-restricting concepts. Thus envisaged, Nietzsche's reflections on history are an extension of his reflections on Tragedy. If we are to understand the aim of his "Use and Abuse of History" (1874), we must first understand something of the work out of which it grew, *The Birth of Tragedy*.

ᴥᴥ§ Myth and History

In 1886 Nietzsche wrote a new preface to *The Birth of Tragedy*, which had originally appeared in 1871. The preface was entitled "Versuch einer Selbstkritik" (Essay in Self-criticism), and in it Nietzsche named the two points of view which, in retrospect, he could see had been the true targets of his youthful polemic. These targets were Irony and Romanticism. "I was then," Nietzsche said, "beginning to take hold of a dangerous problem . . . the problem of scholarly investigation. For the first time in history somebody had *come to grips* with scholarship!" (5). He viewed Irony as the principal attribute of scholars; under the guise of "the 'inquiring mind,'" Irony had been spread over the whole world of thought and imagination as "a clever bulwark erected against the truth" (4–5). "Had this perhaps been your secret, great Socrates?" Nietzsche asked. "Most secretive of ironists, had *this* been your deepest irony?" (5) As for Romanticism, it had been incarnated for the young Nietzsche in Richard Wagner and his music. The intervening years, however, had taught Nietzsche at least one thing: "to adopt a hopeless and merciless attitude toward that 'German temper,' ditto toward German music, which I now recognize for what it really is: a thoroughgoing romanticism, the least Greek of all art forms, and, over and above that, a drug of the worst sort" (13).

The name of Nietzsche is of course associated with that rebirth of interest in mythic thinking which occurred at the end of the last century, and especially with the myth of "eternal return," which Nietzsche opposed to the Christian myth of redemption and the bourgeois doctrine of progress. Löwith, for example, insists that, although the myth of eternal recurrence was set forth in *The Joyful Wisdom* only as the basis of an *ethical imperative*, in

Thus Spoke Zarathustra, the idea was offered as "a metaphysical truth" (*Meaning*, 216–17). In fact, Löwith says, the doctrine of eternal recurrence forms "the fundamental thought in [Nietzsche's] latest work" (219).

Another view of Nietzsche's thought sees him as the creator of another myth, that of the endless exchange between the Dionysiac and Apollonian faculties in man, and hence as the defender of a dualistic philosophy, a Manichean conception of life which is not cyclical in its whole movement, but open-ended, an oscillation in place.

Both views are plausible, and each has its implications for a proper understanding of Nietzsche's thought about history. But I contend that neither the doctrine of eternal recurrence nor that of the Dionysiac-Apollonian dualism leads to an understanding of Nietzsche's thought about historical existence, historical knowledge, and the historical process. The two myths are products of a prior critique of historical knowledge, the results of Nietzsche's efforts, first of all, to translate history into an art, and, second, to translate aesthetic vision into an apprehension of life in Tragic and Comic terms *simultaneously*.

Nietzsche's purpose as a philosopher was to transcend Irony by freeing consciousness from all Metonymical apprehensions of the world (which bred the doctrines of mechanical causality and a dehumanizing science) on the one hand and all Synecdochic sublimations of the world (which bred the doctrines of "higher" causes, gods, spirits, and morality) on the other, and to return consciousness to the enjoyment of its Metaphorical powers, its capacity to "frolic in images," to entertain the world as pure phenomena, and to liberate, thereby, man's poetic consciousness to an activity more pure, for being more self-conscious, than the naive Metaphor of primitive man.

Thus, in *The Birth of Tragedy*, Nietzsche opposed two kinds of false Tragic sensibility: that which interprets the Tragic vision in the Ironic mode, and that which interprets it in the Romantic mode. His demolition of these two false conceptions of Tragic consciousness provided him with the means of reinterpreting Tragedy as a *combination* of Dionysiac and Apollonian insights, as Tragic apprehensions of the world being discharged in Comic comprehensions of it—*and* the reverse. His remarks on historical consciousness, scattered throughout all his works, but addressed most profoundly in "The Use and Abuse of History" and *The Genealogy of Morals*, were meant to carry out the same surgical operation on the historical thought of his own time. History, like Tragedy, has its false as well as its true, its killing as well as its liberating, aspects. And we shall see that, for Nietzsche, the false varieties were Ironic and Romantic, while the true version was that combination of Tragedy and Comedy which he tried to effect in *The Birth of Tragedy out of the Spirit of Music*.

Marx had sought to reintroduce the concepts of law and causation into historical reflection, but in such a way as to make possible a heroic confrontation of the evils of his own present and a hopeful projection of man into his possible future. Nietzsche was motivated by the same desire for a rebirth of heroism in an age of mediocrity and cultural resignation, and he was concerned to re-establish, on new grounds, a basis for an optimistic projection of man into a future. But his strategy was precisely the opposite of Marx's. For, whereas Marx tried to justify a Promethean conception of humanity's tasks for the future by a revision of the concepts of law and causality in history, Nietzsche tried to achieve this same kind of justification through the demolition of these very concepts.

At the beginning of what he called his most "historical" work, *The Genealogy of Morals*, Nietzsche said: "Fortunately I learned in good time to divorce the theological prejudice from the moral and no longer to seek the origin of evil *behind* the world" (151). Most of the killing illusions of modern, no less than of primitive, man arose as a result of a tendency toward Metonymical reductions of *events* into *agencies*, or of "phenomena" into "manifestations" of imagined "noumenal" substances.

For, just as popular superstition divorces the lightning from its brilliance, viewing the latter as an activity whose subject is the lightning, so does popular morality divorce strength from its manifestations, as though there were behind the strong a neutral agent, free to manifest its strength and contain it. But no such agent exists; there is no "being" behind the doing, acting, becoming; the "doer" has simply been added to the deed by the imagination—the doing is everything. The common man actually doubles the doing by making the lightning flash; he states the same event once as cause and then again as effect. The natural scientists are no better when they say that "energy *moves*," "energy *causes*." For all its detachment and freedom from emotion, our science is still the dupe of linguistic habits; it has never yet got rid of those changelings called "subjects." [178–79]

To dissolve belief in these imagined noumena, substances, spiritual agents, and the like, was Nietzsche's principal aim as a philosopher. To expose the illusions produced by what was, in the end, only a *linguistic* habit, to free consciousness from its own powers of illusion-making, so that the imagination could once more "frolic in images" without hardening those images into life-destroying "concepts"—these were Nietzsche's supreme goals as a teacher of his age.

The most dangerous of these life-destroying concepts are those which constitute the basis of all morality: good and evil. By means of Metonymy men create agents and agencies *behind* phenomena; by means of Synecdoche they endow these agents and agencies with specific qualities, and most especially the *quality* of *being something other* than what they *are*. It is small wonder, Nietzsche said, that "repressed and smoldering emotions of vengeance and hatred" take advantage of the superstition of noumenal beings behind phenomena and "in fact espouse no belief more ardently than it is within the discretion of the strong to be weak, of the bird of prey to be a lamb" (179). By this "sublime sleight of hand which gives weakness the appearance of a free choice and one's natural disposition the distinction of merit" (180), the weak are identified as the strong, the rancorous as the generous of spirit, and the "evil" as the "good."

In Nietzsche's view, the supremely "Ironical" nature of his own age had at last exposed these sleights of hand as nothing but manipulations of language for the benefit of the weak of the earth. As a result, the age stood poised on the brink of chaos, confronted the prospect of a nihilism more terrifying than anything that primitive man may be supposed to have confronted at the dawn of human consciousness. As he said at the end of *The Birth of Tragedy*:

Here we have our present age, the result of a Socratism bent on the extermination of myth. Man today, stripped of myth, stands famished among all his pasts and must dig frantically for roots, be it among the most remote antiquities. What does our great historical hunger signify, our clutching about us of countless other cultures, our consuming desire for knowledge, if not the loss of myth, of a mythic home, the mythic womb? [137]

The vaunted "historical consciousness" of the age was thus a symptom of the triumph of the Ironic mode of comprehending the world. But it was also more. For "historical consciousness," Nietzsche argued, is itself one of the sustaining powers of the current illness, the basis of "morality" itself.

The Birth of Tragedy ends with a discussion of the opposition of the "historical sense" to "mythic" consciousness. Nietzsche wanted to free man not from myth but from those "illusions" of which "history" or the "historical process" was representative.

It may be claimed that a nation, like an individual, is valuable only insofar as it is able to give to everyday experience the stamp of the eternal. Only by doing so can it express its profound, if unconscious, conviction of the relativity of time and the metaphysical meaning of life. The opposite happens when a nation begins to view itself historically and to demolish the mythical bulwarks that surround it. [139]

Such terms as "history" and "historical process" were "fictions," which Nietzsche rigorously distinguished from "myth." His purpose was to determine the extent to which man could once more, but this time self-consciously, re-enter the world of mythic apprehensions and reclaim the freedom which Metaphorical consciousness alone permits to human life.

The second essay of *The Genealogy of Morals* begins with a discussion of the phenomenology of "promising"—that is to say, the human process of "remembering" an oath or an obligation *across* time, of carrying into "the present" a commitment made in "the past" so that this present becomes, not a "future," but a recapitulation of that earlier "past." Nietzsche opposed to this power of "remembering" the power of "forgetting" or "oblivion." This power, he said, permits man to "shut temporarily the doors and windows of consciousness" to distracting memories of past states, so that he can "go into" his present *freely*, can respond to, and take action in, a situation with perfect clarity of vision and strength of will. The power of remembering makes man unheroic—that is to say, *predictable*.

Now this naturally forgetful animal, for whom oblivion represents a power, a form of strong health, has created for itself an opposite power, that of remembering, by whose aid, in certain cases, oblivion may be suspended—specifically in cases where it is a question of promises. [189–90]

The result is the creation of a "memory of the will"—not a mere "passive succumbing to past impressions," but a "continuing to will what has once been willed, . . . so that between the original determination and the actual performance of the thing willed, a whole world of new things, conditions, even volitional acts, can be interposed without snapping the long chain of the will." But all this presupposes, Nietzsche said, a consciousness which has been conditioned to "separate necessary from accidental acts; to think causally; to see distant things as though they were near at hand; to distinguish means from ends." In short, the unheroic man is he who "must have become not only calculating, but himself calculable, regular even to his own perceptions." Only thus is he able "to stand pledge for his own future as a guarantor does." (190)

It is obvious that Nietzsche saw the capacity of man to prolong an act of will made in one temporal instant into some future instant, this capacity to remember, as a dangerous power. For him it was the equivalent of a posture vis à vis the future to that which is manifested in historical consciousness vis à vis the past. Self-binding morality or "conscience" was merely a specific form of historical consciousness. And the problem for Nietzsche was how to break the power of the will to consistency, which all forms of thinking that are not Metaphorical in nature impose upon man.

The Birth of Tragedy, Nietzsche said, was an attempt to analyze the Tragic spirit of Classical Greece in purely *aesthetic* terms, to view it as a creation of a faculty of which "music" was another manifestation; and, above all, to distinguish pure Tragedy from its false or demented "moralizing" counterparts. It is obvious that, for him, the true Tragic spirit, that which informed the work of Aeschylus, Sophocles, *and* Aristophanes, as against that of Euripides and the writers of the New Comedy, was a product of pure Metaphorical consciousness. The Tragic spirit was betrayed, he thought, by Euripides and the New Comic writers on the one hand and by Socrates and Plato on the other, by the "reduction" of the meaning of the Tragic *agon* to causal terms or its "inflation" to moral terms. That is to say, Tragedy was betrayed when the meaning of the play was conceived to reside in some "principle" other than the sheer musical interplay of the Apollonian image-making power and the Dionysiac explosions of those images. In the same way that the "meaning" of (nonrecitative) music lay in the sheer *combina-*

tion of melody, rhythm, and harmony, so, too, pure Tragedy was nothing but an *image* of the exchange of Apollonian forms and Dionysiac insights as they functioned to effect man's entry "into," and his exit "from," his "present" *at the appropriate times.*

For Nietzsche, the Greeks had been the first to appreciate how much human life depended upon man's mythopoeic faculties, his ability to dream a dream of health and beauty in the face of his own imminent annihilation. Greek culture in its golden age had, he believed, developed in full consciousness of the fictive foundations on which it rested. He likened this culture to a temple raised on piles sunk in the viscous mud of the Venetian lagoon; it provided an illusion of permanency and self-sufficiency, therefore allowed life to go on, but colored every act performed inside the edifice with a controlled awareness of life's essential tenuousness, its awful finitude.

But Greek culture was no easy escape into an idyll, no simple flight from the primal chaos. In Tragic art the Greeks found a way to remind themselves that human culture was at best a complex of illusions, that it was at most a delicate achievement, that beneath it lay the void from which all things came and to which they must ultimately return, that a given complex of illusions had to be constantly tested and replaced by new ones, and that a creative life was possible only when chaos and form were encompassed by a larger awareness of their mutual interdependence. Greek culture in its golden age, Nietzsche maintained, forewent the impulse to find *the* ideal world in order to enjoy the benefits of *an* ideal world. The Greeks raised human life above a "savage" barbarism, but they did not aspire to an impossible ideality. They achieved a precarious balance between perfect form and total chaos by keeping awareness of both possibilities consistently alive to consciousness.

Tragic art thus reflects their abandonment of any impulse to *copy* the actual or real, whether conceived as an ideal sphere of essences beyond space and time or as the infinite number of phenomena offering themselves to the senses in space and time. Tragic art is both realistically illusionist and creatively destructive of its own illusions. By transforming the horror of the primal void into beautiful images of superior human lives and then destroying them, Tragedy destroys the old dreams upon which human culture is based and clears the ground for the construction of new dreams by which new human needs can be satisfied. The life of the free individual is given scope for creative illusion-making in the interstices between alternating systems of illusions, and the cultural endowment which protects man's vision from the darkness of the abyss is kept from hardening into a sheath, because Tragedy constantly reminds men that every *form* is nothing but a purely human creation, even while offering it as a basis for movement into the future. Thus, Tragic art is the dialectical art *par excellence.* It alone is capable, Nietzsche argued, of both impelling man to heroic collisions with reality and reclaiming man for life after those collisions.

All of this is based upon Nietzsche's belief that man's peculiar strength, as well as his besetting weakness, is his consciousness. Consciousness at once allows man to construct a peculiarly human life and undercuts the impulse to change that life once it is constructed. Because he can look into the nature of things man can act in specifically human ways, but to look too deeply into the nature of things, to understand too much, destroys the will to act. "In order to act," Nietzsche said,

> we require the veil of illusion; such is Hamlet's doctrine, not to be confounded with the cheap wisdom of a John-a-dreams, who through too much reflection, as it were a surplus of possibilities, never arrives at action. What . . . in the case of Hamlet . . . overbalances any motive leading to action, is not reflection but understanding, the apprehension of truth and its terror. . . . The truth once seen, man is aware everywhere of the ghastly absurdity of existence . . . nausea invades him. [*The Birth of Tragedy*, 51]

Fortunately, however, Nietzsche continued, man also has a capacity to *forget* what he knows—more, an ability to *deny* what he knows; he has an ability to dream, to frolic in images, and to clothe the terror, pain, and suffering caused by consciousness of his own finitude in dream-like intimations of immortality. He can bewitch himself, *escape into a Metaphor*, provide a believable order and form for his life, act as if the Metaphor were the truth, and turn his awareness of his imminent destruction into an occasion for heroic affirmation. In this ability to enchant himself, to discharge Dionysiac insights in Apollonian images, lies man's ability to outstrip himself, to act rather than merely contemplate, and to *become* rather than merely *be*.

In *The Birth of Tragedy*, Nietzsche characterized this uniquely human capacity for self-delusion in a brilliant reversal of figures which is reminiscent of the sun Metaphor at the beginning of Hegel's *Philosophy of History*: "After an energetic attempt to focus on the sun," he wrote, "we have, by way of remedy almost, dark spots before our eyes when we turn away. Conversely, the luminous images of the Sophoclean heroes—those Apollonian masks—are the necessary productions of a deep look into the horror of nature; bright spots, as it were, designed to cure an eye hurt by a ghastly darkness" (59–60). Later on, in *The Genealogy of Morals*, Nietzsche would make an idea implicitly contained herein explicit; he would define the impulse to beauty as a reflex to a prior awareness of the ugly. The important point to note for the time being is that for Nietzsche the beautiful was not a reflection of a transcendental realm or an interiorization of it but a *reaction* to it, a creation of the human will to life alone, a reflex action to the discovery of the truth of the world—that is, that it had no truth. This is what Nietzsche meant by his dictum "we have art in order not to die of the truth"—that is, in order not to die of the realization that there is no single, all encompassing truth.

One aim of *The Birth of Tragedy* was to explicate the Tragic *agon* without recurring to either ethical or religious (in the sense of transcendental) categories. Nietzsche wanted to show that the dialectical process by which a human being moves from mere existence through alienation to reconciliation with the world is a function of comprehensible aesthetic impulses alone. Earlier writers—and especially Hegel—had seen Tragic art as a product of the conflict between the willful individual and the social order or the cosmic process, between *aidos* on the one hand and *nomos, moira,* or *physis* on the other. And the catharsis which attended contemplation of the hero's fall had been seen as illuminative of some morally significant truth about the nature of the universe, as pointing to a vague, but real, transpersonal meaning for life. Even Schopenhauer had seen Tragedy as conducing to recognition of *the fundamental truth* that " 'twere better not to have been born at all."

Nietzsche condemned the false pessimism of the latter view no less than the false optimism of the former, and found the essence of the spirit of Tragedy in the heightened awareness it gave to the conflict between man's apprehension of the essentially chaotic nature of existence and his ability to go on living in self-manufactured dreams. Thus envisaged, Tragic art was a product of man's movement toward the abyss from which he had sprung through the testing of images that had previously sustained him *and* a countermovement back into a new set of images charged with a suppressed awareness of the illusory character of *all* form. This *movement* from chaos to form *and back* distinguishes Tragedy from other forms of *poesis* (such as the epic and lyric) and from all *systems* of knowledge and belief (such as science and religion). All other prospects on human existence tend to freeze life in an apprehension of either chaos or form; only Tragedy requires a constant alternation of the *awareness of chaos* with the *will to form* in the interest of life. "Apollo overcomes individual suffering by the glorious apotheosis of what is eternal in appearance: here beauty vanquishes the suffering that inheres in all existence, and pain is, in a certain sense, glossed away from nature's countenance" (102). By contrast, Dionysus "makes us realize that everything that is generated must be prepared to face its painful dissolution. It forces us to gaze into the horror of individual existence, yet without being turned to stone by the vision: a metaphysical solace momentarily lifts us above the whirl of shifting phenomena." We now see, Nietzsche continued, the "struggle, pain, the destruction of appearances, as necessary, because of the constant proliferation of forms pushing into life, because of the extravagant fecundity of the world will." (102–3) As a result of these two experiences of the phenomenal world, the one which sees the eternally beautiful in the transient, and the other which sees the eternally transient in the beautiful, we emerge from the contemplation of the Tragic *agon* with a Comic acceptance of life: "Pity and terror notwithstanding, we realize our great good fortune in having life not as individuals, but as part of the life force with whose procreative lust we have become one" (103).

Obviously Nietzsche advocated not an art in which either Dionysus or

Apollo finally triumphed but one that assumed their mutual interdepend-ence. It is true that he believed that his own age had forgotten Dionysus and given itself over to an excessive worship of Apollo, the will to form *at any cost*. But the cost was not difficult to calculate, Nietzsche believed; the promotion of the delusion of a permanent form and order was destructive of life itself. And only if men were reminded of Dionysus and his claims on all forms of life would it be possible to abandon those forms which had out-grown their usefulness and to create others more responsive to life's manifold needs and interests.

Nietzsche did not, of course, advocate the worship of Dionysus alone; the total triumph of Dionysus, the will to chaos, over Apollo, would lead to a regression to that "savage barbarism" from which the Greeks had elevated themselves only by the cruelest exertions. But the unchallenged rule of the Apollonian faculties in man meant rigidity, oppression, repression, the life of the sleepwalker. Without the Apollonian capacity to dream the dream of Parnassus, man could not live; but the impulse to take a specific form for reality, to turn the capacity to make images against man himself, was ulti-mately as destructive of human life as the rule of Dionysus. Moreover, the unchallenged rule of Apollo portended a reaction of the most violent sort when Dionysus once more asserted his rights.

According to Nietzsche, the most destructive form of illusionism is that which transforms an image into a concept and then freezes the imagination within the terms provided by the concept. All form is ultimately *Metaphori-cal*, not substantive, Nietzsche argued, and, as creatively used, by the Tragic poet, for example, the Metaphor serves as "a representative image standing concretely before him in lieu of a concept" (55). A character in a play is not, then, merely "an assemblage of individual traits laboriously pierced together, but a personage beheld as insistently living before the poet's eyes, differing from the image of the painter in its capacity to continue living and acting" (*ibid.*). This dynamic image-making power is a gift of both Apollo and Dionysus, and is accordingly a *living* synthesis of form and movement, structure and process. The image formed by the poet who understands the uses of Metaphor is a product of Apollo's ability to tranquilize the individual by "drawing boundary lines" in, through, or around the essential chaos; but the poet knows that the image contained in the Metaphor must be exploded by Dionysus, "lest the Apollonian tendency to freeze all forms into Egyptian rigidity" (65) triumph completely and cut off the accesses to life-sustaining powers. When an image becomes frozen into a concept, life in general does not suffer (for life itself cannot be denied), but *human* life does. The hypostatization of either Apollo or Dionysus is destructive of humanity, for humanity can exist only on the boundary line which divides the realms of the two gods. In this scheme, human consciousness acts as a kind of make-weight between two great powers; by throwing their meager forces, now to one, now to the other, men keep the two gods from destroying each other and thrive in the space between them, like Israel between Assyria and Egypt. But sometimes, unhappily, the results are as disastrous as those that befell Israel.

The death of the Tragic sense in ancient Greece, Nietzsche maintained, resulted from the triumph of Irony ("cold, paradoxical ideas") over "Apollonian contemplation" on the one hand and of Romantic "fiery emotions" over "Dionysiac transports" on the other. These betrayals of the Tragic spirit were promoted by Socrates and Euripides. In Socrates, "the Apollonian tendency hardens into logical schematism"; in Euripides, there was "a corresponding translation of the Dionysiac affect into a naturalistic one." (88)

The Socratic betrayal was especially destructive, for it inspired a false optimism in man. This optimism was based on the three Socratic illusions: "Virtue is knowledge; all sins arise from ignorance; only the virtuous are happy" (*ibid.*). Under the influence of these illusions, men were inspired to believe "that thought, guided by the thread of causation, might plumb the farthest abysses of being and even correct it" (93). This was a fatal turning in Greek cultural life, for it set the Greeks on the *fruitless* quest for *final* truths and *total* control over life. In the process, Dionysus, who "makes us realize that everything that is generated must be prepared to face its painful dissolution," was forgotten (102).

Even the failure of the Socratic attempt to make men good by making them rational did not force the Classical world to see the folly of this quest for absolutes. In Plato they found a thinker who could succor their folly, turning their attention from life as lived here on earth to the pursuit of a "goodness," "truth," and "beauty" which supposedly existed *beyond* time and space and which could be attained only by the *denial* of every animal impulse in the human body. This Platonic belief prepared the way for Christianity, which completed the degradation of man by denying him the power of both the will and the reason to achieve the final rest and stability envisioned by Socrates. In the Christian hope for a final salvation, men found a substitute for the reason which had failed them, but only by denying their will to live in the here and now. The triumph of Christianity represented a flight into a peculiarly oppressive kind of anti-idyll, an idyll not of joy but of suffering, founded not on the "belief in a primordial existence of pure, artistically sensitive men" but on the belief in man's essential sickness, weakness, and inadequacy.

This line of thinking provided the bases for Nietzsche's "underground" history of Western man. Since the time of the Greeks, Nietzsche maintained, the history of Western man has been the history of self-induced illnesses. Since that time, man, once a bridge between chaos and form, has assumed the aspect of a slaughtered bull strung between the poles of his own self-delusion. At one pole stands Christianity, with its denial of life's claims on man and its insistence that man find his goals in another world, which will be revealed to him only at the end of time; at the other pole stands Positivist science, which delights in dehumanizing man by reducing him to the status of a beast, conceiving him as a mere instrument of mechanical forces over which he can exercise no control and from which he can find no release. And the history of Western man since the decline of the Tragic spirit describes an alternation of these two life-denying tendencies; first one, then the other, takes its turn at degrading man.

Thus the history of Western consciousness appears to be nothing but an oscillation in place, a Sisyphean eternal return of two, equally destructive conceptions of man's capacities for living and thinking, a cycle of life-denying possibilities, with no hope of escape in the offing. Later on, in *The Genealogy of Morals*, Nietzsche would find a positive worth in all this human self-mutilation in the growth of an intellectual acuteness which, when turned upon the sustaining myths of science and religion, would reveal the poverty of them both. In *The Birth of Tragedy*, however, he was content to point to the *fact* of the annihilation of religion by science and of science by critical philosophy as evidence of a millennial historical *process* of de-mythification and cultural degradation. And he accounted for the heightened historical self-consciousness of modern man by noting the dissolution of all mythic fundaments, repressive as well as liberating, at the hands of science. Running through this cycle, this oscillation, he noted, are evidences of a genuine development, a *progressus*, though thus far only a negative one, the destruction of self-delusion by the instruments of self-delusion themselves, historical consciousness and criticism. Thus, according to Nietzsche, the plot of this history is Ironic, since the very factors that have destroyed man's capacity to enjoy life have now been turned upon themselves. And the outcome is Ironic, in a specific sense, for man now *lives Ironically*, in the full awareness of his own destitution, both of myth and of criticism.

Nietzsche concluded his essay by noting that life does not and cannot justify itself; *it* has no need to do so. Only man feels a need to justify his existence, because only man, of all the animals, is conscious of the absurdity of his being. And, Nietzsche argued, only art can justify life to man, but not any "realistic" art, not an art that is merely imitative of nature. Photographic realism is only another form of science. What is needed, he held, is an art that is aware of its *metaphysical purpose*; for only art, not philosophy or science, can offer a metaphysical justification of life for man. "Art is not an imitation of nature, but its metaphysical supplement, raised up beside it to overcome it" (142). Moreover, art provides the only transcendence that man can hope for, and it provides this not only by creating the dream but by dissolving the pseudo reality of the dream that has atrophied. True art at once tells man " 'Just look! Look closely! This is your life. This is the hour hand on the clock of your existence' " (*ibid.*), and at the same time transmutes all ugliness and discord into an "aesthetic game which the will, in its utter exuberance, plays with itself" (143).

What is man, Nietzsche asked, if not "an incarnation of dissonance"?

And, if man is this, he needs a marvelous illusion to cover this dissonance with a veil of beauty. Nietzsche saw his own time as having reached the term of a long process of human self-alienation; it was ready to enter into a new period of destructive criticism of all of its atrophied illusions. This period of destruction portended an era of violence and discord such as the Western world had seen before only in the Hellenistic Age, when, in the face of the dissolution of the Tragic sense, men had started down the long road of self-mutilation which had made them "modern." Thus, he said:

Today we experience the same extravagant thirst for knowledge, the same insatiable curiosity, the same drastic secularization, the nomadic wandering, the greedy rush to alien tables [as the Hellenistic age], the frivolous apotheosis of the present or the stupefied negation of it, and all *sub specie saeculi*—like symptoms pointing to a comparable lack in our own culture, which has also destroyed myth. [139–40]

But *he* faced the future with optimism: "Whenever the Dionysiac forces become too obstreperous," he wrote, "we are safe in assuming that Apollo is close at hand, though wrapped in a cloud, and the rich effects of his beauty will be witnessed by a later generation" (145–46).

This reference to the alternation of Dionysiac and Apollonian processes by generations figures the idea of history which underlies much of Nietzsche's thought. As noted earlier, it is sometimes held that Nietzsche regarded history as describing a cyclical movement, a movement of eternal recurrence, as an antidote to the naive notions of linear progress current in his own time. No such simple thought even approaches the truth. In the first place, even in *The Birth of Tragedy*, Nietzsche distinguished between the Dionysiac spirit of "*savage* barbarism" and the Dionysiac spirit of the post-Homeric Greeks, and imagined a *progressus* from one to the other through an intermediary, Apollonian or epic, phase of culture. The differences between these three stages in the development of the will to life might be characterized as the differences between will in itself, will for itself, and will in and for itself; these were the "immediate stages" of the Tragic spirit for Nietzsche. They would correspond, in Kierkegaardian terms, to the stages of will-dreaming, will-awakening, and will-willing. The will conscious of itself *as will* provides the basis of pure Tragedy. In short, we have here a *growth* of consciousness *in the will itself*.

Moreover, in Nietzsche's schema, the decline of Greek Tragedy was followed not by a fall *back* into "savage" barbarism but rather by a movement *forward* into decadence, which itself went through three stages: Hellenistic, Roman, and Christian—that is, scientific, military, and religious phases. These phases were seen by Nietzsche as decadent because, instead of releasing the will to the work of either destruction or creation, each of them chastized the will, disciplined it, and ultimately turned its powers against itself.

Modern Western civilization, in Nietzsche's view, is undergoing this process in reverse, to be sure: from "Christian" other-worldliness, to "Roman" militarism, to "Hellenistic" criticism, to a new Tragic age, and thence, presumably, into a new barbarism. But, Nietzsche believed, the new barbarism would differ from the original one by the extent to which men would gain a kind of freedom and power which they had never enjoyed in the old, savage one. Nietzsche's Superman, as he himself said, would be no mere destroyer, but a creator as well, one who lives his *life* as a work of art, who incarnates *in himself* the dissonance and form which the Greeks had been able to incarnate only in images on the Tragic stage.

If this is a cyclical idea of history, it is a very strange "cycle" indeed. For Nietzsche, the way down and the way up were only superficially the same path; his conviction was that we go down in order to emerge purified, cleansed, and divested of our earlier life-destroying illusions. In short, for Nietzsche the whole history of Western man since primitive times was *one great progressive* movement from mere existence, through alienation, to reconciliation, just as the Tragic *agon* on the stage was. But the reconciliation he envisioned was not with "nature" or with "society" but with the self. And the profit of that *agon* was to be found in the attainment of a new level of self-consciousness by which a Zarathustra-like Superman plays his game with chaos.

As thus envisaged, history is not, therefore, a dialectical movement tending toward an absolute beyond time and space. The only "absolute" which Nietzsche recognized was the free individual, completely liberated from any spiritual-transcendental impulse, who finds his goal in his ability to outstrip himself, who gives to his life a dialectical tension by setting new tasks for himself, and who turns himself into a human exemplar of the kind of life which the Greeks thought could be lived only by the gods.

It can easily be seen that Nietzsche's interpretation of the spirit of Tragedy begins with a denial of both the Romantic and Ironic conceptions of the nature of reality. Second, it consists of a conflation of the conventional conception of Tragedy with that of Comedy, so that the two truths separately taught by each of these are now combined into a single multiplex acceptance of life and death. Next, this Tragicomic vision is drained of all moral implications. The Tragicomic vision is identified with "the spirit of music"—that is to say, with nonrecitative music, music which makes no statement *about* the world but simply exists alongside the world of experience as pure form and movement. The verbal and literary counterpart of the spirit of music is Metaphor. By Metaphorical identifications, phenomena are transformed into images that have no "meanings" outside themselves. As images, they simply resemble and differ from whatever surrounds them. In Metaphor, the *principium individuationis* is asserted and denied at one and the same time, as it is in mythic thinking. And in order to re-enter the world of myth, without with heroic action appears impossible, Nietzsche counseled the revision of the concept of Tragedy in purely Metaphorical terms. The return to Metaphorical consciousness would be a rebirth of innocence. It would entail a repudiation of the Metonymical and Synecdochic modes of consciousness, the abandonment of the search for agents and agencies behind phenomena and the endowment of them with spiritual qualities in such a way as to diminish the value of human life.

Nietzsche sought to return man to a direct confrontation with the phenomenal world, with his vision purified but his capacity to manufacture creative illusions intact. He believed that man's capacities for Metaphorical transformations of the world of experience alone can purge both memory and forgetfulness of their potentially destructive effects in human life. The paradigm of Metaphorical consciousness, the capacity to see resemblance in difference and difference in resemblance, served, in turn, as the model of the Dionysiac-Apollonian image which Nietzsche used as the organizing principle of his "history" of the rise and fall of the Tragic spirit.

This "history" was written in an Ironic tone; Nietzsche addressed his audience with a combination of concern and disdain. With respect to its object, which is the Tragic spirit, however, it is anything but Ironic. For the "history" of the spirit of Tragedy is at once Tragic and Comic, Tragic in its plot structure but Comic in its implications. The history of the rise and fall of the Tragic spirit is emplotted as an *agon* which creates the conditions for a return to the "joyful wisdom" of the Comic consciousness. Although written in the glow of Nietzsche's admiration of Schopenhauer and Wagner, the work ends on a note quite alien to either of these "Romantics," a Comic note, which celebrates the liberation of human consciousness from both causality and formal specification, from both pessimism and naive optimism.

But all of this anticipated the fully worked out philosophy that appeared in later works, especially in *Thus Spoke Zarathustra, Beyond Good and Evil,* and *The Genealogy of Morals.* My immediate interest is in Nietzsche's conception of how historical thought can contribute to the ushering in of the new age and what he believed was necessary to give to historical thought the liberating power of Tragic art. I must turn, therefore, to the historiographical coda which Nietzsche provided for *The Birth of Tragedy,* "The Use and Abuse of History."

∽§ *Memory and History*

In *The Birth of Tragedy* Nietzsche located *human* life between a consciousness of chaos and the will to form; in "The Use and Abuse of History" he examined the implications of this idea under the aspect of time. "The Use and Abuse of History" is concerned with the dynamics of remembering and forgetting, which Nietzsche saw as the unique attribute of the human animal.

The Tragic *agon* which takes place on the Greek stage is, after all, timeless; it exists outside the temporal sphere. The man who is to live his life as a work of Tragic art must do so in the constant awareness of the passage of time; he must *live in history*. The problem, therefore, is to determine how the sense of history, the sense of time's passage, acts both creatively and destructively in the peculiarly human dialectic of remembering and forgetting.

Although Nietzsche often spoke as if man's ability to act hinges upon his ability to forget—that is, upon his ability to rid himself of consciousness and to respond to animal instinct alone—in reality Nietzsche believed that human *forgetting* is quite different from animal *oblivion*. It does not really make sense to speak of an animal's capacity to forget, because an animal has no prior impulse to remember. The beast of the field, Nietzsche noted at the beginning of "The Use and Abuse of History," lives in an eternal present, knowing neither satiety nor pain, without consciousness, therefore, and without the peculiarly human impulse to forget, which is an act of will.

Thus, Nietzsche wrote, man, reflecting on the beasts of the field, may ask the beast: " 'Why do you look at me and not speak to me of your happiness?' The beast wants to answer—'Because I always forget what I wished to say'; but he forgets this answer, too, and is silent; and man is left to wonder." And man "wonders also about himself—that he cannot learn to forget, but hangs on the past; however far and fast he runs, that chain runs with him." (5) In short, man lives *historically*; he is aware of his continual becoming, or his unbecoming, of the dissolution of all his presents into a *fixed past*. The past is constantly before man as an image of things done, finished, complete, unchangeable. The intractability of this past is the source of man's dishonesty with himself and is the motive power behind his own self-mutilation.

Man would like to "go into" his present, to live it fully and immediately; this is his dominant impulse. But "the great and continually increasing weight of the past . . . presses down and bows his shoulders." This past travels with man; it is "a dark invisible burden that he can plausibly disown, and is only too glad to disown in converse with his fellows—on order to excite their envy." But man envies the beast, who carries no such burden with him, or the child, "that has nothing yet of the past to disown and plays in a happy blindness between the walls of past and future." (*Ibid.*)

The child differs from the beast, however, in that it may enjoy this memoryless paradise only for awhile. As soon as it learns the words "once upon a time," it is exposed to all of the "battle, suffering, and weariness of mankind" and to the knowledge that human existence is really only "an imperfect tense that never becomes a present." Death alone brings "the desired forgetfulness" to man; "it abolishes life and being together, and sets the seal on the knowledge that 'being' is merely a continual 'has been,' a thing that lives by denying and destroying and contradicting itself." (*Ibid.*, 5–6)

The problem for the creative man is *to learn to forget*, to "stand on a single point . . . without fear or giddiness"—*not to deny the past* and himself as he

was in the past, *but to forget it.* The extreme case of remembrance of things
past would be "the man ... who is condemned to see 'becoming' everywhere."
(6) Such a man would—like Roquentin in Sartre's *Nausea*—no longer believe in his own existence, but would instead see everything fly past in an
eternal succession and lose himself in the stream of becoming. Without forgetfulness no action is possible, no life is conceivable, "just as not only light
but darkness is bound up with the life of every organism" (6–7). *Mere* life is
possible without remembrance, as the example of the beast shows, but "life
in any true sense is absolutely impossible without forgetfulness" (7).

These passages reveal an aspect of Nietzsche's thought which is often overlooked in contemporary analyses of it. Nietzsche was considering a peculiarly
human problem, the problem of learning to forget, which is not an *animal*
problem at all; learning to forget presupposes the prior ability to remember,
which is man's alone. In short, in this essay the historical consciousness is
presupposed; it does not have to be accounted for but is merely assumed.
Later on, in *The Genealogy of Morals,* Nietzsche undertook to explain, on
historical and psychological grounds, how this ability to remember took root
in man; but in "The Use and Abuse of History" he took it for granted and
asked what it implies for the living of a creative human life. The "problem"
of the beast is that it does not remember; the "problem" of man is that he
remembers all too well. Out of this capacity to remember his past all specifically *human* constructions arise. It is not a matter of man's *needing* memory;
it is the glory and perdition of man that he irredeemably *has* memory. Therefore, he *has* history, whether he wants it or not. The question, then, is whether
this capacity to remember has not been overdeveloped and become a threat to
life itself. And it is not so much a matter of destroying history as of learning
when man is justified in forgetting it:

Cheerfulness, a good conscience, belief in the future, the joyful deed—all depend,
in the individual as well as the nation, on there being a line that divides the
visible and clear from the vague and shadowy: we must know the right time to
forget as well as the right time to remember, and instinctively see when it is necessary to feel historically and when unhistorically. [*Ibid.*]

Therefore, the "point that the reader is asked to consider" is that "the unhistorical and the historical are equally necessary to the health of an individual, a community, and a system of culture" (7–8).

It is necessary to stress that Nietzsche located the problem of the worth of
history (and, *a fortiori,* of memory) in the problem of the value or need
which it serves. Remembering, he insisted, is, like seeing, always a remembering of *something,* not a generalized activity; remembering is therefore an act
of will, with a purpose or aim or object. Moreover, man chooses to remember
in a particular way, and the way he chooses to remember a thing is evidence of

whether his attitude with respect to himself is destructive or constructive. A *look* back at his past is a way of defining his present and his future; *how* he sculptures the past, the kind of image he imposes upon it, is preparatory to launching himself into the future. He may decide either to stride heroically into the future or to back into it, but he cannot avoid it. The problem, then, is to purge this capacity for remembering of any self-destructiveness which might inform it. Forgetfulness, too, is a human power, a peculiarly human one. The beast does not *will to forget*, but merely enjoys a state of temporal unconsciousness. By contrast, man both forgets and remembers, and this dichotomy is a uniquely human one; human forgetting is different from animal forgetting, for it is required to erase the memory traces that permit a man to linger uncreatively over his own past life.

As a critic of his own time, then, Nietzsche asked how a creative forgetfulness can be built up in opposition to the overpowering urge to remember which undercuts the will to act creatively, and the degree to which historical consciousness itself can be turned to the service of man's innovating power, his power of self-transcendence. This means that historical knowledge itself must be tied to a prior power, or, as Nietzsche put it: "Historical study is only fruitful for the future if it follows a powerful life-giving influence—only, therefore, if it is guided and dominated by a higher force, and does not itself guide and dominate" (11–12). Nietzsche's ultimate purpose, then, was—like that of Hegel and Marx—to draw historical knowledge back within the confines of human needs, to make it the servant of human needs rather than their master. For life *does need* the service of history, he said; only an excess of history hurts life.

Nietzsche thus granted that man needs history, and in three ways: "In relation to his action and struggle," as an aid to his conservative and reverential capacities, and as a soothing balm to his suffering and desire for deliverance. These three needs in man generate three kinds of history: Monumental, Antiquarian, and Critical. All three nurture—and threaten—peculiarly human faculties.

Monumental history provides exemplars of human nobility and teaches that, since a great thing once existed, it was therefore possible, and so *might be* possible again. Monumental history, history studied above all as the story of great men—in Carlylian fashion—can use the past to condemn the pettiness of the present and project the historian himself into the battle for a better future. Yet this approach to history has its flaws; it can be delusory. Its main weakness is that it depicts effects at the expense of causes; it proceeds by false analogies to find a *common greatness* in every great *individual*. Hence, it obscures the "real historical nexus of cause and effect," destroys the essential difference of all great things, and tends to romanticize the past. As a goad to life, in fact, Romantic novels can serve the same purpose as Monumental history; and, in the hands of a weakling, this kind of history can be turned against the present and future. It can undermine the self-confidence of living men by teaching them that one need not strive for greatness, since all forms of greatness have already been achieved in the past.

The impulse to flee the present in an attitude of pious reverence for the past has its extreme form in Antiquarian history, which, however, has its distinctive characteristics and also its creative and destructive sides. Creatively, Antiquarian history engenders a respect for origins; it is like the "feeling of the tree that clings to its roots, the happiness of knowing one's growth to be not merely arbitrary and fortuitous but the inheritance, the fruit and the blossom, of a past that does not merely justify but crowns the present—this is what we nowadays prefer to call the real historical sense" (19). But, in excess, this Antiquarian attitude tends to level things through *indiscriminant appreciation* of everything, however great or small. Moreover, it places a special value on anything old, *just because* it is old, and inspires a feeling of distrust for anything that is new or departs from the conventional. When "the spring of piety is dried up," the Antiquarian attitude may persist and give itself over completely to the preservation of what is *already* living and oppose the creation of *new* lives (20).

The antidote to both of these kinds of history—the Monumental, which, creatively, points men toward the future on the basis of respect for past greatness and, destructively, undermines their impulse to greatness; and the Antiquarian, which, creatively, engenders a pious respect for the origins and, destructively, opposes the present need or desire—is Critical history. Critical history arises in the impulse to "break up the past, and apply it, too, in order to live" (42). The Critical historian is concerned to "bring the past to the bar of judgment, interrogate it remorselessly, and finally condemn it" (*ibid.*). The Critical historian possesses the power to penetrate through the myths of past greatness and values, to tread the pieties underfoot, and to deny the claims of the past on the present. To be sure, the Critical spirit, too, has its destructive side, which, when carried too far, ends in a deification of the present triviality by default, by having shown that *nothing* is noble. As Nietzsche said later on, "the historical audit brings so much to light that is false and absurd, violent and inhuman, that the condition of pious illusion falls to pieces" (*ibid.*). Critical history engenders an "Ironical self-consciousness" when carried to excess (47). It leads to the discovery of the terrible truth that "everything that is born is *worthy* of being destroyed," and this can lead to the conclusion "better were it then that nothing should be born"—to Schopenhauerian pessimism and disgust with life (*ibid.*). As Nietzsche warned, "It requires great strength to be able to live and forget [what Critical history teaches] how far life and injustice are one" (21).

Thus, according to Nietzsche, the dangers of historical consciousness are to be found in the *excesses* of Antiquarian, Critical, and Monumental history: archaicism, presentism, and futurism, respectively. What is needed is some synthesis of all three ways of reading the past, not an escape from the past, for the past cannot be escaped.

For as we are merely the resultant of previous generations, we are also the resultant of their errors, passions, and crimes; it is impossible to shake off this chain. Though we condemn the errors and think we have escaped them, we cannot escape the fact that we spring from them. At best, it comes to a conflict between our innate, inherited nature and our knowledge, between a stern, new discipline and an ancient tradition; and we plant a new way of life, a new instinct, a second nature, that withers the first. It is an attempt to gain a past *a posteriori* from which we might spring, as against that from which we do spring —always a dangerous attempt, as it is difficult to find a limit to the denial of the past, and the second natures are generally weaker than the first. [*Ibid.*]

All forms of history constantly remind us of this fact; yet we persist in the effort to create such "second natures" and to cultivate them. When we succeed, Nietzsche said, the Critical historian is justified, for he has shown us that this "first nature" was once a "second nature"—"and that every conquering 'second nature' becomes a first" (22).

This threefold division of the forms of historical consciousness can be viewed as an analysis of the modes of Metonymy, Synecdoche, and Irony respectively. It is obvious that, for Nietzsche, a Monumentalist historiography conceives the world in terms of the categories of contiguity and division, the isolation of great men from one another and from the mass, in terms of inferior and superior causal *agencies* in the historical process. Monumentalism is creative when it stresses the achievements of great men, but destructive when it stresses the *differences* between past and present or future greatness. By contrast, Antiquarian historiography is history conceived in the mode of Synecdoche, of continuities and unifications, of relationships between everything that ever existed and whatever presently exists. It makes everything equal in historical value and significance. It is creative when it reminds men that every present human being is a resultant of things past, and destructive when it makes of all present things *nothing but* consequences of past things. By contrast, Critical historiography is history in the mode of Irony, historical thought carried out in the conviction that everything is frail and worthy of being condemned, that there is a flaw in every human achievement, truth in every falsity, and falsity in every truth. This mode of conceiving history is creative when it acts in the service of present needs and undermines the authority of the past and the future. It is destructive when it reminds the present actor in the historical drama that he, too, is flawed and ought not to aspire to heroic stature or revere *anything*.

Nietzsche's proposed antidote for all these forms of historical consciousness in their extreme, or destructive, aspects is historical consciousness operating in the mode of Metaphor. His notion of history as a form of art is a notion of history as a Tragic art, and, moreover, as that pure Tragic art which he defended in *The Birth of Tragedy out of the Spirit of Music*. History conceived in the Metaphorical mode is really what is behind his defense of what he called the "superhistorical" and "unhistorical" points of view in the last section of "The Use and Abuse of History."

In Part IV of "The Use and Abuse of History," Nietzsche argued that history can serve life by becoming a form of art. He insisted that the tendency to turn history into a science is fatal to its life-giving function. "The knowledge of the past is desired only for the service of the future and the present, not to weaken the present or undermine a living future." History conceived as a life-serving form of art will be directed, not to the service of truth or justice, but rather to "objectivity." However, by "objectivity" Nietzsche did not mean the "tolerance" of the humanist or the "disinterestedness" of the scientist; he meant instead the self-conscious "interestedness" of the artist.

When he spoke of "historical objectivity," Nietzsche said, he was thinking of

a certain standpoint in the historian who sees the procession of motive and consequence too clearly for it to have an effect on his own personality. We think of the aesthetic phenomenon of the detachment from all personal concern with which the painter sees the picture and forgets himself . . . ; and we require the same artistic vision and absorption in his object from the historian. [37]

But, Nietzsche insisted,

it is only a superstition to say that the picture given to such a man by the object really shows the truth of things. Unless it be that objects are expected in such moments to paint or photograph themselves by their own activity on a purely passive medium! [*Ibid.*]

On the contrary, he maintained, objectivity is "composition" in its highest form, "of which the result will be an artistically, but not historically, true picture," because:

To think objectively, in this sense, of history is the work of the dramatist: to think one thing with another, and weave the elements into a single whole, with the presumption that the unity of plan must be put into the objects if it is not already there. [37–38]

This implies that historical wisdom, to be distinguished from historical knowledge or information, is dramatistic insight, fabulation or, as I have called it, "emplotment." In fact, Nietzsche maintained, "There could be a kind of historical writing that had no drop of common fact in it and yet could claim to be called in the highest degree objective" (38). And he quoted Grillparzer's remark that history is nothing but the manner in which the spirit of man apprehends facts that are obscure to him, links things together whose connection only heaven knows, replaces the unintelligible by something intelligible, puts his own ideas of causation into the external world, which can perhaps be explained only from within; and assumes the existence of chance where thousands of small causes may be really at work. [*Ibid.*]

Yet, Nietzsche warned, this conception of "objectivity" must be used with caution. One must not assume that there is some "opposition" between "human action and the process of the world" (38–39). They are the *same* thing!

Again, one must not look for some subject *behind* the phenomena. The phenomena are themselves the subjects which the historian is seeking. The historian, in fact, ceases to be instructive when he *generalizes* about his data. While in other disciplines "the generalizations are the most important things," because "they contain the laws," the historian's generalizations, inso-far as they might even legitimately lay claim to the status of laws, are unim-portant, because "the residue of truth, after the obscure and insoluble part is removed, is nothing but the commonest knowledge. The smallest range of experience will teach it" (39). It would be as if the value of the drama were supposed to reside only in its final scene. The value of the historian's work does not lie in its generalizations, but rather,

On the contrary, its real value lies in inventing ingenious variations on a prob-ably commonplace theme, in raising the popular melody to a universal symbol and showing what a world of depth, power, and beauty exists in it. [*Ibid.*]

The fine historian must have the power of coining the known into a thing never heard before and proclaiming the universal so simply and profoundly that the simple is lost in the profound and the profound in the simple. [40]

The historian thus conceived is the master of Metaphorical identifications of objects that occupy the historical field. By transforming familiar things into unfamiliar ones, by rendering them "strange" and "mysterious" once more, the "universal" is revealed to exist in the "particular" and the "particular" in the "universal." The "simple" is hidden in the "profound" and the "pro-found" in the "simple." But this hiding is at the same time a revelation, a revelation of man's power to go into his present and do what he will with history.

What are the principles by which such a historical consciousness ought to be guided? Nietzsche was quite specific in his answer to this question: "You can explain the past only by what is most powerful in the present." "The lan-guage of the past," he said, "is always *oracular*: you will only understand it as builders of the future who know the present . . . only he who is building up the future has a right to judge the past." But this judgment of the past would not yield any rules for predicting the future: "You have enough to ponder and find out in pondering the life of the future; . . . do not ask history to show you the means and the instrument in it." But, by "thinking himself back" to his true needs, the creative man finds the ground on which to let all the "sham necessities go." (*Ibid.*) Through the destruction of that "ironical self-consciousness" fostered by conventional historical scholarship, the grounds for a new, heroic historical vision can be forged.

The kinds of historical consciousness from which Germany, in particular, and Europe, in general, were suffering took three forms, in Nietzsche's view: Hegelianism, Darwinism, and the so-called philosophy of the unconscious, as represented by Eduard von Hartmann. Hegelianism—as Nietzsche knew it—was rationalistic and presentist; it turned "practically every moment into a sheer gaping at success, into an idolatry of the actual for which we have now discovered the characteristic phrase, 'adapt ourselves to circumstances' " (52). Darwinism conflated the history of nature and history of man in such a way as to produce the same effect; it allowed a given generation of men to believe that they were the final goal and end of the whole cosmic process—and to rest content with what they presently were rather than to strive to be something better. The Hartmannian doctrine of the unconscious made of a ceaseless, mysterious *becoming* the motive power of history, which took all of man's responsibility for himself away from him and vested it in an overriding power which he must merely serve, but never strive to control or dominate. (56–57) Such a doctrine, Nietzsche maintained, yields a fantastic parody on history, for it denies history itself. It produces an image of history as a senseless ebb and flow of metaphysical forces. In such a view, man "has nothing to do but to live on as he has lived, love what he has loved, hate what he has hated, and read the newspapers he has always read. The only sin for him is to live otherwise than he has lived" (58). Hartmann's philosophy denies the truths known to the ego and submits to the demands of the id, to use Freudian terms. It requires " 'the full surrender of the individual's personality to the world-process,' for the sake of his end, 'the redemption of the world' " (*ibid.*).

Hartmann's doctrine of the sovereignty of the unconscious is, then, just as dangerous as Hegel's doctrine of the "World Spirit" and Darwin's apotheosized Nature. It represents a hardening of the will to form to the detriment of the will to life. All such general schemata must be eschewed, Nietzsche repeated, if history is to serve the needs of living men: "The time will come when we shall wisely keep away from all constructions of the world-process, or even of the history of man—a time when we shall no longer look at masses but at individuals who form a sort of bridge over the wan stream of becoming" (59). At that time, he predicted, "The task of history" will be to mediate between great individuals, "and even to give the motive and power to produce the great man" (*ibid.*). Then it will be recognized that "the aim of mankind can lie ultimately only in its highest examples" (*ibid.*). The kind of broad

tolerance which Rankean historism, taken in excess, induces in a man is ultimately harmful: "To take everything objectively, to be angry at nothing, to
love nothing, to understand everything—makes one gentle and pliable" (53).
It can even be fatal. But "fortunately history also keeps alive for us the memory
of the great 'fighters against history,' that is, against the blind power of the
actual," whatever it may be (54).

Ultimately, Nietzsche concluded, the antidote to the "malady of history"
must be history itself. It is another Irony that the cure for a historicized culture
must be homeopathic: "For the origin of historical culture, and of its absolutely radical antagonism to the spirit of a new time and a 'modern consciousness' must itself be known by a historical process. . . . science must turn
its sting against itself" (51). When history itself shows the historical origins of
a historical culture, the way will be open to the attainment of that "unhistorical" or "superhistorical" vantage point from which the myth-making powers of
art can do their work. What is the unhistorical? It is merely "the power of art,
of *forgetting* and of drawing a limited horizon around oneself" (69). And what
is the superhistorical? It is merely the power to turn "the eyes from the process
of sheer becoming to that which gives existence an eternal and stable character—to art and religion," Dionysus and Apollo together (*ibid.*). In sum, "The
unhistorical and the superhistorical are the natural antidotes against the overpowering of life by history; they are the cures of the historical disease" (70).

Once we have wrapped ourselves in art and myth, we may be able to return
to the creative study of history "and under the guidance of life make use of the
past in that threefold way—Monumental, Antiquarian, or Critical," for, "All
living things need an atmosphere, a mysterious mist, around them. If that veil
is taken away and a religion, an art, or a genius [is] condemned to revolve
like a star without an atmosphere, we must not be surprised if it becomes
hard and unfruitful, and soon withers" (44).

Modern culture is like this: it has lost all feelings of strangeness or astonish-
ment; it is pleased at everything and therefore neither loves nor hates anything
in its own interest. The result is a generation of men who have become home-
less, doubting all ideas, all moralities. Knowing that "it was different in every
age," the historically oriented man also knows that "what you are does not
matter" (45). Thus, since art is opposed to history, only "if history suffers
transformation into a pure work of art" will it be able to "preserve instincts
and arouse them" (42). But a vision of history "that merely destroys without
any impulse to construct will in the long run make its instruments tired of
life; for such men destroy illusions, and he who destroys illusions in himself
and others is punished by the ultimate tyrant, Nature" (*ibid.*).

Nietzsche's "Use and Abuse of History" is more analytical in its method
than most of his work; it implicitly invests more confidence in conventional
philosophical criticism than the increasingly dithyrambic mode of his later
creations. Yet, appropriately, this analytical work is ultimately only destruc-

tive. In itself it offers little notion of what a Tragic artistic historiography might look like. To be sure, since it is composed in the aura of Nietzsche's *Birth of Tragedy*, an example of such historiography could be supposed to be present to the consciousness of the essay's potential readers. In fact, the two works are complementary, and "The Use and Abuse of History" may be seen as a retrospective ground-clearing operation; it prepares the way for the new kind of historiography displayed in *The Birth of Tragedy*. But the latter work makes possible, by creating the desire for it, only a Tragic art of the sort that appeared in Greece during the fifth century B.C. It asserts the need for a new historical account of Greek Tragedy and moves toward the provision of such an account. It even sets Tragedy over against history as currently conceived as the *means* to the construction of such a new historical account of Greek Tragedy.

But this juxtaposition of ancient Greek Tragedy to the various forms of modern poetic vision (including the Wagnerian, which, at the time, Nietzsche still honored) is primarily only that, a juxtaposition. The process by which the Greek Tragic vision was transmuted into the degenerate modern poetic vision remains obscure. Even while Nietzsche lamented the decline and fall of ancient Tragedy and named the modern historical consciousness as its antitype, he did not, in *The Birth of Tragedy*, provide a theory of historical process by which the transformation of the former into the later can be explained. He was on the verge of such a theory, however; this much is shown by the wrecking operation undertaken in "The Use and Abuse of History" and by the theory of the dialectic of remembering and forgetting which underlies his distinction among the various forms of historicism—the Monumental, the Antiquarian, and the Critical—and, within them, among their creative and destructive forms.

Still, in "The Use and Abuse of History" Nietzsche merely told what a creative, a life-serving, historiography would *not* be; he did not say what it would look like. Would it be structural or narrative, synchronic or diachronic, in conception? Would it be a "story" of individual men in contest with fate, or an assessment of a concluded sequence of events, or, again, a Metaphorical evocation of heroic possibilities? Nietzsche said that it could be all these things simultaneously, or any of them singly or in combination, depending on the life needs of men *as the historian conceives them*. In short, Nietzsche vested the authority to determine both the purpose of a given historical work and the form it will take in the historian's own sense of the life needs of his time. The historian is prohibited only from deifying the past at the expense of the present and the present at the expense of the future—that is to say, from writing uncritical Monumental or uncritical Antiquarian history, or, conversely, unheroic and irreverent Critical history. The model of such a life-serving historiography was offered by Nietzsche himself in a work which all but closed his career, *The Genealogy of Morals*.

◄§ Morality and History

The Genealogy of Morals (1887) can be read as an application of
Nietzsche's proposed "superhistorical" method to a problem at once historical
and philosophical. It seeks to determine the origin and the meaning of morality, of man's moral sense, his conscience, his belief in such qualities as "good"
and "evil." The essay begins with a criticism of the Rousseauist conception of
history, in which a humanity that is basically "good" is seen as having been
corrupted by a "fall" into the social state. On the contrary, Nietzsche argued,
man is not *basically* anything; and, if he has fallen into any condition, it is
into "goodness," from which derive all of the peculiarly human discontents of
the man-animal. However, in this essay Nietzsche offered a schema for emplotting the history of Western morality in such a way as to permit prediction
of an imminent release of man from his constricting "goodness." This release
represents, as it did for Marx, a liberation from the "social" condition. But
Nietzsche did not envision it as a release into "community." Rather, he saw it
as a release from all necessary association with other men, a dream of individual self-sufficiency which is nothing other than anarchy. He called this anarchic
condition "heroism" or "superhumanity," but it is anarchy nonetheless. Moreover, it is an anarchy made more terrible by the dissolution of all "values"
that are presumed to underlie it.

This is not to say that Nietzsche, any more than Rousseau or Marx, denied
the necessity of the social stage as a preliminary to the final, creative (or
heroic) stage. On the contrary, he held that man needed this second stage in
order to sharpen his peculiarly human attributes, his *human* will and reason
(167). But Nietzsche saw this social stage, the stage of self-denial, will-
lessness and reasonableness, as having been dissolved by man's own critical
powers and as preparing man for the breakup of reason and society, thus
releasing the will to a new and higher kind of "barbarism" in which the individual would live his own life as a work of art. Thus, he wrote his history in
the voice of the *eiron*, but he emplotted it as a kind of Comedy.

The first essay in *The Genealogy of Morals* examines the dichotomies "good
and evil" and "good and bad." It opens with an attack upon the English
utilitarian moralists, whom Nietzsche ironically calls "historians of ethics"—
that is, scholars who merely recount conventional ethical attitudes without
subjecting them to any criticism whatsoever. Actually, he said, they have all
been "quite deserted by the true spirit of history. They all, to a man, think
unhistorically." (159)

But what does it mean to "think historically"? In this case, it is to think
oneself back into the consciousness of a free, noble, and strong aristocracy
which takes unto itself the right to "name" those things that please it and
those that do not:

The origin of the opposites *good* and *bad* is to be found in the pathos of nobility and distance, representing the dominant temper of a higher, ruling class in relation to a lower, dependent one. The lordly right of bestowing names is such that one would almost be justified in seeing the origin of language itself as an expression of the rulers' power. They say [Metaphorically], "This *is* that or that"; they seal off each thing and action with a sound and thereby take symbolic possession of it. [160]

The language of nobility is therefore direct, innocent, undevious, naive; it names things without dissimulating, musically as it were, without *second* thoughts.

By contrast, the language of the weak is always a language of second thoughts, of devious intentions, and of secret aims. "When a noble man feels resentment, it is absorbed in his instantaneous reaction and therefore does not poison him." But, Nietzsche said, let us imagine how the "enemy" is conceived by the rancorous, repressed, weak man. He must conceive the "enemy" as "a fundamental idea," as "the Evil one," and "then as a pendant he has conceived a Good one—himself." (173)

Here the difference between the noble man and the weak man is conceived in terms of a distinction between those able to think Metaphorically and those constrained to think conceptually. The former use the language of art; the latter use that of science, philosophy, or religion.

For support of these generalizations, Nietzsche turned to etymology, the histories of the terms "good," "bad," and "evil," and argued that the terms for "good in all languages indicate the social class origin of *all* values" (162). The rebellion against the egoistic amorality of the primal aristocracy is led by a new anti-aristocracy, the leaders of which—the priests—branch off from the primal aristocracy of the strong and develop into its opposite. This new aristocracy of the herd has as its prime attribute the essential quality of the weak wherever they appear—that is, rancor. But it establishes its power over both the masses and the strong by a linguistic strategem; it simply *calls* its rancor "love."

This rancor has its origins in the repression and sublimation of the will to power of the members of the herd. As sublimated, this rancor takes the form of a transvaluation of noble attributes: whereas the noble man designates his own actions as "good" and those which differ from his own as "bad," the weak man begins by designating the actions of his betters as "evil" and his own as "good." Thus the dichotomy "good and bad" is supplanted by the dichotomy "good and evil"; and, whereas the first dichotomy is completely amoral, being merely an assertion of the experience of either the pleasure or the pain felt by the individual, the second is quintessentially metaphysical and moralistic, attributing a qualitatively evil *substance* to actions which differ from those of the person or group doing the defining.

Nietzsche sought to go beyond the metaphysical moralism implied in the language of "good and evil" by taking his stand on the idea of *health*, which he defined as any direct and immediate expression of emotion. Health is to the physical organism as Metaphorical consciousness is to the mental state. Where an emotion does not find direct and immediate outlet, he noted, it creates a fund of dammed up energy which expresses itself indirectly, as rancor. This rancor, in turn, expresses itself in mental rather than physical activity, specifically *in a search for the cause* by which the damming up can be explained, and it finds it—in complete justification—in the strong. But, in order to explain his *own* weakness, the rancorous man charges the strong man with possessing more than *mere* strength—the attribute, strength, is thus translated into a *quality*, evil.

The transformation of an attribute (such as strength or weakness) into a quality (such as evil or patience) is effected by a linguistic sleight of hand. In Section XIV of the first essay in *The Genealogy of Morals*, Nietzsche ironically described how this transvaluation of values occurs; it is all linguistic. The weak transmute "weakness into merit. . . . Impotence, which cannot retaliate, into kindness; cowardice into humility," and so on (180). Thus, the whole history of morality is seen as a product of the operations of Metonymical and Synecdochic consciousness at the expense of the "innocent" Metaphorical apprehension of the world. The search for causes and essences— for agencies behind, and qualities beyond, the phenomena captured in images by Metaphorical language—generates the two instruments of oppression which man turns upon himself: science and religion.

Nietzsche did not see the full extent to which he was utilizing a tropological theory of language to account for morality and culture in his "history" of both in *The Genealogy of Morals*. Almost as an afterthought, in a note appended to the first essay, he suggested the following question for further consideration: "What light does the science of linguistics, especially the study of etymology, throw on the evolution of moral ideas?" (188). He had answered this question in his first essay, in his discussion of the extent to which the Metonymical and Synecdochic dimensions of poetic language serve as the motors of consciousness, in its self-repressing operation, throughout history. The full development of these linguistic powers had resulted, in the end, in the Ironic consciousness from which his age and civilization were suffering. He did not realize that, by taking his stand on the conception of the essential creativity of Metaphorical language, he was begging the question of the part played by Metaphor itself in man's propensities for self-repression. But this linguistic historicism, which accords to Metaphorical consciousness a purely creative function, gave Nietzsche a base from which to criticize the historical consciousness in its various forms (Metonymical, Synecdochic, and Ironic) in his own age.

Nietzsche had been trained as a philologian, which meant that the transformations of language must have been present in his thought as a model for understanding the transformation of consciousness itself. This suggests that his conception of the cycle through which consciousness passes may well have been a projection of his conception of the linguistic cycle that passes from Metaphor through Metonymy and Synecdoche to Irony. The return to the innocence of consciousness was, then, necessarily conceived in terms of a return to the Metaphorical stage of language. In any event, it is obvious that the whole problem of remembering and forgetting, promising and binding oneself over to a fictitious past or future, was tied up in his mind with the fallacies of Metonymical and Synecdochic apprehensions of the world. The "fall" into "goodness," into morality and self-mutilation, was, in the end, nothing but a fall into the further reaches of linguistic possibility.

The second essay in *The Genealogy of Morals*, on "guilt," "bad conscience," and "related matters," begins with a re-examination of the uniquely human power of remembering. And here, as earlier, Nietzsche described memory as a kind of perverse willfulness by which men bind themselves over to a *specific* future as well as to a *fixed* past. This capacity to bind oneself over to a specific future and a fixed past is precisely what is meant by conscience, he argued. The capacity to remember gives to an oath taken in the past the power to bear upon and to determine the present and the future. The oath taken, remembered, and adhered to imposes a *kind* of order on human life, but one quite different from that imposed upon it by the faculty of forgetting. The faculty of forgetting allows us to live in a present; it functions "to shut temporarily the doors and windows of consciousness; to protect us from the noise and agitation with which our lower organs work for or against one another; to introduce a little quiet into our consciousness so as to make room for the nobler functions and functionaries of our organism which do the governing and functioning" (189). When we "forget" the past and future, we can "see" the present clearly. When oblivion is suspended by remembrance, "specifically in cases where it is a question of promises," the will becomes chained to a prior condition and desire; and it continues to affirm that condition and desire, even at the expense of its own health (189–90).

In short, the capacity to promise is of precisely the same nature as the capacity to remember. By promising, one wills forward, to impose a fictitious form on the future; by remembering, one wills backward, to impose a fictitious form on the past. For Nietzsche, the important point about both promising and remembering was the *interest* in the light of which these fictitious forms are imposed on the future and the past respectively. Bad conscience is nothing but the incapacity to accept one's past acts as one's own, the impulse to view them as products of some other agent or agency than one's own will, to see them as manifestations of some "quality" above, or superior to, one's own being. Good conscience, by contrast, is nothing but the power to say that, whatever happened or will happen in the future, happened or will happen by my own agency, as a manifestation of my own qualities. Creative forgetting, Nietzsche held, is at the same time creative remembering. For creative forgetting is nothing but a remembering of one's own will, one's own powers and talents. And it is with whole generations as it is with the individual. To be oneself is to deny the obligations which both past and future lay upon one, except for those obligations that one chooses for oneself and honors simply because one finds them "good." In the second essay of *The Genealogy*, Nietzsche took up the question which he had begged in "The Use and Abuse of History": "How does one create a memory for the human animal? How does one go about to impress anything on that partly dull, partly flighty human intelligence—that incarnation of forgetfulness—so as to make it stick?" (192). Discover the answer to that question, he said, and one not only solves the riddle of conscience, but one solves the riddles of society, culture, and destructive historical consciousness at the same time. The rest of *The Genealogy of Morals* is an essay on the history of culture, society, and morality in terms of a psychological theory of repression and sublimation. In it the sense of *a* single, irredeemable past and terror are identified as being essentially the same thing.

The creation of memory can be effected only by pain, Nietzsche said; it follows, then, that culture memory, like personal memory, is a product of pain, not of pleasure.

Whenever man has thought it necessary to create a memory for himself, his effort has been attended with torture, blood, sacrifice. The ghastliest sacrifices and pledges, including the sacrifice of the first-born; the most repulsive mutilations, such as castration; the cruelest rituals in every religious cult (and all religions are at bottom systems of cruelty)—all these have their origin in the instinct which divined pain to be the strongest aid to mnemonics. [193]

In the beginning of human history, when the memory of mankind was still less strongly developed, the most terrible methods of memory arousal were called for: "The severity of all primitive penal codes gives us some idea how difficult it must have been for man to overcome his forgetfulness and to drum into these slaves of momentary whims and desires a few basic requirements of communal living" (*ibid.*). By the cruelest methods the individual was taught to remember a few "I won'ts" which "entitled him to participate in the benefits of society; and indeed, with the aid of this memory, people eventually 'came to their senses' " (194).

What, then, is the origin of bad conscience? Nietzsche found a clue in the fact that the term "guilt" (*Schuld*) has its origins in a term signifying a material relationship, "to be indebted" (*Schulden*). In short, the idea of guilt arises not in any late doctrine of the freedom of the will but in the notion of *compensation*. The relation between damage and pain, he said, arose "in the contractual relation between creditor and debtor, which is as old as the notion of 'legal subjects' itself and which in its turn points back to the basic practices of purchase, sale, barter, and trade" (195). The creditor receives one kind of payment from the debtor by the pleasure he gets in inflicting pain. The nature of that pleasure is aesthetic: it is the pleasure which comes from being able to *exercise power* over another, a pleasure which makes the punisher feel "noble," superior to the defenseless victim. Basically it is sadistic. And sadism, Nietzsche maintained, is the basis of all "artificial" hierarchies. (196)

Nietzsche saw the origin of the state in the debtor-creditor relationship. In primitive times, he held, "the commonwealth stood to its members in the relation of creditor to debtor" (203–4). Originally, anyone who refused to pay his debts or who laid hands on his creditor was simply outlawed; increasingly, however, it became the practice merely to put a specific price on the crime. In short, as society grew richer, it translated a sadistic pleasure into a commodity with an exchange value. Pain, given or received, can be stored up, drawn upon, taxed, nationalized, or socialized. Nietzsche even contemplated the possibility of a society so rich in accumulated pain that it would have no need to punish its criminals, but would merely forgive them. This would be the millennium for society as *historically* constituted.

All of this was only Ironically suggested, however, for Nietzsche's real purpose was to use the notion of the capitalization of pain to account for the emergence of the idea of justice out of an intrinsically amoral human existence. In reality, he argued, "To speak of right and wrong *per se* makes no sense at all. No act of violence, rape, exploitation, destruction, is intrinsically 'unjust,' since life itself is violent, rapacious, exploitative, and destructive and cannot be conceived otherwise" (208). How, then, does one account for the appearance of the idea of justice at the beginning of civilized existence?

Justice, Nietzsche argued, was originally an instrument used by the strong to diminish the rancor of the weak. Regulation of rancor

is accomplished by wresting the object of rancour from vengeful hands, or by substituting for vengeance the struggle against the enemies of peace and order, or by devising, proposing, and if necessary *enforcing* compromises, or by setting up a normative scale of equivalents for damages to which all future complaints may be referred. [207]

The establishment of such a body of equivalents—that is, of law—divests the vengeful act of its character as a *personal* slight and its particularity and transforms it into an *objective* relationship. And this transformation effects a change in the very nature of perception itself:

Thus the rules deflect the attention of their subjects from the particular injury and, in the long run, achieve the opposite end from that sought by vengeance, which tries to make the viewpoint of the injured person prevail exclusively. Henceforth the eye is trained to view the deed ever more impersonally—even the eye of the offended person, though this, as we have said, is the last to be affected. [208]

In short, justice has its origin in an arbitrary differentiation between "right" and "wrong" actions, and its effect is to reorient the perceptions of eveyone, both the offended and the offender, so that the very feeling of selfhood is neutralized. This led Nietzsche to the conclusion that "from a biological point of view legal conditions are necessarily exceptional conditions, since they limit the radical life-will bent on power and must finally subserve, as means, life's collective purpose, which is to create greater power constellations." And its long-range effect on the species, he maintained, is to bring about "man's utter demoralization and, indirectly, the reign of nihilism." Legality, he insisted is a "weapon against struggle" itself. [*Ibid.*]

This passage on the origin of justice is crucial to an understanding of Nietzsche's psychologistic approach to cultural history. That Nietzsche himself was aware of the connection is shown by the fact that it is followed immediately by a discussion of the way by which the historian is able to penetrate through the cloud of ideology which engulfs every culture's self-image and its own appraisals of its spiritual principles. Thus, in Chapter XII of the second essay in *The Genealogy of Morals*, Nietzsche set forth the ontological basis of true historical method. He began with the following observation:

There is no set of maxims more important for an historian than this: that the actual causes of a thing's origins and its eventual uses, the manner of its incorporation into a system of purposes, are worlds apart; that everything that exists, no matter what its origin, is periodically reinterpreted by those in power in terms of fresh intentions; that all processes in the organic world are processes of outstripping and overcoming, and that, in turn, all outstripping and overcoming means reinterpretation, rearrangement, in the course of which the earlier meaning and purpose are necessarily either obscured or lost. [209]

This passage constitutes nothing less than a rejection of the Mechanistic, Organicist, and Contextualist conceptions of historical explanation, at one and the same time. The historical process is seen to be not a process at all but a series of moments, each of which is related to what came before it and what will follow it by the intentions of the agents on the scene at that time. The idea is to destroy not only all teleology but all causality as well.

What Nietzsche did here was to disengage the "evolution" of a thing from its "uses" by those in power at any given time, locating the "meaning" of that evolution in the intentions of those who control the instruments of public perception in the present. In place of a sequence of cause-effect relationships as the model for viewing the evolution or development of any given biological or social phenomenon, Nietzsche substituted the notion of a set of retroactive confiscations. Thus, he said, "the whole history of a thing, an organ, a custom, becomes a continuous chain of reinterpretations and rearrangements." These reinterpretations and rearrangements "need not be causally connected among themselves," but may "simply follow one another," which means that the *evolution* "of a thing, a custom, an organ" is not necessarily its "*progressus* towards a goal, let alone the most logical and shortest *progressus*, requiring the least energy and expenditure." It is, rather, "a sequence of more or less profound, more or less independent processes of appropriation, including the resistances used in each instance, the attempted transformations for purposes of defense and reaction, as well as the results of successful counterattacks." And he added that, if "forms are fluid, their 'meaning' is even more so." (210)

When unpacked, these cryptic remarks provide important insights into Nietzsche's conception of the semantics of all historical processes. As he summarized it, the argument reduces to the contention that "partial desuetude, atrophy, and degeneration, the loss of meaning and purpose—in short, death —must be numbered among the conditions of any true *progressus*, which latter appears always in the form of the will and means to greater power and is achieved at the expense of numerous lesser powers." This amounts to nothing less than an affirmation of the conventional notion of Tragedy: "The scope of any 'progress' is measured by all that must be sacrificed for its own sake." And Nietzsche even said: "To sacrifice humanity as mass to the welfare of a single stronger human species would indeed constitute progress." (*Ibid.*)

Yet, it would be wrong to conclude too hastily that what Nietzsche called "this point of historical method" is exhaustively describable in terms of the conventional notion of Tragedy. The context in which it was expounded suggests that it was offered primarily as an alternative to the bourgeois notion of "adaptation," which dominated much of the thought about evolutionary processes current in Nietzsche's time. Nietzsche was concerned to put the concept of *activity* in place of the concept of *adaptation* in thought about evolutionary process, whether in society or in nature. (211)

This commentary on historical method permitted Nietzsche to return to his analysis of the relationship between pain and conscience. He noted that punishment increases fear, circumspection, control over the instincts, that it rests at the base of civilized existence, and that it has remained the basis of civilization since the beginning. The infliction of pain even serves as the nexus of a secret bond between the criminal and his judge, who, by *punishing* the criminal for his crimes, shows him that no action, even murder, is in itself wrong; only those actions which are committed under certain circumstances are wrong. This is the liberating discovery made by Stendhal's Julien Sorel in *The Red and the Black* during his trial by a "good" society. The response of Julien Sorel to his condemnation by "moral men" is to deny the right of others to prescribe morality for him. He insists that there is no such thing as substantive evil; and he will not admit to a "bad conscience." He discovers that "bad conscience" is learned. And so it was with Nietzsche: "Bad conscience [is] . . . a deep-seated malady to which man succumbed under the pressure of the most profound transformation he ever underwent—the one that made him once and for all a social and pacific creature" (217). Behind the formation of this bad conscience lies a systematic damming up of the instincts, and a resulting "interiorization" which alone "provides the soil for the growth of what was later called man's *soul*" (*ibid.*). The presumed existence of this soul is in turn the origin of man's impulse to self-mutilation through the invention of all those "spirits" which are imagined to resent the existence of animal impulses in man. Here, too, is the origin of religion. As Nietzsche said: "the phenomenon of an animal soul turning in upon itself, taking arms against itself, was so novel, so profound, mysterious, contradictory, and pregnant with possibility, that the whole complexion of the universe was changed thereby. The spectacle . . . required a divine audience to do it justice" (218). And so the gods were invented to serve as the eternal audience before which this drama of cosmic mutilation could be played out, its "nobility" assured and its "value" authenticated.

It is remarkable how closely Nietzsche's account of the origins of society, conscience, and religion corresponds to Marx's account of it in *The German Ideology*. But there is a significant difference: whereas Marx grounded all of these in the exigencies of human survival and accounted for them by the condition of scarcity which both required the division of labor and led to the unequal distribution of goods produced, Nietzsche located the impelling principle in a psychological factor, the will to power, a force which he considered greater than the will to life and which accounted not only for man's domination and exploitation of other men but also for his own capacity to destroy himself. How else could one account for the excesses of the exploiting class even in the midst of plenty, or the positive acceptance by the exploited classes of their condition of servitude, if not by a psychological predisposition in humanity in which the giving of pain is experienced as a positive pleasure and the receiving of it is conceived as a necessity among those who have no other choice? How else could one account for the self-repression of animal instincts and their twofold expression in the dichotomous relation of "good and bad" on the one hand and "good and evil" on the other? Finally, how could one account, beyond the confines of any merely exploiter-exploited relationship, for that transvaluation of values by which the "good and bad" dichotomy, which must have prevailed among the strong in the beginning of human history, was supplanted by the "good and evil" dichotomy of the weak, which has triumphed everywhere in the historical period? Nietzsche's answers to these questions are all contained in the psychological theory of repression which he developed out of the basic concept of the will to power, and which marks him as a historical psychologist as great, if not greater, than Freud himself.

I say "if not greater than Freud himself" because, in his account of the origin of conscience in humanity, Nietzsche did not require, as Freud did in *Totem and Taboo*, the postulation of a generalized primal "crime" by which a socially conditioned experience such as the Oedipus complex is lived through by the entire species. He found the basis for the emergence of conscience in a purely aesthetic impulse in the strong and the similarly aesthetic response of the weak to this impulse, both of which were expressions of the single, shared will to power of the species. Thus, Nietzsche postulated for the beginning of human history a warrior aristocracy dominating by terror a larger, amorphous, and shiftless mass of subjects. These aristocrats necessarily and instinctively imposed form on this mass, which allowed Nietzsche to hail them as the "the most spontaneous, most unconscious" artists that ever existed. But, instead of working on what have since become conventional artistic materials, these primitive artists worked on men themselves. Bad conscience arose not in them but in their subjects, who, impelled by a will to power every bit as strong as that of their masters, but impeded from expressing it directly, had this instinct driven underground, turned against themselves, to become, in the form of the declaration "I am ugly," a basis for defining the idea of the beautiful. Hence, the idea of "the beautiful," like that of "the good" and that of "the true," is a product of the consciousness which does not act, but is acted upon. Those who are live good, true, and beautiful lives have no need of these concepts; for such concepts are only ways of characterizing what bad, false, and ugly things *are not*. The "concepts" of the good, the true, and the beautiful are, therefore, products of *fractured* wills, of individuals who find in their actual degradation, as contrasted with their natural aspiration to power and enjoyment of life, a distinction between *what is* and what *ought to be*. Nietzsche described the transvaluation of this original consciousness into conscience in the first essay of *The Genealogy*. In the second essay he showed how this transvaluation was translated into the basis of social morality.

Here again Nietzsche was as austere as Marx, and characteristically more psychologistic. And again he anticipated Freud. But Freud conceived the origin of conscience to lie in the economics of sexuality, in the struggle of the sons of the clan for the available women monopolized by the father, and in the subsequent murder of the father by the sons. But then, strangely, Freud invoked the notion of a kind of stockbroker mentality in primitive man by which the sons suddenly perceived the long-range interest of dividing up the women among themselves, setting proprietorial rights over them, and justifying this confiscation by the improvisation of totemic religion.

Nietzsche, characteristically, subordinated the sexual impulse to the power drive, which Freud himself might have done had he not been obsessed by the need to find evidence of the universality of the Oedipus complex. Nietzsche found the origins of social conscience in a simple power relationship. Just as the idea of responsibiltiy in the individual was inspired by the systematic inculcation of a debtor mentality, so, too, the moral continuity of society is seen as a function of a debtor-creditor relationship, *which is imagined to exist between the generations, between living men and their forebears*.

Among primitive peoples, Nietzsche noted with considerably more insight than Freud, each generation feels a sense of *juridical* obligation to the ancestors that is much stronger than any *emotional* one. "Early societies were convinced that their continuance was guaranteed solely by the sacrifices and achievements of their ancestors and that these sacrifices and achievements were required to be paid back." But, of course, Nietzsche said, they could never be fully repaid. In fact, a curious—but perfectly understandable—logic operated in primitive society by which any success among the living actually increased their dependence upon the dead: "the fear of the ancestor and his power and the consciousness of indebtedness increase in direct proportion as the power of the tribe itself increases, as it becomes more successful in battle, independent, respected and feared. Never the other way around." By contrast, failure, decline, defeat, work in the other direction, leading to a diminution of respect for the ancestors, but not necessarily to rebirth, for regeneration is a function solely of the break with the feeling of indebtedness to anyone but one's self. Thus, "Following this kind of logic to its natural term, we arrive at a situation in which the ancestors of the most powerful tribes have become so fearful to the imagination that they have receded at last into a numinous shadow: the ancestor becomes a god. Perhaps this is the way all gods have arisen, out of *fear*." (222)

And just as man has inherited from his primitive ancestors the notions of good and bad, "together with a psychological penchant for hierarchies, so he has inherited from the tribes, together with the tribal gods, a burden of outstanding debt and the desire to make final restitution" (223). This is the origin of all those redemptive religions which have cut the Gordian knot with the ancestors by ascription of both individual responsibility and individual guilt to men, but which in the process have set as a price on this redemption the abandonment of the fruits of the earth for all time. Thus, Nietzsche said, Christianity represents the triumph of the highest sense of indebtedness and guilt ever conceived. He saw the consummation of Christianity, however, as an occasion for joy.

If we are right in assuming that we have now entered upon the inverse development, it stands to reason that the steady decline of belief in a Christian god should entail a commensurate decline in man's guilt consciousness. . . . a complete and definitive victory of atheism might deliver mankind altogether from its feeling of indebtedness to its beginnings, its *causa prima*. Atheism and a kind of "second innocence" go together. [225]

◄§ Truth and History

It would appear, then, that the sense of generational obligation and "historical consciousness" amount to the same thing. The capacity to "remember" lies at the heart of both. And the escape from generational obligation entails an escape from historical consciousness. If men are not to die of the debtor mentality that keeps them from living for themselves alone, remembering must be replaced by a selective forgetfulness.

In the third essay of *The Genealogy*, "What Do Ascetic Ideals Mean?"

Nietzsche sketched a history of the effects of man's capacity for self-mutilation on mankind in general. He saw the development of ascetic ideals as indicative of a special human power—not, to be sure, a spiritual power, but an impulse of the human will, "its fear of the void" (231). Man's will, he said, requires an *aim*. All willing is a willing of *something*. And where an aim is lacking, the will may take the void itself *as* its goal. Thus, when men are unable to give vent fully to their animal passions, they are capable of making of necessity a virtue and of turning chastity into a goal, purpose, or ideal value. And ascetic ideals, the deification of pain and mutilation, are born.

The whole realm of higher culture is, according to Nietzsche, a product of the sublimation of this ascetic impulse. In art, this impulse reaches its apogee in the notion of the will-less artist, the disinterested spectator of the world of the sort postulated by Kant, for whom beauty is, of all things, "disinterested pleasure," as if there could ever be such a thing. Schopenhauer gave to this Kantian conception of the beautiful a specifically decadent turn by glorifying beauty as a "release from the will" and a "sedative of the will." Against this view of the beautiful, however, Nietzsche opposed the Stendhalian notion of it as "precisely the excitement of the will, of 'interest,' through beauty" (240). Thus, the triumph of Kantian and Schopenhauerian aesthetics was the sign of the triumph of intellect *over* will, of man's repressive capacity over the will to power, of the ideal of the spectator over that of the actor. It was, in short, the triumph of the concept over the image. As such it constituted the cause of the Ironic consciousness that characterized the culture of the time.

But, Nietzsche claimed, this ascetic culture, with its ideal of disinterestedness, is merely a dodge by which the philosophers express their own inverted will to power. The "virtues" of the philosophers, Nietzsche argued, are merely means to the end of self-expression considered as pure intellection, the only form of expression open to the repressed man. Thus interpreted, philosophy as it has descended from Plato is little more than an extension of the original perversion of the Apollonian will to form. One ought not to fault what the philosophers have been able to achieve, Nietzsche argued, and he admitted that a certain asceticism is necessary to any strenuous intellectual activity. (247) But it is necessary, he insisted, to determine whether the gain in intellectual power has been worth what it has cost in animal energy, for "Nothing was ever bought more dearly than the small portion of human reason and freedom that is now our pride" (250). Yet Nietzsche was more interested in asking how the substitution of intellection for animal energy arose and what it portended for the future of the culture that it sustained.

If the impulse behind philosophizing is ultimately an aesthetic one—that is, if the urge to philosophize has its origin in the desire to impose form on the world—how does one account for the fact that the philosopher conventionally assumes an ascetic countenance and even a belief in ascetic values? It all began—Nietzsche surmised—as a means of surviving the wrath of the priests in ascetically oriented religious cultures. The philosopher is by nature the enemy of the priest, but, since in the beginning he lacked the prestige of the priest, he had to assume a priestly disguise. Unfortunately, the disguise soon seized the actor and transformed the philosophical impulse to freedom from religion into a new kind of religion every bit as ascetic as that against which it had originally arisen. And the result was that a genuinely life-serving philosophy disappeared.

This is shown by the triumph of a sadistic impulse in philosophy no less than in art. Just as modern art eulogizes the will-less artist, so, too, modern philosophy eulogizes the hobbled thinker. Surely, Nietzsche said, it is the height of sadistic pleasure "when reason in its self-contempt and self-mockery decrees that the realm of truth does indeed exist but that reason is debarred from it," as in the thought of Kant (254–55). The philosophical ideal of his own time, Nietzsche said, imagines a "pure, will-less, painless, timeless knower" with the objective of attaining a "pure reason, absolute knowledge, absolute intelligence" (255). But all these concepts, Nietzsche held, "presuppose an eye such as no living being can imagine, an eye required to have no direction, to abrogate its active and interpretative powers—precisely those powers that alone make of seeing, seeing *something*." This ideal obscures the fact that "all seeing is essentially perspective, and so is all knowing. The more emotions we allow to speak in a given matter, the more different spectacles we can put on in order to view a given spectacle, the more complete will be our conception of it, the greater our objectivity" (*ibid.*). The will to truth, then, is essentially a way of denying the apprehension of the truths of things. The will to truth, like the ideal of "objectivity" which conceives objectivity as the perception of the will-less knower, is the enemy of both truth and will.

Significantly, for my purposes, Nietzsche took modern historians as the very incarnation of this ideal of the will-less knower. They place themselves before the historical past as will-less and thoughtless "mirrors" of events: "They reject teleology; they no longer want to 'prove' anything; they disdain to act the part of judges . . . ; they neither affirm nor deny, they simply ascertain, describe" (293). These "objective" historians have a decadent counterpart in such "aesthetes" as Renan. This is the "epicurean, philandering kind, who ogles life as much as he does the ascetic ideal, who wears the word 'artist' like a kid glove, and who has entirely engrossed the praise of contemplation" (293–94). These spectators *par excellence*, Nietzsche said, possess the "hypocritical 'fairness' of impotence" (295).

But Nietzsche saw European culture as having reached the outer limits of its own alienation. Something had been gained; the will had been saved, even if only for the void. That is what the ascetic ideal is all about finally. It is a "revulsion from life, a rebellion against the principal conditions of living. And yet, despite everything, it is and remains a *will*." It only remains to raise this will-to-nothingness to self-consciousness, to make it a program rather than an expedient, to strike out and to destroy with the powers of this over-refined intellect all of the burdens placed on man by his ascetically induced sensibilities. This and this alone would release the will to a positive willing. In that work of destruction and creation history, too, would have a part, by becoming the superhistorical art displayed by Nietzsche himself in his *Genealogy of Morals*.

It should now be apparent that *The Genealogy of Morals* is a historico-psychological account of the origins of the trinity of conventional humanism: the beautiful, the good, and the true; an analysis of the role that conventional historical consciousness has had in sustaining belief in their substantive reality; and a call by example to the formation of a new, purified, and life-serving historical consciousness by which this burden of substantialism can be thrown off. This new life-serving historicism presupposes a new psychology which encompasses will, as well as reason and the senses, as its subject matter, and makes the dynamics of the will its central object. Lying beneath and sustaining this envisioned psychology is the conviction that man is primarily an image-making animal, an animal which imposes form on the chaos of the sense impressions that bombard him in any merely animal apprehension of his world, and makes his images for a purpose. But this purpose is presumed to be individual and subjective and to have its sole possible end *in* the world, not outside it. Moreover, in Nietzsche's thought, this purpose has been completely liberated from any obligation to the powers that preceded it, exist with it, or will follow it. It finds its practical limitations not in any abstract forces that are conceived to underlie or inform it, or that emerge in the world process as a whole, but solely in the will's own actions, in the interplay with other purposes pursued by other wills which have been similarly liberated from abstract constraints and therefore are similarly free. Neither spirit, society, the state, modes of production, nor culture can lay any claim on this will; least of all can the priests restrain it. For, although spirit, society, the state, modes of production, and culture may be said to exist, they are seen solely as the products of humanity, of its power and of its plastic capacity. As for God, He cannot be said to exist at all; although He may be seen as a product of human imagination, He can be dismissed as only that, and dissolved by an act of the imagination itself.

Nietzsche thus used historical consciousness to sever the last bonds that link men to other men in *shared* enterprises. He envisaged the ultimate dissolution of history itself, and more radically than Marx had done. Like Marx, he perceived beyond the rubble left by that dissolution the formation of a new humanity. But it would not be conscripted to the service of either a new community or a purified culture, for Nietzsche had dissolved the concepts of community and culture, along with those of the past and future, in the interest of creating the autonomous individual. For Nietzsche, there was only the present. Man is alone in it, and he is charged with the responsibility of living every present as if it were to be his eternity. Such is the import of the myth of "eternal recurrence" taught by Zarathustra.

Conclusion

Nietzsche's purpose as a philosopher of history was to destroy the notion that the historical process has to be explained or emplotted in any particular way. The very notions of explanation and emplotment are dissolved; they give place to the notion of historical representation as pure story, fabulation, myth conceived as the verbal equivalent of the spirit of music. Yet this conception of historical representation has its own conceptual underpinnings; it presupposes a lexicon, a grammar, a syntax, and a semantic system by which the historical field can be provided with a number of possible meanings.

When Nietzsche surveyed the historical field he found there only manifestations of the operations of the human will, and he grouped these manifestations into basically two kinds: those of strong men and those of weak men. The syntax of the relationships between these two kinds of historical agents is complicated, however, by the fact that the basic law governing them, the will to power, is mediated by a uniquely human faculty, consciousness. Man's capacity for reflection, and, above all, his ability to *name* things, to confiscate things by linguistic means, results in the erection of a second *illusory world*, alongside the original world of pure power relationships. The history of culture thus appears as a process in which the weak vie with the strong for the authority to determine how this second world will be characterized. And the history of human consciousness describes a process in which the original *imaging* of the world in terms of the categories "good and bad" gives place to different ways of *conceptualizing* it in terms of the categories of "good and evil" on the one hand and the categories of "cause and effect" on the other. Thus, the history of human consciousness can be emplotted as a "fall" out of the original, Metaphorical mode of apprehending the world into the Synecdochic and Metonymical modes of comprehending it. Nietzsche described this "fall" as a transition from music, poetry, and myth into the arid worlds of science, religion, and philosophy.

There is, however, an intrinsic Irony in this "fall," for the full cultivation of the Synecdochic and Metonymical modes of comprehension works to the disadvantage of both. Religion denies art, science denies religion, and philosophy denies science, so that modern man is hurled farther into the depths of a specifically Ironic consciousness, is deprived of faith in his own reason, imagination, and will, and is finally driven to despair of life itself.

In Nietzsche's view, this despair accounted for his own age's obsession with history. The modern historicist mentality is a product of the hope that the past might provide models for comportment in the present, or that the hypostatized "historical process" might by its own operations effect the redemption which man longs for. Failing these, it becomes a distraction, a pastime, a narcotic. Historical thought in the modes of Metonymy, Synecdoche, and Irony, then, not only is a symptom of the malady of modern man but also is a sustaining cause of that malady, for historical consciousness in these modes simply *reminds* man of his enthrallment to forces and processes outside himself, his obligations to past and future generations, his bondage to powers greater or lesser than himself. Historical consciousness prohibits man from "going into" his present and thus reinforces the very condition it is intended to surmount. The immediate problem, then, is to dissolve the authority of all the inherited ways of conceiving history, to return historical thinking to a poetic, and specifically Metaphorical, mode of comprehending the world— that is to say, to promote a capacity for creative *forgetting*, so that thought and imagination can respond immediately to the world lying *there* before it as a chaos, to be done with as current desire and need require.

The return of historical thought to the Metaphorical mode will permit liberation from all efforts to find any definitive meaning in history. The elements of the historical field will be seen to lend themselves to combination in an infinite number of ways, in the same way that the elements of perception do to the free artist. The important point is that the historical field be regarded, in the same way that the perceptual field is, as an occasion for image-making, not as matter for conceptualization. In the process, the very notion of a historical semantics is obliterated. Even the chronicle of events is deprived of its authority as a limiting condition on what the historian may do in his construction of his images of the past. Just as poetry is itself the means by which the rules of language are transcended, so, too, Metaphorical historiography is the means by which the conventional rules of historical explanation and emplotment are abolished. Only the lexical elements of the field remain, to be done with as the historian, now governed by "the spirit of music," desires. The dissolution of the notion of a historical semantics is, at the same time, the dissolution of the dream of a method by which history-in-general can be endowed with any sense at all. The historian is liberated from having to say anything *about* the past; the past is only an occasion for his invention of ingenious "melodies." Historical representation becomes once more all *story*, no plot, no explanation, no ideological implication at all—that is to say, "myth" in its original meaning as Nietzsche understood it, "fabulation."

Yet, this conception of historical knowledge does have specific ideological implications, and they are those of Nihilism, as Nietzsche himself recognized. Any attempt to interpret Nietzsche's thought as a purer and more consistent form of the conventional ideological positions—Conservative, Liberal, Reactionary, Radical, or even Anarchist—must face the fact that, in his conception of history, the prospects of any *community* whatsoever are sternly rejected. In Nietzsche, no historical grounds exist for the construction of any specific *political* posture except that of antipolitics itself. Thought is liberated from responsibility to anything outside the ego and will of the individual, whether past, future, or present. In this respect Nietzsche merely represents a heroic affirmation of the Ironic condition of the culture of his own age.

He saw in such heroic affirmation a means to the liberation of the creative imagination from restrictions placed on it by thought itself. Thus, his envisioned rebirth of Metaphorical consciousness resists regression to the specifically Romantic world view it appears to require. A thinker like Michelet, himself the practitioner of a Metaphorical historiography, was still convinced of the possibility of extracting the essential meaning of history from the whole set of Metaphorical identifications that structured the stories he told. Behind Michelet's wager on the Metaphorical method lay the conviction that humanity, freed from the grip of false conceptualizations of its nature and processes, would still possess the potential to form itself into communities of love and mutual respect. Nietzsche left the world in its fractured condition, divided between the strong, who are destined to dominate it in the fuure, and the weak, who are fated to serve as the "material" out of which the liberated artists of power will fashion their "works of art." This condition of schism is not only accepted but positively affirmed as a desirable condition. Historical thought has been purged of its illusions; the products of its dreams have been transformed into concepts, but have been delivered over to the service of the will to power; and humanity has been consigned to the operations of a world in which artistic decorum alone stands between it and the descent into a dreadful night where Death is king.

The specifically "Radical" nature of Nietzsche's idea of history can now be characterized. He represents a repudiation of the efforts both to explain history and to emplot it as a drama with any general meaning. He advocated an emplotment of the historical process as Tragedy, but he so redefined the concept of Tragedy as to deprive it of any *moral* implication whatsoever. The explanatory strategies that Ranke, Marx, Tocqueville, and even Burckhardt advocated went by the board, since explanation was no longer of any concern to him. Explanation, like emplotment, is only a tactic, not an end or goal aspired to by the historian.

Nietzsche's position on all these matters was closest to that of Burckhardt, but he carried the implications of Burckhardt's conception of history as an art form beyond anything that the latter would have accepted. Burckhardt was still inspired by the notion of the "sublime" as a control on what perception was permitted to find in the historical, as in the visual, field. In Nietzsche the notion of the "sublime" is replaced by that of the "beautiful," and the beautiful is defined as anything that the sovereign will finds "good" to it. The "good," in turn, is contrasted not to "evil" but only to the "bad"—that is to say, to that which the sovereign will finds unpleasureable in experience.

Thus, like philosophy, science, and religion itself, historical knowledge is submitted to the rule of the pleasure principle. It is a supreme Irony that Nietzsche, the enemy of the "aesthetes" of his own time, not only ended by deifying a purely aesthetic conception of history but also subordinated the aesthetic sensibility to the imperatives of the will to power, thereby rendering those aesthetes more arrogant and more dangerous than they would have been without this subordination.

It is here that the basis of Nietzsche's fundamental opposition to Hegel can be found. Whereas Hegel saw historical consciousness as the ground for mediating between aesthetic and moral impulses in man, Nietzsche set up a dichotomy between aesthetic sensibility and morality and then proceeded to find a way of releasing the former from the latter by the dissolution of historical consciousness itself. In the process, however, he took up and pushed to its conclusion an insight which underlay all of Hegel's thinking about historical knowledge—that is, the extent to which the rules governing thought about history had their origins in linguistic habits and conventions themselves. But in setting up a dichotomy within language itself, by radically opposing poetic to conceptual language, and by viewing the latter as a "fall" from the innocence of the former, he precluded any possibility of finding a ground on which artistic insights and scientific knowledge could be turned to the single task of making sense out of the historical process and determining man's place in it. In separating art from science, religion, and philosophy, Nietzsche thought that he was returning it to union with "life." Actually, he provided the grounds for turning it against *human* life, for, since he regarded life as nothing but the will to power, he wedded the artistic sensibility to that will and turned life itself away from that knowledge of the world without which it cannot produce anything of practical benefit to anyone.

Chapter 10

Croce: The Philosophical Defense
of History in the Ironic Mode

∿§ *Introduction*

I have noted the Ironic component in the work of all philosophers of history,
and I have indicated how it differs from the Irony that is implicitly present in
every historian's attempt to wrest the truth about the past from the documents. The historian's Irony is a function of the skepticism which requires
him to submit the documents to critical scrutiny. He must treat the historical
record Ironically at some point in his work, must assume that the documents
mean something other than what they say or that they are saying something
other than what they mean, and that he can distinguish between saying and
meaning, or there would be no point in his writing a history. He could simply
compile a collection of documents and let them figure forth their own truth
in their own terms. To be sure, the historian's Irony may be only a tactical
tool, functioning as a methodological element in the preliminary stage of
research, and becoming progressively dissolved as the "truth" or "truths" contained in the documents become clear. Once he thinks he has extracted the
truth from the documents, he may then abandon his Ironic posture and write
his histories in one or another of the modes I have analyzed, in the firm conviction that he is telling *the truth about* "what really happened" in the past,
with more or less Ironic condescension toward his audience, but not with

respect to what he himself now "knows." The historian *may* maintain an Ironic attitude vis à vis his materials on the one hand and his audience on the other; but, when he maintains an Ironic stance with respect to his own enterprise, as Burckhardt did, the result is history emplotted as Satire, in which Irony is raised to a principle of historical representation.

The case of the philosopher of history is different from that of the historian. The philosopher of history assumes an Ironic (or, if one wishes, a skeptical) attitude, not only with respect to the historical record, but with respect to the whole enterprise of the historian as well. He seeks to determine the extent to which a given historian's work (and, indeed, the whole historiographical enterprise) may still be undergirt by unacknowledged presuppositions or assumptions—that is to say, to identify the *naive* element in historical thinking, the extent to which a given historical work has failed to maintain a critical attitude *with respect to itself*. Thus, although philosophy of history remains Ironical with respect to any given historian's work, its aim is to expose to consciousness, to criticize, and to eliminate the possibility of an Ironical historiography.

Any given historical work—indeed, all historical works—may be adjudged flawed or a failure to some extent, but the philosopher of history wants to show that, in spite of this fact, one need not take an Ironic view with respect to the historiographical enterprise as a whole, that grounds for confidence and belief in the utility of historical thinking for life are possible. Even Nietzsche, who viewed all products of thought Ironically, purported to save historical thinking for life by reducing it to the same fictional level as science and philosophy, grounding it in the poetic imagination along with these, and thereby releasing it from adherence to an *impossible* ideal of objectivity and disinterestedness. Thus, as I have said, even though it begins in Irony, philosophy of history seeks to go beyond Irony, to discover the grounds on which the historian might eliminate the Ironic element in his *account* of the past and purport to tell, with perfect self-confidence, "what was actually happening" in that past. At least, such was the case with the best philosophers of history of the nineteenth century.

Hegel sought the way beyond Irony in historical thinking through a Synecdochic analysis of the different forms of historiography as a preliminary to a dialectical synthesis of their various *kinds* of findings in a philosophical history. Marx sought the way to a philosophical history through a Metonymical analysis and Synecdochic synthesis of the facts contained in the historical record and the work of other historians so as to replace the relativism of ideologically motivated historiography with a nomological system of explanation. Nietzsche, on the other hand, sought a way out of the Irony of the historical thinking of his own day by pushing the Ironic position to its logical conclusion, asserting the essentially Metaphorical nature of *all* knowledge of the world, and dissolving all doubt by establishing the superiority of poetic insight over all other forms of comprehension.

These different critical strategies gave to the three philosophers of history their justification for emplotting history-in-general as Romantic Comedy or Comic Romance, but more "realistically" than their counterparts in historiography, insofar as each was at the same time permitted to assert the essentially "Tragic" nature of every finite historical existent. In Hegel, Marx, and Nietzsche the tension between a Tragic and a Comic vision of the world process was manitained, even though it was enclosed within, and finally resolved by an appeal to, the conception of human knowledge which each assumed to be the most authoritative form of truth: philosophical, scientific, and poetic respectively.

With Nietzsche, however, the categories of analysis began to dissolve. The "forms" which Hegel found in history, no less than the "laws" found by Marx, were defined by Nietzsche as *nothing but fictions*, products of the poetic imagination, more or less useful or convenient for the living of a particular *kind* of life, but in no way adequate to the discovery of the truth of human life. For Nietzsche, full authority for determining which "forms" and which "laws" will be treated *as if* they are the "truth" is vested in the sovereign ego or will, which admits no law except its own life interests or will to power. Nietzsche even dissolved the distinction between the Comic and the Tragic visions of life. In his thought Tragedy is conceived as being of two general kinds: the conventional Ironic kind, which teaches resignation to "things as they are"; and the new, Comic, Apollonian-Dionysiac kind, which teaches a radical overcoming of all situations in the service of the life force alone. In short, Irony is assimilated to Tragedy, and Tragedy to Comedy, in such a way as to make the distinctions between them inconsequential, in the same way that the distinctions among science, philosophy, and poetry are dissolved by their progressive assimilation to the last-named.

But thought about history still remains severed, fragmented, internally wounded. Among historians there is general agreement on the impossibility and undesirability of searching for laws of historical causation, but division over whether historical knowledge is knowledge of the general (of types) or knowledge of the particular (of individualities) persists. Moreover, on the matter of the emplotment of the historical process, there is disagreement over whether history is to be emplotted in the mode of Romance, Comedy, Tragedy, Satire, or some combination of these.

Then, over against the historians stand the philosophers of history, who in general deny the attempt at explanation by description and anticipate the Ironic consequences of a historiographical convention without any firm theoretical base for the defense of the descriptions actually offered as explanations in the narratives. But there is no agreement among these philosophers of history over what this theoretical base should consist of.

Hegel argued for the authority of the Synecdochic mode of characterizing the historical field, of explanation by typological classification and emplotment by a combination of Tragedy and Comedy. Marx argued for the

Metonymical mode, with explanation by nomological or causal analysis and emplotment—as in Hegel—by a combination of Tragedy and Comedy. Nietzsche defended the Metaphorical mode, with explanation by artistic intuition and emplotment in the combination of Tragedy and Comedy unique to his theory of the former *mythos*. It remained only for a philosopher of history to reflect on this severed condition of historical consciousness and to conclude that historical knowledge itself *was nothing but* the existential projection of the Ironic mode to complete the cycle of possible historical attitudes in the philosophy of history that had been lived through in historiography in the transition from Michelet to Burckhardt. The problem would then be: how could one live with a history explained and emplotted in the Ironic mode without falling into that condition of despair which Nietzsche had warded off only by a retreat into irrationalism? The philosopher of history who tried to solve this problem, within the terms set by this analysis of the situation at which historical thinking had arrived by the 1880s, was Benedetto Croce, the most talented *historian* of all the philosophers of history of the century.

✑§ Philosophy of History as Criticism

Croce did not start out as a philosopher, or even as a professional scholar. He never finished the university, and he never held an academic position. As a matter of fact, his opinion of the academic culture of his time was very much like that of Nietzsche and Burckhardt, bordering on contempt. He was—like Burckhardt—a gentleman-scholar, an amateur who had turned to the study of history as an escape from private suffering and the boredom of public life. His early work was antiquarian in the strict sense of the term, more archaeological than historical, consisting of studies of the folklore, life, and architecture of old Naples. In 1893, however, Croce entered the field of philosophy of history, with an essay entitled "History Subsumed under the General Concept of Art." His defense and elaboration of the ideas set forth in this essay launched him on his career as a philosopher. For the next ten years he defended the concept of art which his defense of the notion of history as an art-form had led him to expound in this essay.

In 1902 Croce published his *Aesthetics as a Science of Expression and General Linguistic*, one of the most influential books of its generation. This was followed, in 1905, by *Logic as a Science of Pure Concept*; in 1908 by *Philosophy of the Practical: Economics and Ethics*; and in 1917 by *Theory and History of Historiography*. The four works taken together constitute what Croce called the "Philosophy of the Spirit," which he regarded as a kind of *summa humanistica* for the modern world. It is significant that the first work of the tetralogy was inspired by the necessity of defending a position originally taken in philosophy of history—that is to say, history considered as a form of art—and that the last work, the capstone of the system, as it were, is nothing but a sustained analysis of the nature of historical knowledge.

The structure of the two books is the same, consisting of a theoretical discussion of the main issues, in aesthetics and historiography respectively, followed by a history of previous thinking on the subjects dealt with. Both the theoretical and historical sections of each work are elaborated with a self-confidence and certainty of judgment that are either magisterial or maddening, depending upon the reader's assessment of their justification. The important point is that Croce consistently presupposed the absolute adequacy of his own "Philosophy of the Spirit" for the spiritual needs of his age. From within the interior of this philosophy, he looked out at contending systems and back to preceding ones with that same Ironic gaze which the great cynics have shared with the great fanatics. Croce *knew* (or always claimed to know) precisely "what is living and what is dead" in any position that differed from his own. Yet he tacitly denied that anyone might be able to divine what was living and what was dead in his own system because his own philosophy was quintessentially an organon of "criticism," a critical philosophy *par excellence*; hence it was critical of itself as well as of other philosophies, and hence it guarded against the "false pessimism" and the "false optimism" which had brought every previous system to the ground.

The journal which Croce founded in 1902 and edited until a year before his death in 1952 was called, characteristically, *La Critica*; and in its pages Croce maintained a critical watch over the domain that he had staked out for himself in *Aesthetics* and the other books of the "Philosophy of the Spirit" which followed it. And as a matter of fact, Croce had taken the Ironic element which is present in every critical operation and had raised it to the status of a metaphysical and epistemological principle, by appeal to which the whole cultural endowment of the nineteenth century, and especially its Radical elements, could be assessed, found wanting, and consigned to "history." His problem, as he well knew, was to establish this Ironic position as the sole possible "wisdom" of the modern age without hurling thought into the skepticism and pessimism which a consistently Ironic world view inevitably promoted.

Croce's essays in cultural history always began and ended in the apprehension of the essentially *flawed* nature of every human undertaking; his was a philosophy which found the inadequacy in everything in the past, so that men would find it possible to live with the inadequacies of the present. He was especially tough-minded when it came to the assessment of nineteenth-century European civilization, the conceptions of history which inspired it (especially the doctrine of progress), and the theories of history promoted by its best thinkers. He was willing to admit that nineteenth-century historical thinkers represented an advance over Enlightenment, Renaissance, Medieval, and Classical thinkers. But, in the final analysis, for all the vaunted historicity of the age, he found very little in its historical thought and writing that he could commend unqualifiedly.

The "historical" section of his *Theory and History of Historiography* reads like a litany of errors, misconceptions, overextensions, and blunders. His criticism of the historical thinkers of the age was characteristically Ironical: the philosophers of history had very little "historical" sense; the historians lacked in "philosophical" understanding. While condemning the nefarious "philosophy of history," Croce argued, the historians of the age had remained captive to its illusions, writing histories that derived their form from the "philosophies of history" buried deep within the consciousness of those who prided themselves most on their objectivity and empiricism. Yet, ironically, he also argued that this *simultaneous rejection of*, and *submission to*, the philosophy of history, which marked the work even of Ranke himself, contained a germ of justification.

For, ironically, Croce maintained, history *was* philosophy and philosophy *was* history, and one could not do history without philosophical consciousness, anymore than one could do philosophy without historical consciousness. The nineteenth century had failed because it had not understood the true nature of these activities. All that was required to straighten out the matter, then, was to clarify the true natures of philosophy and history, establish the distinctions between them, and then combine them to make a saner, healthier world view than the nineteenth century had been able to imagine.

Croce purported to show that history was the "matter" of philosophy, just as philosophy was the "method" of history. The nefarious "philosophy of history," which Croce often called a "*contradictio in adiecto*," was in reality a pleonasm. For, in Croce's view, "history was nothing but philosophy," while "philosophy was nothing but history." The concrete *content* of philosophy was historical in nature, just as the *form* of historical propositions was properly provided by the categories of philosophical understanding.

To be sure, Croce insisted that philosophy had its own *method*, which was logic, "the science of pure concept." And history utilized a method uniquely its own in the investigative work that preceded the composition of the historical narrative. Historians had to use philological methods for criticizing the documents, and preconceptual, "intuitive," or artistic, insights for apprehending the objects, that occupied the historical field. This meant that historical knowledge *began* in the artistic apprehension of the particularities that inhabited the historical field, and in this phase of its operations its proper method was that of "art," which was to say "intuition." But, Croce argued, history went on to render judgments on the nature of the particularities discerned in the field. And these judgments were "synthetic a priori" ones, which is to say, characterizations of particularities in terms of the general concepts explicated in philosophy, not combinations of existential statements with the general causal laws that are presumed to govern the relationships between the objects posited by intuition. The important point was that scientific knowledge did not enter into the conception of historical knowledge at all. What began in an *aesthetic* apprehension of the historical field ended in a kind of *philosophical* comprehension of it.

◆§ *"History Subsumed under the General Concept of Art"*

In order to understand what Croce had in mind, it would be well to consider in some detail the essay of 1893 in which he first set forth systematically his notions of the relationship between history and art. The essay should be read within the context of the debate then underway, especially in Germany, between the Neo-Kantians, led by Wilhelm Windelband, and the Neo-Hegelians, led by Wilhelm Dilthey, over the epistemological status of historical knowledge. Briefly, Windelband maintained that historical knowledge was distinguished from scientific knowledge, not by the *objects* that it took to study, but by its aim or goal. Historical knowledge was "idiographic" or "picture-making," while scientific knowledge was "nomothetic" or "law-contriving." Dilthey, on the other hand, argued that history belonged to the *Geisteswissenschaften*, or "sciences of the spirit," while such disciplines as physics and biology belonged to the *Naturwissenschaften*, or "sciences of nature." The differences between these two kinds of sciences arose from the fact that they involved different objects of study, the products of the human spirit (mind, will, and emotions) on the one hand and the products of purely physico-chemical processes on the other. Croce's essay of 1893 was meant to contribute to this debate.

Collingwood has claimed great originality for the 1893 essay, arguing that it took the debate between Dilthey and Windelband far beyond the point to which they had brought it, developing it especially in the line begun by Dilthey. Actually, it did nothing of the sort. It *apparently* shifted the ground of the debate over the nature of history from science to art, but, while doing so, it defined art in such a way as to differentiate it hardly at all from that "idiographic science" invoked by Windelband as the science of the individual.

Like Windelband, Croce held that there were two kinds of cognition, one generalizing and conceptual, the other individualizing and intuitive, in its methods. But, instead of calling these two modes of cognition different kinds of sciences, as Windelband was inclined to do, Croce called the former science and the latter art. The tactic was effective because it struck at a presupposition shared by both Vitalists and Mechanists, who, whatever their differences, agreed that art was less a form of knowledge than an "expression" of, or "response" to, the world, and not a cognitive activity at all. Croce supposed that Mechanists regarded the aesthetic experience as a "vibration" of the senses, while Vitalists viewed it as a manifestation, either direct or sublimated, of animal impulses. For the former, art was a registering of reality; for the latter it was a senseless flight from reality. Croce denied both views. Instead, he defined art as a kind of knowledge, knowledge of the world in its particularity and concreteness, a knowledge that was different from, but complementary to, the conceptual knowledge of the world provided by science.

The essay of 1893 turns upon a dichotomy and a distinction. The dichotomy is drawn within consciousness between knowledge as science and knowledge as art; the distinction is drawn between art in general and the art of history in particular. Both the dichotomy and the distinction arose from Croce's objection to Positivism. The principal error of the Positivists, Croce said, was to assume that *all* valid knowledge was scientific in nature. In fact, Croce maintained, the greater part of human wisdom is not scientific at all, but merely conventional, commonsensical, or at best pragmatic rules, which arise from mankind's performance of the daily tasks needed to keep body and soul together. The Positivists knew that scientific knowledge differed *formally* from conventional or commonsensical wisdom, but they did not see that this made it a different *kind* of knowledge. Science properly understood was a way of comprehending the world conceptually; it was "the search for general truths by means of concepts." ("Storia ridotta," 16) The other way of comprehending the world—that is to say, the nonconceptual, immediate, and individualizing way—was not a science at all, but art, with standards of truth and verification different from, but every bit as rigorous as, those honored in science.

Thus, in Croce's view, art and science were different, not to say diametrically opposed, *modes of cognition.* As he put it: "Either one does science, . . . or one does art. If one subsumes the particular under the general, one is doing science; if one represents the particular as such, one is doing art" (23–24). The two modes of cognition were differentiated by the forms which they gave to their respective perceptions of the world; and, since it appeared obvious that history "elaborated no concepts" whatsoever, since it neither looked for nor entertained general laws, but merely "told what happened," it could not be characterized as a science in any significant sense at all (17–19).

The desire to place history among the sciences sprang, Croce believed, from two false beliefs: that all knowledge had to be scientific knowledge and that art was not a mode of cognition but merely a stimulant to the senses or, conversely, a narcotic. To straighten out the matter, it was necessary only to show that art was *nonconceptual knowledge of the world,* knowledge of the world in its particularity and its concreteness, to point to the fact that history was a similar kind of knowledge of the world, and then to distinguish history from art in general on the basis of the *content* of their representations.

Up to this point, as I have said, Croce had not carried the debate over the nature of historical knowledge beyond the point at which Dilthey and Windelband had brought it. He had merely substituted the term "art" for that of "idiographic science," which Windelband had used to characterize historical disciplines. Collingwood erred, therefore, when he suggested that Croce was closer to Dilthey than to Windelband in his general view of the matter, for Croce still had not distinguished between the possible objects of the modes of cognition differentiated by him as art and science. To Croce, as against Dilthey, the difference between the two lay in the *direction* taken in the process of inquiry, *from intuition of the world* in its particularity *to representation of the world* as a congeries of particulars in the case of art, *from intuition of the world* in its particularity *to subsumption of the particulars under concepts* in the case of science, not in any difference between their objects. Croce's original contribution came when he tried to distinguish between art in general and the art of history in particular on the basis of different kinds of intuitions, the intuition of the *possible* in the case of art in general, the intuition of the *actual* in the case of history. For him, as for Aristotle, the distinction between art in general and the art of history in particular lay in a difference in aim. Whereas art in general sought to intuit the *total possibilities* of individual existence, the art of history sought to determine what had *actually* crystallized as existential particularities in the world. In short, the difference between art and history lay in an epistemological, not an ontological, distinction.

In order to sustain this argument, Croce recurred to his earlier dichotomization of art and science. "In science," he said, "the content is the whole: science seeks to reduce every single manifestation of the real to the category in which it has a place. The aim of science is to reduce the whole to concepts" (30). Art, too, sought to represent the whole, since it was a mode of cognition; but, instead of trying to *reduce* the whole to a limited set of concepts, art tried to *inflate* it by discovering all the possible forms existence might take. Whereas science pursued a course toward the general and universal, art *circumscribed* distinct areas of reality while suppressing awareness of others, in order to *represent* those circumscribed more clearly and distinctly. Science wants to know everything, Croce said; but, while "it is important to know the laws of reality," it is neither necessary nor desirable to know everything at once or to gather data indiscriminately. Art circumscribes the world of experience, heightening our sensibilities to certain parts of it, while reducing our sensibilities to other parts, and showing us what the circumscribed parts consist of individually and directly.

The question then became: How do we know what parts of the world we *ought* to want knowledge of? On what principle do we choose an area of the world for circumscription and representation in its immediacy and individuality? Croce rejected the sensualist, rationalist, and formalist answers to these questions; neither "pleasure," "ideality," nor "formal consistency" made an object per se an aesthetic object. Instead, he took his stand on what he called "the aesthetics of concrete idealism," the theory which had descended from Hegel and had found its most elegant modern expression, in Croce's view, in the theories of Karl Koestlin.

Koestlin, Croce said, had shown correctly that "the content of aesthetics is the interesting: whatever interests man as man, whether from a theoretical or practical side, whether thought, sentiment, or will, what we know and what we do not know, what delights us and saddens us—in short, the entire world of human interest" (32–33). More important perhaps, Koestlin had shown that, the more generalized the interest, the greater the aesthetic value of the content. Thus, a hierarchy of interests could be constructed. At the apex of this hierarchy were those contents which touched upon man as man; below these were those which had to do with man as a member of a particular race, nation, or religion; then came those which bore upon man as a member of a specific class or group; and so on, down to those which had to do with a man only insofar as he was an individual. In sum, the content of art was "reality in general in the extent to which reality arouses interest in various forms, intellectual, moral, religious, political, and the aesthetic properly so called" (33). The content of art, then, Croce concluded, was anything that did not bore men, or everything that "interested" them, for whatever reason.

Leaving aside the Schopenhauerian cast of this definition of the content of art as "the interesting" as such, not to mention the implicit assimilation of philosophy and science to aesthetics, I see here the basis for Croce's later attempt to define "true" historicism as humanism rendered historically self-conscious, for Croce's definition of the content of art is nothing but the humanist "nihil humani a me alienum puto" restated in somewhat different terms. For him, the content of art and the content of human knowledge reduce to the same thing: everything that is humanly interesting. It is not surprising, therefore, that he defined the "historically interesting" as anything that has already happened—that is, the actual rather than the possible. This was pure Aristotelianism, even in its terminology, for in Croce's view, history "stands as the representation of what really happened over against [representation of] the possible" (35).

This meant that, whereas the artist was permitted to project, on the basis of imagination, the world of events which might have occurred or might yet occur, the historian was limited to the representation of events that had actually taken place. The artist had to respect certain criteria of truth, to be sure, but these criteria were to be found in what the imagination permitted him to envision. By contrast, the historian was governed by criteria of truth presupposed by the attempt to represent the actual. Thus, the historian's principal danger was not falsification but imagination, unfounded speculation, flights beyond the facts contained in records of past actualities—that is to say, philosophy of history in any form.

Since the historian's main task is representation of the actual, his sifting of the documents is merely preparatory to the fulfillment of his principal aim: narration. Research, the criticism of documents, interpretation of the documents, and understanding them—all this was *propaedeutic* to the construction of the narrative; and none of this was history properly so-called, any more than an artist's preliminary sketches and drafts could be properly called works of art. Where there is no narrative, Croce said, there is no historiography. In short, historians did not write in order to "explain"; they wrote in order to "represent," to tell what had actually happened in the past—just as Ranke had said they must try to do.

To be sure, Croce conceded that, in the majority of cases, the historian did not succeed in producing anything like a perfect narrative; great masterpieces were as rare in historiography as they were in painting, and finally just as imperfect in their approximations to the ideal type of the genre. This was especially so in history, because the historian worked under the imperative to tell the truth about past events in the face of incomplete evidence. In the greater number of cases, Croce said, historians would have to remain content with what were essentially "preparatory studies or fragmentary expositions marred by discussions, doubts, and reservations." The historian had to look at the world in the partial light of the new moon, "not in the fullness of the noonday sun, like the artist." (38) Thus, one could point to many *perfect pages* of history but not to a single *perfect work*. The sole imaginable perfect history could be written by God alone; but, since there was no God, the historian had to take His place as best he could. He should work, however, with the Faustian awareness that "the book of the past is sealed with seven seals" (39). To the historian, Croce said, it was given "to break a seal here and there and to read some part of that book," but it would never be revealed to him in all its fullness (*ibid.*).

It is difficult not to think of Croce's "revolution" in historical sensibility as a retrogression, since its effect was to sever historiography from any participation in the effort—just beginning to make some headway as sociology at the time—to construct a general science of society. But it had even more deleterious implications for historians' thinking about the artistic side of their work. For, while Croce was correct in his perception that art is a way of knowing the world, and not merely a physical response to it or an immediate experience of it, his conception of art as literal *representation* of the real effectively isolated the historian as artist from the most recent—and increasingly dominant—advances made in representing the different levels of consciousness by the Symbolists and post-Impressionists all over Europe.

Croce's conception of art was dominated by the presuppositions of Renaissance perspectivism—that is to say, by *visual* figuralism. Although he regarded the imagination as the source and origin of the aesthetic apprehension of the world, his distaste for Vitalist irrationalism and Positivist abstractionism led him to view nonrepresentational art as merely bad art or, what amounted to the same thing in his view, as representation of the "ugly," and hence not art at all.

Croce had a dead ear for music, and in poetry his taste ran to classical forms. Romanticism in all its manifestations was to him merely want of form, or imperfect art. And so his resistance to any kind of post-Impressionistic, Symbolist, or Expressionistic art is understandable. Like most Mediterranean aestheticists, he valued line over color, chiaroscuro over painterly effects. Where there was no line, there was no art, for art was the dawing of a line through the chaos of sense impressions, the imposing of a form on the formless reality given to sense, the carving out of stable, concrete images in a world that threatened to fall into meaningless process at every instant. Thus, for him, if art was a mode of cognition and history was a form of art, it followed that historical representations were "true" only insofar as they were "clear" and "accurate" representations of the real—that is to say, the only acceptable epistemological basis for historiography was an empiricism of the sort that Ranke had construed as the sole acceptable principle of historical research.

To be sure, Croce did not accept the precritical principles, or enabling postulates, of Ranke's brand of empiricism; and, in his *History as Thought and as Action* (1938), he criticized Ranke for his lack of "clarity" and his want of philosophical self-consciousness. But, finally, the execution of Ranke's work, not its basic purpose, offended Croce. Ranke was a fuzzy thinker who used imperfectly defined concepts for rendering his judgments on specific epochs, individuals, institutions, and values of the past and present. However, in his desire *merely* to "tell what happened" in its individuality and concreteness, as it *really* happened, in a pleasing *narrative form*, Ranke carried out the task which made history a specific form of art and not a form of philosophy, science, or religion.

In his later work, Croce stressed the link between historical knowledge and philosophy, but even here he subserved his conviction that history was a *clear* representation of the real in its concreteness and particularity. Philosophy was, he began to maintain in the early 1900s, the "method" of history, for it provided the critical concepts by which adequate historical judgments could be rendered. But these judgments were singular in nature, limited to finite, discretely delineated segments of the historical past; in no case could they be extended to serve as judgments on history-in-general. For history-in-general was, like "philosophy of history" itself, a contradiction in terms in Croce's philosophical economy. Why he held this view, which undercut the authority of both sociology and philosophy as possible guides to the construction of a science of history, was already evident in the essay of 1893.

In the essay of 1893 and the defenses of it which appeared in the nine years following, Croce continued to maintain that art was a form of cognition and that history could be subsumed under the general concept of art. But it became increasingly clear to him that, if art in general was the representation of the *possible,* and history was the representation of the *actual,* there must be some criterion by which the historian could distinguish between the possible and the actual. To what criterion did the historian appeal when he said to the Romantic novelist: "What you say happened in the Middle Ages is only a figment of your imagination; what you tell us is interesting, and it might possibly have happened, but it did not happen as you believe it to have happened, but in *this* way. *This* is what *really happened* in the Middle Ages"?

Rankean historism held that this criterion was provided by the documents, but a great Romantic novelist might know the documents as intimately as the historian, might have included in his narrative everything that appeared in the documents in its integrity, and might have appealed to his imagination only to provide the interstices of the narrative, to provide transitions and junctures, and to give to the whole the pleasing form demanded by his readers. Moreover, did not the historian himself have to provide transitions and junctures by some imaginative act, and did he not desire to give to his narratives the same wholeness and internal consistency aspired to by the novelist?

The conflict between the Romantic novelist and the historian arose most crucially at precisely the point where imagination was forced to take over from the chronicle, at the point where it was necessary to ask: "What do the facts given in the chronicle *mean?*" And if the historian were going to be permitted to say, as he often did say, to the Romantic novelist: "What you say *might* have happened, it *could* have happened, but it *did not* happen in the way that you say it did," then there had to be some knowledge of how the world "really" operated, by which such a judgment, even in the face of lack of evidence to decide the issue either way on factual grounds, could be made and decided in favor of the historian. In short, historical judgment required appeal to some theory of how "reality" functioned, a knowledge of the world, and, more specifically, a knowledge of the world of human affairs, which gave to the historian a sense that the world which appeared to him as past was *probably what it appeared to be to him* and not what it was *imagined to be by the novelist.*

As Croce conceived it, there were two possible candidates for the role of arbiter of what was real and what was only imaginary in history: Materialism and Idealism, or, more specifically, Materialism in its Marxist form and Idealism in its Hegelian form. Both offered fully articulated philosophies of history which claimed to provide rules by which the historian could distinguish between significant and insignificant data in history and by which a precise "meaning" could be ascribed to any sequence of historical events in any sector of society or culture. Both claimed to go beyond the Rankean attempt merely to tell *what had happened* and to supply a conceptual apparatus by which to tell not only *why it happened* but also *what it portended* for the future of mankind.

Given Croce's conviction that history was an intuitive apprehension of reality in its individuality and concreteness, it is obvious why he could not accept the views of either Marx or Hegel in their entirety. But he could not ignore them, for theirs were the main alternatives to an inadequate defense of history's autonomy by Ranke and to an inadequate defense of the aestheticist conception of history offered by Nietzsche. Marx and Hegel at least regarded history as the cognitive activity which it was, even if they did not recognize that it was a form of art; Nietzsche recognized it as a form of art but did not comprehend that it was also a form of cognition. A criticism of the conceptual apparatus of Materialism and Idealism, by which too restrictive a form was given to historical knowledge, was therefore necessary. By transferring the conceptual apparatus of Materialism *up*, from below the world, and that of Idealism *down*, from above the world, it might be possible to locate them in the middle range of existence—between matter and mind —where man operated and made his history, to reveal them as the *sociological generalizations* and *philosophical universals* that they respectively were, and thereby to establish their correct functions in the rendering of historical judgments.

✎§ The Aesthetics of Historical Consciousness

Against the fashionable aesthetic theory of his time, which *set art over against* science, philosophy, and history, Croce sought to establish art as the basis of all cognition, and hence as the primitive moment in all characterizations of reality—philosophical, scientific, and historical alike. But his ultimate purpose was to remove history from the ambiguous position, between art on the one hand and science on the other, in which it had been placed by the principal historical theorists of his time. What he did, of course, was to remove it from one ambiguous position, between art and science, only to place it in another, between art and philosophy.

History is not, Croce insisted in his *Aesthetics*, a specific mode of consciousness but a *combination* of two distinct modes, artistic consciousness and philosophical consciousness. In order to defend this conception of history, Croce had to draw a rigorous distinction, amounting almost to a dualistic opposition, between art and philosophy. Art was *nothing but* intuition; philosophy was *nothing but* the science of pure concepts. Historians employed concepts to give form and order to their intuitions. Therefore, history had no "form" peculiar to its possible modes of expression. It was not a "form" at all.

History is not form, but content: as form, it is nothing but intuition or aesthetic fact. History does not seek laws nor form concepts; it employs neither induction nor deduction; it is directed *ad narrandum, non ad demonstrandum*; it does not construct universals and abstractions, but posits intuitions. [44]

This did not mean that historians did not "use" concepts; they had to do so in order to "posit" intuitions—that is to say, to construct propositions about what had actually happened in the past. But this was a funcion of the fact that the historian had to use language, and, moreover, *prose* discourse rather than poetic expressions, in order to render his truths. The important point was that history did not *seek* laws, did not *form* concepts, did not *construct* universals or abstractions. It used the concepts of ordinary language to characterize its data, to tell its stories, or construct its dramas. But these concepts, as Croce made clear in the *Aesthetics*, were nothing but the rules of grammar and syntax that were necessary for the construction of meaningful sentences in ordinary language. To confuse these rules with laws, universals, or abstractions, and, more particularly, to imagine that these rules might be extracted from the narratives actually written, in order to serve as the basis for a putative *science* of history, was not only to misinterpret the nature of historical knowledge but to display a profound misunderstanding of the nature of language as well.

In the concluding chapter of the theoretical section of his *Aesthetics*, Croce undertook to justify the subtitle of that work: "As Science of Expression and of General Linguistic." Historians of historical thinking have tended to overlook the importance of one side of Croce's work by stressing the "expressive" notion of art which is signaled in the subtitle and ignoring the implications of the "linguistic" aspect. But, while it is important to emphasize Croce's conception of history as a form of art, and art as a form of expression (rather than as a simple reflex action), it is equally important to note Croce's insistence on what he called "The Identity of Linguistics and Aesthetics." As he put it in the concluding chapter of the *Aesthetics*, "Philosophy of language and philosophy of art are the same thing" (234). This implies that, for Croce, linguistics provided the model by which what we mean by "historical knowledge" is to be understood. For, if linguistics provides the model of what we mean by art, and history is a form of art, it follows that linguistics gives us a model for comprehending what is meant by historical knowledge. Croce's theory of language, then, lies at the heart of his whole philosophy of history.

Croce's theory of language is holistic, Organicist, and ultimately mimetic. As he put it: "Expression is an indivisible whole. Noun and verb do not exist in themselves, but are abstractions made by our destroying the sole linguistic reality, which is *the proposition*" (240). This means that the clue to understanding language is syntax. Words, or their components, phonemes and morphemes, or grammatical rules do not provide the key to understanding language, but whole sentences, or their equivalents, do.

By the term "proposition," Croce said he meant "an organism expressive of a complete meaning, from an exclamation to a poem" (*ibid.*). And he went on to argue that language is identical with speech, that it is impossible adequately to distinguish between formal rules of language and the speech actually used in discourse: "Languages have no reality beyond the propositions and complexes of propositions really written and pronounced by given peoples for definite periods" (241). From this he concluded that it is impossible to construct a normative grammar for any language, a model language for all languages, or a classification of languages. He even maintained that "translation" from one language to another, or of a proposition from one form of expression to another, is impossible because the only linguistic reality is that which is spoken by individual speakers of that language in the construction of completed propositions.

No two propositions are the same, since the very utterance of any word retroactively "transforms" the meanings of all the words that have come before it (238). This means that languages develop by something like that process of confiscation and reinterpretation which Nietzsche claimed was the most important aspect of historical understanding of all processes in both nature and history.

This theory of language has important implications for the understanding of Croce's aesthetics and, *a fortiori*, his theory of history, for it directs attention to the syntactical dimensions of both—that is to say, to the rules of combination by which the basic units of the linguistic system (lexical and grammatical) and of the historical system (individual men and their institutional groupings) are to be comprehended as dynamic processes. Normally, such rules of combination are thought of as "laws," linguistic or social as the case may be. But Croce denied that linguistic syntax is comprehensible as a "rule-governed" operation. All linguistic usage is "rule-changing" by its very nature. He obliterated the distinction between language and speech. The only language there is, is that which is actually spoken. And the utterance of any sentence is such that it always changes the *entire* linguistic endowment of the speech community in which it is uttered, in the same way that, in the utterance of a sentence, each successive word transforms retroactively the function of all the words coming before it until a period or exclamation point is put at the end. The sentence thus contrived constitutes a closed universe of meaning, *the* meaning of which is *nothing but* the form of its utterance.

So, too, in his theory of art as intuition (perception), which is at one and the same time expression, and as expression, which is at one and the same time an intuition, where there is no intuition, there can be no expression, and vice versa. The *meaning* of the work of art is the *form* that it finally assumes when the artist is finished with it. It has no meaning outside itself; it is *pure* expression, the representation of an intuition governed only by the notion of what is imaginably possible. It can be a product of pure fantasy or an attempt to report an imaginative response to external reality. One ought not ask of the art object, then, if it is "true" or "good" or "useful," but only if it is "beautiful." And the criterion of beauty here appealed to is precisely the same as that used to determine whether a sentence is meaningful or not—that is to say, whether it expresses an intuition adequately or not.

Each work of art stands to every other work of art in precisely the same relationship that every sentence ever uttered stands to every other sentence. We can ask only whether it was possible to utter such a sentence and, if it was possible to utter it, how it bears upon, modifies, changes, or augments the syntactical possibilities of the linguistic protocol that a whole set of artistic statements represent.

Every new work of art represents a retroactive redefinition of every work of art that preceded it, for it represents—if it truly is a work of art and not an uncontrolled ejaculation of emotion—a contribution to our knowledge of what this linguistic protocol is capable of permitting artists to say. Thus, each new work of art represents a filling out of our knowledge of what is possible for the human spirit to imagine and is, therefore, a further justification of our faith in our imaginative powers.

And the same is true of historical works. Each new one represents a filling out of the possibilities of expression of the linguistic protocols of the form of expression called "historical," that combination of art and philosophy by which intuitions are simultaneously affirmed and judged under the categories of the probable or verisimilar. History is concerned not with possibilities but with actualities, with what actually happened. Hence, it requires some rule by appeal to which imagined intuitions can be distinguished from real ones. Historical statements are not merely expressions of an intuition, but expressions of intuitions of *actualities*, or, to be more precise, actualizations. History deals in *real* events, in facts, rather than in *imagined* events. It therefore requires a syntax of its own by which to contrive its statements about what the facts mean. And this syntax is nothing but the rules of ordinary prose discourse of the culture or civilization to which the historian himself belongs.

In some way that is unclear, ordinary language represents to Croce the memory of the wisdom of the race. One can say about historical events only what it is possible to say in the ordinary prose discourse of one's native language. And Croce, like Wittgenstein later, but with a different intention, held that what cannot be said, cannot be said; and it cannot be whistled or danced either. This is the basis of Croce's hostility to all forms of jargon or technical language which might be introduced into a historical account. Much more than representing a simple confusion of science, philosophy, or religion with history, the introduction of any form of artificial terminology into historical discourse represented for him an undeniable evidence of historiographical illiteracy, a want of understanding of the syntax of historical discourse, a failure of faith in the adequacy of ordinary language to represent the real world actually lying before consciousness as a set of concrete actulizations or matters of fact.

The philosopher might reflect on thought as expressed in language and dilate on the nature of the concepts by which thought constructed coherent and logically consistent systems of explanation and understanding. Indeed, in logic, which Croce defined as the science of *pure* concepts, the philosopher possessed a methodology and a syntax for the expression of the conceptual truths discovered by such reflection, *verités de raison* as against the *verités de fait* in which the historian dealt. But the application of the truths derived by logical analysis of pure concepts to the truths derived by intuition of concrete facts, in order to force them into the patterns of logical entailment provided by philosophical reflection, produced nothing but errors, monstrosities, or fantasies. All errors in history, no less than in artistic criticism, begin, Croce said, "when we try to deduce the expression from the concept" (59). We can find "likenesses" between individual works of art, but these are "family likenesses" (119), not generic or typical ones. In history, as in art, we simply "employ vocables and phrases; we do not establish laws and definitions" (63).

This conception of ordinary prose discourse as the paradigm of historical discourse constitutes nothing less than a defense of common sense as the "theory" or "method" of historical synthesis. It provides not only a model of the form that all historical statements must take, but also a model of the nature of the whole historical process. The historical process is like a sentence still in process of being articulated. We live, as it were, within a cosmic sentence not yet completed, the ultimate meaning of which we cannot possibly know, since we do not know what "words" will be spoken in the future, but the order and harmony of which we can infer from our own ability to make sense of what has "been spoken" thus far in accordance with the canons of common sense and our ability to characterize "what happened" in ordinary speech. What we can derive from reflection on the words that have already been spoken is the grammar and syntax of that "spirit" which manifests itself and, as it were, speaks through human thought and action, though to distinguish between this "spirit" and its manifestations in human thought and action would be a mistake, in Croce's view, precisely analogous to that mistake which arises when we try to distinguish between what a work of art *is* and what it *means*. Its being *is* its meaning.

And as it is in the realm of art, so it is in the realm of historical being. Men *are* what they think, feel, and do; what they think, feel, and do *is* their history. This history is the only "nature" they have. And the only meaning that their history has is to be found in what memory preserves of *what* they thought, felt, and did and what the historian, reflecting on memorials of the past, is able *to say* about what they thought, felt, and did in terms acceptable to common sense and expressible in ordinary educated discourse. The only critical principles that the historian can use in the construction of his narratives, and the only critical principles that can be invoked to assess their adequacy, are those of "verisimilitude and of probability" (47).

◆§ *The Nature of Historical Knowledge: The Justification of Common Sense*

Historical analysis is nothing but the attempt to determine what is the most credible evidence. But what, Croce asked, is "the most credible evidence, save that of the best observers, that is, of those who best remember and (be it understood) have not desired to falsify" (*ibid.*). And from this it follows, he admitted, that the case of the historical skeptic is rendered plausible, since the certainty of history is "never that of science" (48). The certainty of the historian is considerable, but undemonstrable. "The conviction of the historian is the undemonstrable conviction of the juryman, who has heard the witnesses, listened attentively to the case, and prayed Heaven to inspire him. Sometimes, without doubt, he is mistaken, but the mistakes are in a negligible minority compared with the number of occasions when he gets hold of the truth" (*ibid.*). And this permitted Croce to conclude:

That is why common sense (*buon senso*) is right against the intellectualists, in believing in history, which is not a "fable agreed upon," but that which the individual and humanity remember of their past. [*Ibid.*]

One *could*, "in a spirit of paradox," doubt that Greece or Rome ever existed, or that Alexander lived or that a Revolution broke out on July 14, 1789, in France. But against such doubt, Croce raised the following objection: " 'What proof givest thou of all this?' asks the sophist, ironically. Humanity replies 'I remember' " (49).

This is not quite tantamount to saying, with the authors of *1066 and All That*, that the only important facts are those one can remember, but it comes close to it. It does suggest, by linking historical wisdom with common sense and the common memory, that the only thing that can count as a historical fact is that which common sense itself can credit as a "genuine" intuition of the "true" reality. It does not quite absolve historical thinking from any obligation to the critical principles of philosophy and science, especially inasmuch as Croce specifically conceded to philosophy the knowledge of the noumenal world figured in the phenomena credited by common sense as historical reality; but it comes close to that too. The point is that historical thought is definitively disengaged from the kind of typological operations that one associates with the social sciences on the one hand and from the kind of nomological analyses that one associates with the physical sciences on the other. (48ff.) Both of these kinds of comprehension are relegated to the status of *something other than* common sense, which they most certainly are meant to be, but at the same time they are denied entry into historical reflection or are admitted into it only as forms of error.

"True science," Croce said, "cannot be anything but Philosophy." The natural sciences are "not perfect sciences: they are complexes of knowledge, arbitrarily abstracted and fixed." (49) The "concepts of natural science are, without doubt, most useful, but one cannot obtain from them that *system* which belongs only to the spirit" (50–51). From this Croce concluded that the only "pure and fundamental forms of knowledge are two: the intuition and the concept; or Art and Philosophy" (52). History has a place *between* these two pure forms of knowledge, being "as it were, the product of intuition placed in contact with the concept, that is, of art receiving in itself philosophic distinctions, while remaining concrete and individual." All other forms of knowledge are, he insisted, "impure, being mingled with extraneous elements of practical origin." (*Ibid.*)

And, in fact, Croce maintained that all scientific generalizations are comprised of pseudo concepts, while all social-scientific ones consist of pseudo typifications. About the nature of the real world, he believed only what common sense permitted him to believe—namely, that there are only individual entities in the universe and that all characterizations of those entities which assert anything more than what common sense and ordinary speech permit one to say about them are "fictitious." History is not "a fable agreed upon," to be sure, but religious "myths," scientific "laws," and social-scientific "generalizations" are "fabulous" in nature. The most that they can claim is convenience or utility for the prosecution of certain practical tasks. Their authority is limited, therefore, temporally and spatially in a way that historical narratives are not. Like great art, great history (history that is the product of a noble intuition) is eternally valid.

Great history is eternally valid, but inevitably flawed. Moreover, it is hobbled in a crucial way, for Croce denied that historical knowledge can contribute significantly to anything other than our understanding of the past. It can never render any judgment of a specifically historical nature on "the present," because the historian himself always exists in the interior of a process which resembles an incomplete sentence. That same combination of common sense, the memory of the race, and philosophical self-consciousness which permits the historian self-confidently to report his "intuitions" of the past cannot be used to render a judgment on the nature of his own world, because, in the present, as in the *whole* historical process, there is no *completed* action for him to intuit or to perceive.

Croce himself remained true to this restriction. All of his own historical works, filled with judgments of the widest ranging sorts and on the most profound subjects, end in ambiguity as they approach the historian's own present. And the same is true of the historical sections of his theoretical works, such as the *Aesthetics* and *Theory and History of Historiography*. In these works the history of thought about aesthetics on the one hand and about history on the other is laid out with perfect confidence, the periods are delineated and characterized, the nature of the transitions from one to another period is defined, and the meaning of the whole process is set forth. But the concluding chapters of these works always end in praise of Croce's own "Philosophy of the Spirit" as the principal repository of the wisdom of both philosophy and common sense for living men. And what this philosophy teaches is that neither philosophy nor history can offer counsel for living the individual present life, except in the general categorical imperative to live it *somehow*.

✌§ The Paradoxical Nature of Historical Knowledge

Thus, for example, Croce's most important contribution to historical thought, *The Theory and History of Historiography*, ends with a paradox. In the concluding chapter of the book, Croce surveyed the historical thought of the past century, exposing the dualisms, antitheses, and conflicts which characterized efforts to relate history to art and science, to reconcile history and philosophy of history, to mediate between Idealism and Positivism, and so on. At last, however, he asserted, all these dualisms have been transcended in a new philosophy, which will provide the basis for a "new historiography."

This new philosophy was, of course, nothing other than Croce's own "Philosophy of the Spirit," which he had been elaborating in a succession of books and articles since the early 1890s. Croce characterized this philosophy at the end of his book on historical theory. He offered it as a world view which resolves all paradoxes by simply identifying their conflicting elements as different aspects or moments of a single "spirit." Thus, it *appears* to provide the basis for a Comic conception of history. For example, Croce wrote:

In the philosophy that we have delineated, reality is affirmed to be spirit, not such that it is above the world or wanders about the world, but such as coincides with the world; and nature has been shown as a moment and a product of this spirit itself, and therefore the dualism (at least that which has troubled thought from Thales to Spencer) is superseded, and transcendency of all sorts, whether materialistic or theological in its origin, has also been superseded with it. [312]

This "spirit," according to Croce, has all the attributes of both physical nature and consciousness. It is "both one and diverse, an eternal solution and an eternal problem, and its self-consciousness is philosophy, which is its history, or history, which is its philosophy, each substantially identical with the other" (*ibid.*). And this marvelous identification of things or concepts that are thought to be antithetical, or mutually exclusive, apparently derives from the fact that "consciousness is identical with self-consciousness—that is to say, distinct and one with it at the same time, as life and thought" (312–13). This recognition of the unitary nature of consciousness, of spirit, and of knowledge is what sanctioned, in Croce's view, his hope for a general rebirth or transformation of historical consciousness, evidence of which Croce purported to see all about him—in his own work, but also in that of others, such as Friedrich Meinecke.

At the same time, however, Croce said, it is impossible "to write the history of this philosophy and of this historiography," because it constitutes the style or life form of a whole epoch; and, since this epoch, or period, is not *closed*, but is just opening, "we are not able to describe its chronological and geographical outline, because we are ignorant as to what measure of time it will fill, . . . [and] what extent of countries it will include" (313–14). Moreover, he insisted, "we are unable to limit *logically* what may be its value outside these considerations," because the man of the present is unable yet to describe the limitations of the new philosophy and new historiography, which limitations *will stem precisely from the solutions* they provide for the questions or problems delineated by them. "We are ourselves on the waves and we have not furled our sails in port preparatory to a new voyage." (314)

Thus, the new philosophy permits the men of Croce's time to look forward to a new age of achievement in thought and culture, and to contrive a "new historiography" absolutely superior to any that came before it. But at the same time they are not permitted to turn this new historical consciousness on the study of their own age. Historical consciousness is advanced by being provided with a new philosophical and theoretical basis, but, paradoxically, the evidence of its advancement is found to reside in the recognition that historical consciousness can say nothing about the age in which it achieves this advance. The tone is Comic, yet reserved; the mood is optimistic, but qualified. The Irony is manifest, but benign.

This conception of the condition of Western historical consciousness anticipated Croce's characterization of European culture and society after World War I. His *History of Europe in the Nineteenth Century* (1931) carried an epilogue in which he was constrained to admit that all the forces of violence, sadism, irrationalism, materialism, and egotism that had existed in the nineteenth century appeared to have re-emerged from World War I strengthened rather than diminished.

Even pessimism and the voices of decadence, which were heard in pre-war literature, are now heard once more, and are preaching the downfall of the West or even of the human race, which, after trying to rise from the animal to man, is about to relapse (according to the new philosophers and prophets) into the life of the beast. [353]

All this was "a fact," Croce said, and it would be useless to deny it or to restrict its significance to one country, social group, or circle of intellectuals. But precisely *because* it was "fact" it offered an occasion for hope. As fact, this condition "has to fulfill a function in the development of the spirit, in social and human progress, if not as a direct creator of new values, at least as material and stimulus for the strengthening, deepening and widening of ancient values" (353–54). This "function," however, could be seen only by some *future* historian, "who will see before him, when it has reached the end of its period, the movement in which we are engaged and whatever it will have led to." But "it cannot be known and judged by us for the very reason that we are engaged in the movement." We shall be able, Croce said, to observe and understand "many things," but we can never perceive "that one which has not yet occurred and the history of which it is in consequence not given us to conceive." (354)

Thus, it appears that, although we can know *that* we represent a new age in both consciousness and practice, we are debarred, by virtue of our very participation in it, from knowing what this new age might consist of. *We can render no responsible judgment on the age in which we ourselves are actors or protagonists.* Moreover, Croce said that *it does not matter* that we are so restricted in our capacity to render a judgment. What "matters" is

that we should take part in [our own historical age] not with contemplation of what cannot be contemplated, but with action according to the role that is incumbent upon each one of us and which conscience assigns and duty commands. [*Ibid.*]

Croce forebade only that which had already been "transcended," the myths of the nineteenth century: Activism, Communism, Transcendentalism, Chauvinism, and so on. In the 1920s, however, he took the revival of these forms of irrationalism as evidence of an essential "energy," a will to a future, and therefore as occasions for actions on behalf of a new life for "liberty." And his history of the nineteenth century closes on the note that had been sounded in the *Theory and History of Historiography*—that is to say, with an admonition to suspend any judgment of the whole while dealing practically, on a day-to-day basis, with its various aspects.

All this, rapidly outlined, is *not prophecy*, for that is forbidden to us and to everyone for the simple reason that it would be vain, *but a suggestion* of what paths moral consciousness and the observation of the present may outline *for those who* in their guiding concepts and in their interpretation of the events of the nineteenth century *agree with the narrative given of them in this history.* [362; italics added]

Others, governed by other ideals, would see the situation differently and accordingly would act differently. Whatever path they choose, however, "if they do so with a pure mind, in obedience to an inner command, they too will be preparing the future well" (*ibid.*). One cannot fault them, whatever path they take, for,

A history inspired by the liberal idea cannot, even in its practical and moral corollary, end with the absolute rejection and condemnation of those who feel and think differently. It simply says to those who agree with it: "Work according to the line that is here laid down to you, with your whole self, every day, every hour, in your every act; and trust in divine Providence, which knows more than we individuals do and works with us, inside us and over us." Words like these, which we have often heard and uttered in our Christian education and life, have their place, like others from the same source, in the "religion of liberty." [*Ibid.*]

&§ *The Ideological Implications of Croce's Idea of History*

Croce was much criticized by Liberals, Radicals, and even Conservatives for the ambiguity of his moral position with respect to the "new forces" that dominated the life of his time, especially Fascism, which he resisted by his example but could not fault unequivocally on principle. Because it was a "fact," it therefore had to be considered to be a factor in the new life that would presumably take shape "beyond" its transient career. What, his critics asked, was the use of a "self-consciousness" that was at once "philosophical" and "historical," if it could render no judgment on anything except that which was *eternal* on the one hand and *past* on the other, and vested the authority to act as one pleased in the present, in the conviction that, whatever one did, if one acted with sufficient "inner" conviction, one would contribute ultimately to a freer life in the future? What had happened to the moral self-certitude and the optimism of the philosopher who had announced before the war the birth of a new consciousness, superior to anything produced in the nineteenth century by virtue of its supersession of all dualism and all transcendence?

Actually, Croce's critics failed to register adequately the qualification he had placed on philosophy's capacity to know reality and history's power to represent it truthfully. At the conclusion of his *Theory and History of Historiography*, Croce denied that men could judge with any certitude the nature of their own age. In his *Philosophy of the Practical*, the present is remitted to the governance of the fourth of the "moments" in which spirit manifests itself other than as the good, the true, and the beautiful. Croce called this fourth moment of the spirit, which he claimed was his most original contribution to philosophy, the moment of the "practical." In the actual living of their lives men could hope for no direction from art, philosophy, history, or science. They had to be governed by their apprehension of their own interests, needs, and desires, governed only by their intuition of the "practicality" or "impracticality" of any given project they might be considering as a course of action. Artistic sensibility gave them the world lying before them in individual "intuitions" or perceptions organized as forms. Science permitted them to organize these intuitions under the categories of cause-effect relationships for the prosecution of certain practical tasks. Philosophy, the science of pure concepts, gave to them the critical powers to utilize these intuitions for other, unpractical, purely intellectual purposes. Historical knowledge permitted them to contemplate previous human efforts to comprehend the world and to act in it and against it, and provided the material for the consideration of the operations of human thought and action in different times, places, and circumstances so as to permit generalizations about the nature of consciousness (or spirit) in conceptual (philosophical) terms.

But history could not provide direction for action in the present, because history as a form of knowledge was knowledge only of the *particular*, never of the *universal*, and not even of the *general*. Those who tried to generalize about the whole set of particular facts that made up the historical account, by abstraction or statistical aggregation, in the manner of sociologists, actually engaged in a pseudo-scientific form of reflection. Their generalizations had to be assessed in terms of the practical considerations that motivated them to arrange a given group of facts in one way rather than another. The authority of such generalizations, then, was not historical, but *only* sociological.

It was much the same for those who sought to submit the data of history to conceptualization in such a way as to extract a "universal" content from their phenomenal form as a chaos, in the manner of Hegel or Comte. Here, too, the kind of authority that was actually being appealed to was nonhistorical, and specifically philosophical. Even though the conceptual organizing principles of the analysis might be turned upon historical facts, and the generalizations contrived might be attended by what were purported to be illustrative examples of its principles taken from history, in reality, Croce maintained, one could neither conceptualize history nor generalize from it. Historical knowledge was *nothing but* knowledge of particular events in the past, data raised to the status of knowledge by virtue of the historian's identification of them as classes of phenomena and organized as elements of a narrative. As such, history was a *combination* of philosophical knowledge (knowledge of concepts) and art (intuitions of particulars).

Historical accounts were *nothing but* sets of existential statements, of the form "something happened," linked together so as to constitute a narrative. As such, they were, first, *identifications* (of *what* happened) and, second, *representations* (of *how* things happened). This meant that, finally, history was a *special* form of art, which differed from "pure" art by virtue of the fact that the historian disposed the categories of "real-unreal" in addition to the normal artistic categories of "possible-impossible." The historian as a dispenser of knowledge could take thought only as far as the assertion that such and such had happened or had not happened. He could never dilate on *what might have happened* in the past *if* so and so had *not* happened, and more important, on what *might yet happen* in the future *if* one did so and so in the present. The historian never spoke in the present tense or subjunctive mood, but only in the simple past (more precisely, the Greek aorist) tense and the declarative mood.

Whereas the poet organized his intuitions in terms of the categories of possibility-impossibility, the historian organized his intuitions under the categories of probability-improbability, but these were the only differences. The class of subject matter (intuitions) was the same for both, and their aims (the representation of these intuitions) were similar. Because their means of representation (language) was the same, their "methods" were identical. The method which poetry shared with history was nothing but the syntactical rules of ordinary speech.

The implications of this conception of historical method were truly significant for the debate over history into which Croce entered in the early 1890s. This notion of historical method implied that historical knowledge could never be used to illuminate present situations or to direct action in the future. Historical consciousness could not, *à la* Hegel, serve as the mediating ground between private and public interests, between tradition and present desire, between innovative and conservative elements in the current cultural order. It could not, *à la* Marx, be appealed to as a means of gaining a perspective on the true nature of the current social or historical situation, so that the relative "realism" of alternative programs of action in that present could be assessed. And it could not, *à la* Nietzsche, provide the grounds for a fictional construction of the world on the basis of which the over-reaching or superseding impulses of the will could be released for their work of construction or destruction, as the case might be.

History "taught" nothing at all, Croce maintained; and the only thing that the theory of history could legitimately teach was that while history gave information about the past, it could never say anything about the true nature of the present world. It could give insights into what had been vital and what had been moribund in any given *past* age, but it could say nothing about what was living and what was dead in the *present* age. Men might determine what was creative and what was destructive in their own age on the basis of privately held preconceptions about what the world was or ought to be, on economic, religious, philosophical, political, or psychological grounds; but they could never find any justification for any course of action by appeal to history.

Their study of the past, of history, might even have its origins in some present interest, problem, or concern; in fact, Croce argued, *all* interest in the past was a function of such present concerns or problems. But insofar as such concerns and problems *dictated* the *form* that knowledge of the past took in a historical narrative, they could only generate errors.

Even though the historian might take present concerns as the point of departure for his investigations of the past, he was not permitted to deduce any general conclusions from the study of the past or to derive implications from the past for the present. For, since historical knowledge was nothing but knowledge of the particular presented in a narrative account of what had actually happened in the past, one could not draw any general conclusions from its study except possibly the manifestly Ironic conclusion that

history is not an idyll, neither is it a "tragedy of horrors" but a drama in which all the actions, all the actors and all the members of the chorus are, in the Aristotelian sense, "middling," guilty-non-guilty, a mixture of good and bad. [*Hist. as the Story of Liberty*, 60]

Or, as Croce put it in *Theory and History of Historiography*:

Not only . . . is history unable to discriminate between facts that are good and facts that are evil, and between epochs that are progressive and those that are regressive, but it does not begin until such antitheses have been superseded and substituted by an act of the spirit which seeks to ascertain what function the fact or the epoch previously condemned has fulfilled—that is to say, what it has pro- duced of its own in the course of development, and therefore what it has pro- duced. And since *all facts* and epochs are productive *in their own way*, not only is not one of them to be condemned in the light of history, but *all are to be praised and venerated*. [90; italics added]

In aestheticizing history, Croce de-ethicized it, although, to be sure, he thought of himself as having raised it to that level of moral self-consciousness which was the highest man might aspire to as a scholar, of having raised it to a position "beyond good and evil," and, in fact, of having permanently de-ideologized it.

Later philosophers of history, laboring under the felt necessity to provide some historically justified condemnation of the totalitarian regimes of the twentieth century, naturally regarded this position as morally agnostic or as a tactical move to discredit the "scientific" historiography of the Marxist Left. And so it appears from my perspective. But it should be remembered that Croce's aim at the time was precisely to deprive history of the authority claimed for it by *all* sectors of the ideological spectrum and to return his- torical studies to the status of an important, but ultimately *second-order*, form of cognition. This aim served well the interests of established social classes and groups, for whom any conceptual analysis of the social and his- torical processes constituted a threat insofar as it might permit the rendering of any judgment on what they regarded as their "natural" position and privileges. If history could be disengaged from political polemics, from science, from philosophy in its traditional forms, and from religion also, and returned to the sanctum of "art," it could be domesticated as a factor in current ideological conflicts.

But, in order for this domestication to be effective, it was necessary to domesticate art itself, to remove from it the "Dionysiac" impulses Nietzsche had put at the very center of the artistic sensibility. Thus, the domestication of historical thought which Croce carried out required, finally, the defense of an aesthetics that was utterly incapable of even recognizing *as art* the whole achievement of post-Impressionism in painting and of the Symbolist movement in literature. Croce showed how historical thinking could be released from an Ironic attitude *with respect to the past*, how it could be rendered ingenuous, even pietistic, where the past was concerned, but only at the expense of forcing the historian to assume the most extreme Irony with respect to everything in his own social and cultural present.

This led many of Croce's followers to conclude that his was a purely relativistic theory of historical knowledge, since, even though the end product was "philosophical" in nature, the original insights on which this knowledge was based were "artistic." But Croce's intentions were anything but to enthrone relativism in place of the naive empiricism of the conventional historian on the one hand and the metahistorical speculations of the philosophers of history on the other. His principal philosophical battles were fought out on the ground of aesthetic theory. From the first to the last, Croce's aim was to redefine the nature of artistic insights in such a way as to constitute them as the basis of whatever knowledge men might have of the real world.

This accounts, in part, for the extreme hostility, amounting to contempt, which Croce showed for Burckhardt in his *History as the Story of Liberty* (1938), a hostility which was much greater than that which he showed for Ranke, whom he condemned only for the naiveté of his "philosophical" understanding. Burckhardt had not erred in viewing history as a form of art; he had erred in his conception of what art was by seeing it as a form of play or narcotic. In a sense, then, Croce's original enemy was Nietzsche and his kind of philosopher, who had misunderstood the nature of art, viewing it as fantasy or inebriant, and who had, as a result, betrayed his generally truthful insight into the "artistic" basis of all knowledge.

I can now characterize the nature of Croce's criticism of all the historians and philosophers of history that preceded him. This criticism followed the method of isolating in a given historian's work the Synecdochic (typological), Metonymical (causal), and Metaphorical ("poetic") elements in it; of determining the roles these modes of consciousness played in dictating the form of the narrative and its content; of designating these modes of conceptualization as the causes of the historian's departure from his proper role as a composer of narratives constituted of concrete facts on the one hand and common sense guided by proper (Crocean) philosophical principles on the other; and, finally, of differentiating between "what is living" and "what is dead" in the thought of the historian or philosopher of history under consideration. This critical principle on the level of epistemology gave to Croce a criterion for identifying errors of emplotment. The narrator is permitted to emplot the historical process not as if it were a Romance, a Tragedy, or a Satire, but only as if it were a Comedy cast in the tone of Irony, Ironic Comedy, or Comic Satire, as the case may be.

The appropriate form of all historical emplotment is Comic inasmuch as the historian is constrained always to show what was living and growing, reproducing and shooting forth, even in the most "decadent" circumstances; he must write of what managed to go on living, even under the most oppressive conditions. He must show that "in death there is life just as in life there is death," but with emphasis on the former paradox rather than on the latter, since "history" is about life and not about death except as a factor *in* life. The Ironic element stems from the fact that "life is death" also, and that everything which is born must die, but not Tragically, since death is a "fact" of life and, like all facts, must be seen as an "occasion" for life's own preservation.

But, again, the historian must not celebrate "life" itself too enthusiastically, must not emplot his histories as if real and enduring resolutions of social conflicts had been achieved or could ever be achieved. Croce refused to begin or end his own major historical works in considerations of what other historians would regard as "epochal" events, in the strict sense of that term, *epokhē*, "stoppage, station, *fixed* point in time." His histories—like Burckhardt's—are *all transition*, low-keyed, gradualistic, low-mimetic, and do not have any inaugurations or resolutions to speak of.

For example, his *History of Europe in the Nineteenth Century* begins *after* the fall of Napoleon, in the drab atmosphere of the Restoration, and ends *before* World War I, in the equally drab atmosphere of the Edwardian age. Croce's intention was to destroy the impression that any teleological process, such as those associated with the *mythoi* of Romance, Comedy, and Tragedy, is at work. The effect was to render unimportant everything that "enthusiasts" thought important, and to elevate the drabber and more mundane aspects of everyday life to the status of genuine achievements, against whatever the irrationalists and intellectualists of the time might have thought of them.

If the "Liberal Age" (1871–1914) seemed "prosaic," Croce said, it was so only because the intellectualists, irrationalists, Socialists and decadents were incapable of appreciating the achievements of the ordinary man, working as best he could to carry out his daily chores and duties. If "false ideals" had come to predominate in the practical life, this was in large part due to the failure of the intellectualists and critics, the poets and philosophers of the age, to embrace warmly and sympathetically the carriers of the age's practical life (*History of Europe*, 323). "False ideals," "irrationalism," "spiritual enfeeblement," and "inner confusion" "might have been overcome by criticism and education" or might simply have "worn themselves out" had they not been fanned to new life by imperialist rivalries on the international scene (*ibid.*).

Thus, World War I appeared not as an "epochal" event but as a result of the combination of a general moral malaise on the one hand and the operations of an irrational will to power on the other. And, far from being a new departure in European affairs, the war, "which had been announced to the peoples with the promise of a general catharsis, in its course and in its end was completely untrue to its promise" (350). Thus, the war itself was not Tragic, either in its outbreak or in the course it ran; it was only *pathetic*. Croce viewed it, as he viewed the whole history of the century preceding it, with the pathos of Irony. This pathos was benign, however, for in his view, the war—like the age which preceded it—offered another "occasion" for creative endeavor. As such, it was to be (qualifiedly) revered and (qualifiedly) criticized at one and the same time, which was all the historian and the philosopher could do.

✒ The Critical Method Applied: The Domesticating Effect of Irony

Explanation as common sense, emplotment in the mode of Ironic Comedy—these represent the essence of Croce's idea of history. The anti-intellectualist and anti-Radical biases are manifest. This idea of history underlies his criticism of all the major philosophers of history that preceded him, the most of important of which were, in his view, Hegel and Vico, who represented examples of the errors of "philosophical" and "poetic" historical thinking respectively. But before Croce embarked on his criticism of Hegel and Vico, he confronted Marx, who represented, to his mind, the most pernicious effort to construct a "scientific" history in nineteenth-century thought. The differences between the way that Croce dealt with Marx on the one hand and the way he dealt with Hegel and Vico on the other are instructive. They demonstrate the essentially domesticating nature of all of his thought about history.

✒ Croce contra Marx

Croce came to grips with Marx only after 1895, when his teacher Antonio Labriola, having abandoned his original Herbartianism, reappeared on Croce's horizon as an advocate of Dialectical Materialism in philosophy and Socialism in politics. Croce claimed to have accorded Marx an open hearing, but, given the position on the "artistic" nature of historical knowledge at which Croce had arrived by 1893, Marx had as little chance of positively affecting Croce as Lenin had of converting the Russian aristocracy. Croce appears to have taken Marx seriously only because Labriola was his advocate. This made the repudiation of Marxism an emotional strain, for it entailed the repudiation of his former "master" Labriola; but the issue was intellectually determined from the beginning. Marx's whole enterprise, which was to fashion laws of historical development, was alien to Croce's conception of history as the study of reality in its individuality and the writing of history as narrative. Still, the encounter with Marxism is instructive, for in it the critical strategy that Croce would apply to every philosophy of history he encountered ever afterward is clearly revealed; moreover, the psychological character of its use as a repetition-compulsion, similar to that used by the defenders of Old Europe against any Radical creed, is clearly manifested.

Croce's first response to his study of Marxism was to dub it "doubly fallicious": in the first place because it was "materialistic"; in the second place because it conceived "the course of history according to a predetermined design" that was little more than a "variation of the Hegelian philosophy of history" (*Come nacque*, 28). Croce granted that Marx's emphasis on the importance of economic forces in human life had been salutary, given the remoteness of the current generation of academic scholars from the realities of the daily life of the masses. But in the end Marxism was neither a valid philosophy of history nor a respectable philosophy in general. It was merely a "canon of empirical interpretation, a recommendation to historians to give attention . . . to economic activity in the life of peoples and to the naive or artificial fantasies caused by it," nothing more and nothing less (30).

Labriola took exception to Croce's conclusions. He accused Croce of being "an intellectual," of being "indifferent to the battles of life," of being interested only in "debates of ideas in books," and, most cuttingly, of being "an industrious man in studying and in writing only in order to escape the boredom which menaced him" (27–28). He also accused Croce of being a slave to a purely *"formal* presupposition, or rather a prejudice" which he could not surmount and which had led him to predecide the issue between himself and Marx.

In response to Labriola's criticisms, Croce returned to the study of Marx's economic and philosophical doctrines. But he emerged from these studies with a judgment that was even harsher than his original one. As an economist, Croce said, Marx had not founded a new doctrine; his work was interesting primarily because it illuminated the relation between workers and owners in capitalist society—that is to say, because of its *historical information* alone. As for the doctrine of surplus value, this was a "result of an eliptical comparison between an abstraction, the completely worker society, which functioned as a type, and [an actual] society, that of private capital" (31). And as for Marx's claim to be both a philosopher and a scientist, he was neither. If he was anything, Croce maintained, Marx was "an arrogant political talent, or perhaps a revolutionary genius, who had given impetus and consistency to the workers' movement by arming it with a historiographical and economic doctrine constructed specifically for it" (37). Actually, Croce went on to say, if Marx had wanted an example of a pseudo science and a pseudo philosophy or a class ideology, he need not have gone to Descartes, Spinoza, Kant, or Hegel to find one: "he had only to look at his own work" (*ibid.*). In the end, Croce held, Marx was nothing but the creator of a new religion, an apostle to the proletariat, but with a gospel that was only destructive, since it threatened "all the ideality of human life" (*ibid.*).

Labriola again responded to Croce's criticism, this time directing his attack at the ideological, and specifically bourgeois, prejudice in it. Actually, Labriola said, Croce was arguing with himself, not with Marx; his sole interest was in the *use* he could make of Marxism, not in finding out what Marxism was all about. Had this not been the case, he noted, it would have been absurd for Croce to maintain that Marx had been unaware precisely and fully of what he was doing. (39) But Croce took refuge in the office of the philosopher. Labriola, he said, was himself interested in the use that could be made of Marxist theories in order to realize the aims of Socialism, while he, Croce, was obliged to determine "what was living and what was dead" in it from a purely philosophical, or theoretical, viewpoint. And the sole "living" element in Marxism was its reminder to historians to take economic activity into account in their studies of the human past. By contrast, the "dead" elements were the economic theory of surplus value, which purported to expose the injustice of capitalist economic practices, and the philosophical-historical doctrine of Dialectical Materialism, which provided a rationale for the revolutionary transformation of capitalist society.

Croce later argued that the "crisis of Marxism" which erupted in the late 1890s provided empirical proof of its philosophical inadequacies. The revisionist dispute was a necessary outcome of a philosophically sophisticated examination of Marx's doctrines. As long as Marxism was studied only by autodidactic workingmen and their enthusiastic intellectual supporters, its philosophical inadequacies remained unexposed. As soon as sophisticated critics like Sorel, Bernstein, and Croce himself turned to an examination of it, Croce said, its philosophical authority dissolved. Not even the recrudescence of Marxism between 1917 and 1938 changed Croce's views on the matter. Writing in the latter year, he said that the revival of Marxism merely reflected the propaganda activities of the Bolsheviks and the low level of philosophical culture which prevailed in Russia.

Croce claimed partial credit for what he took to be the definitive dissolution of Marxism as a philosophical and scientific theory. He continued to write against it, but always in the same vein. In effect, his critical method functioned as a form of cultural innoculation which was much more effective than the wholesale repudiation of nineteenth-century anti-Marxist critics. By granting Marxism a minimal relevance to the study of history, it was possible to appear open-minded about it while simultaneously excising from it the very doctrines which made it a distinctively Radical world view. This tactic of granting that there was something "living" in every attempt to explain history, and of designating as "dead" whatever it was that gave to the attempt the aspect of a new or Radical movement, was the strength of that new historicism of which Croce was the leading twentieth-century theoretician. Ultimately, it was a form of castration by historicization; it permitted a class and a culture under attack from within and without to treat everything inimical to it as if it were already "dead," as if it had already been consigned to history, its place established and its authority as a creed for living men negated.

ᴥᔭ Croce contra Hegel

In retrospect, Croce's repudiation of Marxism appears inevitable. Given his temperament, his class loyalties, and his conviction that history was a form of art, the rejection of Marx appears predictable before the event. His encounter with Hegel is somewhat more difficult to characterize. Croce had been a kind of Idealist from the beginning, even though he had regarded himself as a "realistic" Idealist—that is to say, an Idealist who denied the existence of any transmundane sphere of essences standing over against the world given by sense perception. What, then, did his realistic Idealism consist of? Croce gave his answer to this question in 1906, in his book *What is Living and What is Dead in Hegel's Philosophy*, which moved him one step closer to consolidation of his final position by that process of qualified rejection which characterized him and his age.

In Croce's judgment, Hegel was and remained *the* philosopher, as Schopenhauer had been to Burckhardt. To Croce, Hegel was a *naturally* philosophical intelligence; in fact, if anything, he was *too* philosophical, for he treated universals—that is, *a priori* concepts—which were the sole possible objects of philosophical reflection, as principles of historical interpretation. Hegel had not seen that philosophy is concerned solely with concepts and the formal relations among concepts; that philosophy has its own organon, logic, the science of pure concepts; and that philosophical generalizations have to be limited to concepts and can never be extended to cover events. Hegel's attempt to descend from the knowledge of concepts to actual—natural, social, human—events by deduction, to try to impose a pattern on historical events, was as mistaken as Marx's attempts to treat empirical social and economic generalizations as universals. Marx's generalizations were valid only insofar as they covered actual social and economic practices in a given historical society; Hegel's generalizations covered the much wider field of the mind's operations. But neither could be used as an instrument of historical generalization, where the universalizing impulse was permitted only under the most carefully qualified conditions.

Still, Hegel opened the way to a distinctively modern, because it was a historically self-conscious, humanism. In principle, Hegel had been the consistent enemy of all transcendentalism, the immanentist *par excellence* and hence an essentially historicist thinker. Above all, he had seen through the fallacies of every monistic and dualistic solution to the problem of the relation between appearances and reality. Hegel had discovered that the sole object of thought and action was not some unitary submundane structure of which mind was an epiphenomenon, nor some transmundane spirit of which matter was a weak reflection or manifestation, nor, finally, a fractured totality divided between mind and matter or between spirit and body. The "universal" object sought by philosophy from the beginning was not *beyond*, *beneath*, or *below* human experience; it was the world itself in its concreteness.

At the same time, however, Hegel had conserved the truths—the *partial* truths—contained in both monism and dualism. The unity of the world perceived by monists and the sets of opposites postulated by dualists were valid conceptions of the world. But the unity and the opposition were different aspects of the single, evolving or developing reality. The world was both one and internally differentiated. The unity of the world did not contradict the fact of its internal opposition; rather, the world was *a unity with opposition within it*. (Croce, *Saggio*, 15)

This internal differentiation of the parts within the whole accounted for the world's capacity to evolve, and made of the world a becoming, a history. Unity and opposition thus appear in Hegel's thought as aspects of a totality which has three moments: being, nothing, and becoming (17). The subsumption of unity and opposition, being and nothing, affirmation and negation, to a third term, "synthesis"—that is, becoming—was the glory, as well as the burden, of Hegelian philosophy. In the truth of this perception lay the efficacy of the Hegelian dialectic as the logic of reality; at the same time, Hegel's mechanical application of his threefold schema to the data of nature and history generated all of those false totalistic systems of which Croce and his generation were the irreconcilable enemies.

According to Croce, Hegel's interpreters had uniformly misunderstood him. They had overlooked Hegel's Tragic conception of reality and seen only his optimism (40); they had taken this sublime, transpolitical vision for conservatism (44–45); and they had consistently viewed him as an idealist, when in reality he was one of the purist historicists who had ever lived (46–47). Among earlier philosophers only Vico had come close to anticipating Hegel's insights in profundity and amplitude (50–52). There was, however, an error at the heart of Hegel's whole system: the attempt to apply the *philosophical truth* contained in the discovery that reality was both one and internally differentiated to actual events in the world. "In Hegel's system," Croce said, "where the infinite and the finite are fused into one, and good and evil constitute a single process, history is the reality of the Idea, and the spirit does not exist outside of its historical development." This insight rendered every fact of history, because it was a "fact of the idea," a "sacred" fact to Hegel. This forced historians to give to every fact the same sympathy and the same serious study and promoted a genuinely historicist appreciation of history. This was the "healthy" side of Hegel's philosophy, but it had to be distinguished rigorously from the "sick" side, which consisted of the attempt to apply the threefold schema of the dialectical model to the analysis of the relations among the many concrete facts that make up history. This "sick" side generated that host of "philosophies of life"—from "neurotic mysticism" and "insincere religiosity," through an "antihistorical barbarism," to "Positivism" and the "new Jacobinism"—which afflicted Europe at the dawn of the twentieth century. (48–54)

According to Croce, therefore, in order to salvage "what was living" in Hegel, it was not enough merely to distinguish Hegel the philosopher from Hegel the historian and scientist, as conventional Hegelian scholarship had sought to do (54). On the contrary, Hegel's errors as historian and scientist were the results of a fundamental *philosophical* mistake. This mistake had to be exposed, and Croce claimed to expose it by use of the critical method which he called the method of *distinzione*—that is to say, "discrimination"— and which would constitute the basis of his general philosophy and his philosophy of history for the next half-century.

The method of "discrimination" required the recognition that while *concepts* could be *opposed*—for example, as good to evil or right to wrong— *things* could be only *distinguished* from one another. This did not strike at the essential unity of the whole; it merely suggested that different ways of characterizing the whole were necessary when speaking of things and when speaking of concepts. "For example," Croce said,

we speak of the spirit or spiritual activity in general; but we also speak at every moment of the particular forms of this spiritual activity. And while we consider them all to be constitutive of the complete spirituality . . . , we are concerned not to confuse one with the other; thus we criticize anyone who judges art by moral criteria, or morality by artistic criteria, or truth by the criteria of utility, and so on. [56]

If, in the process of trying to grasp the whole, we are inclined to forget the necessity of "discrimination," we have only to *look* at life in order to be reminded of it immediately. For "life" always presents itself to us as *spheres of activity*, which are extrinsically distinguished one from another, as economic, scientific, moral, and artistic, and as *individual men*, who are distinguished one from another by their callings as poets, workers, statesmen, philosophers, and so on. Not even philosophy *exists* per se, but is always offered as a specific aspect of philosophy: as aesthetics, logic, ethics, and so on. Indeed, the whole of philosophy is internally distinguishable; each philosophy is *a* philosophy distinct from every other.

The whole series of distinct entities which make up the historical process, Croce went on to say, constitutes "a nexus and a rhythm" which ordinary theories of classification cannot adequately characterize. In conventional systems of classification, one postulates a concept and then introduces another concept extraneous to the first; then the two concepts are used as the basis of a division. The second concept is used, Croce said,

almost as a knife with which one cuts a cake (i.e., the first concept) into so many pieces, which remain separated from one another. The procedure yields the result, the disappearance of the unity of the universal. Reality is torn into so many extraneous elements, each of which is indifferent to the others; and philosophy, the thought of the unity, is rendered impossible. [57]

Croce called the correct way of discriminating between the individual entities that make up the reality and of uniting them at the same time into a unity the "classificatory schema of degrees," the credit for which he gave to Hegel. In this schema individual entities are united, not extrinsically and indifferently, but by the "implication" of a lower degree in a higher one. This classificatory schema was the source of Hegel's power of relating such different subjects as literature, law, morality, politics, religion, and so on. In philosophical analysis it was triumphant, for in it the primary concepts of thought were both opposed to one another and united dialectically.

Hegel showed that the fundamental modalities of human experience have to be studied with different conceptual apparatuses. Thus:

The true does not stand to the false in the same relationship in which it stands to the good; nor the beautiful to the ugly in the same relationship in which it stands to philosophical truth. Life without death and death without life are two opposed illusions, whose truth *is* life, a nexus of life *and* death, [a combination] of itself *and* of its opposite. But truth without goodness and goodness without truth are not two illusions which are annulled in a third term: they are false conceptions which are resolved in a nexus of degrees, in a nexus in which truth and goodness are distinct and at the same time united. So too goodness without truth is impossible, as much as it is impossible to will the good without thinking; truth without goodness is possible, but only in the sense which conforms with the philosophical theory of the precedence of the theoretical spirit over the practical, with the theorems of the autonomy of art and the autonomy of science. [61–62]

This theory of individual entities serves as the basis of Croce's organismic holism, which in turn is the basis of his simultaneous rejection and acceptance of every theory of the whole in the history of philosophy. "The organism," he said, is a struggle of life against death; but the members of the organism are not therefore in struggle one against the other, the hand against the foot, or the eye against the hand. Spirit is development, history, and therefore being and non-being together, that is, becoming. But the spirit *sub specie aeterni* which is the subject of philosophy, is ideal history, eternal and extra-temporal, the series of eternal forms of that birth and death, which, as Hegel said, is itself never born and never dies. [62]

To forget this *"punto essenziale,"* Croce warned, is to run the risk of falling into egregious error.

But Hegel had forgotten it; he had failed to keep clear the difference between opposites and distinctions (*distinti*). "He conceived the nexus of gradations in the mode of dialectical opposites; and applied to this nexus the triadic form which is proper [only] to the synthesis of opposites" (64). In other words, he applied to history a mode of analysis appropriately applied only to philosophical concepts. "The theory of distinctions and the theory of opposites became the same thing for him" (*ibid.*). The result was that, in his accounts of the history of philosophy, of nature, and of history properly so-called, Hegel tried to reduce the complex data of their fields to the triadic schema of thesis, antithesis, and synthesis. And, in four chapters of his essay on Hegel, Croce chronicled what he called "The Metamorphosis of Errors" in the fields of philosophy, art and language, natural philosophy, and history in Hegel's work.

Croce's critique of where Hegel's philosophy of history went wrong has special importance for the present study. Needless to say, it hinged upon the charge that Hegel, having failed to perceive the autonomy of art, had necessarily failed to understand the autonomy of history. But, in this critique, Croce stressed the dialectical relationship of the concept of history to the concept of philosophy. "History," he wrote, "differently from art, presupposes philosophical thought as its basis" (89); that is to say, history presupposes the whole which is reality in its concreteness. But, he went on, "like art, history finds its material by intuition" (*ibid.*)—that is to say, by perception of individual concrete entities. And this is why, he concluded, "history is always narration" (the telling of a story), "and never theory and system, even though it has its basis in theory and system" (*ibid.*). This is why one could insist that historians study the documents on the one hand and clearly formulate their ideas of reality and life on the other, "especially those aspects of life which they take up for historical treatment" (89–90). This permitted Croce to say that historiography could never be anything but "scientifically rigorous" in one of its aspects—that is, in its preliminary gathering of its data—even while it remained "a work of art" in the other—that is, in its narration of what it had found. But the content of the historical narrative had to be distinguished from its form. "If all the works of history," Croce noted, "were reduced to their simplest expression," it would be possible to express them all in the form of the "historical judgment," the paradigm of which is "something happened (e.g., Caesar was murdered, Alaric devastated Rome, Dante composed the *Divine Comedy*, etc.)" (90). Analysis of these propositions, Croce maintained, reveals that each of them contains "an intuitive element, which functions as a subject, and logical elements, which function as predicates. The former would be, for example, Caesar, Rome, Dante, the *Divine Comedy*, and so on; the latter, the concepts of murder, of devastation, of artistic composition, and so forth," (*Ibid.*)

The point was that history could yield a "conceptual science" of a purely empirical nature, a sociology, if one decided to build toward a theory of types and classes of historical phenomena; but such a science could not be substituted for the conceptual science that underlies and constitutes the data themselves—that is to say, philosophy. Also, Croce granted, historical considerations *could* issue in philosophy if one decided to pass from the particular to the "theoretical elements" which underlie and make possible a consideration of the particular. But the barrier between reflection on the universal and perception of the particular is insurmountable. Thus, he said, one either does philosophy or one does history; a "philosophy of history" is a contradiction in terms. The attempt to produce such a monstrosity could result only in the negation of the kind of history written by the historians, which was, in Croce's view, precisely what Hegel's philosophy of history amounted to.

Hegel had tried to remain true to the facts, but his dedication to his effort to "conceive" history dialectically betrayed his aim at every turn. From it issued the fragmentary and temporary value that he accorded to every nation, religion, people, and individual he dealt with; to him, the negative element always overrode the positive element in their accomplishments. They were inevitably *aufgehoben* (transcended, annulled), and hence had to be adjudged failures *in the end*. From this also issued the providentialism that Hegel inserted into his accounts of the past in the form of "the cunning of reason," which permitted him to hold that all error was a *kind* of truth, all evil a *kind* of goodness, all ugliness a *kind* of beauty, and vice versa. He could find no way out of his dilemma. His counsel to historians to study the documents and remain true to the facts was "only words" if, "in the face of his established principles, there was no way of making use of facts and documents." (94)

In order to justify his use of philosophical concepts to detect the "meaning" of history, Hegel was forced to make one *reduction* after another: of history of the spirit to history of the state, of civilization in general to civilization in a given time and place, of individual men to the status of instruments of reason, and so on (95–97). Hegel failed to recognize that, "Just as reality has neither nucleus nor shell, but is of a single cast, as the internal and the external are the same thing, . . . so too the mass of facts is a compact mass, which cannot be divided into an essential nucleus and an inessential shell" (98). Thus, "starved for history and nourished by history," Hegel's philosophy became an ambiguous legacy for subsequent historical thinking (*ibid.*). Because he had rendered all events "sacred" by interpreting them as concrete manifestations of the Idea, he inspired a whole generation of great historians to sympathetic re-creations of past epochs and ages. But, because he taught that the manifestations of the spirit could be subjected to the same conceptualization, to the same logical manipulation, as that to which spirit in its abstract form could be subjected, he also inspired that mass of "petulant and comic disparagers of history" who rejected the authority of the facts and made of the historical record whatever it pleased them to make of it (*ibid.*).

Thus, in the end, Hegel failed to escape from the dualism that was his avowed enemy. This dualism was revealed most blatantly in his dichotomization of Spirit and Nature. In Hegel's genuine thought, "Spirit and Nature are two realities: the one existing before the other, or the one serving as the basis of the other, but in any case the one distinct from the other" (131). In order to bring these two realms together, Hegel was forced to postulate a third reality, the Logos, the universal Reason which was at once the basis and the end of both Spirit and Nature. Had Hegel conceived Spirit and Nature only as concepts, which they were, and not as two "concrete realities," he would have seen that the triadic schema was inapplicable to them. And he would have been able to avoid the panlogism which he tried to read into every aspect of both history and nature, and which left no place for the "irrational" anywhere in the world.

Thus, Hegelianism remained an unresolved combination of a philosophy of mind on the one hand and a philosophy of matter on the other. Whereas the term "nature" has a specific content—that is, "the totality of nature, as described by the physical, and mathematical" theories produced by the sciences—and the term "spirit" also has such a specific content—that is, "on the one side, psychology, and on the other philosophy of law, of art, religion, and of absolute spirit or Idea"—the term Logos has no proper content at all (132). It is merely an abstraction of an abstraction—that is, reason considered abstractly and "given on loan to" nature and spirit, distorting and restricting them, and used to criticize the inadequacies of all other philosophies. In his attempt to provide the term "Logos" with a specific content, Hegel went to history and ended by conceiving history and Logos as the same thing.

But, Croce maintained, history is not merely Logos—that is, Reason; it is also Unreason; more precisely, it is where human reason and human unreason reveal themselves in an interplay which *makes* history. But this history is not a discernible totality; it is merely the sum total of the various human acts that display the tension between Reason and Unreason in man. These acts are individual and unique, and, while reflection on them can yield general theories of Reason on the one hand and of Unreason on the other— that is to say, philosophy and psychology respectively—neither philosophy nor psychology can serve as the general science of man by which the specific character of a given human act can be predicted in advance of its actual happening.

History, therefore, always tends to overthrow the generalizations about man constructed by philosophy, psychology, and sociology, or at least it requires endless revision of their generalizations. For history always reveals new data about the interplay of Reason and Unreason in man which generalizing sciences are unable to anticipate. Historians have to use philosophical, sociological, and psychological generalizations to characterize specific historical acts—that is, to join subject to predicate in a concrete judgment. But this joining of subject to predicate in a given historical judgment is itself an intuitive, or aesthetic, operation. By such an operation, the historian gives clarity, order, and form to an area of the historical record that was formerly obscure, disorderly, and chaotic. He does the same thing that the artist does, even though his statements deal with *actual* rather than with *possible* events; and he constantly suppresses his imagination by a philosophical judgment on his own perceptions, so that the real is separated from the merely apparent that his imagination always seeks to substitute for the evidence contained in the documents.

What, then, was "living" and what was "dead" in Hegelianism?- Croce's answer to this question consolidated his resistance to every attempt to make sense of the historical record by appeal to presumed universals or generalizations. On the one hand it was necessary to preserve and to cultivate Hegel's basic insights: his notion that the object of philosophical reflection was the total reality, the concrete universal; his conviction that the dialectic of opposites was the proper instrument of philosophical reflection; and his doctrine of the degrees of reality, which permitted belief in both the autonomy of the various forms of the spirit and their necessary connection and unity. On the other hand, however, it was necessary to repudiate every form of panlogism, every attempt to render reality in its empirical manifestations subject to subsumption under the rules governing Reason *in abstracto*, and hence any attempt to construe *historical reality* dialectically. In short, while affirming the rule of Reason over philosophy and granting its authority as policeman of any use of concepts in historical judgments, it was imperative to deny Reason's authority to construe history-in-general. History had to be protected from the unrestricted use of artistic imagination, scientific generalization, and philosophical conceptualization simultaneously. Historical judgment presupposed clear philosophical concepts (such as good, evil, beauty, truth, utility, and the like) and consisted of combinations of concepts and empirical facts. The facts were discerned by artistic intuition, the concepts constructed by philosophical reflection, but their combination was a specifically historiographical activity, the paradigm of which was that *this* happened at *that time and place*, an activity which neither artistic intuition nor philosophical reflection *alone* could authorize.

On the basis of a number of specific historical statements, it was possible to generalize, and to say, for example, that in *certain types* of times and places, *certain types* of things tend to happen, and to arrive at sociology thereby. But to treat such generalizations as either laws or universals was what Ryle has lately called a "category mistake"; these were *abstractions from* individual historical judgments, *not statements about what actually happened everywhere at all times and places.* Such generalizations could not be substituted for philosophical statements about concepts, the sole universals, or for sets of discrete historical judgments about what had actually happened. Historical knowledge stopped with the recovery of the record of past human actions, of what men had *already* done; it did not go on to dilate on what they were currently doing or what they might or ought to do in the future.

Other kinds of judgments might be used to render account of the meaning of current events, political judgments, moral judgments, economic judgments, and the like; but these could claim no sanction from history. They were proposals, plans, projects offered to men for the organization of their lives here and now, not secured *knowledge.* These proposals, plans, projects, and so on, had to win human approval in the marketplaces and parliaments of nations, on their own merits and according to their apparent relevance to present problems; they sought a false authority when they were justified by an appeal to history, or when they were offered as necessary conclusions from the study of history. History was thus put into quarantine as a guide to present activity and future aspiration. The only thing that history taught was that man had it in him to be *anything* he purposed. The dangers of trying to draw lessons from history were therefore obvious, and they were nowhere more obvious than in the misuse of history made by the thinker whom Croce regarded as the greatest genius produced by modern Italian culture, Giambattista Vico, the subject of Croce's most difficult critical enterprise, *The Philosophy of Giambattista Vico* (1911).

Croce contra Vico

In his *Aesthetics,* Croce credited Vico with having redeemed poetry from the lower reaches of the spirit to which Plato had consigned it. Vico, Croce said, "for the first time revealed the true nature of art and poetry" (277). This revelation took the form of the discovery that "poetry comes before the intellect, but after feeling" (*ibid.*). Plato, like his modern "vitalist" and "irrationalist" counterparts, had confused poetry with feeling. Men feel, Vico said, before they observe; their observation is directed by, or has its occasion in, their feeling. It thus follows, Croce said, that, "poetry being composed of passion and feeling, the nearer it approaches to the *particular,* the more true it is, while exactly the reverse is true of philosophy" (277–78). Here, Croce concluded, "we have a profound statement of the line of demarcation between science and art. *They cannot be confused again*" (278).

Vico's conception of the difference between poetry and history was, Croce continued, "a trifle less clear," so unclear, in fact, that Vico ended "by identifying poetry and history" (279). This identification gave Vico his basis for first comprehending the nature of myth as "the spontaneous vision of the truth as it appears to primitive man" (*ibid.*), and yielded to him thereby his insight into the imagination as the *creative* mode of consciousness (281). At the same time, however, it led him to confuse the "ideal history of the human spirit," conceived as the succession of the eternal stages of the search for truth, with the real history actually lived through by individual men at different times and places in the past. Thus, although Vico could be credited with genuinely original and true insights into the nature of art and poetry, and above all with his discovery of the identification of poetry with language, he still fell prey to the nefarious "philosophy of history." Just as Marx had mistakenly dreamed of a *science* of history and Hegel of a *philosophy* of history, Vico dreamed of, and thought he had found, a *poetics* of history. To criticize Vico, then, meant to separate the aesthetic insights in his philosophy from the application of those insights to the study of history as a methodology. And this is what Croce undertook to do in his book on Vico in 1911.

In Chapter III of *The Philosophy of Giambattista Vico*, entitled "The Internal Structure of the New Science," Croce set forth the critical principles which guided him in his final reading of Vico. Vico's whole system, Croce explained, actually comprises three different "classes of inquiry: philosophical, historical, and empirical; and altogether it contains a philosophy of the spirit, a history (or congeries of histories), and a social science." (37–38) The first class of inquiry is concerned with "ideas" on fantasy, myth, religion, moral judgment, force and law, the certain and the true, the passions, providence, and so on—in other words, with "all the . . . determinations affecting the necessary course or development of the human mind or spirit" (*ibid.*). This first section, Vico's aesthetic theory, was valid and true. To the second class belong Vico's outline of the universal history of man after the Flood, the origins of the different civilizations, the description of the heroic ages in Greece and Rome and the discussion of custom, law, language, and political constitutions, as well as of primitive poetry, social class struggles, and the breakdown of civilizations and their return to a second barbarism, as in the early Middle Ages of Europe. Finally, the third class of inquiry has to do with Vico's attempt to "establish a uniform course (*corso*) of national history" and deals with the succession of political forms and correlative changes in both the theoretical and practical lives, as well as with his generalizations about the patriciate, the plebs, the patriarchal family, symbolic law, metaphorical language, hieroglyphic writing, and so forth.

Croce's argument is that Vico confused these three types of inquiry, ran them together in his reports, and committed a host of "category mistakes" in the process of setting them out in the *Scienza nuova*. The obscurity of the *Scienza nuova* results, he maintained, not from the profundity of the basic insight, but from an intrinsic confusion—that is to say, from the "obscurity of his [Vico's] ideas, a deficient understanding of certain connections; from, that is to say, an element of arbitrariness which Vico introduces into his thought, or, to put it more simply, from outright errors" (39). Vico had failed to see correctly the "relation between philosophy, history, and empirical science" (40). He tended poetically to "convert" one into the other. Thus, he treated "philosophy of the spirit" now as empirical science, now as history; he treated empirical science sometimes as philosophy and sometimes as history; and he often attributed to simple historical statements either the universality of philosophical concepts or the generality of empirical schemata. The confusion of concepts with facts and vice versa—unexceptionable in a poet—was disastrous for Vico the historian. For example, Croce noted, when Vico lacked a document, he tended to fall back upon a general philosophical principle to imagine (poetically) what the document *would have said had he actually possessed* it; or, when he came upon a dubious fact, he confirmed or disconfirmed it by appeal to some (imagined) empirical law. And, even when he possessed both documents and facts, he often failed to let them tell their own story—as the true historian is bound to do—but instead *interpreted them to suit his own purposes*—that is, to suit his own willfully contrived sociological generalizations.

Croce professed to prefer the most banal chronicle to this willful manipulation of the historical record. He could forgive Vico for the numerous factual errors which riddled his work. Imprecise in small matters, Vico made up for it by his comprehensiveness of vision and his understanding of the way the human spirit operated to create a specifically human world. But Croce could not forgive the cause of Vico's confusion, his poetic identification of philosophy with science and history. This "tendency of confusion or . . . confusion of tendencies" was fatal to Vico's claim to have founded a "science" of culture and was the cause of his "fall" into "philosophy of history" (43). An adequate reading of Vico, therefore, required a careful separation of the philosophical "gold" in his work from the pseudo-scientific and pseudo-historical dross in which it was concealed. And Croce proceeded to this task of separation (or transmutation, for this is what it really was) in the chapters that followed with a single-mindedness exceeded only by his confidence that, in his own philosophy, he possessed the philosopher's stone, which permitted the correct determination of "what is living and what is dead" in any system. Anxious to judge, and even to forgive, Vico in the light of the *scholarly* standards that prevailed in the eighteenth century, Croce was unwilling to extend this historicist charity to Vico's *philosophical* endeavors.

A perfect example—and a crucial test—of Croce's critical method appears in Chapter XI of *The Philosophy of Giambattista Vico*, where Vico's law of civilizational change, the so-called law of the *ricorso*, is examined. Briefly summarized, this law states that all pagan peoples must pass through a specific "course" of social relationships with corresponding political and cultural institutions and that, when the course is complete, they must, if they have not been annihilated, retrace this course on a similar, though significantly metamorphosed, plane of existence or level of self-consciousness. If they are destroyed at the end of the cycle, they will be replaced by another people who will live through the course in the same general sequence of stages and to the same general end.

Croce maintained that his "law" is nothing but a generalized form of the pattern which Vico thought he had discovered in Roman history. Vico gratuitously extended this law to cover all pagan societies, which forced him to press the facts into a pattern which applied only, if at all, to the Roman example. This "rarefaction" of Roman history into a general theory of cultural dynamics revealed Vico's misconception of how empirical laws are generated, Croce claimed. Instead of generalizing from concrete cases and thereby contriving a summary description of the attributes shared by all instances of the set, against which the differences among the instances could be delineated, Vico sought to extend the general characteristics of the Roman set to include all sets that *resembled* the Roman in their pagan character. The inadequacy of Vico's law was shown, however, by the large number of exceptions to it which even Vico had to admit existed. If Vico had not been led astray by his loyalty to his biased reading of Roman history, the "empirical theory of the *ricorsi*" would never have been forced to concede so many exceptions to its operations. And, freed from the necessity of forcing other societies into the pattern provided by the Roman example, Vico might have been able to apply the general truth contained in the theory of the *ricorsi* to their several histories.

The general truth implicitly contained in the theory was a philosophical one—namely, that

the spirit, having traversed its progressive stages, after having risen successively from sensation to the imaginative and rational universal, from violence to equity, must in conformity with its eternal nature retrace its course, to relapse into violence and sensation, and thence to renew its upward movement, to recommence its course. [136]

As a general guide to the study of specific historical societies, this truth directs attention to "the connection between predominantly imaginative and predominantly intellectual, spontaneous and reflective periods, the latter periods issuing out of the former by an increase in energy, and returning to them by degeneration and decomposition." But the theory describes only what happens *generally* in all societies; it neither prescribes what must happen at particular times and places nor predicts the outcome of a particular trend.

Such generalizations as those permitted by Croce, such as that which states the relationship between "predominantly imaginative and predominantly intellectual . . . periods," are, Croce said, "to a great extent quantitative and are made for the sake of convenience" (134). They have no force as law. Vico stood convicted, therefore, of an error and a delusion: he erred in trying to extend an empirical generalization to all classes that *resembled* that to which the generalization could be legitimately applied; and he was deluded by the hope of treating a philosophical insight as a canon of historical interpretation which would be valid for all societies at all times and places.

Croce considered two possible objections to this criticism of Vico. On the one hand, he said, it might be argued that Vico did account for the exceptions to his law by referring to external influences or contingent circumstances which caused a particular people to halt short of its term or to merge with, and become a part of, the *corso* of another people. On the other hand, he noted, on the basis of Croce's own interpretation of the true value of the "law," it might be held that, since the law really deals with the "corso" of the spirit and not with that of society or culture, no amount of empirical evidence can serve to challenge it. Croce summarily dismissed the second objection as irrelevant. "The point at issue," he said,

is . . . precisely the empirical aspect of this law, not the philosophical: and the true reply seems to us to be, as we have already suggested, that Vico could not and ought not to have taken other circumstances into account, just as, to recall one instance, anyone who is studying the various phases of life describes the first manifestations of the sexual craving in the vague imaginings and similar phenomena of puberty, and does not take into account the ways in which the less experienced may be initiated into love by the more experienced, since he is setting out to deal not with the social laws of imitation but with the physiological laws of organic development. [*Ibid.*]

In short, Vico's "law" either obtains universally—like the "physiological laws of organic development"—or it does not; one exception is enough to disconfirm it.

This was a curious line for Croce to take, however, for it required that he apply to Vico's "law" criteria of adequacy more similar to those demanded by Positivists than to those required by Croce's own conception of physical-scientific laws as expounded in his *Logic* (1909). Here he had criticized Positivists for failing to see that the function of laws in science was "subserving," not "constitutive" (204). The laws of physical science, he said, were nothing but fictions or pseudo concepts, contrived by men or groups of men in response to needs generated by practical projects in different times and places, the authority of which was limited, therefore, to the duration of the projects themselves. Croce specifically denied that the natural sciences predicted in any significant sense; belief in their predictive power represented the resurgence of a primitive desire to prophesy or to foretell the future, which could never be done. Such beliefs rested upon the baseless assumption that nature was regular in all its operations, when in reality the only "regular" phenomenon in nature was that of mind in its effort to comprehend nature (228). The so-called "laws of nature" were constantly being violated and excepted. From this it followed that, far from being able to claim predictability, the natural sciences were much more dependent upon a *historical* knowledge (of nature) than even the human sciences, which at least had the constant phenomena of mind from which to generalize.

But, if this is the true nature of law in the physical sciences, it must also be the true nature of whatever laws are possible in the social sciences; and, this being the case, what possible objection could there be to Vico's use of the law of the *ricorsi* to characterize the evolutionary process of all societies and to direct research into them with the extent of their deviation from the Roman model in view? The objection would seem to lie solely in Croce's hostility to any attempt to treat society and culture, which he took to be products of spirit, *as if* they were mechanically determined effects of physical causes. In trying to characterize the operations of spirit in their concrete manifestations, in the social forms they took, in terms of laws, Vico seemed to be unwittingly materializing or naturalizing them, and thereby depriving them of their status as creations of spirit. At least, that is the way Croce saw it. Vico treated society and culture as if they were products of an invariable material process (thereby, by the way, betraying his misunderstanding of the true nature of nature); and Croce demanded of him that, once he opted for this treatment, he be consistent and truly regard the process as invariable. Hence we have the thrust of Croce's appeal to the analogy of anyone "studying the various phases of life" who must limit himself to a consideration of "the physiological laws of organic development" and not deal with the "social laws of imitation" (*Phil. of Vico*, 136).

But the analogy betrays Croce's bias in the criticism. For, to follow the analogy out correctly, what is at issue in Vico's case is not a mixture of laws operating in one process with laws operating in another, but the convergence of two systems, each of which is governed by similar laws, the one cancelling out or aborting the operations of the other. For example, even a person studying the various phases of life need not be confused by the fact that a given individual does not reach puberty but, let us say, dies. The death of a person before puberty does not disconfirm the "physiological laws of organic development"; it merely requires that, if we want to explain the failure to reach puberty, we must invoke other laws, specifically those which account for the death of the organism, to explain why the prediction that puberty would *normally* occur was not borne out.

So it is with civilizations. Our characterization of the "course" we predict they will follow is not vitiated by any given civilization's failure to complete such a course if the failure can be explained by invocation of another law, that covering the disintegration of civilizations short of their normal term.

Thus, no number of societies failing to complete the *corso* described by the Roman model used by Vico as an archetype can serve to disconfirm Vico's "law," for the "law of the *ricorsi*" is not a "law" at all; it is merely a theory or an interpretation—that is to say, a set of laws the utility of which, for predictive purposes, requires specification of the limiting conditions within which the laws apply. In principle there is nothing at all wrong with Vico's having chosen the Roman example as a paradigm of civilizational growth against which the growth of all other civilizations known to him, the Jewish and Christian excepted, could be measured. It is perfectly good social-scientific procedure, however imperfectly the procedure was carried out in Vico's case. What Croce objected to was *any* kind of social-scientific procedure, for, by his lights, it represented an effort to treat a product of "free" spirit as causally determined. And so he applied an impossibly rigorous standard of adequacy —a standard he himself had specifically repudiated in his rejection of the claims that Positivists had made for the physical sciences—to Vico's effort to construct a science of societies. This inconsistency in Croce's use of the concept of "law" can be explained only by his desire to claim Vico's sanction for his own manner of philosophizing while denying any claim by modern social scientists to follow out Vico's manner of social analysis.

A better case can be made for Croce's criticism of Vico's efforts to construct a universal history, or philosophy of world history. Here a genuine mixture of categories appears to have occurred. On the one hand, Croce correctly pointed out, Vico wanted to use the theory of the *ricorsi* as the model for *all* civilizational growth; on the other, he wanted to except the Jewish and Christian examples by attributing to them respectively a special memory and a special capacity for renewal, which precluded the termination of their histories before the end of the world. This distinction *was* gratuitous, and Croce was apparently correct in locating it in the conflict between the Christian believer who lurked within Vico's breast and the social scientist who had triumphed in his head. But, as most of Vico's commentators have pointed out, even this inconsistency does not negate the effort, consistently pursued in the social-scientific side of his work, to construct a universal philosophy of history. Croce himself admitted as much when, commenting upon Vico's attempt to draw similarities between Homer and Dante, he granted that such classifications were the necessary bases of any true history; for, as he put it, "without the perception of similarity how would one succeed in establishing the differences?" (156). But here again he deplored the search for similarities as an end in itself; the urge to classify, to construct types, he said, had prohibited Vico from carrying out the historian's task, that of "representing and narrating" (257).

Croce's essentially Ironic stance with respect to the thought of Marx, Hegel, and Vico is revealed not only by his insistence upon his own ability to distinguish between what was living and what was dead in their conceptions of history but also by his consignment of "living" parts of their theories to separate, and indeed even isolated, sectors of the life of the mind. His treatment of Marx was exceptional, inasmuch as he did not even grant to him the status of a significant thinker. In Croce's estimation, Marx had contributed only a reminder to historians to take account of the economic factor in the life of men. Croce permitted Hegel a permanent place in the history of philosophy because of his contributions to logic and the theory of the human sciences, but denied him any genuine achievement as a philosopher of history. Croce acknowledged Vico's permanent contribution to aesthetic theory, but denied him any talent at all as either a historian or a social theorist. What this amounted to was a distancing of the entire effort of past thinkers to raise historical thought to the status of a science, however the term "science" was conceived.

At the same time, while defending the notion that history was a form of art, Croce carried out an operation by which history was prohibited from contributing to that process of imaginative creativity, or creative imagination, which he admitted to art in general. The poetic truths of historiography were rendered prosaic precisely by the degree to which they were consigned to criticism by common sense and to characterization in terms of ordinary language.

✌§ History as Bourgeois Ideology

What lay behind this general, if qualified, rejection of every previous philosophy of history and this qualified, if general, Idealism which Croce finally came to rest with as the basis for his own historical studies? More important, what does the general recognition of Croce's authority as a spokesman for Liberal-humanistic culture in the first quarter of the twentieth century tell us about the mood, the fears, and the aspirations of this age all over Europe? In my view, both questions can be met by a single answer: For a significant segment of cultivated European society between about 1900 and 1930, a society threatened by what appeared to be the progeny of Marx on the one hand and the heirs of Nietzsche on the other, a society which could find little to hearten it in either Ranke or Burckhardt, the main models for the historical thought of the academy, Croce seemed to be offering a genuine alternative, an idea of history that was at once progressive and socially responsible.

In many respects, Croce was trying to do for classical Liberalism what Ranke had done for classical Conservatism a half-century earlier—that is, hedge it around with arguments against Radicalism in any form. He remained a Liberal in his conviction that society and culture could not maintain the form and content of any of their specific incarnations but had to change.

But in his conviction that all change had to be gradual, unplanned, and the spontaneous result of the efforts of individual men to mediate among received traditions, present exigencies, and future aspirations, he spoke especially for most of the troubled Liberals of his generation. In presenting history as the eternal return of man to the task of constructing an arena in which he could display his individuality, Croce soothed the fears of those sons of the bourgeoisie for whom individualism was an eternal value; in presenting historical knowledge as knowledge of human individuality, he provided a barrier against premature assimilation of that individuality to the general truths of science on the one hand and the universal truths of philosophy on the other.

But he did more. He sensed the power of that mood of *senescens saeculum* which gripped the generation of the 1890s. His whole system was a sublimate of his generation's awareness of the passing of an age, the Age of Europe, of humanism, and of that combination of aristocratic and bourgeois values which gave to the ruling groups of nineteenth-century Europe their distinctive life style.

European intellectuals entered the twentieth century with the conviction that, since every total system of explanation had a flaw in it, despair could claim no more authority over men than optimism; that, with the contest between despair and optimism being a draw, optimism was as justified as despair—and much more comforting. But there was more to Croce's option for optimism. He had won a right to it in an actual struggle with death itself; he had literally fought his way back from the grave in his early manhood; and his victorious emergence from the grave gave him, he felt, an unerring eye for whatever was "still living" in anything that was superficially moribund. This is perhaps why his histories are dominated by a search for the shoots of life reappearing on the battlefield of frustrated hopes and dashed aspirations. His own life had taught him that time itself, when lived as history, is "its own mystic Dionysus, its own suffering Christ, redeemer of sins" (*Hist. as the Story of Liberty*, 28).

Only two striking images occur in Croce's rare public reflections on his own complex, and complexly obscured, private life. One is the image of Vesuvius, which in wintertime slumbered quietly beneath a cap of snow, but which was silently gathering power for its eruption when Naples and the Neapolitans were least prepared for it. According to Nicolini, Croce used this image to characterize himself. The other image was that of a pacific monastic cloister, whose high walls blocked out the noise of the public world and gently echoed the fall of water from a fountain, a place pervaded by the scent of lemon trees. This image represented the retreat to which Croce desired to retire when his ascetic schedule of work and thought had exhausted him.

The two images are, of course, complementary. They conjure up visions of darkness, chaos, and violence on the one hand and light, order, and repose on the other. I shall forgo the temptation to interpret them in a Freudian manner as phallus and womb, not because Croce condemned every effort at psychoanalytical historiography, calling it "valet's history" and deriding its practitioners as pseudo scholars seeking a cheap interpretation without the work required by true historical comprehension; but because, in accordance with this prejudice, Croce refused to reveal enough about his private life to permit muster of the kind of detailed evidence that alone can render a psychoanalytical interpretation convincing. In any case, private evidence is not needed to divine the general cast of Croce's psyche and the experiences which gave it its peculiar physiognomy. Croce's public pronouncements, which run to more than eighty volumes, provide ample clues to the import of these two images for his total world view. They figure the main categories of Croce's philosophy; they telegraph the psychological problems for which the philosophy constituted the solutions.

Beneath these images lay Croce's experience of death and return from death; above them rises the attempted unification of life and death in which individual vitality is merged with the universal experience of death as the solution to philosophy's eternal problem. There was good reason for Croce to attempt such a merger. After all, Croce had lived through a number of entombments and rebirths: first, as the successor to a child bearing his name who had died before he was born; second, as one who had risen from entombment in the ruins of an earthquake; then, as a prisoner of melancholy who had been liberated by the young philosopher Labriola in Rome; and, finally, as a prisoner of the "caves" of the archives in Naples who had released himself to the light of philosophy. All this provided ample reason for the mature man, the author of The Philosophy of the Practical (1908), to write: "In truth, there is no need to oppose a eulogy of Life with a eulogy of Death since the eulogy of Life is also a eulogy of Death; for how could we live, if we did not die at every instant?" In that same work Croce defined "cosmic progress" as nothing but the "continuous triumph of Life over Death" and life as sheer "activity," the "unfolding of activity upon passivity. . . . In every new situation the individual begins life all over again." The ultimate reality, the "God" which men had sought since the beginning of human time, was not an external force but merely this regenerative power in man, "that activity which is both Life and Death." (252)

The human capacity to "return," the regenerative power in man, was, in Croce's view, both the source of man's glory and the cause of his uniquely human suffering. For him, no less than for Hegel, Marx, and Nietzsche, man's "confinement" in the life-and-death cycle was also man's "privilege," the basis of his aristocracy. The identification of life with death and the reverse permitted Croce to turn his guns upon the enemies of life and the negators of death alike—that is to say, upon mere pessimists and mere optimists indifferently. Thus, he wrote in The Philosophy of the Practical:

This conception of reality, which recognizes the indissoluble link between good and evil, is itself beyond good and evil, and consequently surpasses the visual angles of optimism and pessimism—of optimism that does not discover the evil in life and posits it as an illusion, or only as a very small or contingent element, or hopes for a future life (on earth or in heaven) in which evil will be suppressed; and of pessimism, that sees nothing but evil and makes of the world an infinite and eternal spasm of pain, that rends itself internally and generates nothing. [251]

This conception of the paradoxical unity of life with death was Croce's antidote to utopian Radicalism and Reactionary despair in historical thinking. This conception had its psychological origins in his own personal experience of both life and death. That experience was definitive in his intellectual development; it also made him the perfect spokesman for a civilization which, from the end of the nineteenth century on, would descend into death again and again, and "eternally return," neither as Marxist proletarian nor as Nietzsche Superman, but as the same combination of aristocratic Idealism and middle-class practicality. These, in fact, were the social equivalents of Croce's main abstract philosophical categories: the principle of Life was nothing but a sublimation of aristocratic heroism; that of Death was nothing more than the bourgeois acceptance of practical exigency. The interplay of the two constituted Croce's conception of culture, and the story of that interplay was his idea of history.

CONCLUSION

In my analysis of the main forms of historical consciousness of the nineteenth century, I have utilized a general theory of the structure of the historical work. I have maintained that the style of a given historiographer can be characterized in terms of the linguistic protocol he used to prefigure the historical field prior to bringing to bear upon it the various "explanatory" strategies he used to fashion a "story" out of the "chronicle" of events contained in the historical record. These linguistic protocols, I have maintained, can be further characterized in terms of the four principal modes of poetic discourse. Using the tropes of Metaphor, Metonymy, Synecdoche, and Irony as the basic types of linguistic prefiguration, I have discussed the modes of consciousness in which historians can implicitly or explicitly justify commitment to different explanatory strategies on the levels of argument, emplotment, and ideological implication respectively. Drawing upon the "world hypothesis" theory of Stephen C. Pepper, I have identified four different theories of truth (or combinations of them) in the historical thinkers studied: Formism, Mechanism, Organicism, and Contextualism. Following the theory of fictions of Northrop Frye, I have identified four different archetypal plot structures by which historians can figure historical processes in their narratives as stories of a particular kind: Romance, Tragedy, Comedy, and Satire. And, using the theory of ideology worked out by Karl Mannheim, I have discerned four different strategies of ideological implication by which historians can suggest to their readers the import of their studies of the past for the comprehension of the present: Anarchism, Radicalism, Conservatism, and Liberalism.

I have suggested that a given historian will be inclined to choose one or another of the different modes of explanation, on the level of argument, emplotment, or ideological implication, in response to the imperatives of the trope which informs the linguistic protocol he has used to prefigure the field of historical occurrence singled out by him for investigation. I have suggested, in short, an elective affinity between the act of prefiguration of the historical field and the explanatory strategies used by the historian in a given work.

These correlations of the tropological strategies of prefiguration with the various modes of explanation used by historians in their works have provided me with a way of characterizing the styles of given historians. And they have permitted me to view the various debates over how history ought to be written, which occurred throughout the nineteenth century, as essentially matters of stylistic variation within a single universe of discourse. Moreover, they have permitted me to abandon the usual categories for designating the different "schools" of historical writing which appeared during the century, categories conventionally taken from more general cultural movements, such as Romanticism, Idealism, and Positivism, and specific ideological movements, such as Liberalism, Radicalism, and Conservatism. I have argued, in fact, that simply to designate the work of a given historian as "Romantic" or "Idealist" or "Liberal" or "Conservative" obscures more than it reveals about the dynamics of the thought processes that led him to compose his histories in a particular way. My analytical method permits me to specify, on different levels of engagement—epistemological, aesthetic, ethical, and linguistic—precisely wherein a given historian's "Liberalism" or "Romanticism" or "Idealism" consists and to what degree it actually determined the structure of the works he wrote.

Moreover, I have claimed that my approach to the problem of nineteenth-century historical consciousness permits me to ignore the distinction, now little more than a precritically accepted cliché, between proper history and philosophy of history. I believe I have penetrated to the metahistorical level on which proper history and speculative philosophy of history have a common origin in any attempt to make sense out of history-in-general. I have suggested that proper history and speculative philosophy of history are distinguishable only in emphasis, not in their respective contents. In proper history, the element of construct is displaced to the interior of the narrative, while the element of "found" data is permitted to occupy the position of prominence in the story line itself. In speculative philosophy of history, the reverse is the case. Here the element of conceptual construct is brought to the fore, explicitly set forth, and systematically defended, with the data being used primarily for purposes of illustration or exemplification. I conclude, therefore, that every philosophy of history contains within it the elements of a proper history, just as every proper history contains within it the elements of a full-blown philosophy of history.

Once these relationships are understood, it becomes possible, in my view, to distinguish between the proper historian and the philosopher of history on the basis of the second order of consciousness in which the latter carries out his efforts to make sense of the historical process. The philosopher of history seeks not only to understand what happened in history but also to specify the criteria by which he can know when he has successfully grasped its meaning or significance. Properly understood, then, philosophy of history is a commentary not only on the historical record but also on the activity by which a given encodation of the historical field can be permitted to claim the status of knowledge. In my view, it is no accident that the outstanding philosophers of history of the nineteenth century were, with the possible exception of Marx, quintessentially philosophers of language. Nor is it an accident that Hegel, Nietzsche, and Croce were all dialecticians. For, in my view, dialectic is nothing but a formalization of an insight into the tropological nature of all the forms of discourse which are not formally committed to the articulation of a world view within the confines of a single modality of linguistic usage—as the natural sciences became after their commitment to Metonymical usage in the seventeenth century.

I have suggested that the nonscientific or protoscientific nature of historical studies is signaled in the inability of historians to agree—as the natural scientists of the seventeenth century were able to do—on a specific mode of discourse. History, like the human sciences in general, remained indentured to the vagaries, but also to the generative capability, of natural language throughout the nineteenth century—and it is so indentured today. As a result, historiography has remained prey to the creation of mutually exclusive, though equally legitimate, interpretations of the same set of historical events or the same segment of the historical process. What the present study shows is that, within a given tradition of discourse, in which a shared set of problems and a common body of contents are taken as the crucial problems to be solved over a given period of time, at least four possible interpretative strategies may be employed, consistent with the types of linguistic protocols sanctioned by the dominant tropes of ordinary speech. I have argued that the types of historiography produced by the nineteenth century correspond, on the metahistorical level, to the types of philosophy of history produced during that same age.

Whereas the master historians of the nineteenth century *wrote* history in the modes of Metaphor, Metonymy, Synecdoche, and Irony, the philosophers of history *wrote about the writing of history* from positions articulated from within the same set of modalities. What made the philosophers of history appear to be scientizing or aestheticizing historiography in Radical ways were their efforts to impose upon historical reflection the linguistic protocols sanctioned by a specific tropological usage. Hegel, Marx, Nietzsche, and Croce all offended conventional historians by their attempts to provide a technical language in which either to talk about history or to talk about historians' talk about history.

The master historians of the nineteenth century intuited that history could not become either a rigorous science or a pure art until the epistemological and aesthetic concepts that underlay the composition of their narratives were clarified. And many of them recognized that, in order to qualify as a science, history would have to be provided with a technical language by which to communicate findings. Without such a technical language, general syntheses similar to those in the physical sciences would be impossible. Yet no single linguistic protocol succeeded in carrying the day among the historians (or among the social sciences in general) in the way that mathematics and logic had done in the physical sciences from the time of Newton on. Since history resisted every effort to formalize discourse, historians were committed to the plurality of interpretative strategies contained in the uses of ordinay language thoughout the nineteenth century.

I do not know whether the four interpretative strategies I have identified exhaust all the possibilities contained in language for the representation of historical phenomena. But I do claim that my typology of interpretative strategies permits me to account for the prestige enjoyed by historians and philosophers of history during different periods of nineteenth-century thought and among different publics within a given period of that thought. I maintain that the link between a given historian and his potential public is forged on the pretheoretical, and specifically linguistic, level of consciousness. And this suggests that the prestige enjoyed by a given historian or philosopher of history within a specific public is referable to the precritically provided linguistic ground on which the prefiguration of the historical field is carried out.

In my view, no given *theory* of history is convincing or compelling to a given public solely on the basis of its adequacy as an "explanation" of the "data" contained in its narrative, because, in history, as in the social sciences in general, there is no way of pre-establishing what will count as a "datum" and what will count as a "theory" by which to "explain" what the data "mean." In turn, there is no agreement over what will count as a specifically "historical" datum. The resolution of this problem requires a metatheory, which will establish on metahistorical grounds the distinctions between merely "natural" phenomena and specifically "historical" phenomena.

It is often said, of course, that historical data consist of all the artifacts, monuments, and documents created by men, and that the problem of historical thinking is to classify the forms of these phenomena and to account for their appearances in historical time by identifying the motives or intentions behind their creation. But, it is not only difficult to distinguish between a natural and a historical phenomenon in certain crucial cases (in wars, for example); it is also difficult to distinguish, in the determination of motives, between a generally animal impulse in a specific historical agent and the specifically human forms that such an impulse may assume. Much depends on how far one wants to pursue the inquiry into motive and intention. One can try to penetrate to the interior of consciousness, where motives and intentions merge first with psychological, then with biological, and ultimately with physico-chemical processes in the depths of human being. But this would expose thought to the threat of an infinite regress. The decision of a conventional historian to take the statements of conscious intention of historical agents at face value is neither more nor less legitimate than the decision of the Materialistic Determinist to reduce conscious intention to the status of an effect of a more basic, psycho-physical cause, or that of the Idealist to interpret it as a function of a more general "spirit of the age." These decisions originate in more basic conceptions of the form that historical theories are conceived to have to take. Thus, historians necessarily disagree not only over the question "What are the data?" but also over the form of the theories by which those data are constituted as "problems" and are then "resolved" by being merged with them to make up "explanations."

In history, I have argued, the historical field is constituted as a possible domain of analysis in a linguistic act which is tropological in nature. The dominant trope in which this constitutive act is carried out will determine both the kinds of objects which are permitted to appear in that field as data and the possible relationships that are conceived to obtain among them. The theories that are subsequently elaborated to account for changes that occur in the field can claim authority as explanations of "what happened" only insofar as they are consonant with the linguistic mode in which the field was prefigured as a possible object of mental perception. Thus, any theory which is framed in a given mode is foredoomed to failure in any public which is committed to a different mode of prefiguration. A historian such as Marx, employing a Mechanistic explanatory theory, has no authority in a public which is precritically committed to the prefiguration of the historical field in the mode of Irony, Synecdoche, or Metaphor. Similarly, a historian such as Burckhardt, who was precritically committed to a prefiguration of the historical field in the Ironic mode, has no authority in a public which is precritically committed to the prefiguration of the historical field in the Metonymical mode. These precritical commitments to different modes of discourse and their constitutive tropological strategies account for the generation of the different interpretations of history which I have identified in this study of nineteenth-century historical consciousness.

It would have been tempting to try to correlate the four basic forms of historical consciousness with corresponding personality types, but I decided against this for two reasons. One is that present-day psychology is in the same state of conceptual anarchy that history was in the nineteenth century. In my view, it seems probable that an analysis of contemporary psychological thinking would reveal the same set of interpretative strategies (each posing as the definitive science of its subject) which I discovered in my analysis of historical thinking. That is to say, since psychology has not attained to the kind of systematization which characterizes the physical sciences, but remains divided into contending "schools" of interpretation, I would probably have ended by duplicating the findings I arrived at in my study of historical thinking.

But, more important, I deny that much is added to the understanding of a given writer's thought by the revelation of the personality type which supposedly underlay and gave form to his work. To reveal the "Radical personality" *behind* Marx's "Revolutionary theories" does not seem to me to clear up in any significant way either the problem of the *specific form* his writings took or the *appeal* those writings have had to publics of both a "Revolutionary" and a generally "Liberal" cast of mind. As for the so-called psychobiographical approach to intellectual history, I note the following problems. When it is a matter of dealing with a thinker or writer of manifest genius, the application of a theory such as psychoanalysis, which was devised for the study of neurotics and psychotics, appears to be a mistake. After all, a neurotic is one who by definition is unequipped to sublimate successfully the obsessions which constitute the complex that determines the structure of his personality. In the case of geniuses such as Hegel, Marx, Tocqueville, Michelet, or even Nietzsche, however, *their works* are evidence of their sublimative capability. A study of the biographies of such geniuses might account for their interest in certain kinds of problems, but it would do little to help us understand the specific forms of their works, the specific relations between theory and data which exist in them, and the appeal that these works have for those publics whose psychological proclivities differ from those of the authors.

I have therefore limited the present study to an analysis of the relation between the manifest level of historical narratives, where the theoretical concepts that have been used to explain the data are deployed, and the latent level, considered as the linguistic ground on which these concepts are precritically constituted. This has been sufficient to permit me to characterize, in what I take to be a value neutral and purely formal way, the different interpretative strategies that were elaborated by nineteenth-century historians and philosophers of history. Moreover, it permits me to explain why it is that, although nineteenth-century historical thinkers studied carefully and completely, within the limits of their several competences, the same "data" in the historical record, they came to such different and seemingly mutually exclusive conclusions about the meaning and significance of those "data" for their own times. By constituting the historical field in alternative ways, they implicitly committed themselves to different strategies of explanation, emplotment, and ideological implication by which to discern its true "meaning." The "crisis of historicism" into which historical thinking entered during the last decades of the nineteenth century was, then, little more than the perception of the impossibility of choosing, on adequate theoretical grounds, among the different ways of viewing history which these alternative interpretative strategies sanctioned.

As thus envisaged, the history of nineteenth-century historical thinking can be said to describe a full circle, from a rebellion against the Ironic historical vision of the late Enlightenment to the return to prominence of a similar Ironic vision on the eve of the twentieth century. The classic age of European historical thought, from Hegel to Croce, represented an effort to constitute history as the ground for a "realistic" science of man, society, and culture. This realism was to be founded on a consciousness that had been freed from the inherent skepticism and pessimism of late Enlightenment Irony on the one hand and the cognitively irresponsible faith of the early Romantic movement on the other. But, in the works of its greatest historians and philosophers of history, nineteenth-century Europe succeeded in producing only a host of conflicting "realisms," each of which was endowed with a theoretical apparatus and buttressed by an erudition that made it impossible for one to deny its claim to at least provisional acceptance.

The prestige of the various thinkers I have studied has waxed and waned with transformations in the moods of the publics that read them. In turn, these moods sanctioned the prefiguration of the historical field in different modalities of discourse. One ought not say, therefore, that Michelet's conception of history was refuted or overturned by the more "scientific" or "empirical" or "realistic" conception of Ranke; or that the work of Ranke, in turn, was nullified by the even more "scientific" or "realistic" Tocqueville; or that all three of these were set in the shade by the inherent "realism" of Burckhardt. Nor is it possible to say, with any theoretical certitude, that Marx was more "scientific" than Hegel in his approach to history, or that Nietzsche was more "profound" in his dilations on historical consciousness than either of these. For what was at issue throughout the nineteenth century, in history as in both art and the social sciences, was the form that a genuinely "realistic representation of historical reality" ought to take. Nor, finally, can one say, with any confidence in the judgment, that there was genuine progress in the evolution of historical theory from the time of Hegel to that of Croce, for each of the master historians and philosophers of history I have studied displayed a talent for historical narrative or a consistency of vision that made of his work an effectively closed system of thought, incommensurable with all the others appearing in contention with it.

I could, from a commitment to a particular conception of science, insist that Tocqueville was a more "scientific" historian than Michelet or Ranke, or that Marx was a more "realistic" social theorist than either Hegel or Croce. But, in order to render such a judgment, I would have to ignore the fact that *on historical grounds alone* I have no basis for preferring one conception of the "science" of history over the other. Such a judgment would merely reflect a logically prior preference, either for the linguistic mode in which Tocqueville and Marx prefigured the historical field or for the ideological implications of their specific figurations of the historical process. In the human sciences, it is still a matter not only of expressing a preference for one or another way of conceiving the tasks of analysis but also of choosing among contending notions of what an adequate human science might be.

Yet, reflection on the evolution of nineteenth-century historical sensibility does permit me to locate present-day historiography within a specific phase of the history of historical consciousness in general. Much of the best historical reflection of the twentieth century has been concerned, like its counterpart in the early nineteenth century, to overcome the condition of Irony into which historical consciousness was plunged at the end of the nineteenth century. In my view, this concern accounts for the popularity of present-day speculative philosophy of history as well as for the revival of interest in the work of the great historical theorists of the pre-Ironic period: Hegel, Marx, and Nietzsche. Although contemporary academic historiography remains locked within the Ironic perspective that produced the crisis of historicism in the late nineteenth century, and continues to lament any interest in speculative philosophy of history on the part of nonprofessionals and professionals alike, historical thinking in general continues to generate systems of "historiology" which challenge the Ironic perspective.

Modern historical thought attacks this Ironic perspective from two sides. It seeks to overcome its inherent skepticism, which passes for scholarly caution and empiricism, and its moral agnosticism, which passes for objectivity and transideological neutrality. In the work of writers and thinkers as different as Malraux, Yeats, Joyce, Spengler, Toynbee, Wells, Jaspers, Heidegger, Sartre, Benjamin, Foucault, Lukács, and a host of others, contemporary historical thinking sets alongside the Irony of professional historiography, and as possible alternatives to it, conceptions of the historical process which are cast in the modes of Metaphor, Metonymy, and Synecdoche, each with its own strategies of explanation and each with an ideological implication that is unique to it. When it is a matter of choosing among these alternative visions of history, the only grounds for preferring one over another are *moral* or *aesthetic* ones.

The late R. G. Collingwood was fond of saying that the kind of history one wrote, or the way one thought about history, was ultimately a function of the kind of man one was. But the reverse is also the case. Placed before the alternative visions that history's interpreters offer for our consideration, and without any apodictically provided theoretical grounds for preferring one over another, we are driven back to moral and aesthetic reasons for the choice of one vision over another as the more "realistic." The aged Kant was right, in short; we are free to conceive "history" as we please, just as we are free to make of it what we will. And, if we wish to transcend the agnosticism which an Ironic perspective on history, passing as the sole possible "realism" and "objectivity" to which we can aspire in historical studies, foists upon us, we have only to reject this Ironic perspective and to will to view history from another, anti-Ironic perspective.

Such a recommendation, coming at the end of a work which professes to be value neutral and purely Formalist in its own reflections upon historical thinking in its classic age, may appear inconsistent with the intrinsic Irony of its own characterization of the history of historical consciousness. I do not deny that the Formalism of my approach to the history of historical thought itself reflects the Ironic condition from within which most of modern academic historiography is generated. But I maintain that the recognition of this Ironic perspective provides the grounds for a transcendence of it. If it can be shown that Irony is only one of a *number* of possible perspectives on history, each of which has its own good reasons for existence on a poetic and moral level of awareness, the Ironic attitude will have begun to be deprived of its status as the *necessary* perspective from which to view the historical process. Historians and philosophers of history will then be freed to conceptualize history, to perceive its contents, and to construct narrative accounts of its processes in whatever modality of consciousness is most consistent with their own moral and aesthetic aspirations. And historical consciousness will stand open to the re-establishment of its links with the great poetic, scientific, and philosophical concerns which inspired the classic practitioners and theorists of its golden age in the nineteenth century.

BIBLIOGRAPHY

❧ *Works Analyzed in the Text*

Burckhardt, Jacob. *The Age of Constantine the Great*. Translated by Moses Hadas. Garden City, N.Y.: Doubleday Anchor Books, 1956.
———. *Briefe*. Edited by Max Burckhardt. Bremen: Carl Schünemann Verlag, 1965.
———. *Der Cicerone: Eine Anleitung zum Genuss der Kunstwerke Italiens*. Basel: Schweighauser'sche Verlagsbuchhandlung, 1855. English version: *The Cicerone: An Art Guide to Painting in Italy for the Use of Travellers and Students*, bk. III. Translated by A. H. Clough. London: T. Werner Laurie, n.d.
———. *The Civilization of the Renaissance in Italy*. Translated by S. G. C. Middlemore. London: Phaidon Press, 1960.
———. *Force and Freedom: An Interpretation of History*. Edited by James Hastings Nichols. New York: Meridian Books, 1955. A translation of *Weltgeschichtliche Betrachtungen*.
———. *Judgements on History and Historians*. Translated by Harry Zohn. Boston: Beacon Press, 1958.
Carlyle, Thomas. "On Biography." In *Critical and Miscellaneous Essays: Collected and Republished*, vol. III. Boston: Brown & Taggard, 1860.
———. "Boswell's *Life of Johnson*." In *ibid*.
———. "On History." In *A Carlyle Reader: Selections from the Writings of Thomas Carlyle*, edited by G. B. Tennyson. New York: Modern Library, 1969.
Croce, Benedetto. *Aesthetic as Science of Expression and General Linguistic*.

Translated by Douglas Ainslee. London: Macmillan, 1909. Italian version: *Estetica come scienza dell' espressione e linguistica generale*. Palermo: Sandron, 1902; Bari: G. Laterza, 1908.

————. *Come nacque e come morì il marxismo teorico in Italia (1895–1900)*. Bari: Laterza, 1938.

————. *Filosofia della pratica: Economia ed etica*. Bari: Laterza, 1957.

————. *History: Its Theory and Method*. Translated by Douglas Ainslee. New York: Harcourt and Brace, 1923. Italian version: *Teoria e storia della storiografia*. Bari: Laterza, 1917.

————. *History as the Story of Liberty*. Translated by Sylvia Sprigge. New York: Meridian Books, 1955. Italian version: *La Storia come pensiero e come azione*. Bari: Laterza, 1954.

————. *History of Europe in the Nineteenth Century*. Translated by Henry Furst. New York: Harbinger Books, 1963. Italian version: *Storia d'Europa nel secolo decimonono*. Bari: Laterza, 1943.

————. *Logica come scienza del concetto puro*. 3rd ed., rev. Bari: Laterza, 1917.

————. *The Philosophy of Giambattista Vico*. Translated by R. G. Collingwood. New York: Russell & Russell, 1913. Italian version: *La Filosofia di Giambattista Vico*. Bari: Laterza, 1911.

————. *Saggio sullo Hegel, seguito da altri scritti*. 3rd ed., rev. Bari: Laterza, 1927.

————. "La Storia ridotta sotto il concetto generale dell' arte." In *Primi Saggi*. 3rd ed., rev. Bari: Laterza, 1951.

Droysen, Johann Gustav. *Grundriss der Historik*. In *Historik: Vorlesungen über Enzyklopädie und Methodologie der Geschichte*, edited by Rudolf Hübner. Munich: R. Oldenbourg, 1958. English version: *Outline of the Principles of History*. Translated by E. Benjamin Andrews. Boston: Ginn & Co., 1893.

Hegel, Georg Wilhelm Friedrich. *The Phenomenology of Mind*. Translated by J. B. Baillie. 2nd ed., rev. London: George Allen & Unwin, 1961.

————. *The Philosophy of Fine Art*. Translated by F. P. B. Omaston. 4 vols. London: G. Bell & Sons, 1920. German version: *Werke*, vols. XIII–XV: *Vorlesungen über die Ästhetik*. Frankfurt am Main: Suhrkamp Verlag, 1970.

————. *The Philosophy of History*. Translated by J. Sibree. New York: Dover Publications, 1956. German version: *Werke*, vol. XII: *Vorlesungen über die Philosophie der Geschichte*. Frankfurt am Main: Suhrkamp Verlag, 1970.

Heine, Heinrich. *Mein wertvollstes Vermächtnis: Religion, Leben, Dichtung*. Edited by Felix Stössinger. Zurich: Manesse Verlag, 1950. English translations cited in the text are from *The Poetry and Prose of Heinrich Heine*, selected and edited by Frederick Ewen. New York: The Citadel Press, 1948.

Herder, Johann Gottfried. *Ideen zur Philosophie der Geschichte der Menschheit*. Darmstadt: Melzer, 1966. English translations cited in the text are from *Herder on Social and Political Culture*, translated by F. Barnard. Cambridge, Cambridge University Press, 1969; *Reflections on the Philosophy of History of Mankind*. Translated by T. O. Churchill and edited by Frank E. Manuel. Chicago: University of Chicago Press, 1968.

Humboldt, Wilhelm von. "Über die Aufgabe des Geschichtsschreibers." In *Gesammelte Schriften*, vol. IV, edited by Albert Leitzmann. Berlin: B. Behr's Verlag, 1905. English version: "On the Historian's Task." *History and Theory*, 6 (1967): 57–71.

Kant, Immanuel. *On History*. Edited with an introduction by Lewis White Beck. Indianapolis and New York: Library of Liberal Arts, Bobbs-Merrill Co., 1963.

Mably, Gabriel Bonnet de. *De la manière de l'écrire l'histoire*. Paris, 1789.

Marx, Karl. *Capital*. Translated by Eden and Cedar Paul. London: Dent & Sons, 1962. German version: *Das Kapital: Kritik der politischen Ökonomie*. Vol. XXIII of Karl Marx and Friedrich Engels, *Werke* (Institut für Marxismus-Leninismus beim ZK der SED). Berlin: Dietz Verlag, 1962. English translations of fragments cited in the text are from *Karl Marx: Selected Writings in Sociology and Social Philosophy*, translated by T. B. Bottomore. New York: McGraw-Hill, 1956.

―――. *The Civil War in France*. In Karl Marx and Frederick Engels, *Selected Works*. New York: International Publishers, 1969.

―――. *The Class Struggles in France, 1848 to 1850*. In Karl Marx and Friedrich Engels, *Basic Writings on Politics and Philosophy*, edited by Lewis S. Feuer. Garden City, N.Y.: Doubleday & Co., 1959.

―――. *The Eighteenth Brumaire of Louis Bonaparte*. In Marx and Engels, *Selected Works*. Fragments cited in the text are from Feuer, ed., *Basic Writings*.

―――. *The German Ideology*. English translations cited in the text are from Bottomore, ed., *Karl Marx: Selected Writings*, and Feuer, ed., *Basic Writings*.

―――. Preface to *A Contribution to the Critique of Political Economy*. In Bottomore, ed., *Karl Marx: Selected Writings*.

―――. "Theses on Feuerbach." English translations cited in the text are from Bottomore, ed., *Karl Marx: Selected Writings*.

―――― (with Friedrich Engels). *Manifest der kommunistischen Partie*. In vol. IV of Karl Marx and Friedrich Engels, *Werke* (Institut für Marxismus-Leninismus beim ZK der SED). Berlin: Dietz Verlag, 1959. English translations cited in the text are from Feuer, ed., *Basic Writings*.

Michelet, Jules. *Histoire de la révolution*. Paris, 1888. English version: *History of the French Revolution*. Translated by George Cocks and edited by Gordon Wright. Chicago and London: University of Chicago Press, 1967.

―――. *Oeuvres complètes*, vol. XXV: *Précis de l'histoire moderne*. Paris: Ernest Flammarion, n.d.

Nietzsche, Friedrich. *The Birth of Tragedy out of the Spirit of Music*. Translated by Francis Golffing. New York: Doubleday & Co., 1956. German version: *Die Geburt der Trägodie aus dem Geist der Musik*. Stuttgart: Alfred Kröner Verlag, 1964.

―――. *The Genealogy of Morals: An Attack*. Translated by Francis Golffing. New York: Doubleday & Co., 1956. German version: *Werke*, vol. VII: *Zur Genealogie der Moral*. Leipzig: Alfred Kröner Verlag, 1910.

―――. *The Use and Abuse of History*. Translated by Adrian Collins. Indianapolis and New York: Library of Liberal Arts, Bobbs-Merrill Co., 1957. German version: *Vom Nutzen und Nachteil der Historie für das Leben*. Basel: Verlag Birkhäuser, n.d.

Novalis [Friedrich Philipp von Hardenberg]. "Christendom or Europe." In *Hymns to the Night and Other Selected Writings*, translated by Charles E. Passage. Indianapolis and New York: Library of Liberal Arts, Bobbs-Merrill Co., 1960.

Ranke, Leopold von. "A Dialogue on Politics." In Theodore von Laue, *Leopold Ranke: The Formative Years*. Princeton: Princeton University Press, 1950.

————. "The Great Powers." In *ibid.*

————. *History of Civil Wars and Monarchy in France.* Translated by M. A. Garney. 2 vols. London, 1852.

————. *History of the Latin and Teutonic Nations, 1494–1514.* Translated by P. A. Ashworth. London, 1887.

————. *History of the Ottoman and Spanish Empires.* Translated by Walter A. Kelly. London, 1843.

————. *History of the Popes, Their Church and State, and Especially of their Conflicts with Protestantism in the Sixteenth and Seventeenth Centuries.* Translated by E. Foster, 3 vols. London, 1853–56.

————. *History of Reformation in Germany.* Translated by S. Austin. 3 vols. London, 1845–47.

————. *The Theory and Practice of History.* Edited by Georg G. Iggers and Konrad von Moltke, with new translations by Wilma A. Iggers and Konrad von Moltke. Indianapolis and New York: Bobbs-Merrill Co., 1973.

Schopenhauer, Arthur. *The World as Will and Idea.* In *The Philosophy of Schopenhauer,* edited by Irwin Edman. New York: Modern Library, 1928.

Tocqueville, Alexis de. *Democracy in America.* Translated by Henry Reeve, revised by Francis Bowen, and now further corrected and edited, with a historical essay, editorial notes, and bibliographies, by Phillips Bradley. 2 vols. New York: Vintage Books, 1945.

————. *The European Revolution and Correspondence with Gobineau.* Edited and translated by John Lukács. New York: Doubleday & Co., 1959.

————. *Memoir, Letters, and Remains of Alexis de Tocqueville.* 2 vols. London: Macmillan & Co., 1861.

————. *Oeuvres complètes,* vol. XII: *Souvenirs.* Edited by J.-P. Mayer. Paris: Gallimard, 1964.

————. *The Old Regime and the French Revolution.* New translation by Stuart Gilbert. New York: Doubleday & Co., 1955.

Vico, Giambattista. *The New Science.* Translation of the third edition (1744) by Thomas Goddard Bergin and Max Harold Fisch. Ithaca, N.Y.: Cornell University Press, 1968.

Vico, Jean-Baptiste. *Principes de la philosophie de l'histoire.* Translated by Jules Michelet. Paris: Colin, 1963.

Voltaire. *Discours sur l'histoire de Charles XII.* Paris, 1831.

————. *Philosophical Dictionary.* In *Works: A Contemporary Version.* Revised and modernized new translation by W. F. Fleming. London: The St. Hubert's Guild. n.d.

◄§ Works on Historiography, Philosophy of History, and Critical Theory Referred to in the Text

Auerbach, Erich. *Mimesis: The Representation of Reality in Western Literature.* Translated by Willard Trask. Princeton: Princeton University Press, 1968.

Barthes, Roland. *Michelet par lui-même.* Paris: Editions du Seuil, n.d.

Benveniste, Emile. *Problems of General Linguistics.* Translated by Mary Elizabeth Meek. Coral Gables, Fla.: University of Miami Press, 1971.

Burke, Kenneth. *A Grammar of Motives.* Berkeley and Los Angeles: University of California Press, 1969.

Cassirer, Ernst. *The Philosophy of the Enlightenment.* Translated by Fritz C. A. Koelln and James C. Pettegrove. Boston: Beacon Press, 1955.

Collingwood, R. G. *The Idea of History.* New York: Oxford University Press, 1956.

Danto, Arthur C. *Analytical Philosophy of History.* Cambridge: Cambridge University Press, 1965.

Dilthey, Wilhelm. *Gesammelte Schriften,* vol. I: *Einleitung in die Geisteswissenschaften: Versuch einer Grundlegung für das Studium der Gesellschaft.* Edited by Bernard Groethuysen. Stuttgart: R. G. Teubner, 1959.

————. *Gesammelte Schriften,* vol. VII: *Der Aufbau der geschlichtlichen Welt in den Geisteswissenschaften.* Edited by Bernard Groethuysen. Stuttgart: R. G. Teubner, 1958.

Dray, William H., ed. *Philosophical Analysis and History.* New York: Harper & Row, 1966.

Foucault, Michel. *The Order of Things: An Archeology of the Human Sciences.* New York: Pantheon Books, 1971.

Frye, Northrop. *The Anatomy of Criticism: Four Essays.* Princeton: Princeton University Press, 1957.

Fueter, Eduard. *Geschichte der neueren Historiographie.* Munich: Oldenbourg, 1911. French version: *Histoire de l'historiographie moderne.* Translated by Emile Jeanmaire. Paris: Alcan, 1914.

Gallie, W. B. *Philosophy and the Historical Understanding.* New York: Schocken Books, 1968.

Gombrich, E. H. *Art and Illusion: A Study in the Psychology of Pictorial Representation.* London and New York: Phaidon Books, 1960.

Gooch, G. P. *History and Historians in the Nineteenth Century.* Boston: Beacon Press, 1959.

Gossmann, Lionel. *Medievalism and the Ideologies of the Enlightenment: The World and Work of La Curne de Sainte-Palaye.* Baltimore: The Johns Hopkins Press, 1968.

————. "Voltaire's Charles XII: History into Art." *Studies on Voltaire and the Eighteenth Century,* 25 (1963): 691–720.

Hartmann, Geoffrey. *Beyond Formalism: Literary Essays, 1958–1970.* New Haven and London: Yale University Press, 1971.

Henle, Paul, ed. *Language, Thought, and Culture.* Ann Arbor: University of Michigan Press, 1966.

Herodotus. *The Histories.* Translated by Aubrey De Délincourt. Hammondsworth, Middlesex, and Baltimore: Penguin Books, 1959.

Iggers, Georg G. *The German Conception of History.* Middletown, Conn.: Wesleyan University Press, 1968.

Jakobson, Roman. "Linguistics and Poetics." In *Style in Language,* edited by Thomas A. Sebeok. New York and London: Technology Press & John Wiley, 1960.

────── (with Morris Halle). *Fundamentals of Language.* The Hague: Mouton, 1956.

Lacan, Jacques. "The Insistence of the Letter in the Unconscious." In *Structuralism,* edited by Jacques Ehrmann. New York: Doubleday & Co., 1970.

Laue, Theodore M. von. *Leopold Ranke: The Formative Years.* Princeton: Princeton University Press, 1950.

Lemon, Lee T., and Reiss, Marion J., eds. *Russian Formalist Criticism: Four Essays.* Lincoln: University of Nebraska Press, 1965.

Lévi-Strauss, Claude. "Overture to le Cru et le cuit." In *Structuralism,* edited by Jacques Ehrmann. New York: Doubleday & Co., 1970.

──────. *The Savage Mind.* London: Weidenfeld & Nicholson, 1966.

Liard, Louis. *Enseignement supérieur en France, 1789–1893.* 2 vols. Paris, 1894.

Lovejoy, Arthur O. "Herder and the Enlightenment Philosophy of History." In *Essays in the History of Ideas.* New York: G. P. Putnam's Sons, 1960.

Löwith, Karl. *Meaning in History: The Theological Implications of the Philosophy of History.* Chicago: University of Chicago Press, 1949.

Lukács, Georg. *The Historical Novel.* Translated by Hannah and Stanley Mitchell. London: Merlin Press, 1962.

Mannheim, Karl. "Connservative Thought." In *Essays in Sociology and Social Psychology,* edited by Paul Kecskemeti. London: Routledge & Kegan Paul, 1953.

──────. *Ideology and Utopia: An Introduction to the Sociology of Knowledge.* Translated by Louis Wirth and Edward Shils. New York: Harcourt, Brace & Co., 1946.

Mill, John Stuart. "Nature." In *Essential Works of John Stuart Mill,* edited by Max Lerner. New York: Bantam Books, 1961.

──────. "Utility of Religion." In *ibid.*

Mink, Louis O. "The Autonomy of Historical Understanding." In Dray, ed., *Philosophical Analysis and History.*

──────. "Philosophical Analysis and Historical Understanding." *Review of Metaphysics,* 21, no. 4 (1968): 667–98.

Momigliano, Arnaldo. "A Hundred Years after Ranke." In *Studies in Historiography.* New York: Harper Torchbooks, 1966.

Neff, Emery. *The Poetry of History: The Contribution of Literature and Literary Scholarship to the Writing of History since Voltaire.* New York: Columbia University Press, 1947.

Pepper, Stephen C. *World Hypotheses: A Study in Evidence.* Berkeley and Los Angeles: University of California Press, 1966.

Popper, Karl R. *The Poverty of Historicism.* London: Routledge & Kegan Paul, 1961.

Poulet, Georges. *Studies in Human Time.* Translated by Elliot Coleman. Baltimore: The Johns Hopkins Press, 1956.

Sonnino, Lee A. *A Handbook to Sixteenth Century Rhetoric.* London: Routledge & Kegan Paul, 1968.

Stern, Fritz, ed. *The Varieties of History: From Voltaire to the Present.* New York: Meridian Books, 1956.

Valéry, Paul. *The Outlook for Intelligence*. Translated by Dennis Folliot and Jackson Mathews and edited by Jackson Mathews. New York and Evanston: Harper Torchbooks, 1962.

Walsh, W. H. *Introduction to the Philosophy of History*. New York: Harper Torchbooks, 1958.

Weintraub, Karl J. *Visions of Culture*. Chicago and London: University of Chicago Press, 1966.

Wellek, René. *Concepts of Criticism*. New Haven and London: Yale University Press, 1963.

White, Hayden V. "The Burden of History." *History and Theory*, 5, no. 2 (1966): 111–34.

———. "Foucault Decoded: Notes from Underground," *ibid.*, 12, no. 1 (1973): 23–54.

INDEX